D0275635

THE 1948 OLYMPICS

HOW LONDON
RESCUED
THE GAMES

The 1948 Olympics

How London rescued the Games

Bob Phillips

Published in Great Britain by
SportsBooks Limited
1 Evelyn Court
Malvern Road
Cheltenham
GL50 2JR

Cover design by Alan Hunns

Cover photographs from Action Images

Photographs in plate sections from Getty Images

A catalogue record for this book is available from the British Library.

ISBN 9781899807 54 3

Printed and bound in England by
Cromwell Press.

Mixed Sources
Product group from well-managed
forests and other controlled sources
www.fsc.org Cert no. TT-COC-2082
© 1996 Forest Stewardship Council
FSC

This book is dedicated to the memory of Alfred Nakache, who competed at the Olympic Games of 1936 and then survived, against the most appalling odds, to take part again in 1948.

CONTENTS

FOREWORD

By Sir Roger Bannister

A T THE TIME of the 1948 London Olympics I was only 19 and I felt, probably wrongly, that I was too young for the full Olympic exposure. In those days, when we were vastly undertrained by today's standards, there was a widely held notion that too much racing when one was young was wrong, physically and psychologically. No one believes that now! At any rate, I turned down the invitation to join the Olympic "possibles" – who in those days of rationing received extra food parcels. I was then invited to be a minor official. So, as it were, I had a front seat to see what the Games meant to the competitors, their countries, the press and the spectators.

As a result my whole view on sport was changed from a jumbled striving of individual athletes and sports to a new and higher kind of unity that can combine men's and women's highest endeavours. I began to see a debt of loyalty I had previously owed to Oxford to a whole new world of sport in which I now felt a small part, of which the Olympic Games were the pinnacle, rejuvenated every four years by the celebration of each Olympics.

Over the years since 1948 that feeling has never left me. Despite the undoubted cheating, rows and corruption common to all human affairs, and incidentally equally rife in the Ancient Greek Olympics, I have continued to hold an idealist view of the overall benefits of the Olympic Games.

Bob Phillips has every qualification to write this history of the London Olympics and their significance for the young people competing who, after all, are those for whom this festival is designed. He learnt his sports writing first from the McWhirter twins and their magazine, *Athletics World*, then graduated to national newspapers and the BBC athletics commentary team.

I recommend this book most warmly and wish it every success.

The Breathless Tale of
the Forgotten Flag

ROGER BANNISTER WAS appointed assistant to the Great Britain team commandant, Colonel EA Hunter OBE, at those 1948 London Olympics and his presence of mind and fleetness of foot were to prove of vital importance to the dignity of the British contingent at the opening ceremony. Bannister told the story in his biography, *First Four Minutes*, published by Putnam in 1955:

"One anxious moment stands out. On 29th July 1948, the day of the opening ceremony, the Commandant and I were about to drive over to the Stadium. We had been told that a car carrying the flags of all the nations was to drive along the line of assembled teams just before they marched into the Stadium. In this way there would be no danger of any team forgetting its flag. As we were leaving Uxbridge my eyes caught sight of an old Union Jack which we had used for minor flag-raising ceremonies. We kept it rolled up in a corner of the office. I suggested we should take it with us, 'just in case'.

"On arrival at Wembley we saw the car park was crowded and we left it to the driver to find a place. The Commandant and I made our way to the British team. The flags for the parade had just been handed out – there was no flag for the British team. A mistake had been made. In another twenty minutes the British team, parading last as host nation, would enter the Stadium. The whole ceremony culminated in placing the flags of the various countries in a semi-circle round an athlete who would take the Olympic oath on behalf of all competitors.

"The Commandant ordered me to find the flag we had brought from Uxbridge. He gave me a jeep and a British army sergeant. Together we tore off towards the car park. We drove furiously through the crowds which still packed the approaches to the Stadium. I kept my hand on the hooter so it sounded continuously. We reached the car park. There were thousands of cars and to find ours in time seemed an impossibility.

"Everyone stared as we rushed round like madmen up and down the lines of cars. It took us ten minutes to find our car. It was locked, so I smashed the window with a stone while the sergeant restrained a policeman who wanted to arrest me.

"Seizing the flag, I rushed back to the jeep, and we set off for the Stadium. But the entrances were blocked by last minute arrivals and the jeep was soon hemmed in on all sides. Hooting was useless. Time was perilously short, and I could see the British team having to parade without a flag. I jumped out of the jeep. Using the flag as a battering ram, with brass spike foremost, I charged through the crowd and reached the British team just before they marched into the Stadium".

PREFACE

"Surpassing in magnificence any previous home of the Games"

The senior administrator's tribute:

"The great test was taken; and the organisation rose gloriously to the supreme challenge. The visitors were housed and fed; the athletes were made at home in camps where every care was taken of their waking and sleeping hours. Wembley Stadium itself, where day after day huge crowds assembled, surpassed in magnificence and convenience any previous home of the Games. All the other Olympic venues, too, were splendidly organised both from the spectators' and the competitors' point of view. Torquay I found much nicer than Nice; Henley recaptured the atmosphere of the old, old days; while at Aldershot and Sandhurst competitions went on in the friendliest manner ... on behalf of the International Olympic Committee and all participants at the Games I say a hearty 'Thank you' to Britain." – *J Sigfrid Edström, President of the International Olympic Committee, writing in the British Olympic Association's Official Report of the 1948 London Olympic Games.*

The daily newspaper columnist's opinion:

"Britain has risen from her austerity and proved that we have the will, if not the rations, to fight and swim, row and run. We have been beaten in most events but never disgraced. Stout McCorquodale ran like a lion and the wee Scots lassie, Cathie Gibson, proved that her heart was almost as big as herself. Slim dainty ballet dancer Maureen Gardner sped over the hurdles to lose by a touch. Laurel wreaths are out of fashion. Silver-gilt medals will tarnish. But the youth of 1948 have met and sent a glow around the world." – *Ian Coster, writing in the London Daily Mail.*

The medal-winning competitor's recollection:

"Coming second was not as important as it is today. You were so thrilled to have done what you did. You didn't get the coverage that you get today, where it's only to do with money. We weren't celebrities, because there was no TV where you were on every week. I think it was more fun then. We were all friends, and I don't think they are now. I don't think I would like to be taking part now." – *Dorothy Tyler, silver-medallist in the 1948 Olympic high jump (as she had also been in 1936), reminiscing in the year 2000.*

The teenage spectator's enthusiasm:

"I was 16, still at school, and my father gave me tickets for the athletics as a Christmas and birthday present combined and found me 'digs' at Kensal Green. I travelled every day on the Underground. There was tremendous excitement in the air at Wembley. It was a terrific thrill for me to be there, and I'm sure that everyone there felt the same. The war was only just over. England was a mess. There was rationing and no money, and the winter of 1947 had been awful. It was so cold that at boarding school we wore overcoats under the blankets when we went to bed. People today really have no idea what it was like. So the Olympics were something marvellous. There was colour and pageantry and the buzz each day grew bigger and better, and no amount of rain – and, oh, how it rained! – could spoil it." – *David Thurlow, later to become a professional journalist and leading athletics historian.*

The academic expert's appraisal:

"No one expected that the Games could be mounted otherwise than austerely. The result showed how little the festival needs an elaborate and grandiose setting. The cynic would probably point out that the number of nations participating was limited. Some of the potentially obstreperous among them were excluded. Others had not yet come into existence." – *Professor HA Harris, eminent Olympic historian.*

The broadcaster's review:

"The BBC's faithful viewer in the Channel Islands, 180 miles away, where reception is variable, was able to get pictures of excellent entertainment value." – *The Radio Industries Council, reporting on the coverage for the country's 80,000 owners of television sets.*

Author's Introduction

"It was all very different, of course ... the true spirit of amateur athletics"

THIS IS NOT an encyclopaedic chronicle of every result attained by the 4,071 competitors at the 1948 Olympic Games. If anyone really wants to know who finished last in the marathon that sort of detail can be gleaned from the British Olympic Association's Official Report, though I admit that copies can only rarely be found these days through the internet or on the shelves of second-hand bookshops and will cost you more than 100 times the seven shillings and sixpence (37½ pence) for which they originally sold. There's also the Games Organising Committee's report, all 776 pages of it, for which you will pay some £360 (550 euros). Actually, now I come to think of it, the identity of the man who finished last in the marathon *is* to be found by any diligent reader in the following pages.

Rather, this book is intended to be an informative and entertaining account of how it was that London, battered and bruised, came to be chosen to stage those Games so soon after the end of the Second World War, and what happened when the Games took place. Of course, there is as much discussion of the achievements of the champions at Wembley and the other venues as is hopefully relevant and helpful, but the broader intention is to set the whole affair in a social, political and economic perspective. Many of the competitors had harrowing wartime experiences to tell, including a Jewish deportee, a German army deserter and a survivor of a Japanese prisoner-of-war camp.

The entire Games cost some three-quarters of a million pounds to stage – equivalent, perhaps, to some £77 million in today's terms – and they made a modest profit. The competitors were all amateurs, or at least declared themselves as such, allowed to receive no more than their out-of-pocket expenses. No fortunes were to be made by them, nor by meeting promoters or equipment manufacturers; no prize money was won, no percentages of athletes' earnings were handed over to agents, coaches and managers. Sparse accommodation was provided in barrack-rooms, college dormitories and converted school classrooms. Food parcels from North America and the old Empire eked out the meagre menus. The richer teams brought their own provisions. Vouchers for the Underground were issued to athletes for them to make their own way to the stadium, or they rode in double-decker buses or even hitched a ride from helpful passing motorists or lorry-drivers.

This is entirely unlike 21st-century sport. As one member of the British team was to recall wistfully very many years later – "it was all very different, of course, compared with the Olympics of these days, but it did seem to me to be athletics at its best, and it was the last occasion, I believe, that everyone was acting in the true spirit of amateur athletics".

The stark evidence of the statistics shows that the best of athletics and the 16 other sports at the Olympics of 1948 was not in the same intrinsic class as at all the Games since, but mere facts and figures tell no more than part of the story. It is a natural temptation for an author concentrating his attentions on one segment of history to project the idea that his subject of choice is somehow of very special significance, even perhaps unique, but the fact is that the Olympic Games of 1948 were the last of an era. Within four years they were to change out of all recognition; most significantly because of the entry at last of the USSR and the widespread development of state aid for sport there and in other Communist-bloc countries. In the pages that follow will be found the personal testimony of numerous 1948 competitors – often poignant, often amusing, never pretentious or self-seeking – who have recorded for posterity what it was like to be a champion or merely an "also ran" in those far-off days of austerity and amateurism.

Robert Edelman, the American author of the most comprehensive study of the rise of Soviet sport, has written: "If the clock is stopped at any given point in time during the evolution of an institution such as the Olympic Games, evidence can be found of both the perpetuation of past practices and attitudes and the anticipation of those of the future. Inevitably this was true of the London Games of 1948. The general adherence to amateurism and the cautious approach towards media coverage and commercial sponsorship reflected a continuing attachment to the past. Still dominated athletically and administratively by Western Europe and North America, and not yet feeling the full extent of Cold War rivalries, the London Olympics might, ironically, be described as the last prewar Games."

A further striking feature of these Games is their size – or, to be more accurate, lack of it. The number of sports and the number of events were far fewer than today. Some disciplines such as mountain biking and beach volleyball had yet to be invented. In women's athletics there was no race beyond 200 metres and no pole vault, triple jump, hammer throw or all-round competition. In swimming the butterfly stroke was still thought of as a variation of the breaststroke and there were no medley races. In cycling there was no individual track pursuit or road time-trial, and nothing for women. Nor were there were women competing in equestrianism, rowing or shooting, and in fencing and gymnastics they had only one event each.

The restriction to 17 sports was not for lack of interest. During 1947 the International Olympic Committee received applications from a motley collection of administrators of other disciplines for inclusion at the 1948 Games – archery, baseball, gliding, women's hockey, lacrosse, roller-skating, rugby football, table-tennis and volleyball most prominent among them – and rejected them all. Proposals of an even more fanciful nature were received, and also turned down, from the international governing bodies of chess, dancing, model yachting and polo. Yet, at the same time, the anomalies remained of one of the sports at the Games being entirely restricted by its rules to commissioned officers in the armed forces and of a code of "amateurism" which still allowed a newspaper rowing correspondent to take part in his sport, and win a gold medal, and the director of the world's most renowned riding-school to compete in equestrianism.

So far as coverage of the competitions in this book is concerned, I took the policy decision to include the results of all finals (in some cases summarised), on the basis that anyone competing in a final has some bearing on the ultimate result and the eventual distribution of medals. This approach inevitably leads to anomalies because there were as few as six finalists in some of the athletics events, whereas there were other sports in which no eliminating rounds were held at all. There were, for example, 123 men taking part in the gymnastics competition, which was drawn out over a period of three days. So far as possible the full names, or the familiar names, of all competitors are given, but it should be noted that in 1948, and for some years afterwards, only initials and surnames were usually given in British newspaper and magazine reports, and even the list of participants in the organising committee's official report does not contain full names.

As a further point of style, surnames of Spanish origin are followed by family names, and, though these are usually omitted in reports, I have included them for clarity's sake. Thus the Mexican diver, Joaquin Capilla Pérez, is mostly referred to elsewhere as "Joaquin Capilla" but is given his full name here. I have also used familiar first names, such as Bill, Bob, Tom, when it is obvious what the abbreviations stand for, but not when the derivation is more obscure. Thus, to take another diver as an example, the Dutchwoman, Jacoba Floor, is listed as such, and not as "Cobie Floor", by which she was familiarly called. Some women competitors were known by both their maiden and married names, of which the most famous of all Dutch Olympians, Fanny Blankers-Koen, is a prime example, and have been listed accordingly.

A selection of the long list of the books and other publications to which I have made reference in the course of research will be found on other pages, and I have had great help from a number of National Olympic Committees and their archivists, websites and publications; particularly those of Argentina, Australia, Austria, Bahamas, Belgium, Bermuda, Canada, Denmark, Estonia, France, Great Britain, Holland, Hungary, Lithuania, Luxembourg, Mexico, New Zealand, Norway, Poland, Portugal, Spain, Sweden, Uruguay, Venezuela and the USA.

Those individuals to whom I owe most for help and encouragement are Neil Allen, Les Crouch, Stan Greenberg, Dave Terry and David Thurlow.

Neil was the highly regarded athletics and boxing correspondent of *The Times* and a contributor to the monthly *World Sports* magazine who set new standards in British sports journalism from the 1960s onwards. His interviews with Dame Mary Glen Haig, Don Scott and Bert Bushnell form an integral part of this book.

Les is a fellow track "nut" who I first met, appropriately, on a crowded bus making its way through the streets of Rome to the Olympic Stadium in 1960, and who has carried out detailed research into the origins of the 1948 Games. Stan has published his own *Olympic Almanack* and has generously shared his knowledge with me. Dave is a world-respected authority on the origins of numerous sports and possessor of a vast library of relevant literature. David, also a much-respected professional journalist, has been the main contributor for a number of years to the historical and statistical athletics journal which I edit and has recorded a series of interviews with retired international athletes from as far back as the 1920s which are of inestimable value. For many of those elusive first names I am indebted to Bill Mallon (USA), one of the world's foremost Olympic scholars, and his colleagues, Arild Gjerde (Norway) and Jeroen Heijmans (Holland), who have intensively researched the subject. My thanks, also, for his support to the publisher, Randall Northam, of SportsBooks, who again I have known for a long time from his journalistic involvements.

I would also like to note the help of Tineke Derksen (Holland), Harry Gordon (Australia), Ove Karlsson (Sweden), Robert Ladner (Austria), Peter Matthews, Cindy Slater (USA), Cynthia Stinger (USA) and Joanne Watson. They have all, in their different ways, provided a significant input for this book. I hope they think the effort was worthwhile, and I hope you do, too.

Bob Phillips, Boutières, France, 2007.

Chapter 1

HOW THE GAMES WERE WON

"A challenge to British grit"

LONDON WAS NOT the obvious choice of venue for the 1948 Olympic Games. Nor was it even a logical, or a sensible, choice. This is readily apparent with the benefit of some 60 years of hindsight. In 1946, when the decision was announced, many a heart sank at the prospect. Yet it took not 60 years but a mere matter of minutes after the Games had ended, as the Olympic flame was doused at the closing ceremony, for a collective sigh of relief to be breathed and for the realisation to dawn that London had done itself proud.

These were the first Games to be held after the end of World War II, and there were numerous other cities far better qualified to be the hosts. Stockholm and Lausanne, for example, had both benefited from cosy neutrality during the war years. Paris had been liberated, more or less unscathed, in 1944. The American cities of Baltimore, Chicago, Detroit, Minneapolis, New York, Philadelphia, San Francisco – far removed from the battle zones – were jostling in line, all of them eager to open their doors, and they might well have offered as an incentive to defray the travelling expenses for their European poor relations, though the cost of sending the US team to London was met through public fund-raising. Yet it was never a contest. Battle-weary, bomb-scarred London was chosen as if by divine right.

There was no mass gathering of International Olympic Committee (IOC) members in some exotic location to hear sophisticated presentations of facility construction and financial calculation from eloquent chiefs of delegations, supported by their retinue of technical experts, revered ex-champions, and even presidents and prime ministers. There was no pondering of respective merits, no weighing of issues, no back-room politicking to shift support from one contender to another as the next round of voting loomed. In effect, London was elected unopposed, and the origins of that curious decision can be traced back to a decade or more before the 1948 Games opened.

London's destiny was very largely decided by one member of the International Olympic Committee, J Sigfrid Edström, and nobody questioned the autocratic nature of the process. After all, who was going to deny the gift of an Olympic Games to the city which had defied the might of Hitler's waves of bombers and rocket missiles? This was to be an Olympic Games to revive the joys of sporting endeavour and to celebrate a resumption of peace and freedom. London was the symbolic setting – and even if it was no more than sentiment which decided the issue, then London had much of that in its favour, and Stockholm, Lausanne, Paris, New York, Chicago, Detroit, San Francisco, and anywhere else for that matter, had little or none by comparison. For the abandoned Games of 1940 and 1944 a cosmopolitan array of other cities had at various times declared an interest (Alexandria, Barcelona, Budapest, Buenos Aires, Dublin, Montreal, Rio de Janeiro, Rome, Toronto), but they, too, had dropped by the wayside despite the obvious appeal of many of them.

To understand how London was favoured it is necessary to appreciate that at its beginning there was a very definite sense of protocol, rather than preferential treatment, about the selection process. Memories were all too fresh of the 1936 Games in Berlin where Hitler and his cohorts had strutted and blustered in vain search of "Aryan supremacy", and though the Germans had won more medals than anyone else they had been firmly put in their place in the Olympic Stadium by the marvellous achievements of an Afro-American athlete named Jesse Owens. It was the relentless flag-waving and hideous chanting which left a deeply scarring impression.

Such frenzied nationalism was not at all what the Olympic mandarins wanted. The next Games of 1940 had originally been allocated to Tokyo, though not without misgivings concerning the country's remoteness and militancy, which were exacerbated when Japan's confrontation with China escalated into war in 1937. The IOC's qualms were laid to rest when the Japanese organising committee decided in July 1938 that because of what they described as "protracted hostilities with no prospect of immediate peace" both the Summer Games and the Winter Games, which were due to be held in Sapporo, would have to be cancelled. The task of finding alternative candidates prepared to take on such a huge commitment at short notice was surprisingly easy because the IOC soon made a willing recruit for the Summer Games of Helsinki, which had unavailingly applied in 1927 for the 1936 Games and then lost the vote for 1940 to Tokyo, 36 to 27. The offer by Garmisch-Partenkirchen to host the Winter Games, as they had in 1936, was also eagerly accepted.

No country was surely more suited to stage the Summer Games than valiant little Finland, which had achieved its first successes in 1912 as a subjugated part of the Russian Empire and then after independence had produced the famed "Flying Finns" of the 1920s and 1930s: the craggy, remorseless distance-runners whose supremacy was perfectly personified by Paavo Nurmi, the expressionless "Executioner of the Stopwatch", who had won Olympic gold medals galore in the

1920s and set world records beyond count (well, actually nine gold medals and 34 world records, to be precise). It seems inconceivable, but even the start of the Second World War in September of 1939, and then that winter's "White War" between Finland and the USSR, did not immediately persuade the IOC to abandon plans for the Games, and it was only Germany's invasion of Denmark and Norway in April 1940 which at last sounded the death-knell. Helsinki declared the Games forfeited at the end of that month. To be absolutely fair to the IOC, there had been some widespread political and public feeling, or at least some hope, before then that the so-called "phoney war" against Germany would not last long.

The IOC executive had resolutely convened two months earlier in Paris, and in the absence of a full meeting of delegates, which would have taken place during the now cancelled Helsinki Games, London was selected as the venue for the 1944 Games by 20 votes to 11 for Rome, two for Detroit and one for Lausanne. Despite the war, this invitation was not only anticipated but welcomed in London. It should be noted that the IOC was not then, nor is it now, a freely elected democratic body. It was unashamedly patrician in its constitution and its rules stated that it could select "such persons as it considers qualified to be its members, provided that they speak French or English and are citizens of and reside in a country which possesses a National Olympic Committee". Its members were regarded as "ambassadors from the IOC to the sporting organisations of their respective nations" and were without exception drawn from the socially superior ranks of their respective countries. Of the 39 newcomers to IOC membership during the 1930s, there were three Princes (of Denmark, Japan and Liechtenstein), a Marquess, a Baron, a Pasha (military commander), three Counts and four Generals.

The Marquess was, in fact, Lord Burghley, the sixth Marquess of Exeter, who had been elected in 1933, having won eternal sporting fame as the Olympic 400 metres hurdles champion of five years before, and had been president of the Amateur Athletic Association since 1936 (and would continue to be so for 40 years). Among those who joined him in the IOC hierarchy was an American, Avery Brundage, who had no title to his name but who had made his fortune in the construction business. Brundage, like Lord Burghley, had competed in the Olympics, though with rather less success, placing sixth in a track and field pentathlon competition in 1912, and was eminently qualified for IOC election, according to the requirements laid down by the French founder of the modern Olympic movement, Baron Pierre de Coubertin, that all members be "independent financially" and "without active political connections". Lord Burghley, as it happens, had briefly been a Member of Parliament in the early 1930s but that was seen as no bar.

Great Britain had first thrown its hat into the Olympic rings in 1936 when an alternative bid to that of Tokyo was made by the Lord Mayor of London and the British Olympic Association for the 1940 Games. This, though, was a half-hearted effort, designed more as a symbolic voice of protest against Japanese militarism than as a serious offer, and was withdrawn within a few weeks. Two years later

Lord Aberdare, on behalf of the BOA, offered London again as an emergency alternative for 1940, and from 1938 onwards Lord Burghley, then aged 33, had campaigned vigorously in support of London as a future Olympic venue, which meant in all probability that in the manner of the time and circumstances he had discreetly said the right things at the right time to the right people. He was to find an ally in Brundage, who as president of the US Olympic Committee since 1929 was to have a very major influence in the eventual decision regarding the choice for the 1948 Games, though not necessarily the key one, as will be explained in due course. Needless to say, the strictures of war meant that the 1944 London Games were abandoned, just as their 1940 predecessors had been, but again the IOC – astonishingly – was not hurried into a decision even as Europe was being torn apart around them.

The power of attorney of the IOC had been reduced effectively by then to Edström, the acting president who had assumed the position in 1942 when the incumbent president, Count Henri de Baillet-Latour, of Belgium, died after 17 years in office. Edström was Swedish and the IOC headquarters since 1922 were also in neutral territory in Lausanne, in Switzerland, at the quaint parkland address of "Campagne Mon-Repos". He was therefore able to travel and communicate much more freely than his colleagues, though even allowing for this freedom of movement his attitude to the conflict going on around him could perhaps be described as cavalier, at best. In a letter to Count de Baillet-Latour in 1939 he stated, "It certainly is sad for our Olympic cause that this World War has started" (!), and early the next year he again regaled the Count with the airy observation that "I do not see why we men of sport should have to bow our heads too much to the war".

Edström is a pre-eminent figure of sports administration in the 20th century. Born in 1870, he had been educated in Gothenburg and Zurich. In 1896 he had gone to the USA to work for the Westinghouse electrical manufacturing company in Pittsburgh and had then become chief engineer of the Zurich tramway system and president of the leading firm of electrical manufacturers in Sweden. He was one of the organisers of the 1912 Olympics in Stockholm and took the lead in founding the International Amateur Athletic Federation (IAAF) that year, remaining as its president until 1946, when he was succeeded by Lord Burghley. He was elected to the IOC in 1920, became a member of the executive board within a year, and was made vice-president in 1931. The IOC said of him in a homily written in 1962, 10 years after his retirement at the age of 82, that "he was able to handle effectively all the complicated problems which arose after the Second World War". It was Avery Brundage who succeeded him as IOC president in 1952 and his reign lasted 20 years, often in controversial circumstances, but that is a story for another time and place.

Such was Edström's optimism – or was it mere insularity? – that he was still of the belief in 1943 that London could go ahead with the Games the next year. How he could possibly have envisaged this is beyond understanding. To indulge in pure speculation, London could presumably have put on some sort of Games, had there been the will to do so. Football, cricket and athletics had all continued since 1939 as welcome diversions for the beleaguered public and as valuable fund-raisers for the war effort, and so there was some sort of structure of facilities and officialdom still in place. Whether any competitors from abroad could have actually got to London is another matter, though it is worth remarking that the great Swedish middle-distance runner, Gunder Hägg, had made a transatlantic voyage to the USA in the summer of 1943 – albeit a tortuous adventure lasting 25 days in a tanker vessel – for a series of races, stopping off in London for a day or so to train with a young British miler named Doug Wilson in Hyde Park in the shadow of the batteries of anti-aircraft guns and the canopy of protecting barrage balloons.

Maybe Edström somehow believed that the Ancient Greek custom of a laying-down of arms during an Olympic celebration could be invoked with Nazi approval. Certainly, he was keen to the point of obsession that the 50th anniversary of the founding of the modern Olympic movement, which led to the inaugural Games of 1896, should somehow be marked during 1944, and a ceremony was held that year in Lausanne, with Germany among those few countries represented.

From the purely mundane sporting point of view, there would have been a surprising number of qualified competitors to produce a Games of some quality, as activity had been sustained at a high level in the USA, for instance, where the AAU (national) and NCAA (national collegiate) championships in athletics continued uninterrupted, and there were plenty of athletes of Olympic calibre who were still at college or were serving in the armed forces on home soil. The national 220 yards title was won that year by a prodigious Texas high-school student named Charley Parker, and had he had the opportunity to go to the 1944 Olympics he might now be regarded in hindsight as one of the great heroes of the Games instead of having slipped into obscurity. Even in Europe it was almost a matter of business as usual, with a full season of athletics action in neutral Sweden, in Finland, and in occupied countries such as Denmark, France and Holland. That was also the case in South and Central America. Even in England the pre-war world mile record-holder, Sydney Wooderson, whose army service was restricted to the home front because of poor eyesight, competed frequently and had the opportunity to run the mile distance again in a very respectable time of 4min 12.8sec to support the "Aid to Russia Fund".

Towards the end of 1944 the future looked distinctly brighter. The Allied armies had landed on the Normandy coast on D-Day, 6 June. The Red Army was pushing the Germans back in the East. Paris had been liberated, and Prime Minister Winston Churchill and General de Gaulle, leader of the Free French, had together strolled down the Champs Elysées on Armistice Day, 11 November, celebrating the end of World War I. This next war seemed as good as won, and among the many spirits to be revived was that of Olympism. The three leading members of the British Olympic Association – Lord Aberdare, Lord Burghley and Sir Noel Curtis-Bennett – issued a declaration of faith that same month of

November to the effect that the first post-war Olympic Games should be hosted by London. Then, within a few weeks of peace being declared in Europe in May 1945, Edström wrote to Lord Aberdare, coolly advising him that "Brundage and I have agreed that we shall have the next Games in London". It was, in all essence, a *fait accompli*, though one or two formalities still needed to be observed and Lord Burghley accordingly made a visit to Stockholm that October. Maybe it could be said of Edström, then aged 74, and in his youth a fine sprinter with a best 100 metres time of 11.0sec, that in this instance he was quick off the mark ... but he could be confident that there was no zealous official at his back about to fire the recall pistol.

Before the year was out the IOC delegates, emerging from their wartime hiatus, had dutifully followed Edström's lead, even though they had apparently been offered the alternative of Lausanne (presumably because of its IOC connections) to vote for if they so chose. Maybe the suggestion of Lausanne was merely for form's sake, and there is certainly no evidence that Edström gave the IOC delegates any great encouragement in that direction. The Lord Mayor of London formally applied on behalf of his city to host the Games, as he was required to do, and by February of 1946 had received the inevitable letter of acceptance of the bid. The voluminous correspondence in which Edström indulged gives no clue as to why he was so committed to London, when it would have seemed obvious that his own country could offer a far more suitable venue. Nor is it apparent why Brundage – with so many American would-be hosts at hand – should have also strongly supported London.

The answer would seem to be the "London effect". Sweden, basking in untroubled affluence, was perhaps not considered to be an appropriate destination for the representatives of impoverished countries which were recovering from war and would then be discovering how "the other half" had lived. As for the far-distant cities of the USA, it was thought to be too costly a venture for European nations, and maybe the wily Brundage saw that by backing London's emotive cause he could not be seen to be favouring any one of his compatriots. He could also cite the fall-back argument that the USA had staged the Games as recently as 1932, in Los Angeles. Brundage and Lord Burghley played a vital role, but Edström, at the seat of IOC power, was the man who "won" the 1948 Games for London.

Norman Baker, the US-based academic who has written extensively about Olympic politics, believes that part of the reason for the choice of London was the city's previous commitment to the abandoned 1944 Games but that the more significant factor was the economic one. The motivation for support of London, he wrote, "was reinforced by the fact that the majority of alternative host cities were located in the United States, and there were severe doubts about the practicalities and costs of trans-Atlantic travel and the impact that this could have on the number of participants. This was a serious consideration in an era when, numerically, European nations predominated within the Olympic movement".

Now that London had "won" the right to stage the Games, the much more demanding task was to be ready on schedule. Little more than two years remained before the Olympic flame was to be lit, and it is unimaginable that any prospective candidate in the 21st century would ever have contemplated so truncated a timescale. The magnitude of the Games is now such that any successful bidding city, such as London for 2012, needs all of the seven years' advance notice which it is given to complete (hopefully) its preparations. Even allowing for the lower expectations of the latter 1940s, these London Olympic Games of 1948 were going to be characterised, unappealingly but unavoidably, as the "Austerity Games".

The historian, Paul Addison, has written graphically of Britain's "black and white images of hardship and high endeavour" at this time: "The right to live in peace had been dearly paid for at the risk of life and limb, and the mere fact of physical survival was something to celebrate. Yet the conditions of everyday life were shabby and constricting. Work, though plentiful, was slow to bring the longed-for rewards of an ideal home with a chicken in the pot and a Morris Ten in the garage". The Education Act of 1944 had raised the school-leaving age to 15, but secondary education for all could still not be implemented throughout the country, for the simple reason that the required new schools were not yet built. Such basic commodities as meat, bread, even potatoes, were severely rationed. Government-sponsored poster-boards across the country carried the woeful message, "We're Up Against It. We Work Or Want. A Challenge To British Grit".

The war had cost Britain £7,000 million – a quarter of the nation's wealth – and so the fact that these Olympic Games would have that subtitle of "Austerity Games" went without saying. The dictum of "Austerity" in every walk of life was firmly lodged in the national consciousness by Olympic year. Sir Stafford Cripps had been appointed Chancellor of the Exchequer by the Labour Prime Minister, Clement Attlee, in November of 1947, and Cripps's economic policy was based, in the words of the historian, LCB Seaman, on the principle that "salvation could only come through the organised re-conversion of the whole nation to the lost Victorian gospel of Work and Sacrifice". Production targets were demanded of industry; employees were made aware that seeking higher wages was selfish; the country was taught to realise that it was "living on tick" until exports improved.

Not all of life, though, was grim. As another eminent historian, Arthur Marwick, has explained: "Britain lay in a crepuscular zone with the shadows of night as firm upon the landscape as the heartening hints of the rising sun ... tracts of London, Merseyside, the Midlands, Plymouth and Clydeside, and many historic towns besides, lay desolate. Yet in other areas new factories, new roads, new bridges gave an air of bustle and prosperity which had been lacking for a generation." The basic economic reality was that even after the depredations of war British people were still better off than any in the world except those of the USA, Canada and neutral Sweden and Switzerland.

Leisure activities provided some solace from the humdrum of everyday life, and more so than at any other time in Britain's history. That finest of cricket writers, Neville Cardus, seems to have caught the stoic mood of the era perfectly in writing of one match: "I went to Lord's to see a pale-faced crowd, existing on rations, the rocket bomb still in the ears of most folk – to see this worn, dowdy crowd watching Compton. The strain of long years of anxiety and affliction passed from all hearts and shoulders at the sight of Compton in full flow, sending the ball here, there and everywhere, each stroke a flick of delight, a propulsion of happy, sane, healthy life. There was no rationing in an innings by Compton."

As with Denis Compton's batting, neither was there "rationing" of the bewildering footballing skills of Stanley Matthews nor of the remarkable running ability of the baggy-shorted, unassuming little Sydney Wooderson. Matthews made one of his many international appearances for England against Scotland at Hampden Park in April 1948, where there was a huge crowd, and he recalled of the pre-match ceremonies: "When Field Marshal Montgomery of Alamein stepped on to the pitch, 135,000 voices sounded like a million. The roar was deafening and continued for the best part of the presentation of the teams. Monty made a point of chatting to Tom Finney and Scotland's Willie Thornton, both of whom had served under the Field Marshal in the Eighth Army in North Africa."

England played 24 wartime matches against Scotland or Wales, and no doubt the 5-3 home win at Wembley in 1943, in particular, brought much-needed pleasure to the massed crowd at a particularly depressing juncture of the war. At the White City Stadium, in London, in August of 1945, Wooderson had taken on one of the great Swedes, Arne Andersson, in a mile race, when 50,000 packed the stands and thousands more were locked out. Andersson's illustrious compatriot, Gunder Hägg, resumed acquaintance at that same meeting in a two-mile race with Doug Wilson, his Hyde Park training companion of two years previously.

The hunger for sport was insatiable, and this was long before the era of armchair viewing. That hunger was sated by competing in sport or actually going to watch it, not staying at home for it to be served up on the small screen. Sport simply was not available in that form. Television was still in its infancy in Britain and when the BBC's Director of Outside Broadcasts started to draw up his budget in 1947 for the next year's Olympic Games, recognised as the most important event to have been covered by television to that date, it was in the knowledge that, according to the Radio Industries Council, there might be only 80,000 or so sets to receive the pictures and the commentary. As the eventual cost for the 64 hours and 27 minutes of programmes was some £180,000, and the estimated number of viewers was half-a-million or so, the BBC could be said to have paid dearly for their output.

Every sports stadium and ground in the country was packed. On a single April day in London in 1948 "some 100,000" were at the FA Cup Final at Wembley, while another 23,000 were at Twickenham for the annual seven-a-side rugby union tournament, and 5,000 at Park Royal for an England v USA women's hockey match. Also that afternoon five London football clubs – Chelsea, Crystal Palace, Queen's Park Rangers, Tottenham Hotspur and West Ham United – were playing at home to thronged terraces. The week before, the Amateur Cup final between Leytonstone and Barnet had drawn 59,605 people to Stamford Bridge. Later that month "as many people as could be squeezed into the ground" were at Worcester to see the Australian cricketers begin their tour (having brought with them 200 cases of tinned meat as a gift to the British people) and Don Bradman make a century. The 83,260 crowd at the Manchester United v Arsenal match of 17 January 1948 remains a League record to this day.

On 1 May, some 92,000 people – most of them presumably Northerners on a day excursion, apart from King George VI and Queen Elizabeth in the guest-box – saw Wigan win the Rugby League Cup final at Wembley. The same week there were 10,000 who cheered on the boxers in the ABA finals and on 15 May there were 16,000 who were privileged to be at Southend when the Australian batsmen scored 721 against Essex, and Bradman, as was his habit, made another century. Oh, yes, and there were another 25,000 at the Yorkshire–Lancashire cricket match that day, 25,000 for Middlesex v Sussex, and 20,000 for Notts v Surrey.

One good reason for all this enthusiasm was that there was not a great deal else on which to spend money. Cars, petrol, housing, clothing, food and other consumable goods were all severely rationed and in some cases almost unobtainable. So entertainment, at the cinema as well as on the sporting field, was the outlet for people who had "six years of grief, boredom, frustration and slaughter to make up for", as the historian, Paul Addison, expressed it. Even so, there were to remain doubts about the attractiveness of the Olympic Games for the British public until the Games themselves actually began.

This anomaly was to be explained by Norman Baker, who in 1994 published a study entitled *Olympics or Tests: The Disposition of the British Sporting Public, 1948*. The "Tests" in question were those to be played by England against the visiting Australian cricketers, and Baker wrote: "Tests with Australia were part of the so very attractive familiar routine of 'domestic' sporting competition. The Olympics were simply not seen in comparable terms. They were not part of that routine, that familiar pattern. They were an international event staged in Britain, not a British event. Impressive and attractive though they might be once they actually arrived before the British public, the Olympics were not relished in anticipation by the majority of sports followers in Britain."

The more imponderable factor was the international political situation. This year of 1948 was the start of the "Cold War". In June of 1947 the US Secretary of State, General George Marshall, had unveiled plans for a recovery programme which would entail $12,500 million-worth of aid to 16 countries in Western Europe. The USSR, which had already had close control of Poland and Rumania since 1945, began to seal up what Churchill had so chillingly described as the "Iron Curtain" and access to Berlin was closed off by Soviet troops on 24 June 1948. The "Berlin Airlift" began soon after, flying in tons of goods each day in American and British transport planes to service the city. In Czechoslovakia there had been a Communist coup in February.

Apart from all the economic and political crises which faced the Games organisers, including a national newspaper campaign during 1947 to have the Games cancelled altogether, there were some delicate matters of public relations to be considered. How were the visiting competitors and spectators to be treated? The prospect of substantial revenue from the influx of tourists was a major reason for continuing Government support, but what would be the reaction of the local populace? As Norman Baker has explained: "The rationing of food and a critical shortage of housing persisted for much longer after the war than had been anticipated and thus became the objects of a volatile public debate. To accord too much privilege for foreign visitors would garner hostility from an austerity-stricken British public. On the other hand, to expose competitors to the full rigours of post-war British life would surely provoke international controversy."

Thus ideas for an "Olympic village" were abandoned and competitors were put up in existing military barracks, colleges and schools. They were given the same extra rations available for workers in heavy industry and allowed to bring their own provisions. Because of currency restrictions, many European visitors could not afford the hotel accommodation available, but there was a good response to an appeal by the organisers to householders to provide low-cost bed and breakfast.

The Royal Air Force barracks at Uxbridge and West Drayton and an ex-Army convalescent encampment in Richmond Park would house some 3,900 competitors and officials. Middlesex County Council made available classrooms in 18 of their schools for temporary conversion into men's dormitories. Three private colleges were opened up for women. Room also had to be found for 200 equestrian competitors at Camberley and for 400 yachtsmen in Torquay. The Henley oarsmen were put up in schools in Henley itself and in High Wycombe and the women canoeists in relative splendour at a Henley hotel.

The weekly ration available to the British public consisted per person of one ounce (28gm) of bacon, eight ounces (226gm) of sugar, two ounces (56gm) of tea, two ounces of cheese, 13 ounces (368gm) of meat, seven ounces (198gm) of butter or margarine, 2½ pints (1.2lt) of milk, four ounces (113gm) of preserves, four ounces of sweets, 63 ounces (1,786gm) of bread and one egg. Recognising that this would hardly sustain the Olympic visitors, help was sought from abroad, and among the contributions gratefully received were 100 tons (100,000kg) of fresh fruit and vegetables from Holland, 160,000 eggs from Denmark and 20,000 bottles of mineral water from Czechoslovakia. No doubt some Britons wondered how such countries, which had also been involved in the war, had such largesse to spare.

Very late in the day, a financial problem loomed when large numbers of cancellations of bookings, said to be as much as £120,000-worth, flooded in from the USA, mostly because of the deteriorating political situation in Berlin, with its distinct threat of war against the USSR. Tickets totalling 2¼ million had been printed, with half of them going abroad, but the boxing and swimming finals had already sold out by the end of June and the Amateur Athletic Association reported that its allocation had been oversubscribed by 158,000 applications. Nearer the start of the Games as many as 13,000 athletics tickets were available for some days, but in the end the estimated attendance for the eight days of competition on the track at Wembley was 668,000, to all intents and purposes a complete sell-out. Where the tourists failed to come, the locals happily took their seats.

The IOC had meanwhile been grappling with the thorny issue of who exactly was to be invited to the Games. The USSR, which had yet to compete at an Olympic Games, had been fulsomely encouraged by the IOC to set up an Olympic Committee, the only means by which it could become eligible to take part, but declined to do so and would therefore be absent. Whether this was a purely political decision or a tactical one – deeming that Soviet sportsmen and sportswomen were not yet ready to take on (and beat) the world – can only be guessed at, though there are accounts that the Soviet leader, Stalin, was prepared to sanction entry of a team but that when he called together the nation's sports leaders and they were unable to assure him of victory across the board he decided to wait until 1952. Whatever the reason, the boycott was inconsistent with the fact that a USSR athletics team had been generously welcomed to Oslo for the 1946 European Championships, though actually ineligible to take part because they were not affiliated to the International Amateur Athletic Federation, and had significantly won five of the eight women's titles on offer. Soviet weightlifters and wrestlers had also won international titles during 1946 and 1947.

Germany and Japan would not be asked, though their Olympic Committees were said by each country to be restored, and the influential Avery Brundage, for one, had voiced the opinion, if only in passing, that both countries ought to be included. It could hardly be said that the IOC acted unconstitutionally in this matter, for the simple reason that there appeared to be no constitution to break. The October 1946 bulletin of the IOC listed two members from Germany and three from Japan, and there was even a representative of Lithuania, now absorbed into the USSR, who was living in exile in Germany. The list of National Olympic Committees also included Germany and Japan, though no addresses were given. An application from a newly-formed Lithuanian committee "in exile in England", which must have been submitted more in hope than expectation, was refused in 1947, and before the end of the year the IOC announced brusquely, and with some disregard for simple grammar: "Invitations will be sent out by the Organising Committee to participate in the 1948 Games early in the New Year. Germany and Japan will not be included."

Some international sporting relations had very quickly been re-established with Germany, and the British record for the javelin had been broken twice in meetings in Cologne and Düsseldorf in September 1945 by a London policeman, Denis Jacobs, who was on secondment duty. Then, in 1947, a combined Oxford and Cambridge Universities athletics team made a tour, competing against a German Universities selection, among others. The case for the Japanese was less tenable. Edström was perversely pressing for their inclusion, presumably oblivious to the idea that the presence of Japanese competitors in London after the treatment which their country had meted out to Allied prisoners-of-war would certainly not have been wholeheartedly welcomed by the British public.

Austria, Hungary and Italy – all of whom had been enemies of the Allies for all or part of the war – were found to be acceptable. So, too, were Portugal, Spain, Sweden, Switzerland and Turkey, which as neutral countries had supplied materials to the Germans. Rumania declined the invitation, presumably under Soviet pressure. Israel, which had declared its independence from Palestine in May of 1948, was denied entry because of the lack of an Olympic Committee, which conveniently avoided upsetting the Arab nations. Another minor dispute – though not so minor for the competitors affected – concerned the team from what was then called Eire, which included members of the internationally unrecognised National Athletic & Cycling Association of Ireland, who were not allowed to compete. Some of the Irish competitors withdrew in protest at the ban on their team-mates.

The Israeli request was debated long and hard as late as the executive committee meeting of the International Olympic Committee in London on 26 July, three days before the Games were to officially open, and the very fact that there was so much discussion of the matter is significant in itself. There should have been no need for any lengthy deliberations. "No National Olympic Committee, no Games place" was the IOC's hard-and-fast rule, but their description of the Israeli application as "a demonstration of political propaganda", and their dismissal of the alleged presence of two would-be women competitors in London as "no more than a pretext", smacks of being a pretext in its own right.

Among the most poignant ironies of all this political manoeuvring were the starkly contrasting experiences of two javelin-throwers, Herma Bauma and Janis Stendzenieks. Bauma was an Austrian woman but was the official holder of the German record, as Austria had been annexed in 1938 by Germany, and would be able to compete in London (and would win the gold medal). Stendzenieks was a Latvian refugee (or "displaced person", as he and the nine million other Europeans then in the same predicament were euphemistically known) living in exile in Lincoln, but was barred, though he could have won the men's javelin (and was actually in the stadium to see the title taken with a distance considerably less than he had achieved earlier in the summer). In athletics alone there were at least 40 potential medallists – even potential winners in a number of cases, such as Stendzenieks – who were thus excluded from the Games.

So far as those who were going to run the Games were concerned – as opposed, of course, to running in them – the choices of Viscount Portal of Laverstoke DSO MVO as president and Lord Burghley as chairman of the organising committee were logical enough. Since 1936 Viscount Portal had been president of the British Olympic Association (BOA) and Lord Burghley chairman of its council. The Organising Committee, a nucleus of which had met as early as March of 1946 under Lord Burghley's chairmanship, also included Lord Aberdare and Sir Noel Curtis-Bennett, who had been IOC members since 1929 and 1933 respectively. All of them had served under Viscount Portal's chairmanship on the "Investigating Committee for the 1944 Olympic Games" which had first met in December 1938; so their planning processes had something of a head start.

Other members of the Organising Committee were Jack Beresford, CB Cowley, Alderman Harold Fern OBE JP, Ernest Holt OBE, John Eaton Griffith CBE, Colonel Evan A Hunter OBE, J Emrys Lloyd OBE, CJ Patteson CMG, Arthur Porritt CBE FRCS, Stanley Rous CBE and RB Studdert, and there was a wealth of administrative experience among their numbers.

Beresford was the legendary oarsman who had won five Olympic medals, including three golds. Cowley was an executive of the London Press & Advertising Agency. Alderman Fern had been honorary secretary of the Amateur Swimming Association since 1921 (and of the Southern Counties' ASA for 16 years prior to that appointment). Holt had become honorary treasurer of the BOA in 1946, having held the same post and then that of honorary secretary of the Amateur Athletic Association from 1932 to 1947. Eaton Griffith had less obvious credentials as a vice-president of the International Lawn Tennis Association but was the Government's nominee, having served as chairman of the European Coal Organisation until its dissolution at the end of 1947. Colonel Hunter had been secretary of the BOA since 1925.

Emrys Lloyd, the committee's legal adviser, was in the unique position of also being a competitor, having taken part in fencing in the 1932 and 1936 Games and being selected again not only for the 1948 events but as the team's flag-bearer at the opening ceremony. Patteson was a Canadian IOC member who was an executive of the Canadian Pacific Railway Company working in London. Porritt, the Olympic 100 metres bronze-medallist for New Zealand in 1924 and an IOC member since 1934, was now the King's Surgeon. Rous had been secretary of the Football Association since 1934, in which capacity he had, bizarrely, attended a match in which neutral Sweden had hosted German-occupied Denmark in 1943. Studdert was managing director of the Army & Navy department-store chain which would provide much-needed office space.

The Great Britain team's commandant was to be Lieutenant-General Sir Frederick Browning KBE CB DSO, Comptroller of the Household of Her Royal Highness Princess Elizabeth, who had been Chief of Staff to Lord Mountbatten and Military Secretary to the War Office, and was married to the novelist, Daphne du Maurier. He had served in action throughout the war and was responsible for the unforgettable remark to Field Marshal Montgomery concerning the airborne landings, "But, sir, I think we may be going a bridge too far". A much more egalitarian note was struck by the choice as athletics team captain of another seasoned campaigner, as this was Bill Roberts, a self-made man from industrial Salford who had won a 4x400 metres relay gold medal in Berlin and then served in the "other ranks" as an aircraft fitter with the RAF during the war.

From the outset in 1946 the Organising Committee was in favour of Wembley Stadium as the main venue – particularly for the athletics events, but also for football, gymnastics, hockey and showjumping, plus boxing and swimming in the Empire Pool Arena and fencing in the Palace of Engineering, which were both adjoining – rather than the White City Stadium at Shepherd's Bush, though the latter's proprietors were invited to submit their bid and duly did so. This preference for Wembley might, on the face of it, seem surprising because the White City had the weight of history on its side, and not to say a ready-made track, though its cinder surface was regarded as notoriously slow, and had been the venue for the previous London-organised Olympics of 1908. When the 1934 British Empire Games had been staged in London, the athletics events had been held at the White City and the boxing and swimming at the Empire Pool.

The annual Amateur Athletic Association (AAA) Championships – which were, in effect, a championships of England open to the world – had moved from another London venue, Stamford Bridge, to the White City in 1932 after the track had been refurbished. International two-a-side matches were regarded from the 1920s onwards (and even into the 1960s) as the major fixtures of the season outside the quadrennial Olympics, European Championships and British Empire Games, and Great Britain had competed against France at the White City in 1933, 1935, 1938, and again in 1946, against Germany in 1933 and 1937, and against Norway in 1938. The traditional post-Olympic British Empire v USA match had taken place there in 1936, and the vast crowd which gathered that day to see Jesse Owens and Britain's 4x400 metres relay heroes was said to have numbered 93,000.

Wembley Stadium, of course, had its own legacy of high-level sporting achievement. It had been built in 300 days at a cost of £750,000 for the British Empire Exhibition of 1924. The first turf had been cut by the Duke of York (later King George VI) in January of 1922 and the facilities were ready just in time (four days before, to be exact) for the famous 1923 FA Cup Final for which some 250,000 people turned up and the official attendance was 126,047, many of them spilling on to the pitch and holding up play before they were nudged back by police horses including the most noticeable, a white horse called Billy, ridden by PC George Scorey.

FA Cup finals had been played there ever since, as had England's home matches against Scotland, though not the fixtures with Ireland or Wales. Numerous other sports, particularly weekly greyhound-racing and speedway-racing, had been held there. There had been 90,000 in the stadium for an England v Scotland football match in October of 1944 (almost the very same time when thoughts of a 1948 Olympics were beginning to stir). There were more than 60,000 members of the Wembley speedway supporters' club and 85,000 watched one match against West Ham. Such was the earning power of Wembley Stadium that the 1948 Olympic organisers were to pay the owners £92,500 (equivalent to some £6 million in 21st-century values) in compensation for lost revenue while the track was built and the athletics events took place. Despite these honourable credentials, the reason for Wembley's preferment can be credited to one man.

That man was Arthur Elvin, managing director of the stadium company since 1927, whose overtures to the Games' organising committee were so effective that by January of 1948 he had become Sir Arthur Elvin and had been appointed to the General Purpose Committee, also chaired by Viscount Portal. His conversion of the Games decision-makers to his cause had not been an overnight sensation; far from it, he had cannily established relations with the BOA as early as 1937, and when the IOC held its 1939 Congress in London, which was to be the last for seven years, Elvin put on an evening of dinner and entertainment at the stadium for the delegates. No doubt, the honoured guests gazed down that June evening from the comfortable hospitality boxes which usually housed well-heeled greyhound-racing pundits and were duly impressed by the greensward spread below them, upon which 7,000 members of the Women's League of Health and Beauty, under the direction of Prunella Douglas-Hamilton, were putting on a display described as being "filled with whirling, leaping and dancing figures – a joyous sight for all present". The IOC members were also treated at Wembley to an indoor ice-skating exhibition by Britain's European champions, Cecilia Colledge and Graham Sharp, and by six-year-old Jennifer Nicks, who would herself become an Olympic competitor in 1948 and 1952.

The entire Congress "was pervaded by an atmosphere of hospitality", according to the report by a German member, Carl Diem, in the IOC bulletin of July 1939. The delegates had also attended the Aldershot Military Tattoo, the King's birthday parade along Whitehall, and official dinners put on by Viscount Portal, the British Olympic Association and the Foreign Office. Ironically, there was a cinder track buried beneath the ground at Wembley which had only had brief usage soon after the stadium had opened.

It was, in fact, only because of Elvin's acute sense of a business opportunity that Wembley remained available as a potential Olympic venue. His first humble involvement had been as a tobacco-kiosk manager at the British Empire Exhibition who had then bought up other sales franchises on the site. After the exhibition closed in 1925 the stadium was little used and run-down and the owners bankrupt, but Elvin saw a business opportunity and bought the property for a bargain price of £150,000 in 1927 with one intention in mind – to stage greyhound-racing. This sport had been invented in the USA in 1890 and had been introduced with some success at Belle Vue, in Manchester, in 1926, and Elvin had decided that there was a profitable future in it. He raised capital of £230,000, of which £180,000 was from public subscription, spent £100,000 on a track, car parking and access roads, and was ready to stage the first meeting by 10 December of that same year of 1927.

To Elvin's delight, and that of his backers, 90,000 people turned up for the opening venture and liked what they saw. Within five months Elvin and his Wembley Stadium Ltd had recouped its investment and was making money. There is no need to go into any great detail about why greyhound-racing became so popular, other than to say that it was a sport for the masses, more readily accessible and cheaper than horse-racing and which provided more comfortable spectating than football. Meetings three times a week attracted regular crowds of 80,000, and Wembley was saved. The British sports historian, Mike Cronin, who has made a study of the subject, has concluded that, but for the dogs, "the stadium would have been torn down in the late 1920s".

As Sir Arthur Elvin's work staff were digging deep, and he was digging into his own pocket to pay for a £120,000 pedestrian promenade from the nearest underground railway station to the stadium gates, the general economic situation in Britain was further worsened by the appalling weather. The winter of 1946–47 was the harshest for 50 years, with much of the country snow-covered from December to March, and the situation was described bleakly by the historian, LCB Seaman: "These four months of meteorological misery were marked by something like complete industrial breakdown. Factories had to shut through lack of coal, and by early February two million men were out of work. In December coal supplies to factories were cut by 50 per cent. In February coal supplies were stopped altogether for all industrial users in the South-East, the Midlands and North-West, and it became an offence to use electricity in the home between 9 a.m. and midday, and 2 p.m. and 4 p.m."

Britons, whose basic needs such as housing, clothing, bread, potatoes, fruit and vegetables were in desperately short supply, could well have been forgiven for thinking "we fought a war for this?". A splendidly entertaining anecdote of particular relevance is to be found in the autobiography of the singer, artist and bon viveur, the late George Melly, serving in the Royal Navy in 1946, whose ship was sent to Copenhagen for a courtesy visit. He recalled of one meal supplied by their hosts: "There was tray upon tray of Danish pastries and cakes bursting with real cream. How can this be, I asked myself, as I wolfed down a second plate. Denmark was occupied and we weren't, and yet only a year after the end of the war they've got all the cream cakes they want, and we've still got butter rationing. It was a question we were to ask ourselves for several years to come." The inimitable Melly was not the sporting type, in any polite drawing-room sense of the term, but maybe even Britons of a sports-minded nature could have been forgiven for thinking that contemplating inviting the world to an Olympic Games in such frugal times was an extravagance bordering on madness.

"Madness" was not a concept which Viscount Portal and his committee colleagues would have entertained as they dutifully made their plans and juggled their figures. The Government had made it clear from its first approval of the Games project in 1945 that no money would be forthcoming from them to meet the costs, which eventually amounted to some £760,000 – the equivalent of £77 million in 21st-century monetary values – but this was not without its humorous aspect. The predecessor to Sir Stafford Cripps as the Labour Government's Chancellor of the Exchequer had been Hugh Dalton (more formally, Edward Hugh John Neale Dalton, later Baron Dalton of Forest and Frith in the County Palatinate of Durham), who had been educated at Eton and King's College, Cambridge, and he was later to recall in his diary the following tale of what he called, presumably tongue-in-cheek, "a new declaration of Government policy which I made on the Olympics".

He wrote: "I had been informed by the President of CUBC (Cambridge University Boat Club), who had the great sense to belong to my old college, that in the Olympics the Boat Crews would have to row in old British boats with old British oars against foreign crews in new British-built boats with new British-built oars ... I was, however, very glad to inform them that that very day before leaving London I had been in touch with the Admiralty, as well as with the Secretary of State for Air, who was not only an old King's man and an old President of the Union but also an old Olympic captain, and I was able now to say that the Admiralty would give special consideration to providing, as a most exceptional case, suitable boats and oars for the British crews in the Olympics."

Whether, in fact, the Admiralty was ever able to fulfill this promise is not recorded, but if they did so it was not without its reward. As will be related in due course, the rowing events at the Games were to make a very considerable contribution to the British team's efforts. With a Viscount at the helm, and a Socialist Chancellor to assist who could draw on such a valued old boys' network, the Games were surely in good hands. Now it was time for those Games to begin, however austere they might be on the sidelines.

The Olympic historian, Ernest A Bland, writing early in 1948, caught the doughty mood of the capital: "The face of London has greatly changed in the 40 years which have elapsed since last the Olympiad was held in this country. In fact, in no such period of her long and illustrious history has it changed so much, except, perhaps, when smitten by the Great Fire and the Plague. She stands now, stained and untidy, having gone through two major wars and several economic crises. But her voice, as personified in Big Ben, has not been silenced, and it calls with courage a gallant welcome to some five thousand athletes and maybe a quarter-of-a-million of their followers. They may not see her in festival dress. They may have to scrum for their food. They may find a tight pack in their hotels. But they will come!"

On the track, the pitches, river and sea, and in the covered arenas, the competitors – of whom there would actually be some 4,000 or so from 59 countries – would ensure that there was nothing "austere" in their endeavours. Baron de Coubertin, founding father of the Modern Games, had died in 1937, but hopefully his spirit would prevail. In 1906 he had proclaimed: "The Olympic Games are not just an ordinary world championship but a quadrennial festival of universal youth; 'the springtime of mankind', a festival of supreme efforts, multiple ambitions, and all forms of youthful activity celebrated by each succeeding generation." A festival of supreme efforts is just what the Games of 1948 gave full promise of being.

Chapter 2

LET THE GAMES BEGIN

But where is "poor little Sydney"?

THE LEADER ARTICLE in *The Times* of Wednesday 28 July, the day before the Games were to open, loftily turned its attention to the burning (in the literal sense) issue of the moment: "Even among those who have not become, to use an almost unavoidable phrase, Olympic-minded, there is one event in the Games which has captured the imagination – the carrying of the lighted torch from distant Olympia to the Stadium at Wembley." Then the article concluded emphatically, "Nearly everyone knows the runner they would like to see." No name needed to be mentioned because the man in question was the nationally renowned Sydney Wooderson, who had set world records for 800 metres, 880 yards and the mile before the war and had additionally performed the remarkable feat of winning the European Championships 1500 metres in 1938 and the 5000 metres – in the only race of his career at the distance – eight years later.

Wooderson had retired from track competition after 1946 but was still one of the fittest men in the country at the age of 33, as evidenced by the fact that only the previous March he had won the National cross-country title over a gruelling hilly course of 10 miles in length at Graves Park, in Sheffield. There was no doubting his credentials and his aptitude for the task, but unfortunately for him there were other considerations which were kept secret – and, worse than that, he was to receive the shabbiest of treatment at the hands of organising committee members who otherwise had carried out as exemplary a task in the lead-up to the Games as could be hoped for. The bald facts are that Wooderson was told beforehand that he would be the final bearer of the torch into the stadium and would light the flame. He arrived on the day fully expecting to carry out the privileged task, only to be then informed that he was not wanted and someone else would take his place.

This was no last-minute decision. The choice of torch-bearer was supposed to be a secret, and even the immediate family of Commander Bill Collins, who had brilliantly organised the 3,590-man relay from the ancient kindling site at Olympia, in Greece, did not know until the day of the Opening Ceremony. Others certainly were aware, because Ernest Holt, on behalf of the Games organising committee, had written to the chosen man on 7 July, giving him detailed instructions as to what to wear: "You should be attired in white, and I would suggest that you use lightweight rubber shoes, spikes not being necessary. The pace round the Stadium would be moderate without being too fast or too slow. It is all part of the 'play' and will require a certain amount of acting to make it effective. Collins will no doubt have discussed this with you, and if you would turn up one Sunday morning at Motspur Park you and I could discuss it further."

The recipient of the letter was an athlete whose abilities, though respectable, were far inferior to those of Wooderson. He was John Mark, a quarter-miler who the previous Autumn had been listed among the 13 "possibles" for Olympic selection at 400 metres and the 4x400 metres relay but had not shown the form during the 1948 season to merit being in the team. What he did have in his favour, as it transpired, was that he was tall and blond. He was also president of the Cambridge University Athletic Club, and as Lord Burghley – who may well have been influential in the choice – had occupied the same post 20 years before, this could only have stood Mark in good stead. The charm of Wooderson, as everyone knew, was that he was unassuming, bespectacled and diminutive off the track, but as soon as he stepped on to it he ran like a demon. The brave little solicitor's clerk from Blackheath Harriers had cruelly been passed up at the last moment for an Adonis. Even the reserve was a future Cambridge man, Angus Scott, who at least was a rather better runner than Mark and was to take part in the 1952 Olympic 400 metres hurdles.

Wooderson's biographer, David Thurlow, has delved into the matter in great depth and has discovered from Commander Collins's papers that a search had been going on for a tall and blond athlete since at least April of 1948, though there is no clue as to who was responsible in the first place for the decision that this was the type of man most suitable for the occasion. Various candidates who were said to fit the bill as regards tallness and blondness had been suggested but had been found wanting, and the Games organising committee eventually agreed at their meeting of 24 June to make an approach to Mark "subject to him not being included in the British team". The issue was resolved eight days later when Mark was eliminated in the heats of the 440 yards at the AAA Championships, which acted as Olympic trials, and by 6 July he had agreed to carry the torch.

How heartless it was of the organisers that Wooderson was not told then that they had changed their minds. Characteristic of Wooderson's self-effacedness, it was not until more than half a century later, in a discussion with David Thurlow, that Wooderson mentioned the subject, and as he was then approaching his 92nd birthday it was understandable that he was unable to remember with whom he had had the relevant conversations, though he believed that it was Lord Burghley and Commander Collins. Wooderson died in 2006.

While Wooderson was kept in the dark, others were in the know. Harold Abrahams was one of the bastions of British athletics; an historic winner of the 100 metres at the 1924 Olympics, AAA committee member since 1926, co-founder of the British Amateur Athletic Board in 1931 and honorary treasurer since 1946, IAAF delegate since 1934, prolific radio broadcaster and newspaper columnist – and another Cambridge man. He had also been appointed assistant manager for the Great Britain athletics team at Wembley, but this responsibility did not preclude him (or, for that matter, the senior team manager, Jack Crump) from voicing his opinions in print right up to the eve of the Games, and during and after them, and in one preview article he wrote puckishly of the torch-bearer's "secret" identity, "I do not think I shall be far short of the mark in suggesting that he will be some runner who might at one time have been included in Great Britain's team". It is doubtful whether there were many astute readers, however knowledgeable they may have been about athletics, who would have been alerted by the play on the word "mark". Mark had run his best 440 yards of the year on 10 July at Motspur Park – where, irony of ironies, Wooderson had set his pre-war world records – but even by the modest standards of British quarter-miling in 1948 a time of 49.4sec did not merit any headline attention.

The game was at last thoroughly given away when The Rt Hon Philip Noel Baker MP, Secretary of State for Commonwealth Relations, contributed an article entitled "The Olympic Games In Perspective" to the BOA's Official Report, published later in 1948 by the highly-regarded monthly magazine *World Sports*, their official organ. Noel Baker's specific qualification for writing was that he had run in the Games of 1912 and 1920, when he won a silver medal as team captain. Even more admirably, he was also to become in 1959 the only Olympian to be awarded the Nobel Peace Prize. Noel Baker wrote of John Mark that he appeared in the stadium "tall and handsome like a young Greek god". It should be noted that Noel Baker had also attended Cambridge University, and he had been the Government's Air Secretary who had been approached by his fellow-minister, Hugh Dalton, on the college old boys' network regarding the provision of new boats for the British rowing team.

No press report of the opening ceremony made any reference to Wooderson's absence – not even in *The Times* – but then the media of that era was far less inclined to enter into controversy, particularly after a day's joyous celebrations which were of such importance to British self-esteem, of which the historian, Correlli Barnett, was to be of rather sharper opinion in his evaluation: "Their beliefs and myths about themselves as a nation were the misleading products of romantic historical nostalgia and unshakeable self-satisfaction." In the purely sporting context, a future much-respected athletics correspondent of *The Times*, Neil Allen, still a teenager in 1948, hit the nail on the head when he wrote almost 50 years later: "For me, deliberately choosing so-called Greek-god figures for an

Olympic opening ceremony smacks far too much of a Berlin ubermensch feast for the propaganda lens of a Leni Riefenstahl, but then having once been privileged to have shaken the hand of diminutive heroes like Stanley Matthews, Gordon Richards and Jimmy Wilde, I wouldn't have picked any of them to decorate an heroic frieze at the Acropolis either." Neil Allen makes a further telling point which shows up the Olympic organisers of 1948 in a poor light compared with their Finnish successors: "I can never forget what happened four years later in Helsinki when a rotund balding 55-year-old trotted round the track and the capacity crowd bellowed the immortal name of Paavo Nurmi, Finland's track hero as Sydney Wooderson was ours."

Maybe in the throes of their euphoria, the press and public in that August month of 1948 could be excused for not associating Mark's appearance with that of the German 1500 metres runner who had brought the torch into Berlin's Olympic Stadium 12 years before and who was the very personification of the Aryan ideal, but the knowledge of hindsight leaves a bitter taste in the mouth. It is astonishing that the Games organisers, all of them staunch defenders of the establishment faith, should have taken as their model an image created by the country against which they had been fighting for six years and which had been brought to universal attention by Fräulein Riefenstahl's dramatic but disturbing film of those Nazi-traduced Games. Even so, it was perhaps realistic of Queen Elizabeth (later the Queen Mother) to say, as she is reputed to have done, when she was told of the choice of John Mark, "Of course, we couldn't have had poor little Sydney doing it". Mark, who became a doctor and practised in Hampshire, died in 1991, unacknowledged by the sporting press, having kept his thoughts on the torch business to himself for a lifetime.

Commander Collins's organisational efficiency had ensured safe passage to Britain of the torch on its 3,160-kilometre journey, even through regions where a civil war was in process, and via Lausanne, where Madame la Baronne de Coubertin, widow of the founding figure of the Modern Olympics, presided over a ceremony of honour at his graveside. The single mishap of note occurred, embarrassingly, immediately on arrival on English soil. Half a minute after being brought ashore at Dover from the Royal Navy frigate, HMS *Bicester*, the torch flickered out and remained unlit for as much as three minutes. Whether or not the hapless bearer at that time, a Chief Petty Officer Herbert Barnes, was clapped in irons for the misdemeanour has not been recorded, but once the torch was re-lit the relay proceeded without a hitch through packed and enthralled crowds from then on.

One of the bearers as it reached the streets of South London was a former Scottish cross-country international, Alick Pirie, a stalwart of the local Harriers club, who was accompanied by his 17-year-old son, whose experience of running then had most notably included school cross-country races as enemy aircraft flew overhead. More than a dozen years later, after a tempestuous career as a world record-breaker and Olympic medallist in constant conflict with authority,

Gordon Pirie was to recall passionately: "As I waited that sunny morning so long ago I shook with excitement. Then, when my father put the torch into my hand, as if symbolically passing on the great spirit of a champion to the next generation, I was surprised to find it was hot. I ran through the cheering crowds at Reigate, Surrey, and the flame seemed to draw my very soul on to the start of a great journey down the years. It was the start, too, of a personal crusade to make British athletics match up to the best in the world."

So the torch eventually arrived at Wembley Stadium, borne aloft by J W E Mark, whose diet had been fortified, incidentally, by food parcels sent from Greymouth, in New Zealand, the home town of the Oxford-educated New Zealand hero of the Berlin Olympics, Jack Lovelock. It is doubtful whether more than a very few of the 84,000 crowd recognised Mark when he strode on to the track – other than the organising committee members, who needed no telling, and maybe a few of his fellow medical students at St Mary's Hospital who had irreverently mocked him in the weeks before by trotting round him with flickering cigarette-lighters held on high and had now come along to see the real thing. What was of more importance even than Sydney Wooderson's feelings as he watched from the stadium seat which he had paid for himself was that everything passed off right – and it did. Philip Noel Baker, writing for the official report, might have been expected to see the best in the occasion, but there is no doubting the heartfelt enthusiasm of his reaction to Mark's appearance:

"No one who saw it will forget that thrilling spectacle. The Stadium, perfect in proportion, its green turf encircled by the smooth red track; its rising tiers gay with the suffused colours of the 80,000 people in their summer clothes; the teams in white, red, green and blue lined up across the centre; the massed bands in scarlet, the choirs in white behind; 7,000 pigeons filling the great arena with the beating of their wings and the flickering of their shadows on the ground. It was to this moving scene that the torch-bearer came. Tall and handsome like a young Greek god, he stood for a moment in the sunshine, held the torch aloft to salute the concourse, then ran in perfect rhythm round the track, saluted again, and lit the Flame in the bowl where day and night it burned until the Games were done."

Newspapermen in their more immediate reports for the following day's editions were moved to similar lyricism. John Macadam, a bombastic columnist for the *Daily Express*, which unashamedly described itself on each day's front page as "The World's Greatest Newspaper", had earlier dismissed the prospect of the Games with the wearied observation of one who had seen it all: "So round it comes again – Olympiad! – with all the flag-waving and the houha and the squabbles." Yet the opening ceremony inspired him to express (no pun intended) a shade more optimism: "The applause rose to one of our most valued philosophies: that 6,000 athletes running and jumping together in regimented contest in some way advance the cause of peace. A solemn reflection: the fact that never yet has it proved even remotely right in no way spoils the blessed thought. The air was full of amity and brotherhood. I was so recently in Berlin, where those principles of love are not too strikingly in evidence. Maybe I am sour. However, if mankind can solve its frustrations by running and jumping and diving; if only just one of the world's bedevilments can be sorted out on the strictly physical level – why, nobody will be more full of astonished pleasure than I." His figure of 6,000 competitors was something of an overstatement, but there was no doubting the passion of his views.

James Cameron, also writing for the *Daily Express*, was as far-travelled and as sceptical as his colleague, Macadam, but still concluded: "Even the tired men and the cynics, wearied for years by false symbols and phoney goodwill talk, said: This must mean SOMETHING. Not much, not the Millennium, but something. You cannot usher 59 nations into an arena, make them mingle in a split-minute schedule, give them a common salutation, without something profitable emerging, big or little as it may be. The cheer-leaders may be labouring after a vain thing, but yesterday's Opening Ceremony gave one that momentary excitement, that perennial glimpse of co-operation, that passing feeling that men might one day succeed where States and Governments always fail."

Ian Coster, for the *Daily Mail*, was content to revel in the unaccustomed splendour of it all: "It was unreal, un-English, a scene of colour and light and warmth – specially warmth – with an India-like sun blazing down on the bright green turf and red-brown surround. London and the weather were putting on a supreme show. Banked round Wembley was massed humanity – countless men, women's summer frocks – all reduced to a shimmer of pastel shades. Wembley was a garden. The scarlet of the massed bands of the Guards was like a great bed of wallflowers and, back of them, the white frocks of the massed choirs were like a field of stocks." The front page of his newspaper carried a headline which could well have been made use of in wartime but now had an altogether more welcome meaning – "The Hour Has Struck".

The London correspondent of the *Manchester Guardian* was enraptured. "The scene inside the great stadium had a lightness and a delicacy that one has never before witnessed in England," he wrote. "Not a dark garment was to be seen except the morning coats of the Olympic committee-men. The stands were like a gigantic hanging garden of mixed stocks, whose colours were pastel-blue and pink." William D Clark, a feature writer for the Sunday newspaper, *The Observer*, commented wittily: "As our bus proceeded down the Harrow-road it did indeed seem that austerity had triumphed over any admonitions to put out more flags. The most festive sign on the route rather bleakly announced 'Welcome to the Olympic Games. This road is a danger area'. It was a surprise, then, to find that in spite of the lack of publicity or official blarings some 85,000 people had managed to hear the good news – or bush telegraph – and turn up at the Wembley Stadium."

Allison Danzig, an observant and urbane staff writer for the *New York Times*, provided a transatlantic perspective which cut incisively to the heart of the matter: "For the British, forgetting for the moment the pinch and plainness of their struggle for revival, it was an occasion comparable with other great pageants that stud their history. For weeks London had seemed cold and indifferent to the great spectacle being mounted in its midst. Ticket sales were slow. Newspapers had space for the test cricket and dog- and horse-racing, but little for the Olympics. Visiting correspondents were baffled by the aloofness and bungling of the British press relations staff. Liaison and co-operation were lacking between home and visiting officials. Few flags, pennants, bunting or window-dressing were to be seen in the city. It seemed that one of the worst flops in the history of the Games was in the making.

"But all of that proved misleading. It was the British way of doing things, of refusing to become excited or to be stampeded into anything smacking of hoopla. In the end the public showed it knew a good thing."

The message had been made clear. No hoopla, please, we're British!

Certainly no hoopla from His Majesty King George VI, Patron of the British Olympic Association, who was invited by the President of the IOC after the march-past of the competing countries to open the Games with the obligatory brief statement: "I proclaim open the Olympic Games of London celebrating the fourteenth Olympiad of the Modern Era." The Olympic Flag, with its five inter-laced rings of blue, yellow, black, green and red, representing the five Continents, which had been put to use for the first time at another hurriedly-organised post-war Games (those of Antwerp in 1920), was raised. The pigeons were released into the cloudless London sky. A salute of guns was fired. The Olympic Flame arrived and the "Sacred Olympic Fire" (the IOC's official description) was lit.

The Olympic Oath on behalf of all of the competitors was taken by Wing-Commander Don Finlay, who had won medals for the 110 metres hurdles at the 1932 and 1936 Games and would compete again in the next day or so at the age of 39. He stood ramrod-straight as one would expect, resplendent in his jaunty beret, blue blazer and white slacks, and pronounced: "We swear that we will take part in the Olympic Games in loyal competition, respecting the regulations which govern them and desirous of participating in them in the true spirit of sportsmanship, for the honour of our country and the glory of sport." The exhortation has remained, in essence, the same ever since.

The national anthem was played. The teams marched out. The Games could now begin.

The previous day in the House of Commons, the Prime Minister, Clement Attlee, had said of the tense situation sparked off by the Berlin Airlift that "the Government were fully determined to take any measure in defence of the realm which seemed necessary to meet the situation". Having attended the Olympic opening ceremony, he then departed on holiday to the west coast of Ireland to play golf. He was staying in a remote estate cottage but left instructions that a message could be taken on his behalf by telephone at the gatekeeper's lodge, if need be.

No one raised an eyebrow at such insouciance. No hoopla, please, we're British!

Chapter 3

YOUTH AND AGE

Wembley's wartime divide

THE COMPETITORS FROM the 59 nations who paraded round the Wembley track on the sweltering hot afternoon of the Opening Ceremony were, not to put too fine a point on it, a mixed bunch – a conglomeration of as yet inexperienced youngsters, who were the representatives of the first post-war sporting generation, and resilient survivors from pre-war years, who had picked up the pieces of their sporting lives and hoped now to achieve at the age of 30-plus at least some measure of what had been the high ambitions of their early 20s.

Of the British contingent of 313, twenty had competed in the 1936 Games – seven athletes, seven fencers, two wrestlers, an oarsman, a swimmer, a water-polo player and a yachtsman – and as between them they were to win two of Britain's three gold medals, plus a silver and a bronze, their contribution to the meagre 1948 haul was beyond value. The bronze-medallist road-walker, Tebbs Lloyd Johnson, had been competing since the early 1920s. Don Finlay, of course, had won hurdles medals at the two previous Games. The fencing captain, John Emrys Lloyd, had also been a competitor in 1932. The talents of others, like the sprinters, Dorothy Manley and Alastair McCorquodale, who won silver medals, and a 15-year-old, Elinor Gordon, who would go on to win a swimming bronze in 1952, had only surfaced (particularly apt for the last-named) a few months before the Games.

The configuration of most other countries was much the same. Among the USA's athletes were a 40-year-old marathon man, Johnny Kelley, who had also been in Berlin and would still be competing at the distance in 1975, and Henry Dreyer, who had won his first national title in 1935, though by now still no great age for a hammer-thrower at 36. Another of the many US track and field champions was a 17-year-old, Bob Mathias, who won the 10-event decathlon despite not having tackled the event for the first time until a month or so before.

In the women's foil fencing the gold medal would be taken by the 41-year-old Hungarian winner from 1936, Ilona Elek, and the bronze by the 36-year-old

Austrian winner from 1932, Ellen Müller-Preis, though both were far junior to Ivan Osiier, of Denmark. He had been born in 1888, eight years before the first Modern Olympics, had first competed in the Games in 1908, had won a silver medal at the 1912 Games, and was making a comeback at the age of 59. A Norwegian yachtsman, Magnus Konow, had also competed in the 1908 Games. Sven Thofelt, épée team bronze-medallist for Sweden (and modern pentathlon champion 20 years before), was aged 44. Yet Christian d'Oriola, one of the French gold-medallists in this sport where guile and longevity go hand-in-hand, was only 19. The average age of Finland's men's gymnastics team was 33, and the best of them was 40. A 12-year-old girl, Lisia Macchini, competed for Italy in this sport, and a 13-year-old girl, Talia Gonzalez, swam for Brazil.

The Games gold-medallists would range from a 56-year-old yachtsman, Paul Smart, of the USA, to a 17-year-old swimmer, Thelma Kalama, also of the USA, who was four months younger than Bob Mathias. Britain's medallists included a 17-year-old swimmer, Cathie Gibson, and among her team-mates in the pool was Norman Wainwright, exactly twice her age, who had won his first national title when Miss Gibson was aged two.

An act of faith translated into reality

The Times carried this report on the morning of Thursday 29 July.

"An act of faith on the part of a city and a country that have felt to the full the strains of war and the stringencies of peace will be translated into reality. The Olympic programme today branches off from the cinder track into the basket-ball field, the stretches of river where rowing eights can exercise themselves, the sea where yachts catch the breeze, and the ground on which Association football is played. Equestrian events establish a moral superiority over the chariot races which thrilled crowds beginning to confuse sports with circuses, bicycles climb and zoom to victory, canoes are paddled, and hockey teams bully off. White, red, yellow and black races compete, and it is charming to read that a team from Hawaii, where to pick a lotus would seem an intolerable strain, is to engage itself in the exacting task of lifting a weight."

There was not, of course, any team from Hawaii at the Games, because the chain of islands had been part of the USA since 1898, but the writer for *The Times* must surely have known that and was simply exercising his prerogative to employ poetic licence. Two members of the US weightlifting team were Hawaiian-born, and one of them, Harold Sakata, won a silver medal. His father was a Japanese immigrant and his mother was an American of Japanese origin, and he became much more famous in later life as the actor who played the role of "Oddjob" in the James Bond film, *Goldfinger*.

Chapter 4

THE PROSPECTS FOR SUCCESS

How many golds for Britain?

THE IMPRESSION FORMED by the correspondent of the *New York Times* that the British newspapers were giving little attention to the Games, even in the last few weeks leading up to their opening, was not a false one. Even so, this did not necessarily mean that there was a lack of interest on the part of the editors and their reporters in their offices ranged along London's Fleet Street. Newsprint factories were operating at only 35 per cent of their capacity because of the shortage of paper supplies, and such limited space as the sports writers had at their disposal was devoted, understandably, to what had happened the previous day, rather than to conjecture as to what might happen in the future. *The Times* carried only eight pages a day, with a profusion of worrying international crises taking precedence in their coverage.

There were, of course, other time-honoured sporting distractions in Britain that July to vie with the prospects for the forthcoming Olympic Games. Not least of them were the Australian cricketers, who as previously mentioned were drawing in huge crowds at every match as they despatched the efforts of weary English bowlers to all parts of the boundary and often way over it. Henry Cotton had won the Open golf championship for the third time, having previously done so in 1934 and 1937. Four days before the Games opened Freddie Mills beat Gus Lesnevich, of the USA, at the White City for the world light-heavyweight boxing title, and was the first Briton since 1905 to hold the title undisputed. Gordon Richards was in the process of becoming champion jockey for the 21st time since 1925. Two Americans, Bob Falkenburg and Louise Brough, won the singles titles at Wimbledon.

The preview by *The Times* on the morning of the first day of Olympic competition on Friday 30 July appeared only in the third column of the Sporting News in its broadsheet coverage. The first column was concerned with the England v Australia Fourth Test which had begun at Headingley the previous day and the second column with the scores in all the county matches which were taking place.

Athletics: "Do not expect Britain to win a lot of titles"

Despite the paper shortage, there were worthy attempts at producing comprehensive form-guides to the Games events some significant time in advance, though their contents often betrayed a lack of knowledge of what was happening in sport outside British shores. The best of them, containing a fine appreciation of what was going on elsewhere, was a compact 112-page handbook edited by the athletics correspondent of the London *Evening News*, Jack Oaten. He had a well-deserved reputation for sound judgement, and his preview of the athletics events struck exactly the right note of realism and cautious optimism.

"Much was heard during 1947, and no doubt will continue to be heard this year, about Britain's poor chances," he wrote. "There are plenty who consider our prospects of success very remote and think that we are foolish to challenge the world's best while still crippled, athletically speaking, as a result of the war. This is not a view to which those responsible for finding and preparing a British team will subscribe. Neither is it mine, though I would sound one important note of warning. Do not expect Britain to win a lot of titles. If your criterion of success or failure is going to be based on the table of first places won by nations, then you are doomed to a big disappointment. But failure to win a lot of Olympic championships is definitely not the signal for another outcry about a British sports debacle."

Towards the end of 1947 a list of 183 men and women had been drawn up by the British Amateur Athletic Board as Olympic "possibles", but of these only 12 men had even ranked in the top 30 in the world in their events during the year and only six women in the top 20. If a higher level of top-10 ranking was to be taken as the criterion for possibly winning an Olympic medal then there were only three men who could be so considered, though all but one of the women also fulfilled this requirement. It should be explained that such detailed facts and figures of annual performances were put together only as the result of painstaking research many years later by members of the international Association of Track & Field Statisticians, which was not formed until 1950, and at least part of this information would not have been available to Jack Oaten at the time. Even so, Oaten obviously had some accurate data to hand because he was absolutely correct when he said that there had been 18 Americans who had run 100 yards in 9.6sec (the mark of world class) that year. It would only be early in the following year, though, that some form of reliable international ranking-lists became available and these were made full use of in the seeding of the heats at Wembley.

Oaten was not immune to the inherent male chauvinism of the era because his assessment of British chances made no reference whatsoever to the women, an oversight he was perhaps to regret in the light of history, and in his "men only" article he picked the high jump, marathon and two walking races "as our strongest suits". His hopes lay with the brilliantly talented Scottish high-jumper

Alan Paterson, who would not turn 20 till the following June; with the durable Midlands marathon-runner Jack Holden, about to celebrate his 41st birthday, and Britain's finest cross-country man of the 1930s; and with a gaggle of walkers which included Harry Churcher, Harry Forbes, Bert Martineau, Charlie Megnin and Rex Whitlock (brother of the 1936 50 kilometres winner). It is no reflection on Oaten's powers of prediction that not one of these did, in fact, win a medal, and the best performances among them were to be those of Churcher and Martineau, who each got fifth places.

On the contrary, it is to Oaten's credit that he suggested: "In my view the most heartening thing for the future of British athletics would not be to win three gold medals and fail miserably in all the other events, but to win none, and instead place finalists in, say, half of the 23 events. Nothing could better prove that our planning in 1946 and 1947 had been on the right lines, and that our youngsters are of the right stuff." This fond hope was to be realised because Britain's men had finalists (or placings in the first dozen in straight finals) in 12 of the 23 events, though whether this compensated for the apparently meagre haul of a silver medals won by 38-year-old Tom Richards in the marathon and by the 4x100 metres relay team and a bronze medal by 48-year-old Tebbs Lloyd Johnson in the 50 kilometres walk, rather than the three golds hoped for, is a matter of conjecture. Richards and Lloyd Johnson were clearly not the "youngsters" Oaten had in mind.

It was not just in such otherwise commendable publications that women athletes suffered prejudice. Their programme contained only nine events – 100 metres, 200 metres, 80 metres hurdles, 4x100 metres relay, high jump, long jump, shot, discus and javelin. Great Britain was to contribute eight finalists, a far higher ratio than the men had achieved, and to win four silver medals. Curiously, but for the presence of a certain Dutch lady, there would have been accumulated the very three British gold medals that Oaten had asked for ... but that is one of the most enduring stories of these Wembley Olympic Games of 1948 which will be related at length in the section of this book devoted to the athletics events.

So far as the other Olympic sports were concerned, the British "experts" were mostly groping in the dark, but a valiant effort was made in a 270-page volume entitled *The Sports Book: Britain's Prospects in the Olympic Games and in Sport Generally*, published early in 1948, and edited and compiled by James Rivers. The Olympics actually occupied only 113 of the pages and the articles were limited to athletics, boxing, cycling, football, modern pentathlon, rowing, swimming and wrestling. No attempt was made to come to grips with the complexities of basketball, canoeing, equestrianism, fencing, gymnastics, hockey, shooting, weightlifting or yachting, Maybe the publisher's budget was exhausted by the star-studded list of writers already signed up, including the ubiquitous Harold Abrahams for athletics, George Whiting for boxing, WJ Howcroft for swimming and Hylton Cleaver for rowing.

Abrahams, like Jack Oaten, qualified with the utmost care all of his predictions. The Trinidad-born sprinter, McDonald Bailey, "seems assured of a place in the final", Abrahams surmised. Another sprinter, Jack Archer, "might reach the final, but he will have to be at his best to do so". Derek Pugh at 400 metres "might just reach a final". Of the 800 metres men – John Parlett, Harold Tarraway, Tom White – Abrahams thought "two of these three good enough to reach an Olympic final". Of the marathon and walks, Abrahams was more confident: in Jack Holden "we have a potential winner"; for the 50 kilometres walk "I regard an Olympic victory here as a possibility". As for the chances of the double-medallist high hurdler, Don Finlay, "We should be immensely proud if he reaches the last six". Harry Whittle, at 400 metres hurdles, "will, I expect, reach the final". High jumping of Alan Paterson's standard "is an extremely ticklish business", Abrahams observed arcanely, then added, "But the fact that I can be contemplating a possible victory for Great Britain is a tremendous thing".

The other events were summarily dismissed, and probably rightly so. The hop step and jump (now known as the triple jump) "is not up to Olympic standard" ... "I am sorry to say that while our performers at the discus and javelin are showing improvement they have still some way to go to reach international performances" ... "We have no class performers in the shot and pole vault". Only the imposingly-named Scottish hammer-thrower Duncan McDougal Munro Clark received any form of commendation, though there was no suggestion from Abrahams that Clark would be a medal contender, and rightly so.

Abrahams dealt briefly but enthusiastically with the women's events, suggesting "a very fine chance" for Maureen Gardner to earn Britain's first women's Olympic athletics title in the 80 metres hurdles. He also said of the sprinter Winnie Jordan, "I confidently expect her to finish in the first three" and that the relay team "will give a very good account of themselves". Discussing the high-jump chances of Dorothy Tyler, who as a 16-year-old had won silver in Berlin, Abrahams said, "It would be a fine achievement if she was in at the kill". Less obviously, he suggested that Margaret Lucas "might well obtain a place in the discus".

Similar to Oaten's conclusions, this all added up to not very much in terms of medals: perhaps gold in the marathon, 50 kilometres walk and women's hurdles; perhaps a medal of sorts in both high jumps and the women's 100 metres. Abrahams was unapologetic, even waspish, in a summing-up which sounded as if a barrister was addressing a jury – but then, of course, a barrister was exactly what Abrahams was in his professional life outside athletics:

"If you are rather an exacting person, and I think 'exacting' rather a polite word to use, you will doubtless be disappointed. For my own part I think we have made a very remarkable recovery in this country from the war years. I think the all-round standard of our athletes shows every promise of being higher than it was in the years immediately preceding World War II, but I am fully alive to the kind of opposition which we shall be faced in the Olympic Games, and while I should naturally be disappointed if we did not gain at least a couple of Olympic victories,

I shall not be at all surprised. Nor should I regard such a result as indicative of decadence or anything else.

"If our athletes succeed in bettering their previous best performances, I hope our public will give them due recognition. It is not fair just to look at a victory and be elated, or witness a defeat and be depressed. The real merit of a victory can only be properly assessed by a careful and honest examination of all the facts. Many an athlete who has failed to get a place in one Olympiad would have been a winner in a previous one. Many a runner who has finished second or third has deserved more praise than a winner on another occasion." Abrahams, and other scribes, would have cause to echo those words on numerous Olympic occasions during the years to come.

The best-informed sports enthusiasts in Britain were the subscribers to *World Sports*, which had established itself in pre-war years and had been revived in December 1947. It carried the description "Official Magazine of the British Olympic Association", which rather suggested that it might be taken up with staid official policy statements, but under the editorship of Cecil Bear it was, in fact, a lively and astonishingly informative publication with an authoritative line-up of contributors, including Harold Abrahams, Victor Barna, Denzil Batchelor, Neville Cardus, Henry Longhurst and Willy Meisl. There were also regular articles on "Women in Sport" by Susan Noel, innovatory colour photographs and artists' impressions, and a lengthy "Round the World" column.

Where else could any avid reader in Aberdeen, Altrincham or Aldershot learn in a single issue of what was happening in such sporting spheres as golf in Australia, skating in Austria, boxing in Belgium, ice-hockey in Canada, football in Germany, swimming in Japan, athletics in New Zealand or cross-country running in the USA? Throughout the months of 1948 leading up to the Games, *World Sports* published a stream of articles about the selections being made and the hopes being held out for the London Games by numerous of the competing countries.

Another of the athletics contributors was the Great Britain team manager, Jack Crump, who seemed to find little difficulty in combining his official duties with a profitable journalistic career, though one wonders what the reaction was of the athletes who would be under his command at Wembley when they read his predictions for gold medals in the July issue of the magazine. He forecast no fewer than seven titles for his team – Jack Holden in the marathon, Harry Churcher and Harold Whitlock in the walks, Maureen Gardner in the hurdles, Dorothy Tyler in the high jump, Joan Shepherd in the long jump, and the women's 4x100 metres relay team. His comments clearly showed that he believed that his was a realistic assessment, not mere wishful thinking, but it must have been a heavy burden to bear for those he had singled out. It is one matter to be branded as a favourite by the popular press; quite another matter, though, to know that your own team manager has publicly proclaimed that you should win. As it happens, Crump was not only wrong on those seven counts but correctly selected no more than eight of the 32 eventual winners.

The national newspapers were much more circumspect and *The Times* preview of 28 July restricted itself to suggesting that Holden and Churcher were "the two men most likely to give Britain an athletics victory". The correspondent for the *Manchester Guardian* hesitated even to give his blessing to the much fancied Holden, admitting to "a horrid sneaking fear that the Koreans will prove victorious, as in 1936". Of Britain's women he was more hopeful, saying of Holland's multiple world record-holder Fanny Blankers-Koen, that in the high jump she "may have to yield" to Dorothy Tyler and that in the hurdles she "may meet her match" in Maureen Gardner.

Much more space was given by the same writer to another issue entirely, and one otherwise disregarded by the scribes. In nostalgic vein he wrote, "Few women in a lifetime command at the same time such strength, perfect physical balance and co-ordination of mind and muscle, and unlike many field-event specialists she remained essentially feminine". The object of his affections was the German winner of the discus throw at the 1936 Games, Gisela Mauermayer, and he underscored his message by continuing, "Beautiful again was the only word for the running of Fräulein Krauss and Fräulein Dollinger. This year's Olympic Games will be the poorer for the absence of the Germans, and above all for the loss of the German women".

The *Daily Express* had started an entertaining "Olympic Scrapbook" column on 17 July, but rather than surmise about who would win the gold medals the newspaper's chief sports writers, John Macadam and Frank Rostron, preferred to concentrate on such "human interest" stories as how the 6ft 3in (1.90m) tall American woman discus-thrower, Frances Kaszubski, would fit into her billet bed, or what was being done to prevent the extra rations for competitors being diverted onto the black market. One item of constructive news that slipped through from Rostron's pen was that the Jamaican quarter-miler, Herb McKenley, had casually knocked off a timing of 30.1sec for 300 yards in training, only three-tenths slower than his own world record.

Boxing: "1948 will see us back on the list of Olympic champions"

George Whiting, the boxing correspondent of the London *Evening Standard* newspaper, was not only authoritative but witty, beginning his article with the observation that "Britain started this Olympic boxing business way back in 1908, and we so far forgot our traditional 'after you' attitude in international sport as to win all five of the weights". He soon made it clear that he expected no such run of success 40 years later: "All that, however, was in spacious days when we were an acknowledged power in world sport. The subsequent record does not look anything like as good."

No British boxer had won an Olympic title since 1924, and Whiting explained why: "In the days before world competition became so keen nobody bothered much about Olympic boxing until a few weeks before our men were due in the ring. A few weekends at a country camp, plus their ordinary club training, were considered ample preparation for eight men seeking the highest boxing honours the world can offer." Now, Whiting happily reported, the Amateur Boxing Association "have approached their problems in a more business-like frame of mind for the Games of 1948".

Not that medals were now guaranteed. There was another perennial problem with which the ABA could not necessarily deal. Whiting wrote, "The fleshpots of the professional ring have always been a temptation to working-class lads who make up the bulk of Britain's amateur boxers – especially so during the recent boom – and the swift switch from cutlery to cash on the part of their stars will always be a major headache for the ABA". Yet Whiting remained optimistic. "The prospect of winning an Olympic silver-gilt medal, however, has stayed the hand of a number of our 'great unpaid', " he added, and his conclusion was that "I feel certain 1948 will see us back on the list of Olympic boxing champions".

The fighters he had in mind to break the 24-year fast were a featherweight, Peter Brander, and a welterweight, Johnny Ryan, who had won the European title the previous year in Dublin. Brander, said Whiting, "is the personification of the style that has made British amateur boxing world famous". Ryan might well have quaked at the praise heaped on his shoulders, because Whiting stated categorically of him that if he "fails to qualify for, and win, the Wembley welters, it will be the biggest disappointment that the game in this country has suffered for years". George Whiting and "the game", as shall be revealed, were to be disappointed.

Cycling: "We can win all five titles ... but there is a big 'if' "

The slogan devised by the National Cyclists' Union, who were responsible for selecting the British team, smacked of either supreme confidence or blind faith – "Not a single Olympic cycling title must leave this country." The only obvious candidate for a gold medal was the reigning world amateur sprint champion Reg Harris, and history was otherwise not on the NCU's side. At the Games of 1932 and 1936 three gold medals had been won by France, two each by Germany, Holland and Italy, and one by Australia. The return for Britain, which had not won a cycling gold since 1920, was a silver and two bronzes.

WJ Mills, pre-eminent among British cycle-racing writers of the time, asked the obvious rhetorical questions: "Are the Union over-optimistic? Can we possibly win all five cycling titles? Have we the cyclists capable of it? Are the Union going the right way in selecting and training the teams?" Surprisingly, Mills's response was entirely positive, even if carefully qualified. "We *can* win all the five cycling titles", he wrote, "but there is, of course, a big 'if'."

Reg Harris was that rarest of beings among Britain's Olympic team – an outstanding favourite to win, and almost certainly as much so by overseas opinion. In Paris the previous year he had beaten Dutchman Cor Bijster in two straight races to win the world title. Harris, said Mills, "has the speed, track-craft and experience of international racing; he has, moreover, a burning ambition to win an Olympic title". The man he had faced in the world final – "the only man capable of giving Harris a run for his money in a sprint race" – had since turned professional and so was out of the reckoning. "There is nobody on last year's form capable of beating Harris", declared Mills, and who could argue with him?

It was a curious anomaly of the Olympic track cycling programme that the three other events – the 1,000 metres time-trial, the 2,000 metres tandem sprint and the 4,000 metres team pursuit – were not actually contested that often. None of them had even figured in the World Championships ever since they had begun in 1893; an individual pursuit had been introduced in 1946 but was not on the Olympic programme. Mills thus had very little to go on in assessing Britain's chances, but he had a stab at it.

The tandem might have held out some prospect, as it was an event which seemed to particularly appeal to the British. Gold medals had been won at the Olympics of 1906 and 1920 and silver in 1908, 1928 and 1932. At the time of writing, Mills firmly believed that Harris, who had won the 1947 British title with Alan Bannister, would concentrate only on the sprint at the Herne Hill track, in South London, where the Olympic cycling events would be held, and believed that Britain's hopes of winning with another pairing were "based on the weakness of our opponents, rather than on the strength of our entry". As it happens, Harris and Bannister were to contest the Olympic event, and with some considerable success.

The time-trial should be won, in Mills's view, "by any rider who can clock 1min 13sec", and this was a particularly keen observation because it was to transpire that he was only half-a-second out in his calculation. The Italians, he warned, "have strong reserves of time-trial men ... the French, too, will field a good man ... but the surprise of the day may well come from far-off Uruguay". The team pursuit had been won in Berlin on a fast wooden track by France in 4min 45sec, but Mills believed that "inside five minutes, perhaps as fast as 4min 50sec" would suffice on the slower Herne Hill surface. "Have we four men who can do this?" he asked, and his honest reply was that "we don't know yet". Again his prediction was spot-on because the title was to be won in 4min 57.8sec. Mills's summing-up of track gold-medal chances was "sprint 100%, tandem sprint 90%, time-trial 90%, team pursuit 90%", which seemed to suggest one gold and three other medals, silver or bronze.

The road race was to be held on a circuit course in Windsor Great Park, and the previous year's World Championship event in similar circumstances at Rheims, in France, hardly bode well for Britain's Olympic chances. Victory had gone to the aptly-named Alfio Ferrari, of Italy, and the best of the Britons was

George Fleming, who had finished 12th and then announced his retirement at the season's end. The salutary lesson from Rheims was that teamwork won road races and, as Mills pointed out, Fleming had been the only one of the British quartet to match the "terrifically fast speed" from the start and then "alone, he had to contend with teams of four men in which, in accordance with normal race tactics, the 'star' man was being nursed by the other three, all willing to sacrifice their chances just to get one man home".

Football: "You can't win on bread and jam!"

Oh dear! The prospects for Britain's national game were grim, and it was what was lacking on the dining-room table as much as on the playing-pitch that was at fault. "There is an old Welsh proverb to the effect that 'you can't win a prize-fight on bread and jam!'" wrote one of the country's leading football writers, Norman Acland. "The same applies to football. So, as national prestige is concerned, the population at large would not complain if the Minister of Food made special concessions to the players training for the Olympic matches. We may take it for granted that our rivals will live off the fat of the land."

Extra food rations were, indeed, made available for all those selected for Britain's Olympic team, and so presumably the dietary deficiency was compensated for, but there was another problem of economics with which the British team would have to cope in the Games tournament. Together with France and Eire, Britain was the only country in Europe which had not accepted the principle of "broken time" payments – compensation for lost wages – for amateur players. The gulf of opinion on the matter was so wide that England and the other home countries had withdrawn from FIFA, the world governing body, in 1928 and had not returned to the fold until 1946. For the same reason there had been no British team at the Olympics in 1924 and 1928 and when an appearance was made in 1936 (there had been no football at the 1932 Games) it had not been auspicious.

By 1948 the organisation had improved considerably but the prospects perhaps only marginally. Matt Busby (later Sir Matt), manager of Manchester United, had been put in charge of the team and a series of trials and then internationals had been played during May, June and July with mixed fortunes. In the last of the matches on 25 July there was a victory against France, 3-2 in Nantes, but overall there was no great cause for jubilation because the GB team performances had been greeted mutedly as the "triumph of simple courage and teamwork over artistry", and it was the British team's 17-year-old Scottish goalkeeper, Ronnie Simpson, towards whom the main praise was directed. One member of the 22-man squad, Peter Kippax, already had experience of playing at Wembley, having been an amateur member of the Burnley side which lost to Charlton Athletic 1-0 in the 1947 FA Cup Final.

The Olympic opposition would include the full international teams of

Denmark, Sweden and Yugoslavia. The England professional XI, including Raich Carter, Tommy Lawton, Wilf Mannion and Stanley Matthews, had lost 1-0 to Switzerland in Zurich the previous year, and as Matthews himself recalled later the Swiss were "not considered a power in European football". They were not even entered in the Olympic tournament. All Britain could do regarding the Olympics, wrote Norman Acland, was "to hope for the best".

Rowing: "Short of money, short of boats, and a starvation diet"

Self-evident it may have been, but the thought was worth repeating. "The one great problem which makes long training for Olympic rowing so difficult in Great Britain is that men cannot practise rowing by themselves, when the intention is that they shall race with seven (or three) others ... Any first-class eight *must* be got together in good time and must be trained and coached as a combination. Only so can unison be acquired." The author was the country's foremost rowing writer, Hylton Cleaver.

At the previous year's European Championships, held on Lake Lucerne, Cleaver pointed out, one of the titles had been won "by Italy, a country defeated in war, yet able to finance a fine national crew, and to train it on good food". For the Championships, Cleaver added despairingly, "Great Britain, the country which saved the world, could provide only two mediocre crews, short of boats, short of money, and trained on a starvation diet". Racing-shells in Britain were subject to a luxury tax; timber for oars was in short supply; and foreign travel was severely restricted.

No stick-in-the-mud, Cleaver gave great attention to the fact that the stretch of the River Thames used for the Henley regatta, and to be used again for the Olympics, was "not so good a course as can be expected on the Continent". Only two crews had been able to row in each event at Henley over the years, and though this would be expanded to three for the Games the capacity was still far short of the standard six crews for Olympic events of the past. Cleaver also believed that there would be an inherent advantage for crews in the outside stations because the course was upstream and the adverse current was stronger in the centre.

Yet there were some encouraging pointers for the Games. In the Henley coxless pairs the veterans from pre-war years, "Ran" Laurie and Jack Wilson, had beaten their Australian opponents by three lengths to repeat their victory of 1938. On the other hand, just as Hylton Cleaver had feared, the double sculls pairing of Bert Bushnell and Richard Burnell had been brought together with only a fortnight to train after Bushnell had been passed over for the single sculls selection, and there was honour to defend here because Jack Beresford and Leslie Southwood had won for Britain in Berlin. Beresford, one of the very greatest of all British oarsmen, and Southwood had dead-heated with an Italian pair at Henley in 1939 and would have been strong contenders for another Olympic win the next year. Beresford would be one of the team coaches at the Henley Olympic regatta, and maybe his presence would inspire a copyist.

It might have been thought that a sport dominated in Britain by Oxbridge would be at some advantage when it came to facilities and finance, but even the privileged varsity men suffered the same practical problems as everyone else in Britain. As Cleaver pointed out, "Rowing coaches in this country can no longer give their men such hard work and long mileage in training as they used to because of present-day rations".

Swimming: "Foolish to even consider winning several titles"

The European Championships in swimming had been revived in 1947 in Monte Carlo after a gap of nine years. The star of the meeting had been a Frenchman, Alex Jany, who won both the 100 and 400 metres freestyle; the latter in world-record time. Britain's single success in the programme of six events for men and five for women had come in the men's 200 metres breaststroke, won by Roy Romain. This gave some sort of pointer for what would happen in the Wembley Pool when Olympic titles were at stake – but perhaps not much. The American men and the Danish and Dutch women were the world power, and they would be the ones to beat.

Britain's last Olympic medals had been bronze for the women's backstroke and the relay in Los Angeles in 1932, so what reason was there to hope for anything better this time? WJ Howcroft, a renowned coach as well as a journalist, was not optimistic.

"Throughout the world, during the war years, other races, white, black and yellow, have been developing, coaching and training their young people to an exceptionally high degree of proficiency. Here in Europe France, Hungary, Sweden, Denmark, Holland and Belgium have made a big advance, especially with their women swimmers. In the Middle East Egypt, Palestine and Lebanon are three countries where swimming has made giant strides. Russia, since she has joined the International Swimming Federation, is eligible for the London Olympiad – and from figures in my possession the Soviet representatives are likely to hold their own against the rest of the world. In the Far East Korea, China, India and Ceylon are possible Olympic contestants, but the greatest surge of progress is in Latin America. No less than eight countries south of the Panama Canal have already contacted the International Swimming Federation for information in connection with the Games in London."

The USSR, as we know, was not to make an appearance in London – except for numerous "technical observers" at all the sporting venues – but that made no difference to Howcroft's terse summary of Britain's status in the pool: "Britain, carrying the handicap of several war years, will do well if their representatives reach the final of three or four events." The only two home swimmers he regarded as being in the "Olympic reckoning" were Roy Romain and the 17-year-old Scots girl Cathie Gibson, who had placed second in the European Championships 400 metres freestyle and 100 metres backstroke. "Physically, Romain has everything," Howcroft wrote. "He is 6ft 4in in height with powerful shoulders and long tapering limbs. He has the ideal physique for the exhausting butterfly stroke ... On paper Miss Gibson's chance appears to be hopeless when compared with the American star Ann Curtis, who is credited with 5min 7.6sec, but the big Californian girl is a developed swimmer with many years of racing and training experience. On the other hand, Miss Gibson is a newcomer who only took the crawl stroke seriously in the Autumn of 1946."

Though not hopeful of immediate success, Howcroft struck a rousing note for the future. "Even if we fail to raise a winning flag at Wembley our entry in the Games will have served one decidedly useful purpose," he wrote. "Through the country, from Plymouth to Aberdeen, there are promising young swimmers, virtually unknown outside of club circles, working hard and training seriously. Ninety per cent of these unknowns will improve as a direct result of the Olympic incentive."

This was a welcome message that could equally apply to every other Olympic sport. Whatever Britain's Olympic team of 1948 achieved, there were many, many others taking part in various sports who would surely be inspired by the very presence alone of the Games in their midst.

Wrestling: Now it was time to be "put through the mill"

Though largely known to the public as a professional stage spectacle, wrestling had as much right as any other sport to serious consideration. In fact, in Olympic terms, only athletics was its equal, because both disciplines had figured most prominently in the Ancient Greek Games, the known origins of which went back to 776 BC, and wrestling's history could be traced to much earlier than that to cave drawings from 3000 BC. As Britain had not won a wrestling gold since 1908, nor any medal at all since 1928, prospects of coming away with some reward this time seemed rather remote.

Yet the British Amateur Wrestling Association was not only undaunted but probably as far-sighted as any of the home governing bodies for an Olympic sport. A scheme had been set up in 1946 whereby the best wrestlers regularly met each other in competition and for training, and a tough programme had been laid out under the direction of chief coach Vic Bensen, based on the principle of "devil take the hindmost". George MacKenzie, the Association's secretary, was one of Bensen's assistants and explained: "Suitable and selected contestants were introduced into the teams for the purpose of displacing the lower graded of the provisional team. So the training has progressed with the leaders of the team having to fight and train hard all the time to retain their places against those just below them in the table."

Both Bensen and MacKenzie had a wealth of competitive experience to call upon. Bensen had won 13 national titles between 1919 and 1934, including three different weights in 1926; MacKenzie had won seven national titles and had competed in all five Olympic wrestling tournaments from 1908 to 1928, and he forecast that the London Olympics would attract "the greatest assembly of wrestlers that the world has ever seen, for never before have so many countries signified their intention of sending wrestlers".

The most prominent among them would be the USA, Sweden, Turkey, Finland and Egypt. International competition had been resumed after the war with European Championships for freestyle wrestling in Stockholm in October of 1946 and for Greco-Roman wrestling in Prague in April 1947, and Sweden had won five titles and Turkey four. Regrettably absent would be the USSR, which had won the three heaviest Greco-Roman weight categories. World Championships had been held between 1904 and 1922 but would not resume until 1950.

MacKenzie was making no promises. Not once did he suggest a medal was in the offing. Britain's wrestlers had prepared as best they could, and MacKenzie warned: "I do not feel that we have a team to carry off Olympic honours ... but I do feel sure that the team we have in the making – and I write as one who has been through the mill a number of times (five Olympic Games) – is an improving team and one that will give Great Britain a result as good or even better than we have ever had in any previous Olympiad."

That was actually a curious claim by MacKenzie because in 1908, as he would have known himself for having been there, Britain had won three of the five freestyle titles. The Greco-Roman style was then almost universally preferred and the home wrestlers had faced only a handful of opponents. The return of the Games to London 40 years on would be a very different prospect.

No great hopes of medals for Britain could be gleaned from a study of form in the other Olympic sports. The tale was so often a familiar one. Britain had been the inventors of so many of the modern Olympic sports and in years gone by had led the world in levels of achievement, but now the world had moved on, and ahead.

The basketball title would surely go to the USA, where the game had been invented in 1891, and Britain would have to settle for simply taking part and hoping for a consolation win in one of the qualifying matches. The first canoe races had been held on the River Thames in 1867, but there had been no competition of any kind in Britain from 1939 to 1947.

Showjumping in Britain was in decline and the three-day event had never been contested in the country before; so equestrian ambitions were severely limited. British women had won silver medals in fencing in 1924, 1928 and 1932, but the best prospects now lay with one of the men, John Emrys Lloyd.

Gymnastics in Britain lacked apparatus, facilities and coaches. Britain had won the Olympic hockey in 1908 and 1920, but India had taken every title since and there had not even been a British team at the Games for 20 years. In 31 different Olympic shooting finals since 1920 Britain had won only one gold and two silvers – all in 1924. The military-dominated modern pentathlon had oddly been very largely a preserve of neutral Sweden, and there was no reason to suppose that would change.

Yet there was a gleam of light on the horizon – literally so. Far away from London, where the Atlantic waves rolled on to the Devonshire shoreline and lapped against the seafront at the elegant resort of Torquay, the yachting events would include the Swallow class for the first time, and Britain had won a bronze in the similar Star class in 1936. At the other end of the scale Britain would be defending the 6-metre title won in Berlin. Could it be that the "little ships" which had performed such heroic deeds at Dunkirk in 1940 would again come to Britain's rescue?

Chapter 5

THE ARTISTIC VIEW OF OLYMPIC SPORT

C OMPETITION OF THE most sedentary and civilised kind at the 1948 London Games began on 15 July, a fortnight before the opening ceremony, with an "Olympic Sport in Art" exhibition at the Victoria and Albert Museum. Eight first prizes were awarded in various categories of architecture, literature, music, painting and sculpture, and were won by contestants from Austria, Finland, France, Great Britain, Italy, Poland and Sweden. The tradition of holding cultural events at the Games had begun with the Ancient Greeks, and the late Baron Pierre de Coubertin, "founding father" of the Modern Games, had been a vigorous supporter of its continuation.

Britain's "champion" was a deaf-and-dumb member of the Royal Academy, Arnold Thomson, who had been born in Bangalore, in India, and who had established a national reputation as a designer of posters for the Ministry of Information during World War II. His painting of a naked, severely burned RAF crewman being tended by a nurse in a saline bath remains one of the most moving of artists' interpretations of the horrors of war. Thomson received his Olympic prize for his oil painting of a bout at the London amateur boxing championships, and his work was inspired by personal experience because he had been a boxer himself in his youth. In similar vein, a prize for a poem entitled "Rhythme du Stade" went to a young Frenchman, Gilbert Prouteau, who had been a candidate for an Olympic place in the 110 metres hurdling event.

There was also a direct thread from Prouteau back to the 1896 Games, where a fellow-athlete had won a literary prize. George Stuart Robertson (later Sir George Stuart Robertson QC) was an Oxford undergraduate who had travelled to Athens on his own initiative after spotting an advertisement for the Games in the window of the travel agents, Thomas Cook's, but as his preferred event, the hammer throw, was not on the programme he had instead taken part in the shot and discus and in the lawn-tennis tournament. He had also put his classical training to good use by composing a Greek ode in the style of Pindar, and when he recited this at the Games he was presented with an olive branch and laurel wreath by the admiring King of the Greeks.

Chapter 6

THE 59 COMPETING COUNTRIES

The countries entered in the Games were:

Afghanistan, Argentina, Australia, Austria, Belgium, Bermuda, Brazil, British Guiana, Burma, Canada, Ceylon, Chile, China, Colombia, Cuba, Czechoslovakia, Denmark, Egypt, Eire, Finland, France, Great Britain, Greece, Holland, Hungary, Iceland, India, Iran, Iraq, Italy, Jamaica, Korea, Lebanon, Liechtenstein, Luxembourg, Malta, Mexico, Monaco, New Zealand, Norway, Pakistan, Panama, Peru, Philippines, Poland, Portugal, Puerto Rico, Singapore, South Africa, Spain, Sweden, Switzerland, Syria, Trinidad & Tobago, Turkey, Uruguay, United States of America, Venezuela, Yugoslavia. *Note: British Guiana now Guyana, Burma now Myanmar, Ceylon now Sri Lanka, Czechoslovakia now Czech Republic and Slovakia, Eire now Ireland.*

The 13 countries which had been represented at the first Modern Olympic Games in Athens in 1896 had been Australia, Austria, Bulgaria, Chile, Denmark, France, Germany, Great Britain, Greece, Hungary, Sweden, Switzerland and the USA. Six of these – Australia, France, Great Britain, Greece, Switzerland and the USA – were to maintain an unbroken Olympic link by competing again in London in 1948. Competing for the first time were British Guiana, China, Iran, Iraq, Jamaica, Korea, Puerto Rico, Singapore, Syria and Trinidad & Tobago. Cuba had entered officially for the first time, having been represented by individuals in 1904.

The International Olympic Committee gives the number of competitors at the 1948 Games as being 4,104 (3,714 men, 390 women). These figures, and the total of 59 competing countries, beat the previous record participation of 4,066 competitors (3,783 men, 328 women) and 49 countries in Berlin in 1936. The

British Olympic Association lists a slightly different figure for women competing in London (385) and this may be due to varying numbers in the 11 teams which took part in gymnastics, where up to eight competitors were allowed per nation.

Other figures have been quoted for the number of competitors at various times over the years, but very recent research by members of the International Society of Olympic Historians – most notably by the US authority, Bill Mallon – has arrived at totals of 4,071 for London (3,678 men, 393 women) and 3,954 for Berlin (3,625 men, 329 women), and these can now be regarded as the authoritative version.

The number of competitors entered by each country in 1948 is as follows, in order of the size of teams, and showing the overall totals with the numbers of men and the numbers of women listed consecutively in brackets:

Great Britain 313 (266, 47), USA 300 (262, 38), France 284 (248, 36), Argentina 199 (188, 11), Italy 183 (164, 19), Sweden 174 (155, 19), Switzerland 171 (165, 6), Denmark 159 (141, 18), Belgium 148 (129, 19), Holland 137 (103, 34), Hungary 126 (106, 20), Finland 123 (118, 5), Austria 114 (88, 26), Canada 104 (89, 15), Mexico 88 (81, 7), Yugoslavia 86 (75, 11), Egypt 85 (85, 0), Norway 80 (77, 3), India 77 (77, 0), Czechoslovakia 76 (63, 13), Australia 75 (66, 9), Brazil 70 (59, 11), Spain 64 (64, 0), Eire 62 (61, 1), Uruguay 59 (59, 0), Greece 57 (56, 1), Turkey 57 (56, 1), Chile 53 (49, 4), Cuba 53 (53, 0), Portugal 47 (47, 0), Korea (45, (44, 1), Luxembourg 45 (42, 3), Peru 41 (41, 0), Iran 35 (35, 0), Pakistan 35 (35, 0), South Africa 32 (31, 1), China 26 (26, 0), Afghanistan 25 (25, 0), Philippines 24 (24, 0), Poland 23 (19, 4), Iceland 19 (16, 3), Jamaica 13 (9, 4), Bermuda 12 (10, 2), Iraq 11 (11, 0), Puerto Rico 9 (9, 0), Lebanon 8 (8, 0), Ceylon 7 (7, 0), New Zealand 7 (6, 1), Colombia 6 (6, 0), Trinidad & Tobago 5 (5, 0), British Guiana 4 (4, 0), Burma 4 (4, 0), Monaco 4 (4, 0), Liechtenstein 2 (2, 0), Malta 1 (1, 0), Panama 1 (1, 0), Singapore 1 (1, 0), Syria 1 (1, 0), Venezuela 1 (1, 0).

The Official Report of the Games organising committee includes a list of 4,689 "competitors", but these are presumably those who originally entered, and if so this indicates that there was a "drop out" rate of some 15 per cent, either before teams set off on their journeys to England or after they had arrived.

Chapter 7

THE SPORTS AT THE 1948 GAMES

THE ORGANISERS WERE required by the International Olympic Committee to hold six of the 17 sports – athletics, boxing, cycling, fencing, swimming and wrestling. The other 11 sports decided upon were the same as at the 1936 Games – basketball, canoeing, equestrianism, football, gymnastics, hockey, modern pentathlon, rowing, shooting, weightlifting and yachting.

How the medals were shared

Countries are listed in order of total medals gained and in alphabetical order where scores are equal.

	Gold	Silver	Bronze	Total
United States of America	38	27	19	84
Sweden	16	11	17	44
France	10	6	13	29
Italy	8	12	9	29
Hungary	10	5	12	27
Great Britain	3	14	6	23
Denmark	5	7	8	20
Finland	8	7	5	20
Switzerland	5	10	5	20
Holland	5	2	9	16
Australia	2	6	5	13
Turkey	6	4	2	12
Czechoslovakia	6	2	3	11
Argentina	3	3	1	7
Belgium	2	2	3	7
Norway	1	3	3	7
Egypt	2	2	1	5

Mexico	2	1	2	5
South Africa	2	1	1	4
Austria	1	–	3	4
Canada	–	1	2	3
Jamaica	1	2	–	3
Korea	–	–	2	2
Panama	–	–	2	2
Portugal	–	1	1	2
Uruguay	–	1	1	2
Yugoslavia	–	2	–	2
Brazil	–	–	1	1
Ceylon	–	1	–	1
Cuba	–	1	–	1
India	1	–	–	1
Iran	–	–	1	1
Peru	1	–	–	1
Poland	–	–	1	1
Puerto Rico	–	–	1	1
Spain	–	1	–	1
Trinidad & Tobago	–	1	–	1

How wartime affected the medal count

At the Berlin Games of 1936 the USA had failed to win more medals than any other country for the first time since 1912, when they had tied with the hosts, Sweden. Germany's meticulous preparations – designed, of course, to prove racial as well as sporting supremacy – brought its team 89 medals in Berlin to the USA's 56, but Germany's absence from London, together with that of Japan, and of Estonia, Latvia and Lithuania (now absorbed into the USSR), meant that 116 medals were available, as it were, for redistribution, allowing for one or two changes in programme. That the USA should come top again in the medals table was therefore no surprise, and the obvious beneficiary was Sweden, taking full advantage of wartime neutrality in coming second. Sweden had totalled between 20 and 29 medals in the Games from 1924 to 1936 and in London boosted their score to 44.

On the face of it, the most unexpected improvement was made by France, whose total of 29 medals was their highest since 1924, when the Games were in Paris and 38 medals were won. It has to be borne in mind, though, that sport in France had continued largely unhindered throughout the German wartime occupation, and the same reasoning could be applied to Denmark's haul of 20 medals, compared with their previous best of 13 in 1920. A country which should obviously have benefited from wartime neutrality was Switzerland, and certainly its gold-medal count was much higher than in Berlin – five, compared with one

– but the overall medals total was not much increased, from 16 to 20, and in 1924 Swiss competitors had won more golds (seven) and more medals (25).

Great Britain's performance, even if the mass of silver medals suggested that their representatives were best at being "good runners-up", was actually an exceptional one. In 1936 Britons had won 14 medals (four gold, seven silver, three bronze), and the total scores in previous years had been 16 in 1932, 20 in 1928, 34 in 1924, 43 in 1920 and 41 in 1912. Britain had thus done better in 1948 than in any Games since 1924, and better by a sufficient margin that it could not simply be put down to an expansion of the programme. Figures before 1912 do not really mean very much because the London Games of 1908 was packed out with a huge variety of additional events in which most, if not all, of the competitors were British and they won 147 medals!

Strangely, nowhere in the British Olympic Association's Official Report of the 1948 Games is there any mention at all of the Great Britain team's overall achievements in comparison with previous years. This is a pity. These bald figures told an encouraging tale. Curiously, even though "league tables" were discouraged, the BOA produced a "specially compiled chart" in which each country was awarded seven points for a first place, five points for a second, four points for a third, three points for a fourth, two points for a fifth, and one point for a sixth, and 41 of the 59 competing countries qualified for inclusion. The leaders were as follows:

1	USA	547.5pts
2	Sweden	308.5
3	France	206
4	Hungary	183.1
5	Italy	166
6	Great Britain	162
7	Finland	153.75
8	Switzerland	135.6
9	Denmark	129
10	Holland	107.

Chapter 8

A Woman's Place

is ... on the rostrum

WOMEN HAD NOT been allowed to compete in the Ancient Greek Olympics, nor even to attend, apart from chosen priestesses, and their role in London in 1948 was still a minor one. They provided less than 10 per cent of the competitors and were restricted to athletics, canoeing, fencing, gymnastics and swimming. Yet it was a woman – the great all-round Dutch athlete Fanny Blankers-Koen, winner of four gold medals – whose name is still, some six decades later, the one which is most closely associated with the Games, and who perhaps more than any other single person has played her part in leading women towards the sporting emancipation which they deserved.

Even so, women had already been taking part in the Games in Paris in 1900, and making history in so doing. It was long thought that the first woman gold-medallist was a British tennis-player, Charlotte ("Chattie") Cooper, who won the ladies' singles and shared in the mixed doubles title with Reginald Doherty, the outstanding player of his generation. Now, though, it has been established that in strict chronological order at those 1900 Games the first woman winner was Madame la Comtesse Hélène de Pourtalès, of Switzerland, a crew member of the 6-metre-class yacht, *Lerina*, skippered by her husband, Comte Henri de Pourtalès.

Miss Cooper kept fit by running up and down stairs at home and might well have been a champion sprinter, had such an opportunity existed for her. Additionally, there were two other women who competed on even terms with men in 1900. Madame Filleul Brohy and Mademoiselle Marie Ohnier, of France, took part in the croquet tournament in the company of 10 men, though without winning medals.

Golf was also part of the 1900 programme and 19 women played in their own championship, won by Margaret Abbott, from Chicago, who had taken up the game two years before and was now an art student in Paris. She was accompanied by her mother, who also reported on her daughter's success as the correspondent of the *Chicago Tribune* newspaper. A photograph which is believed to be of Miss Abbott on the course confirms the description quoted by the French

Olympic historian, Professor André Drevon, that she was "tall, very elegant and very beautiful". The Olympic Games events of 1900 had many competitors (11,542 took part in gymnastics events alone!) and they were stretched out in a disorganised fashion over most of the year. The golf tournament was held at Compiègne, north of Paris, and it is perfectly possible that Miss Abbott – in common with many competitors in other sports – would have had little or no idea that she was taking part in an Olympic event.

Further notable successes by women were achieved in archery at the 1908 London Games, where 53-year-old Sybil ("Queenie") Newall won from Charlotte ("Lottie") Dod, famed as a Wimbledon tennis champion and later as a golfer. Then, in 1912 in Stockholm, women daringly bared their legs for the first time in Olympic competition to take part in freestyle swimming events at 100 metres and the 4x100 metres relay, where a 17-year-old, Bella Moore, was in Britain's winning team. A 20-year-old Australian, Fanny Durack, had persuaded her country's reluctant selectors to send her and she obliged by winning her event and breaking the world record. In 1928 athletics for women made a belated appearance, and world records were set at 100 metres by 16-year-old Betty Robinson, of the USA, and at 800 metres by Lina Radke, of Germany, but after the latter race some of the contestants appeared to be exhausted and the chauvinistic IOC hierarchy took the opportunity to ban any women's race further in distance than 200 metres for the next 32 years! For the athletics programme in London in 1948 the 200 metres, long jump and shot were added to the six events contested in Berlin.

Of the 59 countries competing in 1948, 32 included women in their team – most notably, Great Britain, USA, France, Holland, Austria, Belgium, Italy, Sweden and Canada. There were 14 countries which won women's medals in athletics (nine events), canoeing, fencing, gymnastics (all one event each) and swimming and diving (seven events), as follows: USA 12 (five gold, four silver, three bronze), Denmark eight (three gold, three silver, two bronze), Holland eight (five gold, one silver, two bronze), Australia five (two silver, three bronze), Great Britain five (four silver, one bronze), Austria four (one gold, three bronze), France four (two gold, two bronze), Hungary four (two gold, one silver, one bronze), plus Italy two silver, Czechoslovakia one gold, Argentina and Finland each one silver, Canada and Sweden each one bronze. Four of Holland's gold medals and both of France's were each won by a single woman.

A close study of the numbers of women entered reveals some surprisingly low figures for emancipated countries such as Australia (nine), Switzerland (six), Finland (five), Norway (three) and South Africa (one), and this is a subject which is perhaps worth a whole study in itself. Some countries had every reason to be grateful to the representation of the "weaker sex" in their ranks. Australian women, outnumbered more than seven to one by their male team-mates, won five of the country's total of 13 medals. The Dutch women won half of their country's 16 medals, including all five golds. Austrian women won all but one of their country's five medals.

Chapter 9

THE COST ...
AND THE PROFIT

T HE SECTION OF the Official Report of the Organising Committee of the 1948 Olympic Games, published in 1951, devoted less than one of its 776 pages to the matter of "Receipts and Expenditure", with a brief introduction:

"The following statement of Receipts and Expenditure to 31 December 1949 is not completed owing to certain contingent liabilities remaining outstanding, but it is anticipated the final accounts will show an approximate profit of £29,000, subject to tax and to the publication of the Official Report:

RECEIPTS

Gross revenue from the sports	£545,628
Housing, feeding and transport of competitors	£174,097
Miscellaneous income	
(less outgoings directly chargeable thereto)	£41,963
	£761,688

EXPENDITURE

Technical charges and equipment (including staff wages)	£121,741
Temporary works at Wembley and other venues	£78,120
Wembley Stadium Ltd – Compensation	£92,500
Works and services provided by Government departments	£118,033
Housing, feeding and transport of competitors	£164,644
Transport	£37,925
Insurance against cancellations	£7,821
Equipment of British team	£10,884
Administrative charges (including professional fees)	£90,557
Payment to the International Olympic Committee	£5,000
Entertainment	£3,638

Permanent record of winners at main stadium (provision)	£1,000
Office furniture (amount written off)	£405
Balance, being excess of Income over Expenditure, subject to income tax, profits tax, publication of the Official Report, and certain contingent liabilities	£29,420
	£761,688

In 21st-century terms £29,420 is equivalent to approximately £3 million; £761,688 is equivalent to approximately £77 million.

Chapter 10

RECOVERING FROM THE WAR

Athletics: Empire Stadium, Wembley, 30 July to 7 August

T HE WAR YEARS had put an end to the Olympic aspirations of a host of athletes, and it needed the example of just one race to adequately illustrate the point. At the 1940 US championships the 1500 metres was won in a time only one-tenth slower than Jack Lovelock's world-record 3:47.8 at the Berlin Olympics four years before. The relatively unknown runner who came so close to making history was Walter Mehl, a 24-year-old student at Wisconsin University, and just behind in second place was Glenn Cunningham, the Olympic silver-medallist. Mehl had made a huge improvement on what he had previously achieved, and the next year he ran one of the fastest indoor miles ever, but he then went into the armed forces and never competed seriously again. Cunningham – one of the greatest of all middle-distance runners of the 1930s – retired at the age of 30 as soon as he realised that there was no chance for him to run in another Olympics.

Yet there was much more athletics activity during the war years than might have been imagined – to the extent that 122 world records were broken between 3 September 1939, when war was declared in Europe, and 8 August 1945, when Japan surrendered. Such was the normality of the bureaucratic processes of the sport that even during such years of conflict 88 of those performances were duly considered by the International Amateur Athletic Federation (IAAF) to have been achieved in the regulation circumstances which would entitle them to be officially ratified.

The majority of the new world records were set in the USA, where competition continued at a high level, or in neutral Sweden, but other new standards were reached in Finland, France, Holland, Italy, South Africa, Switzerland, the USSR – and even in Germany, where the 400 and 800 metres world record-holder from before the war, Rudolf Harbig, ran the fastest-ever 1000 metres, and other ratified performances were achieved in the 30 kilometres walk and in the women's javelin. Some of the advances in performances made during those war years were even of very considerable historical significance.

The great Swedish runners Gunder Hägg and Arne Andersson set 21 world records between them at distances from 1500 to 5000 metres between 1941 and 1945. They took it in turns to reduce Lovelock's 1500 metres record by almost five seconds (30 metres or so in terms of running distance) to 3:43.0 and Sydney Wooderson's mile record of 4:06.4 from 1937 by exactly five seconds to 4:01.4 – thus bringing the mythical four-minute mile into prospect. Hägg also improved the 3000 metres record from 8:09.0 to 8:01.2 and became the first man to beat 14 minutes for 5000 metres, with a time of 13:58.2 which took more than 10 seconds off the previous best. Another landmark was passed in the 3000 metres steeplechase in Sweden when Erik Elmsäter broke nine minutes. In Finland Taisto Mäki became the first man to beat 30 minutes for 10,000 metres in 1939, a fortnight after war had been declared, and his fellow-countryman, Viljo Heino, improved this hugely to 29:35.4 in 1944.

The 1940s was an era in which imperial distances on the track, such as 100, 220, 440 and 880 yards and one mile, two miles, three miles and six miles, were still recognised as standard events throughout the USA and the British Empire, and for world-record purposes. It was not, in fact, until 1976 that the IAAF decided to "go metric" and abandon events at imperial distances for official purposes, with the exception of the time-honoured one mile. In the field events measurements were still made in feet and inches in countries which had not adopted the metric system (and still are in the 21st century in the USA), and so the achievements of two Americans carried particular significance.

In the high jump, Lester Steers took the record up to 6ft 11in (2.11m) and had actually jumped 7ft 0½in (2.15m) in a reliably measured "exhibition" event to become the first "seven-footer". In the pole vault, Cornelius ("Dutch") Warmerdam made seven improvements on the pre-war record of 14ft 11in (4.54m), passing the 15ft mark in 1940 and reaching 15ft 7¾in (4.77m) two years later. Steers was competing more than a quarter of a century before the now ubiquitous Fosbury flop was devised and used the "straddle" technique, clearing the bar face down. Warmerdam had none of the advantages of the catapult effect of the modern fibreglass pole, which was yet to be invented, and was the last man to set a world record with a bamboo pole. Steers's record stood for 12 years and Warmerdam's for 15, and they remain two of the greatest athletes in the history of their events. Neither, sadly, ever had the opportunity to compete in an Olympics.

Of the 34 women's world records set during the war years seven would be to the credit of Fanny Blankers-Koen, of Holland, at 100 yards, 100 metres, 80 metres hurdles, high jump and long jump, plus a share of two more in relays. She became the first woman to officially beat 11sec for 100 yards (10.8) and she also, remarkably, broke the high-jump record three times in one meeting (1.67m, 1.69m, 1.71m), and took the long-jump record from its pre-war 6.12m to 6.25m. She might even have done something about the modest standards at 400 metres and 800 metres, had she set her mind on it. At the latter distance an unappreciated Soviet woman, Yevdokiya Vasilyeva, had improved the record in isolation from 2:16.8 to 2:12.0. Blankers-Koen, as we know, would get her Olympic chance, but the 800 for women would not come back on to the Olympic programme until 1960, thus denying Vasilyeva hers. In any case, the USSR obstinately remained unaffiliated in the Olympic year of 1948, but when at last they joined the fold Vasilyeva had the belated consolation of official recognition for a time of 2:13.0.

Had there been an Olympic Games of 1944, then Hägg, Andersson, Heino, Elmsäter, Steers, Warmerdam and Blankers-Koen would all have made very worthy champions, fit to stand comparison with any in Olympic history. There would also have been a place of honour in the memory for the likes of Americans such as John Wilson and Ken Wiesner in the high jump and Earl Audet in the shot, or Adolfo Consolini and Giuseppe Tosi, of Italy, in the discus, and Sven Eriksson, of Sweden, in the javelin. The names of Wilson, Audet and Eriksson are long since forgotten by all but a handful of zealous statisticians, but the others would live to fight another day – even if Wiesner would have to wait until the Games of 1952, when he won a silver medal.

The three years which elapsed between the end of the war and the staging of the 1948 Games were quite extensive enough for another wave of top-class athletes to come and go. In those days, long before the professionalism of the sport, three years or less was an average lifespan for international athletes to realise at least some of their potential before turning their attentions to the rather more vital long-term consideration of earning a living. During 1946 and 1947 athletes at the top of the world rankings included such Americans as Elmore Harris at 400 metres, Johnny Fulton at 800 metres, Dave Albritton in the high jump, and Bob Fitch in the discus (for which he broke the world record), but none of them ever came remotely into the Olympic reckoning. Nor, for that matter, did a 23-year-old sergeant in the Women's Royal Air Force, Margaret Ring, the leading high jumper in Britain in 1947 but who failed to approach that form again, or a brilliantly talented Oxford undergraduate, John Wilkinson, whose sprinting career was to be consequently marred by injury, and whose colourful life would have merited an Ealing Studios screenplay.

So Olympic year arrived, and for some of the American athletes the toughest battle of all would be simply to qualify for the team. Since 1908 an Olympic Trials had decided the US selections, and it would be the first three in each event who would automatically go to Wembley, regardless of temporary indisposition on the day of any would-be champions. Such extravagance was affordable because of the abundance of talent available in many events, but tales were legion over the years of the fine athletes – even potential Olympic gold-medallists – who had failed to win a place and had perforce stayed at home while lesser beings took the Olympic honours. The same was bound to happen again when the leading US athletes, who had qualified via the NCAA (national collegiate) or AAU (national) championships, came together at the Northwestern University's Dyche Stadium in Evanston, Illinois, on 9 and 10 July, less than a month before the Olympics opened.

Some were injured and did not get to the trials at all, including the world's fastest miler of the year, Gil Dodds, and the high-jump silver-medallist from 1936, Dave Albritton. Amongst the surviving hopefuls were many who had waited through the war years for their chance. Barney Ewell had won the AAU 200 metres in 1939 and 100 metres in 1941, and Charley Parker the 200 in 1944. Cliff Bourland had been 400 metres champion in 1941 and 1942. Bill Hulse had won the 800 in 1943 and 1500 in 1944 and held the US mile record. Others were hoping to renew the Olympic experience. Joe McCluskey, now 37, had won the first of his nine national steeplechase titles in 1930 and had been the Olympic bronze-medallist in 1932 and a finalist again in 1936. Ernest Crosbie had competed in both 1932 and 1936 at the 50 kilometres walk. Then there was marathon man Johnny Kelley and hammer thrower Henry Dreyer from the Berlin Games.

The most prominent of the victims of the sudden death selection process was the world's finest high hurdler, Harrison ("Bones") Dillard, who had won 82 successive races before losing at the AAU championships and then getting everything wrong in the trials final, hitting several barriers hard, and eventually coming to a halt at the eighth. Fortunately for Dillard, he had also qualified to run the 100 metres at the trials and earned his place on the team by managing third place in a race won by Ewell in a time of 10.2 which equalled the world record held by Jesse Owens, among others. Charles Fonville threw the shot a mere 16.49m, having set a world record and been the only man to exceed 17m during the season (and, what is more, in 12 competitions), and placed fourth – so was out. Fred Johnson, the national long-jump champion, suffered the nightmare of three fouls – and so he, too, was out.

Barney Ewell, now aged 30, also qualified at 200 metres, where he and the winner, Mel Patton, both equalled Jesse Owens's world record of 20.7 set at the Berlin Games, and Cliff Bourland was third in that race. Ernest Crosbie, who had finished a valiant last in the Berlin walk, won his third successive Olympic trial, while Henry Dreyer was second in the hammer and Johnny Kelley was chosen for the marathon on the basis of three races run in 1947–48 – so they would all go again to the Games. Other hopes were firmly dashed. The one-time teenage prodigy, Charley Parker, was last in his 100 metres heat and fourth in the 200 final. Bill Hulse was sixth at 1500 metres. Joe McCluskey was fifth in the steeplechase.

By contrast, there were also those for whom Olympic selection came as a welcome bonus or even a complete surprise. John Deni had missed qualifying in the 1936 50 kilometres walk trial by one second and was assured of a place this time only when the athlete with whom he had tied for third place was disqualified. A

19-year-old high jumper, George Stanich, had so little confidence in his ability to win a trip to Europe that he tore up the passport-application forms given to him beforehand, but he beat his personal best by two inches and finished second to an aptly-named 18-year-old, Vern McGrew. In the high hurdles final, Clyde Scott benefited from Dillard's mishap and then from Ed Dugger hitting the last hurdle when looking set for the vital third place. Bill Burton got a surprising third place in the discus with a personal best. Bob Likens, who had narrowly qualified for the javelin trials by placing sixth in the AAU championships, had then retired because he had a wife and two children to support but had been persuaded by his father-in-law to continue and placed second to Martin Biles, who had been NCAA champion in 1940–41 and AAU champion in 1943–44.

There were 32 university and college students in the team, 24 members of clubs (including seven from Los Angeles AC), seven who were unattached, and one in the Armed Forces. There had, in effect, been an adverse benefit from the intervention of war. US athletics teams at the Olympics in the past had very largely consisted of students who mostly retired after graduation, in many cases never having developed their sporting talent to the full, and this would be true again for many more Games until professionalism was introduced in the 1980s. The number of athletes who had made a comeback, determined not to let the loss of years thwart their Olympic ambitions, meant that this US team would be more mature, and therefore stronger, than ever before.

Women's athletics was still very much the poor relation in the US and five of the team came from southern universities and the other six from sponsored clubs in the north-east. The US Olympic Committee required qualifying standards for selection in each sport, and those for athletics were based on the eighth-placed performance in each event at the Berlin Olympics. Only 10 athletes achieved that at the women's one-day trials at Providence, Rhode Island, on 12 July, but the USOC then allowed all winners to be selected, plus Jean Walraven. The second-placed woman in the 80 metres hurdles, Nancy Cowperthwaite Phillips, turned down her selection because she had just got married.

Few other countries had any selection problems which would require as radical a solution as had been devised for Americans in the men's events. Perhaps the Swedes, with five of the 10 fastest 1500 metres runners in the world, needed to ponder awhile over their choice. Maybe the Finns, with four of the six fastest at 10,000 metres, gave more than a moment's thought to their decision. In Britain it seemed rather a case of hoping that some of those who were not really of international calibre but would fill out the team would find inspiration on the day.

The Amateur Athletics Association Championships, at the White City Stadium, on 2 and 3 July – which were, in effect, championships of England open to the world – provided the British Amateur Athletic Board selectors with their conclusive evidence, but nine of the 19 titles went to overseas athletes. Australians, perhaps inspired by their all-conquering cricket compatriots, won the 100 yards,

440 yards, high jump, long jump and triple jump. The "Flying Dutchman", Willy Slijkhuis, took the three miles with ease. Irishmen won the shot and discus. The Latvian refugee, Janis Stendzenieks, won the javelin. The margins of British defeat were embarrassing in some instances – more than 30ft (nine metres) in the javelin.

Depressingly, despite Britain's fine cross-country tradition, the two miles steeplechase was won in very slow time and the monthly magazine, *Athletics*, rightly commented that "we are obviously a long way behind world class in this event". This was patently apparent to the spectators and "most cheers went to the Army runner, Signalman FS Hewitt, who captured the crowd's imagination with his brave if seldom successful attempts to clear the obstacles, particularly the water-jump". Even so, the first three men home in this entertaining but unathletic spectacle were all duly selected to run at Wembley.

Encouragement, though, came from the performances of John Parlett, at 880 yards, and Bill Nankeville, in the mile, in beating strong foreign opposition, and there was a startling victory in the 120 yards hurdles for an 18-year-old pupil at Barrow Grammar School, Joe Birrell, ahead of two very good Aussies. Among the long list of those who had been named as Olympic "possibles" the previous year were 15 pre-war internationals, and eight of them were selected for Wembley: Bill Roberts for the 400 metres and 4x400 metres relay, Stan Cox at 10,000 metres, Jack Holden for the marathon, Don Finlay for the 110 metres hurdles, Harry Askew in the long jump, Jim Nesbitt and Laurence Reavell-Carter in the discus, and Norman Drake in the hammer. Also in the team, though not originally "possibles", were Tebbs Lloyd Johnson for the 50 kilometres walk and Dick Webster for the pole vault. Roberts, Finlay, Reavell-Carter, Drake, Lloyd Johnson and Webster had all competed at the 1936 Berlin Games.

Bill Roberts, now aged 36, was named as team captain and his life story was a fascinating one which would surely have made the ideal subject for a working-class version of *Chariots of Fire*. He had been born in the back streets of the Northern industrial city of Salford, had left school at 14, and had worked his way up from messenger-boy to manager of a timber-yard alongside the Manchester Ship Canal. He had taken up athletics as a youngster in the 1920s, and inspired by the example of an illustrious Salford Athletic Club colleague, Walter Rangeley, the Olympic 200 metres silver-medallist in 1928, he had finished second in the 1934 British Empire Games 440 yards, and had then taken part in unforgettable finals at 400 metres and 4x400 metres at the Berlin Olympics.

At 400 metres, his team-mate Godfrey Brown had lost the gold to Archie Williams, of the USA, by a matter of centimetres and Roberts himself had missed the bronze by a similar margin behind another American, Jimmy LuValle. The US selectors had then, overconfidently, left Williams and LuValle out of their relay team and the British quartet of Freddy Wolff, Godfrey Rampling, Roberts and Brown famously won by a long way, and it is questionable as to whether even a full-strength US team would have challenged the inspired victors that day. In the individual event Brown and Roberts had run times of 46.68 and

46.87 respectively, which would remain unsurpassed by any other Briton until 1958. Brown had attempted a comeback for the 1948 Olympics but was sadly eliminated in the AAA heats.

Roberts – also an accomplished musician and dance-band leader in his spare time – made the long journey to Australia for the 1938 Empire Games despite being told a few days before his departure that he would lose his job if he went. When he recalled this phase of his life more than 60 years later, he was adamant that his decision had been right: "My view was that if selection for the Games turned up it was my duty, nothing less, to run for England. I'd run for Great Britain in international matches, and we'd won the relay gold in Berlin. Whether you lost your job or not, you answered the call." Roberts won the 440 yards at the Empire Games and, after wartime RAF service, during which he often ran challenge races for "beer money" against unsuspecting army rivals, he got back into a rather more formalised type of competition, and his lion-hearted anchor stage for the 4x400 metres at the 1946 European Championships in Oslo had brought Britain the silver medals.

Winners from the Women's AAA Championships, held at Chiswick on 26 June, included Winnie Jordan at 100 metres, Sylvia Cheeseman at 200 metres, Maureen Gardner in the hurdles and Dorothy Tyler (née Odam, the 1936 Olympic silver-medallist) in the high jump. All were duly selected, and their team manager, Mrs Winifred Hughes, expressed some quiet confidence in their abilities. "I feel sure we shall find some of them well placed in the finals," she wrote in *Athletics* magazine. "Up to the present we have had only one woman placed in an individual Olympic event and that is Dorothy Odam, who will be competing again in the high jump, and we shall all be surprised if she does not equal, if not better, her 1936 performance ... Taken all round I believe we shall have good reason to be proud of our girls."

Allowing for dual qualifications in some cases, London and the Home Counties provided 32 of the 65 male members of the team; the Armed Forces and the North seven each; the Midlands and Scotland six each; Achilles (the club for Oxford and Cambridge University graduates) five; Northern Ireland three; the Channel Islands, Ireland and Wales one each. Perhaps the most surprising (not to say mystifying) selection was that of Donald McKenzie for the 4x400 metres relay squad, who had run some useful times at 100 and 220 yards but had no performances at all of any significance at 440 yards!

The Home Counties provided 15 of the 20 female members of the team; the Midlands three; the Armed Forces and the North one each. Dora Gardner, aged 36 and like Tyler a pre-war high-jump international, was named team captain.

The USA team for Wembley was as follows:

MEN

100 metres: Harrison Dillard (Baldwin-Wallace Coll), Barney Ewell (unattached), Mel Patton (Uni of Southern California)

200 metres: Cliff Bourland (Los Angeles AC), Ewell, Patton

400 metres: Dave Bolen (Uni of Colorado), George Guida (Villanova Uni), Mal Whitfield (Ohio State Uni)

800 metres: Herb Barten (Uni of Michigan), Bob Chambers (Uni of Southern California), Whitfield

1500 metres: Clem Eischen (Washington State Uni), Don Gehrmann (Uni of Wisconsin), Roland Sink (Uni of Southern California)

5000 metres: Clarence Robison (Brigham Young Uni), Curtis Stone (unattached), Jerry Thompson (Uni of Texas)

10,000 metres: Herman Goffberg (Shanahan Catholic Club), Edward O'Toole (New York AC), Fred Wilt (unattached)

Marathon: Johnny Kelley (Boston Edison Employees' Club), Ollie Manninen (Boston AA), Ted Vogel (Boston AA)

3000 metres steeplechase: Bob McMillen (Los Angeles AC), William Overton (Alabama Polytechnic Uni), Browning Ross (Villanova Uni)

10,000 metres walk: Henry Laskau (Maccabi AC), Fred Sharaga (92nd Street YMHA), Ernest Weber (German-American AAC)

50 kilometres walk: Ernest Crosbie (White Horse Social Club, Baltimore), John Deni (Pittsburgh Boys' Club), Adolf Weinacker (Michigan State Uni)

4x100 metres relay: Eddie Conwell (unattached), Dillard, Ewell, Patton

4x400 metres relay: Bolen, Guida, Arthur Harnden (Texas Agricultural & Mechanical Uni), Whitfield

110 metres hurdles: Bill Porter (Northwestern Uni), Craig Dixon (Uni of California at Los Angeles), Clyde Scott (Uni of Arkansas)

400 metres hurdles: Dick Ault (Uni of Missouri), Roy Cochran (Los Angeles AC), Jeff Kirk (Uni of Pennsylvania)

High jump: Dwight Eddleman (Uni of Illinois), Vern McGrew (Rice Uni), George Stanich (Los Angeles AC)

Pole vault: Richmond ("Boo") Morcom (New Hampshire State AA), Bob Richards (Uni of Illinois), Guinn Smith (San Francisco Olympic Club)

Long jump: Herb Douglas (Uni of Pittsburgh), Willie Steele (San Diego State Uni), Lorenzo Wright (Wayne Uni)

Triple jump: Bill Albans (unattached), Bob Beckus (Los Angeles AC), Erkki Koutonen (unattached)

Shot: Jim Delaney (San Francisco Olympic Club), Jim Fuchs (Yale Uni), Wilbur Thompson (Los Angeles AC)

Discus: Bill Burton (US Army), Victor Frank (Yale Uni), Fortune Gordien (Uni of Minnesota)

Hammer: Bob Bennett (unattached), Henry Dreyer (New York AC), Sam Felton (Harvard Uni)

Javelin: Martin Biles (San Francisco Olympic Club), Bob Likens (San Jose State Uni), Steve Seymour (Los Angeles AC)

Decathlon: Bob Mathias (unattached), Irving Mondschein (New York Pioneer Club), Floyd Simmons (Los Angeles AC)

WOMEN

100 metres: Audrey Patterson (Tennessee State Coll), Mabel Walker (Tuskegee Institute), Lillian Young (Forrestville Playground AC)

200 metres: Mae Faggs (New York Police Athletic League), Nell Jackson (Tuskegee Institute), Patterson

80 metres hurdles: Theresa Manuel (Tuskegee Institute), Bernice Robinson (Washington Park AC), Jean Walraven (North Olmstead-Westlake AC)

4x100 metres relay: Faggs, Jackson, Manuel, Patterson, Walker, Young

High jump: Alice Coachman (Albany State Coll), Emma Reed (Tennessee State Coll), Robinson

Long jump: Reed, Walraven, Young

Shot: Dorothy Dodson (JT Dempsey Hurricanes), Frances Kaszubski (North Olmstead-Westlake AC)

Discus: Dodson, Kuszebski

Javelin: Dodson, Manuel

The Great Britain team for Wembley was as follows:

MEN

100 metres: Ken Jones (Newport AC), Alastair McCorquodale (London AC), Emmanuel McDonald Bailey (Polytechnic H)

200 metres: John Fairgrieve (Achilles Club), McCorquodale, Paul Vallé (Army & Enfield AC)

400 metres: Les Lewis (Borough Road College & Walton AC), Derek Pugh (South London H), Bill Roberts (Salford AC)

800 metres: John Parlett (Dorking St Paul's AC), Harold Tarraway (Southampton University & London AC), Tom White (Lincoln Wellington AC)

1500 metres: Dick Morris (Milocarian AC), Bill Nankeville (Army & Old Woking AC), Doug Wilson (Polytechnic H)

5000 metres: Jack Braughton (Blackheath H), Bill Lucas (Belgrave H), Alec Olney (Thames Valley H),

10,000 metres: Stan Cox (Southgate H), Steve McCooke (East Antrim H), Jim Peters (Essex Beagles)

3000 metres steeplechase: Peter Curry (Achilles Club), Rene Howell (Polytechnic H), Geoffrey Tudor (Achilles Club)

Marathon: Jack Holden (Tipton H), Stan Jones (Polytechnic H), Tom Richards (South London H)

10,000 metres walk: Harry Churcher (Belgrave H), Jim Morris (Surrey AC), Ron West (Cambridge H, Kent)

50 kilometres walk: Tebbs Lloyd Johnson (Leicester Walking Club), Bert Martineau (Surrey Walking Club), Rex Whitlock (Metropolitan Walking Club)

4x100 metres relay: Ken Anderson (Liverpool Police), Jack Archer (Loughborough College & Notts AC), Fairgrieve, Jack Gregory (Crusaders AC, Dublin), Jones, McCorquodale, Vallé, Alan Watt (Shettleston H)

4x400 metres relay: Tom Collier (Small Heath H), Ken Crowe (Manchester AC), Terry Higgins (RAF & Herne Hill H), Lewis, Donald McKenzie (Edinburgh University), Martin Pike (Polytechnic H), Pugh, Roberts

110 metres hurdles: Ray Barkway (Achilles Club), Joe Birrell (Barrow GS), Don Finlay (RAF & Milocarian AC)

400 metres hurdles: Michael Pope (London AC), Ron Unsworth (Manchester AC), Harry Whittle (Reading AC)

High jump: Adegboyega Adedoyin (Queen's University, Belfast), Alan Paterson (Army & Victoria Park AAC), Ron Pavitt (Polytechnic H)

Pole vault: Dick Webster (Army & Milocarian AC)

Long jump: Adedoyin, Harry Askew (Achilles Club & Jersey AC), Whittle

Triple jump: Sid Cross (Birchfield H), Robert Hawkey (Darlington H) Allan Lindsay (St Andrew's Uni)

Shot: John Giles (Southgate H), Harold Moody (South London H)

Discus: Ernest Brewer (Old Rutlishians AC), Jim Nesbitt (Royal Ulster Constabulary), Laurence Reavell-Carter (RAF)

Hammer: Duncan Clark (Royal Ulster Constabulary & Wellpark H), Ewan Douglas (RAF), Norman Drake (Blackpool & Fylde H)

Javelin: Morville Chote (Army & Achilles Club), Malcolm Dalrymple (London AC)

Decathlon: no selections made

WOMEN

100 metres: Doris Batter (London Olympiades), Winnie Jordan (Birchfield H), Dorothy Manley (Essex Ladies AC)

200 metres: Sylvia Cheeseman (Spartan Ladies AC), Margaret Walker (Spartan Ladies AC), Audrey Williamson (Women's Royal Army Corps & St Gregory's AC, Cheltenham)

80 metres hurdles: Bertha Crowther (Middlesex Ladies AC), Maureen Gardner (Oxford Ladies AC), Joan Upton (Spartan Ladies AC)

4x100 metres relay: Batter, Cheeseman, Gardner, Jordan, Manley, Maureen Pletts (Airedale H), Walker, Williamson

High Jump: Crowther, Dora Gardner (Middlesex Ladies AC), Dorothy Tyler (Mitcham Ladies AC)

Long jump: Margaret Erskine (Birmingham Atalanta AC), Lorna Lee (Tonbridge AC), Joan Shepherd (Essex Ladies AC)

Shot: Margaret Lucas (Epsom & Ewell H), Bevis Reid (Mitcham Ladies AC), Elspeth Whyte (Epsom & Ewell H & London Uni)

Discus: Lucas, Reid, Whyte

Javelin: Gladys Clarke (Birchfield H), Marian Long (Epsom & Ewell H)

The athletics world records on the eve of the 1948 Olympics

MEN

100 metres: 10.2 Jesse Owens (USA), Chicago 20 June 1936; 10.2 Hal Davis (USA), Compton, California, 6 June 1941; 10.2 Lloyd La Beach (Panama), Fresno, California, 15 May 1948; 10.2 Barney Ewell (USA), Evanston, Illinois, 9 July 1948

200 metres: 20.7 Jesse Owens (USA), Berlin, 5 August 1936; 20.7 Mel Patton (USA), Evanston, Illinois, 10 July 1948; 20.7 Barney Ewell (USA), Evanston, Illinois, 10 July 1948. Note: Until 1951 world records were recognised for times set on straight courses or round a turn. The official world record was 20.3 for 220 yards (201.17 metres) set on a straight course by Owens, Ann Arbor, Michigan, 25 May 1935. Lloyd La Beach (Panama) also ran 20.3 for 220 yards (timed at 20.2 for 200 metres en route), Compton, California, 4 June 1948, but this was not ratified.

400 metres: 45.9 Herb McKenley (Jamaica), Milwaukee, 2 July 1948. Note: McKenley had also set a world record for 440 yards (402.34 metres) of 46.0 (equivalent to 45.7 for 400 metres), Berkeley, California, 5 June 1948.

800 metres: 1:46.6 Rudolf Harbig (Germany), Milan, 15 July 1939

1500 metres: 3:43.0 Gunder Hägg (Sweden), Gothenburg, 7 July 1944; 3:43.0 Lennart Strand (Sweden), Malmö, 15 July 1947

5000 metres: 13:58.2 Gunder Hägg (Sweden), Gothenburg, 20 September 1942

10,000 metres: 29:35.4 Viljo Heino (Finland), Helsinki, 25 August 1944

3000 metres steeplechase: 8:59.6 Erik Elmsäter (Sweden), Stockholm, 4 August 1944. Note: because of variations in courses official records were not recognised until standardisation in 1954, but Elmsäter's time was the best recorded under the rules applied to Olympic competition.

Marathon: 2:25:39 Yun Bok Suh (Korea), Boston, Massachusetts, 19 April 1947. Note: Because of variations in road terrain official records were not recognised.

10,000 metres walk: 42:39.6 Werner Hardmö (Sweden), Kumla, 9 September 1945. Note: A time of 42:31.0 by Václav Balsán (Czecholsovakia), Prague, 24 October 1945, was not officially ratified.

50 kilometres walk: 4:34:03 Paul Sievert (Germany), Munich, 5 October 1924.

110 metres hurdles: 13.7 Forrest Towns (USA), Oslo, 27 August 1936; 13.7 Fred Wolcott (USA), Philadelphia, 9 June 1941. Note: Harrison Dillard (USA) set a world record for 120 yards (109.73 metres) hurdles of 13.6, Lawrence, Kansas, 17 April 1948. This time would be regarded by statisticians as equivalent to the same 13.6 for 100 metres hurdles.

400 metres hurdles: 50.6 Glenn Hardin (USA), Stockholm, 26 July 1934

4x100 metres relay: 39.8 USA (Jesse Owens, Ralph Metcalfe, Foy Draper, Frank Wykoff), Berlin, 9 August 1936

4x400 metres relay: 3:08.2 USA (Ivan Fuqua, Edgar Ablowich, Karl Warner, Bill Car), Los Angeles, 7 August 1932. Note: University of California (John Reese, Fay Froom, Clarence Barnes, Grover Klemmer) set a world record for 4x440 yards of 3:09.4, Los Angeles, 17 June 1941, equivalent to 3:08.2 for 4x400 metres. University of Southern California (Warren Smith, Howard Upton, Cliff Bourland, Hubie Kerns) was second, also in 3:09.4, but the time was taken on only one watch and was not ratified.

High jump: 6ft 11in (2.11m) Lester Steers (USA), Los Angeles, 17 June 1941

Pole vault: 15ft 7¾in (4.77m) Cornelius Warmerdam (USA), Modesto, California, 23 May 1942. Note: Warmerdam also cleared 15ft 8¼in (4.79m) indoors, Chicago, 20 March 1943, but indoor performances were not then recognised for world-record purposes.

Long jump: 26ft 8¼in (8.13m) Jesse Owens (USA), Ann Arbor, Michigan, 25 May 1935

Triple jump: 16.00m Naoto Tajima (Japan), Berlin, 6 August 1936

Shot: 58ft 0 ⅜in (17.68m) Charles Fonville (USA), Lawrence, Kansas, 17 April 1948

Discus: 180ft 2⅜in (54.93m) Bob Fitch (USA), Minneapolis, 8 June 1946

Hammer: 59.00m Erwin Blask (Germany), Stockholm, 27 August 1938

Javelin: 78.70m Yrjö Nikkanen (Finland), Kotka, 16 October 1938

Decathlon: 7,900 points Glenn Morris (USA), Berlin, 7–8 August 1936.

Note: this performance was scored on the 1934 Tables then in use. On the current 1985 Tables Morris's score would be 7,254 points.

WOMEN

100 metres: 11.6 Helen Stephens (USA), Kansas City, 8 June 1935; 11.6 Stanislawa Walasiewicz (Poland), Berlin, 1 August 1937. Note: Fanny Blankers-Koen (Holland) ran 11.5 in a race against men, Amsterdam, 5 September 1943, and this time was not ratified. The official handbook of IAAF records, published in 2003, notes of Walasiewicz that "by today's criteria it is 99 per cent certain that she would not have been admitted to women's competitions".

200 metres: 23.6 Stanislawa Walasiewicz (Poland), Warsaw, 4 August 1935. Note: the best performer otherwise was Helen Stephens (USA) who ran 23.2 for 220 yards on a straight course, Toronto, 2 September 1935, and 24.1 for 200 metres round a turn, Wuppertal, 19 August 1936.

80 metres hurdles: 11.0 Fanny Blankers-Koen (Holland), Amsterdam, 20 June 1948

4x100 metres relay: 46.4 Germany (Emmy Albus, Käthe Krauss, Marie Dollinger, Ilse Dörffeldt), Berlin, 8 August 1936

High jump: 1.71m Fanny Blankers-Koen (Holland), Amsterdam, 30 May 1943

Long jump: 6.25m Fanny Blankers-Koen (Holland), Leiden, 19 September 1943

Shot: 14.38m Gisela Mauermayer (Germany), Warsaw, 15 July 1934: Note: Tatyana Sevryukova (USSR) achieved 14.89m, Frunze, 14 October 1945, but this was not ratified because of the USSR's non-affiliation to the IAAF.

Discus: 48.31m Gisela Mauermayer (Germany), Berlin, 11 July 1936. Note: Nina Dumbadze (USSR) achieved 50.30m, Sarpsborg, Norway, 29 August 1946, not ratified for the same reason as applied to the shot.

Javelin: 48.21m Herma Bauma (Austria), Vienna, 29 June 1947: Note: Klavdiya Mayuchaya (USSR) achieved 50.32m, Moscow, 23 September 1947, not ratified for the same reason as applied to the shot and discus.

Of these world record-holders 13 would be at Wembley: Ewell, Patton, Dillard and Bourland (all USA); Strand, Elmsäter and Hardmö (all Sweden); La Beach (Panama), McKenley (Jamaica), Heino (Finland), Yun Bok Suh (Korea), Blankers-Koen (Holland) and Bauma (Austria).

Chapter 11

ATHLETICS

Emil sets off along the golden road.
Elspeth is just glad to be there

The first day – Friday 30 July

The day's programme: 11 a.m. High jump qualifying; 2.30 p.m. 400 metres hurdles heats; 3 p.m. 100 metres heats; 3.30 p.m. Discus (women) final; 4 p.m. 800 metres heats; 4.30 p.m. High jump final; 5 p.m. 400 metres hurdles semi-finals; 5.30 p.m. 100 metres quarter-finals; 6 p.m. 10,000 metres final.

I T WAS NOT a good start to the afternoon. The barriers had been set out wrongly for the opening track event, the 400 metres hurdles heats, and it took 35 minutes to put things to rights. A slow hand-clap and more than a murmur of the phlegmatic wartime refrain, "Why are we waiting?", was heard from the restless crowd, but when the action at last got under way the sun-baked spectators were soon treated to some quality athletics.

The opener of the six hurdles heats, with only the first two finishers in each to qualify for semi-finals later in the day, was won by Roy Cochran, of the USA, and his time of 53.9 – taking it nice and easy – was far faster than two of the three Britons soon to be seen on the track had ever achieved. It must have been a poignant experience for Cochran because the previous occasion he had run in London was in August of 1939 at the White City Stadium, when he had won the 440 yards hurdles at the British Games in 52.7, and a week or so later he had shared in one of the very last world records to be set before the outbreak of war as a member of a USA 4x800 metres relay team in Paris.

The fastest heat-winner in 53.6 was the powerful but awkward-looking Duncan White, of Ceylon, who had run in the 1938 British Empire Games. The other Americans, Dick Ault and Jeff Kirk, and all three Frenchmen (Jacques André, Jean-Claude Arifon, Yves Cros) got through, together with John Holland (New Zealand), Rune Larsson (Sweden), Ottavio Missoni (Italy), Bertil Storskrubb (Finland) and Harry Whittle (GB). The slower of the Britons, Michael Pope and Ron Unsworth, were eliminated but far from disgraced. They ran personal best times of 55.3 and 55.1 respectively, and Pope's memories of the occasion were of the fondest when asked to relate his experiences almost 60 years later:

"The draw for the heats was put up on a noticeboard, and as soon as I saw that I'd got the European champion, Storskrubb, of Finland, as well as John Holland, of New Zealand, who'd come second in the AAA, I knew there was not a snowflake's chance of getting any further, but I thought that with a bit of luck I might run faster than ever before, and that's what I managed to do. So I was happy with that.

"It was all very different, of course, at Uxbridge, where the team was, compared with the Olympics of these days, but it did seem to me to be athletics at its best. It was the last occasion, I believe, that everyone was acting in the true spirit of amateur athletics. Nobody bothered two pins about what is now sometimes called 'austerity'. The Canadians sent us food parcels, and we were all perfectly comfortable and everyone had enough to eat. We went to bed early. We did a lot of training. The important thing was to do your very best on the day."

Pope was then 21 and had taken up 400 metres hurdling only while serving with the Royal Tank Regiment in Germany the previous year. Returning to civilian life, he won the 440 hurdles at the start of the Olympic season for the Amateur Athletic Association (AAA) representative team in their annual match against Cambridge University and was encouragingly told by the British team manager, Jack Crump, "If you keep this up, you may get into the Olympic team". By modern standards, Pope's training was alarmingly slight, as he recorded in his diary no more than 61 sessions throughout 1948. He became a music student the next year and continued to run for his club until 1953. Ron Unsworth was even more of a novice than Pope, and recalls that he was persuaded to take up hurdling by a generous-hearted Harry Whittle, who early in 1948 made the cheery observation, "I've got an easy event here. Why don't you try it?"

The 100 metres had attracted 69 entries, though this was by no means a record, as there had been 87 in Paris in 1924, which had required 17 first-round heats. Here, at Wembley, 12 heats needed to be drawn, from which the first two in each would go into the quarter-finals later in the day. It could not be said that there were any real shock failures in the first round, though it might have been thought odd that Walter Pérez, of Uruguay, who had run 10.4 in the seaport capital of Montevideo a month before, could now manage only 11.0 to finish third in heat 10. Timing standards varied significantly throughout the world in this era when almost invariably hand-held watches were used rather than automatic devices, but maybe Pérez was simply injured, unwell or overawed – all of which are recurrent and contagious Olympic complaints.

Despite the seeding the winning heat times varied from 10.4 (Dillard, of the USA) to 11.0 (Fayos, of Uruguay), and so far as the prospects were concerned all that seemed to be proved was that Dillard was in cracking form – not that anything else would be expected from an American sprinter. The automatic times which were not revealed to the public, nor for that matter even discovered in the archives until 27 years later, were invariably slower and the fastest of these was a 10.6 by John Treloar, the Australian winner of the 100 yards ahead of Britain's best at the previous month's AAA Championships.

It did rather seem that the newly constructed track was conducive to quality sprinting, because Dillard's 10.4 equalled the time of McDonald Bailey in a club race the previous month, the fastest ever on British soil. The 100 metres, of course, was very rarely run in Britain, but even at the predominant 100 yards Bailey's British all-comers' record was 9.6, which he had achieved twice in legal conditions in 1947 and which was the equivalent to a 10.4 for 100 metres. It was not until 10 July that removal of Wembley's existing greyhound-racing circuit and its fencing, lighting and electric-hare apparatus had begun, and laying of the track had been completed just a day or so in time for the sprinters to step on to it. The surface was, of course, cinders – no all-weather tracks would be in use in Britain for another 20 years – and its condition would be entirely at the mercy of the weather.

The form of automatic timing in operation at Wembley was unlike anything else before or since. Margins in hundredths of a second were given for those finishing behind the winner but no such precise times were given for the winners themselves. The timing was done by eight watches, above each of which was a solenoid with a core touching the watch's button. When the trigger of the starter's gun was depressed an electrical circuit was completed and a current started the watches. At the finish a photo-cell was used and a current again passed through to stop the watches. The system failed on a number of occasions, apparently because of insufficient electrical contact, but the data it produced has allowed many of the times for athletes to be established which would otherwise have gone unrecorded. Only the times for the first three in each shorter-distance track event were ever published by the Games organisers, and it was the assiduous work of the late Bob Sparks, president of the Association of Track & Field Statisticians, which eventually brought the missing performances to light.

The average difference between the hand times and automatic times for the dozen heat-winners in the first round of the 100 metres was just under 0.2sec, confirming the belief expressed by Harry Hathway, one of the official timekeepers at Wembley and a leading practitioner for 20 years, that the principal fault with human timekeeping was the tendency to anticipate. Numerous pre-war British international athletes were officiating with Hathway in various capacities at Wembley, including the 1932 Olympic 800 metres champion Tommy Hampson, a press steward; the 1924 hammer bronze-medallist Malcolm Nokes, a judge for the throwing events; the 1936 800 metres finalist Brian MacCabe, a recorder; and the leading sprinter of the 1930s Cyril Holmes, who was a marksman.

The first of the field events to be decided on this opening day was the women's discus, and this would also be the first of the Wembley competitions to be critically affected by absentees, though only a few of the most knowledgeable of spectators in the stadium would surely have been aware of the fact. This was where the USSR boycott would bite deep, and it would do so again in the days to follow. The Georgian-born Nina Dumbadze had won the European discus title in 1946 and set an unofficial world record of 50.50m the same year. Two months before the 1948 Olympics she had come close to her best with a throw of exactly a metre less. In normal circumstances no one could possibly have threatened her for the gold medal; not even the No.2 Soviet thrower, Klavdiya Tochonova, who was almost four metres behind at 45.63.

Without these two, or a third Soviet woman, Yelizaveta Bagryantseva, who had thrown 44.20, the Olympic competition would be minor league stuff, and the stark evidence of the results cannot be argued with. Micheline Ostermeyer, of France, won at 41.92, and Edera Cordiale-Gentile, of Italy, was second at 41.17. Not even the Olympic Games record, set in Berlin at 47.63 by the official world record-holder Gisela Mauermayer, was remotely challenged. Curiously, no qualifying round was held and all 21 competitors took part in an unnecessarily prolonged final. Mme Ostermeyer was admiringly described by one French writer as *"grande, solide, svelte, distinguée"* – which needs no translating! She was 1.78m (5ft 9in) tall and weighed 65kg (11st 8lb).

But then Olympic titles are won on the field of play, not in the dusty columns of ranking-lists, and it was hardly the fault of Ostermeyer that better throwers than her were not there on the day. In any case, hers was to be one of the most appealing stories of these Games, because regardless of the intrinsic merit of her throwing she has particular distinction as surely the only Olympic champion to also be a celebrated concert pianist. In 1946 she had placed second in the European Championships shot-put and had won the premier piano prize at the Paris Conservatory.

Fifty years after the 1948 Olympics she made a nostalgic return visit to Wembley with a group of fellow-French competitors from that year and there she met up with Neil Allen, the experienced Olympic journalist, who was keen to refresh his memories of that occasion of long ago when he had been an agog 15-year-old among the crowd. He soon discovered that the discus success had come about by chance.

"When I had been selected for the London Olympics in the shot and high jump they decided to let me compete in the discus, too", Madame Ostermeyer explained. "After all, there were no Russians competing and '*on ne sait jamais*'. I can see now that it was quite amazing that I should be the winner in my 'new' event, even though I insist it was through practising rather than competing that I had acquired the 'hands and fingers' sensation of throwing. But to become an Olympic champion, to win a gold medal with an honest throw of 41 metres 92, ahead of the Italian favourite, Gentile, was a special present."

In fourth place in the women's discus was Jadwiga Marcinkiewicz, of Poland, making her third Olympic appearance at the age of 36, having placed third in 1932 and second in 1936 under her maiden name of Wajsowna. She had also set nine world records, including two in succession at the "Women's World Games" at the White City Stadium, in London, in 1934. The Dutchwoman Anna Panhorst-Niesink, in sixth, improved one place on her Berlin showing when she was 17.

Britain's trio of Bevis Reid, Margaret Lucas and Elspeth Whyte were 14th, 19th and 20th respectively of the 21 competitors, which on the face of it seems of no great import, but there was an abiding memory of the occasion for the coach of one of the women. Kenneth Sandilands ("Sandy") Duncan was an international sprinter and long jumper before the war but had to withdraw from the Berlin Olympic team because of a hamstring injury. He was invited to go instead as a member of the headquarters staff, and thus began a long and distinguished career in sports administration. Later in 1948 he was to become general secretary of the British Olympic Association and he was one of the officials in the stadium at Wembley, acting as a judge of the jumping events. He had also been coaching a number of Olympic "possibles", among them Elspeth Whyte, and despite her modest showing both she and he were delighted that she had got into the team.

Miss Whyte, then a 21-year-old student at London University, was by no means obviously a natural for her events. "She was very small", Sandy Duncan recalled more than half a century later, "and we had no proper weightlifting in those days. I got her somehow to lift a men's 16lb hammer, and it worked well enough for her to get selected. I think you'll find she finished last in the shot at Wembley and 20th out of 21 in the discus, but she competed in the Olympic Games, and very, very few of us can claim that."

The official film of the Olympic Games devotes a rather disproportionate amount of time to the women's discus, featuring a repetitive succession of throws by most of the finalists. Such undeserved attention serves only to show that almost without exception the technique adopted by the competitors was rudimentary and lacking in any real power or zest. Weight-training was virtually unknown in those days even for male exponents of the throwing events, and there is little evidence that the women in this event were throwing on anything more than natural ability. Nina Dumbadze was sadly missed.

The six first-round heats of the 800 metres, with the leading four in each to go through to the next day's semi-finals, should have been largely a formality – and certainly started that way when the fastest man of the year, Marcel Hansenne, of France, won the opening race from the AAA champion, John Parlett, and the new Australian record-holder, 20-year-old Bill Ramsay, with an Argentinian, a

---

Discus (women) result: 1 Micheline Ostermeyer (France) 41.92m, 2 Edera Cordiale-Gentile (Italy) 41.17, 3 Jacqueline Mazéas (France) 40.47, 4 Jadwiga Marcinkiewicz (Poland) 39.30, 5 Charlotte Haidegger (Austria) 38.81, 6 Anna Panhorst-Niesink (Holland) 38.74, 7 Majken Åberg (Sweden) 38.48, 8 Ingeborg Mello de Preiss (Argentina) 38.44, 9 Frieda Tiltsch (Austria) 37.19, 10 Paulette Veste (France) 36.84, 11 Frances Kaszubski (USA) 36.50, 12 Gudrun Arenander (Sweden) 36.25, 13 Petronella Roos-Lodder (Holland) 36.15, 14 Bevis Reid (GB) 35.84, 15 Marianne Schläger (Austria) 34.79, 16 Dorothy Dodson (USA) 34.69, 17 Ljubica Gabric-Calvesi (Italy) 34.17, 18 Pak Pong Sik (Korea) 33.80, 19 Margaret Lucas (GB) 33.02, 20 Elspeth Whyte (GB) 32.46, 21 Julija Matej (Yugoslavia) 30.25.

Korean and an Egyptian out of the picture. However, in the next heat there was a most unfortunate incident when Doug Harris, of New Zealand, and Herluf Christensen, of Denmark, collided, and the Dane collapsed to the ground. He was left untended for some time, which greatly incensed the public nearest to him, and when at last he was taken off to hospital it was discovered that he had broken his leg. Christensen had been the eighth fastest among the entrants at 1:51.0 and would certainly have entertained hopes of reaching the final.

John Parlett was soon joined in the next round by his team-mate, Tom White, but the third Briton, Harold Tarraway, had a much tougher task in heat five and only slipped through by a fraction in fourth place. The 6ft 4in (1.93m) tall Arthur Wint received as warm a reception as anybody by winning the fourth heat; though he was representing Jamaica he had served as a Flight Lieutenant with the RAF during the war and was now a London University medical student and a very familiar figure on British tracks. Much the fastest qualifying times of 1:52.8 and 1:52.9 were recorded by the US trials winner, Mal Whitfield, and the leading Swede, Ingvar Bengtsson, in the last heat, but they smacked of wild extravagance because there were only five starters and a time of almost 10 seconds slower would still have sufficed.

The first of the field events was now to be decided: the men's high jump. Here Britain had high hopes of the 20-year-old Scot, Alan Paterson, who was 6ft 6in (1.98m) tall, had placed second in the 1946 European Championships, and had set a national record of 6ft 7½in (2.01m) the previous year, but the odds seemed to favour the even more youthful Americans Vern McGrew and George Stanich, who had both cleared 6ft 8¼in (2.04m) in their Olympic trials. After all, 23 of the 30 leading high jumpers in the world for the year were Americans, and so McGrew, Stanich and their team-mate, Dwight Eddleman, had overcome immense opposition to even get to Wembley. History was also on their side because Americans had won the Olympic men's high-jump gold at every Games but one since 1908 – and the exception was a US-trained Canadian, Duncan McNaughton, in 1932. The world record had been held unbroken since 1895 by 11 successive Americans.

The morning's qualifying round for the high jump was supposed to have reduced the entry of 27 competitors to a manageable number, but the required height of 1.87m was failed by only seven men, including Britain's Ron Pavitt (though Pavitt, an early exponent in Britain of the "straddle" style, was to do much better with fifth place at the 1952 Games). The final came as something of an anticlimax as none of the Americans were in their best form – and, nor for that matter, were many of the others. McGrew, suffering from nerves, could go no higher than 1.80m. Paterson and his splendidly titled Nigerian-born team-mate Prince Adegboyega Folaranmi Adedoyin cleared 1.90m but failed at 1.95m. By then five men were left in the competition, and the only one to clear 1.95m at the first attempt was an entirely unforeseen Norwegian, Bjørn Paulson, who had never figured even in the European top 50 before Olympic year. Then at 1.98m the single success was by the Australian record-holder, Jack Winter, and he was thus Olympic champion.

The event had been held in difficult circumstances, with the distraction of the 10,000 metres going on and the approach surface to the high-jump bar breaking up. In the absence of any official transport, Winter had hitched a ride to the stadium in the morning and had stayed there all day. On his final jump he felt a sharp pain in his back and knew he could go no higher. He was a 23-year-old bank clerk from Perth, Western Australia, and it was a welcome return to Britain for him as he had served there with the Royal Australian Air Force during the war, earning his pilot's wings at the age of 18. He was training to fly Wellington bombers when the war ended and filled in some of his time while waiting to be sent home by working as a film extra, appearing in *Caesar and Cleopatra*.

On two counts this win of his was out of the ordinary: he was the first Australian gold-medallist in athletics since his unrelated namesake, Nick Winter, had won the triple jump in 1924; and he was the last man to win the Olympic men's high jump with the antiquated and inefficient "Eastern cut-off" style by which the jumper cleared the bar in what was more or less a seated position. Already, the world record-holder, Les Steers, had shown the way with his face-down "straddle", which raised the body's centre of gravity much higher above the bar, and the "Fosbury Flop" would change the whole manner of high-jumping at the Olympics 20 years on. Winter persevered with his outdated technique and won again at the British Empire Games of 1950.

He was one of many Australians selected for the Games who raised their own money for the venture, and he later recalled one hazardous fund-gathering effort when he and the sprinter Shirley Strickland, also a West Australian, stood in a boxing-ring listening to an appeal on their behalf and then sheltering their heads from the shower of two-shilling pieces which the fight fans threw in appreciation.

It is one of the continuing joys of Olympic competition that second place could be taken by a complete outsider like Paulson, who no doubt felt much less weight of expectation on his shoulders than did, say, his American and British opponents. Paulson was a law student in Oslo who had only two seasons of serious competition behind him, and had come to Wembley as the No.3 Norwegian high jumper, having never beaten either of his compatriots. But he had equalled his personal best and then won his one and only national title three weeks later. He retired after the 1950 season to concentrate on his studies and became a respected lawyer and then public prosecutor in the city of Stavanger.

High jump result: 1 Jack Winter (Australia) 1.98m, 2 Bjørn Paulson (Norway) 1.95, 3 George Stanich (USA) 1.95, 4 Dwight Eddleman (USA) 1.95, 5 Georges Damitio (France) 1.95, 6 Art Jackes (Canada) 1.90, 7= Alan Paterson (GB), Hans Wahli (Switzerland) 1.90m, 9= Alfredo Jedresic (Chile), Pierre Lacaze (France), Göran Widenfelt (Sweden) 1.90, 12 Adegboyega Adedoyin (GB) 1.90, 13 Birger Leirud (Norway) 1.80, 14= Hercules Azcune (Uruguay), Lloyd Valberg (Singapore) 1.80, 16 Vern McGrew (USA) 1.80, 17 Kuuno Hönkönen (Finland) 1.80, 18 Gurnam Singh (India) 1.80. No height cleared – Bjørn Gundersen (Norway), Nils Nicklén (Finland)

The Americans Eddleman and Stanich were initially announced as having tied for third place before a recount gave Stanich the bronze medal on the "fewer misses" rule in use for the first time at an Olympics. It is really rather difficult to understand why the officials should have made such an elementary blunder, though they claimed the rules were "ambiguous", and it was not the only mistake of the day. Charitably, it could be said that at the opening session of the most important athletics meeting ever to be held in Britain, taking place in a stadium which had only briefly been used for the sport more than 20 years before, and with officials under the spotlight of public scrutiny for the first time in the best part of a decade, mistakes were likely to happen.

For the first time at an Olympics, seeding of heats had been introduced. This was based on the statistical researches of the two pre-eminent experts, Roberto Quercetani, of Italy, and Don Potts, of the USA, but even the most careful of calculations beforehand are not able to allow for what happens once competition gets under way. Accordingly, there appeared to be an anomaly in the semi-finals of the 400 metres hurdles as the Italian Missoni, who had been born in what is now Croatia, had qualified in a time of 53.4 in the second semi-final, whereas the 52.5 by Arifon, of France, and Kirk, of the USA, had failed to get them through in the first semi-final. Yet there were four heat-winners in the second semi-final and only two in the first, and on the basis of heat times the draw seemed fair enough. The fact is that for no obvious reasons one qualifying race can often be markedly faster than another in Olympic competition.

Missoni, who had been a prisoner-of-war in North Africa and had been repatriated in a seriously ill condition, had worked wonders to get to the final; Arifon, who had given up smoking for Olympic year, might have been tempted to light up again in frustration.

It had been the first three in each of the two 400 metres hurdles semi-finals who had gone through to the next day's final, and both races had been intensely competitive. The Swede, Larsson, won the first, and his time of 51.9 was sensational, breaking the Olympic record which had stood since 1932. The rather peculiar circumstances in which this record had been set need explaining, because the holder was Glenn Hardin, of the USA, who two years later set a world record of 50.6 which was to stand until 1953, but he had only come second in Los Angeles. The winner had been Bob Tisdall, of Ireland, but he had knocked down a barrier, and the rules then in force meant that a record could not be recognised, though the Irishman kept his gold medal. In fairness, Tisdall's time of 51.7 (electronically recorded as 51.67) should have been reinstated by 1948 as the Games record.

Ault and White qualified behind Larsson, and Cochran promptly ran another 51.9 in the second semi-final, with Cros and Missoni following. Whittle very narrowly missed a place in the final, recording the same time as Missoni, while Kirk, the third fastest man of the year before the Games, and Storskrubb, the European champion from 1946, were the surprising eliminations. Whittle, like Pope and Unsworth, had run his fastest ever time, and so all had certainly "done their very best on the day", as Pope had hoped, to give the British team a creditable start to these onerous Olympic proceedings.

Missoni met his wife Rosita at the Games – she was studying in London and decided to watch the athletics – and they went on to found a world-famous fashion business (Missoni had designed the Italian track team's uniforms).

From the 100 metres quarter-finals 12 men would go through to the next day's semi-finals, with the first three of the six runners in each of the four races to qualify. It would not be until the 1964 Games that an eight-lane track would be brought into standard use. Of the dozen who advanced at Wembley, the USA, Australia and Great Britain each provided three. Dillard, Ewell and Patton won the first three quarter-finals for the USA and the one-man team from Panama, Lloyd La Beach, won the fourth. Apart from the three Australians and three Britons, the others to get through were Rafael Fortún Chacón, of Cuba, and Juan Lopez Testa, of Uruguay. This was only to be expected of the Americans, but relatively untilled ground was being struck by the trio from Central and South America. From those regions only Argentina had previously had an Olympic sprint semi-finalist, and Carlos Bianchi had gone on to place fifth in the 1932 200 metres. The fastest time was Patton's at 10.4 (10.6 automatically), but no one was revealing their true form just yet.

Among those departing was George Lewis, of Trinidad, who had unofficially equalled the world 100 yards record of 9.4 back in 1944 in a race in which McDonald Bailey had placed third. There had been a report that Lewis had run that time again in California three months before coming to Wembley, and he had been described in his homeland as "a potential Olympic 100 metres winner". He would not be alone in having carried the over confident hopes of fellow-countrymen into an Olympic Games.

The climax of the day, when the only track gold medal was to be decided, was the 10,000 metres. There were 27 starters and the fastest of them was Viljo Heino, of Finland. Heino was the latest in a long line of "Flying Finns", maintaining a marvellous tradition which had begun with Hannes Kolehmainen, winner at 5000 and 10,000 metres at the 1912 Olympics, and had been continued by Paavo Nurmi, and then by further Olympic triumphs for Lauri Lehtinen and Gunnar Höckert at 5000 metres and by Ilmari Salminen at 10,000 metres in the 1930s. Heino, who had succeeded another fellow-countryman, Taisto Mäki, with a world record 29:35.4 in 1944, had not been quite as fast since, but then he had not needed to be, winning the 1946 European title from yet another Finn by almost 40 seconds.

Even so, there was a challenge to the seemingly impregnable Finnish domain. Emil Zátopek, of Czechoslovakia, had tried 10,000 metres for the first time only the previous May and had misjudged the pace, going off much too fast but still beating the national record by more than two minutes. Less than three weeks later Zátopek set out again, improved beyond recognition, and agonisingly came within two seconds of Heino's record. With more guidance from the trackside he might well have surpassed Heino because his Czech biographer, František Kožík, was to recall impassionedly of the seething excitement among the spectators: "We are seized with panic because according to our own reckoning even the world record might have been broken ... but down there in the centre no one seems to realise it."

The others in the pre-Olympic 10,000 metres rankings were far behind Heino's 29:35.4 and Zátopek's 29:37.0. Only five others, all from Scandinavia, had broken 31min: Könönen (Finland) 30:10.8, Heinström (Finland) 30:11.0, Stokken (Norway) 30:24.4, Albertsson (Sweden) 30:26.4, and Dennolf (Sweden) 30:50.0. The six-mile times by the British trio (equivalent to a minute slower for 10,000 metres) were 30:07.0 for Jim Peters, 30:08.4 for Stan Cox, 30:27.6 for Steve McCooke, and maybe on that basis Peters or Cox could manage a place in the first ten.

The race thus held out every promise of being a strictly two-man affair, and nothing that happened early on gave any reason to change that view. Heino went straight into the lead from Albertsson and Heinström, covering the first kilometre in 2:55.6, well inside world-record pace and which, if sustained, would lead to a winning time of around 29:20. At 2000 metres, reached in 5:52.0, the schedule was precisely the same. At 3000 metres (8:51.0) it had dropped a shade but was still faster than Heino in his world-record run. Zátopek was at that stage back in an unobtrusive 17th position, but within two laps he had moved up to fourth and during the next kilometre he went into the lead. Heino was in front again at halfway, but in the stiflingly hot conditions the pace had slowed (14:57.0 at 5000 metres), and when Zátopek increased the tempo only marginally from 3min 5sec to 3min 3sec for successive kilometres it was too much for Heino, who stepped off the track after 16 laps.

Zátopek ploughed remorselessly on, alone and untested in the tortuous head-wagging, shoulder-rolling, grimacing manner which was to become so familiar over the next few years, and the effect on the crowd was electrifying. Among them was a 16-year-old David Thurlow. "I was high up near the scoreboard about 180 metres from the finish," he recalled. "When Zátopek began to run away the crowd went mad, cheering him on – 'Zá-to-pek! Zá-to-pek!' – so superb was he. Most of us had never seen front-running like that. When Heino stepped off the track it just did not seem possible."

Of the next five behind Zátopek only the Algerian-born Frenchman Alain Mimoun-o-Kacha was able to improve on his previous best time, undoubtedly suffering less than the others in the heat. Subsequently abbreviating his surname, Mimoun was to find himself in a similar situation behind the "Czech Locomotive" on further occasions in European Championships and Olympic Games races. Mimoun was the first North African to achieve an Olympic medal in a distance track race, though another Algerian-born Frenchman, Boughèra El Ouafi, had won the marathon in 1928. Mimoun was finally to receive just reward for his patience by winning the Olympic marathon himself in 1956.

Zátopek had first come to public notice when finishing fifth in the 1946 European Championships 5000 metres as a relative novice a long way behind Britain's Sydney Wooderson, and he had progressed by 1947 to running the second fastest ever 5000 metres of 14:08.2 and 10 of the 12 best times of the year – the other two being by Heino. The Wembley 5000 metres was still to come, and Zátopek was clearly now regarded as very likely to be the first man since the Finn Kolehmainen, in 1912, to achieve the 5000–10,000 double. Not even Nurmi had managed that, though he had won the 1500 and 5000 within the hour at the 1924 Games!

Zátopek's winning time was well outside the world record but beat the previous Olympic best of 30:11.2 set by Janusz Kusocinski, of Poland, in 1932, and another youthful spectator among the wildly excited crowd to be vividly impressed by Zátopek's triumph that day was the then 17-year-old Gordon Pirie, who would later set world records and would race against Zátopek and even beat him. For his 1961 autobiography, Pirie was to compose the following tribute:

"I instantly recognised him as the embodiment of an ideal for myself as I saw him scorch through the 10,000 metres field. From that day he has never ceased to be my greatest inspiration and challenge and my firm friend. My whole life was focussed on the resolve to beat him. And one day I did. Zátopek was a phenomenon and an all-time great. That year at Wembley he burst through a mental and physical barrier. He showed runners that what they had been content with up to then was nothing to what could be achieved."

The British trio all performed most commendably. Cox ran the equivalent of his best time for six miles. Peters was close to his best. All that is known of the Ulsterman, McCooke, is that he completed the course. To say that Steve McCooke was one of the less privileged runners in the race is a masterpiece of understatement. He was the father of six children and an agricultural labourer by trade who would receive no wages while he was away. He later related his straitened circumstances: "When I set off for London I had thirty shillings in my pocket. There was no sponsorship in those days. That thirty bob had to last me a fortnight. I was there fifteen days and when I got back my wife asked me for two shillings and I had to tell her I had tuppence left." The monetary details really need no explaining, but thirty shillings would now be £1.50 and "tuppence" would be much less then one penny.

McCooke and many of his fellow-competitors were disgracefully served by the officials, who lost count of the laps and were unable to record any of the times after eighth place, nor even any of the finishing positions after 11th, other than the last man. Apparently, they were bedazzled by the sight of Zátopek and became irretrievably confused! Even the results which were produced may not be correct after the medal placings because Cox was to recall more than 50 years later: "Harold Abrahams insisted that I had run a lap too many. He repeated it in his radio report, but there has never been any means of proving it one way or the other because there was no film. If he was right I would have been fourth in a much faster time." If Abrahams was correct, Cox might have actually been second.

Farcically, when the result was announced there were further errors. The Swede Dennolf, was placed fourth and the Belgian Everaert sixth. The Norwegians appealed on behalf of Stokken that he was fourth, and this was supported by Dennolf himself. Everaert pointed out that he was not sixth but had retired from the race, but the officials refused to believe him and were only finally persuaded when the Belgian team management confirmed Everaert's honest admission! Lataster, the Dutchman, was told that he was disqualified for running one lap short and it was not until the year 2002, when he was 80 years old, that Lataster learned he had later been reinstated.

One theory for the muddle is offered by Les Crouch, a former chairman of Britain's energetic body of enthusiasts, the National Union of Track Statisticians, who suggested in an article for the bulletin of the International Society of Olympic Historians that the officials may have simply forgotten that they were in charge of a 10,000 metres race (25 laps of the track) and thought that it was a six-mile race (24 laps), and so the bell for the last lap was rung a lap too soon! At least one finisher would have been unaffected by the bell-ringer's mistake: Luo Wen Ao, of China, was a deaf mute.

For Zátopek this was the first of what were to be many gold medals. It was also an historic victory in the sense that it was the first by an athlete from a communist-led Eastern European regime, and there would be an avalanche of those across the range of Olympic sports as the USSR and its satellites wholeheartedly embraced the principles of state aid for sport in the 40 years to come until the walls started to crumble. Zátopek was a lieutenant in the Czech Army at the time of his Wembley success, and promotion would follow regularly during his athletics career.

What a contrast that was to the experience of not only McCooke but also of Stan Cox. He was one of only three athletes who had competed for Britain in both the last pre-war international match – a fraught affair against Germany in Cologne a fortnight before hostilities began – and the first international after the war, versus France in Paris in September 1945. The other two, incidentally, were the sprinter Cyril Holmes and an Australian-born shot-putter, Alan Bandidt. Cox served as

---

10,000 metres result: 1 Emil Zátopek (Czechoslovakia) 29:59.6, 2 Alain Mimoun-o-Kacha (France) 30:47.4, 3 Bertil Albertsson (Sweden) 30:53.6, 4 Martin Stokken (Norway) 30:58.6, 5 Severt Dennolf (Sweden) 31:05.0, 6 Abdallah Ben Said (France) 31:07.8, 7 Stan Cox (GB) 31:08.0, 8 Jim Peters (GB) 31:16.0, 9 Salomon Könönen (Finland), 10 Edward O'Toole (USA), 11 Fred Wilt (USA). Also finished between 12th and 23rd positions – Ricardo Bralo (Argentina), Eusebio Guiñez (Argentina), Luo Wen Ao (China), Pat Fahy (Eire), André Paris (France), Steve McCooke (GB), Josef Lataster (Holland), Harry Nelson (New Zealand), Jakob Kjersem (Norway), Constantino Miranda (Spain), Gregorio Rojo (Spain), Mannie Ramjohn (Trinidad & Tobago). André Paris (France) was known to be 23rd. Did not finish – Robert Everaert (Belgium), Herman Goffberg (USA), Viljo Heino (Finland), Evert Heinström (Finland)

a sergeant with the RAF in Iraq and then in France and Germany after D-Day, returning to his job as a storeman with the Standard Telephone & Cable Company, but he had to take a day's unpaid leave to run in the Olympic 10,000 metres, no small matter for a family man with a wife and two children to support.

Cox, like his 10,000 metres team-mate Jim Peters, moved up to the marathon in later years, and Peters set three world best performances in 1952 and 1953, with Cox also inside the previous fastest on the first occasion. However, they suffered traumatic experiences in major championship races, both failing to finish at the 1952 Olympics (where Zátopek won on his debut at the event) and in a heatwave-affected Empire & Commonwealth Games race in 1954. After taking up officiating Cox narrowly escaped death when he was struck during a competition by a javelin which missed piercing his heart by a quarter of an inch.

The Olympic 10,000 metres fourth-placer Martin Stokken, of Norway, would go on to achieve the rare feat in 1952 of competing in both the Winter and Summer Olympics, placing sixth in the 18 kilometres cross-country ski race at Oslo and 10th at 10,000 metres on the athletics track in Helsinki. Also taking part in the Helsinki 10,000 metres would be Zátopek, winning one of his three gold medals at those Games, and Mimoun, inevitably again second. Gordon Pirie was seventh, and he would also be fourth at 5000 metres to Zátopek, Mimoun and Herbert Schade (Germany). Mimoun and team-mate Abdallah Ben Said were the first North African-born distance-runners to make an impression in Olympic track events, but it would not be until 1960 when a totally unheralded Ethiopian, Abebe Bikila, won the first of his two Olympic marathon titles, that the realisation would begin to dawn of what Africans might achieve in distance-running.

Athletics. The second day – Saturday 31 July

Dillard, the part-time sprinter, wins gold. Lloyd Johnson, the old-time walker, wins bronze.

The day's programme: 10 a.m. Hammer qualifying; 11 a.m. Long jump qualifying; 11 a.m. Pole vault qualifying; 1.15 p.m. 50 kilometres walk; 2.30 p.m. Javelin (women) final; 2.30 p.m. 100 metres semi-finals; 2.45 p.m. 100 metres (women) heats; 3.15 p.m. 800 metres semi-finals; 3.30 p.m. 400 metres hurdles final; 3.30 p.m. Hammer final; 3.45 p.m. 100 metres final; 4 p.m. 5000 metres heats; 4.45 p.m. Long jump final.

SIX GOLD MEDALS TO be decided. Hot weather again, and this was not good news for the 50 kilometres walkers, who would be setting out at a most unwelcome hour of the afternoon. There were 23 members of the "heel-and-toe" brigade who lined up for their long trudge through the streets of the Middlesex suburbs of Stanmore, Edgware and Mill Hill and out into the Hertfordshire countryside via Radlett, Aldenham and along the Watford bypass. The winner would not be expected back until towards six o'clock in the evening. The favourite was the European champion from Sweden, John Ljunggren, but Britain had a title to defend, and the Berlin gold-medallist's brother, Rex Whitlock, was there and would naturally like to keep it in the family. Comparing times set on varying courses was difficult, but a notable absentee would be a Latvian named Liepskalis, who had recorded 4hr 35min 49sec in 1947. The first news to be relayed back to the stadium was encouraging. Though Ljunggren already had a long lead at 10 kilometres, Rex Whitlock and Bert Martineau were together for Britain in third place.

Back on the track the 100 metres semi-finalists were the first to assemble and the women javelin-throwers the first in the field. Dillard, looking more and more like a serious sprinter, and therefore a gold-medal threat, won the first semi-final from Ewell, and McCorquodale delighted the crowd by taking the qualifying third place from one of the Australians, John Bartram. Patton and LaBeach were first and second in the other semi-final, and McDonald Bailey was third for Britain ahead of another Australian, John Treloar. This was splendid stuff from the British in direct contrast to their decisive beating by Treloar at the AAA Championships. Not since 1928 had Britain produced an Olympic finalist in the men's sprints, when Jack London and Walter Rangeley had each won silver, and not since 1924 had there been *two* Britons in a sprint final, when Eric Liddell had won a bronze at 200 metres and the 100 metres champion, Harold Abrahams, had been sixth and last. Would it be too much to hope for another medal this time?

The first heat of the first round of the women's 100 metres brought the packed crowd their first sighting of Fanny Blankers-Koen and she duly won by a large margin in 12.0. By now the rain had arrived, but it was summer, after all, and British spirits refused to be dampened. Winnie Jordan, whose first Women's AAA national title win had been in 1937, qualified with a second place, and then Doris Batter and Dorothy Manley each won their heats. Manley's time was an impressive 12.1, and the crowd's reaction was ecstatic. There was another hearty cheer shortly after three o'clock when it was learned that at 20 kilometres in the walk Whitlock and Martineau were still the closest to Ljunggren, though not very close.

The first three in each of three 800 metres semi-finals would go through to the final, and Parlett courageously responded to the challenge by running 1:50.9 to break his personal best and finish close behind Hansenne and Whitfield. The other winners were Bengtsson and the American, Barten. The USA would have three men in the next day's final, France two, and Denmark, Great Britain, Jamaica and Sweden one each. Among those eliminated was Josy Barthel, from Luxembourg, who would fare better at 1500 metres the following week, reaching the final, and far better at the next Olympics, when he would astonish everyone except possibly himself and his astute German coach, Woldemar Gerschler, by winning the gold. Also eliminated in the 800 metres semi-finals was the New Zealander who had led the 1947 world rankings, Doug Harris.

Harris suffered the worst of misfortunes. The Achilles tendon in his left leg had been spiked in the collision which had happened in his heat and it tore just as he was starting his final effort behind Wint and Bengtsson. He hopped away from the track in agony and was taken off on a stretcher and then to St Mary's Hospital, where at least he had the consolation of being in the safest of hands as he was tended by his fellow-countryman Sir Arthur Porritt. Harris later said that he had felt capable of running 1min 46sec in the final, and such a bold claim must inevitably sound presumptuous in view of the fact that the world record had stood at 1:46.6 to Germany's Rudolf Harbig (also coached, incidentally, by Woldemar Gerschler) since 1939, but the New Zealander was an immensely talented athlete whose potential was forever to remain unrealised. He had started a physical education course at Loughborough College, and after recovering from his horrendous injury he easily beat Arthur Wint the following year in the British universities' championships, but recurring leg problems prematurely put an end to his career.

The 400 metres hurdles finalists came on to the track: Cros in lane one, Missoni in two, Cochran in three, Ault in four, White in five, Larsson in six. Larsson's running in the semi-final suggested he could threaten Cochran, but the Swede went off far too leisurely in the outside lane and left himself with more than enough to do in the finishing straight. Cochran, hurdling in his characteristically smooth and relaxed style, won with ease and settled the issue regarding the Olympic record with a time of 51.1, which was only half a second outside Glenn Hardin's 12-year-old world record. Cochran tends to be overshadowed by Hardin in the event's history but deserves better. He had said after the US trials that he could have run "50 seconds flat, if necessary, to win", and few could doubt his ability to do that. He had a best time of 46.7 for 400 metres on the flat and would figure in the US 4x400 team later in the Games.

Cochran, a father of two, had spent three years in the US Navy, and there is an intriguing twist to his tale because his brother and coach, whose unusual first name was Commodore, and who was 17 years the older of the two, had also won Olympic gold – in the 4x400 metres relay in 1924! Roy Cochran (his full first names were LeRoy Braxton) had been born the ninth of ten children in Richton, Mississippi, and had won the US AAU title as a novice 20-year-old in 1939. The ungainly Ceylonese, White, was the revelation of the race, having improved from a pre-Games best of 53.0 set in his national championships, and he would go on to win the Empire Games title two years later. Sitting at home, and no doubt frustrated when he heard news of the result, was a fine American hurdler, George Walker, who had run 51.9 in the US trials but had finished fourth.

As the finalists for the 100 metres finished their preparations on the warm-up strip of track outside the stadium, there was another welcome report from the walk. Ljunggren was leading by almost five minutes at halfway in a time of 2:12:17 – inside world-record pace – but Whitlock and Martineau were still second and third.

The line-up for the 100 metres from the inside lane was Patton, Ewell, LaBeach, McCorquodale, Bailey, Dillard, and it could be argued that this was as good a sprint field as had ever been brought together. Jesse Owens's world-record 10.2 had been equalled by LaBeach (twice) and Ewell within the previous three months. In 1947 Patton had become the first man to run 100 yards in 9.3, erasing Owens's 9.4, and had done that same time again in Olympic year. Dillard was obviously a sprinter of comparable class but had never had the opportunity to prove it while concentrating on hurdling. McCorquodale's achievement in reaching an Olympic final in only his second year of competition was nothing short of amazing. McDonald Bailey, born in Trinidad but resident in Britain since joining the RAF during the war, had been denied a chance to run in the 1946 European Championships, where he would surely have won both the 100 and 200, but was suffering here from a throat infection.

The most dramatic part of the final came after the race was over, when Ewell set off on a cavorting dance of delight round the first bend of the track. Whether he genuinely believed he had won, or whether this was force of habit from trying

---

400 metres hurdles result: 1 Roy Cochran (USA) 51.1, 2 Duncan White (Ceylon) 51.8, 3 Rune Larsson (Sweden) 52.2, 4 Dick Ault (USA) 52.4, 5 Yves Cros (France) 53.3, 6 Ottavio Missoni (Italy) 54.2. Automatic timing gave the winner's time as 51.3 and the margins behind the winner as being White 0.76sec, Larsson 1.00, Ault 1.26, Cros 2.18, Missoni 2.85.

to influence the decision of hapless judges in the tight finishes so common in the USA, does not matter much. The fact is that Dillard, in the lane nearest to the crowd, had led all the way and was the new champion. Ewell was second, LaBeach third, and McCorquodale had missed a medal by just two hundredths of a second. Dillard's hand time was 10.3 to prove that he was the one who found the extra metre, his margin of victory. Patton, underweight because of problems with English cooking, was a listless fifth. The surprise of the race for those who followed the sport closely was not so much that Dillard had won – after all, he had been the joint fastest man in the world the previous year at 100 metres with a time of 10.3 – but that Patton had lost.

What is more, who could possibly have imagined that the untutored Scots-born rugby footballer and cricketer who had first come to notice when winning the Army 100 yards in 9.9 as a 21-year-old Lieutenant in the Coldstream Guards would within a year complete an Olympic 100 metres final the best part of a metre ahead of a world record-holder? So little was known of Alastair McCorquodale that even *The Times* in its Games preview of three days previously had spelt his name as "McCorquindale", though they did manage to correct it by their next edition. Perhaps only his coach could have nursed such dreams of Olympic renown. He was Guy Butler, who had some considerable experience of Olympic success himself, having won silver and bronze at 400 metres and gold and bronze for the 4x400 metres relay at the 1920 and 1924 Olympics. Butler never had the chance to see what his immensely talented protégé could do in the fullness of time. McCorquodale retired at the season's end to devote his attentions to the rather more important matter of the family printing business and confined his sporting activity to the cricket field. One of the McCorquodale firm's major print contracts would be for the 776-page official report of the 1948 Olympic Games Organising Committee.

In 1951 the twins, Norris and Ross McWhirter, who were journalists, magazine publishers and the leading British athletics historians of the era, wrote a ground-breaking book entitled *Get To Your Marks!*, which traced the development of the sport in both a British and a worldwide context. One of their exercises was to rank the top 10 British sprinters of all-time in order of merit, based on their best performances and their achievements in major championships, and they listed McCorquodale as No.1 for 100 yards and 100 metres even ahead of the 1924 Olympic champion, Harold Abrahams.

The women javelin-throwers had meanwhile been working their way through the successive rounds, and the winner to emerge was Austrian Herma Bauma, aged 33, who had placed fourth in Berlin, but there were rather more

---

100 metres result: 1 Harrison Dillard (USA) 10.3, 2 Barney Ewell (USA) 10.4, 3 Lloyd LaBeach (Jamaica) 10.6, 4 Alastair McCorquodale (GB), 5 Mel Patton (USA), 6 Emmanuel McDonald Bailey (GB). Automatic timing gave the winner 10.5 and the margins behind him as being Ewell 0.06sec, LaBeach 0.09, McCorquodale 0.11, Patton 0.17, McDonald Bailey 0.31. No official times were taken for fourth, fifth and sixth places, and this shortcoming was to be repeated in numerous races at Wembley.

nuances to this occasion than the 82,000 crowd – with the possible exception of a very few avid enthusiasts among them – could possibly have realised. By 1938, when her country was annexed, Bauma had become a German citizen and she resurfaced in competition in 1941 and then as German national champion in 1942. Whatever the political niceties, Austria had been allowed back into the Olympics, and Bauma was worth her win. She had set an official world record of 48.21m in 1947, and though this was less than had been achieved by one Soviet thrower, Lyudmila Anokhina, in 1945 (48.39) and by another, Kladiya Mayuchaya (50.32), later in 1947, the fact is that there was only 29 centimetres between the best throws of the three world leaders in 1948, all from the USSR, and Bauma in fourth place. Bauma set a further world record of 48.63m a month later. The silver medal at Wembley went to another 33-year-old, Kaisa Parviainen, who came from the ancestral home of javelin-throwing, Finland, and had improved on a national record which she had set 13 years before. At least one of her javelin-throwing fellow-countrymen would hope to do better in defence of national honour in five days' time.

Bauma, rewarded with a coveted teaching appointment when she returned home, had beaten the Olympic record from 1936, but otherwise the standard was ordinary, at best. Even so, the two British women entered still filled the last two places. A British woman had also been last in Berlin. In seventh place at Wembley was a former handball player from Czechoslovakia, who would soon become rather better known as Mrs Zátopek and would win gold for herself at the Helsinki Games of 1952.

The irrepressible Mr Zátopek was back on the track for the 5000 metres heats and in characteristic fashion ran far faster than was necessary to qualify, chasing home the Swede, Erik Ahldén, when a time half a minute slower would have been quite enough. But then that was Zátopek's style – always giving of his best. All but one of the 12 finalists would be European. They included Albertson and Stokken, third and fourth in the previous evening's 10,000 metres, but not Mimoun, sixth in his heat, and not any of the British trio. Alec Olney had run his best ever three miles at the AAA Championships in second place to the "Flying Dutchman", Willy Slijkhuis, despite being knocked off the track, but had lost that form for whatever reason and went out in the slowest of the heats.

This was all a far cry from Sydney Wooderson's masterful European Championships win at the 5000-metre distance only two years before, and Wooderson at 33 could still have been a strong Olympic contender. Although he had won the 10-mile National cross-country title earlier in the year, he had given

---

Javelin (women) result: 1 Herma Bauma (Austria) 45.57m, 2 Kaisa Parviainen (Finland) 43.79, 3 Lily Carlstedt (Denmark) 42.08, 4 Dorothy Dodson (USA) 41.96, 5 Johanna Teunissen-Waalboer (Holland) 40.92, 6 Johanna Koning (Holland) 40.33, 7 Dana Ingrova (Czechoslovakia) 39.64, 8 Elisabeth Dammers (Holland) 38.23, 9 Gerda Schilling (Austria) 38.01, 10 Ingrid Almqvist (Sweden) 37.26, 11 Melania Sinoracka (Poland) 35.74, 12 Theresa Manuel (USA) 3.82, 13 Nicole Saeys (Belgium) 31.77, 14 Marian Long (GB) 30.29, 15 Gladys Clarke (GB) 29.59

up track racing to concentrate on his career as a solicitor, and his shoal of British records from 800 to 5000 metres would remain beyond reach until another decade began. At least the news from the walk was exciting: Ljunggren leading by more than eight minutes at 35 kilometres, and clearly heading for gold, bar a disaster, but Whitlock still second and now Lloyd Johnson moving up to third.

In the morning's hammer-throw qualifying round thirteen men had achieved the necessary 49 metres. Leading them was the new world record-holder from Hungary, Imre Németh, whose heave of 59.02m the previous month had improved a minuscule two centimetres upon a 10-year-old mark by Germany's 1936 Olympic silver-medallist, Erwin Blask. If it seems hardly possible that measurements of such fine distinction could be made regarding 16lb balls of iron being flung through the air and thumping into soft turf over a distance of more than 60 yards, then so be it; world records were made to be broken, and Németh had cut it almost as fine as could be conceived. Three throwers from Germany and two from the USSR who all ranked in the world's top 10 were noticeably absent from the proceedings, including the 1936 Olympic champion, Karl Hein, throwing as well as ever. Among the failures was a Finn, Reino Kuivamäki, who had apparently been regularly exceeding 55 metres in training, and had even reportedly reached 58.20, very close to the world record, with one throw – but could not manage 49 metres here. Even the strongest of men are known to weaken under Olympic pressure.

Németh, whose name translates as "German" in his native Hungarian, won the final, though still almost half a metre short of Hein's Games record, and when he returned home to Budapest the gold medal must have seemed a nice bauble to dangle in front of his 21-month-old son's eyes. A cheerful Yugoslav, Ivan Gubijan, was unexpectedly second and the bronze went to an American left-hander, Bob Bennett, by just seven centimetres from his team-mate, Sam Felton, while the third American, Henry Dreyer, was ninth, as he had been in 1936. The exuberant Felton was in the habit of wearing a straw boater when competing but had refrained from doing so on this occasion. For Bennett it had been a long wait, because he had been the No.2 thrower in the world in 1940. Greater patience still was required of the leader in the rankings that same year as he was a German, Karl Storch, who would have been a strong challenger in 1948, had he been allowed to compete, but at last won a silver medal in 1952.

Contrary to what might be supposed, Németh was not the first thrower from a Communist-controlled country to win an Olympic throwing event, as Hungary was still ruled by a coalition government in 1948, but he founded a dynasty which was to prosper under the new regime to come to power the following year. Németh, who had been born in the town of Košice (then part of Czechoslovakia), himself progressed the world record to 59.57m and then 59.88, and he coached a fellow-countryman, József Csermák, so astutely that he performed the ultimate feat of winning the 1952 Olympic title with the first 60-metre throw in history. Németh was third, and his achievements clearly made a lasting impression on his young son, named Miklós: he grew up to win the Olympic javelin gold medal 28 years after his father's title success.

Németh's victory also marked a new departure in hammer-throwing as it finally put an end to the strong Irish influence which had endured since the 1880s. The event could trace its history back to mediaeval times, and most prominently numbered among its exponents had been King Henry VIII. Then in the 19th century it became a feature of athletics meetings in Ireland. Irish-born Americans had taken every Olympic title from 1900 to 1920 and Dr Pat O'Callaghan had then won for Ireland in 1928 and 1932. O'Callaghan might well have added a third title in 1936 but was prevented from competing by an internal dispute between rival sports governing bodies. The 1920 champion, Pat Ryan, had held the official world record from 1913 to 1938, but O'Callaghan had well beaten it in 1937, without the performance ever being ratified, and another Irishman, Bertie Healion, who had been AAA champion in 1938 and 1939, was reputed to have exceeded 200ft (61 metres) more than once with "exhibition" throws after taking up professional wrestling.

The morning's qualifying round of the long jump had produced a banal result, with only four men reaching the modest standard of 7.20m. So the next eight, including all three Britons, were added to make up the 12-man final. The American trio of Willie Steele, Herb Douglas and Lorenzo Wright appeared to be in a class of their own – all of them highly accomplished sprinters – and Steele settled the issue with his very first jump in the final, clearing 7.825m. No one else got remotely close in what was really a very moderate competition. Theo Bruce, who had served in the Royal Australian Air Force in Britain during the war, was a surprising second ahead of Douglas, and fifth, sixth and seventh places were all taken by athletes who had also competed the previous day: Adedoyin for Britain, Damitio for France and Whittle again for Britain. No Briton had ever finished higher than Adedoyin in an Olympic long-jump final since the Irishman, Peter O'Connor, had won the silver at the 10th anniversary Games of 1906.

Jesse Owens, the Berlin Olympic champion, still held the world record at 8.13m from 1935 and would continue to do so for another twelve years, but the eminent American coach, J Kenneth Doherty, was to write of Willie Steele in 1953 that "it may well be that he was an even greater broad jumper than Owens"

Hammer result: 1 Imre Németh (Hungary) 56.07m, 2 Ivan Gubijan (Yugoslavia) 54.27, 3 Bob Bennett (USA) 53.73, 4 Sam Felton (USA) 53.66, 5 Lauri Tamminen (Finland) 53.08, 6 Bo Ericson (Sweden) 52.98, 7 Teseo Taddia (Italy) 51.74, 8 Einar Söderqvist (Sweden) 51.48, 9 Henry Dreyer (USA) 51.37, 10 Svend-Aage Fredriksen (Denmark) 50.07, 11 Duncan Clark (GB) 48.35, 12 Johan Houtzager (Holland) 45.69, 13 In Kang Whan (Korea) 43.93.

Long jump result: 1 Willie Steele (USA) 7.825m, 2 Theo Bruce (Australia) 7.555, 3 Herb Douglas (USA) 7.545, 4 Lorenzo Wright (USA) 7.45, 5 Adegboyega Adedoyin (GB) 7.27, 6 Georges Damitio (France) 7.07, 7 Harry Whittle (GB) 7.03, 8 Felix Würth (Austria) 7.00, 9 Harry Askew (GB) 6.935, 10 Enrique Kistenmacher (Argentina) 6.80, 11 Edward Adamczyk (Poland) 6.735. Baldev Singh (India) also qualified but was injured and did not compete.

("broad jump" being the term used to describe the event in the USA). Owens himself had had the opportunity to appreciate Steele's talents at close hand because Steele had marginally fouled on a jump of 26ft 10in (8.17m) at the US Olympic trials, for which Owens was a long-jump official, and had won the event at 26-2 (7.97).

Steele was a teenage prodigy who had come back after Army war service to fulfil his great promise, having cleared 25-7½ (7.81) in 1942 at the age of 18, the longest jump in the world for the year. He was the world leader again in 1946–47–48 with a best of 26-6 (8.07) which only Owens had ever exceeded. Steele's runway speed was ideal – he had done 9.7 for 100 yards in April of 1948 – but his jumping technique was by no means perfect, as he had a tendency to throw himself off to the side as he landed in the pit, and he might well have been capable of achieving something very much further. He was certainly reputed to have gone beyond 27ft (8.23m) several times in training, but he was plagued by injuries and was carrying an ankle ailment at Wembley which restricted him to only two jumps. He never competed again after his Olympic victory, and when he died in 1989 the world record stood at the legendary 8.90m achieved by Bob Beamon in the 1968 Olympics.

Shortly after the long jump had got under way the next bulletin from the walk brought mixed blessings. Whitlock had dropped out, burned off by Ljunggren's fast pace, but Lloyd Johnson had moved up and was second at 40 kilometres and had actually narrowed the lead by 95 seconds, though there was no serious prospect of him making up the enormous amount of tarmac which separated him from the Swede. At 45 kilometres Johnson was still second, though only half a minute or so ahead of a Swiss.

Still, all's well that ends well. Ljunggren duly came back into the stadium to win the walk, and it was more than six minutes before the next two arrived, but one of the figures to be espied was the tall, spare frame of Tebbs Lloyd Johnson, striding manfully in for the bronze medal. Lloyd Johnson had won his first national title 21 years before, had finished 17th in Berlin, and now at the age of 48 was earning Britain's first medal of the Games. He had cannily worked his way through the field: 13th at 10 kilometres, eighth at 20 kilometres, fifth at 25 kilometres, and into the first three from 35 kilometres onwards.

Lloyd Johnson had been competing for 28 years and attributed his longevity to a healthy lifestyle and exceptional lung capacity. He refused to accept that British athletes were at a disadvantage because of rationing: "I think the food excuse for our being overshadowed by foreign athletes is much overstressed. In my own case, not being one of the original 'possibles', I received no extra food concessions whatsoever and trained entirely on the normal rations available to everyone. I honestly think that if the monotony of such a diet could be overcome one could perfectly well train on bread, butter and jam." He lived to the age of 84.

It was a triumph of true British grit, of seeing it through to the very end; the very spirit, in other words, of Dunkirk, the Blitz and D-Day. There was a spring in the step, and maybe a sympathetic rumbling in the stomach, of the British spectators as they made their way out of the stadium that night. The fifth-placed Bert Martineau had briefly appeared as a novice walker in 1937, had done nothing through the war years, and had then re-emerged in 1947.

Predominance in road walking had thus passed from British to Swedish hands. Tommy Green and Harold Whitlock had won the Olympic 50 kilometres walk for Britain in 1932 and 1936 respectively, and Whitlock had won again at the 1938 European Championships in Paris. John Ljunggren had succeeded Whitlock as European title-holder in 1946 ahead of two Britons, Harry Forbes and Charlie Megnin, and was unquestionably one of the very best road walkers of his generation. He was aged 28 at the time of his Olympic win and continued to compete at a high level for many more years to come, setting six world records between 1951 and 1953, including 4:29:58 for a track 50 kilometres. He was second in the 1950 European Championships – with his brother, Verner, third to complete the first such pairing to win championship medals in the same event – and ninth, third, second and 16th at the Olympics through to 1964! He took part in 499 races during his career, winning 315, finishing second in 101 and third in 33.

Freddy Blackmore, with the knowledge and experience of an Olympic walks judge, was fulsome in his praise for Ljunggren. Writing in the monthly magazine *Athletics*, he stated: "Let it be at once acknowledged that a walker of true Olympic quality has succeeded Green and Whitlock, even though we are naturally disappointed one of our representatives did not retain the only individual athletic title won by Great Britain in 1936 – with the result that we now have none. However, 'true Olympic quality' is the reason why. Ljunggren started out in the manner of the man who meant to win the race, walking confidently and competently at a pace which quickened questions as to whether he might last the distance but none with regard to his mode of progression."

In the 21st century times of under 3hr 40min for the 50 kilometres walk are required to win major championships, but the rules have changed completely, and Ljunggren and his contemporaries, who seem positively pedestrian by comparison, would not even recognise the modern means of progression as being race-walking at all. Nor could Lloyd Johnson possibly have imagined that the sport in Britain would be so far reduced in stature as to be practised by only a handful in the 21st century, whereas there were 279 entries for the national 20 miles race in 1948.

---

50 kilometres walk result: 1 John Ljunggren (Sweden) 4:41:52, 2 Gaston Godel (Switzerland) 4:48:17, 3 Tebbs Lloyd Johnson (GB) 4:48:31, 4 Edgar Bruun (Norway) 4:53:18, 5 Bert Martineau (GB) 4:53:58, 6 Rune Bjürstrom (Sweden) 4:56:43, 7 Pierre Mazille (France) 5:01:40, 8 Claude Hubert (France) 5:03:12, 9 Enrique Villaplana (Spain) 5:03:31, 10 Tage Jönsson (Sweden) 5:05:08, 11 Henri Caron (France) 5:08:15, 12 Ernest Crosbie (USA) 5:15:16, 13 Sándor László (Hungary) 5:16:30, 14 Salvatore Cascino (Italy) 5:20:03, 15 John Deni (USA) 5:28:33, 16 Adolph Weinacker (USA) 5:30:14. Did not finish – Sixto Ibañez (Argentina), Rex Whitlock (GB), Sadara Singh (India), Valentino Bertolino (Italy), Francesco Pretti (Italy), Per Baarnaas (Norway), Gerhard Winther (Norway).

Athletics. The third day –
Monday 2 August

"My dear, do you mind very much if we turn you into a sprinter?" the coach enquired ... and a medal-winner was in the making

The day's programme: 11 a.m. Discus qualifying; 2.30 p.m. 200 metres heats; 2.30 p.m. Pole vault final; 3.30 p.m. Discus final; 3.30 p.m. 100 metres (women) semi-finals; 4 p.m. 800 metres final; 4.15 p.m. 200 metres quarter-finals; 4.45 p.m. 100 metres (women) final; 5 p.m., 5000 metres final.

IT WAS A matter of "never on a Sunday" for sport in Britain in those far-off days. So the Olympics took a brief respite, and the finalists for the 800 metres and 5000 metres and the semi-finalists for the women's 100 metres had plenty of time to recover during the August Bank Holiday weekend from their earlier exertions ... and plenty of time, too, to dwell on the rigorous challenge to come. The Olympic Games, with its series of races, its glare of publicity and expectation, its unfamiliar herding together for days on end in crowded team accommodation, brought far more pressure to bear than most athletes ever suffered anywhere else in a competitive lifetime. Some would crack under the strain.

The 200 metres began with twelve first-round heats, and Ewell, LaBeach, McCorquodale and Patton from the 100 metres finalists were out on the track again, but Patton had run indifferently in that race – buckling under the pressure, perhaps? – and so Ewell seemed to be the favourite. Herb McKenley, of Jamaica, had some remarkable times to his credit from the previous year, including 20.2 for 220 yards (201.17 metres, and therefore worth 0.1sec faster for the metric distance) on a straight course and 20.4 round a curve, both declared wind-assisted, but would he treat this event as no more than a warm-up? He had the 400 metres, in which he was world record-holder, and the 4x400 relay still to come. McKenley and the American third string, Cliff Bourland, were much the fastest heat winners in 21.3, but there would be quarter-finals less than two hours later on the rain-soaked track, and that was where the real sorting-out would take place.

The pole vault and discus were also to be decided on this Monday, and the rain which fell steadily all afternoon, getting heavier towards the evening, would not be at all to the liking of anyone except possibly the distance-runners. Before activity began it was perhaps timely to reflect that from the nine events already concluded over the two previous days the USA had won three gold medals, and Australia, Austria, Czechoslovakia, France, Hungary and Sweden one each. There had been other medals for Ceylon, Denmark, Finland, Great

Britain, Italy, Norway, Panama, Switzerland and Yugoslavia. Four continents were represented, and Africa, too, if you counted Algerian-born Alain Mimoun: athletics was truly living up to its image as the universal sport at the heart of the Olympic movement.

The three semi-finals of the women's 100 metres confirmed beyond all doubt that, short of falling flat on her face, which was not beyond a possibility in the gathering gloom, Blankers-Koen would take the gold. She won the first semi-final in 12.0. Dorothy Manley, for Great Britain, and Viola Myers, for Canada, each won the other two in 12.4. It was merely a question of wondering by how great a margin the victory would be fashioned. Even allowing for the conditions, some of the other semi-final performances, as slow as 13.4sec, were far removed from international standards. The fault lay with the restrictions imposed on the organisers by a six-lane track. Too many races were producing too many sub-standard qualifiers. There had been 38 competitors in the first round, which was two too many to have had six heats, with the first two going through from each. Seven heats would have produced 14 semi-final qualifiers, also two too many!

The nine finalists for the 800 metres were Whitfield, Barten and Chambers (all of the USA), Hansenne and the appealingly named and maybe even appetisingly named Chef d'Hotel (both of France), Holst-Sørensen (Denmark), Parlett (Great Britain), Bengtsson (Sweden) and Wint (Jamaica). The British almost had a right to call the event their own because the Olympic title had been won by Albert Hill in 1920, by Douglas Lowe in 1924 and 1928, and by Tommy Hampson in 1932, and it was to Parlett's credit that he was being thought of in those terms. Yet his best of 1:50.9, set in the semi-finals, was a long way short of the 1:48.3 which the Frenchman, Hansenne, had run in June, while Holst-Sørensen was the European champion and had run 1:48.9 during wartime.

Bengtsson had won a tune-up race just before the Games in 1:49.4. Whitfield, who invariably ran no faster than it took to win, had been the US trials winner in 1:50.6, one-tenth ahead of Barten. Wint had run 1:50.0 the year before. Bare statistics never tell the whole story, but this intricate aspect of the sport could not be expected to be a strong point with press or the public, and Parlett, whether he liked it or not, was being tipped for a medal, even the gold. It was 16 years to the day since Hampson had last won for Britain, in the process becoming the first man to break 1min 50sec.

It was a splendid race, though the line-up at the start had been an odd one, with the runners close to the first bend and not in staggered lanes, so that those on the outside – particularly Parlett in lane nine – had to cut in, and there was an unseemly scrabble for the best tactical positions. Chef d'Hotel, born in the Western Pacific island of New Caledonia, which had been a convict settlement in the 19th century, and then Hansenne led through the first lap, covered in 54.2sec, working to a preconceived French plan.

Whitfield went to the front after the bell in the fluent style which had earned him the nicknames of "Marvellous Mal" and "Swivel-Hips" but was strongly challenged by Wint's giant strides in the home straight and held on by just a couple of metres to win in 1:49.2. Hansenne had kept enough in reserve to secure third place. Parlett ran himself to exhaustion, perhaps paying the price for his fast semi-final, and was a long way back in eighth position. Even *Athletics* magazine, which perhaps should have been more understanding, described his performance as "a great disappointment to the home crowd" and criticised his tactics, and Harold Abrahams later reflected that it was "against judgment" to have believed that Parlett might spring a surprise. Undeterred, Parlett lived to fight another day, because in 1950 he was to achieve the impressive feat of winning the British Empire 880 yards and the European Championships 800 metres six months apart.

Parlett's recollection of the race half a century later is that a misunderstanding at the start had cost him dear. He was friendly with Hansenne of France, who had drawn him out to a personal best in the France v GB match the previous year, and Hansenne spoke to him as they were lining up. "If I had understood his French I might have done better," Parlett explained. "I was drawn number nine and he was eight and said something. I realised afterwards he was saying that his mate, Chef d'Hotel, from an inside position would go off and lead the pack, and we should follow behind. Lacking experience of both the French language and Olympic finals, I rushed off and got crushed in the mob."

Whitfield was then a sergeant in the US Air Force and later saw active service flying missions in the Korean war but still found the time for athletics training and to compile one of the greatest competitive records in history. From 1948 to 1954 he lost only three times at 800 metres or 880 yards, and though he rarely pushed himself to the limit he gave a remarkable demonstration of his speed and stamina in a meeting at Eskilstuna, in Sweden, in August of 1953. First of all he broke the world record for 1000 metres – a non-championship event but highly prized on the Continent – and then two hours later was only one-tenth outside the 400 metres world record with a time of 45.9. The year before Whitfield had again beaten Wint for the Olympic 800 metres title.

McKenley ran another 21.3 in the first of the four quarter-finals of the 200 metres. Bourland, La Beach and Patton won the next three, and the astonishing McCorquodale knocked four tenths off his previous best with a 21.6 on Patton's heels. Also through to the semi-finals for Britain was McCorquodale's successor as Army sprint champion, Second Lieutenant Paul Vallé, a member of the Enfield Athletic Club who had made something like 10 metres-worth

---

800 metres result: 1 Mal Whitfield (USA) 1:49.2, 2 Arthur Wint (Jamaica) 1:49.5, 3 Marcel Hansenne (France) 1:49.8, 4 Herb Barten (USA) 1:50.1, 5 Ingvar Bengtsson (Sweden) 1:50.5, 6 Bob Chambers (USA) 1:52.1, 7 Robert Chef d'Hotel (France), 8 John Parlett (GB), 9 Niels Holst-Sørensen (Denmark). The automatic timing for the winner was 1:49.3 and the margins behind him were 0.28sec for Wint, 0.78 for Hansenne, 1.04 for Barten, 1.56 for Bengtsson, 2.82 for Chambers, 4.89 for Chef d'Hotel, 6.97 for Parlett, 7.06 for Holst-Sørensen. No official times were recorded for seventh, eighth and ninth places.

of improvement since being beaten by a clubmate earlier in the season at the Middlesex county championships.

The draw for the women's 100 metres final had Jones (Canada) on the inside, then Thompson (Jamaica), Blankers-Koen, Strickland (Australia), Myers (Canada) and Manley (GB). Manley ran like Dillard had from the same lane and gave Blankers-Koen a much closer contest than anyone might have expected. The officially-timed margin was three-tenths, 11.9 to 12.2, but automatic timing gave only 0.20 difference, and in the photographs and on the film it looks even closer.

The official Olympic film shows clearly that there were no more than two real sprinters in the race. Blankers-Koen and Manley were the only ones who ran with fire and lack of inhibition. The rest just looked far too dainty. This was a marvellous breakthrough for Manley, because she had only taken up sprinting that same year, and the background to how this came about is well worth explaining in some detail.

Her coach was the avuncular Sandy Duncan and he later described the circumstances in which their association had started: "In the build-up to the 1948 Olympics I coached the sprinter, John Fairgrieve, among others. Then one day a girl came up to me to be coached in the high jump. She was doing the 'scissors' and didn't seem to have much future in that. So I asked to have a look at her on the track and immediately said, 'My dear, do you mind very much if we turn you into a sprinter?' Thank goodness she agreed because she ended up as Britain's silver-medal winner behind the great Fanny Blankers-Koen."

While her athletics future was being transformed, Miss Manley was dealing with acute personal worries because her fiancé was seriously ill in hospital, and she was visiting him and training five days a week while commuting daily from her home in Manor Park, in Essex, to her full-time job as a shorthand typist in the City of London. Her memory of the Olympic final was to remain crystal-clear, and she related it again to the esteemed athletics writer, David Thurlow, when he interviewed her for an issue of the statistical and historical journal, *Track Stats*, in 2005:

"I was notoriously bad at starting, but on this occasion I think I got the best start of my life. In fact, I was away so well, and was in front of Fanny, that it went through my mind that I had made a false start, and I expected that we would be recalled. Now, I should not have been thinking that, and I obviously lost a little bit, but it would not have made any difference because Fanny would still have beaten me. She was much faster and stronger than any of us. I was second and I was so excited, overjoyed, and then there I was on the podium getting the silver medal. I was still a bit dazed and I was so emotional that I did not notice the Union Jack being hoisted. It's something I've always regretted."

Now Mrs Hall, she went on to a bronze medal in the 1950 European Championships 200 metres, again won by Blankers-Koen, and a gold at 4x100 ahead of Holland, with "you know who" on the anchor stage, before a poisoned thyroid gland brought her running career to an end. In 1973, after the death of her first husband, she married her fellow-Olympian and European champion John Parlett. Her feelings about her athletic achievements were very much down-to-earth, as evidenced by her further recollections of her Olympic experience: "I did not think of myself as a champion. I just thought, 'That's not me.' There was no great build-up at the time. I did not expect to get gold and I was just happy to be taking part. Someone said I did not put everything into it, that I did not have the 'win at all costs' attitude, and I said I did because I enjoyed it so much."

The Ancient Greek art of discus-throwing was being practised all afternoon and a pair of sturdy Italians, Adolfo Consolini and Giuseppe Tosi, were once again proving themselves particularly adept. They had been in the forefront of the event throughout the war years, and they had placed 1-2 in the 1946 European Championships. The fact that two Italians were so dominant is not as surprising as it might at first seem. Consolini was a farmer's son and had begun competing as a 20-year-old in 1937, visiting England the next year to win the AAA title. He had the example to inspire him of a fellow-countryman, Giorgio Oberweger, who had taken the bronze medal in Berlin, and also had early guidance from one of the leading American coaches of the day, Boyd Comstock, who had been employed by the Italian Federation and is famously said to have remarked of Consolini in a letter to his fellow-coach in the USA, Dink Templeton, "I've got a spaghetti-eater over here who will throw that thing 200 feet."

Throwers from the USA came and went – such as Archie Harris and Bob Fitch, world record-breakers in 1941 and 1946, and Al Blozis, killed on active service in 1945 – and in Olympic year the most serious transatlantic challenger would be Fortune Gordien, who had won the AAU and NCAA titles for the second successive year and then the US trials. Prior to the Olympics the season's bests were 54.78m for Tosi, 54.54 for Gordien and 53.61 for Consolini. It had all the makings of a desperately close contest.

Consolini had first strike by breaking the Olympic record with 51.08 in the qualifying round, an extended affair involving 31 throwers, of whom 19 fell by the wayside. Prominent among the casualties were Oberweger and two of the Americans, Victor Frank and Bill Burton. Also sent back to the dressing rooms, with their services no longer to be required, were all three Britons, which was disappointing but not all that surprising. Neither of the Britons in Berlin in 1936 had qualified for the final, including one of the 1948 trio, Squadron Leader Laurence Reavell-Carter, and before then no thrower had even been thought worth sending since the "free-for-all" 1908 London Games, when there were two discus competitions and seven British participants – none of

---

100 metres (women) result: 1 Fanny Blankers-Koen (Holland) 11.9, 2 Dorothy Manley (Great Britain) 12.2, 3 Shirley Strickland (Australia) 12.2, 4 Viola Myers (Canada), 5 Patricia Jones (Canada), 6 Cynthia Thompson (Jamaica). Automatic timing gave the winning time as 12.2 and the margins behind the winner as being Manley 0.20sec, Strickland 0.39, Myers 0.43, Jones 0.49, Thompson 0.67. No official times were taken for fourth, fifth and sixth places.

whom qualified for either final. In a largely dismal record of British field-events endeavour over a period of 40 years, the discus remained the most dismal event of all. The situation *would* improve dramatically: at the 1956 Olympics Mark Pharaoh would be fourth.

Tosi beat Consolini's record with 51.78 in the first round of the final, but Consolini went ahead in the next round by exactly a metre and Gordien clinched third place in round three. Consolini's enviably accomplished style of throwing was described in a book written jointly by the respected US coaches Payton Jordan and Bud Spencer as a "replica of a spinning-top, whereby the body's centre of gravity changed a minimum, all forces co-ordinated in centrifugal rotation, and moving the discus through a wide arc with increasing speed".

A Greek, Nikolaos Syllas, managed seventh place in defence of his national legacy and he had also been sixth in Berlin. Even when a traditional "Greek style" competition had been held at the inaugural 1896 Games in Athens the winner had been an American, Robert Garrett, who had never previously seen a Greek discus but promptly broke the Greek-held "world record". Greece, it seemed, would have to settle merely for the honour of having invented the whole Olympic business.

The USA did not actually have a divine right to win the pole-vault title, though it must have seemed that way to any other aspiring medallists, assuming there *were* any. Americans had won the Olympic pole-vault at every Games since 1906, when a Frenchman, Fernand Gonder, had been successful. Americans had also held the world record since 1898, apart from brief incursions by Gonder and a disconcertingly versatile Charles Hoff, from Norway, whose only appearance in an Olympic final was at 800 metres in 1924. Nothing seemed likely to shake American predominance in 1948 as 16 of the top 20 vaulters in the world were from the USA, including Earle Meadows, the 1936 Olympic champion. At the US trials, Meadows had been beaten into sixth place, but the defence of the American tradition seemed safe in the hands of Bob Richards and Richmond ("Boo") Morcom, who between them could offer four AAU national wins among their credentials, and their team-mate Guinn Smith, who had tied for the NCAA title in 1941 before going into the Army Air Corps and as a captain being awarded the Distinguished Flying Cross. In the event, it was a much closer-run thing than they, or anyone else, might have imagined.

The rain fell steadily. Smith and Morcom were nursing knee injuries and Richards was not quite ready yet (though he would be in 1952 and 1956, winning the gold at both Games). Smith, using a new Japanese-made pole, only got over 3.95m and 4.10 at his second attempts. At 4.20 he cleared at his first try, but so, too,

Discus result: 1 Adolfo Consolini (Italy) 52.78m, 2 Giuseppe Tosi (Italy) 51.78, 3 Fortune Gordien (USA) 50.77, 4 Ivar Ramstad (Norway) 49.21, 5 Ferenc Klics (Hungary) 48.21, 6 Veikko Nyqvist (Finland) 47.33, 7 Niklaos Syllas (Greece) 47.25, 8 Stein Johnson (Norway) 46.54, 9 Arvo Huutoniemi (Finland) 45.28, 10 Uno Fransson (Sweden) 45.25, 11 Hermann Tunner (Austria) 44.43, 12 Eduardo Julve (Peru) 44.05.

did a Finn, Erkki Kataja, sporting a woollen hat, who would have been much more familiar with the prevailing weather than his Californian rival and was performing very close to his personal best of 4.25. It was after 6.30 in the evening that Smith, Kataja and Richards tried 4.30 and only Smith made it, at his last attempt.

Such performances seem derisory by modern standards, where six-metre vaults with highly flexible fibreglass poles are not uncommon, but these men were for the most part competing with the type of bamboo pole with which the peerless Cornelius Warmerdam had held the world record at 15ft 7¾in (4.77m) since 1942 (and would continue to do so until 1957) and were landing in sand-pits. Bamboo poles had some flexing qualities but would soon be replaced by safer poles made of blended alloy metals, and the courage of these men of the 1940s fully matched that of their 21st century inheritors, even if their heights did not. The renowned US coach, Dink Templeton, believed that Smith could become the second man to clear 15ft, saying of him: "In pull-up, push-off and approach Guinn Smith comes nearer than the other vaulters to Warmerdam's model." Smith, though, retired after his Olympic triumph.

All of the first eight places had been taken by Americans and Scandinavians, and the Norwegian, Kaas, in fourth place had a dual qualification, having been born in New York. Some confusion was caused by the Puerto Rican duo whose names were identical. One of them helpfully added a roman numeral "I" to aid identification, but he was not No.1 by nature because both he and his team-mate cleared the same height. Britain had no part in the final as Dick Webster, son of one of the very few British coaches to have encouraged field events in the pre-war era, was unable to emulate his unexpected achievement of finishing equal sixth with a British record in Berlin 12 years before.

The 5000 metres final brought Zátopek face to face with three Swedes, three Finns, an American, a Belgian and a Norwegian, but it was the two others among the dozen runners for whom he would certainly have had most regard: Gaston Reiff, of Belgium, and Willy Slijkhuis, of Holland. Zátopek had lost to both of them in 3000 metres races the previous year, and though he had won a 5000 metres less than two months before the Olympics in 14:10.0, and in the process had run the Dutchman into the ground (he did not finish), Zátopek would have assumed that matters might be different with an Olympic title at stake.

Zátopek's tactics were in sharp contrast to those he had adopted for the 10,000 three days before. He led from the start as the rain poured down, but the pace was no more than severely testing, rather than deliberately destructive. The time at 2000 metres was 5:38.0 – on schedule for 14:05 – and only world record-holder Gunder Hägg had ever run faster than that. What a pity it was

---

Pole vault result: 1 Guinn Smith (USA) 4.30m, 2 Erkki Kataja (Finland) 4.20, 3 Bob Richards (USA) 4.20, 4 Erling Kaas (Norway) 4.10, 5 Ragnar Lundberg (Sweden) 4.10, 6 Richmond Morcom (USA) 3.95, 7= Hugo Gollers (Sweden), Valto Olenius (Finland) 3.95, 9= Victor Sillon (France), José Vicénte I (Puerto Rico), José Vicente Barbosa (Puerto Rico) 3.95, 12 Allan Lindberg (Sweden) 3.80.

that Hägg was absent, banned three years earlier for infringing the archaic amateurism rules.

The next kilometre was much slower (2:55.0), and when Reiff moved ahead the Czech seemed to have no answer. Perhaps even he, for all his draconian training sessions of as many as 60x400 metres efforts, was feeling the strain in his third race of the Games. The fourth kilometre took 2:52.0 and Reiff was on his own, leading Slijkhuis by 30 metres and Zátopek by twice that. The race seemed over, and it was not until the last lap that Zátopek, from 50 metres down, began to make any impression on the man who was thought to be champion-elect by everyone in the stadium – bar Zátopek. The last 200 metres was phenomenal: gaining on Reiff with every stride to the frenzied excitement of the crowd, Zátopek closed to within a yard or so. Unfortunately for the 10,000 metres champion, the finishing line intervened and Reiff had clung on to win. A classic photograph of the end of the race tells the whole story: Reiff, arms spread as if in despair, staring agonisingly over his shoulder at the fearsome spectacle of the red-vested pursuer bearing relentlessly down on him.

Reiff had the look of the vanquished; Zátopek that of the victor; but it was Reiff who had the gold, and deservedly so for his brave mid-race effort. The silver had to suffice for Zátopek, and it must be said that he had not run the most sensible of races. There had been no reason for him to bear the brunt of the inclement weather and lead his two main rivals, though his intention had surely been to blunt the finishing-speed of both Reiff and Slijkhuis, whose 1500-metre times were far better than his. If he felt he had to lead, he should have gone at a faster pace, or he should have varied the pace. When Reiff attacked at 3500 metres Zátopek should have hung on to him grimly at whatever cost, in the knowledge that the Belgian was known to be vulnerable when put under pressure. But then it is, of course, much easier for those who only stand and stare to run the race from a cosy vantage-point on the sidelines!

Reiff himself explained it all later as if he always had matters under control. "The weather was bad," he recalled. "It had been raining for many hours. I have to say that I had no alternative but to follow Emil, to attach my wagon to the Czech locomotive, so that I could eventually finish the race with a sprint and have a chance of victory. After 3500 metres of the race Emil was still in front and it seemed to me that he was showing signs of tiredness. At that moment I said to myself, 'If he slows down the Dutchman, Slijkhuis, would become a danger and could beat us in the sprint', because Slijkhuis had beaten me in the heats. So I thought, 'I am going to increase the pace. I am going to make as if to pass Zátopek and that will force him to go faster.'

"Emil, of course, did not want anyone to pass him. Never, in any race, had he let a rival go by. He accelerated for 500, 600 metres, then again he gave signs of weariness, and I took advantage of that by accelerating again. To my great surprise I realised that he had lost ground, and I soon had a lead of 30 metres or so. I could already see myself as Olympic champion, but I had not given thought to the unshakeable nature of Zátopek, and little by little he came back. At 300 metres from the finish I looked back and I registered that he was no more than 20 metres behind. I gave it my maximum effort and in the home straight I again looked round and Zátopek was at a dozen metres.

"I heard the hubbub of the crowd and I did not know whether it was in recognition of me winning or whether it was for Zátopek closing on me. It was only a few metres from the line that I saw Zátopek about to pass me. Then I found a last burst of energy. I wanted to be Olympic champion and I accelerated, accelerated as much as I could, and took one metre fifty, two metres. It was truly very hard. The home straight there was the toughest of my whole career, but it was with absolute joy that I crossed the line and knew I was Olympic champion."

The official Olympic film of the race is poorly edited, showing Reiff at one moment on Zátopek's heels and the next some 40 or 50 metres ahead, rather than the 30 metres described by Reiff, but the finish is shown in its entirety. Reiff's version differs from the actuality, but who needs worry about that? To hear the thoughts that were going through an athlete's mind in the last few seconds of an Olympic triumph is far more important than whether or not they were strictly accurate. Reiff's nonchalance about his manner of victory was justified a month later when he beat Zátopek again at 5000 metres, 14:19.0 to 14:21.2, in the Czechoslovakia v Belgium match in Prague.

Win or lose, Zátopek made an unforgettable impression on all those who saw him at Wembley. Typical of the numerous youngsters whose enthusiasm for and dedication to sport was to be forever fired by Zátopek's example was a 16-year-old who had travelled down to London with a dozen team-mates from the Lancashire club, Radcliffe Harriers. They camped near Hounslow and made their way to the stadium each day by underground train. Now in his latter 70s, Harold Ogden recalls the experience with unabated pleasure, and he certainly learned a lesson from it because he soon became a good enough cross-country runner to place eighth in the national youths' championship the following year.

"I was mad on all sports. I'd been interested in athletics since 1943 and was so upset that Sydney Wooderson wasn't running in the Olympics. But it was Zátopek who was my hero, as I'd known about him since he ran in the European Championships in 1946. Heino, of Finland, was expected to win the 10,000 metres, but when Zátopek went away and won it had a big effect on everyone who watched it. I still can't understand his tactics in the 5000 because if he'd stayed closer to Reiff he was bound to have won. A day or so later I was walking along the Charing Cross Road, and there coming towards

---

5000 metres result: 1 Gaston Reiff (Belgium) 14:17.6, 2 Emil Zátopek (Czechoslovakia) 14:17.8, 3 Willy Slijkhuis (Holland) 14:26.8, 4 Erik Ahldén (Sweden) 14:28.6, 5 Bertil Albertsson (Sweden) 14:39.0, 6 Curtis Stone (USA) 14:39.4, 7 Väino Koskela (Finland) 14:41.0, 8 Väino Mäkelä (Finland) 14:43.0, 9 Marcel Vandewattyne (Belgium), 10 Martin Stokken (Norway), 11 Helge Perälä (Finland). Did not finish – Evert Nyberg (Sweden). Automatic timing gave the margin between Reiff and Zátopek as 0.26sec. No times were recorded for 9th, 10th and 11th places.

me was a bunch of athletes in tracksuits, Zátopek amongst them. I got his autograph, but I was so overwhelmed that I can't for the life of me remember what I said to him!"

Reiff, whose village birthplace was near the battlefield of Waterloo, was a very fine athlete, setting an exceptional world record for 2000 metres less than two months after his Olympic success and the next year becoming the first man to break eight minutes for 3000 metres, but for all that he was not in the class of Zátopek. Zátopek was to establish himself as one of the very greatest of all distance-runners – and in the opinion of many who saw him, including this author, *the* greatest – and despite the constriction of living in a Communist regime he charmed the world with his cheery personality and his readiness to help opponents with advice. A marvellous story about him is told by Neil Allen, who met up with him at the British Embassy in Prague in the mid-1960s. Because the state police did not like the idea of their citizens conversing too long with foreigners Zátopek invited his English guest to join him on a car-ride round the city and talked at length about his London Olympic adventure.

"It was a liberation of the spirit," he confided in his slow but fluent English. "After all those dark days of the war, the bombing, the killing and the starvation, the revival of the Olympics was as if the sun had come out. I went into the Olympic village and suddenly there were no more frontiers, no more barriers, just the peoples meeting together. It was wonderfully warm. Men and women who had lost five years of the full life were back again, and there were the young ones, too.

"I never really saw London then, though I have done since. You know, I became so worried as I realised that I had a good chance in the 10,000 metres. I would say to myself again and again, 'Oh dear, there is Heino, of Finland, and all the others. Maybe I can win, but maybe I cannot.'. Of course, to your public I was not a name until after my 10,000 metres victory. Then, perhaps, they took me to their hearts a little when I ran that incredibly stupid tactical 5000 metres against Reiff, of Belgium. Suddenly, I was saying, 'Here is the last lap and maybe I can win.' But I had been too stupid. The crowd at London cheered for me, but when I got back to Czechoslovakia they asked, 'How could you be so stupid? How did it happen?' "

Years later, when another legendary record-breaking distance-runner, Ron Clarke, who never won an Olympic title, visited Zátopek in Prague he discovered after his departure that his host had slipped one of his Olympic gold medals into his baggage as a parting gift. The cry of "Zá-to-pek! Zá-to-pek! Zá-to-pek!" rang to the rafters of stadiums round the world to salute every step that Zátopek took. When he died at the age of 78 a host of Olympic heroes travelled from around the globe to honour his memory.

Athletics. The fourth day – Tuesday 3 August

One-two-three in the shot. A different kind of one-two-three in the water.

The day's programme: 10.30 a.m. 10,000 metres walk heats; 11 a.m. Triple jump qualifying; 11 a.m. Shot qualifying; 3 p.m. 80 metres hurdles (women) heats; 3.30 p.m. 200 metres semi-finals; 3.30 p.m. Triple jump final; 3.45 p.m. 110 metres hurdles heats; 4 p.m. Shot final; 4.15 p.m. 3000 metres steeplechase heats; 5 p.m. 80 metres hurdles (women) semi-finals; 5.15 p.m. 200 metres final.

THREE MEN'S TITLES were to be decided – 200 metres, triple jump and shot – but the day began with what were really superfluous heats of the 10,000 metres track walk. There were 19 competitors who could well have been accommodated in a straight final, but maybe the officials thought that judging would be difficult with such numbers. This was an event which had caused problems in the past because of walkers "lifting" – that is failing to keep at least one foot in contact with the ground at all times – and it would create so many difficulties again in 1952 that it was abandoned thereafter in favour of a 20 kilometres road walk, where the pace would be slower and, hopefully, fairer.

At Wembley, though, it was an event with major interest for Britain because it was thought that there was a real chance of a medal, even gold. The British trio of Harry Churcher, Jim Morris and Ron West went through safely enough to the final, though John Mikaelsson, of Sweden, had the fastest time. A South African, Kalie Reyneke, had produced sensational performances on home tracks, but his technique was so much a matter of controversy that the national selectors had studied his action on newsreel film under a microscope before they were satisfied – only to find their faith misplaced when he was among the six disqualifications at Wembley. Also unable to satisfy the judges were all three Americans, including Henry Laskau, who, born in Berlin in the midst of World War I, had been a 1500 metres runner before escaping the Nazi persecution of Jewish people in 1938. For the day's finals British interest would be restricted to finding out whether McCorquodale or, far less likely, Vallé would qualify at 200 metres, but there were also the hurdlers to see for the first time, and these were events for which Britain held high hopes.

Maureen Gardner won her 80 metres hurdles heat in 11.6, but she had just seen Fanny Blankers-Koen break the Olympic record with 11.3 to show everyone else exactly what they were up against. Less than an hour later it was the turn of the men, and some grief was caused by the British participants. Wing Commander Don Finlay, of the RAF, now a distinguished silver-haired 39-year-old, led at the final barrier in his 110 metres hurdles heat but then went tumbling and thus lost all hopes of reaching a third Olympic final. Harold Abrahams reported that "the groans as he fell headlong and rolled over and over were a pathetic conclusion to a brilliant career", though the indomitable Finlay actually was to have a year or more yet of fine athletic achievement left in him. Joe Birrell, the teenage AAA winner, faded out of contention after hitting a hurdle in his heat. Those Olympic nerves were in full jangle mode.

In between the hurdles events the first of the two 200 metres semi-finals had featured McKenley, Patton and Ewell, which gave Vallé no chance and he finished a distant though honourable fourth ahead of a Brazilian and a South African as McKenley won in 21.4. McCorquodale had a better chance in the second semi-final, and it was close between five of the six runners, but he just lost out to Bourland (21.5), LaBeach and Les Laing, from Jamaica, who had served in the RAF and was well known to British fans as a member of the Chiswick-based Polytechnic Harriers club. Laing would have been running for Britain in the Games had Jamaica not entered. Only one tenth of a second separated McCorquodale in fifth place from LaBeach in second.

The triple jump (or hop, step and jump as it was then called, and more properly so) suffered from the absence of Japan. The Japanese had totally dominated the event in the 1930s, and successive world records had been set in winning Olympic titles by Chuhei Nambu in Los Angeles and by Naoto Tajima in Berlin, whose jump of exactly 16 metres was still unsurpassed, and would not be for another three years. The morning's qualifying had seen 13 men over the requisite 14.50m – and the early exit of 16 others, including Sid Cross, Allan Lindsay and Robert Hawkey, who formed the gallant but outclassed British trio.

The gold and silver medals were decided in the first round of the final to the advantage of Ahman, of Sweden, and Avery, of Australia, respectively, and no one else got anywhere near for the rest of an unexciting competition. This event, like the track walk, was not one in which the Americans then excelled because it was only contested in Olympic year, for whatever reason, by colleges and universities. At least Ahman had literally risen to the occasion, setting a personal best of 15.40m, while Avery, a New South Wales police officer, was maintaining an Australian heritage: Nick Winter had won the event in 1924 and Jack Metcalfe, the Australian team manager at Wembley, had placed third in 1936.

Having said that, it was not a particularly exhilarating event, but it ought to be added that it could have been very different. One of the most intriguing competitors in the final was a 6ft 1in (1.86m) tall Indian named Henry Rebello, variously described as being aged 17 or 21, who was credited with an official national record of 15.29 from the previous February but was also said to have achieved 15.86 – a performance which had been exceeded only by Tajima's world record. At a special warm-up meeting for Olympic athletes at the Motspur Park track, in Surrey, less than a month before the Wembley final, Rebello had beaten Avery with a leap of 48ft 10in (14.88), achieved while wearing baggy flannel trousers to deliberately hamper his performance because the pit was too short for him to make an all-out effort.

The Indian team management was so confident of Rebello winning the Olympic final that they had arranged in advance a celebratory dinner, but at the very moment that he was about to take his first jump a series of presentation ceremonies for the medallists in wrestling began. Rebello was required to wait half an hour, according to one report, and when at last he set off down the runway he tore a leg muscle and had to be carried off on a stretcher. That was, to all intents and purposes, the end of his career, though he did compete again in India the following year.

Less than a fortnight after the Olympic final, Keizo Hasegawa, of Japan, cleared 15.62, but by the time the Japanese were invited back at the 1952 Games their superiority had waned and the new champion and record-holder was a Brazilian whose very name rang out with the resonant rhythm of the event – Adhemar Ferreira da Silva. He won Olympic gold in both 1952 and 1956 and took the world record to 16.56, and no one could possibly have foreseen such a future for the 20-year-old who placed eighth at Wembley.

The shot had been won by a German in 1936 but on every previous occasion from 1896 onwards, bar one, by Americans. This time the US world record-holder, Charles Fonville, had been a principal victim of his country's "do or die" trials system, which mattered to him but not to the medal prospects, as there were eight other Americans in the leading 10 in the world. The sole intruder was an Estonian, Heino Lipp, kept out of the Games by the wilfulness of his Soviet masters, and faint hopes of any challenge to the US faded further when the best remaining non-American, Roland Nilsson, of Sweden, was eliminated in the qualifying round.

The final was a cakewalk. Between them the Americans – Wilbur Thompson, Jim Delaney and Jim Fuchs, who had all set personal bests in their trials the previous month – had 13 puts beyond 16 metres, and the furthest that anyone else could do was 15.43 by a Pole, Mieczyslaw Lomowski, Thompson, who at 6ft (1.83m) tall and weighing 15st 7lb (89kg) was a mere stripling by 21st-century standards in the event, was the winner at 17.12, though he had been beaten in the US trials by the similarly built Delaney, and maybe his advantage was mental, rather than physical. The following year Thompson explained to a coaches' conference in the US his practised routine, and though his terminology was somewhat on the formal side his recipe for success was readily apparent: "There must be a consistency of action in practice. This is necessary as it is desired to

---

Triple jump result: 1 Arne Åhman (Sweden) 15.40m, 2 George Avery (Australia) 15.365, 3 Ruhi Sarialp (Turkey) 15.025, 4 Preben Larsen (Denmark) 14.83, 5 Geraldo de Oliveira (Brazil) 14.825, 6 Valdemar Rautio (Finland) 14.70, 7 Les McKeand (Australia) 14.53, 8 Adhemar Ferreira da Silva (Brazil) 14.49, 9 Åke Hallgren (Sweden) 14.485, 10 Bill Albans (USA) 14.31, 11 Helio Coutinho da Silva (Brazil) 14.31, 12 Won Kwon Kim (Korea) 14.25, 13 Lennart Moberg (Sweden) 14.215. Henry Rebello (India) no recorded jump.

John Mark, a Cambridge University quarter-miler who did not qualify for Great Britain's Olympic Games team, proudly holds the torch at the opening ceremony. The packed crowds were unaware that the country's best known athlete, Sydney Wooderson, by then retired, should have had the honour.

Gordon Pirie, then aged 17 (right), shares in the Olympic torch relay. Eight years later he was a silver-medallist at the Games.

Captain John W Anderson, Avery Brundage, President of the United States Olympic Committee, and John McGovern, counsellor of the Olympic committee, raising the Olympic flag aboard the steamship 'America' enroute to London.

100 metres winner Harrison Dillard, of the USA (right), is congratulated by runner-up Barney Ewell. Great Britain's Alastair McCorquodale, fourth, is in the background.

Jamaica's Arthur Wint, who served in the Royal Air Force during World War II, wins the 400 metres.

But Wint had to settle for silver in the 800 metres as Mal Whitfield (USA) won gold. Marcel Hansenne of France was third.

Wembley's rain and mud. Henry Eriksson, of Sweden, is congraulated on his 1500 metres triumph.

Gaston Reiff, of Belgium, is helped after his 5000 metres win.

Czechoslovakia's Emil Zatopek finished second in the 5000 metres but was not to be denied in the 10,000 metres.

Automatic timing was in use at Wembley, but judging of the track events was still entrusted to a bevy of officials.

The marathon runners leave Wembley Stadium's famous twin towers behind them. Great Britain's Tom Richards, who won the silver medal, is third in the leading group.

Roy Cochran, of the USA, wins the 400 metres hurdles.

Bill Porter, of the USA, celebrates his 110 metres hurdles victory with silver medallist and fellow countryman Clyde Scott.

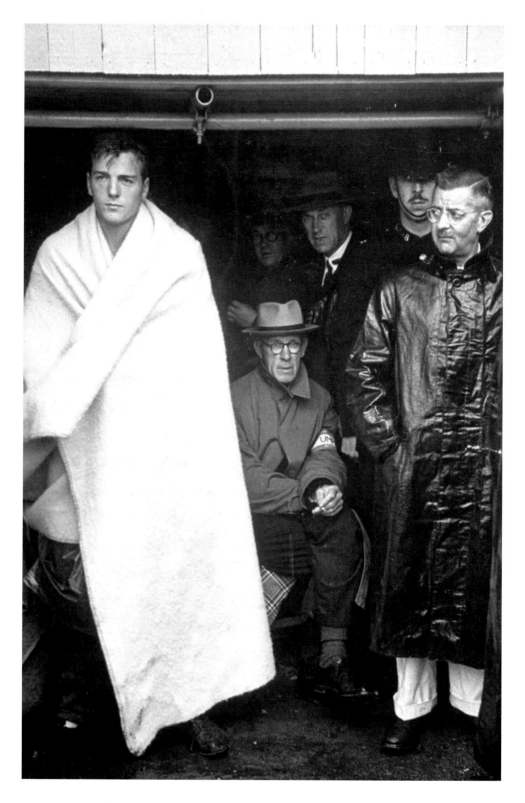

Bob Mathias, of the USA, shelters from the rain during his progress to decathlon gold.

But there was no such creature comforts for two of his fellow competitors.

Guinn Smith, of the USA, fails at 4.40m in the pole vault but he had already won with 4.30. Note that one of the judges in smoking!

have a nerve pattern so established that after a certain sequence of events the put is started automatically."

Delaney and Fuchs had each led in the opening two rounds with Olympic records of their own, and Fuchs was to become one of the great exponents of the event over the next two years, winning 88 consecutive contests and taking the world record up to 17.95. John Giles, a strapping ex-Guardsman who had been "volunteered" for the event in true Army fashion while serving in Germany, had given Britain some hope for the future by setting an English native record of 14.79 in the qualifying round at Wembley, though he could not reproduce that form in the final.

There was a worrying moment for Maureen Gardner and her thousands of supporters in the 80 metres hurdles semi-finals when she stumbled and only just qualified in third place. The other heat was won, inevitably, by Mrs Blankers-Koen in a far faster time.

McKenley had the least favoured inside lane for the 200 metres final, with Patton in lane two, LaBeach in three, Ewell in four, Bourland in five and Laing in six, and Patton found his form at last to win from Ewell and LaBeach, who were therefore repeating their 100 metres placings. Ewell had been generally regarded as the likely winner after Patton's indifferent running in the 100, but Patton had the advantage into the home straight and held on through to the finish. Asked to describe the race, Patton replied laconically, "I'd been studying Barney's method of running the 220 and I discovered just where he turned it on in most of his races. So I just turned it on a little sooner and got an early jump on him."

The official times were 21.1 for both Patton and Ewell, but the margin of victory was clearer than that, as the automatic timer was to reveal. LaBeach had been born in Panama of Jamaican immigrant parents who had gone there to work on the canal-building project, and two of his brothers, Byron and Sam, were fine sprinters; the former representing Jamaica in the 1952 Olympics. Lloyd LaBeach could now claim to be one of the most successful Olympic "teams" in history, having won two medals as his country's sole representative in any sport.

Patton had been accorded the very rare privilege for an athlete of being featured on the cover of *Time* magazine the previous week (in succession to Igor

---

Shot-put result: 1 Wilbur Thompson (USA) 17.12m, 2 Jim Delaney (USA) 16.68, 3 Jim Fuchs (USA) 16.42, 4 Mieczyslaw Lomowski (Poland) 15.43, 5 Gösta Arvidsson (Sweden) 15.37, 6 Yrjö Lehtila (Finland) 15.05, 7 Jaako Jouppila (Finland) 14.59, 8 Čestmír Kalina (Czechoslovakia) 14.55, 9 Konstantinos Yataganas (Greece) 14.54, 10 Witold Gierutto (Poland) 14.37, 11 John Giles (GB) 13.73, 12 Sigfús Sigurdsson (Iceland) 13.66.

---

200 metres result: 1 Mel Patton (USA) 21.1, 2 Barney Ewell (USA) 21.1, 3 Lloyd LaBeach (Panama) 21.2, 4 Herb McKenley (Jamaica), 5 Cliff Bourland (USA), 6 Les Laing (Jamaica). Automatic timing for the winner was 21.3 and the margins behind him were 0.05sec for Ewell, 0.20 for LaBeach, 0.24 for McKenley, 0.27 for Bourland and 0.72 for Laing. No official times were recorded for fourth, fifth and sixth places.

Stravinsky and Howard Hughes) as part of their Olympic preview coverage. Memorably, a *Time* writer had said of Patton that he "looks fragile enough to be bowled over by the smell of locker-room sweat … he is tall and thin like the hand of a stopwatch". Such training aids as lifting weights were almost unheard of in the 1940s, and sprinters of that era were long and lean – or short and lean – and not the muscular powerhouses of the 21st century.

The American academic, Dr Don Potts, was universally regarded as the leading authority on the sprints, having made a close study of all the great champions from the late 19th century onwards, and in 1954 he published his findings regarding the "World's Fastest Humans", based on their best times and their competitive records at 100 yards, 100 metres, 200 metres and 220 yards. He rated Patton behind only Jesse Owens. Equal third were Ralph Metcalfe, a triple Olympic medallist in 1932 and 1936, and Hal Davis, who set world records at 100 yards and 100 metres in the war years. LaBeach (the only non-American listed in the top six by Potts) was fifth and Ewell sixth.

Thus the Wembley men's 100 and 200 metres finals, even if the times were unexceptional, can be regarded as having brought together more great sprinters than any other Olympics had previously done. Patton, the father of a two-year-old daughter when he won at Wembley, had taken a job as a shoe-repairer to help pay his way through university and eventually earned a Master's degree. His credentials as a master sprinter were to be emphatically confirmed in a single afternoon in 1949 when he ran 100 yards in 9.1, with an assisting wind of 2.9 metres per second, not much over the 2.0-metre limit for official record recognition, and a world record 20.2 for 220 yards on a straight track.

This fourth day of Wembley athletics finished on a low note for Britain, and even the un-named correspondent of *Athletics*, presumably the editor, PW ("Jimmy") Green, could find nothing positive to suggest about the performances of the British competitors involved. "The less said about the home runners in the 3000 metres steeplechase the better," he wrote. "They were hopelessly outclassed."

A profitable change of direction was to be made by one of the Wembley steeplechasers who was among the also-rans. The US trials winner in only his second race at the distance had been 20-year-old Bob McMillen, despite falling at the last water-jump. In the first of the three heats at Wembley he fell in the water three times, finished last but one, and swore to concentrate on miling instead. It was a good move. He was to win the 1500 metres silver medal at the 1952 Games.

Athletics. The fifth day –
Wednesday 4 August

A Finnish film actor, a French concert pianist, and Mrs Blankers yet again.

The day's programme: 11 a.m. Javelin qualifying; 11 a.m. Long jump (women) qualifying; 11 a.m. Shot (women) qualifying; 2.30 p.m. Javelin final; 3 p.m. 80 metres hurdles (women) final; 3.15 p.m. 110 metres hurdles semi-finals; 3.30 p.m. 400 metres heats; 4.30 p.m. 1500 metres heats; 4.30 p.m. Long jump (women) final; 5 p.m. Shot (women) final; 5 p.m. 110 metres hurdles final; 5.15 400 metres quarter-finals.

HALFWAY THROUGH THE athletics programme; 17 gold medals had been distributed; 16 still to be contested. The USA had won seven titles, Sweden two, and Australia, Austria, Belgium, Czechoslovakia, France, Holland, Hungary and Italy one each. None yet for Britain, but there were still hopes, though most of them now rested on the slim chances of Mrs Blankers wearying of winning. Three field events would be decided this Wednesday – only the very faintest prospect of any British success there – and two hurdles finals. None of the British male hurdlers had progressed, but Maureen Gardner had.

The javelin qualifying distance of 64 metres seemed a reasonable enough target, but it confounded all but four of the competitors. An American, Martin Biles, led with 67.68, a shade unexpected as no US thrower had ever won anything better than bronze in this event. The others to advance automatically were two Swedes (Berglund and Petersson) and a Finn (Rautavaara), and that made much more sense as between them Sweden and Finland had won six of the seven gold medals on offer since 1908. Not for the first time, nor for the last, some of the qualifiers in throwing events would fail to reproduce their form in the final, and Biles was to be no better than sixth when the gold medal was at stake, Petersson ninth and Berglund tenth.

One of the non-qualifiers was Malcolm Dalrymple, who had set a British record of 210ft 9½in (64.25m) a couple of months previously but was more than 10 metres short of that at Wembley. His father, Jock, had also been a British record-holder and had competed in the 1924 Olympics. Malcolm Dalrymple was an engineering factory worker in Bedford and one of only two AAA junior champions of 1939 who revived their athletics careers to a sufficient level to qualify for the 1948 Games – the other being Martin Pike in the 4x400 metres relay – and his Wembley showing was a great disappointment to him, as he still recalled at the age of 82:

"On my first effort I was given a 'no throw' and I argued the matter with the judge, who I knew because he happened to be the sports master at Bedford Modern

School. I believed I had thrown far enough to qualify for the final. To this day I still can't see how my foot had crossed the line, but the judge said it had, and then my other two throws were not as good." Dalrymple had trained after work by throwing in the street until his employers gave him an extra hour at lunchtime, so long as he made up the time later in the evenings. "No one in Britain really knew much about the javelin," he remembered. "When we went up to the park to train, even the cricketers would stop to watch what we were up to."

In the final Rautavaara – who, being Finnish, no doubt had rather better training facilities at his disposal than did Dalrymple – got off the one big throw that he needed to win in the first round, though it was not actually that big – 69.77, almost three metres short of the Olympic record from 1932. Rautavaara was a film actor by profession, and he had been a leading man in world javelin-throwing since 1937, with a best throw of 75.47 in 1945.

Dr Steve Seymour, an osteopathic surgeon, achieved the best ever result for the USA with the silver. He had first figured in the world rankings in 1942, and when he joined the US Army in 1944 he kept up his training by throwing dummy hand-grenades while stationed at Fort McArthur, in Texas. He had then served in the Middle East and had changed his javelin-throwing technique after suffering an elbow injury in helping to quell a riot in Egypt. He had created a stir a year before the Olympics by winning the AAU title with a throw of 248ft 10in (75.84m), which beat the US record by more than 14ft. The Hungarian bronze-medallist, Várszegi, was the longest-serving of the medallists, having also placed eighth in 1936.

Americans were thought to be not proficient at the event because they had been brought up from childhood as baseball pitchers, which did not suit the javelin technique. Maybe so, but they were obviously learning fast because they were to take the gold and the silver in Helsinki four years later, much to the amazement of their hosts, and the next year to deprive the Finns of the world record they had monopolised since 1930 (though the 12th and last man in the Wembley final was to briefly get it back for Finland in 1956). The absent Latvian refugee Janis Stendzenieks, who a couple of months before had thrown further than Rautavaara's gold-medal effort, was apparently a tearful spectator in the Wembley stands. It would not be until 1992 that the Olympic organisers found a way of allowing stateless athletes into the Games, when a Yugoslav shot-putter competed under the title of "Independent Olympic Participant". It was a simple enough idea that was long overdue when finally put into practice. Also missing was Sweden's Sven Daleflod, who was ill but who had recovered by the following month and won three competitions with throws beyond 71 metres.

Javelin result: 1 Tapio Rautavaara (Finland) 69.77, 2 Steve Seymour (USA) 67.56, 3 József Várszegi (Hungary) 67.03, 4 Pauli Vesterinen (Finland) 65.89, 5 Odd Mæhlum (Norway) 65.32, 6 Martin Biles (USA) 65.17, 7 Mirko Vujačić (Yugoslavia) 64.89, 8 Bob Likens (USA) 64.51, 9 Gunnar Petersson (Sweden) 62.80, 10 Per-Arne Berglund (Sweden) 62.62, 11 Lumir Kiesewetter (Czechoslovaka) 60.25, 12 Soini Nikkinen (Finland) 58.05.

For the eagerly anticipated 80 metres hurdles final Blankers-Koen and Gardner were alongside each other in lanes two and three. The other finalists were Strickland (Australia), Oberbreyer (Austria), Lomská (Czechoslovakia) and Monginou (France), but they were understandably not paid too much heed by the packed crowd as the athletes made their preparations and dug their starting-holes. It was a wonderful race – one of the very best of the entire Games – and to many of the spectators without a direct view of the finish line it must have seemed, if only momentarily, that Gardner had won the long-sought-after gold.

For once Blankers-Koen had not been in command from the start, and the reason may be gleaned from the official Olympic film, which shows that Gardner inadvertently moved before the gun was fired. Maybe Blankers-Koen saw this out of the corner of her eye and thought there would be a recall. Certainly the gun should not have been fired, though in any case no advantage was gained and Blankers-Koen soon took the lead from Gardner and Strickland. Then, over the last barrier and on the short run-in, Gardner made an immense effort and seemed to have closed the gap. However, Blankers-Koen had just held on as both were credited with a time of 11.2, which only Blankers-Koen herself had ever beaten with her world-record 11.0 of the previous June. The automatic timer was to reveal many years later when its secrets were uncovered that the difference between gold and silver was 0.05sec, equivalent to half a metre or so.

The men's high hurdles semi-finals told a familiar tale of American supremacy. Dixon won the first in 14.2. Porter equalled the Olympic record in winning the second from Scott, 14.1 to 14.2. The next fastest time was 14.5 by the Australian, Gardner. The line-up for the final later on was Dixon, Porter, Lidman (Sweden), Triulzi (Argentina), Gardner and Scott. Gardner was a remarkable athlete, so short-sighted that he could barely see from one flight of hurdles to the next and his basic speed was negligible, with a 100 yards best of merely 10.3sec. Lidman, aged 33, whose European record of 14.0 from 1940 was to last for 16 years, was one of only two finalists at Wembley to have also qualified for a track final in Berlin (the other was Blankers-Koen, who ran in the 4x100 metres relay in 1936), where he had placed a close fourth, but neither he nor Gardner would be in the reckoning this time.

As if according to a well-thumbed Hollywood script, the three Americans left the others far behind and Porter moved through from third to get the verdict over Scott, who was running in the outside sixth lane which had already nurtured gold and silver in the men's and women's 100 metres finals. The hand times were seriously at fault because Porter was given 13.9, Scott and Dixon 14.1, and yet

80 metres hurdles (women) result: 1 Fanny Blankers-Koen (Holland) 11.2, 2 Maureen Gardner (GB) 11.2, 3 Shirley Strickland (Australia) 11.4, 4 Yvette Monginou (France), 5 Maria Oberbreyer (Austria), 6 Libuše Lomská (Czecholsovakia). The automatic timer gave Blankers-Koen's time as 11.4 and the margins behind her as 0.05sec for Gardner, 0.10 for Strickland, 0.59 for Monginou, 0.64 for Oberbreyer, 0.68 for Lomská. No official times were recorded for fourth, fifth and sixth places.

there was only 0.09sec between the three of them on the automatic device. Dixon, whose mother was Scottish, had no doubt when asked some 50 years later about what would have happened if Harrison Dillard had not fallen in the US trials race: "He was the best hurdler in the world in '48. If he had made the team, he would have won it easily."

Porter, at 6ft 3in (1.90m) tall, was perfectly built for the 3ft 6in hurdles, and his performance was inevitably to be judged in the light of Dillard's absence. This is by no means fair because the new champion was a very worthy one. He had brought Dillard's long unbeaten sequence to an end at the AAU championships in June and had then run an automatically-timed 13.90 in the US trials, which was possibly as fast as Dillard's hand-timed best of 13.6. Dillard ran 13.9 on four occasions in subsequent races during August and September in Europe to prove that he had not lost the hurdling knack. Porter, though still only 22 years old, was the father of two children and retired after the Olympics, like so many of his team-mates who also had livings to earn.

The first and second rounds of the 400 metres went according to plan, though it seemed rather excessive on the part of Arthur Wint, running his fourth and fifth races in six days, to produce the fastest times of 47.7 on each outing. In the second of these Bill Roberts just lost out on a semi-final place in what seemed to be much the toughest race of the four, and *The Times* paid the hero of Berlin a fine tribute: "The gallant effort of Roberts, the 36-year-old British captain, in a heat of the 400 metres behind Whitfield, the American, earned the generous applause it deserved. Although he did not survive the second round he ran better than anyone had a right to expect, and it was nice to see several of his fellow-competitors congratulate him on a second worthy effort in one afternoon."

Roberts had been given the responsibility of team captaincy by British manager Jack Crump ahead of more obvious candidates like Wing Commander Finlay and had made an unintentionally spectacular impression when he gave an introductory speech at the RAF Uxbridge barracks where the athletes were lodged. He had taken up pipe-smoking and when he gestured to emphasise a point his hand thumped against his side and set light to a box of matches in his pocket!

The four 1500 metres heats decided the composition of the 12-man final to be run the following day. The three Swedes and the Dutchman, Slijkhuis, who had won the 5000 metres bronze, were the winners. Čevona, of Czechoslovakia, also went through, and after Zátopek's achievements any Czech on the track was going to be taken very seriously. The 800 metres bronze-medallist Hansenne, of

---

110 metres hurdles result: 1 Bill Porter (USA) 13.9, 2 Clyde Scott (USA) 14.1, 3 Craig Dixon (USA) 14.1, 4 Alberto Triulzi (Argentina), 5 Peter Gardner (Australia), 6 Håkon Lidman (Sweden). Automatic timing gave Porter's time as 14.2 and the margins behind him as 0.04sec for Scott, 0.09 for Dixon, 0.51 for Triulzi, 0.59 for Gardner, 0.66 for Lidman. No official times were taken for fourth, fifth and sixth places.

Athletics. The sixth day – Thursday 5 August

On the way to 400 metres gold ... and then the roof fell in

The day's programme: 10.30 a.m. Decathlon 100 metres; 11.30 a.m. Decathlon long jump; 3 p.m. 400 metres semi-finals; 3 p.m. Decathlon shot; 3.30 p.m. 200 metres (women) heats; 4 p.m. Decathlon high jump; 4.15 p.m. 3000 metres steeplechase final; 4.45 p.m. 400 metres final; 5 p.m. 200 metres (women) semi-finals; 5.30 p.m. Decathlon 400 metres.

THE DECATHLON WOULD decide the best all-round athlete of the Games: 100 metres, long jump, high jump, shot and 400 metres to be contested on this Thursday; then the 110 metres hurdles, discus, pole vault, javelin and 1500 metres the following day. The athletes would be in action until far into the evening and the weather might turn out to be dreadful again. It was going to be a long, hard haul before the gold medal would be decided. So it seemed bizarre that a 17-year-old American high-school student should be the favourite for the title in this most arduous of competitions.

The outcome would be decided on the basis of a statistical table which gave 1,000 points for what were considered to be performances of the highest quality and lower scores for every performance inferior to those. The 1,000-point marks had been set as follows: 100 metres, 10.5sec; Long jump, 7.70m; Shot, 15.70m; High jump, 1.97m; 400 metres, 48.0sec; 110 metres hurdles, 14.6sec; Discus, 48.99m; Pole vault, 4.20m; Javelin, 69.98m; 1500 metres, 3min 54.0sec.

Bob Mathias had won the US trials in only his second decathlon, and he had never even heard of the event until his coach entered him for one which happened to be taking place two months before the Olympics in nearby Los Angeles. Mathias had won there with a score of 7,094 points. The world record had been set by the USA's Glenn Morris at 7,900 points at the 1936 Olympics, and as only 15 others in the world had ever beaten 7,000 points in the next dozen years it was apparent that Mathias had made the transition from promising teenage hurdler to world-class decathlete in the space of 48 hours.

Mathias then improved to 7,222 at the trials at the end of June, and there would be only four other 7,000-plus scorers to face him at Wembley. One of them was Argentina's Enrique Kistenmacher, who had already taken part in the long-jump final the previous Saturday, and he started the 10-event test with a 10.9 for 100 metres and a 7.08m in his speciality to establish an early lead. With only the semi-finals and final of the 400 metres, the heats and semi-finals of the women's

200 metres and the final of the steeplechase taking place on the track, the decathletes would be the centre of attention for much of the day. There were 35 of them in all, a ridiculously large number, but there were no qualifying standards for entry into Olympic events at that time.

Before the afternoon's athletics had started the spectators were treated to a bonus in the form of an "exhibition" lacrosse match. It was the prerogative of Games organisers to include a demonstration of a non-Olympic sport, and so an All-England team captained by Lieutenant Commander John Whitehead, who had won the Distinguished Service Cross and bar during the war, met the Rensselaer Polytechnic team from Troy, New York, which had been touring England, and whose captain was the leading US scorer, Dayman "Demon" Jordan. The match ended amicably in a 5-5 draw and was described by the honorary secretary of the English Lacrosse Union as "one of the best exhibitions of lacrosse seen in England for a long time". Lacrosse had actually figured on the Olympic programme in St Louis in 1904 and again in London in 1908 when Canada beat Great Britain 14-10. Lacrosse had also been an exhibition sport in 1928 and 1932 and was to be so again in 1984.

The idea of holding both the semi-finals and final of such a gruelling event as the 400 metres within less than two hours seems ludicrous now, but it was a standard feature of the Games until 1956 – and it did not seem to have done past champions much harm. Eric Liddell had won in 1924 for Britain with an official world record of 47.6; Bill Carr, of the USA, had set another world record of 46.2 in 1932; Archie Williams, also of the USA, had run 46.5 in 1936. Even so, when Arthur Wint won the first Wembley semi-final in 46.3 and his Jamaican team-mate, Herb McKenley, the second in 47.3, it seemed as if it was McKenley who was being much the more sensible of the two in saving his energies. The British, for whom Godfrey Brown's silver medal in 1936 was but a fond memory, had no one in the semi-finals.

For the final the line-up from the inside was Bolen (USA), McKenley, Wint, Whitfield (USA), Curotta (Australia) and Guida (USA). Whitfield and Wint had taken gold and silver at 800 metres, and not since 1920 had anyone appeared in both 400 and 800 finals, when the English-born Bevil Rudd, of South Africa, had won gold and bronze. McKenley, as befits the sprinter-type, went off very fast and led by a good six metres into the straight, but to the astonishment and mounting excitement of the spectators Wint began to gain ground with his nine-foot stride and with 50 metres or so to go cruised past the now struggling McKenley to win rather easily in 46.2 (actually 46.3 by automatic timing). The 18-year-old Australian Curotta had given his all to qualify and was well out of it, while Guida was clearly favouring an injured leg and could not even break 50sec. Whitfield, the 800 metres champion, got the bronze. Bolen, the other American in fourth place, later became a distinguished diplomat, serving as US ambassador to Botswana, Lesotho and Swaziland.

McKenley was the world record-holder at 400 metres (45.9) and at 440 yards

(46.0, equivalent to 45.7 for 400 metres) and was well accustomed to running the first half of his races almost flat out, though not necessarily of his own volition. For both the 400 and 440 records he had passed halfway in 21.0, and he admitted, "I did not quite fully understand just how to control my speed". His account of the Wembley race to a coaches' conference in California a few years later was graphic and almost painfully frank:

"I was determined to run about 45.6 and set about it quite calmly. I knew exactly what I had to do. The pistol fired and we were off. I was in lane two and when I reached the 200 metres mark I had passed Morris Curotta, of Australia, who was on the outside lane. I knew I must have been running well since Curotta's running is patterned something after mine. Feeling more relaxed and less fatigued than any other time I could remember, I decided to keep up the same effort without any thought of relaxing my shoulders or arms.

"I felt almost as good at the 300 metres mark and decided then to go into my kick. The result was that at about 40 or 50 metres from home the roof fell in, as it were, and all I could do was hold on as best I could. This is not intended as an alibi, nor to detract from Arthur Wint's magnificent performance, but I do feel that with a little better distribution of speed I not only would have finished better but would definitely have run a faster time – although I might not have won." McKenley had passed 200 metres in 21.4 and Wint in 22.2. Their second halves took exactly 25 and 24 seconds respectively.

There was a curious underlying story to this race. In circumstances which were by no means inconceivable the gold medal could have been Britain's, rather than Jamaica's. When the list of British "possibles" for the Games athletics had been published towards the end of the previous year the British Amateur Athletic Board had appended a footnote that Wint and McKenley, together with another Jamaican, Les Laing, and the Trinidadian, Emmanuel McDonald Bailey, would "be considered for selection should their own countries not require their services". This proposal was based on the fact that any citizen of a country within the Empire was regarded as British.

So far as Wint, Laing and McDonald Bailey were concerned, this declaration of intent had a perfect logic to it, as they all lived in and had competed for Great Britain. McKenley's case was rather different because he had gone to university in the USA during the war years and had never been a resident of Britain, though no doubt he would have given serious thought to running in the Olympics for Britain if Jamaica did not enter a team. The Jamaican officials sent in their Olympic entry forms early in 1948 and that put an end to such wishful thinking. It had been a

---

400 metres result: 1 Arthur Wint (Jamaica) 46.2, 2 Herb McKenley (Jamaica) 46.4, 3 Mal Whitfield (USA) 46.9, 4 Dave Bolen (USA) 47.2, 5 Morris Curotta (Australia) 47.9, 6 George Guida (USA) 50.2. The automatic time showed 46.3 for Wint and the margins behind him as being 0.23 for McKenley, 0.66 for Whitfield, 0.90 for Bolen, 1.77 for Curotta and 4.50 for Bolen.

nice idea while it lasted. McDonald Bailey decided his own destiny, eventually opting for Britain even though Trinidad & Tobago also decided to take part. Wint later qualified as a surgeon at St Bartholomew's Hospital, in London, and served as Jamaican High Commissioner in Britain from 1974 to 1978.

The decathletes had moved on to the shot where the Pole, Gierutto, who had reached the final of the individual event, had much the best effort of 14.53. Next came the high jump in which five men tied at 1.86, and as the three eventual medallists were among them this event can now be seen, in the wisdom of hindsight, as a sort of watershed. The 400 metres would finish off the first day, and maybe finish off the hopes of some of the 33 weary competitors still left in.

Of course, no day's athletics at these Wembley Olympics should be complete without a win for Fanny Blankers-Koen – after all, she had already been first across the line in six races spread over the previous Saturday, Monday, Tuesday and Wednesday – and she duly obliged again with a first-round 200 metres success in 25.7. The real news was that four of the other heats were won in faster times by a South African (25.3), a Briton (25.4), an American (25.5) and a Jamaican (25.6). Was the great lady feeling the strain? Was there hope yet for her rivals, who might otherwise have been forgiven for seeing only a silver lining on the horizon?

The responses later in the day to those questions were a firm "no" and once more "no". Blankers-Koen won her semi-final in 24.3; the second semi-final was a dead heat between Audrey Williamson, of Great Britain, and Shirley Strickland, of Australia, in 24.9. Another Briton, Margaret Walker, also qualified. Could either of them do better than Manley or Gardner? It seemed unlikely.

The steeplechase, as fully expected, was a private affair sorted out among the Swedes, including Erik Elmsäter, who had run the first sub-9min clocking four years before. That performance would survive as a world record until 1951, though to be absolutely precise the time was regarded as no more than a "world best performance". For reasons known only to the IAAF hierarchy, they declined to recognise the event for record purposes until 1954, despite its having been run at a standard distance of 3000 metres at every Olympics since 1920. The problem was that some other steeplechase races were being held without the requisite seven water-jumps and 28 barriers, but it still seemed that officialdom was throwing the baby out with the bathwater, if the analogy can be excused. Elmsäter was an army officer and one of that select band who had also competed in the Winter Olympics, having placed 19th in the 18-kilometre cross-country skiing and ninth in the combined event (skiing and ski jumping) at St Moritz earlier in 1948.

The gold-medallist for Sweden was Thore Sjöstrand, whose surname, perplexingly, was pronounced something like "Where-strond", ahead of his team-mates, Elmsäter and Hagström, as the expected challenge from the Spanish-born Frenchman, Raphael Pujazon, who had won the European title on his debut at the event in 1946, evaporated when he dropped out with two laps to go. A Finn, Siltaloppi, might well have split the Swedes but fell at the last water-jump while in third position. There was no doubting the calibre of Sjöstrand, who became the second sub-nine-minute man before the season was out and had six of the best 12 performances of the year, but this was the first and only men's track event at Wembley in which the absence could be felt of a genuine contender from the USSR.

The winning time was 9:04.6, and a month later Aleksandr Pugachevskiy won his national title in Kharkov in 9:06.4 and would certainly have been in the reckoning for an Olympic medal. In third place to him in the USSR championships race was Vladimir Kazantsev, who would go on to reduce the world best to 8:49.8 and then 8:48.6 in 1951–52 and would be Olympic silver-medallist in Helsinki behind an American, Horace Ashenfelter, and ahead of the Briton, John Disley. The fanciful notion that the USA and Great Britain would collect Olympic steeplechase medals the next time round would have been laughed to scorn in 1948.

It was after 10 o'clock at night and lagging more than 4½ hours behind schedule, when the decathletes returned to the track for their 400 metres races. Kistenmacher, the best sprinter in the competition, was more than a second faster than anyone else with a time of 50.5, though this was obviously wrong and should have been 50.2 or so because his automatic timing was better by one tenth. The disparity was worth a dozen points, and even this small amount might make some difference because he now led at halfway with 3,897 points, but only very narrowly from Heinrich (France) with 3,880, and the three Americans were in close attention: Mathias 3,848, Simmons 3,843 and Mondschein 3,811.

3000 metres steeplechase result: 1 Thore Sjöstrand (Sweden) 9:04.6, 2 Erik Elmsäter (Sweden) 9:08.2, 3 Göte Hagström (Sweden) 9:11.8, 4 Alex Guyodo (France) 9:13.6, 5 Pentti Siltaloppi (Finland) 9:19.6, 6 Petar Šegedin (Yugoslavia) 9:20.4, 7 Browning Ross (USA), 8 Constantino Miranda (Spain) 9:25.0, 9 Robert Everaert (Belgium), 10 Aarne Kainlauri (Finland), 11 Roger Chesneau (France). Did not finish – Raphael Pujazon (France). The automatic timer also showed 9:04.6 for the winner and the margins behind him were 3.81sec for Elmsäter, 7.54 for Hagström, 8.94 for Guyodo, 15.39 for Siltaloppi, 16.08 for Segedin, 19.42 for Ross, 22.00 for Miranda, 24.04 for Everaert, 26.89 for Kainlauri, 27.45 for Chesneau. No official times were taken for 7th, 9th, 10th and 11th places.

Athletics. The seventh day – Friday 6 August

A gruelling race? A shade too gruelling a race? Not for one woman.

The programme: 10.30 a.m. Decathlon 110 metres hurdles; 11.30 a.m. Decathlon discus; 2.30 p.m. Decathlon pole vault; 4 p.m. 4x100 metres relay heats; 4.30 p.m. Decathlon javelin; 4.30 p.m. 200 metres (women) final; 5 p.m. 1500 metres final; 5.30 p.m. 4x400 metres relay heats; 6.30 p.m. Decathlon 1500 metres.

THE FINALS FOR the 1500 metres and the women's 200 metres and the heats of the relays left the decathletes again centre stage for much of the day, but unfortunately the weather *was* dreadful, just as had been feared. The spectators huddled into their raincoats, only too familiar with such a typical British summer, and the athletes found what shelter they could from the downpour as the hours wore on. It would be another late night for the all-rounders, and probably past a 17-year-old's normal bedtime before they would be finished. The best of the hurdlers in the decathlon were Simmons, of the USA, and Mullins, of Australia, each of them splashing through the puddles in a commendable 15.2, and that put Simmons in the overall lead. Others, like the Belgian, Dayer, who struggled home in 19.7, had real trouble with this event, and three of them did not complete the distance at all.

The discus and pole vault served to swing the decathlon firmly in favour of Mathias, the teenager in only his third competition, and with two events to go he had a useful lead – 6,192 points, to 6,027 for the Frenchman Heinrich. Kistenmacher was still third at 5,952, but the other Americans, Simmons (5,900) and Mondschein (5,875), were in close attendance. The discus was not without incident because the marker for a throw of 145ft or so (44.20m) by Mathias was knocked over, and after half an hour's fruitless search in the rain the officials abandoned their efforts and gave him credit for 44 metres. The competition was already slipping far behind schedule before this further delay.

The women's 200 metres finalists, from the inside lane, were Robb (South Africa), Blankers-Koen, Strickland (Australia), Walker (GB), Williamson (also GB) and Patterson (USA), but there was only ever one runner in the race for gold. Blankers-Koen won by an enormous margin, eight-tenths of a second, and her time of 24.4, confirmed by the automatic system, on cinders which were rain-soaked, even half-flooded, was probably worth 23.8 or better in decent conditions. Times of under 24sec had only ever been achieved (both in 1935) by the dubious Polish woman Stanislawa Walasiewicz in a race against men and the 1936 Olympic champion, Helen Stephens, twice on straight tracks which gave an advantage of several tenths of a second.

The silver medal went yet again to a Briton, but whereas the other runners-up to Blankers-Koen at 100 metres (Dorothy Manley) and in the hurdles (Maureen Gardner) were to continue on to further international successes Audrey Williamson remains something of an enigma. This was her one and only appearance for Great Britain, and though she continued competing for at least another six years it was at no higher than inter-services' level. She was a career officer in the Women's Royal Army Corps, rising to the rank of captain during this time.

She had won the Army 100 yards in 1947 on the same day that Lieutenant Alistair McCorquodale had done so in the men's race, but she was not even listed among the 10 Olympic "possibles" at 100 metres and seven at 200 metres named at the year's end. She gained her Olympic place by finishing third in the Women's AAA 220 yards to Sylvia Cheeseman and Margaret Walker, and so was very much regarded as No.3 for the event, but she improved some five metres at Wembley from a previous 220 yards best of 25.6 to a semi-final time of 24.9, albeit wind-assisted.

Not a great deal of attention was given to her achievement, which was less than generous. Jack Crump, writing in the official British Olympic Association report, paid brief tribute, referring to "a tremendous effort in the last 10 metres". The correspondent for *The Times* commented dismissively: "Miss Williamson did well to gain the second place in such a gruelling race – a shade too gruelling for women, as many thought." Male chauvinism? Or genuine concern?

Williamson had overtaken the American, Patterson, and the Australian, Strickland, in those closing stages of the race, and it was Patterson who was given the decision for the bronze medal – of great historical significance as this was the first medal ever to be won at the Olympics by an Afro-American woman – but there was a sequel many years later which showed conclusively that it was Strickland who actually came third. In 1975, when the then president of the Association of Track & Field Statisticians, Bob Sparks, gained access to the Wembley photo-finish pictures, the relevant one for the women's 200 metres showed beyond any possible doubt that Strickland had crossed the line 0.85sec behind the winner and Patterson 0.86 behind.

It is difficult to understand how such a mistake could have been made at the time by the officials responsible. Surely the photograph was studied in some detail after the race to establish not only the third place but also the second place of Williamson? Both Strickland and Patterson wore white vest and shorts, but for obvious reasons there could hardly have been confusion in identifying them. To compound the felony, neither the IOC nor the IAAF have ever done anything about properly amending their records, which continue to show in their results Patterson as third, though acknowledging in footnotes that she wasn't. It is too late now to compensate Shirley Strickland (later Mrs de la Hunty), who became one of the greatest of all women athletes, winning seven Olympic medals (officially), including hurdles gold in 1952 and 1956, and setting 10 world records. She died in 2004 at the age of 79. Mrs de la Hunty herself had declined to take up the matter when encouraged to do so by Australian officials after the mistake had been discovered.

The 4x100 metres relay heats had produced no real surprise, with the USA fastest at 41.1 ahead of Italy (41.3), Great Britain and Hungary (both 41.4), though the draw did not favour the Australians, whose team looked to have real medal potential but who were eliminated in 41.5, whereas Canada went through in another heat in 42.3. The US team included the long-jumper, Lorenzo Wright, on the second stage, something of a surprise as the obvious choice would have been Eddie Conwell, who had placed fourth in the US trials 100 metres, but it made no difference. None of the Italian quartet had run in the individual 100 or 200 metres, though two of them were potential semi-finalists, and having been kept back specifically for the purpose it must have been a long and anxious wait for them all week to at last get on to the track.

The 1500 metres final would be one of the pivotal events of the Games, regardless of result. Next to the 100 metres, it had always been the most keenly awaited of contests, and its past champions had been among the greatest of athletes – Nurmi in 1924, Beccali in 1932, Lovelock in 1936, all of them world record-holders. In 1900, 1912 and 1920 the race had been won by Britons; firstly, by a railway engine-driver, Charles Bennett; then by an Oxford University oarsman, Arnold Jackson, in world-record time; finally, by an ex-soldier who had survived the slaughter of the First World War, Albert Hill. Though wearing the colours of his native New Zealand in Berlin, Lovelock had learned his racing skills during the 1930s as an Oxford University undergraduate. It was 12 years to the day since his Olympic triumph.

Bill Nankeville, the AAA champion and sole British qualifier, thus carried something of a burden, though no one seriously expected either he or anyone else to challenge the Swedes. The great wartime record-breakers, Hägg and Andersson, were missing, banned for infringing the amateurism rules, but there were plenty more of their countrymen to take their places. The six fastest 1500 metres runners of all time were Swedish and three of them were in the Wembley final: Strand, who had equalled Hägg's 3:43.0 world record the previous year;

---

200 metres (women) result: 1 Fanny Blankers-Koen (Holland) 24.4sec, 2 Audrey Williamson (GB) 25.1, 3 Shirley Strickland (Australia), 4 Audrey ("Mickey") Patterson (USA), 5 Margaret Walker (GB), 6 Daphne Robb (South Africa). The automatic timer also read 24.4 for Blankers-Koen and the margins behind her were 0.80sec for Williamson, 0.85 for Strickland, 0.86 for Patterson, 1.19 for Walker, 1.25 for Robb. Patterson was incorrectly awarded the bronze medal with a hand time of 25.2. No official times were recorded for fourth, fifth and sixth places.

Eriksson, fourth fastest at 3:44.4; Bergkvist, sixth fastest at 3:46.6. Only one other finalist had ever broken 3:50, but he *was* a Czech named Čevona and so might just turn out to be a speedier version of Zátopek. Others in the race were Jørgensen (Denmark), Johansson (Finland), Hansenne (France), Slijkhuis (Holland), Garay (Hungary), Barthel (Luxembourg) and Gehrmann (USA).

Hansenne, the 800 metres bronze-medallist, blazed through the first lap in 58.3 but any thoughts that he might use his basic speed to run the rest off their legs evaporated when his second lap took four seconds longer and he reached 800 metres in 2:02.6. The Swedish phalanx then swept by, and Eriksson led at 1200 metres in 3:05.0 and just kept going, with only Strand attempting to follow. Eriksson duly won in 3:49.8, worthy running in the dismal weather conditions, and Slijkhuis repeated the bronze he had won at 5000 metres. Nankeville, sixth in 3:52.6, ran his fastest time, all that could be asked of him. He had survived a wartime factory bombing which killed 135 people and then a road accident in which he broke all his ribs while serving with the army in Germany. Unnoticed in 10th place was Barthel; at the next Olympics he would attract rather more attention. He won.

The USA had not won an Olympic 1500 metres since 1908 and their sole representative this time, 20-year-old Don Gehrmann, also the only non-European in the race, did well enough to finish one place behind Nankeville. Gehrmann went on to compile an immensely impressive competitive record, particularly as an indoor miler, and his recollections almost 60 years later of his one and only Olympic experience take something of an unexpected turn:

"There was no television and not a lot of people in America knew too much about the Games. They weren't a real big deal here, except of course in trying to make the Olympic team. The American Olympic team, with three competitors in each event, was particularly difficult to make, with the thousands of athletes that we have competing here in the United States. I was only young in 1948, and I had the opportunity to run in the trials and happened to have enough sprint in order to win the final, and two other fellows – one from Washington state and one from California – were the athletes with me running the Olympic 1500-meter.

"What was probably the most important thing in my mind with the Olympics of 1948 – really, two things – were the ceremonies, especially the opening ceremony, which were something that was spectacular then, and is even more spectacular now, and otherwise the fact that running in the Games was probably not as important back then as making the American team. Therefore, I did not

1500 metres result: 1 Henry Eriksson (Sweden) 3min 49.8sec, 2 Lennart Strand (Sweden) 3:50.4, 3 Willy Slijkhuis (Holland) 3:50.4, 4 Václav Čevona (Czechoslovakia) 3:51.2, 5 Gösta Bergkvist (Sweden) 3:52.2, 6 Bill Nankeville (GB) 3:52.6, 7 Don Gehrmann (USA), 8 Erik Jørgensen (Denmark), 9 Denis Johansson (Finland), 10 Josy Barthel (Luxembourg), 11 Marcel Hansenne (France) 4:02.0, 12 Sándor Garay (Hungary). The automatic time for Eriksson was 3:50.0 and the margins behind were 0.40 for Strand, 0.48 for Slijkhuis, 1.37 for Čevona, 2.05 for Bergkvist, 2.51 for Nankeville, 4.63 for Gehrmann, 4.65 for Jørgensen, 6.28 for Johansson, 7.14 for Barthel. No official hand times were recorded for 7th, 8th, 9th, 10th and 12th places and no automatic times for 11th and 12th.

have quite the emotion and maybe the motivation that I should have had. The Olympics did not mean as much financially or personally in one's future as they certainly do today."

In contrast to the men's sprint relay, where the chance of a British medal had been clearly confirmed, the qualifying round of the 4x400 caused considerable heartache. There had seemed fair hope that Britain might even challenge for a medal there, too, as the aggregate times, based on current best performances for each of the athletes concerned, worked out at 3:08.3 for Jamaica, 3:09.1 for the USA, 3:13.4 for Italy, 3:13.5 for Sweden, 3:14.3 for Great Britain and 3:15.0 for France.

Two teams from each of three heats would go into the next day's final, and the Americans were never seriously threatened in the first heat, winning in 3:12.6 and leaving Italy and Great Britain to fight it out for the one other place. Missoni gave the Italians a good start and this was maintained by Paterlini and Rocca. Even so, Rocca was only a 48.9 man at best and the first three British runners – Les Lewis, Martin Pike and Derek Pugh – should have been able to keep their team well in contention despite their relative lack of experience and send off their seasoned team leader, Bill Roberts, with a fighting chance on the anchor stage.

Unfortunately, Roberts's team-mates were just not up to it on the day, and as the baton-changing was also far from perfect he was left with too much to do. The situation was exactly the same as it had been at the European Championships in Oslo two years before when Roberts had reduced a huge French lead to a metre or so and earned Britain the silver medals. Here at Wembley he was again setting off a dozen yards down, and he put in a tremendous effort against the Italian, Siddi, who on paper was a second faster and had been kept out of the individual 400 because the Italians rated their chances of a relay medal so highly. Roberts excelled himself, as he always did in relays, and the margin at the end had been brought down to no more than a yard or so, but Italy had qualified in second place in 3:14.0 and Britain had not in third place in 3:14.2. The expert observers, the McWhirter twins, were to later describe this as "the only inept piece of seeding in the entire programme".

As if missing the final by such a fraction was not frustrating enough in itself, Roberts and his team-mates would then learn that France had needed only 3:17.0 to get through behind Jamaica (3:14.0) in heat two and that Finland and Sweden had taken first and second in the third heat in a derisory 3:20.6 and 3:21.0 following the withdrawal beforehand of Australia.

Thus Britain had been eliminated despite accomplishing the fourth fastest time of the 16 competing teams. Roberts, the ex-RAF serviceman, having run the last major race of his life, must have thought that his farewell sortie into the highest levels of a competitive career which had begun back in the 1920s was ending with the sort of bumpy landing which his station commander in wartime days would not have approved of one little bit.

Long after the relay runners had packed their bags, gone back to their barrack-rooms and colleges, and hopefully had a hot bath, the decathletes were doggedly casting their javelins off into the gloomy night air and hoping that there was someone out there to mark their flight. The Scandinavians, inevitably, were the most able among them and a Finn, Mäkelä, had the longest throw of 62.55 which would have done rather well in the individual event two days before. Presumably, Mäkelä had become an all-rounder because he was not even among the dozen best of his country's javelin men, but he was well outside the decathlon medal reckoning. Mathias, with a throw of 50.32, lost some ground to Simmons (51.99), but the difference was worth only 31 points and the gold medal now seemed safe. The value to Simmons was that he had now pulled up to second place: Mathias 6,785, Simmons 6,524, Heinrich 6,457, Kistenmacher 6,451, Mullins 6,418.

After a suitable time for recovery the ultimate 1,500 metres test got under way four hours later than it should have, and it was after 10.30 at night that Mathias finally crossed the line. His time of 5:11.0 was of no great merit – worth 5:35 or so for the mile, which would be good enough to win at almost any school sports day – but decathletes are built for speed and strength, not for running middle distances, and the 1500 metres is usually a purgatory for them. Why have it in the decathlon at all? Well, that's a subject for enquiry in another time and place, but maybe a 400 metres hurdles would be a better climax, and it would certainly provide these marvellous athletes with a more appropriate showcase for their talents and the onlookers with a much more edifying spectacle than that of a group of tired, plodding men.

What a sad reflection it was on the host country that not a single decathlete worthy of selection could apparently be found when such countries as Egypt, India, Liechtenstein and Peru – none of them with any notable athletics tradition – were represented. There had actually been three British "possibles" nominated the previous year, and at the AAA Championship decathlon two months before the Games the best of them, 20-year-old Les Pinder, from Doncaster, had scored only 5,378 points in fourth place, but he would surely have benefited from the Olympic experience. The AAA title-winner was a Dane, Hans Moesgaard-Kjeldsen, working in the shipping business in England, who was selected for Denmark but declined the invitation when his employers would not agree to his having time off from work for the extra training he believed he needed to do himself justice. There was still one British resident in the Wembley event because India's Baldev Singh was a student at Loughborough College.

Bob Mathias's consistency at Wembley can be gauged by the fact that his scores in the first seven events, which took him into the lead, all ranged between 703 points and 859 in value. Having demonstrated such precocious teenage talent, he was to win the Olympic decathlon again in 1952 with a world-record score of 7,887 – and then retire at the ripe old age of 22, which he was later to regret when he realised how far short he had fallen of his full potential. He went into films, starring in a Hollywood adaptation of his life story and in a spoof version of the

1896 Olympics, and he then turned to a prominent career in public life, serving as a congressman from 1966 to 1974, before becoming director of the US Olympic Training Center. When he died in 2006 at the age of 75, the chairman of the US Olympic Committee Peter Ueberroth said of him: "He was a champion in every aspect of life. With his passing the Olympic movement has lost a true friend and America has lost a true hero."

There is no doubting that Mathias is one of the great athletes in history, but pure misfortune – being in the wrong place at the wrong time – can deny others, now long forgotten, the chance of similar glory. The world rankings at the end of 1948 would not show Mathias as No.1. That position was occupied by an athlete named Heino Lipp with a far superior score of 7,780pts achieved a month after Mathias's Olympic triumph. The reason that Lipp was not at Wembley was simple: he was an Estonian and therefore now a citizen of the USSR. Lipp was also a 16.47m shot-putter and would have challenged the Americans in that event, too. Another Soviet athlete, Vladimir Volkov, was compiling a score of 7,229 in Moscow as the Wembley event was taking place and would also, obviously, have been at least a medal challenger.

The silver-medallist from France, Ignace Heinrich, had some wartime experiences to relate, just as did so many of the competitors at Wembley, but his had a very fair claim to being unique. He came from the Alsace region of northeast France and was forcibly conscripted into the German army at the start of the war. He related the subsequent tale as follows: "I deserted from the German army and disguised myself among the French prisoners. I was captured by the Russians and because we were in Eastern Prussia we were treated as French volunteers fighting the Russians. We were treated worse by the Russians than we had been by the Germans. I got away again and was repatriated through Odessa. So then, for me, France was something very special, and I said to myself, 'One day, I will do something to pay thanks'."

Decathlon result: 1 Bob Mathias (USA) 7,139pts, 2 Ignace Heinrich (France) 6,974, 3 Floyd Simmons (USA) 6,950, 4 Enrique Kistenmacher (Argentina) 6,929, 5 Erik Peter Andersson (Sweden) 6,877, 6 Peter Mullins (Australia) 6,739, 7 Per Eriksson (Sweden) 6,731, 8 Irving Mondschein (USA) 6,715, 9 Edward Adamczyk (Poland) 6,712, 10 Godtfred Holmvang (Norway) 6,663, 11 Per Stavem (Norway) 6,552, 12 Örn Clausen (Iceland) 6,444, 13 Yrjö Mäkelä (Finland) 6,421, 14 Pierre Sprecher (France) 6,401, 15 Kjell Tånnander (Sweden) 6,325, 16 Waclaw Kuźmicki (Poland) 6,153, 17 Johannes Sonck (Finland) 6,142, 18 Davorin Marčelja (Yugoslavia) 6,141, 19 Witold Gierutto (Poland) 6,106, 20 Hernan Figueroa (Chile) 6,026, 21 Hercules Azcune (Uruguay) 6,026, 22 Jacques Cretaine (France) 5,829, 23 Fritz Nussbaum (Switzerland) 5,808, 24 Mario Recordon (Chile) 5,732, 25 Lionel Fournier (Canada) 5,590, 26 Albert Dayer (Belgium) 5,586, 27 Oskar Gerber (Switzerland) 5,558, 28 Sayed Mukhtar (Egypt) 5,031. Did not finish – Baldev Singh (India), Gebhard Büchel (Liechtenstein), Josef Seger (Liechtenstein), René Kremer (Luxembourg), Eduardo Julve (Peru), Armin Scheurer (Switzerland), Oto Rebula (Yugoslavia).

Athletics. The eighth and final day – Saturday 7 August

"I knew I could win it. But then I blistered badly and I had to come out."

The day's programme: 3 p.m. Marathon; 3.15 p.m. 4x100 metres relay (women) heats; 3.30 p.m. 4x100 metres relay final; 3.35 p.m. High jump (women) final; 3.45 p.m. 10,000 metres walk final; 4.40 p.m. 4x100 metres relay (women) final, 4.50 p.m. 4x400 metres relay final.

ONLY SIX EVENTS remained, but there were realistic hopes of British medals in all but one of them. The 4x400 metres team had been unjustly treated by the draw in the heats and would not be competing, but Jack Holden in the marathon, Dorothy Tyler in the high jump and Harry Churcher in the walk might even win gold, and the 4x100 relay teams could contemplate medals behind the US men and the Dutch women. The weather had improved, but it was getting hotter and could well cause suffering for the marathon-men, who were setting out on a route which would take them from the stadium along much the same roads as the 50-kilometre walkers to Stanmore, Edgware, Mill Hill, Stirling Corner, Radlett, Elstree and then back to Stanmore for the run-in. At the furthest points, they would be wending their way through country lanes, not the urban sprawl which it would become in the years to follow.

There were 41 marathon starters from 21 countries. The distance would be the bizarre but standard 26 miles 385 yards (42.195 kilometres), which had been devised at the 1908 London Olympics because it happened to be the exact measurement from under the windows of Windsor Castle (so that the Royal children could see the start) to a point opposite the Royal box at the Shepherd's Bush Stadium (so that the Queen had an unobstructed view of the finish). Comparing form when no two courses are the same is a hazardous business, but it seemed clear that the man to beat was Yun Bok Suh, of Korea, who had run the fastest-ever time of 2:25:39 in the classic annual race at Boston, Massachusetts, the previous year. The European champion from Finland, Mikko Hietanen, had finished second on that occasion, exactly four minutes behind, and both Korea and Finland had an Olympic tradition in the event to uphold. Finns had won gold in 1920 and 1924 and a Korean, Kee Chung Sohn, had beaten Britain's Ernie Harper in Berlin – though running under a false name, Kitei Son, and a false flag, that of Japan, because his country had been annexed by the Japanese. He was now coach to Yun Bok Suh.

The annual Polytechnic Harriers marathon over the Windsor to Chiswick course seven weeks before the Games had acted as the trial for Britain's hopefuls, and Jack Holden had won in 2:36:44.6, which hardly seemed to compare with the times at Boston, but Holden was a renowned distance-runner from the famous Tipton Harriers club, in Staffordshire, and he had been England's outstanding cross-country man of the 1930s. At the age of 39 he seemed to be maturing nicely, and his team-mates were Tom Richards, 38, and Stan Jones, 34 – the latter having earned his place by only 10 seconds from a luckless Ulsterman, John Henning. Great Britain had never won the Olympic marathon; the race of 1904 had been won by the Birmingham-born Tom Hicks and that of 1912 by an Ulsterman, Ken McArthur, but both had by then emigrated and were running for the USA and South Africa respectively.

There were only 11 teams entered for the women's 4x100 relay, but three heats were still held by the intransigent organisers, and it all turned out to be rather unfair. France and the USA each finished third in their heats in 48.1 and 48.3 respectively and were eliminated; Italy dropped the baton in the other heat and Austria qualified in second place in 50.0. The line-up for the men's 4x100 was Hungary in lane one, then Holland, USA, Great Britain, Italy and Canada. The USA again had Lorenzo Wright, who had placed fourth in the long jump, on the second stage in place of Eddie Conwell, who had gone down with asthma. Wright was a capable enough sprinter, with a 100 metres best of 10.5 from the previous year, but this was still a puzzling choice by the US management.

Their normal practice in past Olympics had been to bring all the first six from their trials 100 metres, and even to give the fifth and sixth finishers there a place in the relay team. This had caused all sorts of fuss and furore in Berlin when Marty Glickman and Sam Stoller had originally been chosen instead of the 100 metres gold- and silver-medallists, Jesse Owens and Ralph Metcalfe, "to give the other boys a chance" – according to the team coach, Lawson Robertson – but were then replaced on the morning of the heats. This would have seemed a sensible change of mind, except that this was Nazi Berlin and Glickman and Stoller were the only Jewish athletes in the US athletics squad. It seems grossly far-fetched that the US management would have wanted to somehow appease Hitler, but that was the suggestion made in much of the press coverage.

It might have been expected that Don Campbell and Billy Mathis, the other finalists at 100 metres in the 1948 US trials, would have travelled with the team as Games reserves, but this did not happen. Mathis had failed to finish that race and was presumably injured, but the real reason seems to be that though it was a departure from tradition the US selectors believed they already had plenty of talent in other events which they could draft in for the relay, and so only Conwell, fourth in the trials, was named alongside Patton, Ewell and Dillard. It could be presumed that Wright was brought in because he had actually run in the trials 100 metres, though he had finished last in his heat. The long-jump winner, Willie Steele, would have been an obvious candidate but was now carrying an injury. The high hurdlers all had a fine turn of speed, as one might suppose, and Clyde Scott had even run a 9.4 (wind-assisted) and a 9.6 (legal) for 100 yards earlier in the season. Maybe the decision was based on sentiment. Wright had not won a medal, and so he would be given the chance which had been snatched away from Glickman and Stoller 12 years before.

Having said all that, it might also have seemed odd that the chosen quartet had Dillard, the 100 metres winner, running the third stage round the bend and Patton, the 200 metres champion, running the anchor stage along the straight. In defence of the decision it should be noted that the US team coach was Dean Cromwell, who had been in charge at the University of Southern California (USC) for the previous 40 years and knew rather more about relay-racing than most, and it was a USC quartet which had held the current world record for 4x110 yards since 1938. The supremely versatile Dillard, who had also been an outstanding junior at 400 metres hurdles, was to end 1948 with a best 200 metres time only one tenth slower than Patton's. Cromwell knew what he was doing.

Even so, the British started so well in the final that after two stages Gregory was a shade ahead of Wright, only for Dillard to gain something like five metres round the bend on Jones, and Patton came flying down the home straight to clinch a crushing US victory by seven metres or so from the British and the Italians ... but the real drama was only now about to begin. It was a confusing sequel which has never been properly explained, but after a long delay it was announced that the Americans had been disqualified and that the British were the winners. It seemed that the first baton exchange between Ewell and Wright had taken place outside the allowed zone. The US manager lodged a protest, but the organisers went ahead with the medal ceremony anyway, which seemed a strange – if not illegal – action to take.

The best that can be said of this unseemly haste is that because it was the last day of athletics competition it was felt that a ceremony had to take place now or never. It would be churlish to imagine that the British team was rushed on to the rostrum to give the densely packed crowd a home victory to cheer at last. However, if the latter was, indeed, the case, then the spectators reacted with a typical sense of "fair play", as the correspondent of the *New York Times* reported in admiring detail: "The judicial victory awarded the British sprinters was the first time the British crowd had had an opportunity to cheer a triumph by their countrymen. But the Britons disagreed with the judges. They did not want to win even one victory in that way. They gave their loudest cheer to the disqualified Americans ... that is sportsmanship at its best."

Not everyone in the press box was of the same opinion. The *Daily Telegraph* correspondent, Lainson Wood, heard differently to his American colleague because he wrote in his report the following morning that "the cheer that went up from 85,000 mostly British throats when a home success was at last announced will head the cavalcade of my memories". Oddly, he made no reference to any US protest having been lodged, and perhaps no one among the officials had seen fit to inform the press. Even so, there was a plaintive note to his article, headlined "Hollow First For Britain". He wrote: "The fact that Britain's representatives were all better known on the football and cricket field before Olympic training started does seem to symbolise the British attitude towards sport. As an excuse for lack of success in the Games that is, of course, both sloppy and feeble. We are, generally speaking, a long way behind the Americans in technique. Maybe we always shall be, and there are many who prefer it that way."

This was a less than charitable view of the British achievement. It was certainly true that Archer, Gregory and Jones were all fine rugby union wing-threequarters and McCorquodale was more at home in white flannels. Yet Archer had won the European 100 metres title in 1946 before breaking his leg in a rugby match; Gregory was a durable enough sprinter to run again in the 4x100 relay at the 1952 Olympics; and Jones, in between becoming the most capped rugby player in the world, pursued a long and successful track career, which was to conclude with a Commonwealth Games 220 yards bronze medal at the age of 32.

Three days later the gold-medal decision was reversed after a study had been made of the film of the race and it had become clear that there had been no infringement by the Americans. It is surprising, even astounding, that this could not have been done soon after the race had finished, as the official film-makers were providing what was proudly claimed to be "up-to-the-minute" footage on a regular basis for cinema newsreel showing worldwide, and the service was described as being "almost a routine matter" in the organising committee's official report. There were also three television cameras in the stadium sending pictures to the engineering control van and then to the nearby broadcasting centre, and surely their coverage could have been made immediately available? There may have been valid technical reasons why this did not happen, but it is hard to imagine what they could have been. Once the matter was cleared up the British team handed their gold medals over to the Americans and the Italians and Hungarians in turn passed theirs on, but the Americans never had the honour of mounting the victory rostrum. Their medals were presented the following Wednesday to Dan Ferris, secretary of the US AAU, by Lord Burghley, but the four American sprinters did not receive them until they arrived in the post several months later. Wright, the late replacement in the US team, came to a sad end, stabbed to death at the age of 45 in a domestic dispute.

It was a fine effort by the British quartet, especially as the services were lacking of one of their best sprinters, McDonald Bailey, who was unwell. All credit, in particular, to Jack Gregory, who had run the second stage and kept Britain in the lead. Though he had been born in Bristol he was a member of Crusaders Athletic Club, in Dublin, and could have run for Eire at the Olympics in the individual

---

4x100 metres relay result: 1 USA (Barney Ewell, Lorenzo Wright, Harrison Dillard, Mel Patton) 40.6, 2 Great Britain (Alastair McCorquodale, Jack Gregory, Ken Jones, John Archer) 41.3, 3 Italy (Enrico Perucconi, Antonio Siddi, Carlo Monti, Michele Tito) 41.5, 4 Hungary (Ferenc Tima, László Bartha, György Csányi, Béla Goldoványi) 41.6, 5 Canada (Don McFarlane, James O'Brien, Don Pettie, Ted Haggis) 41.9, 6 Holland (Jan Lammers, Johannes Meyer, Gabe Scholten, Johan Zwaan) 41.9. The automatic timing for the winners was 40.7 and the margins behind were 0.71sec for GB, 1.01 for Italy, 1.20 for Hungary, 1.22 for Canada, 1.27 for Holland.

sprints had he so chosen. Instead, he took his chance with Great Britain merely as one of eight being considered for the relay.

As the women's high jump began, the first news came through from the marathon. A Belgian, Gailly, was leading at 10 kilometres, and there would have been some Britons in the crowd who would readily have recognised the name because he had been in England during the war for training as a paratrooper and had competed for the London-based club, Belgrave Harriers. In second place was Luo Wen Ao, of China, who had run in the 10,000 metres, followed by a Frenchman, Josset, and an Argentinian, Guiñez. Holden and Richards were 10th and 14th, a minute or so down. It was early days yet.

The finalists for the 10,000 metres track walk were all from Europe – three Swedes, three Britons, two Italians, a Frenchman and a Swiss. The leading Briton was Harry Churcher, also a Belgrave Harrier, a pre-war product, now aged 37, who had won everything he could in Britain during the months leading up to the Games, including the national title on the road at 10 miles for the second successive year and on the track at two and seven miles, as he had in 1939. He had also broken the 16-year-old world record for the track five miles in cold and blustery conditions, but he now faced formidable Swedish opposition with much faster times to their credit at the Olympic distance.

Werner Hardmö and John Mikaelsson had between them set 38 world records at distances from 3000 metres to 10 miles – the first of them, by Mikaelsson, dating back to 1937 when he won the AAA seven miles title. Hardmö held the official world record for 10,000 metres at 42:39.6, from 1945, and Mikalesson had done 42:52.4 the same year, but it was performances in championship conditions which weighed more in the evidence and Mikalesson had won the 1946 European title in a much slower time of 46:05.2, with Hardmö disqualified after only six laps. Churcher's best was 45:31.6, while the third Swede, Ingemar Johansson, had not a single record to his name but was his country's champion from the previous year. Attention had been carefully drawn to the most telling aspect of the prospects for the event by the leading British authority on the subject, Freddy Blackmore, who had commented: "The competitor who shows 44:50 or upwards and pleases the judges will be the winner." Blackmore would be in the ideal position to report back on who gave the judges the most pleasure as he had been appointed their chief.

Churcher had been cautioned in the heats because of his action, and it may be that his chance of gold had gone before the final even started. Freddy Blackmore's account of the race says it all: "With Harry Churcher proceeding cautiously – even more so after being cautioned again – Mikaelsson set out to walk away with the race. From our point of view he was allowed to have it far too much his own way, his style faultless until the late stages." Churcher's time was little faster than in his heat and his team-mate, Jim Morris, was almost a minute down on his qualifying performance, losing the bronze-medal position late on to Schwab, of Switzerland, just as Lloyd Johnson had lost the silver to another Swiss in the 50 kilometres road walk. Mikaelsson's time was also slower than in his heat (45:03.0), when he had beaten an Olympic record which had stood since 1912.

There was clearly a problem with this event. Of the 19 competitors at Wembley, 11 had been cautioned at least once each and seven had been disqualified. The British-inspired and internationally accepted definition of race-walking for the previous 20 years had been simple enough – "Walking is progression by steps so taken that unbroken contact with the ground is maintained" – but maybe not sufficient for the purpose, especially when translated into other languages. Aware that something needed to be done, the IAAF's walking commission had deliberated the matter during the Games, and their amendment of the rule had been accepted by the full IAAF congress which met after the Games had ended. The amplifying words which were added were "i.e. the advancing foot must make contact with the ground before the rear foot leaves the ground". Unfortunately, this attempt at clarification did not seem to work the oracle.

Schwab, whose father had been the bronze-medallist in the Olympic 50 kilometres walk in 1936, was to win the European title two years later from Maggi and Mikaelsson, but there was not at all a satisfactory outcome to the race as the two British competitors, Roland Hardy and Lol Allen, were disqualified in controversial circumstances after having crossed the line in second and third places. At the 1952 Olympics Mikaelsson retained his title from Schwab and Bruno Junk, of the USSR, but the latter two were blatantly "lifting" in the last 50 metres and should have been disqualified. The event's days were numbered and it never appeared in the Olympic programme again.

By now the marathon runners had passed 25 kilometres. Gailly had led at 20 kilometres by 24 seconds from Luo Wen Ao, with Guiñez and Josset following, and Holden and Richards still 10th and 14th. By 25 kilometres the Chinese runner had retired from the race and Gailly (1:27:27) led from Guiñez (1:28:08), with a Swede, Östling, and another Argentinian, Cabrera, next at 1:28:26 and 1:28:28. The major threat to the long-time leader, though, seemed obviously to come from Heino, the 10,000 metres world record-holder, now seventh at 1:29:04 and presumably eager to make amends for his track debacle eight days before. Holden remained 10th and Richards had moved up and was only four seconds behind him in 11th.

It was now a question of who might have started too fast and would pay the price, as the Chinaman had done, and who was judging the race best. The weather had become sultry and windy – not at all suitable for marathon running – and though the pace was not exceptional, and would produce a time of 2:31 or so for the full distance if maintained, it was still beyond what all but a handful of the runners had ever achieved. The Korean world "record" holder, Yun Bok

---

10,000 metres walk result: 1 John Mikaelsson (Sweden) 45:13.2, 2 Ingemar Johansson (Sweden) 45:43.8, 3 Fritz Schwab (Switzerland) 46:00.4, 4 Jim Morris (GB) 46:04.0, 5 Harry Churcher (GB) 46:28.0, 6 Emile Maggi (France) 47:02.8, 7 Ron West (GB), 8 Gianni Corsaro (Italy), 9 Giuseppe Dordoni (Italy). Disqualified – Werner Hardmö (Sweden). No official times were taken for 7th, 8th and 9th places.

Suh, had moved through to 14th place, four minutes down, and that gap could still be closed, but the Finnish No.1, Hietanen, was already long since out of the reckoning altogether, having dropped from fifth at 5 kilometres to 31st at 10 kilometres and then made the biggest drop of all.

The 4x100 metres for women brought together Australia in lane one, and then Canada, Great Britain, Austria, Holland and Denmark in that order towards the outside. It seemed that the first three Dutch runners, led off by Stad-de Jong, who had been born in Java (now part of Indonesia), only needed to keep within three or four metres of whoever led the race, and Blankers-Koen would ensure the gold medals. Britain had two of their silver-medallists, Manley and Gardner, in the team and it might be that Blankers-Koen would have to chase after Gardner again, just as she had in the hurdles final.

Rather surprisingly, it was Denmark who were in front beyond halfway, and at the final change they were still only a metre or so down on Australia, with Britain, Canada and Holland more or less in a line three or four metres behind. Blankers-Koen, almost inevitably, made up the difference on the Australian, and it has to be said that the British performance was disappointing as the Canadians, all of them teenagers, took the bronze. The final baton exchanges by both the Australians and the British were poor ones and cost them the gold and bronze medals respectively. The valiant Danes, whose anchor runner had been born in Frankfurt-am-Main, in Germany, slipped to fifth.

Of the six finals for the 4x400 metres relay since it was first contested at the 1912 Games the USA had won four and Great Britain two. There was no British team this time to offer a challenge, and even if there had been the hopes would have been for bronze at best. The prime opposition to the Americans on this occasion would come from the Caribbean island of Jamaica, competing for the first time in the Games, and the fact was that the individual times of the runners suggested there was very little to choose between the two countries. Wint, McKenley and Whitfield had finished 1-2-3 in the 400 metres final two days before, which gave an obvious edge to the Jamaicans. Neither Bolen nor Guida, who had also been in that race, were in the US team, but Harnden had run 47.3 and Bourland 47.4 during the preceding months, compared to 47.6 for Jamaica's Rhoden, and the other American would be Cochran, winner of the 400 metres hurdles and capable of as fast as 46.7. The destiny of the race might depend entirely on how the fourth Jamaican, Laing, managed to get round. Like Bourland he had reached

4x100 metres relay (women) result: 1 Holland (Xenia Stad-de Jong, Jeanette Witziers-Timmer, Gerda van der Kade-Koudijs, Fanny Blankers-Koen) 47.5, 2 Australia (Shirley Strickland, June Maston, Elizabeth McKinnon, Joyce King) 47.6, 3 Canada (Viola Myers, Nancy MacKay, Dianne Foster, Pat Jones) 47.8, 4 Great Britain (Dorothy Manley, Muriel Pletts, Margaret Walker, Maureen Gardner) 48.0, 5 Denmark (Grete Nielsen, Bente Bergendorff, Birthe Nielsen, Hildegard Nissen) 48.2. 6 Austria (Grete Jenny, Maria Oberbreyer, Grete Pavlousek, Elfriede Steurer) 49.2. The automatic timing for the winners was 47.6 and the margins behind were 0.09sec for Australia, 0.48 for Canada, 0.55 for Great Britain, 0.63 for Denmark, 1.65 for Austria.

the 200 metres final, but unlike the American he had little or no experience of the longer distance.

All of this conjecture was to quickly count for nothing. The draw from the inside lane was Italy, France, Jamaica, USA, Finland and Sweden. Rhoden gained a couple of yards on Harnden on the first leg, but Bourland went right away from Laing to give Cochran a dozen metres on Wint. The 400 metres champion began to make some slight inroads on the 400 metres hurdles champion along the back straight but suddenly pulled up and fell distraught on to the grass infield, having been seized with cramp. The Italians were already out of it, as Rocca had also suffered an injury, and the rest of the race was a procession. Whether the Jamaicans could have made up the lost ground seems dubious, but they were to find their consolation four years later at the Helsinki Olympics. In one of the most exciting relay races ever run, the same Jamaican quartet beat the USA, including Whitfield again, and broke the world record by over four seconds.

The women's high jump had now been in progress for some 80 minutes, and as there had been 19 starters there was a long way to go yet. Gyarmati, the long-jump winner, was already eliminated, but the Frenchwoman who had won two gold medals, Ostermeyer, was still there, as were all three Britons – Bertha Crowther, Dora Gardner and Dorothy Tyler – together with Steinegger (Austria), Dredge (Canada), Beckett (Jamaica) and Coachman (USA). Coachman's best for the year was 5ft 4¾in (1.64m), while Gardner and Tyler had both cleared 5-4 (1.62).

At 30 kilometres of the marathon Gailly's lead over Guiñez had been reduced to just over half a minute (1:47:01 to 1:47:33) and a second Korean, Yoon Chil Choi, was alongside Cabrera only 20 seconds behind, having moved up from eighth. Richards was running with Heino, seventh and eighth in 1:48:48, but the deeply disappointing news was that Holden was out of the race, crippled by blisters and climbing forlornly into a following car. The Korean No.1, Yun Bok Suh, had slipped back to 16th, and that was surely to be the end of his chances.

By the 35-kilometre point, Yoon Chil Choi had taken the lead (2:06:02). Cabrera, Gailly and Guiñez were next, all within 50 metres or so, and Richards was now fifth and not far behind (2:06:54). Heino had lost three minutes to Richards in five kilometres, and he was certainly not going to figure among the medals. Within the next two kilometres the race changed decisively as Cabrera, Gailly and Richards moved into the first three places and Yoon Chil Choi slowed to a limping walk, with his shoes in his hands, and then inevitably retired. At 40 kilometres Cabrera was five seconds ahead of Gailly and 11 seconds ahead

---

4x400 metres relay result: 1 USA (Arthur Harnden 48.0, Cliff Bourland 47.3, Roy Cochran 47.8, Mal Whitfield 47.3) 3min 10.2sec, 2 France (Jean Kerebel, Francis Schewetta, Robert Chef d'Hotel, Jacques Lunis) 3:14.8, 3 Sweden (Kurt Lundquist, Lars-Erik Wolfbrandt, Folke Alnevik, Rune Larsson) 3:16.0, 4 Finland (Tauno Suvanto, Olavi Talja, Runar Holmberg, Bertel Storskrubb) 3:24.8. Did not finish – Jamaica (George Rhoden, Les Laing, Arthur Wint, Herb McKenley), Italy (Ottavio Missoni, Luigi Paterlini, Gianni Rocca, Antonio Siddi).

of Richards. The official film of the Games gave a great deal of attention to the marathon, and so the style and demeanour of the leading runners is there for all to see: Gailly's resolute stride and easy low arm action; Richards's oddly crabbed but effective action, with his left arm held close to his chest and rarely moving; the moustachioed Cabrera, loping effortlessly along.

The closing stages were intensely exciting and the finish as dramatic as it had been in 1908 when the Italian, Dorando Pietri, had collapsed inside the stadium and eventually been helped over the line by anxious officials, inevitably to be disqualified. Richards caught the others and might even have led briefly, but the film sequence as the runners came along the walkway towards the stadium, hemmed in by the thronged lines of spectators kept in check by a convoy of police motorcyclists, shows Gailly leading by no more than 50 metres at the most from Cabrera, with Richards another 30 metres back and the fourth man, Coleman, of South Africa, in sight, though 150 metres further behind.

Gailly was first to enter the stadium but could scarcely put one foot in front of the other, and Cabrera soon passed him in an unhurried fashion, to be followed by Richards. The Olympic film clearly shows Cabrera wrongly running on the inside of an official as he overtook Gailly, though even those sticklers for the absolute letter of the law would hardly have dared suggest disqualification for such a trivial offence. Cabrera cruised comfortably to the finish, while the expression on Richards's face as he started round the track makes it obvious that he had only just realised Gailly's plight, and so he then determinedly set off after him. Poor Gailly was reduced to a walk more than once, glancing agonisingly behind him, as well he might because the South African, Coleman, had also arrived in the stadium and could, perhaps, have snatched the bronze, had he known the situation earlier.

Coleman had already been a front-rank marathon-runner before the war, winning the 1938 Empire Games title in Australia in a time of 2:30:49.8 – the second best in the world for the year – but he maintained ever after that he had run much faster that same year in the Natal championship event. Unfortunately, he arrived at the finish so much earlier than expected that the timekeepers were still in a nearby café having a cup of tea. Coleman reckoned to have run 2:24, according to his wristwatch, and the world "record" at that time was 2:26:42, set in 1935 by Kee Chung Sohn, who won gold in Berlin the following year.

It was the fifth consecutive Olympics at which an outsider had won the marathon title and the third successive at which a Briton had finished second. Cabrera had not even been thought of beforehand as the leading Argentinian but was not the first man from that country to win, as Juan Carlos Zabala had done so in 1932, ahead of Britain's Sam Ferris. The extent to which the last seven kilometres or so of the race affected the result can be seen by the following table. It shows the leading runners at 35 kilometres behind Yoon Chil Choi and Cabrera and their times, together with their finishing position and the amount of time they lost or gained in relation to Cabrera in the remainder of the race:

3	Gailly 2:06:33, third, lost 39sec	9	Sensini 2:08:56, ninth, lost 2min 12.4sec
4	Guiñez 2:06:37, fifth, lost 1min 37.4sec	10	Kurikkala 2:09:54, 13th, lost 4min 32.4sec
5	Richards 2:06:54, second, gained 8sec	11	Heino 2:09:57, 11th, lost 3min 13.4sec
6	Luyt 2:08:00, sixth, lost 1min 49.4sec	12	Systad 2:11:32, eighth, gained 1min 12.6sec
7	Östling 2:08:04, seventh, lost 2min 15.0sec	13	Larsen 2:11:53, 10th, lost 1min 7.4sec
8	Coleman 2:08:18, fourth, gained 33.6sec	14	Melin 2:11:59, 12th, lost 1min 59.6sec

With Cabrera first, Guiñez fifth and Sensini ninth, Argentina won the unofficial team title, and this was all the more remarkable because apparently none of them had run the distance before – as was also the case with Gailly – and their journey to the Games had hardly been conducive to their final preparations as they had spent three weeks at sea before making their first landfall in Spain. Sensini was thought of as the best of the trio, having won the South American "marathon" title in 1947 at a distance of 32 kilometres and in a time which equated to about 2:35, but he apparently over-trained once he was back on dry land.

Cabrera was a fireman at the time of his Olympic win, but when he returned home he and his wife were given a house by the Peron Government and he went on to qualify as a professor of physical education. He ran 210 races in a career which lasted from the late 1930s to 1957, but only seven of them were major road events. He was Pan-American Games marathon champion in 1951 and sixth in the 1952 Olympics. He was appointed president of the National Olympic Committee but sadly died in a road accident in 1981.

Jack Holden was bitterly disappointed with his failure to finish and the memory still rankled when he was aged 93 and was to recall the race: "I was almost a certainty. I knew I could win it. But then I blistered badly and had to come out. I'd had blisters many times before. They would burst and sting, but I carried on. This time I'd overdone the hardening of them beforehand by pickling them in permanganate of potash and made the skin like leather. It had blistered under the skin and at 17 miles I had to drop out. I was so disappointed that I'd let everybody down."

Holden worked as a groundsman for the Palethorpe sausage-manufacturing company and was one of the first distance-runners – together with Emil Zátopek – to regularly run 100 miles a week in training. Though he wanted to give up racing (but not training) after the Olympics, he was persuaded to continue and within a month won the annual South London Harriers' 30-miles road event by more than 20 minutes, and he then achieved the Empire and European marathon double in 1950. He recalled meeting the two Soviet runners in the dressing room before the European title race and pointing to the number on his back and telling them, "Have a look at this because you'll be looking at it for the rest of the way".

Tom Richards, 38 years old, had been born in Upper Cwmbran, in South Wales, and had come to London in 1936 to find work as a male nurse at Tooting Bec Hospital. His experience of marathon-running was positively encyclopaedic compared with Cabrera and Gailly, dating back to 1939 when he placed fourth in the prestigious annual Polytechnic Harriers' marathon, which he had then won in 1944 and 1945, and placed fourth again in 1946 and third in the AAA championship five weeks later. In 1947 he was second in the Poly, first in the Rugby race organised by the British Thomson Houston electrical company, and second in the AAA (to Holden), all within the space of 70 days. He had finished second again to Holden in the 1948 AAA race.

Unassuming by nature, Richards had also set a world's fastest time for 30 miles on the road in 1945 and he made marathon-running look simple, as he was described by one admiring newspaper correspondent as "gliding over the ground with almost effortless ease". One of his favoured South London training courses took him past a public house at halfway, where he stopped for a refreshing pint of beer before continuing on his way. In the detailed list of refreshments provided for the Olympic competitors, there is no mention of beer, and so we must assume he did without on this occasion. Richards was still road-racing at the age of 62.

Stan Jones was the very last man to finish the marathon, in 30th place, though there were 11 others who did not complete the course. Shortly before his death in 2006 at the age of 91, he recalled: "It was a brute of a day. I was about halfway down the field at six or seven miles, running with the South Africans, Coleman and Luyt, who went on to finish fourth and sixth. But it got harder and harder as the race progressed. I passed Hietanen, who we thought should have won easily, but he dropped out, and then Holden went later. There was little shade, and I felt terribly tired before halfway with my head buzzing. The last two miles were almost a complete blank, but I do remember seeing Dorothy Tyler finishing the high jump. We must have been the last two Brits to use the track!"

A teacher by profession, Jones had started running in 1933 and took up road-racing during the war years, when there was a surprising amount of competition to be had. Over a period of 30 years he was to take part in 181 races of 10 miles or further, of which 135 were at least 20 miles and 87 were at least the marathon distance. He ran the London to Brighton race (52½ miles) on 11 occasions. His last marathon was in 1970, at the age of 55, when he recorded a time of 3:28:29. Coached by Sam Ferris, he ran 60 miles or more a week in training.

Marathon result: 1 Delfo Cabrera (Argentina) 2hr 34min 51.6sec, 2 Tom Richards (GB) 2:35:07.6, 3 Etienne Gailly (Belgium) 2:35:33.6, 4 Johannes Coleman (South Africa) 2:36:06.0, 5 Eusebio Guiñez (Argentina) 2:36:36, 6 Syd Luyt (South Africa) 2:38:11, 7 Gustaf Östling (Sweden) 2:38:40.6, 8 John Systad (Norway) 2:38:41, 9 Alberto Sensini (Argentina) 2:39:30, 10 Henning Larsen (Denmark) 2:41:22, 11 Viljo Heino (Finland) 2:41:32, 12 Anders Melin (Sweden) 2:42:20, 13 Juho Kurikkala (Finland) 2:42:28, 14 Ted Vogel (USA) 2:45:27, 15 Enrique Inostroza (Chile) 2:47:48, 16 Lloyd Evans (Canada) 2:48:07, 17 Gérard Côté (Canada) 2:48:31, 18 Stylianos Kyriakidis (Greece) 2:49:00, 19 József Kiss (Hungary) 2:50:22, 20 Sevki Kogu (Turkey) 2:51:07, 21 John A. Kelley (USA) 2:51:56, 22 Kaspar Schiesser (Switzerland) 2:52:09, 23 Walter Fedorick (Canada) 2:52:12, 24 Olavi Manninen (USA) 2:56:49, 25 Hong Chong Oh (Korea) 2:56:54, 26 Patrick Mulvihill (Ireland) 2:57:35, 27 Yun Bok Suh (Korea) 2:59:36, 28 Sven Håkansson (Sweden) 3:00:09, 29 Jakob Jutz (Switzerland) 3:03:55, 30 Stan Jones (GB) 3:09:16. Did not finish – Luo Wen Ao (China), Mikko Hietanen (Finland), Pierre Cousin (France), René Josset (France), Arsène Piesset (France), Jack Holden (GB), Athanassios Ragazos (Greece), Chota Singh (India), Salvatore Costantino (Italy), Yoon Chil Choi (Korea), Hans Frischknecht (Switzerland). Note: times were recorded to the nearest one-tenth of a second for only the first three and (inexplicably) for seventh place.

As Stan Jones remembered so many years later, the women's high jump was reaching its final stages as he came into the stadium as the last man home in the marathon. Only three women had cleared 1.61 and then Ostermeyer went out, with a bronze to add to her two golds. Coachman, of the USA, and Tyler, of Great Britain, both cleared 1.68 and then failed at 1.70, and the gold went to the American because she got over at the first attempt and Tyler at the second. At the Berlin Games, when Mrs Tyler was 16-year-old Miss Odam, the rules were different and required a jump-off if two athletes cleared the same height, and this she lost to a Hungarian. The mother of two from Mitcham Athletic Club thus ended up at Wembley with her second silver medal.

Dorothy Tyler's career was amazingly durable, lasting 28 years, and including in addition to the Olympic medals two other Olympic appearances in 1952 and 1956, two world records, two Empire Games golds, a European silver and 14 national titles. Her last year of competition was in 1963 and she then went into coaching with her club and took up golf at the age of 48, still playing three times a week when she was 80. Her memories of the Wembley event were candidly modest:

"Coming second was not as important as it is today. You were so thrilled to have done what you did. You didn't get the coverage that you get today, where it's only to do with money. We weren't celebrities because there was no TV where you were on every week. I think it was more fun then. We were all friends, and I don't think they are now. I don't think I would like to be taking part now."

Alice Coachman, too, had served a long apprenticeship, winning 10 successive AAU high-jump titles since 1939, when she had been aged 15, and also champion at 50 metres and 100 metres on eight occasions. At Wembley she created history as the first Afro-American woman to win an Olympic title, and she remembered every detail when interviewed almost 50 years later: "Everyone on the team failed. Only Mickey Patterson got a third place. So here I was, the last person to try to bring America through. There were only three people left in the high jump, Dorothy Tyler, me, and Ostermeyer from France. The people just sat there and watched.

"I did not know I had won. Someone came out there and told me. Someone said, 'Come on.' I looked up and saw 'A. Coachman – USA'. They said, 'Come on, you've got to get on the stand.' So I just took my hair down and brushed it back and went to the stand. I was happy to get my medal awarded to me by King George because I'd read so much about the King and Queen of England ... When we returned home, it was all over. I hung up my shoes after that."

Harold Abrahams gave a detailed account of the closing stages of the high jump event in the next day's *Sunday Times*, which provides an interesting perspective. "Most of the crowd were unaware of the technical rules which made every jump, successful or not, a vital factor in the possible result, for if jumpers tie the failures decide the issue – and Mrs Tyler was behind on failures", he wrote. "At 5ft 5⅜in both girls got over first time. This, as it were, restored Mrs Tyler to her chance of success. Indeed, when I rushed across the ground to the officials and saw the score-card it was plain that Mrs Tyler could win it if both failed completely at the next height for a new Olympic record.

"Again Miss Coachman got over at her first jump. Mrs Tyler failed. Although the crowd didn't know it yet, that was really the end. Dorothy probably did know, but she was not disheartened and at her second attempt the roar of the crowd showed that she had got over."

And so the athletics events at the XIVth Olympic Games came to an end, and on what had become a familiar note for the British: one athlete narrowly failing to win gold, another doggedly determined to finish the course even though in last place. Among the numerous summaries in the British press in the days which followed, it was perhaps a considered comment in the weekly magazine *The Spectator* which most aptly caught the national mood of phlegmatism in adversity. "This time we were bound to be losers, just as we were due to be hosts, and it is perhaps not presumptuous to say that we showed up reasonably well in both capacities."

High jump (women) result: 1 Alice Coachman (USA) 1.68m, 2 Dorothy Tyler (GB) 1.68, 3 Micheline Ostermeyer (France) 1.61, 4= Vinton Beckett (Jamaica), Doreen Dredge (Canada) 1.58, 6 Bertha Crowther (GB) 1.58, 7 Ilse Steinegger (Austria) 1.55, 8 Dora Gardner (GB) 1.55, 9= Annemarie Iversen (Denmark), Simone Ruas (France) 1.50, 11= Shirley Gordon (Canada), Carmen Phipps (Jamaica), Claudealia Robinson (USA) 1.50, 14= Catherine Bourkel (Luxembourg), Anne-Marie Colchen (France), Emma Reed (USA) 1.40, 17= Olga Gyarmati (Hungary), Elisabeth Müller (Brazil) 1.40, 19 Elaine Silburn (Canada) 1.40.

Chapter 12

LOOKING BACK ON THE ATHLETICS

12 records broken, 21 not. But maybe there was more to it than mere records.

HOW GOOD WAS the athletics at the 1948 Olympics? Well, on a score out of 10 the stark answer is "between three and four". Games records were broken in 12 events; conversely, they were not in 22 others. The records that were improved were at 800 metres, 5000 metres, 10,000 metres, 110 metres hurdles, 400 metres hurdles, shot, discus, 10,000 metres walk and women's 80 metres hurdles, high jump, long jump (not previously held at the Games) and javelin.

Should everyone – athletes, organisers, press, public – have been satisfied with that overall outcome? Who can say six decades later? Maybe the simple answer is that the question of how many records had been broken was not the right one to ask in the first place.

The more significant conclusion should perhaps be that the events had gone off reasonably well, despite a fairly lengthy list of official errors. There had been no political issues, no fights, no arguments of consequence, no blatant chauvinism – and all of these cankers had blighted Games in the past, and particularly those of 1908 in London which had been a wrangle between the British and the Americans from start to finish. The Olympic spirit, in a tattered state after the horrendous nationalism of Berlin in 1936, had been revived at an Empire Stadium where the packed crowds – estimated to be 80 per cent British – had responded enthusiastically and generously to a spectacle with which they were not at all familiar: a gathering of athletes from every corner of the globe who were challenging, and for the most part destroying, the last remaining vestiges of the myth of British sporting superiority.

This was not the cosy familiarity of a Test series with the Australian cricketers – those ex-colonial upstarts who had been winning matches with scant regard for the Mother Country's tradition and history ever since the 1880s. Nor was it the satisfyingly insular round of football encounters with the Scots, the Welsh and the Irish, blithely ignoring a World Cup tournament which happened somewhere distant every four years. Nor was it the horse-racing and greyhound-racing for which the punters risked only their money, not their national pride.

Rather, this was a truly international gathering in which even such tiny dots on the map as Ceylon, Jamaica and Panama could glean their harvest-tide of honour. There had, of course, been some measure of international athletics in Britain in the 1930s. Regular matches against France and Germany had been held for a decade or more; others took place with Finland and Norway. The benevolent Sunday newspaper, the *News of The World*, had begun sponsorship of an annual British Games, with invited guests from the USA and the Continent, once the domestic athletics authorities had relaxed their draconian rules regarding payment of expenses. But there had been nothing like the Olympics of 1948 – not even those of 1908, where as many as a dozen Britons had been allowed to enter each event and a sizeable portion of the gold medals in various sports had been too easily earned.

Some of the Wembley champions were coming to the end of careers which had begun in the war years or even before – Eriksson, Porter, Cochran, Smith, Steele, Thompson, Rautavaara, Coachman, Bauma. Others were laying foundation-stones for even greater successes – Dillard, Wint, Whitfield, Zátopek, Németh, Mathias. For a few, Wembley was a major episode in a continually unfolding saga – Reiff, Cabrera, Mikaelsson, Ljunggren, Blankers-Koen, Gyarmati, Ostermeyer. Perhaps no other Games before or since had been witness to so many divergent fortunes. In the biographies of those Wembley champions the theme of "six lost wartime years" so often recurs.

Any comparison between the Wembley Games and those of 12 years before in Berlin throws up the latter in a better light. It makes sense to take the third-place performances as a guide because there can be exceptionally outstanding winners and injured or unwell sixth-placers (in other words, those who were last in the short-distance track races) who distort the image, and on that basis Berlin was better in 16 of the 23 men's events; the exceptions being the 200 metres, 800 metres, 5000 metres, 110 metres and 400 metres hurdles, shot and discus. By contrast, five of the six women's events were better at Wembley.

The leading countries in the athletics medal tables for Berlin and Wembley are as follows:

Berlin 1936

USA 25 medals (14 gold, seven silver, four bronze), Germany 16 (five gold, four silver, seven bronze), Finland 10 (three gold, five silver, two bronze), Great Britain seven (two gold, five silver), Japan seven (two gold, two silver, three bronze), Italy five (one gold, two silver, two bronze).

Wembley 1948

USA 26 (11 gold, five silver, 10 bronze), Sweden 13 (five gold, three silver, five bronze), France eight (two gold, three silver, three bronze), Great Britain seven (six silver, one bronze), Australia six (one gold, three silver, two bronze), Holland six (four gold, two bronze), Italy five (one gold, three silver, one bronze).

The only constant figures here are those of the USA, Great Britain and Italy, all of whom did more or less as well at Wembley as they had in Berlin. Germany and Japan were out of the reckoning at Wembley, and the country which otherwise suffered most in the interim was Finland, whose distance-running supremacy in Berlin (seven medals from the 5000 metres, 10,000 metres and steeplechase) had collapsed. At Wembley their single gold medal and two silvers were won in the javelin for both men and women and in the pole vault. The six "lost years" became six "gained years" for neutral Sweden – and, rather more surprisingly, for France, which had won no medals in Berlin; for Australia, which had won only a bronze; and for Holland, which had won two bronzes. Somebody had to pick up the awards – 23 of them in all – which had been vacated by the Germans and the Japanese.

Caution should be exercised here because it is all too easy to read so much into medal counts, when the difference between bronze and "nothing", otherwise known as fourth place, can be a paltry 0.02 of a second, as it was in the 100 metres at Wembley, or 0.04 of a second as it was in the 200 metres, or 21 points (6,950 to 6,929) as it was in the decathlon. It should also be pointed out that five of Holland's six medals at Wembley were won by just two athletes (and one of them had a quarter-share in the sixth). In 1936 Holland had won two bronzes, both by the same man. Neither medal tally necessarily reflected a genuine rise or fall of national standards.

One comparison which could be made with confidence was that of each Wembley event with the others. So a statistical enterprise which was worth the effort was carried out by the Italian expert, Roberto Quercetani, who worked out the value for each of the men's individual performances at Wembley on the decathlon scoring tables. His unavoidable limitation was that nothing comparable existed for women, for whom an all-round competition would – ridiculously – not be introduced at the Olympics until 1964. Signor Quercetani's compilation read as follows:

1	Wilbur Thompson (USA), Shot, 1,168pts
2	Bill Porter (USA), 110 metres hurdles, 1,142
3	Adolfo Consolini (Italy), Discus, 1,135
4	Arthur Wint (Jamaica), 400 metres, 1,131
5	Jim Delaney (USA), Shot, 1,115
	Herb McKenley (Jamaica), 400 metres, 1,115
7	Roy Cochran (USA), 400 metres hurdles, 1,104

8   Gaston Reiff (Belgium), 5000 metres, 1,105
9   Emil Zátopek (Czechoslovakia), 5000 metres, 1,102
10   Craig Dixon (USA), 110 metres hurdles, 1,099
     Clyde Scott (USA), 110 metres hurdles, 1,099
     Giuseppe Tosi (Italy), Discus, 1,099
13   Jim Fuchs (USA), Shot, 1,084
     Mal Whitfield (USA), 800 metres, 1,078
15   Emil Zátopek (Czechoslovakia), 10,000 metres, 1,081
16   Mal Whitfield (USA), 400 metres, 1,078
17   Arthur Wint (Jamaica), 800 metres, 1,074
18   Harrison Dillard (USA), 100 metres, 1,071
19   Willy Slijkhuis (Holland), 5000 metres, 1,067
20   Marcel Hansenne (France), 800 metres, 1,065
21   Duncan White (Ceylon), 400 metres hurdles, 1,064
22   Fortune Gordien (USA), Discus, 1,062
23   Erik Ahldén (Sweden), 5000 metres, 1,060
24   Rune Larsson (Sweden), 400 metres hurdles, 1,059
25   Henry Eriksson (Sweden), 1500 metres, 1,058

The best events in depth were therefore the shot, 110 metres hurdles (both of them "clean sweeps" for the USA), 400 metres, discus, 5000 metres (the only event with a non-medallist ranked), 400 metres hurdles and 800 metres. The male "Athlete of the Games", usually thought of as being Zátopek, could be said to have been either Thompson, whose performance was worth so much more than anyone else's, or Wint, whose score for two events was better than anyone else's. It should be noted that the walks, relays and the decathlon itself did not figure on the scoring tables, and as Dillard, Cochran and Whitfield also won relay golds they merit higher ranking. Worth further consideration when comparing different performances is the longevity of Games records. Dillard's 100 metres of 10.3 had equalled the time set by fellow-Americans Eddie Tolan, Ralph Metcalfe (both 1932) and Jesse Owens (1936), and it would not be beaten until 1960, while Whitfield equalled his 800 metres record of 1:49.2 in 1952 and the 1.68m high jumps of Alice Coachman and Dorothy Tyler also survived until 1956.

Some of the results of the meetings which took place immediately after the Games make interesting reading. Before the month of August was out better performances than had won Olympic titles were achieved by Dillard (20.8 for 200 metres) and McKenley (46.1 for 400 metres), and also by three Americans in the field events: George Stanich (2.04 for the high jump), Richmond Morcom (4.37 for the pole vault) and Steve Seymour (70.96 for the javelin). These, though, merited only the transitory plaudits of the crowds at those keenly contested international (but medal-less) meetings in Paris, Stockholm and Prague – not a place in Olympic history.

So far as the British were concerned, the hoped-for three gold medals had not materialised, but then experience of the annual ritual-dance of Olympics, World Championships, European Championships and Commonwealth Games which characterises the sport in the 21st century now teaches us that for every three projected successes maybe one will come to reality. Often neglected is the mundane matter which undermines the striking headline: that for every Briton touted by the media as a title favourite, there are others in the USA, Australia, France, or wherever, who are being given the same sort of build-up for that very same gold medal.

Harold Abrahams, the doyen of British athletics writers with unmatched experience of competing in and commenting upon Olympic celebrations ever since 1920, gave his sober assessment as follows: "I do not think there is any cause for recrimination or exaggerated disappointment. Many of our athletes, indeed the majority of them, did as well as any reasonable critic could require, and some of them did better then we had any right to expect." This, of course, was a response to the reaction of others. The "recrimination" and "exaggerated disappointment" had already been widely expressed. Whether it was justified was another matter entirely.

A retrospect of a markedly different kind was composed by Marcel Hansenne, the French 800 metres bronze-medallist and a sports journalist of such a fine literary turn of mind that he was to produce this gloriously-phrased assessment of his personal twin interests: "It is a double-edged job being a runner and a sports writer. The writer can write about the runner, but the runner cannot run away from the writer." In his memoirs of the Games he voiced severe criticisms of the predominantly British spectators at the Empire Stadium. It may be that his judgement was clouded by what he saw as his own relative failure on the track, as he was to recall that, "A quarter-of-an-hour after my defeat in the 800 metres I was very happy. The sadness only came later." Yet what he had to say surely struck some vital chords, uncomfortable reading as it may have made for some. He wrote in the weekly Parisian magazine *But et Sport*:

"No rapport was established between the athletes and the spectators. It was a crowd which did not deserve to see the Games. They did not understand them. I have never seen a public so insensitive as they were to all the grandeur which can result from the Games. Day after day saw them interested only in a small number of athletes: those who wore the British colours. I do not say this to belittle in any way the importance of what happened. Thank God, the athletes, once they were in action, distanced themselves from everything going on around them ... The only good excuse I can give for the British crowd is that after a long and hard ordeal, during which they had conducted themselves heroically, they needed to reassure themselves about their state of health, and that is why, without doubt, they took such a great interest in their own athletes, blindly encouraging them as if athletes from other countries did not exist. They sensed that they were losing their old sense of superiority, and they were trying to cling on to it in a touching manner. But there was no miracle at Wembley. In each event it was the best who won."

This point of view was completely at odds with the conclusion reached in the Organising Committee's Official Report concerning the spectators that "it is not unreasonable to say that they set a standard of impartial generosity which may well stand as a model for all time – a classic example of the Olympic spirit at its best". A correspondent for the *Manchester Guardian* paid even more fulsome a tribute, with a side swipe at officialdom: "Now the medals have been handed out I should like to make honourable mention of the crowds who sat some days through pitiless rain, waiting with supreme patience for the officials to put on an event. The discomfort of these people, without whom Olympics would not be possible, as they spent the long interval between races getting wetter and wetter, had not the slightest effect on the rate of progress, which was either slow or dead slow."

Maybe Monsieur Hansenne, fine writer as he was, expected Gallic fervour rather than Anglicised stoicism. No hoopla, please, we're British.

Chapter 13

THE HARDEST RACE OF ALL: FANNY BLANKERS-KOEN'S OWN STORY

"Nobody could ever have felt less like a champion. My knees trembled. Never had I been so nervous."

THE PERFORMANCES OF Fanny Blankers-Koen at the 1948 Olympics did more to establish the credibility of women's athletics than any other achievements before or since. There had been exceptional woman athletes before her – particularly the Americans, Mildred Didrikson and Helen Stephens, who had been outstanding at the 1932 and 1936 Games respectively – but no one with the supreme all-round ability of the "Flying Dutch Housewife". She was by no means a "cover girl". She gave the impression of raw-boned power. Already a mother of two in 1948, she was just like the neighbour you would meet at the school gates who does rather well in the parents' race on sports day.

Four Olympic gold medals, five European Championships gold medals, 21 world records, winner of all but two of 166 competitions between 1948 and 1950, world No.1 in six different events, she was the first woman to be declared by popular consensus as the outstanding athlete of either gender at an Olympics. When she began competing in the mid-1930s there were no European Championships for women. There were only six events for women at the Olympics of 1936. The 800 metres, her first preference as 17-year-old Francina

Koen, had been struck off the Olympic schedule after 1928. Women athletes were largely ostracised – very rarely competing at the same meetings as men – and amusedly tolerated. Blankers-Koen did most to break down that barrier of male chauvinism.

She was equal fifth in the Berlin Olympic high jump and a member of the Dutch team which was also fifth in the 4x100 metres relay. She was third at 100 and 200 metres in the 1938 European Championships, won by a Pole, Stanislawa Walasiewicz, who by 21st-century criteria would not have been regarded as eligible for women's competition. In 1940 Fanny married her coach, Jan Blankers, who had been a very capable athlete himself, winning the AAA triple jump in 1931 and 1933. She was able to continue competing in German-occupied Holland through to 1944, when she set three of her world records, but was recovering from injury at the time of the first post-war European Championships in 1946 and settled merely for wins at 80 metres hurdles and in the relay.

After 1948 she continued competing for another five years, winning three more European titles in 1950, but at the 1952 Olympics she was not in the best of health and failed to finish the hurdles final. Four years later she was one of a number of leading athletes invited to contribute their Games memories to a book in support of the British Olympic Appeal Fund edited by British journalist Stan Tomlin, the Empire Games three miles champion in 1930. This is her wonderfully graphic account:

"The race that will forever stand out clearly in my mind when I think back to the Wembley Games will be my struggle in the 80 metres hurdles with Maureen Gardner. Eight years have passed, but still when people ask me which was the most memorable race of my career my answer is 'my Olympic hurdles contest in 1948'. I can recall every detail of the two days on which the heats and the final were held. Never shall I forget the day of the heats – Tuesday 3 August. I went to the warming-up track behind Wembley Stadium that morning as the Olympic 100 metres gold-medallist, but nobody could ever have felt less like a champion. My knees trembled. Never had I been so nervous before a race. I wasn't even in the mood to sign my autograph for all those enthusiastic boys and girls who were clamouring for it. I promised them, 'Come back when the race is over'.

"I went through my warming-up as usual, but my mind was not on it. All the time I was waiting for my first glimpse of my rival, Maureen, whom I had never seen before. I had read, of course, that she had a splendid personal best time of 11.2sec, and though I had set the world's record at 11.0sec earlier in the year I knew only too well how many factors can upset form in sprinting races.

"Maureen Gardner arrived by car and made a considerable impression on me when I saw that she had brought her own hurdles. An athlete who carries her own hurdles around must really be in the top class, I thought. There were no other hurdles available on the training track, and because I felt in need of a little practice over the flights before the first heat I summoned up my courage and stepping over to Maureen asked if I could use hers. We shook hands and I noticed immediately that I was not the only one who was nervous. Both of us were on tenterhooks, which was understandable because all the sports-writers of my country had marked me down as favourite for the title and all the British experts had tipped Maureen for the gold medal.

"Just how good Maureen was I was soon to see. In her semi-final she scraped a hurdle and lost her balance, but she still managed to achieve third position and a place in the final. My compatriots encouraged me. 'It will be an easy win for you, Fanny,' said my team-mates. But my husband was more cautious. 'Fanny,' he said, 'no long-jumping for you tomorrow. You must concentrate on the hurdles because this English girl knows her business. An athlete who can recover as Maureen did in the semi-final is obviously a very dangerous rival.'

" 'Concentrate on the hurdles, concentrate on the hurdles, concentrate ...' As I returned to our team quarters in St Helen's School, Northwood, I kept repeating those words. That night I slept far from soundly. In my mind I ran hundreds of 80-metre hurdles races. Now and again my trepidation would be relieved by a consoling thought: 'What does it matter if you lose?' I asked myself. 'After all, you have already won the 100 metres title. Ever since 1936 you have had the ambition to be an Olympic victor. Now you have achieved it. Be satisfied.' And another part of me would answer, 'Why be content? Why should you lose? Maureen Gardner is no better than you are. Go out and win. Of course you can do it.' So, a prey to conflicting hopes and fears, I passed the long night, and the vital day dawned.

"At half past one that Wednesday I arrived at the dressing-room. My husband was waiting for me. 'Did you sleep well?' he asked. I had to be truthful. 'Not very,' I told him. 'But you have eaten well, I hope?' I told a white lie. 'Yes, yes,' I said, but the truth was I had been too keyed up to eat anything.

"Again we made our way to the training track, and somehow I subdued my jangling nerves while I went through my warming-up routine, jogging round the track, limbering exercises and so on. When the time for the final drew near my husband left me because he wanted to see the race from the stand reserved for competitors. But before going he smiled at me and said teasingly, 'You are too old, Fanny.'

"Those five taunting words were spoken in fun but with a purpose. At that time I had never met Jack Crump, the British team manager, although he is now one of my best friends. But in 1948 I was very angry with him for having written that I was too old to make the grade in the Olympics. My husband's joking reminder that some people had written me off as a has-been was a shrewd psychological thrust. It was just the thing to rouse me, to make me go out there and prove to them that even if I was 30 years old and the mother of two children I could still be a champion.

"Too old was I? I would show them. The fateful hour approached and the draw for positions in the final was announced. I was in luck. I had drawn the lane next to Maureen and would be able to keep a close eye on her. But my rising self-confidence was shattered at the start. For one of the very few times in my career I was off to a late start. Just when I was thinking that there was going to be a 'flier' the pistol shot rang out and I was left standing. The rest of the field were a yard ahead of me. What is a yard? What is a fraction of a second? Not much, you may say, but in a race over 80 metres it can mean the difference between defeat and victory.

" 'You are beaten, Fanny. You'll never catch them.' That's what I was thinking, but then I realised that the finishing tape still loomed a long way ahead. I could make up that lost ground. I raced after Maureen, sprinting as I had never sprinted before. How glad I was that we had trained in Holland to meet such a crisis, to keep a cool head and come up with your opponents again after starting with a handicap.

"By the time we reached the fifth hurdle I was level with Maureen, but I was going so fast that I went too close to the hurdle, hit it, and lost my balance. What happened after that is just a blurred memory. It was a grim struggle in which my hurdling style went to pieces. I staggered like a drunkard. Even so, I was fairly confident that I had passed Maureen before the finish, although I was not so sure about Shirley Strickland, who was in the fifth lane and up there with me at the end.

"So it was quite a jolt for me to hear the British national anthem being played when our race was over. Had Maureen then won after all? No – the band were saluting the Royal family, who had just arrived at the stadium. I breathed again, but the suspense was still not over. It was a photo-finish and we had to wait the camera's judgement. As the programme continued, Maureen, Shirley and I glanced continually at the scoring board. Then at last the result came up. The first two ciphers of the winner's number appeared on the board – a six, then a nine. I jumped for joy. My number was 692.

"Maureen and I shook hands. It had been a wonderful race and I was proud to have beaten such a brilliant athlete. We left the ground. My husband was feeling as delighted as I was. 'Well done, Fanny,' he said. 'You aren't too old after all' – and he left his congratulations at that! But there was Geoff Dyson giving Maureen a long, long kiss. Ah well, as somebody standing near said afterwards, 'That's the difference between an engaged couple and a staid old married pair!' "

Geoff Dyson and Maureen Gardner were married the following month. Mrs Dyson again finished second to Mrs Blankers in the 1950 European Championships hurdles. The services of the visionary and articulate Dyson as AAA national coach were lost to Britain when he took up a coaching appointment in Canada in 1961 after a disagreement with the AAA over his conditions of employment. Maureen Dyson tragically died of cancer at the age of 45 in 1974. Fanny Blankers-Koen was voted by the IAAF as its "Woman Athlete of the Century" at the end of 1999. She died in 2003, aged 85.

Chapter 14

THE DEFEATED HERO'S MEMORIES

"I knew I was going to be passed ... it was like the progress of a martyr."

NONE THE WORSE for his galling experience in the last few hundred metres of the Olympic marathon, Belgium's bronze-medallist, Etienne Gailly, was racing again within the month, placing second to Ben Ahmed Labidi, of France, in the Inter-Allies' Championships 5000 metres in Brussels. A couple of weeks later Gailly was back in England and finished second again to Labidi in the services' "Britannia Shield" cross-country race at RAF Halton, in Buckinghamshire. But then perseverance in the face of adversity was clearly a salient characteristic of his, as his wartime tribulations had shown.

He had managed to escape from German-occupied Belgium early in 1943, aged 20, and made his way through France but was arrested in Spain and spent six months in prison. Released to be sent back to Belgium, he managed instead to find his way to England via Portugal and Gibraltar, and joined the Belgian free forces, where he trained as a parachutist and graduated as a second lieutenant. While undergoing training he was a member of the famed London club, Belgrave Harriers, where he was known as "Steve", before taking part in the 1944 airborne landings. Prior to the Wembley Olympics he had never run a marathon, though he had won races at a distance of 32 kilometres. The November 1948 issue of *World Sports* contained Gailly's own story of his Olympic race, and it is the magazine's Continental editor Willy Meisl, a former Austrian football and water-polo international, who is due the credit for having made the approach to Gailly. This is one of the first detailed accounts ever made by an Olympic marathon runner of his experiences.

"Following the tactics which my coach and I had mapped out beforehand, I was determined to run my race without bothering much about my opponents. I was concerned with one thing only – the stop-watch which I carried on my left wrist and which enabled me to control whether or not I was keeping to the pre-arranged timetable. To my surprise, after five kilometres, whilst I had expected to be rather hanging back, I found myself among the leaders.

"Quite contrary to my expectations, the first part of the race had not been very fast. To find myself suddenly in the lead, though I had done nothing but run within schedule, was rather a shock. For a short while a Chinese runner kept me company, but soon I lost him and I was alone. This had not been my intention. I was simply following my timetable, based on a total time of 2 hours 30 minutes. I was not acting the runaway. The others were running more slowly than my coach and I had anticipated.

"I was convinced the others would soon re-establish contact with me. In fact, I was often glancing back, expecting Heino and Holden to appear at my side. I considered them my most dangerous rivals, and it was baffling not to see them coming to the front. When after about 32 kilometres the Korean, Choi, passed me and I could not respond, I asked myself, 'Is he travelling so fast or am I fading?' I had to admit to myself that my strength had left me temporarily. I could only watch how fast Choi was running.

"Although I hated this tiredness, I was not unduly alarmed. I had been alone in the lead for 27 kilometres. Things looked not quite so good now, but after all I felt nothing more than a normal tiredness, which I hoped to soon overcome. Next the Argentinian, Cabrera, passed me. This, however, did not discourage me, not even when he gained some 60 yards on me, because just at this time I felt my rhythm coming back. Almost automatically I closed quickly with Richards, who was running behind Cabrera. No sooner had I got in the Argentinian's slipstream than I decided to spurt without delay. I no longer felt powerless. If at that moment somebody had told me that only two kilometres further on I would fall victim to a truly crushing wave of fatigue, I could not have believed it.

"I passed Cabrera, and having regained the lead I seemed to be travelling really well. Certainly I was tired but quite convinced that I would last the distance. It was then that I committed what was probably my No.1 blunder of the race. To rejoin Cabrera I had to make good some 70 yards. Having achieved this, I drew away from him quickly, perhaps too quickly, because after about one kilometre I had left him 60 yards or so behind. This works out at over 100 metres gained in only two kilometres and may have been too much for me.

"Tiredness made itself more strongly felt up the little hill leading to Wembley Stadium. Still, I felt alright and had no premonition of collapsing. At the very moment, though, when I stepped on to the track exhaustion overcame me like a powerful drug. Immediately after I crossed the normal finishing-line – unfortunately this was not the real finish which lay 400 metres further on – I knew I was going to be passed.

"I cannot deny that this last lap was hard for me. It was like the progress of a martyr. I was horribly weak, and I almost fainted, but I blamed this mainly on my cramped stomach. I still do not think I was really exhausted. It was my stomach which caused the real trouble.

"First Cabrera and then Richards passed me as if they were behind a veil. I was no longer fighting them but that awful overwhelming weakness, wanting more than anything to get to that unbelievably distant finishing-line. I got there. Somehow."

Etienne Gailly tried the same strategy again in the 1950 European Championships marathon in Brussels, leading early on before fading to eighth place. The race was won, as was the Empire Games marathon earlier that year, by Britain's Jack Holden, who had failed to finish the Olympic marathon. Gailly's left foot was seriously injured by a mine while he was on active service with his regiment in Korea the following year and he never raced again. He was killed in 1971, at the age of 48, when he was knocked down by a car.

Chapter 15

THE GIANTS ENTER THE ARENA

Basketball. Harringay Arena, 30 July – 13 August.

THERE WERE PRELIMINARY-ROUND matches which gave no clue whatsoever to the final outcome of the basketball tournament. The USA beat Argentina by only two points, 59-57. China beat Korea by a single point, 49-48. Yet the USA won the gold medals and Korea placed eighth, Argentina 15th and China 18th of the 23 competing nations. The reality was that the Americans were by far the best team, and there was not a great deal to choose between most of the rest. Among the handful of stragglers were the British.

Of the 84 matches, 26 were won by six points or less – of which four required extra time. Five were won by one point, 11 were won by two points and 10 were won by between three and six points. Belgium, in 11th place, figured in six matches which were decided by six points or less, winning three of them. On the other hand, except for their temporary aberration against the Argentinians, the USA won all their encounters by margins of 25 points or more. Eire, in last place, lost theirs by 71-9, 49-22, 88-25, 73-14 and 46-21. Great Britain were little better in 20th place, as their only success was by that 46-21 margin against the Irish.

The summary in the official report of the Games organising committee was written by William Browning, the honorary secretary of the Amateur Basketball Association and the arena manager for the tournament. He lavished praise on the champions: "Of the USA team the salient features were the enormous height of their players and their speed. Normally, men of 6ft 9in to 7ft tall are not fast, but these players had all the agility of bantams! When height is combined with agility, superb ball-control and intelligence, there is no answer. Apart from the match with the Argentine before the USA team had settled down, there was not a team who gave them a close game. As soon as these giants entered the arena, the opposing teams seemed to wilt and fade away."

The USA had also won the inaugural Olympic title in Berlin, where the matches had been bizarrely held outdoors, so that when it poured with rain on the day of the final, and turned the surface of sand into mud, the score against Canada was reduced to 19-8. Mexico had taken the bronze medals ahead of Poland, Philippines and Uruguay. Misguidedly, the FIBA (Fédération Internationale de Basket Amateur) had attempted to introduce a rule midway through the tournament limiting the height of players to 6ft 3in (1.90m), but the Americans objected, as one would expect, and the idea was soon shelved.

It was an opinion worth heeding as the game had been devised in the USA in 1891 by Dr James Naismith, an instructor at the training school of the International YMCA College in Springfield, Massachusetts, who knocked the base out of a fruit-basket and hung it on the gymnasium wall to provide an energetic indoor diversion for the youths in his charge. The enterprise of the Canadian-born Dr Naismith, who gratifyingly presented the medals in Berlin in 1936, was more in the nature of a refinement than an invention as various games bearing some resemblance to basketball had been played since pre-Christian times. Sport owes a debt to the inventive Canadian doctor because one of his pupils devised volleyball in 1895 as a non-contact alternative to basketball.

The first European Championships had been held in Geneva in 1935, and the Baltic nations had shown an immediate aptitude, with Latvia winning that year and then Lithuania succeeding them in Riga in 1937 and in Cannes in 1939. Czechoslovakia had beaten Italy for the 1946 title, again in Geneva, and had, in turn, been defeated by the USSR the next year in Prague. The Soviet boycott of the Wembley Olympics meant, of course, that no Latvians or Lithuanians would be taking part. There had been an England team at the 1946 European Championships, but there were no high hopes for Great Britain's Olympic debut.

A neat link had been forged with the 19th-century origins of the game when Hoylake YMCA, from the Wirral, won the Amateur Basketball Association national championship in 1936 and 1937, but the two leading teams in post-war England were comprised of European exiles and American evangelists. The national champions in 1947 were the Carpathians, winning 48-25 against the Birmingham team, Dolobran, a club for Quakers sponsored by the Cadbury's chocolate-making firm which was to provide six of the Great Britain Olympic squad, and in 1948 the Latter Day Saints beat the Latvian Society 39-30. Basketball was not a game which had yet caught on widely with the British – and maybe the same could still be said all these years hence.

The World Championships would not come into existence until 1950, and so seeding was optimistically based on the 1936 Olympic results, with the four leading teams in Berlin who were among the 23 present in London each heading one of the qualifying groups, in which every country played all the others: Group A – Brazil, Canada, Great Britain, Hungary, Italy, Uruguay; Group B – Belgium, Chile, China, Iraq, Korea, Philippines; Group C – Argentina, Czechoslovakia, Egypt, Peru, Switzerland, USA; Group D – Cuba, Eire, France, Iran, Mexico.

The seeding worked well enough despite its dated credentials, though five of the six teams in Group B tied on points. Brazil and the USA each won all of their five matches, and the eight qualifiers for the quarter-finals were Brazil and Uruguay from group A; Chile and Korea from Group B; Czechoslovakia and USA from Group C; France and Mexico from Group D.

The non-qualifying countries were then assigned, according to their finishing positions, to two other group quarter-finals which would involve, respectively, the teams contesting 9th to 16th places and those contesting 17th to 23rd. The margins between the top eight and the others were very finely drawn in some cases; as an instance, Belgium's loss of two of their matches in Group B by two points (including to one of the qualifiers, Korea) and their success in two by the same margin (including to the other qualifier, Chile). In the end the difference between Chile reaching the last eight and Belgium not doing so was that in their matches against the luckless Iraqis Chile scored 100 points and Belgium only 98! Argentina, having pressed the Americans so close, lost their vital closing group match to the Czechs, 45-41.

By comparison, the remaining matches involving the top eight were largely one-sided, though the bronze-medal playoff was described as "a game teetering with excitement and temperament". The Americans simply got better and better, once they had become accustomed to the international refereeing. Mexico had decisively beaten France in their group match, 56-42, and were unfortunate to be drawn against the USA in the semi-finals, as otherwise they might well have won the silver or bronze medals. The Americas – North, Central and South – provided five of the first six teams in the guise of the USA, Brazil, Mexico, Uruguay and Chile, plus Canada in ninth place. Apart from the surprising French, who had come to the tournament with modest expectations of finishing in the top eight, the only other European team in the leading 10 was Czechoslovakia, though the USSR would presumably have challenged strongly for a medal, had they entered.

For all of the US dominance, other teams made their mark, and perhaps even more indelible a mark. William Browning saw every match in his official capacity and his contribution to the organising committee's official report contained some interesting and clearly constructive comments about styles of play. Browning observed: "Though the USA won the championship, that they played the best basketball to watch may be in doubt, for some of the most scintillating ball-play was that of the Far Eastern teams – Korea, Philippines and China. These three teams were a joy to watch. Though small of stature, their speed and ball-manipulation were an education. How the crowd loved them, and how well they earned the admiration and respect of basketball enthusiasts!"

As in 1936, FIBA made a rule change even as the tournament was progressing, but this time it was positively received. It was decided that no player could remain under his basket for more than three seconds while his team possessed the ball. The official report explained the background: "From the technical point of view, the tournament made it clear that centre-pivot play had slowed the game. There was far too much bringing the ball down slowly and then setting up a play. Match after match revealed the same movement: the tremendous urge to establish a solid defence and to set up an attack around the pivot player."

France, in particular, had benefited from what was described as their "rock-like defence and methodical offensive". The French trainer-manager was Robert Busnel, only 34 years old, who had played in every position on the court since he had taken up the game at the age of 16, and later became president of the French Basketball Federation. France was never to be as successful again in an Olympic tournament. The USA, by contrast, would compile a record 62 Olympic matches without defeat until losing controversially 51-50 to the USSR in the 1972 final.

The US trials for the 1948 Games had been held the previous March and had involved four club teams and four university teams in play-offs at Madison Square Garden. The Phillips 66ers, based at Bartlesville, Oklahoma, who had won the 1948 AAU (national) title, beat the University of Kentucky 53-49, and each provided five members of the selected Olympic squad. Much the tallest among them was Bob Kurland, of the Phillips 66ers, at 7ft (2.13m), who would win a second gold medal in Helsinki in 1952, but by the modern standards of the game his team-mates were not exceptionally big: Gordon Carpenter and Alex Groza were each 6ft 7in (2.01m), Don Barksdale 6-6 (1.98) and Robert Pitts 6-5 (1.95). None of the others were over 6-3 (1.90) and Ralph Beard was only 5-10 (1.77). The 66ers also provided the coach, Omar ("Bud") Browning, presumably no relation to the ABA secretary, and Kentucky provided the assistant coach, Adolph Rupp.

Don Barksdale was the first Afro-American to take part in Olympic basketball and his pathway to the Games had not been an easy one. At high school in California he was prevented by racial discrimination from playing in the basketball team. He graduated in 1941 and went into the US Army, demonstrating his versatile sporting talents during his service by winning the 1944 AAU title in the triple jump. He was named in the "All-American" team of outstanding track and field athletes which would have provided the nucleus of the Olympic selection that year, had there been a Games, and so had missed his chance in one sport, only to grab the opportunity when it came up again four years later in another sport, though he was still the 13th-ranked long jumper in the world in 1947. Of those 1944 "All-Americans", the only other one to win gold in 1948 was the sprinter, Barney Ewell.

Barksdale continued to break down barriers in his later life. After the 1948 Olympics he established a career as a radio disc jockey and then signed a $60,000 contract to play professional basketball for the Baltimore Bullets, later becoming the first Afro-American in the Boston Celtics team. After an ankle injury ended his career, he set up a music-recording company, Rhythm Records, and owned two nightclubs in Oakland, in California. He died in 1993 at the age of 69.

Harringay Arena's 7,000-capacity was never fully taken up, but the matches attracted increasingly larger crowds, from 200 on the first day to 800 on the second, 1,500 on the third, and then an average of 2,500 every evening until the final when over 5,000 people turned up. This was a tribute to the attractiveness of the spectacle and to the curiosity of the untutored spectators because there was not a great deal to cheer from the British point of view. Even so, in the British Olympic Association's report, again written by William Browning, some guarded encouragement is given: "The British team occupied 20th position – no surprise to the officials of the Association, for it was realised our standard of play was far below the rest of Europe. However, Great Britain improved considerably during the Games and by the end of the tournament was playing quite good basketball."

Great Britain's results were as follows: Group A – lost to Uruguay 69-17, to Canada 44-24, to Brazil 76-11, to Italy 49-28, to Hungary 60-23; 17th-to-23rd positions, quarter-finals – beat Eire 46-21; 17th-to-23rd positions, semi-finals – lost to China 54-25; 19th-20th positions, playoff, lost to Egypt 50-18. The Great Britain players were Frank Cole (Dolobran, Birmingham), Trevor Davies (Polytechnic, London), Alex Eke (YMCA, London), Malcolm Finlay (YMCA, London), Colin Hunt (Dolobran, Birmingham), Douglas Legg (Dolobran, Birmingham), Ronald Legg (Dolobran, Birmingham), Stanley McMeekan (Dolobran, Birmingham), Sydney McMeekan (Dolobran, Birmingham), Robert Norris (Polytechnic, London), Lionel Price (Polytechnic, London), Harry Weston (Smethwick), Stanley Weston (Smethwick). Little is known about them, but it would seem that there were three sets of brothers.

One curious occurrence during the Olympic tournament was that the Hungarian team, having qualified for the 9th-to-16th playoffs, withdrew from the tournament because they had apparently run out of money, and currency restrictions prevented them from raising any more. This seems difficult to understand because in at least two other sports – fencing and gymnastics – there were still Hungarian competitors in action on the dates that the basketball players would have been playing. Could not somebody have lent the basketball team the money, or even given it to them, or is there some underlying reason for their early departure from Harringay? Maybe the simple explanation is that there was not enough money to go round the whole Hungarian contingent. So the fencers and the gymnasts, who were likely to win medals (and duly did so), were allowed to stay, while the basketball players, who would be ninth at best, were packed off home.

Basketball results: 1 USA, 2 France, 3 Brazil, 4 Mexico, 5 Uruguay, 6 Chile, 7 Czechoslovakia, 8 Korea, 9 Canada, 10 Peru, 11 Belgium, 12 Philippines, 13 Cuba, 14 Iran, 15 Argentina, 16 Hungary, 17 Italy, 18 China, 19 Egypt, 20 Great Britain, 21 Switzerland, 22 Iraq, 23 Eire.

Quarter-finals – USA 63 Uruguay 28, Mexico 43 Korea 32, Brazil 28 Czechoslovakia 23, France 53 Chile 52. Semi-finals – USA 71 Mexico 40, France 43 Brazil 33. Final – USA 65 France 21. Third-place match – Brazil 52 Mexico 47.

The teams were as follows: USA: Clifford Barker (University of Kentucky), Don Barksdale (Oakland Bittners), Ralph Beard (University of Kentucky), Lewis Beck (Phillips 66ers), Vincent Boryla (Denver Nuggets), Gordon Carpenter (Phillips 66ers), Alex Groza (University of Kentucky), Wallace Jones

(University of Kentucky), Bob Kurland (Phillips 66ers), Ray Lumpp (New York University), Robert Pitts (Phillips 66ers), Jesse Renick (Phillips 66ers), Jack Robinson (Baylor University), Kenny Rollins (University of Kentucky).

France: André Barrais, Michel Bonnevie, André Buffière, René Chocat, René Dérency, Maurice Desaymonnet, André Even, Maurice Girardot, Fernand Guillou, Raymond Offner, Jacques Perrier, Yvan Quénin, Lucien Robuffic, Pierre Thiolon.

Brazil: Luiz Benvenuti, João Francisco Bráz, Alfredo Rodrigues da Motta, Zenny de Azevedo, Ruy de Freitas, Nilton Pacheco de Oliveira, Marcus Vinicius Dias, Affonso Azevedo Evora, Alexandre Gemigniani, Alberto Marson, Guilherme Rodrigues, Massinet Sorcinelli.

Mexico: Angel Acuña Lizaña, Isaac Alfaro Loza, Alberto Bienvenu Barajas, José de la Cruz Cabrera Gándara, Jorge Cardiel Gaitán, Rodolfo Diáz Mercado, Francisco Galindo Chávez, Jorge Gudiño Goya, Héctor Guerrero Delgado, Emilio López Enriquez, Ignacio Romo Porches, Fernando Rojas Herrera, José Santos de Léon.

Chapter 16

BOB KURLAND RECOLLECTS HIS OLYMPIC TRIUMPHS

The man who changed the way basketball was played

I F YOU ARE a 13-year-old boy growing up in St Louis, Missouri, playing basketball comes naturally. "We played any place you could get a rim up or a basket up," recalled Bob Kurland some 70 years later. If, like young Bob, you already happened to be 6ft 6in (1.98m) tall at that age, playing such a game comes more naturally than most, but that does not mean that the route to winning two Olympic gold medals was easy. There have been plenty of exceptionally tall basketball players in the last half-century or so, but none of them has yet matched Kurland's accomplishment of winning gold medals at the Games of 1948 and 1952. Nor has anyone else been honoured with the fulsome citation at the Basketball Hall of Fame in the game's founding place of Springfield, Massachusetts, that "his ability to block and alter opponents' shots changed the way basketball was played".

After graduating from high school in 1942, and now 6ft 9in (2.05m) but still, in his own recollection, "pretty thin and awkward", Kurland went to Oklahoma State University for three days of trials, and the coach there told him, "I've never seen a boy like you before. If you want to get an education and work for an hour or so a day, we'll give you room, board and tuition." Kurland took the scholarship and helped the university team to win the coveted national collegiate title in 1945 and 1946 and was the leading points-scorer in the nation in the latter year. There he learned the fundamental lesson of the game: "You must play as a team, not as five stars. Otherwise you're going to get your butt beaten."

He then joined the Phillips Petroleum Company in Bartlesville, Oklahoma, to play for their team in an industrial league which had been sanctioned by the US governing body of amateur sport, the AAU, before the advent of professional basketball. The Goodyear Tire and Rubber Company and the 20th Century Fox film studios were among the other employers with teams in the league. The "Phillips 66ers" won the 1948 AAU title and were naturally one of the teams invited to take part in the trials from which the Olympic team would be selected.

Five of the Phillips team, including Kurland, by now 7ft (2.13m) tall, were chosen for the Games, but the whole squad then had to set off on a tour to Kansas, Oklahoma and Kentucky to play matches which would raise the money to pay their way to London. The practice together was useful, but Kurland's abiding memory is of a lesson in race relations for the team and the spectators who came to see the matches: "Don Barksdale was the first Afro-American to play Olympic basketball and I had so much admiration for what he achieved. When we played in Kentucky and passed the water bottle along as we sat on the bench I can still remember the gasp from the crowd as it was handed on to him."

Then it was off to New York for the transatlantic liner crossing and a spectacular departure: "Kelly, the oarsman, was in the team, and his sister, Grace, came down to see him off, and she was quite the prettiest thing that anyone had ever seen." (Grace was later to star in such films as *High Noon*, *Dial M for Murder* and *High Society* before marrying Prince Rainier of Monaco.) Arriving in England, the US players then began another tour which took them as far as Edinburgh, playing exhibition matches to raise public awareness of the sport. "There was still, of course, evidence of the bombing," he recalls of his impressions, "but the transport worked. The food was very good. We were comfortable and clean, The people were civil. We certainly weren't disappointed by what we saw and experienced."

The Olympic tournament went according to plan, apart from the narrow victory against Argentina. "We thought we were lucky as hell," Kurland says. "There's times when somebody just nails a lid on the rim and all your co-ordination disappears. Don Barksdale got 15 or 17 points that day and saved our bacon. Otherwise, we felt good about ourselves. We felt there was no reason to lose if we did our best."

The 1952 Games were different, Bob Kurland emphasises. "The Russians had been there in 1948 with their notebooks and their cameras, taking notes and pictures galore. Then when we came to play them in Helsinki they were big, rugged men, some of them quick, and they played with brute strength in a very rough style. Well, we thought, if that's the way it is, we'll play the same way. We really felt that it was our obligation not to lose, that there was a threat to our way of life, and we carried that belief on to the court with us."

The Phillips 66ers were AAU national champions four times from 1946 to 1952 with Kurland's help and won 369 of the 395 matches they played. After retiring from the game he worked for Phillips until 1985, rose to high executive position, and was responsible for the innovation of self-service petrol stations. His reputation as a gold-medal basketball player went everywhere with him, and on one social occasion someone told him, "Bob, you're a legend." Bob Kurland replied unhesitatingly, "If you believe in legends, that is."

Chapter 17

APPEALS, DEMONSTRATIONS ... AND A GOOD FIGHT EVERY NOW AND THEN

Boxing. Empress Hall, Earls Court and Empire Pool, Wembley. 7–13 August.

T HE COMMON PRACTICE when assessing the merits of Olympic boxing is to catalogue the contestants who have gone on to professional stardom, and the "class of '48" passes the examination with an A-plus credit: Pascual Pérez, Vic Toweel, Jimmy Carruthers, Wallace ("Bud") Smith and László Papp most prominent among the "graduates".

The far greater value of the Olympic boxing, though, is surely the opportunity it gives for self-expression to young men from disadvantaged countries, where the provision for learning such sophisticated skills as pole vaulting, swimming the butterfly stroke, or swinging on the asymmetric bars is very much limited, if it exists at all. For the great majority of these youthful fighters the Olympic tournament provides the most meaningful bouts of fisticuffs in which they will ever engage. Among the 39 nations putting boxers into the Wembley ring were Burma, Iran, Lebanon, Pakistan and Peru – none of them noted for their athletes, swimmers or gymnasts.

The most successful countries in the eight weights which were contested came from three different continents. Argentina, Hungary and South Africa each won two titles, while Czechoslovakia and Italy won one each. There were 12 other nationalities among the semi-finalists – in other words, boxers who could have fought for a bronze medal at the very least – from Australia, Belgium, Denmark, Eire, Great Britain, Korea, Poland, Puerto Rico, Spain, Sweden, Switzerland and the USA. The bantamweight bronze won by Juan Venegas was the first ever medal in any Olympic sport for a Puerto Rican, and there would not be another until 1976, also in boxing. Mike McKeon, at middleweight, came closer to a medal than any member of the Irish team in any Olympic sport in 1948 but was unable to take his place for the deciding bout because of injury.

Though each nation was allowed to enter only one boxer per weight, the largest ever Olympic start-list of 206 competitors was assembled, and so a preliminary day's boxing was held at the Empress Hall on Saturday 7 August, where the wrestling had finished only the day before, and while the last of the swimming events were taking place at the Empire Pool. Work went on from midnight Saturday to midday Monday to build a bridge across the Empire Pool on which the ring was placed, and for the rest of the week of competition the reflection of the arc-lights and the multi-coloured flags in the shimmering water would add an exotic splendour to the occasion.

To deal first with those "big names" already mentioned, it can be quickly summarised that Pascual Pérez, of Argentina, became world flyweight champion from 1954 to 1960; Vic Toweel, of South Africa, was world bantamweight champion from 1950 to 1952, losing his title to Jimmy Carruthers, of Australia, who retired unbeaten after 1954; Wallace ("Bud") Smith won the world lightweight title in 1955; László Papp, of Hungary, went on to fashion one of the greatest of all Olympic boxing careers, winning three gold medals, and was then allowed to turn professional and became European middleweight champion in 1957. A Briton, Jack Gardner, had his share of glory in the paid ranks, winning the British heavyweight title in 1950.

The talents of some of these doughty pugilists were not necessarily immediately apparent at Wembley. Pérez, at flyweight, and Papp, at middleweight, both won titles, but none of the other three had even a medal between them. At bantamweight Toweel lost a close decision in his opening bout and Carruthers was unlucky to suffer a cut eye which prevented him taking his place in the quarter-finals against the eventual champion. Smith reached the semi-finals at lightweight but was injured and unable to fight for the bronze. Gardner was beaten in the heavyweight quarter-finals.

Furthermore, neither Pérez nor Papp was the man who made the greatest impression in the Empire Pool ring on the experts. The trophy for the most stylish boxer of the tournament went to George Hunter, the South African winner of the light-heavyweight title, and it was said of him: "Never was an honour more richly deserved. Hunter boxed impeccably, hit correctly with the knuckle part of the closed glove, and showed a pleasing variety of punches." The comments could not have come from a more authoritative source because they were those of George Whiting, the much-respected *Evening Standard* correspondent who composed the boxing article for the British Olympic Association report of the Games.

Great Britain had two beaten finalists – Johnny Wright, who gave Papp a good fight, and Don Scott, narrowly out-pointed by Hunter. This was a reasonably satisfactory return, considering that Britain had not won any Olympic boxing medals since 1924, and in the process Wright was reviving a lapsed middleweight tradition. The title in that division had been won in 1908 by JWHT (Johnny) Douglas and in 1920 and 1924 by Harry Mallin. Douglas also captained England at cricket when they took the Ashes in Australia in 1911–12. His formidable collection of initials stood for "John William Henry Tyler", but he was fondly known as "Johnny Won't Hit Today" because of his defensive qualities as a batsman. It was said of him that "his batting was of the stubborn variety and he was the ideal man to save a match", and his demeanour as a boxer naturally had a somewhat more aggressive character to it.

The Amateur Boxing Association had begun their training programme for the British team a year before the Wembley Games, winning praise for their foresight even from the often critical George Whiting. Groups of as many as 30 boxers were regularly brought together in London, and Harry Mallin and another 1924 gold-medallist, Harry Mitchell, provided their expertise, together with doctors, dieticians and physical training staff. There were at least two significant losses along the way as the temptation of turning professional proved too great for the 1947 ABA champions at bantamweight, Danny O'Sullivan, and flyweight, Jim Clinton. It was certainly worth O'Sullivan's while because he became British champion in 1949 and later fought for a world title.

At the 1947 European Championships in Dublin Johnny Ryan had won the welterweight title, beating a future world champion, Charles Humez, of France, on points, and Clinton, Wally Thom (middleweight) and George Scriven (heavyweight) all got to their respective finals. Great Britain finished a close second to France in the team competition by a margin of 22 points to 19, but these championships were not to provide much of a form-guide for the Olympics to come. The title-winners at heavyweight, Gearoid O'Colmain, of Ireland, and at light-heavyweight, Hennie Quentemeyer, of Holland, were beaten in their first fights at Wembley, and the only European champion to reach a Wembley final was the lightweight Joseph Vissers of Belgium. Yet it was a stupendous achievement for the German-born Quentemeyer to have been at the Olympics at all because even among a host of ex-servicemen competitors his wartime experiences were exceptionally harrowing. He had served as a bomber crew member with the Royal Air Force in the Far East, had been shot down twice, and had survived a Japanese prisoner-of-war camp, where he had worked as a slave labourer on the infamous Burma railway and his weight had fallen to 55kg (8st 8lb).

The 1948 ABA Championships were staged in early May and were the 60th in the series which had begun in 1881 as the first amateur bouts to be staged under the Marquess of Queensberry rules. A packed crowd of 10,000 watched what were, in effect, the final Olympic trials and were to see four of the eight titles go to the armed forces. The winners were Henry Carpenter (Bradfield) at flyweight, Tommy Profitt (LNER Manchester) at bantamweight, Peter Brander (Slough Youth Centre) at featherweight, Ron Cooper (Royal Navy) at lightweight, Max Shacklady (Eccles) at welterweight, Johnny Wright (Royal Navy) at middleweight, Don Scott and Jack Gardner (both Army) at light-heavyweight and heavyweight.

The imposingly named Maximilian Baldwin Shacklady, a scientific instrument maker by profession and the father of two children, provided the upset of the evening by beating the European champion, Ryan, and *The Times* reported of the contest that "Ryan had promised to win the title for a third year in succession, but for all his ring-craft he was worn down by a strong and persistent opponent". Wright beat Tommy Warren, from West Ham, in what was described as "a grand battle between two well-matched men. Seaman Wright was the steadier, and this quality just carried him through against a strong and willing fighter".

Some of the most successful countries at Wembley – Argentina, Hungary, Italy and South Africa – had also been in the forefront of Olympic boxing during the 1920s and 1930s, with 16 gold medals between them. The USA had actually won more titles (six) than any of these at the five Games held in those decades – three of them by future world professional champions Frankie Genaro, Fidel La Barba and Jackie Fields – but oddly did not meet with anywhere near such success at Wembley, where only their welterweight, Horace ("Hank") Herring, won a silver. The previous year Europe had won only one contest in a match with the USA, and that had been by the Spanish flyweight, Luis Martinez, who did not get beyond the quarter-finals at Wembley, losing to the eventual silver-medallist.

Flyweight (up to 51kg)

26 entries, 10 first-series bouts, six boxers received byes to the second series.

The first name out of the box when the draw was made at Earls Court was that of Pascual Pérez, who duly disposed of his opponent from the Philippines in the second round and then went on to beat a South African, a Belgian, a Czech and an Italian to win the title. George Whiting described Pérez as "the man with the punch" and said of the final, "Pérez boxed with excellent judgement, carefully weighing up Badinelli's 'southpaw' peculiarities, scoring freely with his right hand in the second round, and standing up well to his rival's finishing burst in the third".

Pérez, a 22-year-old clerk at the Argentinian parliament in Buenos Aires, had suffered the unsettling experience of being "disqualified" before he had even stepped into the ring. He had been declared over the limit at the weigh-in, but when the matter was queried by Argentina's management it was quickly discovered that the British officials had made a mistake and confused Pérez with his bantamweight team-mate Arnoldo Pares. Badinelli, whose first name was the splendidly apt one for a boxer of "Spartaco", was one of 20 or so Wembley contestants who fought in the less common southpaw style – that is with the right foot forward.

Another who caught Whiting's keen eye in this division was the Korean bronze-medallist Soo Ann Han, "whose streamline boxing and acceleration won him third place and were in keeping with the highest flyweight traditions". Together with a bronze in weightlifting, this was the first medal ever to be won for Korea in any Olympic sport, though Korean-born marathon-runners had taken gold and bronze in the colours of conquering Japan at the 1936 Games. Soo Ann Han fought again in the 1952 Olympics but did not reach the semi-finals. The European champion from Spain, Luis Martinez, and the fourth of the semi-finalists, Frantişek Majdloch, of Czechoslovakia, were also impressive in a division which, in Whiting's view, "was on the most consistently high level of all the eight classes". Britain's entry, Henry Carpenter, from Peckham, in South London, had won his Olympic place by beating a future British professional bantamweight champion, Peter Keenan, in the ABA finals and was thought of as "a definite British hope" but lost on points in his opening bout to a Belgian, Alex Bollaert, who then had the misfortune to encounter Pérez in the next series.

Bantamweight (up to 54kg)

30 entries, 14 first-series bouts, two boxers received byes to the second series.

There was a fine mix of second-series winners – from Australia, Chile, Ceylon and Puerto Rico, along with Europeans from Eire, Hungary, Italy and Spain – but the overall standard, for some reason, did not match that of the flyweights. Maybe the quality would have been better if the South African Vic Toweel, who had won all but two of the 190 previous bouts in his career, had not lost a narrow decision to Pares, in the first series, and the Australian Jimmy Carruthers had not suffered a cut eye which forced him to withdraw from his third-series meeting with the eventual champion Tibor Csik, of Hungary, who was only 18 years old. Both Toweel and Carruthers, as previously mentioned, would go on to the highest professional levels.

The Hungarian gold-medallist had a relatively easy passage, reaching the semi-finals with only one fight which went the distance as his Brazilian opponent in the first series had been disqualified. At least the final, against the Italian Zuddas, was a close-fought contest. Again Britain's interest in this division did not last long as the Mancunian millwright Tommy Profitt was beaten on points in the first series.

Flyweight result: 1 Pascual Pérez (Argentina), 2 Spartaco Badinelli (Italy), 3 Soo Ann Han (Korea). Semi-finals: Pérez beat Frantişek Majdloch (Czechoslovakia) on points, Badinelli beat Soo Ann Han on points. Final: Pérez beat Badinelli on points. Third place: Soo Ann Han beat Majdloch on points.

Bantamweight result: 1 Tibor Csik (Hungary), 2 Giovanni Battista Zuddas (Italy), 3 Juan Venegas (Puerto Rico). Semi-finals: Csik beat Venegas on points, Zuddas beat Alvaro Vicente Domenech (Spain) on points. Final: Csik beat Zuddas on points. Third place: Venegas beat Domenech on points.

Featherweight (up to 58kg)

30 entries, 14 first-series bouts, two boxers received byes to the second series.

Demonstrations by South American spectators against two of the decisions by the judges marred this weight division. When Eddie Johnson, of the USA, was declared the points winner over Basilio Alves, of Uruguay, in the second series, sections of the crowd vented their displeasure by booing for 15 minutes, a fair enough demonstration of popular opinion, but matters got out of hand when Alves's supporters hoisted him on to their shoulders and attempted to charge the table occupied by the jury of appeal. After the semi-final victory of South African Dennis Shepherd over the Argentinian Francisco Nuñez, the latter's fellow-countrymen had to be held in check by a dozen attendants until they were finally calmed by a speech from Argentina's member of the appeal jury.

All this brouhaha detracted from the more conventional entertainment provided from within the ring. George Whiting thought that the title "was won in a workmanlike style" by Ernesto Formenti, of Italy, but had most to say about the beaten finalist, Shepherd, another southpaw who had in turn defeated the American Johnson, in the third series. "Never was there a pluckier or more patched-up puncher, and these Olympics gave us dozens", Whiting wrote in the BOA report. "Shepherd boxed five bouts, in four of which his right eye was badly cut and subsequently stitched and re-stitched. However, in Shepherd's case, fortune certainly favoured the brave. The verdicts he received over Johnson and Nuñez were open to hot debate – and he certainly got it!"

The bronze for Antkiewicz was the only medal won by Poland in any sport at the 1948 Olympics and also the first to have ever been won by that country in boxing. He would go on to get the silver at lightweight at the 1952 Helsinki Games. Antkiewicz suffered from one unexpected problem prior to one of his fights; he fell foul of the British "work to rule" attitude, as his coach, Feliks Stamm, explained: "We had to take a bus to Wembley, and at that very moment the bus driver had a tea break and did not want to go. We had to get there by tube and arrived at the very last moment."

The British representative, Peter Brander, lost to a Frenchman in his opening bout, which came as a severe disappointment as Brander had been thought of as a medal contender. An apprentice electrician from Southampton, he had been enthusiastically hailed after his ABA win as "the personification of the style that has made British amateur boxing world famous". Decribing Brander's defeat in an article for the *Daily Telegraph*, Lainson Wood drew attention to what at the end of the week's boxing would become a major controversy – the perversity of some of the judges: "Apparently impressed by the fact that he must attack all the time

---

Featherweight result: 1 Ernesto Formenti (Italy), 2 Dennis Shepherd (South Africa), 3 Aleksy Antkiewicz (Poland). Semi-finals: Shepherd beat Francisco Nuñez (Argentina) on points, Formenti beat Antkiewicz on points. Final: Formenti beat Shepherd on points. Third place: Antkiewicz beat Nuñez on points.

to win a verdict from a polyglot tribunal of judges, he sailed in recklessly against a taller man with a longer reach. He was cuffed with lefts and rights and stabbed with a left-hander's prodding right for his pains." The man who beat Brander, Mohamed Ammi, had taken up the sport only two years previously and was the French North African champion, but he next came up against the eventual silver-medallist and thus made his exit.

Lightweight (up to 62kg)

28 entries, 12 first-series bouts, four boxers received byes to the second series.

The USA (twice), Great Britain (in 1908), Denmark, Italy, South Africa and Hungary had previously won this title, and three of these countries – Denmark, South Africa and the USA – were to figure in the medal reckoning again this time. A Peruvian had the misfortune to come in overweight for his first-series bout and thus never got to throw a punch at all. For the second series Africa, Asia, Europe, North and South America all had an involvement, though the African in this instance was a South African – and it would not be until 1960 that a boxer from Central or East Africa would win a medal.

As it happens, it was the 19-year-old Gerald Dreyer, from a long-established Transvaal boxing family, who won the Wembley title, and he did so, according to George Whiting, by "boxing in strictly 'traditional' style, and without frills or fancy touches". His opponent in the final was European champion Joseph Vissers, of Belgium, who had been considered fortunate to be awarded the decision against a future professional world champion, Wallace ("Bud") Smith, of the USA, in the semi-finals. Vissers was holding his own with Dreyer until he was knocked down by a left-hander to the jaw in the second round.

The organising committee's official report of the boxing events, couched in much more restrained terms than those of Whiting's pen, described the final thus: "Vissers is a persistent attacker and set about wearing Dreyer down, until a short left to the chin put him down for a count in the second round. Thereafter, there seemed little doubt that Dreyer would finish up the winner." The deceptively frail-looking Danish bronze-medallist, Svend Wad, came in for special praise from this same writer: "His exemplary conduct in the ring was matched by the skilful use of his left hand."

Britain's Ron Cooper, a Royal Navy stoker, kept the fires of hope flickering for his supporters with a first-series points win over a Dutchman, but he then lost to Irishman Maxie McCullagh, and the embers were extinguished. Of their five fights at the four lightest divisions, British boxers had now lost four. By contrast, the Italians had produced three finalists, though their lightweight was a first-series loser.

Lightweight result: 1 Gerald Dreyer (South Africa), 2 Joseph Vissers (Belgium), 3 Svend Wad (Denmark). Semi-finals: Dreyer beat Wad on points, Vissers beat Wallace Smith (USA) on points. Final: Dreyer beat Vissers on points. Third place: Wad declared the winner as Smith withdrew injured.

Welterweight (up to 67kg)

26 entries, 10 first-series bouts, six boxers received byes to the second series.

Julius Torma, Hungarian-born but fighting for Czechoslovakia, was described by George Whiting as "one of the few winners who looked to be in no trouble at any stage of the competition". However, Whiting had no great regard for the overall standard in this division, citing Torma, Hank Herring (USA), Alessandro d'Ottavio (Italy) and Zygmunt Chychla (Poland) as "the best of a not very distinguished company". Torma – "always set for a punch, never caught on his heels" – beat the agile Herring in the final. Chychla lost to d'Ottavio in the third series (quarter-finals) but did rather better four years later in Helsinki by winning the gold.

According to the organising committee report, Torma was "probably the best defensive boxer in the competitions, and he was also a strong attacker. His defensive work was a joy to watch. Without moving his feet, he would sway out of distance or ride any punch that was close enough to be menacing. His sangfroid must have been disconcerting to his numerous opponents and coupled with his general ring-craft proved too much for all of them". Herring "certainly made Torma move around, but his snappy punches did not land often enough to give him the verdict". Britain's Max Shacklady stopped his Danish opponent in the first series but was then outpointed by a Spaniard, Aurelio Cadabeda.

Middleweight (up to 73kg)

25 entries, nine first-series bouts, seven boxers received byes to the second series.

This was a European-dominated division with second-series winners from Belgium, Eire, France, Great Britain, Holland, Hungary and Italy, and just one intruder from Uruguay. Britain's challenger was 19-year-old Ordinary Seaman Johnny Wright, of the Royal Navy, who had first shown promise as a national sea cadets' champion but had not even been remotely thought of as an Olympic "possible" at the start of the year. He unexpectedly won the ABA title and had now beaten a Swiss and an Argentinian in his first two Olympic bouts.

The first of the four qualifiers for the semi-finals was yet one more Italian, Fontana, and he was joined by Papp (Hungary), McKeon (Eire) and then Wright, with a further points win at the expense of a Dutchman. Papp, another of the "southpaws", was a two-handed puncher who had won all three of his fights by knockouts, requiring less than four rounds in total. McKeon had disposed of the European champion from France, Aimé-Joseph Escudie, in circumstances – at least in the ring itself – which met with George Whiting's full approval, as he said of them that they "gave us every kind of firework in a close, spirited, and

---

Welterweight result: 1 Julius Torma (Czechoslovakia), 2 Horace Herring (USA), 3 Alessandro d'Ottavio (Italy). Semi-finals: Herring beat Douglas du Preez (South Africa) on points, Torma beat d'Ottavio on points. Final: Torma beat Herring on points. Third place: d'Ottavio beat du Preez on points.

eminently sporting bout. Too good a bout, in fact, to have been followed by the resignations of French officials after McKeon had been declared the winner".

Papp and Wright won through to the final, and Papp took the title, though it was a close-run thing. Whiting concluded that "with a tightening up in the defence of his chin, Wright might easily have prevailed even over the vigorous Papp". The Hungarian moved down to the light-middleweight division (71kg limit) which was introduced at the 1952 Games and won there and again at Melbourne in 1956. He thus became the first triple champion in Olympic boxing history. In Melbourne he was asked who his toughest Olympic opponent had been and he replied, "That Englishman, Wright, at Wembley."

Even so, writing in the *Daily Mail*, Geoffrey Simpson disagreed with George Whiting's opinion and was adamant that "only Wright's pluck and endurance kept him going ... Wright's spirit in fighting back in the face of sustained punishment won the hearts of the crowd, and his last-round rally was heartening indeed, but the verdict was well won by the Hungarian". Celebrating with a splash the announcement of the decision, Papp's trainer dived fully clothed into the surrounding water.

Wright, who came from Potter's Bar in Hertfordshire, left the Royal Navy in 1949 and boxed as a professional from 1951 to 1953, but he suffered persistent back problems and had only fought for cash 13 times when he retired. He then became a publican in Barnet and subsequently took over the Fallow Buck pub at Clay Hill, Enfield, in Middlesex. Papp moved on from his illustrious career to become the national boxing coach from 1971 to 1992 and died in the year 2003 at the age of 77.

Light-heavyweight (up to 80kg)

24 entries, eight first-series bouts, eight boxers received byes to the second series.

The necessity of reducing entries to a last eight who would contest quarter-finals threw up anomalies in the draw such as at this weight, in which one-third of the starters had the distinct advantage of not being required to take part in the first series. Undeterred, the 21-year-old South African George Hunter eliminated a British-based Jamaican, an American, a Finn (Harri Siljander, who was to win a bronze in 1952) and an Argentinian to reach the final, where his opponent was Britain's military policeman Don Scott, whose shorter route was via a Hungarian, an Italian and an Australian.

Hunter was the winner of a close-fought contest and at the tournament's end was awarded the trophy for the most stylish boxer at any weight. It was a decision with which George Whiting was in complete agreement, and he also had much to say in praise of the beaten finalist: "To have been outpointed – and only narrowly

---

Middleweight result: 1 László Papp (Hungary), 2 Johnny Wright (Great Britain), 3 Ivano Fontana (Italy). Semi-finals: Papp beat Fontana on points, Wright beat Mike McKeon (Eire) on points. Final: Papp beat Wright on points. Third place: Fontana declared the winner as McKeon withdrew because of injury.

outpointed – by the immaculate Hunter was a fitting climax to the carefully-studied boxing of the 20-year-old Scott. The Englishman was handicapped from the start by an injured nose and a nerve-racking spell of insomnia. With a little more devil, Scott might have won the final." For the *Daily Mail*, Geoffrey Simpson again took a different view: "Hunter was the equal of Scott in leading and better by far as a counter-puncher and in-fighter."

Hunter turned professional soon afterwards and the following year won the South African light-heavyweight title, but in a career which continued until 1954 never fought outside his home country.

Heavyweight (over 80kg)

17 entries, one first-series bout, 15 boxers received byes to the second series.

The victim of being "one over the limit" for what would otherwise have been a neat quarter-final series of eight bouts was a Brazilian, Vicente dos Santos, who lost on points to Jay Lambert, of the USA, but even when full-scale action got under way it was not of great note – and almost predictably so. As George Whiting expressively put it: "The big fellows, I am afraid, again failed to provide the thrills so often promised but so rarely achieved by their kind."

The eventual winner was Rafael Iglesias, of Argentina, who produced the only knockout punch of any of the finals when he put his Swedish opponent, Gunnar Nilsson, down on the canvas in the second round. Iglesias, according to Whiting, "saved his hardest and best directed punches" for the final, while Nilsson had already "exceeded the hopes of even his most fervent countrymen" by getting there. Britain's Jack Gardner, a Grenadier Guardsman, started well by knocking out a well-considered Austrian, Karl Ameisbichler, but then lost to Hans Müller, of Switzerland, in their contest to decide a semi-final place. Gardner held the British professional heavyweight title from 1950 to 1952.

In terms of an overall team competition at the boxing tournament (four points for first, three for second, two for third, one for fourth), Italy and South Africa would have been joint leaders with 14pts, from Argentina (11), Hungary (eight) and Great Britain (six).

Light-heavyweight result: 1 George Hunter (South Africa), 2 Don Scott (Great Britain), 3 Mauro Cia (Argentina). Semi-finals: Scott beat Adrian Holmes (Australia) on points, Hunter beat Cia on points. Final: Hunter beat Scott on points. Third place: Cia beat Holmes, stopped in third round.

Heavyweight result: 1 Rafael Iglesias (Argentina), 2 Gunnar Nilsson (Sweden), 3 John Arthur (South Africa). Semi-finals: Nilsson beat Hans Müller (Switzerland) on points, Iglesias beat Arthur on points. Final: Iglesias beat Nilsson, knockout in second round. Third place: Arthur declared the winner as Müller withdrew injured.

It had been a good tournament, but it might well have ended disastrously. Of course, there had been the usual arguments about some of the decisions, erupting into widespread crowd misbehaviour on a couple of occasions, but this was no more than might be expected of such a volatile occasion as Olympic boxing, where variations in standards (more truthfully, competence) of judging can spark off emotive reactions. George Whiting was generous in his praise of the senior officials – JO McIntosh, honorary secretary of the ABA (Amateur Boxing Association); Lieutenant-Colonel Rudyard H Russell, ex-Irish Guards and now honorary secretary-treasurer of the AIBA (Association Internationale de Boxe Amateur); and JM Wyatt, the ABA president and AIBA president of honour. Without them, Whiting said, "Boxing could not possibly have made such an important contribution to the 1948 Games".

Of others who were involved Whiting was less tolerant. "Lastly", he wrote in the BOA report, "there were the referees and judges – those luckless people who by the sheer incompetence of a few of their number brought the Olympic boxing into disrepute, and near to ruin. Only ruthless elimination of the incompetents by a courageous jury of appeal saved the situation. Whether the jury should have been burdened with such an unpopular task, or whether, as seems obvious, the pruning should have been undertaken beforehand, will forever remain a topic in the inner councils of the world's amateur boxing rulers.

"To put it baldly, incompetent refereeing and uninstructed judging, especially in the early bouts, was directly responsible for the encouragement of much slapdash boxing, and for the consequent appeals, protests, arguments, accusations, resignations and demonstrations."

Subsequently, the AIBA published a highly critical report concerning a large number of the 56 judges who presided at the Games and issued wide-scale bans: "It can now be said that one-third of them were below the standard required for international boxing ... in all there were approximately 12 contests in which winners were returned as losers due to bad judging." Of the 37 judges who survived the AIBA "purge", all were from Europe, except for two from Egypt and one each from Argentina, Ceylon, South Africa and the USA. Of 37 referees, the 20 who were retained were all Europeans, other than one from South Africa and one from the USA.

Happily, the organising committee's official report concluded on an encouraging note for those with a sense of boxing history and aesthetics: "It is a tribute to the birthplace of boxing to say that almost all of the winners, and many of those who reached the later stages, owed much to the fact that they boxed in the traditional English style. True, they all showed that they could meet emergencies by 'fighting' when necessary, but there is little doubt that the upstanding straight-punch style is still the basis of good boxing."

Chapter 18

How Don Scott won his Silver Medal

No headlines. No razzamatazz. Just a case of
doing your best.

D ON SCOTT WAS no more than eight years old when his father
bought him his first set of boxing gloves, and it was at the age of
about 15 that the youngster's coach in Derby, Bob Curley, decided
that he might have a future champion on his hands. Just three
years later, in 1946, Scott won the Midland Counties' middleweight title and
reached the semi-finals of the Amateur Boxing Association championships.
National service in the army, as a Corporal physical training instructor in the
Royal Military police, fast-forwarded his progress in the ring, and after winning
his bout in a match between Britain and Denmark at Wembley in 1947 he set his
sights on Olympic selection at light-heavyweight the following season.

"I hadn't even won an ABA title at that stage," he recalled more than half a
century later, "but when you're young – and remember I was still only 19 – the
sky sometimes seems the only limit to your hopes. After all the war years it was a
wonderful relief to think about something as special as the Olympics in our own
country, and not about threatening shadows, like bombing of civilians or young
servicemen being killed or permanently damaged."

In May of 1948 he won his first ABA title at Wembley, surviving a semi-final
knockdown by Jim Alsopp, of Birkenhead, before stopping Jack Sully, from
Wales, in the second round of the final. A match between the Imperial Services
and the ABA followed, with Scott scoring a second win on points over Alsopp.
Scott remembered, "It wasn't like the big headlines and the razzamatazz today,
but even so many years later I can remember finding it hard to appreciate that me,

an apprentice turner from Derby, just doing my national service, was about to box in the actual modern Olympic Games in London."

Troubled by a nose injury, which led to a subsequent operation, he was glad to have a bye in the first round of the Olympic tournament, and he then defeated a Hungarian and the next day beat an Italian and then an Australian to reach the final against South Africa's talented George Hunter. "Two Olympic fights in one day was a bit special," Scott agreed.

"Matter of fact, the night before the final I found I were so marked up that I went to bed with a piece of steak over each eye to reduce the swelling, and I didn't sleep well. Hunter was outstanding, of course, and that's why he got the award as the best boxer all-round. I did my best, and some judges thought I boxed really well."

At the 1950 Empire & Commonwealth Games in Auckland Scott won the light-heavyweight gold medal, and he had some 80 bouts altogether as an amateur. "But I only wish I could have had a more successful career when I turned professional in the spring of 1950," he said regretfully. "Looking back, it was wrong to fight as a heavyweight when I weighed less than 13 stone. Being 6ft 2in tall, when I did go down to light-heavy at least I won the Midlands area title as a pro."

In 2005 he was delighted to be invited to Buckingham Palace for a reception to mark the centenary of the British Olympic Association. "I'd met the Duke of Edinburgh at a reception at the Savoy Hotel after the 1948 Olympics had ended, and who would have thought that a lad from Derby would have seen him again all those years later?" he enthused.

The following February Don Scott died at the age of 77. The man who beat him at Wembley, George Hunter, died the same year, aged 78.

Chapter 19

CROOKED KEELS, AND THE EMERGENCE OF AN OLYMPIC LEGEND

Canoeing. Henley-on-Thames, 11–12 August.

JOHN DUDDERIDGE KNEW very well the magnitude of the task facing him. It was not a question of finding British canoeists capable of challenging for the highest honours – that was a cause long since lost – but of devising a course which would satisfy the needs of the visiting competitors from 15 other countries. In Berlin 12 years before, when canoeing had been introduced to the Olympics, Austria had won three of the nine gold medals, Czechoslovakia and Germany two each, Canada and Sweden one each. The last World Championships had been held in Sweden in 1938, and of the 12 events the home country won five, Germany four, Czechoslovakia two and France one.

Dudderidge, honorary secretary of the British Canoe Union and also the Olympic team manager, had competed in Berlin, where Britain's best performer had been George Lawton, who placed a respectable eighth of 13 in a 10,000 metres race for folding kayaks. This was an event which would not be held at Henley, but Lawton would still be in attendance because he had been appointed assistant to Dudderidge. The main canoe-racing venues in Britain, which had been revived for use only the year before, were at Teddington, in Middlesex, and at Windermere, far off to the north-west of England in the Lake District, but it was eventually agreed that the rowing course at Henley-on-Thames would be the site for canoeing two days after the oarsmen had vacated it.

A claim was later made by Dudderidge in the BOA official report that the decision was "of valuable service to the sport of canoe racing generally, as it brought this form of competition before the wider public gathered to watch the rowing". It has to be said that there was no obvious evidence of any beneficial spin-off, particularly as the narrow stretch of water at Henley was not at all suitable for the kayak events, where the numbers entered were too great to have the usual mass starts and so competitors had to be sent off in time-trial fashion at 30-second intervals. For both those watching and those taking part, it was not easy to gauge exactly what was happening, whereas in Berlin as many as 20 competitors had started abreast and thus provided an exciting spectacle.

It would seem that the underlying reason for having the canoeing events at Henley was purely economical. In these "Austerity Games", where every effort was made, and justifiably so, to use existing facilities and avoid unnecessary expenditure, it made sense to take advantage of the arrangements which had already existed for the annual Henley Regatta or had been specially put in place for the Olympic rowing, whatever the drawbacks for those who would have to make the best of them. There was, at least, a satisfying historic link because the first recorded canoe races had taken place on the River Thames in 1867.

The Olympic canoeing events at Henley divided themselves into two distinct styles – Kayak and Canadian. The Kayak canoes were based on the hunting craft used by Eskimo fishermen and were long, narrow, decked, and with a foot-operated rudder, if desired. In Kayak events competitors are seated and use a double-bladed paddle alternatively on each side of the craft. The Canadian canoes were based on the open birch-bark craft of the Native Americans and no rudders were permitted. In Canadian events competitors are in a half-kneeling position, switching the single-bladed paddle from side to side. The standard distances raced were at 1000 and 10,000 metres, and a women's event at 500 metres was enterprisingly added instead of having a men's relay.

Kayak pairs 10,000 metres result: 1 Gunnar Åkerlund & Hans Wetterström (Sweden) 46min 9.4sec, 2 Ivar Mathiesen & Knut Östbye (Norway) 46:44.8, 3 Thor Axelsson & Nils Björklof (Finland) 46:48.2, 4 Alfred Christensen & Finn Rasmussen (Denmark) 47:17.5, 5 Gyula Andrási & János Urányi (Hungary) 47:33.1, 6 Cornelius Koch & Hendrik Stroo (Holland) 47:35.6, 7 Ludvik Klima & Karel Lomecký (Czechoslovakia) 48:14.9, 8 Hilaire Deprez & Jozef Massy (Belgium) 48:23.1, 9 Walter Piemann & Alfred Umgeher (Austria) 48:24.5, 10 Alfons Jezewski & Marian Matloka (Poland) 48:25.6, 11 Fritz Frey & Werner Zimmermann (Switzerland) 48:33.2, 12 Richard Flèche & Maurice Graffen (France) 50:10.1, 13 Raymond Clark & John Eiseman (USA) 50:26.6, 14 Gerald Covey & Henry Harper (Canada) 53:04.2, 15 René Fonck & Jean Nickels (Luxembourg) 53:46.0.

Kayak singles 10,000 metres result: 1 Gert Fredriksson (Sweden) 50:47.7, 2 Kurt Wires (Finland) 51:18.2, 3 Eivind Skabo (Norway) 51:35.4, 4 Knud Ditlevsen (Denmark) 51:54.2, 5 Henri Eberhardt (France) 52:09.0, 6 Jochem Bobeldijk (Holland) 52:13.2, 7 Czeslaw Sobieraj (Poland) 52:15.2, 8 Alfred Corbiaux (Belgium) 53:23.5, 9 Jan Matocha (Czechoslovakia) 53:51.0, 10 Herbert Klepp (Austria) 55:11.7, 11 Emil Bottlang (Switzerland) 55:33.7, 12 Ernie Riedel (USA) 56:34.5, 13 Marcel Lentz (Luxembourg) 59:58.2.

Canadian pairs 10,000 metres result: 1 Stephen Lysak & Stephan Macknowski (USA) 55:55.4, 2 Václav Havel & Jiří Pecka (Czechoslovakia) 57:38.5, 3 Georges Dransart & Georges Gandil (France) 58:00.8, 4 Karl Molnar & Viktor Salmhofer (Austria) 58:59.3, 5 Bert Oldershaw & William Stevenson (Canada) 59:48.4, 6 Gunnar Johansson & Verner Wettersten (Sweden) 1:03:34.4.

The course for the 10,000 metres races on the first day was made up of four laps of the river, starting downstream in the direction of Temple Island, around which an anticlockwise turn was made to go upstream past the Henley Regatta enclosures to turn again at Rod Eyot Island. The last 2000 metres was a straight run to the finish. So the spectators – such as they were after a morning of heavy and continuous rain – could actually see the kayaks passing on four occasions. All the 16 countries which were entered for the canoeing events were represented in the kayak pairs, except for Great Britain, but Scandinavians were totally dominant, with the Swedes, Gunnar Åkerlund and Hans Wetterström, winning from Norway, Finland and Denmark.

Åkerlund was a carpenter by trade and Wetterström a fireman, and the pair of them were to win the world title two years later and then lose the Olympic gold medal in 1952 by only four-tenths of a second to Finland, with the same Norwegian pairing as at Henley finishing fifth. Wetterström would also be fourth with a different partner when the event was held for the last time at Melbourne in 1956, and the Hungarian gold-medallists there would include the Henley fifth-placer, UránYi.

The same four countries swept the board in the kayak singles, which marked the first Olympic appearance of Gert Fredriksson, who won for Sweden and would become the most successful of all Olympic canoeists, accumulating six gold medals, a silver and a bronze through to the Games of 1960, by which time he was 40 years old. He was then appointed as coach of the Swedish team at the 1964 Games which won gold in the kayak singles and pairs. At Henley, Fredriksson comfortably beat a Finn, Kurt Wires, who would be one of the winning pair at the Helsinki Games, and in fifth place was Henri Eberhardt, of France, who had been a silver-medallist in Berlin. The times in the singles and pairs events reflected the toughness of the course compared with the point-to-point waterway used in Berlin: singles, Berlin 46:01.6, Henley 50:47.7; pairs, Berlin 41:45.0, Henley 46:09.4. Again there was no Briton in the singles event.

The Canadian events at 10,000 metres drew only five competitors for the singles and six for the pairs, and so in both races all set off together. Here the balance of national power was very different and the medals went to Canada, Czechoslovakia, France and the USA. The American crew of Steve Lysak and Steve Macknowski, who were both from Yonkers, New York, took the lead with the very first few strokes in their home-made mahogany canoe, eventually winning by an enormous margin from the Czechs. There was a scare for the winners after the race was over when it was reported that they had collided with one of the buoys at the Rod Eyot turning, but the judges wisely decided that as it was a paddle which had struck the buoy, and no possible advantage could have been gained, the result would stand.

The Swede, Wettersten (not to be confused with his Kayak Pairs compatriot, Wetterström), who was one of the pair who finished a very distant last, fared rather better in subsequent Olympics, placing sixth of nine in the 1000 metres singles in 1956. The Frenchman, Dransart, was to win a silver medal in the 10,000 metres pairs at the 1956 Games with a different partner.

The singles was won by another Czech, František Čapek, and this led to a controversy which far overshadowed any concerns there may have been about the course or the time-trial method of racing. The race, in any case, was something of an experiment because such a distance had not been contested before by Canadian canoes, but it was the craft themselves which were the centre of attention and some consternation. John Dudderidge explained the situation at length in his article for the BOA report:

"In this event there appeared for the first time what came to be described as the 'crooked' canoes. These canoes had been brought over by several European teams, and the chief feature which distinguished them from normal canoes was the curve in their keels. It is usual to build a canoe with a straight keel, so that it runs true. If the keel is curved, it will have a tendency to turn to one side. When a canoe is paddled by one man using a single blade, the drive of the paddle on one side tends to turn the canoe away from the paddling side. This tendency is corrected by the paddler, and skill in making this correction with minimum loss of power is the chief factor in single Canadian technique.

"By curving the keel in the appropriate direction the two turning tendencies can be made to neutralise each other, and the canoe will run straight without need for steering by the paddler. Such a situation will allow the paddler to devote the whole of his strength and effort to forward drive and give him an advantage over an opponent who has to steer as well as drive."

Protests about the "crooked" canoes had been registered before the events had started, but the International Canoe Federation had decided that there was nothing in the rules to prevent their use at Henley. As at the same time they banned them for future competition, this could be said to have been equivocation. Čapek used a "crooked" canoe to win the title and the Czech management generously lent a similar craft to the American Frank Havens, who finished second just over half a minute behind. In third place was Norm Lane, of Canada, almost another two minutes further back in a conventional craft, and one could sympathise with his resigned comment after the race had finished that "I sometimes felt as though I was pushing a barge". Havens won the gold at the 1952 Games and was eighth in 1956, after which the event was discontinued.

The 1000-metre events took place on the second day, with heats for the kayaks in the morning and finals in the evening. The eight who went through to the men's kayak singles final from the 15 starters came from Austria, Czechoslovakia, Denmark, Finland, France, Holland, Norway and Sweden (Fredriksson again). The only non-European entrants in the heats had been Thomas Horton, from the USA, who was eliminated by a decisive margin, and a valiant Briton, Norman

---

Canadian singles 10,000 metres result: 1 František Čapek (Czechoslovakia) 1:02:50.2, 2 Frank Havens (USA) 1:02:40.4, 3 Norm Lane (Canada) 1:04:35.3, 4 Raymond Argentin (France) 1:06:44.2, 5 Ingemar Andersson (Sweden) 1:07:27.1.

Dobson, who finished last but only three-tenths of a second behind a Hungarian. The kayak pairs qualifiers came from much the same countries as in the singles, except that Hungary and Canada took the place of Austria and France. The British pair of Jack Henderson and John Simmons was again last but not desperately so.

There were 10 women competing at 500 metres, from Austria, Belgium, Czechoslovakia, Denmark, Finland, France, Great Britain, Holland, Hungary and Sweden, and the two heats reached a bizarre conclusion as Sweden's Ingrid Apelgren finished last in the second heat in a faster time than the winner of the first heat. The only other required elimination was that of Joyce Richards, of Great Britain, a physical education teacher from Watford, in Hertfordshire, who was almost a quarter of a minute down on fourth place in her heat.

Gert Fredriksson duly won his second gold medal in the kayak singles final with what Dudderidge described as a demonstration of "his superiority and confidence in a striking fashion". In his morning heat Fredriksson had lingered nonchalantly in fourth place until 50 metres from the finish and then swept through to win by one-tenth of a second – all quite unnecessary, of course, because he was already far ahead of the fifth-placed canoeist and would have qualified anyway, but no doubt most unsettling for his opponents. In the final there was never any question of the result, and the superb technique and immense power of the Swede brought him home almost seven seconds ahead of the Dane, Kobberup, with Eberhardt taking the bronze for France to become one of a select few to have won Olympic medals in any sport both pre-war and post-war.

The kayak pairs produced yet another Swedish win and a Scandinavian whitewash as Hans Berglund and Lennart Klingström beat their Danish rivals in an intensely exciting race by only two-tenths of a second, and the first five finishers were separated by no more than 2½ seconds. However, there was an unfortunate sequel to the race when the Hungarians, including Andrási, who had already competed in the 10,000 metres, were disqualified after they had finished in the bronze-medal position for the transgression known as "hanging" – that is following in the wake of another canoe. John Dudderidge went to the pains of commenting in his report that "it is not always easy to avoid the appearance of 'hanging', even when innocent of deliberate intent", and this remark seemed to be as close as maybe he felt was diplomatic to saying that he thought that the decision was a harsh one. The exclusion of the Hungarians let the Finnish pair in for their second bronzes after the 10,000 metres.

The Canadian singles and pairs events again required only straight finals – and "crooked" canoes. Like his winning Czech team-mate in the 10,000 metres singles event, Josef Holeček made use of one of the new canoes and won rather easily from Douglas Bennett, of Canada, who was in a conventional craft. There was no

---

Kayak singles 1000 metres result: 1 Gert Fredriksson (Sweden) 4:33.2, 2 Johan Frederik Kobberup (Denmark) 4:39.9, 3 Henri Eberhardt (France) 4:41.4, 4 Hans Martin Gulbrandsen (Norway) 4:41.7, 5 Willem Frederik van der Kroft (Holland) 4:43.5, 6 Harry Åkerfelt (Finland) 4:44.2, 7 Lubomir Vambera (Czechoslovakia) 4:44.3, 8 Walter Piemann (Austria) 4:50.3.

doubting, though, Holeček's class because he was to take the world title in 1950 and the Olympic gold again at Helsinki in 1952 by almost as great a margin.

The Canadian pairs produced an historic win for Jan Brzák, who had also taken a gold medal in this event with a different partner 12 years before in Berlin. Brzák went on to win the 1950 world title and the silver at the 1952 Olympics with his Henley partner, Bohumil Kudrna. Then in 1955, by now aged 43, Brzák proved his boundless stamina as well as his speed by canoeing some 200 kilometres to Prague in 20 hours with 46-year-old Bohuslav Karlik, who had been the Canadian singles 1000 metres silver-medallist in 1936. The US and French crews which followed Brzák and Kudrna home along the Thames had also taken the gold and bronze respectively at 10,000 metres. The Belgians suffered the mishap of one of their crew members falling overboard.

Denmark was one of the countries in the forefront of campaigning for a women's race to be included at Henley, and so it was just reward that it should be a Danish woman who won the inaugural title. In what may be a unique Olympic occurrence – though it is rare to find anything happening in an Olympic Games which has not taken place in some similar form before – the first four in the final finished in exactly the same order as they had in their heat. Hoff actually made the least advance, from 2:32.2 to 2:31.9, but it was still sufficient to give her victory in a splendidly close contest which more than justified the fight to get women accepted at Henley in the first place.

Sylvi Saimo, of Finland, was to improve precisely 20 seconds in time and six places in the order of finishing to win the gold when the Games came to her home country four years later. Then this event, like so many others across the range of Olympic sports, was to become an Eastern European monopoly (five wins by the USSR and two by the German Democratic Republic) until the boycott-affected Games of 1984 when Sweden won their first gold medals for 20 years.

Despite the unsuitability of the course and the controversy over the "crooked" keels, the canoeing events had gone off well. It was felt that the results would have

---

Kayak pairs 1000 metres result: 1 Hans Berglund & Lennart Klingström (Sweden) 4:07.3, 2 Ejvind Hansen & Bernhard Jensen (Denmark) 4:07.5, 3 Thor Axelsson & Nils Björklof (Finland) 4:08.7, 4 Ivar Mathiesen & Knut Östbye (Norway) 4:09.1, 5 Otto Kroutil & Miloš Pech (Czechoslovakia) 4:09.8, 6 Cornelius Gravesteyn & Willem Pool (Holland) 4:15.8, 7 Gerald Covey & Henry Harper (Canada) 4:56.8. Disqualified – János Toldi & Gyula Andrási (Hungary).

Canadian singles 1000 metres result: 1 Josef Holeček (Czechoslovakia) 5:42.0, 2 Douglas Bennett (Canada) 5:53.3, 3 Robert Boutigny (France) 5:55.9, 4 Ingemar Andersson (Sweden) 6:08.0, 5 Frank Havens (USA) 6:14.3, 6 Harold Maidment (Great Britain) 6:37.0.

Canadian pairs 1000 metres result: 1 Jan Brzák & Bohumil Kudrna (Czechoslovakia) 5:07.1, 2 Stephen Lysak & Stephan Macknowski (USA) 5:08.2, 3 Georges Dransart & Georges Gandil (France) 5:15.2, 4 Douglas Bennett & Harry Poulton (Canada) 5:20.7, 5 Karl Molnar & Viktor Salmhofer (Austria) 5:37.3, 6 Gunnar Johansson & Verner Wettersten (Sweden) 5:44.9, 7 Mike Symons & Hugh Van Zwaanenberg (Great Britain) 5:50.8. Did not finish – Hubert Coomans & Jean Dubois (Belgium), man overboard.

been no different had the new canoes been disallowed, and the overall success of the occasion was a tribute to the British organisers, whose sport had been in complete abeyance from 1939 to 1947. Even the modest performances of the eight British canoeists were no cause for dissatisfaction, as John Dudderidge pointed out: "The British team for the Games had to be forged in less than a year, and as suitable craft had to be built the effective period of preparation was reduced to about six months. The normal period of training for international competition is three or four years, and although the British competitors were not able to hold their own against their more experienced opponents they showed good style, pluck and determination."

Kayak singles (women) 500 metres result: 1 Karen Hoff (Denmark) 2:31.9, 2 Alida van der Anker-Doedens (Holland) 2:32.8, 3 Fritzi Schwingl (Austria) 2:32.9, 4 Klára Bánfalvi (Hungary) 2:33.8, 5 Ružena Koštalová (Czechoslovakia) 2:38.2, 6 Sylvi Saimo (Finland) 2:38.4, 7 Anna van Marcke (Belgium) 2:43.4, 8 Catherine Vautrin (France) 2:44.4.

Chapter 20

ON A BICYCLE BUILT FOR TWO, REG STILL HAS TO SETTLE FOR SILVER

Cycling. Herne Hill and Windsor Great Park, 7–13 August

REG HARRIS WAS as firm a British favourite for a gold medal as any that could possibly be found. His virtues were extolled by all the leading cycle-racing correspondents, among them WJ Mills, editor of the authoritative magazine, *The Bicycle*, who said of him that he "has the speed, track craft and experience of international racing; he has, moreover, a burning ambition to win an Olympic title". The newspaper based in the city where Harris trained, the *Manchester Guardian*, claimed of their favoured son that he "may well be regarded as almost certain to carry off the Olympic title".

Every word of the praise was fully justified. Harris had won the world title in 1947, and the man he beat, Cor Bijster, of Holland, would not be at the Olympics because he had turned professional. Harris had been born in Bury, in Lancashire, and was now 28, having started racing in 1936 at the age of 16. He had come close to losing his life during the war, escaping from a burning tank while serving with the Army in North Africa. He won the first of his numerous national track-cycling titles in 1944 and after the London Olympics would go on to a glittering career which entirely merits the assessment of him as Britain's greatest ever sprint cyclist. He became a professional in 1949 and won the world title that year, and again in 1950, 1951 and 1954. At 36 he was still good enough to reach the final. At 54 he made a comeback and astonishingly won the British title yet again! The one prize that eluded him was an Olympic gold.

The title hopes may well have been lost before Harris even put a foot in a pedal on the Herne Hill track, the South London venue for Olympic track cycling, which had been refurbished after serving as an RAF barrage-balloon site during the war. There was widespread media coverage of a dispute between Harris and the British team management because of his apparent insistence in going his own way in the pre-Games training programme, and a week before the racing was due to start it was reported that he had been summarily dropped from the team. It was only on Thursday 5 August, two days before Harris was due to start racing, that the National Cyclists' Union hierarchy was said to have changed its mind and he was reinstated. But all the wrangling and a furiously divided media campaign could have done nothing for his peace of mind. Oddly, a year or so later it was claimed by WJ Mills in an article in *World Sports* that there never had been any major differences between Harris and officialdom, and that the affair had been largely a newspaper exaggeration, though this version of events does not tally with the recollection of one of Harris's team-mates, Tommy Godwin.

Harris was beaten in the sprint final by an Italian, Mario Ghella, who had been described on the strength of his previous season's form by WJ Mills as not being "in the same class". However, a year can make a lot of difference, particularly as Ghella was still only 19, and Mills was one of the experts who was soon beginning to change his mind once the sprint qualifying rounds had got under way. "It was quite obvious from a study of the preliminary heats", Mills was to write in the BOA official report, "that the final was going to be between Ghella and Harris." The 1000 metres sprint started at the beginning of the home straight and finished at the end of it to make up the full distance of 1000 metres as two laps of the Herne Hill track amounted to 920 metres, but it mattered not in an event in which the two contestants jockey for position from the start on the steep banking at what can be a snail's pace and then hurl all their efforts into what is usually a flat-out last 200 metres.

The sprint competition started on the opening day, Saturday 7 August, and there were 11 first-round heats and five repêchage heats (the latter designed to give the losers a second chance) to reduce the 25 starters to 16 for the eighth-finals. One of the contests, between a Cuban and an Indian, continued for more than 3¼ minutes; the quickest, lasting 1min 42.7sec, involved the same Cuban against a Dutchman. The fastest last 200 metres was ridden in 12.4sec by Clodomiro Cortoni, of Argentina; the slowest in 17.2sec, by Erich Welt, of Austria. Again, this detail was of limited significance. The real racing was still to come, starting with the quarter-finals which were to involve Bazzano (Australia), van de Velde (Belgium), Masanes Gimeno (Chile), Schandorff (Denmark), Ghella (Italy), Harris (Great Britain), Rocca (Uruguay) and Heid (USA). The Chilean was the surprise, having beaten the favoured French champion, Jacques Bellanger, by half a wheel, but finalising the last eight was not as straightforward a process as might have been anticipated.

The first of what sometimes seemed to be interminable delays had been caused when the Uruguayan management protested against the disqualification of their man, Rocca, after a crash in his eighth-final against the Dutchman, Hijzelendoorn. By the time that the objection lodged in favour of Rocca had been considered and upheld, it was decided to re-run the race on the Monday. So only three of the four quarter-finals could be completed on the Saturday, and Ghella, Schandorff and Harris went through, to be joined eventually by Bazzano, who beat Rocca two days later. All of these encounters had been scheduled to be decided as the best of three races but in each case were won in two straight runs.

Olympic history is not always of the greatest help in forecasting who wins next, but it was notable that neither France nor Holland, who between them had won six sprint titles since 1896, were represented at this stage, and nor, of course, was Germany, for whom Toni Merkens had controversially won in 1936 against a Dutchman but had not lived long to enjoy his success, dying in the Second World War fighting on the Russian front. British sprinters, ominously, had occupied second place in 1906, 1908 and 1920 but had reached no finals since.

The semi-finals brought together Ghella against Schandorff and Harris against the Italian-born Bazzano. Ghella again won in two races and set a track record of 11.9sec for the last 200 metres in the latter which confirmed what a strong contender he was. Harris then beat Bazzano. The final came as something of an anticlimax because in the first race Ghella caught Harris by surprise and opened up a five-length lead, with Harris easing up when he realised that he could not win, and then in the second race Ghella led again, held off three attacks by Harris, and won by the best part of two lengths as Harris again slackened off, his chance of gold gone. All the watching and waiting that preceded the final mad dash meant that both races lasted more than four minutes.

On the victory rostrum Harris did not seem too disappointed. On the contrary, he wore a broad smile, and maybe his thoughts had already turned to the attractions of the paid ranks and the prospect of winning the world professional title the following year. He duly did so, becoming the first man to take that title at the first attempt. Before that, though, he was to bow the knee again to Ghella in the amateur sprint at the World Championships in Holland a month after the Olympics. Ghella beat the Dane, Schandorff, in the final, and Harris had to settle for a bronze-medal win over his fellow Briton, Alan Bannister.

Harris was to be voted Britain's "Sportsman of the Year" for 1949 in separate ballots organised by the *Daily Express* and by the *Sporting Record* weekly newspaper. The fruits of his professional success were further apparent from the regular advertisements in the press in which he was shown extolling the virtues of "CurAcho – the Celebrated Spirit Embrocation" and of the Raleigh Lenton

---

Sprint result (1000 metres): 1 Mario Ghella (Italy), 2 Reg Harris (Great Britain), 3 Axel Schandorff (Denmark). Semi-finals: Ghella beat Schandorff 2-0, ¾-of-a-length and three lengths, last 200 metres 12.1sec and 11.9; Harris beat Charlie Bazzano (Australia) 2-0, one length and ¾-of-a-length, last 200 metres 13.7 and 12.7. Final: Ghella beat Harris 2-0, three lengths and 1½ lengths, last 200 metres 12.2 and 12.0. Third place: Schandorff beat Bazzano 2-0, ¾-of-a-length and "lengths", last 200 metres 12.9 and 12.0.

sports bicycle, astride which he was depicted carrying out his road training in natty plus-four trousers and a chunky sweater.

The 4000 metres team pursuit also began on the opening day, and a dress rehearsal the previous year at Herne Hill had provided a useful guide as to what might happen. A French quartet had beaten Great Britain by just over two seconds in 5min 0.4sec, and even though only one of the eight riders in the two teams involved went on to gain Olympic selection the race had given some idea of what level of performance would be needed to win the gold. There was no comparison with the Olympic record of 4:45.0 set by France in Berlin, and nor was there expected to be on the recognisably slow Herne Hill surface. This is an event in which the teams start on opposite sides of the track and each rider in turn takes the lead to maintain optimum speed. The most successful teams are those who best combine their speed with smooth lead-changing.

The starting-points were adjusted for the team pursuit – as they would also be for the 1000 metres time-trial and 2000 metres tandem events – so that the exact 4000 metres distance would be covered, setting off from opposite entrances to the straights. The fastest of the first-round times was 5:03.6 by France, but the only close race in the eight heats was Denmark's win over Australia, 5:04.1 to 5:06.5. The Australians still qualified for the quarter-finals because theirs was the fastest losing time, and they were joined by Belgium, Great Britain, Italy, Switzerland and Uruguay, as well as France and Denmark. Italy had won every Olympic title from 1920 to 1932 and had then placed second to France in 1936. Great Britain, winners in 1908, had been second in 1920 and third in 1928, 1932 and 1936. Two of Britain's Berlin bronze-medallists, Ernie Mills and Charlie King, had been appointed coaches to the quartet chosen to represent Britain at Herne Hill.

France and Great Britain were drawn together in the first semi-final, and the French won decisively, 4:54.4 to 4:59.1. The Italians were actually a second or so slower than the British in beating the surprising Uruguayans in the second semi-final, and it may be that the British would have done better with this draw. Italy included the world champion at the 4000 metres individual pursuit, Arnaldo Benfenati, in their team, and Uruguay had the man whom Benfenati had beaten in that final, Atilio Francois, in theirs. There was no individual pursuit on the 1948 Olympic programme, and nor would there be at any Games until 1964. It would be another 40 years before there would be any women's track cycling.

The team pursuit final lacked nothing in drama, even though both teams were clearly tired after their hard semi-final qualifiers. The Italians were already two lengths up after three laps and double that ahead after seven laps (a time advantage of 2.4sec), but the French wore them down and took the lead two laps from the finish, despite dropping one of their team, to ride out easy winners when the Italians came apart in the closing stages, losing two of their quartet. The British team, which included Alan Geldard, a clubmate of Reg Harris at Manchester Wheelers, produced a faster time in winning the third-place match, in which Uruguay had led by 2.0sec after three laps but were eventually very well beaten. It was the third successive Games that France, Italy and Great Britain had shared the team-pursuit medals and it would happen again in Melbourne in 1956, by which time British quartets would have won six consecutive sets of bronze medals.

Naturally, the French victory at Herne Hill should have been the cause for much rejoicing in the country at the very heart of cycle-racing, but there was one Frenchman who was not at all happy, even though he could claim a lion's share of the credit for the gold-medal success. Paul Ruinart was the manager of Vélo Club de Levallois, whose quartet had won the French national title earlier in the season and could therefore have expected to be chosen *en bloc* for the Games. The authorities of the Fédération Francaise de Cyclisme (FFC), in their wisdom, decided to replace one of the VCL team, Jean Ferrand, with a rider from a rival club, Pierre Adam, of AS Boulogne-Billancourt, and Monsieur Ruinart was still seething about the matter even after the French triumph.

He was interviewed in the next issue of *But et Club*, one of those sepia-printed weekly illustrated sports magazines which flourished in France from the 1930s through to the 1960s, and he pulled no punches. "I knew that Monsieur Revelly, the Games selector, wanted at any price to take only part of the VCL team to form 'his' Olympic team," he ranted. "I even believe that he wanted only two men from my club. I also know, without knowing the reason, which I *would* like to know one day, that Jean Ferrand was on the 'condemned' list. One day I will have my revenge. I hope to go with my VCL team to Herne Hill and win back our track record to prove to the FFC that they have no right to deprive VCL of a title which is theirs by right."

Quel horreur! Monsieur Ruinart even invoked the sacred memory of Joan of Arc in his diatribe against the selectors, quoting the words of her biographer, Lucien Fabre: "The majority of imbeciles who exist in every gathering of mankind finish up by becoming dominant and ruling the others. They submerge the elite, stifle them." Now this, of course, is a sentiment regarding officialdom which is shared by many a coach, manager and competitor in any sport you care to name, but it is not often expressed in public in quite so vehement a manner!

In all probability, the French Federation officials would not have been too surprised at the attack on their integrity. Back in 1936, Ruinart was already manager of the VCL club and was described, as one might have expected, as a dynamic and outspoken personality with radical ideas about training methods. He had lambasted the Olympic management then for demanding that the French sprint and tandem cyclists race off against each other in a last-minute trial before the Games. One reason why Ruinart felt so strongly about the 1948 team-pursuit selection was that another VCL quartet – intact this time – had won the gold in Berlin. In his mind, it was VCL who should have been defending their title, not France hers.

The pre-eminent French cycling writer, René de la Tour, had some sound advice for the irate Monsieur Ruinart, whose temper had been further frayed by the fact that he was not one of a dozen or so club officials invited by the French

Federation to Herne Hill. "Paul Ruinart is a wise man who knows he should be happier with something other than posing for a photograph." wrote de la Tour soothingly. "For example, to have been the real artisan of our first major cycling success in London."

Charles Coste, the captain of the French pursuit team at Herne Hill, kept well clear of the controversy, preferring to talk only about what happened on the track. "Were we ever in danger?" he asked rhetorically. "Not really. Even in the semi-final, when the British had taken the lead after a fast start, it only served to reinforce our confidence. I knew what the four of us could do. We had worked well together on our relay. No one was going to give up in our team. In short, we were ready. We only regret one thing. That the state of the surface at Herne Hill did not allow us to achieve the time which would really indicate the value of our performance."

Coste went on to enjoy a successful professional road-racing career, winning the Paris–Limoges classic in 1953, and then became a race director and journalist before being killed in a plane crash. One of his team-mates, Serge Blusson, had some outstanding road-racing successes, winning the amateur Paris–Evreux race in 1949, which Robert Charpentier had also won in the same year as his Olympic triumph of 1936. Blusson then won Paris–Limoges in his first year as a professional in 1950, the Grand Prix de Plouay in 1953 and the Tour de Picardie in 1957, though his most notable performance was probably finishing third in the Milan–San Remo race of 1952. Milan–San Remo – "La Primavera" – had been the opening one-day classic of the road-racing season since 1907, and is still so more than a century later.

Reg Harris's sprint defeat was by no means the end of his Olympic ambitions. Rather against expectations, he had decided to also ride in the tandem event, which began on the Monday evening, with clubmate Alan Bannister as his partner. Harris and Bannister were unquestionably the best in Britain at this event and had won the 1947 national title, but it was thought that Harris would prefer to concentrate his efforts on the sprint. The 10 countries which entered tandem pairings were Argentina, Austria, Belgium, Denmark, France, Great Britain, Holland, Italy, Switzerland and the USA. Great Britain had won in 1906 and 1920; France in 1908, 1924 and 1932; Holland in 1928; and Germany in 1936.

Harris and Bannister beat Austria and Holland – the latter in a race lasting almost eight minutes – to reach the semi-finals, where they were joined by France, Italy and Switzerland. Like the British duo, the French and Italians had also selected leading sprint specialists as half their teams – René Faye and Ferdinando Terruzzi respectively. The British punctured while leading with 200 metres to

---

4000 metres team pursuit result: 1 France (Charles Coste, Serge Blusson, Ferdinand Decanali, Pierre Adam), 2 Italy (Arnaldo Benfenati, Guido Bernardi, Anselmo Citterio, Rino Pucci), 3 Great Britain (Alan Geldard, Tommy Godwin, Dave Ricketts, Wilf Waters). Semi-finals: France, 4:54.4, beat Great Britain, 4:59.1; Italy, 5:00.5, beat Uruguay (Atilio Francois, Juan de Armas, Luis de los Santos, Waldemar Bernatsky), 5:06.3. Final: France, 4:57.8, beat Italy, 5:36.7. Third place: Great Britain, 4:55.8, beat Uruguay, 5:04.4.

go but went on to beat the French by a length in the re-run, while Italy easily disposed of Switzerland by six lengths. For what it was worth both finalists had produced a fastest last 200 metres of 11.2sec during the course of the qualifying rounds.

The delays which bedevilled the Olympic cycling programme affected the tandem final more than any other, and the third and deciding race was held in almost complete darkness. The British had started well by leading the first race for most of the closing lap and winning by a length. Then the Italians had levelled the score with a two-length win in the second race. The third appearance of the finalists was immensely exciting – for those who could see it! – as the Britons led by almost two lengths down the final back straight and into the banking, only for the Italians to draw level and then edge six inches ahead at the line.

The tandems had always provided immensely exciting racing during their Olympic existence from the intercalated 1906 Games onwards, but the fact was that there was very little tandem-racing even internationally, and only the Germans and the British had been regular practitioners in pre-war years. Even so, the event would survive on the Olympic schedule until 1972 and the Italians were to twice more win gold.

Terruzzi was already 34 at the time of his Olympic success, but he went on to make a very substantial living until he was 50 years old in the bizarre realm of indoor six-day racing, with its interminable laps of the track, enlivened by mad-dash sprints amid all the din of fevered loudspeaker announcements, blaring music and raucous beer-drinkers. Between 1951 and 1964 he won 21 of these quasi-vaudeville bicycle "marathons" with various partners in venues which included Barcelona, Buenos Aires, Copenhagen, Melbourne, Montreal, New York and Paris.

Damp and oppressive weather severely affected times in the 1000 metres time-trial, in which the winner by a clear one second was Frenchman Jacques Dupont, whose time of 1min 13.5sec was slower than the Olympic record of 1:12.0 set by Dutchman Arie van Vliet on Berlin's wooden track in 1936 and far outside the official world record of 1:10.0 held by an Italian, Fabio Battesini, since 1938. Dupont had an even faster time of 1:08.6 to his credit on the Bordeaux track as further proof of how slow was the going on the bitumen surface at Herne Hill. Britain's representative here was Tommy Godwin, who had also been selected for the team pursuit, and he took his second bronze medal behind the Belgian, Nihant. It was later revealed by WJ Mills that Reg Harris had been selected

---

Tandem sprint result (2000 metres): 1 Ferdinando Terruzzi & Renato Perona (Italy), 2 Reg Harris & Alan Bannister (Great Britain), 3 René Faye & Georges Dron (France). Semi-finals: Great Britain beat France, one length, last 200 metres 11.4. Italy beat Switzerland, "lengths", last 200 metres 11.5. Final: Italy beat Great Britain 2-1, lost by one length, last 200 metres 11.1; won by two lengths, last 200 metres 11.3; won by six inches, last 200 metres 11.6. Third place: France beat Switzerland (Jean Roth & Max Aeberli) 2-0, one length and one length, last 200 metres 11.7 and 12.2.

to ride the individual time-trial but was replaced by Godwin a couple of days beforehand.

Dupont, only just turned 20, was known for his attention to detail as "Jacques la Méthode", was the current French champion for both the time-trial and the individual pursuit, and he was also named for the Olympic road race at Windsor Great Park. He was beaten in the individual pursuit final at the World Championships a month after the Olympics by a 17-year-old Italian, Guido Messina, and then emulated his team-pursuit compatriots, Coste and Blusson, by turning his attention to professional road-racing, surviving a serious crash in 1949 and then winning Paris–Tours in 1951 and 1955, the Circuit de l'Indre in 1952 and 1954, and the French national title in 1954.

WJ Mills had eloquently explained the demands of time-trialling in one of his previews of the Olympic cycling: "There are no 'ifs' and 'buts', no question of tactics and strategy ... the art of getting fast '1000' times lies in knowing yourself and your capabilities. From a standing start, and without any assistance whatsoever from the helper, who merely holds you in position on the line, and is not allowed to push you, you have to know just how much strength you can allocate to getting going and what time is necessary for the first 250 metres, so that you can hold your maximum right to the very last metre. Even a fifth of a second too fast in your initial quarter will leave you floundering before the finish." Unintended proof of that was provided by the Italian, Gino Guerra, who passed halfway in 37.8sec to lead Dupont by 0.2 but faded drastically away to ninth place.

Thus there were no gold medals for the British on their home track, but there could hardly be any complaints about the all-round performance. Italy (two golds and a silver), France (two golds and a bronze) and Great Britain (two silvers and two bronzes) had between them totally dominated the four events, leaving only a silver for Belgium and a bronze for Denmark. This all fitted in with the experience of the interwar years during which the sole non-Europeans to win Olympic medals had been the South Africans, third in the 1920 team pursuit, and the Australian time-triallist, Edgar ("Dunc") Gray, who won the bronze in 1928 and the gold in 1932. By the time of the 1952 Olympics the world of cycling was opening up and Australians were to win two golds and a silver on the track and South Africans two silvers and a bronze.

Very largely unnoticed in sixth place in the time-trial was an Australian, Sid Patterson, who had celebrated his 21st birthday the day before and within

---

Individual time-trial result (1000 metres): 1 Jacques Dupont (France) 1min 13.5sec, 2 Pierre Nihant (Belgium) 1:14.5, 3 Tommy Godwin (Great Britain) 1:15.0, 4 Hans Flückiger (Switzerland) 1:15.3, 5 Axel Schandorff (Denmark) 1:15.5, 6 Sid Patterson (Australia) 1:15.7, 7 Jackie Heid (USA) 1:16.2, 8 Walter Freitag (Austria) 1:16.8, 9 Gino Guerra (Italy) 1:17.1, 10 Onni Kasslin (Finland) 1:17.4, 11 Carlos Tramutolo (Uruguay) 1:17.5, 12 Theodorus Blankenauw (Holland) 1:17.7, 13 Jorge Sobrevila (Argentina) 1:17.9, 14 José Leon (Venezuela) 1:18.1, 15 Lorne Atkinson (Canada) 1:20.2, 16= Compton Gonsalves (Trinidad), Reinaldo Paneiro (Cuba) 1:21.5, 18 Adolfo Romero (Mexico) 1:22.7, 19 Rohinton Noble (India) 1:22.9, 20 Wazir Ali (Pakistan) 1:24.8, 21 L K Lewis (British Guiana) 1:25.0.

a few years would become one of the greatest of all track cyclists. He won world amateur titles in the sprint in 1949 and the individual pursuit in 1950 and then became professional pursuit champion in 1952 and 1953. He set a record for the outdoor kilometre from a flying start, with a time of 1min 4.0sec, and from 1959 onwards won numerous six-day races in Australia.

The only road event at the Olympics of 1948 was a massed-start race for men. This was held at Windsor Great Park on a circuit of 11.5 kilometres (more precisely, 7 miles 202 yards) to be covered 17 times for a total distance said to be 195.5 kilometres (119 miles 1,414 yards), though estimates varied slightly, according to which report you read. The event had not been intended originally for Windsor, which was outside the Greater London area, but for Richmond Park, in Surrey, until it was discovered that a Parliamentary Act prohibited any activity there conducted at a greater speed than 20 m.p.h. – even if it *was* the Olympic Games.

A cycle road race at varying distances had been held at every Games except, oddly, the previous London celebration in 1908, and French riders had won it in 1906 (84 kilometres), 1924 (188 kilometres) and 1936 (100 kilometres). Until 1936 the event had usually been organised as a time-trial, and the 1912 version had taken a particularly masochistic form, with the 123 competitors starting at two-minute intervals from two o'clock in the morning and covering no less than 320 kilometres round a lake near Stockholm, completed by the South African winner, Rudolph Lewis, in 10 hours 42 minutes 39 seconds. So, strictly speaking, the only previous massed-start form to go on was that of Berlin, where the Frenchman, Robert Charpentier, had won in a bunch sprint finish from his team-mate, Guy Lapébie. Britain's Charles Holland had shared fourth place with a German and a third Frenchman.

The NCU, Britain's ruling body, had named 12 Olympic road-race possibles at the end of 1947 and the four eventually chosen were Ernie Clements (Birchfield), Bob Maitland (Solihull), Ian Scott (Middlesbrough) and Gordon ("Tiny") Thomas, of the Yorkshire Roads Club. All of them had strong enough domestic credentials, but it was a question as to whether their tactical acumen would match that of the Continentals. National titles had been won by Clements in 1946, Thomas in 1947, and Maitland in 1948 – though Thomas's success by a margin of 1½ minutes turned out to be a moral one only, as he was disqualified for changing a wheel outside a designated area. Scott was a versatile rider who had come close to being selected for the 4000 metres team pursuit on the track. Their confidence was boosted by a crushing win in the prestigious Belgian race, the Grand Prix de Liège, in July, when Thomas and Maitland came in together six minutes ahead of the third-placed home rider.

At this point it is perhaps worth explaining that cycle road-racing is not simply a matter of everyone going as fast as they can, and may the strongest man win. The basic premise is that two or more riders, taking it in turns to lead and therefore share the brunt of the headwind, will always – or almost always – be superior even to a better rider on his own. Furthermore, each team goes into a race with a designated leader, for whom everyone else in the team rides in support. That includes keeping him sheltered from the wind, plying him with food and drink whenever he needs it, chasing after every potential rival of his who threatens to get away, waiting for him if he punctures or has any other problem, and then mounting a concerted effort at the appropriate time to provide a springboard for his victory. The leader of each team is the fastest or the strongest, or the best climber if there is a mountain finish.

For this Olympic race climbing ability was not top of the list of priorities. There was a stretch imaginatively called "Breakheart Hill", about a kilometre from the finishing-line, though it rose not much more than 25 metres in some 400 metres – roughly a 1-in-16 ascent – and would have struck no fear into the hearts of any of the French, Belgians or Italians in the race, for many of whom the ultimate ambition would be to turn professional and tackle the Alps and Pyrenees in the legendary Tour de France, which had first been held in 1903. Even 17 times up this puny Berkshire slope would break none of their hearts.

The World Championship race, which had been held at Rheims, in France, the previous year, had been won by an Italian, Alfio Ferrari, and his success had been attributed by WJ Mills to "superior team help". Britain's best rider had been George Fleming in 12th place, with Clements 21st and Maitland equal 25th. More encouragingly, Fleming had beaten the best of the French riders to win the three-day Paris-to-London race sponsored by the *News Chronicle* newspaper, with Maitland fifth and Clements 10th, but then at the season's end Fleming had announced his retirement to everyone's surprise. Nevertheless, he was to make his modest contribution to preparations for the Games by acting as the "pilot" cyclist for the national 20 miles road-walking championship in Hyde Park in March of 1948 and then assisting at the Games cycle road-race as a steward in the "pits".

There were 101 riders at the road-race start. The maximum of four per team was entered by Argentina, Australia, Austria, Belgium, Canada, Chile, Denmark, France, Great Britain, Holland, India, Italy, Luxembourg, Mexico, Norway, Sweden, Switzerland, Turkey, USA, Uruguay and Venezuela – 21 countries in all. There were three riders each from Finland, Greece, Peru and South Africa; two from Korea; and one each from British Guiana, New Zealand and Pakistan. What a pity, then, that for this splendidly cosmopolitan gathering neither the weather nor the road surface was up to standard. Torrential rain for part of the day limited the numbers of spectators to an estimated attendance of 10,000 to 15,000, rather than the 40,000-to-50,000 hoped for, and the loose gravel caused havoc with tyres. One luckless rider apparently punctured eight times and 107 punctures were reported in all!

Only at the official pit-stops situated in the finishing straight and halfway round the course were riders allowed technical assistance, and if they punctured elsewhere they simply had to do what every common-or-garden cyclist was well used to doing – dismount, change the tyre, and pump up the inner tube. Some of the most enduring images of the official film of the 1948 Olympics, which otherwise is distinctly nondescript, are of cyclists falling off or puncturing whilst the race commissaire cruises serenely past them seated in an open-top Rolls-Royce.

The first lap was covered in 18min 22sec for an average of about 23 miles (39 kilometres) per hour. The leaders were Faanhof, Voorting (both of Holland), Johansson (Sweden) and Suda (Turkey). Anyone watching who had also been in Berlin 12 years before might well have specially noted the surprising presence of the Turk, as a rider from that country named Talat Tuncalp had been involved in the close finish at those Games and had placed equal eighth. Not only that but Tuncalp was again among the starters this time. Perhaps more significant was the presence of the two Dutchmen, who seemed keen to ensure the pace was fast and might be working on behalf of one of their team-mates safely protected in the bunch.

Johansson, for whatever reason, chose to break away on his own in the second lap and was a minute ahead but was then caught on Breakheart Hill by the two Dutch riders. These three worked well together and after seven laps (2:07:43) they had a lead of four minutes, but then Johansson became the first of the day's major victims, puncturing and losing three minutes. It was on the 12th lap, with less than 60 kilometres (37 miles) to go, that the pattern of the race was established when the leaders were caught by a group of nine riders, including Hoobin (Australia), Delathouwer, Wouters (both Belgium), Beyaert (France), Maitland, Thomas (both Great Britain) and – remarkably – Johansson, of Sweden, who had managed to join the chasing group after his mishap.

Prominent casualties at this stage of the race were Rasmussen (Denmark), who punctured, and Rouffeteau (France), who crashed into his manager at the pits while taking refreshment. Faanhof, who had done so much of the work so far, was ill-rewarded with a puncture and dropped out of the reckoning, leaving Belgium and Great Britain as the teams with the advantage in the leading group. Each had two riders, and if either of the pairs worked together they could increase immeasurably the chances of a victory for one or other of them. The classic strategy would now be for one of the Belgians or Britons to constantly sprint off ahead, forcing the other nationalities to chase after him, while his team-mate rode steadily, knowing that the attack was not a serious one. Most notably, the Italian world champion, Ferrari, and his three team-mates had all missed the vital break and were out of contention.

At 15 laps (4:39:32) Beyaert and Maitland were leading the group, and then on the 16th lap Thomas broke away but was chased and caught by Delathouwer. The pair of them had a useful lead of 15 seconds as they made the penultimate climb of Breakheart Hill. It was a good move and could benefit one or other of them, or hopefully set matters up for their team-mates behind. Halfway round the last lap all eight riders were together again, and inevitably there was an easing-off as each of them tried to calculate the decisive moment to make a final effort.

Beyaert was the first to try to get away, but Hoobin led the group back into contact. Then, just before the top of the final rise, with less than a kilometre to go, Beyaert attacked again, quickly got a gap of eight lengths, and none of the others had the strength left in their legs to go after him. Voorting, Wouters, Delathouwer, Johansson and Maitland came in together in that order, with Hoobin and Thomas another two seconds back. It was a good result. All of the leading eight had done their share of the work, and Beyaert was clearly the best of them, with no team-mate there to help him.

For the 22-year-old Beyaert it was one of those races that roadmen dream about. He had been involved in all the right breaks and he had decided that the Dutchman, Voorting, was the one to watch. When Voorting had attacked at the critical moment on the last lap only Beyaert had "got on his wheel", to use the racing parlance, and he described the situation in detail when he met up with the excited French press reporters awaiting him beyond the finishing-line: "I passed Voorting and looked back and saw that all the others were in Indian file and seemed to be taking it easy, just like the Dutchman. In a flash I realised my good luck. The time that it took my opponents to re-group, and the 30 metres advantage which I had at the top of the climb, was enough. I'm going to give the title to my fiancée as a wedding present. At least it did not cost me much!"

The next group of five, led by the world champion, Ferrari, came in almost 3½ minutes down, and among them was a third Belgian, van Roosbroeck, to ensure the team award. There were only 15 other finishers, spread over the best part of the next 20 minutes, but the wait was worthwhile because Ian Scott rode in on his own in 16th place to give Britain the team silver medals ahead of France, whose third scorer was the track time-trial gold-medallist Jacques Dupont. Only Argentina, Italy, Sweden and Switzerland otherwise had scoring teams. The rest had retired, including Britain's Ernie Clements. Among the most battle-scarred of the non-finishers were an Argentinian and a Turk, who had collided and crashed on a particularly dangerous corner and had squared up to each other in rage, with the Argentinian eventually limping mournfully away to the side of the road dragging his wrecked machine and slumping under a tree in tears. In one of the most telling sequences of the official Games film, the commentator cryptically observed, "A story that needs no words."

Also among the non-finishers were all four riders from Canada, Chile, India, Mexico, Turkey, USA, Uruguay and Venezuela, and if it seems odd that so many should come such a long way for so little return, so be it. Another of the quirks of cycle road-racing is that riders will be inclined to "climb off" once they have no further interest in the race – either because they have done their required work on behalf of a team-mate or simply because they have lost all chance of a prominent placing. To the layman it might seem preferable in years to come for a Chilean or a Turk to be able to say that he once came 29th in an Olympic road race, rather than to admit that he failed to complete the course.

All credit, then, to an Australian and two Danes who eventually arrived almost 22 minutes behind the winner for no other glory but a sense of satisfaction. The Australian was Russell Mockridge, who was to win Olympic pursuit and tandem gold medals on the track in 1952. He had taken up cycle-racing because his defective eyesight prevented him from playing ball-games and his elegant appearance at his first race, wearing a sleek white jersey and a pink cap, earned him the nickname, "Little Lord Fauntleroy". As a professional road racer, he won the Tour de Vaucluse, in France, in 1955, but three years later back home in Australia he was killed when hit by a bus during a road race. Mockridge's team-mate Jack Hoobin was to surprise all the Continental aces by winning the world amateur road-race title in 1950.

Among the interested spectators throughout the rainswept afternoon in Windsor Great Park had been the new Olympic marathon champion Delfo Cabrera, supporting his Argentinian colleagues, and the Duke of Edinburgh, in his role as Royal representative, and there is one scene in the official Olympic film which shows the Duke congratulating the bespectacled winner and then one of the British riders. It takes no great lip-reading skills to discern that the Briton is saying "Thanks very much", but there was no such tribute from WJ Mills in his article in the September issue of *World Sports*. In fact, he was scathingly critical of the British tactics – or, rather, the lack of them.

Their cardinal error, according to Mills, was not to give support to Ian Scott, the fastest finisher among them. After puncturing, Scott had chased the leaders on his own for 14 miles and had then had nothing left when the decisive break was made. Mills wrote: "If Maitland, Clements and Thomas had eased and waited for Scott to nurse him back into the field, two things would have happened. First, Clements, our second best sprinter in the team, would have missed the crash which put him out of the race with his rear wheel ripped to pieces. Secondly, Scott would have been 'in at the death'. As it was, Maitland and Thomas survived with the leaders unto the end but as expected had no sprint left to challenge Beyaert."

Beyaert was 22 and his only previous victory of particular note was the Paris–Briare one-day race in 1947. At the World Championships the following month he was eighth as the title was won by Sweden's Harry Snell, who had trailed in 18th at Windsor. Beyaert subsequently had a couple of wins in 1950 as a professional – the Grand Prix d'Isbergues and Paris–Boulogne – and then went to live in Colombia. Dutch silver-medallist Voorting moved on to a much more illustrious professional career, highlighted by stage wins in the Tour de France of 1953 and 1958.

Great Britain's cyclists had served their country well on the track and road, and there was more good news to come later in the year. At the annual Cycle Show at Earls Court it was announced that the British cycle industry had produced two million machines in the past year and 1.5 million of them had gone for export. The star exhibit was the Hercules Kestrel Super Club, retailing at £25 and five shillings – equivalent to about £610 (915 euros) in 21st-century terms.

Road-race individual result: 1 José Beyaert (France) 5hr 18min 12.6sec, 2 Gerardus Voorting (Holland) 5:18:16.2, 3 Lode Wouters (Belgium) 5:18:16.2, 4 Léon Delathouwer (Belgium) 5:18:16.2, 5 Nils Johansson (Sweden) 5:18:16.2, 6 Bob Maitland (Great Britain) 5:18:16.2, 7 Jack Hoobin (Australia) 5:18:18.2, 8 Gordon Thomas (Great Britain) 5:18:18.2, 9 Alfio Ferrari (Italy) 5:21:45.0, 10 Silvio Pedroni (Italy) 5:21:45.0, 11 Alain Moineau (France) 5:21:45.0, 12 Eugène van Roosbroeck (Belgium) 5:21:45.0, 13 Jakob Schenk (Switzerland) 5:21:45.0, 14 Rudolf Valenta (Austria) 5:24:48.0, 15 Jean Brun (Switzerland) 5:26:54.0, 16 Ian Scott (Great Britain) 5:26:57.2, 17 Jacques Dupont (France) 5:28:21.8, 18 Harry Snell (Sweden) 5:28:22.2, 19 Franco Fanti (Italy) 5:29:35.2, 20 Livio Isotti (Italy) 5:31:08.6, 21 Caferino Perone (Argentina) 5:33:15.4, 22 Danete Benvenuti (Argentina) 5:33:15.4, 23 Miguel Sevillano (Argentina) 5:33:15.4, 24 Åke Olivestedt (Sweden) 5:33:48.2, 25 Walter Reiser (Switzerland) 5:34:25.2, 26 Russell Mockridge (Australia) 5:39:54.6, 27 Kristian Pedersen (Denmark) 5:39:57.2, 28 Knud Andersen (Denmark) 5:39:57.2.

Road-race team result: 1 Belgium (Lode Wouters 3, Léon Delathouwer 4, Eugène van Roosbroeck 12) 15hr 58min 17.4sec, 2 Great Britain (Bob Maitland 6, Gordon Thomas 8, Ian Scott 16) 16:03:31.6, 3 France (José Beyaert 1, Alain Moineau 11, Jacques Dupont 17) 16:08:19.4, 4 Italy (Alfio Ferrari 9, Silvio Pedroni 10, Franco Fanti 19) 16:13:05.2, 5 Sweden (Nils Johansson 5, Harry Snell 18, Åke Olivestedt 24) 16:20:26.6, 6 Switzerland (Jakob Schenk 13, Jean Brun 15, Walter Reiser 25) 16:23:04.2, 7 Argentina (Caferino Perone 21, Danete Benvenuti 22, Miguel Sevillano 23) 16:39:46.2.

Chapter 21

THE FORMER DELIVERY BOY WHO CAME BACK WITH TWO MEDALS

Tommy Godwin recalls his track-cycling experiences

TOM McCOOK IS one of those selfless individuals who are the lifeblood of athletics – a long-serving official with one of Britain's most famous clubs, Birchfield Harriers in Birmingham. He seems to know almost everyone who is anyone in the sport. One Saturday afternoon, when I had taken a break from completing the manuscript of this book and was watching a meeting at the National Indoor Arena in the city, our discussion took a different turn. Knowing about my Olympic project, he asked me, "Would you like to meet Tommy Godwin? He's here at a reception." Would I like to meet Tommy Godwin? Indeed I would! "Lead on," I delightedly replied.

We wended our way downstairs and into a vast banqueting suite thronged with people enjoying the hospitality of the generous sponsors. Eventually Tom stopped at a table – presumably for a passing word with yet more of his innumerable acquaintances, I thought – but instead he turned to an elegantly dressed man who looked to be a very healthy 65-year-old and introduced me. This was Tommy Godwin, all of 86 years old, winner of two bronze medals on the Herne Hill cycle-racing track at the 1948 Olympics. If I had been told that he was a veteran of the 1968 Olympics, rather than those of 20 years earlier, I would have readily believed it. Later, away from the buzz and clamour of the lunch tables, he talked impassionedly about his experiences at a decidedly makeshift Olympics, and this is what he told me:

"We had no training camp beforehand, no manager. I wasn't told until the Monday night that I'd be riding the time-trial on the Wednesday. I'd beaten

Ken Marshall, who had been the favourite to get into the team at the start of the season, but they'd named Reg Harris for the time-trial instead, though he hadn't ridden in any of the selection races for that event. Reg was a very fine bike rider, but he didn't come down to train with us and all sorts of excuses were made for him. Bill Bailey, who had ridden in the 1920 Olympics, had been the team manager, but he'd resigned over the business of Reg being suspended and then reinstated, and we had Harry Ryan come in as manager and he knew nothing about time-trialling or my other event, the team pursuit.

"I'd believed for years afterwards that the four of us who rode in the team pursuit had never ridden together before the Games, but I've been told since that we had ridden together – once! The selection was made only three or four days before the event, and we really had absolutely no idea of what we were doing. No one knew which of us was the strong man in the team. The complete lack of organisation for the Olympics was quite typical of what the sport was like in those days. I just regarded myself as a good all-round bike rider, and like everybody else then I did it all by trial and error. We had no knowledge of technology, scientific research, nutrition or physique. We knew nothing about recovery rates. All you had in your favour was a belief in yourself.

"We got the bronze medals, but I still think that if we'd met the French in the final it would have been a very close match for the gold. We should at least have had the silver medals, anyway, because one of the Italians nearly fell off his bike and his manager ran over to the trackside and held him up. The rules stated perfectly clearly that no assistance or pushing was allowed, and so I went over to the officials and protested, but all they said was, 'You can't protest. You weren't riding for the silver medals.' The French and Italians controlled the sport then and so we didn't have our say in the matter."

At the time of the 1948 Olympics, Tommy was working 48 hours a week as an electrician at the BSA factory in Birmingham and his only rewards from the sport were the clocks, watches and canteens of cutlery which he won regularly. Taking to heart the lessons of lack of preparation, he became Britain's first national cycling coach in 1962 and was manager of the Olympic team two years later. "I'd known about coaching from a very early age," he explained. "My parents had gone to the USA and I'd been born there, and so I saw how much the Americans put into coaching and training even at high school. My father had a real love for sport and I remember him asking me when I was only eight years old if I would run in the Olympics. I said, 'Yes, Pop,' but, of course, it turned out to be cycling instead of running."

The family returned to Birmingham in 1932, when Tommy was 12, and it was as a result of his first job after leaving school that the seeds were sown for his future sporting success – he rode a bicycle as a grocer's delivery boy. Married 63 years and a lifelong teetotaller, Tommy retains the upright bearing and brightness of eye of a man who still takes very good care of himself, but no more cycling for him. "The roads round Birmingham are far too dangerous for that," he says.

Chapter 22

GET BACK IN THE RANKS, SERGEANT!

Equestrianism. Aldershot, Camberley and Empire Stadium, Wembley, 9–14 August.

HYLTON CLEAVER WAS a prolific contributor to numerous popular magazines of the late 1940s and early 1950s – *Punch, Men Only, Everybody's, Picture Post*. He was also a correspondent for the London *Evening Standard*, and his speciality was what would have been known in those days as the "upper crust" sports. He wrote largely about rowing, golf, rugby union and equestrian events in an indulgent style, but with occasional sharp thrusts of observation which cut through the high-society image of those pastimes. He had seen the 1908 Olympic marathon as a child, and as a journalist had covered the Berlin Games. He was there again when they returned to London.

In 1951 he wrote a book entitled *Sporting Rhapsody*, a delightfully entertaining medley of his reminiscences, and though some would seem quaintly sentimental and overly patriotic when read again more than half a century later there was often a strain of realism which set everything in a proper perspective. Discussing the Olympic equestrian events, he recalled an heroic painting of a Victorian-era battle charge by the cavalry of the Scots Greys and the foot soldiers of the Gordon Highlanders and made an impassioned plea:

"Why cannot a combined attack of the same kind on the athletes of other countries be launched now, helping us to defy those who in 1948 courteously commended our organisation and our hospitality but went home convinced that we should never win anything again? The moral, surely, is that we must go on horse *and* foot, hot-foot at that, for Helsinki if we are ever to justify our heritage, and when some people argue that horses have no part in Olympic Games I say they have a very vital part, and a far more convincing right to be in the show than any soccer or hockey team."

Britain's horsemen won a team bronze medal in the Prix des Nations show jumping competition at the 1948 Games, never having previously placed higher than seventh. At the 1952 Games the British trio won the gold – the only victory by any representatives of Great Britain in any sport. It is hard to imagine now, when the equestrian events have brought so much subsequent success, but in 1948 Britain's horseback competitors were riding for the most part into uncharted territory. The six equestrian events were to be won by five different countries, but not including the hosts.

The three-day event – dressage, cross-country, show jumping – had produced an unlikely bronze medal for Britain in 1936. The third rider in the team, Richard Fanshawe, accumulated no less than 8,754.20 penalty points, but only one other country, Czechoslovakia, managed to complete a team, and one of their riders took more than 2¾ hours to cover the cross-country course, for which the time limit was 17min 46sec, and so lost 18,130.70 points! Hylton Cleaver wrote of the 1948 three-day event – the first competition of its kind ever to be seen on British soil: "Britain competed in something we had never seen before. We started getting ready late and competed half-trained. We did bravely and we did not succeed."

In show jumping, in which Britain had never won a medal but had gained individual fourth places in 1912 and 1924, standards had fallen alarmingly. Captain GHS Webber, secretary-general of the British Show Jumping Association, summarised the domestic situation in the immediate post-war years in an article which he wrote in 1959, by which time Britain had won their team gold at Helsinki and then bronze at the 1956 Games: "The interest and entertainment had gone out of the jumping due to the sameness, lack of enterprise and initiative in the building of courses. For fear of transgressing the rules and incurring the disfavour of competitors, show executives put up the same few fences round the outside of the ring, with a water-jump down the centre or, in the absence of water, a triple bar. The time element did not come into it in any way, with the result that the test became one of jumping individual fences unconnected with each other".

Dressage, in which the rider is required entirely from memory to put the horse through a 13-minute series of movements designed to test co-ordination and technical skill, took place at the Army's Command Central Stadium at Aldershot on Monday 9 August. Britain had never had the least success in Olympic competition in this discipline and no one was even considered worth entering on this occasion. Sweden had won the individual title in 1912, 1920 and 1924, succeeded by Germany in 1928, France in 1932 and Germany again in 1936. Team-scoring was introduced in 1928 and Germany and France had won the three golds in the same sequence.

The 1948 dressage competition marked the end of an era of exclusivity. Only commissioned officers were allowed to take part, but by 1952 the restrictions had been abandoned and the silver medal went to a Danish woman, Lis Hartel, who was paralysed below the knees after suffering polio in 1944. By 1972, 21 of the 33 competitors would be women. The uniforms worn by the 19 riders from nine countries at Aldershot were those of five Colonels, a Lieutenant-Colonel, a Commandant, a Major, nine Captains, a First Lieutenant and a Lieutenant. Though there were three each from Argentina, Portugal and Sweden – all of them untouched by the recent war – it was decided to leave out the two most advanced exercises from the programme because it was felt that the training of horses and riders would have been too severely disrupted.

The individual gold went to Captain Hans Moser, of Switzerland, riding the Hungarian-bred *Hummer* with Colonel André Jousseaume, of France, second, riding an Anglo-Arab, *Harpagon*, and Captain Gustaf-Adolf Boltenstern, of Sweden, third, riding *Trumf.* Jousseaume's career in this event was of remarkable duration and consistency; he had placed fifth in 1932 and 1936 and would be third in 1952 and fifth again in 1956, riding *Harpagon* on each occasion. By 1956 he was 61, and as France took the team gold at Aldershot, and had also won gold in 1932 and silver in 1936, his collection of medals was brought to five. In seventh place at Aldershot was Austria's Colonel Alois Podhajsky, born in Mostar, in what is now Bosnia. He was the chief instructor at the Spanish Riding School in Vienna and had won the bronze in 1936.

The hidebound rules concerning eligibility led to a ludicrous situation in the team event. Sweden had won the gold by a substantial margin from France and the USA, with their three riders placed in the first six, but it was then discovered some months later that despite his title Lieutenant Gehnäll Persson was merely a non-commissioned officer and the team was disqualified in retrospect. This raises obvious questions which seem never to have been considered by the compilers of the official Games reports.

Surely the Swedes must have known of the rules? Persson's team-mates were a Major and a Captain and it beggars belief that they were not aware of what rank was held by Persson. One of the three dressage judges was Count Carl Bonde, of Sweden, winner of the Olympic title in 1912, and it seems inconceivable that he would have been ignorant of Persson's status. So why was Persson selected? If he was essential to the team, then why was he not conveniently and permanently promoted beforehand? After all, neutral Sweden had not fought a battle for 134 years, and the ability to ride a horse to Olympic standard in the furtherance of national honour might well have been thought to have counted at least as much as knowledge of military strategy when it came to judging Swedish officer material.

Regrettably, the organising committee's official report swept the whole affair as far under the carpet as they could. Nowhere does Persson's name appear in the account of the event or in the results, and there is merely a reference to Sweden to the effect that "one of their team members was not qualified to compete under the rules of the Fédération Equestre Internationale". The British Olympic Association's report, published soon after the Games finished, lists Persson and makes no reference to the matter of disqualification, for the simple reason that at that stage the Swedes were still recognised as having won the gold medals.

The full story puts the whole affair into an even more ludicrous context. Ove

Karlsson, the leading Swedish Olympic historian, investigated the matter and says that Persson's status was discovered "by chance" by Commandant Georges Hector, of France, the 79-year-old secretary-general of the international ruling body, the FEI, since its formation in 1921. He had learned that the Swedes had promoted Persson from non-commissioned officer to second lieutenant for the duration of the Olympic Games, and this was duly reported to the April 1949 session of the IOC in Rome by the FEI president, Baron Gaston de Trannoy, of Belgium, who wanted either the IOC to exact punishment or the FEI to take a decision. It may be that Baron de Trannoy was particularly on the lookout for such a transgression because the matter of non-commissioned officers being ineligible had been raised, somewhat injudiciously, by a Swedish member, Count Clarence de Rosen, at the IOC meeting in St Moritz early in 1948, and the Baron himself was there to retort that the subject should have been discussed by the FEI first.

Bo Ekelund, Sweden's IOC member, claimed that his country had done nothing wrong and accused the FEI of being "old-fashioned, snobbish and anti-democratic". Even so, the matter was handed over to the FEI, who decided to disqualify Persson. At the Swedish National Olympic Committee meeting of December 1949, it was reported that the medals and diplomas awarded had been returned to the London Games organisers, but the supreme irony was that at the FEI congress the previous month the rules for competition had been changed, allowing not only "other ranks" but also civilians, including women, to compete in the future. Women had already been allowed to compete in international dressage competitions – except, inexplicably, the Olympic Games!

Justice was done at long last in 1952, when rank was no longer of any consequence, because the same Swedish threesome of Saint Cyr, Boltenstern and Persson won the team gold, and then, to emphasise the point, won again in 1956. Saint Cyr was individual champion in both those years. Boltenstern had won silver in the 1932 team event and had placed eighth individual that year and would be fourth in 1952 and seventh in 1956. His father, also named Gustaf-Adolf, had won individual silver in 1912. So father and son between them spanned 44 years of Olympic competition.

Sweden's disqualification enabled Portugal to take the bronze – the country's only medal success in 1948 other than a silver in yachting. The Portugese bronze-medallists could between them point to a wealth of Olympic experience, remarkable even by the durable standards of equestrianism. Paes and Valadas would compete again in 1952 and Silva also took part in the Games of 1936 and 1960, though they all appear to be mere novices in retrospective comparison with their compatriots in the showjumping event still to come. Henrique Alves Callado was to compete in every Games from 1948 to 1964 and Hélder Henrique de Souza Martins was making a return to Olympic competition at Wembley at the age of 46 after having taken part in the Games of 1924 (where he won a team bronze) and 1928. One of the US silver-medallists, Bob Borg, was born in the Philippines, as was Franklin Wing, who was to place fourth in the showjumping event.

The three-day event began on Tuesday 10 August with the dressage. All but seven of the 45 competitors were officers in the various armed services, and full teams of three were entered by Argentina, Brazil, Denmark, Finland, France, Great Britain, Italy, Portugal, Spain, Sweden, Switzerland, Turkey and the USA. Not surprisingly, Colonel Jousseaume, who had already won the individual dressage silver, led at the end of the day, but by only two marks (scoring 322 out of a maximum of 400) from Anton Bühler, of Switzerland, with Fabio Mangilli, of Italy, third (315). The best of the British in equal ninth place was Brigadier Lyndon Bolton, a late replacement in the team for the 1936 team bronze-medallist, Lieutenant-Colonel Alec Scott, who had broken an arm in training. Switzerland led the team standings from France and the USA.

The next day came the endurance, speed and cross-country test, covering a distance of 33.5 kilometres (21 miles), which consisted of six kilometres of roads to be covered at a speed of 220 metres a minute (time limit 27min 17sec); 3.5 kilometres of steeplechase, jumping 12 obstacles, at 600 metres a minute (time limit 5min 50sec); 15 kilometres of roads, again at 220 metres a minute (time limit 1hr 8min 11sec); eight kilometres of cross-country, jumping 34 obstacles of a maximum height of 1.20 metres, at 450 metres a minute (time limit 18min); and finally one kilometre on the flat at 333 metres a minute (time limit 3min). The roads and paths used were in the vicinity of the Army site at Aldershot. The steeplechase section was on Tweseldown Racecourse and the cross-country section was specially constructed at Old Dean Common.

Hylton Cleaver described the course in splendidly imaginative detail: "Man and horse had to set out at dawn on a ride by track, road and path of several miles. When this was ended they were sent on a steeplechase. Then came another long hack, on which the man had to nurse his mount and bring it along at a steady, recognised gait, neither too fast nor too slow, in condition neither too hot nor too phlegmatic. Then, without pause, came the point-to-point – a dramatic ordeal by way of towering slopes, down steep gradients, along loose and stony paths,

---

Dressage individual result: 1 Hans Moser (Switzerland) riding *Hummer* 492.5 marks, 2 André Jouseaume (France) *Harpagon* 480, 3 Gustaf-Adolf Boltenstern (Sweden) *Trumf* 477.5, 4 Bob Borg (USA) *Klingson* 473.5, 5 Henri Saint Cyr (Sweden) *Djimm* 444.5, 6 Jean Saint-Fort Paillard (France) *Sous les Ceps* 439.5, 7 Alois Podhajsky (Austria) *Teja* 437.5, 8 Earl Thomson (USA) *Pancraft* 421, 9 Francisco Paes da Silva (Portugal) *Matamas* 411, 10 Francisco Valadas (Portugal) *Feitico* 405, 11 Justo Iturralde (Argentina) *Pajarito* 397, 12 Luis Mena e Silva (Portugal) *Fascinante* 366, 13 Frank Henry (USA) *Reno Overdo* 361.5, 14 Carlos Kirkpatrick O'Donnell (Spain) *Yanta* 353, 15 Maurice Buret (France) *Saint Ouen* 349.5, 16 Humberto Terzano (Argentina) *Bienvenido* 327, 17 Oscar Goulu (Argentina) *Grillo* 281.5, 18 Gabriel Gracida Jarmillo (Mexico) *Kamcia* 248.5. Note: Gehnäll Persson (Sweden), originally sixth with 444 marks, was later disqualified because he was not a commissioned officer, as the rules required.

Dressage team result: 1 France (André Jousseaume 2, Jean Saint-Fort Paillard 6, Maurice Buret 15) 1,269 marks, 2 USA (Bob Borg 4, Earl Thomson 8, Frank Henry 13) 1,256 marks, 3 Portugal (Fernando Paes da Silva 9, Francisco Valadas 10, Luis Mena e Silva 12) 1,182, 4 Argentina (Justo Iturralde 11, Humberto Terzano 16, Oscar Goulu 17) 1,005.5. Note: Sweden (Gustaf-Adolf Boltenstern 3, Henri Saint Cyr 5, Gehnäll Persson 6), originally first with 1,366 marks, was later disqualified for the reason stated above.

over hard commons, across water, walls and gates, and 'ski' jumps which were awesome. The great thing was to be up in time, without flogging the animal or rushing fences. Finally came a gallop-in over the flat."

Despite the impression given by Cleaver, the course was thought by the experts to be rather on the easy side. Even so, Colonel Jousseaume came to grief, suffering two falls, finishing 41st and last, and then being eliminated as his horse was lame. Bühler, the Swiss rider, also fell twice and finished equal 25th. Captain Bernard Chevallier, of France, had a clear round over the cross-country and even gained points with record times to finish ahead of two Americans, Lieutenant Charles Anderson and Lieutenant Colonel Frank Henry. The overall leader was now Captain Alfred Blaser, of Switzerland, from Chevallier and Mangilli. Denmark headed the team scores from the USA and Sweden. The leading Briton in this phase of the competition was Major Peter Borwick, who was 20th.

The final day's show jumping over 12 obstacles cost both Captain Blaser and the Danish team their chances of gold. Blaser knocked down too many barriers, while one of the Danish riders went off course and was disqualified. A passing reference is made in the organising committee's official report which ought really to have been expanded upon at some greater detail: "Some of the markers on the course had been moved, inadvertently, at the last moment and without sufficient warning to competing riders. As a result, some riders had to be disqualified for taking a wrong course, which was hard luck on both the individual riders and their teams." Whether the Danes were happy to settle for a sympathetic but ineffectual murmur of "hard luck" in their ears after three days of strenuous effort, or whether they made any official protest, is not recorded.

Chevallier, Henry and Captain Robert Selfelt, of Sweden, were clearly not affected because they all had clear rounds to take the overall medals. The USA, Sweden and Mexico won the team medals. It was Henry's second and third medals as he had been in the US dressage team which had won bronze. Also in the US three-day team was Colonel Earl Thomson, who had won the individual silver and team gold in 1932 and individual silver again in 1936. Bühler, in 19th, would win individual bronze and team silver in 1960 and would be in the sixth-placed team in 1972. Stahre, of Sweden, in equal 15th place, would win team gold in 1952 riding the same horse, *Komet*. The Finn, Roiha, had been born in Viipuri, as had his showjumping team-mate, Taimo Rissanen, and six other compatriots in various sports. Viipuri had become part of the USSR after the war settlement of 1940 and the entire Finnish population had been evacuated. Finnish troops briefly recaptured the city, but it returned to Soviet hands in 1944 and was now known as Vyborg.

The respective scores at Aldershot of the leading four for each of the three days were as follows:

Chevallier – minus 104, plus 108, 0   = plus 4
Henry – minus 117, plus 96, 0   = minus 21
Selfelt – minus 109, plus 84, 0   = minus 25
Anderson – minus 111, plus 96, minus 11.5   = minus 26.5

J Sigfrid Edstrom, the president of the International Olympic Committee, and the man responsible for London being awarded the Games, presents the medals for the women's 80 metres hurdles. Fanny Blankers-Koen, of Holland, took the gold, with Great Britain's Maureen Gardner second and Australia's Shirley Strickland third.

*Fanny Blankers-Koen also beat a British opponent,
Dorothy Manley, in the 100 metres.*

The *medallists* in the women's discus were Micheline Ostermeyer, of France (centre), *who* won the gold, together with Jacqueline Mazéas, also of France (right), and Edera Cordiale-Gentile, of Italy

*Ahmet Kireçci, of Turkey who won bronze in the freestyle middleweight tournamen**t** in 1936, returned to win gold at Greco-Roman heavyweight.*

Hungary's Károly Takács, the 1938 World champion, lost his right hand as a result of an accident during an army exercise but learned to shoot left-handed and won the rapid-fire pistol event in 1948.

Paul Elvström, of Denmark, (left) the greatest of all Olympic sailors, took gold in the Firefly yachting class. He was also to win in 1952, 1956 and 1960 and carried on competing until 1988. He is congratulated by compatriot Eyvin Schlottz.

The last of the equestrian events at the 1948 Olympics was the Prix des Nations show jumping and was staged as a finale at the Empire Stadium on Saturday 14 August prior to the closing ceremony. The individual gold had previously been won by seven different countries – Belgium (1900), France (1912), Italy (1920), Switzerland (1924), Czechoslovakia (1928), Japan (1932) and Germany (1936). The team title, first contested in 1912, had gone three times to Sweden, and then to Spain and Germany. Curiously, in 1932 no medals were awarded because none of the competing countries finished a complete team. Britain had never won a medal, and there was no particular hope entertained at Wembley that they would do so now. The performance in Berlin had been described as a fiasco. The British team had been the only one to fail to complete the course – "solely through lack of training". For the Wembley event some £4,000 had been raised by the British Show Jumping Association to prepare the team and hopefully make some amends.

The course of 19 obstacles was admitted in the BOA report to be "extremely difficult", and the proof of this was that none of the riders had a clear round and three retired after falling. The three leaders were the Marquis d'Orgeix (France), Uriza (Mexico) and Wing (USA), each with eight faults, when the last rider, Mariles Cortes, also of Mexico, came into the ring. He had already taken part in the three-day event and won a team bronze, and it was obvious that Mexico now had a chance of gold. Their first two riders had incurred 28 faults, and the only other countries for which three riders had survived were Spain, with 56.5 faults, and Great Britain, with 67. These two were assured of medals, but Mexico would win if Mariles Cortes had no more than 28 faults.

Three-day event individual result : 1 Bernard Chevallier (France) *Aiglonne* plus 4 marks, 2 Frank Henry (USA) *Swing Low* minus 21, 3 Robert Selfelt (Sweden) *Claque* –25, 4 Charles Anderson (USA) *Reno Palisade* –26.5, 5 Joaquim Nogueras Márquez (Spain) *Epsom* –41, 6 Erik Carlsen (Denmark) *Ezja* –44, 7 Aecio Morrot Coelho (Brazil) *Guapo* –52, 8= Fabio Mangilli (Italy) *Guerriero da Capestrano*, Fernando Marques Cavaleiro (Portugal) *Satari* –55, 10 Francisco Reyes Carrere (Argentina) *Rosarino* –59, 11 Alfred Blaser (Switzerland) *Mahmud* –59.25, 12 Humberto Mariles Cortes (Mexico) *Parral* –61.75, 13 Ernest van Loon (Holland) *Springsteel* –62, 14 Kai Aage Krarup (Denmark) *Rollo* –65, 15= Olof Stahre (Sweden) *Komet*, Sigurd Svensson (Sweden) *Dust* –70, 17 Peter Borwick (Great Britain) *Liberty* –80.25, 18 Julio Sagasta (Argentina) *Cherenda Cue* –92.5, 19 Anton Bühler (Switzerland) *Amour Amour* –95, 20 Adolf Ehrnhooth (Finland) *Lilia* –110, 21 Earl Thomson (USA) *Reno Rhythm* –114, 22 Raúl Campero (Mexico) *Tarahumara* –120.5, 23 Joaquín Solado Chagoya (Mexico) *Malinche* –123, 24 Adam Hendrik Ten Cate (Holland) *Unique de Genual* –145.5, 25 Fernando Paes (Portugal) *Zuari* –167.5, 26 Fernando Gazapo de Sarraga (Spain) *Vivian* –179.25, 27 Lyndon Bolton (Great Britain) *Sylveste* –182, 28 Mauno Roiha (Finland) *Roa* –202, 29 Santiago Martinez Larraz (Spain) *Fogoso* –202.25, 30 Raimondo d'Inzeo (Italy) *Regate* –223, 31 Renildo Pedro Ferreira (Brazil) *Indio* –250, 32 Pierre Musy (Switzerland) *Franzosin* –250.15, 33 R Emanuelli (France) *Tourtourelle* –303.25. There were 12 non-finishers, including Douglas Stewart (Great Britain) *Dark Seal*.

Three-day event team result : 1 USA (Frank Henry 2, Charles Anderson 4, Earl Thomson 21) minus 161.5 marks, 2 Sweden (Robert Selfelt 3, Olof Stahre 15=, Sigurd Svensson 15=) minus 165, 3 Mexico (Humberto Mariles Cortes 12, Raul Campero 22, Joaquin Solano Chagoya 23) minus 305.25, 4 Switzerland (Alfred Blaser 11, Anton Bühler 19, Pierre Musy 32) minus 404.5, 5 Spain (Joaquim Nogueras Marquez 5, Fernando Gazapo de Sarraga 26, Santiago Martinez Larraz 29) minus 422.5. Note: only five complete teams finished.

The organising committee's official report stated drily that "excitement among the spectators mounted steadily" – presumably no pun was intended – as Mariles Cortes and his horse, *Arete*, reached the 15th obstacle before making a mistake. They finished with only 6.25 faults and both the individual and team golds were won. Uriza won the jump-off for the other medals, with no faults to four each for d'Orgeix and Wing. Mexico's horsemen had done their country proud as the only other Mexican medal success at the 1948 Olympics was a bronze by the highboard diver, Joaquin Capilla.

In the *Daily Express*, John Macadam had only one regret about the day's happenings, and that concerned the closing ceremony of the Games, which followed the completion of the Prix des Nations event, and from which the great majority of the competitors in all the sports were absent because they had already gone home or had started their journeys. "How that great-hearted Wembley crowd, so sporting that they *prayed* the Mexican winner of the final equestrian event over his last hurdles, would have cheered them as they cheered every great athlete, no matter where he came from," Macadam wrote.

There was no great surprise about the Mexican success. Their riders had made a lasting impression at the previous year's New York International Horse Show, and the day after their Olympic success the "special correspondent" of the London Sunday newspaper, *The Observer*, had written: "Finally, in came Mariles. Watching him schooling at Aldershot one had feared for England. Sure enough, there was no relaxation of impulsion and control and *Arete* made as fine a performance as any horse ever did in the Prix des Nations."

The British trio had exceeded all expectations in taking the team bronze medals, and one of the pairings – Harry Llewellyn and *Foxhunter* – would return in 1952 for far greater and everlasting glory as a member of the gold-medal-winning team. The Welsh-born Llewellyn, who had finished second in the famed annual Grand National steeplechase race in 1936, later became Sir Harry Llewellyn Bt CBE. One of his fellow title-winners would be Major Douglas Stewart, who had competed in the three-day event at Aldershot but failed to finish and later became commanding officer of those same Royal Scots Greys who had inspired Hylton Cleaver's hopes for future British success at the Olympics.

Among those who did not complete the course was Italian Raimondo d'Inzeo, who had earlier placed 30th in the three-day event. Together with his brother Piero he would go on to form one of the most famous of showjumping family partnerships. Individually, Raimondo won silver and Piero bronze in 1956, then Raimondo won gold and Piero silver in 1960. As two-thirds of the Italian team they won silver in 1956 and bronze in 1960 and 1964. They also placed fifth in 1968, won bronze again in 1972 when teams were increased from three riders to four, and were competitors once more in 1976.

The Mexican double gold-medallist, Mariles Cortes, placed sixth in the individual show jumping in 1952, but subsequently led a rather more eventful life. In 1964 in Mexico City he shot dead another motorist who had tried to force him

J Sigfrid Edstrom, the president of the International Olympic Committee, and the man responsible for London being awarded the Games, presents the medals for the women's 80 metres hurdles. Fanny Blankers-Koen, of Holland, took the gold, with Great Britain's Maureen Gardner second and Australia's Shirley Strickland third.

Fanny Blankers-Koen also beat a British opponent,
Dorothy Manley, in the 100 metres.

The medallists in the women's discus were Micheline Ostermeyer, of France (centre), who won the gold, together with Jacqueline Mazéas, also of France (right), and Edera Cordiale-Gentile, of Italy

The USA carried all before them in the basketball tournament despite a shaky start.

The glamorous American women in the swimming and diving events attracted the photographers. This is Ann Curtis, winner of two gold medals and a silver in freestyle races.

For the honour of Great Britain. Jack Wilson and 'Ran' Laurie hear the national anthem ring out at Henley at the medal ceremony for the coxless pairs event.

Captains Birger Rosengren, of Sweden, (left) and Miroslav Brozovic, of Yugoslavia, shake hands before the football final. C J Battersby, the technical manager for the football tournament, in the suit tie and next to him is William Ling, of Great Britain, the referee.

Captain Willie Grut of Sweden during the cross country section of his modern pentathlon victory.

Turkey's Talat Tuncalp, who also competed in the cycling road race at Berlin in 1936, wonders why life is so unfair after crashing. The child's bicycle being close by cannot have helped his mood either.

The USA's Sammy Lee and Vicki Draves, who were both Asian-Americans,
between them won three gold medals and a bronze in the four diving competitions.

Captain Alois Blaser, of Switzerland, and his mount, Mahmud, tackle an obstacle during the cross-country section of the three-day equestrian event organised by the army at Aldershot.

(top) László Papp waits to be given his gold medal for winning boxing's middleweight title. Johnny Wright of Great Britain was second with Ivano Fontana of Italy in bronze position.
(bottom) John Davis wins the weightlifting heavyweight title.

Ilona Elek of Hungary, the foil champion from 1936, took gold again.

Ahmet Kireçci, of Turkey who won bronze in the freestyle middleweight tournament in 1936, returned to win gold at Greco-Roman heavyweight.

Hungary's Károly Takács, the 1938 World champion, lost his right hand as a result of an accident during an army exercise but learned to shoot left-handed and won the rapid-fire pistol event in 1948.

Paul Elvström, of Denmark, (left) the greatest of all Olympic sailors, took gold in the Firefly yachting class. He was also to win in 1952, 1956 and 1960 and carried on competing until 1988. He is congratulated by compatriot Eyvin Schlottz.

The last of the equestrian events at the 1948 Olympics was the Prix des Nations show jumping and was staged as a finale at the Empire Stadium on Saturday 14 August prior to the closing ceremony. The individual gold had previously been won by seven different countries – Belgium (1900), France (1912), Italy (1920), Switzerland (1924), Czechoslovakia (1928), Japan (1932) and Germany (1936). The team title, first contested in 1912, had gone three times to Sweden, and then to Spain and Germany. Curiously, in 1932 no medals were awarded because none of the competing countries finished a complete team. Britain had never won a medal, and there was no particular hope entertained at Wembley that they would do so now. The performance in Berlin had been described as a fiasco. The British team had been the only one to fail to complete the course – "solely through lack of training". For the Wembley event some £4,000 had been raised by the British Show Jumping Association to prepare the team and hopefully make some amends.

The course of 19 obstacles was admitted in the BOA report to be "extremely difficult", and the proof of this was that none of the riders had a clear round and three retired after falling. The three leaders were the Marquis d'Orgeix (France), Uriza (Mexico) and Wing (USA), each with eight faults, when the last rider, Mariles Cortes, also of Mexico, came into the ring. He had already taken part in the three-day event and won a team bronze, and it was obvious that Mexico now had a chance of gold. Their first two riders had incurred 28 faults, and the only other countries for which three riders had survived were Spain, with 56.5 faults, and Great Britain, with 67. These two were assured of medals, but Mexico would win if Mariles Cortes had no more than 28 faults.

Three-day event individual result : 1 Bernard Chevallier (France) *Aiglonne* plus 4 marks, 2 Frank Henry (USA) *Swing Low* minus 21, 3 Robert Selfelt (Sweden) *Claque* –25, 4 Charles Anderson (USA) *Reno Palisade* –26.5, 5 Joaquim Nogueras Márquez (Spain) *Epsom* –41, 6 Erik Carlsen (Denmark) *Ezja* –44, 7 Aecio Morrot Coelho (Brazil) *Guapo* –52, 8= Fabio Mangilli (Italy) *Guerriero da Capestrano*, Fernando Marques Cavaleiro (Portugal) *Satari* –55, 10 Francisco Reyes Carrere (Argentina) *Rosarino* –59, 11 Alfred Blaser (Switzerland) *Mahmud* –59.25, 12 Humberto Mariles Cortes (Mexico) *Parral* –61.75, 13 Ernest van Loon (Holland) *Springsteel* –62, 14 Kai Aage Krarup (Denmark) *Rollo* –65, 15= Olof Stahre (Sweden) *Komet*, Sigurd Svensson (Sweden) *Dust* –70, 17 Peter Borwick (Great Britain) *Liberty* –80.25, 18 Julio Sagasta (Argentina) *Cherenda Cue* –92.5, 19 Anton Bühler (Switzerland) *Amour Amour* –95, 20 Adolf Ehrnhooth (Finland) *Lilia* –110, 21 Earl Thomson (USA) *Reno Rhythm* –114, 22 Raúl Campero (Mexico) *Tarahumara* –120.5, 23 Joaquín Solado Chagoya (Mexico) *Malinche* –123, 24 Adam Hendrik Ten Cate (Holland) *Unique de Genual* –145.5, 25 Fernando Paes (Portugal) *Zuari* –167.5, 26 Fernando Gazapo de Sarraga (Spain) *Vivian* –179.25, 27 Lyndon Bolton (Great Britain) *Sylveste* –182, 28 Mauno Roiha (Finland) *Roa* –202, 29 Santiago Martinez Larraz (Spain) *Fogoso* –202.25, 30 Raimondo d'Inzeo (Italy) *Regate* –223, 31 Renildo Pedro Ferreira (Brazil) *Indio* –250, 32 Pierre Musy (Switzerland) *Franzosin* –250.15, 33 R Emanuelli (France) *Tourtourelle* –303.25. There were 12 non-finishers, including Douglas Stewart (Great Britain) *Dark Seal*.

Three-day event team result : 1 USA (Frank Henry 2, Charles Anderson 4, Earl Thomson 21) minus 161.5 marks, 2 Sweden (Robert Selfelt 3, Olof Stahre 15=, Sigurd Svensson 15=) minus 165, 3 Mexico (Humberto Mariles Cortes 12, Raul Campero 22, Joaquin Solano Chagoya 23) minus 305.25, 4 Switzerland (Alfred Blaser 11, Anton Bühler 19, Pierre Musy 32) minus 404.5, 5 Spain (Joaquim Nogueras Marquez 5, Fernando Gazapo de Sarraga 26, Santiago Martinez Larraz 29) minus 422.5. Note: only five complete teams finished.

The organising committee's official report stated drily that "excitement among the spectators mounted steadily" – presumably no pun was intended – as Mariles Cortes and his horse, *Arete*, reached the 15th obstacle before making a mistake. They finished with only 6.25 faults and both the individual and team golds were won. Uriza won the jump-off for the other medals, with no faults to four each for d'Orgeix and Wing. Mexico's horsemen had done their country proud as the only other Mexican medal success at the 1948 Olympics was a bronze by the highboard diver, Joaquin Capilla.

In the *Daily Express*, John Macadam had only one regret about the day's happenings, and that concerned the closing ceremony of the Games, which followed the completion of the Prix des Nations event, and from which the great majority of the competitors in all the sports were absent because they had already gone home or had started their journeys. "How that great-hearted Wembley crowd, so sporting that they *prayed* the Mexican winner of the final equestrian event over his last hurdles, would have cheered them as they cheered every great athlete, no matter where he came from," Macadam wrote.

There was no great surprise about the Mexican success. Their riders had made a lasting impression at the previous year's New York International Horse Show, and the day after their Olympic success the "special correspondent" of the London Sunday newspaper, *The Observer*, had written: "Finally, in came Mariles. Watching him schooling at Aldershot one had feared for England. Sure enough, there was no relaxation of impulsion and control and *Arete* made as fine a performance as any horse ever did in the Prix des Nations."

The British trio had exceeded all expectations in taking the team bronze medals, and one of the pairings – Harry Llewellyn and *Foxhunter* – would return in 1952 for far greater and everlasting glory as a member of the gold-medal-winning team. The Welsh-born Llewellyn, who had finished second in the famed annual Grand National steeplechase race in 1936, later became Sir Harry Llewellyn Bt CBE. One of his fellow title-winners would be Major Douglas Stewart, who had competed in the three-day event at Aldershot but failed to finish and later became commanding officer of those same Royal Scots Greys who had inspired Hylton Cleaver's hopes for future British success at the Olympics.

Among those who did not complete the course was Italian Raimondo d'Inzeo, who had earlier placed 30th in the three-day event. Together with his brother Piero he would go on to form one of the most famous of showjumping family partnerships. Individually, Raimondo won silver and Piero bronze in 1956, then Raimondo won gold and Piero silver in 1960. As two-thirds of the Italian team they won silver in 1956 and bronze in 1960 and 1964. They also placed fifth in 1968, won bronze again in 1972 when teams were increased from three riders to four, and were competitors once more in 1976.

The Mexican double gold-medallist, Mariles Cortes, placed sixth in the individual show jumping in 1952, but subsequently led a rather more eventful life. In 1964 in Mexico City he shot dead another motorist who had tried to force him off the road. In 1972, at the age of 59, he was arrested in Paris for drug-smuggling but died in prison before he could come to trial.

Prix des Nations show jumping individual result: 1 Humberto Mariles Cortes (Mexico) riding *Arete* 6.25 faults, 2 Rubén Uriza (Mexico) *Harvey* 8, 3 Jean-François Marquis d'Orgeix de Thonel (France) *Sucre de Pomme* 8, 4 Franklin Wing (USA) *Democrat* 8, 5= Jaime Garcia Cruz (Spain) *Bizarro*, Eric Sörensen (Sweden) *Biatunga* 12, 7= Max Fresson (France) *Decametre*, Harry Llewellyn (Great Britain) *Foxhunter*, Henry Nicoll (Great Britain) *Kilgeddin* 16, 10= José Navarro Morenes (Spain) *Quorum*, Francisco Pontes (Brazil) *Itaguai*, Alberto Valdes (Mexico) *Chihuchoc* 20, 13 Greger Lewenhaupt (Sweden) *Orkan* 20.75, 14 Dan Corry (Eire) *Tramore Bay* 21.25, 15 César Campos (Argentina) *Santa Fé* 24, 16 Marcelino Gavilán y Ponce de Leon (Spain) *Forajido* 24.5, 17 Fred Ahern (Eire) *Aherlow* 25.5, 18 Henrique Alves Callado (Portugal) *Xerez* 26, 19 Arthur Carr (Great Britain) *Monty* 35, 20 Joachim Gruppelaar (Holland) *Random Harvest* 36, 21 John Russell (USA) *Air Mail* 38.25, 22 José Correia Barrento (Portugal) *Alcoa* 42.5, 23 Taimo Rissanen (Finland) *Viser* 56. There were 21 non-finishers.

Prix des Nations show jumping team result: 1 Mexico (Humberto Mariles Cortes 1, Rubén Uriza 2, Alberto Valdes 10 =) 34.25 faults, 2 Spain (Jaime Garcia Cruz 5=, José Navarro Morenes 10=, Marcelino Gavilán y Ponce de Leon 16) 56.5, 3 Great Britain (Harry Llewellyn 7=, Henry Nicoll 7=, Arthur Carr 19=) 67. Note: only three countries finished complete teams.

Chapter 23

"TO HIT WITHOUT ONESELF BEING HIT"

Fencing. Palace of Engineering, Wembley. 30 July–13 August.

The programme: Men's team foil, first & second rounds 30 July, semi-finals & final 1 August; Women's individual foil 2 August; men's individual foil, first & second rounds 3 August, semi-finals & final 4 August; men's team épée, first & second rounds 5 August, semi-finals & final 6 August; men's individual épée first & second rounds 8 August, semi-finals & final 9 August; men's team sabre first & second rounds 10 August, semi-finals & final 11 August; men's individual sabre first & second rounds 12 August, semi-finals & final 13 August.

N
O SPORT AT the 1948 Olympics other than perhaps the equestrian events and yachting seemed to favour the guile of age and experience to a greater extent than fencing, despite the speed and agility also required of its exponents. Christian d'Oriola, the precocious French winner of the world foil title in 1947 at the age of 18, was an exception, a mere stripling among men. Numerous fencers at Wembley had competed at Olympic level in the 1930s, and some even in the 1920s, but in terms of longevity they all had to give precedence to Dr Ivan Osiier, for whom selection in Denmark's team would entail a nostalgic return trip to London – after an absence of 40 years!

Dr Osiier had competed at the Games of 1908 at the age of 19, and then at those of 1912, 1920, 1924, 1928 and 1932. He had appeared in nine Olympic finals. His one medal had been a silver earned in the individual épée in 1912 which had been won by Paul Anspach, of Belgium, who was also at Wembley in his capacity as president of the sport's ruling body, the Fédération Internationale d'Escrime (FIE). Osiier's wife, Ellen, had been the Olympic foil champion when it was first held for women in 1924.

Fencing itself was, of course, of great antiquity. Evidence has been found of swordsmanship being practised in Egypt in 1360 BC, and the first ruling body for fencing in Britain was "The Corporation of Masters of Defence", which had been established some time before 1540 by King Henry VIII, who also pursued another sporting interest – that of hammer throwing – as well as his six wives. Interest in fencing was revived in Britain in the mid-19th century and the Amateur Fencing Association was founded in 1902, though national championships for the foil and sabre had started four years earlier. The future Sir Winston Churchill was an enthusiastic fencer and had won the Public Schools' foil title in 1892. At the first Modern Olympic Games, in Athens in 1896, there were foil and sabre events for men, won respectively by Emile Gravelotte, of France, and Ioannis Georgiadis, of Greece. The FEI was formed in 1913.

The entries for the various Wembley events were so numerous that the organising committee's official report enthused about "the greatest competition ever staged in the history of the sport". The individual competitors numbered 63 for the foil, 55 for the épée, 51 for the sabre and 39 for the women's foil. There were 16 men's teams entered for the foil, 21 for the épée, 17 for the sabre. No addition would be made to the programme until the women's team foil was introduced in 1960. The épée is the heaviest of the three weapons (770 grammes) and the target area is the whole body. The foil weighs 500 grammes and the upper body only is the target. The sabre also weighs 500 grammes and the target is above the waist, including the head.

Fencing had been largely a European preserve at the Games, with France (10 individual golds, six team golds), Italy (seven individual, eight team) and Hungary (six individual, five team) as the most successful countries in the men's events to be held at Wembley. The women's foil had been won by four different countries in succession – Denmark, Germany, Austria and Hungary. The first European Championships had been held in 1921, elevated to the status of World Championships in 1936, and Italy had won 23 individual and team titles, Hungary 19 and France 17. One British victory had been achieved by Gwen Neligan in 1933. At the 1947 World Championships in Lisbon France had won the individual and team titles for the men's foil and épée; Italy had won the individual and team sabre; Austria the women's individual foil; and Denmark the women's team foil.

The only individual Olympic winners from outside Europe had been the Cubans, Ramón Fonst, for the foil and épée in both 1900 and 1904, and Manuel Diaz, for the sabre in the latter year. There had also been a foil win by a combined Cuba/USA team in 1904, but these Games were held in St Louis and few Europeans took part. Encouragingly, at Wembley there would be competitors from the USA, Canada, Egypt, Cuba, Mexico and six South American countries.

Though there was no one to challenge the longevity of Dr Osiier, there were 11 men and two women who had won medals in 1932 or 1936 and would do so again in 1948 – and in some instances at Games after that. Pre-eminent among them was the Hungarian Aladár Gerevich, who would eventually merit consideration as one of the greatest of all Olympic competitors in any sport, having been a member of the winning sabre team at every Games from 1932 to 1960, by which time he was 50 years old.

Gerevich was to bring his total of medals to 10, with the individual gold at Wembley, plus a bronze (1936) and silver (1952) in that event and another bronze in the team foil (1952). He also figures among the most successful of Olympic families as he married Erna Bogáthy Bogen, who had been foil bronze-medallist in 1932 and whose father, Albert, had won a team sabre silver in 1912. To complete the family tree, Pál Gerevich, son of Aladár and Erna, won team sabre bronze in 1972 and 1980!

A further major contribution to Hungary's dominance of sabre fencing was made by Tibor Berczelly, Pal Kovács and László Rajcsányi, who were all team-mates of Gerevich for the sabre in 1936, 1948 and 1952, and by Kovács again in 1956 and 1960. In Olympic team sabre competition Hungary won 46 consecutive matches from 1924, when they had lost to Italy, to 1964, when they again lost to Italy. In the individual sabre Hungary's finest hour was to be in 1952 when Kovács, Gerevich and Berczelly took the three individual medals in that order of precedence.

Italy's preference was for the épée and their outstanding exponent of the weapon was Edoardo Mangiarotti, who won his first team gold at Berlin in 1936 at the age of 17 and was again in the winning team in 1952, 1956 and 1960. He was also individual épée champion in 1952 and had a sixth gold in the 1956 team foil. He won 13 Olympic medals in all, and a team-mate and individual silver-medallist in 1952 was his elder brother, Dario. Their father, Giuseppe, was a fencing master from Milan who had taught them both from the age of eight and had deliberately converted Edoardo into a left-hander because he believed it would be of advantage to him.

Two other Italians, Aldo Montano and Vincenzo Pinton, won team sabre silvers in 1936 and 1948 (and Pinton again in 1952), and a third, Manlio di Rosa, won team foil gold in 1936 and silver in 1948. Two French gold-medallists at Wembley had also been medal-winners in the same event before the war: René Bougnol, with team foil gold in 1932 and silver in 1936, and Michel Pécheux, with team épée bronze in 1936. All three women's foil medallists at Wembley were fencers of comparable experience, as Ilona Elek, of Hungary, who won the gold, had also been champion in 1936 (and would be silver-medallist in 1952); Karen Lachmann, of Denmark, second at Wembley, had placed fifth in 1936 (and would be bronze-medallist in 1952); and Ellen Müller-Preis, of Austria, had been champion in 1932 and bronze-medallist in 1936.

Britain's women had outshone their male counterparts in individual competition with silver medals in 1924 for Gladys Davis, in 1928 for Muriel Freeman, and in 1932 for Heather Guinness, familiarly known as "Judy". The

British men had also won silver in the team épée in 1906, 1908 and 1912, including Edgar Seligman on each occasion. Seligman, described as "the pioneer of modern British fencing", made his fifth and final Olympic appearance in 1924 at the age of 57 and continued to give service to the sport as a coach, judge and administrator. The profusion of facts and figures may not be easy to absorb but they are essential to the understanding of the traditions of the sport.

The AFA Championships had only been resumed in 1947 and therefore almost all of Britain's selected fencers had started their careers in the 1930s. The veterans were needed because only 51 of the 109 clubs in existence in 1939 had survived the war years. The men's captain, John Emrys Lloyd, a graduate of King's College, Cambridge, had won the Amateur Fencing Association (AFA) national junior foil title in 1926 and the first of his seven senior titles in 1928. He was sixth in the Olympics of 1932 and 1936. He had also placed third in the World Championships of 1931 and 1933. He had served with the RAF during World War II, and now at 39 he found himself back among many old friends.

The Games venue was the "Palace of Engineering" at Wembley, and it was not the most salubrious of choices because it had been built for the Empire Exhibition of 1924 and had subsequently been used as Government offices. The organising committee's report was somewhat ambivalent in its opinion of the facilities, stating in one sentence no more than that they "proved adequate" and in the next that "the central piste, on which all the finals were fought, with its steeply-banked seating, giant scoreboard and national flags overhead, was declared by visitors to be the best fencing arena yet seen"; or, at least, that's what it was claimed that the visitors had said. In any case, it seems reasonable to presume that the London organisers' policy of making do with whatever buildings were readily available, and keeping the costs of conversion or adaptation down to the minimum, worked well enough so far as fencing was concerned.

For the individual foil, the French and Italians, who between them had won all but one of the 10 previous Olympic titles, were expected to dominate. France had their youthful world champion d'Oriola, together with René Bougnol and Jehan Buhan; Italy's three were the Nostini brothers, Giuliano and Renzo, and Manlio di Rosa, leaving Edoardo Mangiarotti to concentrate on the épée. Britain's hopes lay with Emrys Lloyd. The first round consisted of eight pools, with the top four in each qualifying, and the winners were di Rosa and Giuliano Nostini for Italy, Emrys Lloyd and René Paul for Great Britain, d'Oriola and Buhan for France, Cetrulo for the USA and Tessi for Uruguay.

In the second round of four pools, di Rosa, Giuliano Nostini, d'Oriola and an Argentinian, Galimi, each had six wins. Emrys Lloyd was equal second in his pool, but Paul and the third Briton, AR Smith, were eliminated. This left 16 men to contest the semi-finals in two pools: all three French, all three Italians, two Americans, two Belgians, one each from Argentina, Denmark, Egypt, Great Britain, Hungary and Sweden. Buhan won the first pool from d'Oriola, Ruben (Denmark) and Emrys Lloyd; Maszlay (Hungary) won the second from Bougnol,

Valcke (Belgium) and di Rosa, who beat Cetrulo in a barrage and was therefore the only Italian finalist.

The final was a triumph for France as Buhan had only 14 hits against him in winning all of his seven bouts and d'Oriola (who was, incidentally, a cousin of a medal-winning horseman Pierre Jonquères d'Oriola) took the silver with five wins. Emrys Lloyd lost the bronze to Maszlay only on hits against as both won four bouts. Charles-Louis de Beaumont, the honorary secretary of the AFA, provided the account for the British Olympic Association's report and was fulsome in his praise of the gold-medallist: "Of medium height, and very rapid in the conception and execution of his attacks, he adapted his game extremely well to his different opponents ... his brilliantly intelligent and controlled foil play was in the highest tradition of the French school."

In the team foil event each of four fencers met each of their opponents, and France began its defence of the title in an undemanding fashion, overwhelming Eire and then Canada by 16-0 scores, while Italy, the silver-medallists from 1936, dealt with Greece in the same manner. Great Britain got through narrowly against Holland, winning on fewer hits against (58 to 63) after each had won eight bouts. The semi-finals consisted of two pools each of four teams, with the first two in each pool going on to the finals: Argentina, Belgium, Hungary and Italy in the first pool; Egypt, France, Great Britain and the USA in the second pool.

Italy beat Argentina 11-5 and Hungary 9-2 and Belgium beat Hungary 10-6, but the pool ended abruptly when the Argentinians disputed the result of their first bout against Belgium and withdrew in protest. Accurate judging of whether or not hits had been made would become easier when electrical apparatus was introduced to the Games in 1956. The British quartet was beaten very narrowly on hits against by the Americans, 8-8 (60-64), and did well enough against France, losing 10-6, but were eliminated with Egypt. The finalists were thus Belgium, France, Italy and the USA, and the gold medals were decided in an immensely exciting match between France and Italy in which France had led 6-3 but Italy had won five of the last seven bouts, only to lose on hits received, 60 to 62.

France had made use of six fencers and had won 85 of their 112 bouts, led by Jehan Buhan (20-6), André Bonin (16-4) and Jacques Lataste (15-5). By a

---

Individual foil result: 1 Jehan Buhan (France) bouts 7-0, hits 35-14; 2 Christian d'Oriola (France) 5-2, 29-18; 3 Lajos Maszlay (Hungary) 4-3, 25-22; 4 John Emrys Lloyd (Great Britain) 4-3, 23-29; 5 René Bougnol (France) 3-4, 28-26; 6 Manlio di Rosa (Italy) 3-4, 22-27; 7 Paul Valcke (Belgium) 1-6, 23-31; 8 Ivan Ruben (Denmark) 1-6, 15-33.

Team foil result: 1 France (André Bonin, René Bougnol, Jehan Buhan, Christian d'Oriola, Jacques Lataste, Adrian Rommel) matches 3-0, bouts 28-18; 2 Italy (Manlio di Rosa, Edoardo Mangiarotti, Giuliano Nostini, Renzo Nostini, Giorgio Pellini, Saverio Ragno) 2-1, 28-15; 3 Belgium (Raymond Bru, Georges de Bourguignon, Henry Paternoster, Paul Valcke, André van de Werve de Vorsselaer, Edouard Yves) 1-2. 19-27; 4 USA (Daniel Bukantz, Dean Cetrulo, Dernell Every, Silvio Giolito, Nathaniel Lubell, Austin Prokop) 0-3, 14-29. Match results – France 11 USA 5, Italy 11 Belgium 5, Belgium 9 USA 7, France 8 Italy 8 (60-62), France 9 Belgium 5, Italy 9 USA 2.

quirk of the competition, Italy had not been required to complete earlier matches and so had contested only 95 bouts, winning 73, and actually had the two most successful fencers in Edoardo Mangiarotti (17-3) and Giuliano Nostini (13-2). All of the Belgians except one (Edouard Yves) had also been in the team placed equal fifth in 1936, and of these Raymond Bru had waited even longer for a medal, having been in the fourth-placed team in 1928. For Great Britain, Emrys Lloyd won 11 of his 16 bouts. From 1974 to 1978 he would serve as president of the AFA.

The individual épée followed a similar format to the individual foil: a first round of eight pools, a second round of six pools, and 18 qualifying for the two semi-final pools. By that penultimate stage there were still 12 countries represented – Argentina, Belgium, Brazil, Colombia, France (all three of their representatives), Great Britain, Italy (also all three), Luxembourg, Norway, Sweden, Switzerland and the USA. Encouragingly for Britain, the national épée champion, Dr Ronald Parfitt, won six bouts, and the only other competitor to do so was Norman Lewis, of the USA, each of them heading their semi-final pools. The reigning world champion from France, Edouard Artigas, competed only in the épée team event.

Fencing – like running – is a discipline in which pacing yourself to last the distance is all important, and Lewis and Parfitt ended up in the lowest two places of the 10 finalists. For the third successive Games (and for the next three to come) Italy provided the winner but, in this instance, somewhat against the odds. Luigi Cantone had been a late replacement in the event for Dario Mangariotti, who had injured a foot in the team contest, and had then lost his first two bouts to Dario's brother, Edoardo, and to the other Italian, Carlo Agostoni, before winning all of his remaining seven.

The final took 5½ hours to complete and de Beaumont described the event as "the severest competition of the meeting". Modesty prevented the writer from elaborating on that point, but de Beaumont himself was one of the Britons who took part and had lost a three-way barrage in the second round. Born in Liverpool, his impressive full name was Charles-Louis Leopold Alfred de Beaumont and in 1931 he had been appointed Britain's representative to the FIE and was honorary secretary of the AFA for 20 years from 1936 until he became president. He had been the national épée champion in 1936–37–38 and had been captain of the British team at the Berlin Olympics. During the war he had served as a wing commander with the RAF and had been awarded the MBE.

He said of Cantone that he was "certainly the best épéist on the day ... a left-hander of medium height, he preserved his orthodox style throughout". He also demonstrated what de Beaumont described as "the efficacy of the cardinal rule of épée fencing – to hit without oneself being hit". The silver medal was only finally decided by a barrage after Zappelli, of Switzerland, and Edoardo Mangiarotti had each finished with identical results of five wins, 17 hits against and 20 scored. The fencers in fourth and fifth places also each had five wins.

The favourites for the team épée, as for the team foil, were France, Italy and Sweden, and they all had an easy start. The French went through to the second round without a fight when Chile withdrew. Italy beat Brazil 14-2 and qualified automatically when Brazil lost their next match in that pool to Great Britain. Sweden needed only eight bouts in their single match for a winning lead over Greece. The four second-round pools involved Hungary, Italy, Norway and Poland in pool one; Denmark, Egypt, France and Great Britain in pool two; Argentina, Sweden and Switzerland in pool three; Belgium, Luxembourg and the USA in pool four.

Italy had two more overwhelming wins of 14-1 v Poland and 12-2 v Norway, and there was no requirement for a match against the other qualifiers from that pool, Hungary. France had rather more of an energy-sapping time, beating Denmark 12-4, Great Britain 12-3 and Egypt 8-5. As the Egyptians also lost only 8-6 to Denmark, having beaten Great Britain 11-5, they could be said to have not had the best of the draw. Argentina and the USA each lost their first two matches in the remaining groups, and so there was an easy passage for Sweden, Switzerland, Belgium and Luxembourg, who needed only one match apiece to qualify.

The all-European semi-finals brought together Belgium, Denmark, France and Switzerland in pool one, and Hungary, Italy, Luxembourg and Sweden in pool two. France were very surprisingly beaten by Belgium, and beaten easily, 10-5, but the Belgians had already lost 7-6 to Denmark and were then outscored on hits against after a 7-7 draw with Switzerland, and so were eliminated. The second pool was far less competitive as Sweden began by crushing Hungary 15-0, and after Italy and Sweden had in turn beaten Luxembourg the Italians quickly ran up an 8-1 winning margin against the Hungarians, enough to qualify them without any further bouts.

France and Italy started well in the final by respectively beating Sweden 11-4 and Denmark 12-4. Then when the Italians took a 4-1 lead in the third match against the French the gold medals seemed decided, but the French rallied magnificently and won 10 of the remaining 11 bouts. Victory over Denmark gave France the title, and their star performer here was the 1938 world champion,

---

Individual épée result: 1 Luigi Cantone (Italy) bouts 7-2, hits 24-15; 2 Oswald Zappelli (Switzerland) 5-4, 20-17; 3 Edoardo Mangiarotti (Italy) 5-4, 20-17; 4 Henri Guérin (France) 5-4, 20-19; 5 Jean Radoux (Belgium) 5-4, 19-20; 6 Henri Lepage (France) 4-5, 19-20, 7 Carlo Agostoni (Italy) 4-5, 22-21; 8 Emile Gretsch (Luxembourg) 3-6, 16-22; 9 Norman Lewis (USA) 3-6, hits against 24; 10 Ronald Parfitt (Great Britain) 2-8, hits against 23. Note: only "hits against" were recorded for Lewis and Parfitt in the official results.

Team épée result: 1 France (Edouard Artigas, Marcel Desprets, Henri Guérin, Maurice Huet, Henri Lepage, Michel Pécheux) matches 3-0, bouts 31-10; 2 Italy (Carlo Agostoni, Luigi Cantone, Antonio Mandruzzotto, Dario Mangiarotti, Edoardo Mangiarotti, Fiorenzo Marini) 2-1, 25-21; 3 Sweden (Per Carlsson, Frank Cervell, Carl Forssell, Bengt Ljungquist, Sven Thofelt, Arne Tollbom) 1-2, 18-26; 4 Denmark (Erik Andersen, René Dybkaer, Kenneth Flindt, Mogens Lüchow, Jakob Lyng, Ib Benjamin Nielsen) 0-3, 12-29. Match results – France 11 Sweden 4, Italy 12 Denmark 4, France 11 Italy 5, Sweden 8 Denmark 7, Italy 8 Sweden 6, France 9 Denmark 1.

Michel Pécheux, who won all 11 of his bouts in the three matches which constituted the final and 25 out of 30 in total. The Swede, Sven Thofelt, now aged 44, had also been in the silver-medal team in 1936 and has the rare claim to being outstanding in two different sports, because he was the 1928 Olympic champion for the modern pentathlon, which includes fencing among its five disciplines. His son, Björn, was to compete in the 1960 Olympic modern pentathlon. Agostoni, of Italy, had been the épée individual bronze-medallist in 1932.

Hungary had won the Olympic individual sabre title at every Games they had contested since 1908 and had taken three of the first four places in Berlin. Who, then, could hope to beat their Wembley trio consisting of the prolific Gerevich, Kovács and Berczelly, who had figured in the winning sabre teams of 1936 and again in the previous couple of days at Wembley? The world title had actually been held for the past decade by the Italian, Aldo Montano, who had won the last pre-war championship in 1938 and the first post-war championship in 1947, but he competed only in the team event at Wembley. Gerevich had been world champion in 1935 and had been succeeded by Kovács in 1937.

The eight first-round pools saw the elimination of the durable Dr Osiier, now aged 59, and of Britain's 46-year-old Arthur Pilbrow, but the British champion, Roger Tredgold, who had been a team-mate of Pilbrow's at the Berlin Games and was a psychiatrist by profession, went through in style, winning all four of his bouts, and was joined by Robin Brook, a director of the Bank of England. Those into the semi-finals were all the three Hungarians, together with three Italians, three Americans, two French, and one each from Austria, Denmark, Egypt, Mexico and Poland. Tredgold was beaten by the Mexican, Haro Oliva, in a barrage, and Brook was fifth in his group.

Haro Oliva then created the surprise of the semi-finals by eliminating the Hungarian, Berczelly, after another barrage. Gerevich, Kovács (both Hungary), Daré, Pinton (both Italy), Nyllas, Worth (both USA) and Lefevre (France) were the other qualifiers. The final was the last event to be decided and was described by de Beaumont as "a fitting climax to the tournament, providing a first class exhibition of swordplay". Gerevich won all of his seven bouts, though pressed hard by Kovács, who had led 4-2 in their encounter, and 31 of the 32 sabre bouts he contested at the Games.

Hungary had not lost a sabre team match at the Olympics since 1924, and with four of the Berlin team available again it seemed unlikely that anyone would bar their way on this occasion. De Beaumont's succinct comment that "the supremacy of the Hungarians was never seriously challenged" says it all. They had a bye in the first round and needed only one match in the second round, beating Egypt 9-2, to reach the semi-finals, in which they were joined in the first pool by Argentina, Belgium and Poland. The second pool brought together France, Holland, Italy and the USA. The British quartet had been eliminated after losing 11-5 to the USA and 9-4 to Italy.

Hungary marched on through the semi-finals, 15-1 v Argentina and 12-3 v

Poland, and the third match of the final, in which they beat Italy 10-6, decided the title, but the Italians resisted stoutly. The score was 4-4 at halfway and de Beaumont said of the encounter that it was "a magnificent display of modern sabre fencing". The USA lost the silver medals by the narrowest of margins, drawing 8-8 in the closing match with Italy and being "out-hit" 61 to 59. Hungary also provided two of the US bronze-medallists because Tibor Nyllas and George Worth (whose original name was György Vitez) had both been born in Budapest. One of their team-mates, Miguel de Capriles, had been born in Mexico City.

The entrants for the women's foil included four of the first six in Berlin: Ilona Elek (Hungary) first, Ellen Müller-Preis (Austria) third, Karen Lachmann (Denmark) fifth and Jenny Addams (Belgium) sixth. Müller-Preis had also won under her maiden name of Preis at the age of 19 in 1932 and Addams had placed sixth in 1928 as a 19-year-old and fourth in 1932. Elek, already 29 when she made her Olympic debut, had been European champion in 1934 (with her sister, Margit, second) and 1935 and Addams European champion in 1930. Müller-Preis, by now a mother of two, had become the first post-war world champion in 1947.

Elek, Müller-Preis, Lachmann and Elek's sister, Margit, won their first-round pools, but among those eliminated was Britain's Elizabeth Arbuthnot, who had also competed at the 1936 Games. The other two Britons – Mary Glen Haig and Gytte Minton – both went on to the semi-finals, for which all three Hungarians qualified, together with Müller-Preis, Lachmann and Addams. Ilona Elek and Müller-Preis each won her semi-final pool and were joined for the final by Lachmann, Glen Haig, Filz (Austria), Cesari (Italy), Cerra (USA) and Margit Elek.

Ilona Elek, in the words of de Beaumont, "fought throughout with a forcefulness and *brio* which the years have left undimmed, but she was closely pressed by Karen Lachmann, of Denmark, whose more classical style was much admired, and who actually received less hits in the final pool". Elek beat Lachmann 4-2 in the last and deciding bout. Lachmann had been born in Peking (now Beijing) and Müller-Preis has the particular distinction for a 1948 Olympian of having been born in Berlin. Müller-Preis became Professor

---

Individual sabre result: 1 Aladár Gerevich (Hungary) bouts 7-0, hits 35-18; 2 Vincenzo Pinton (Italy) 5-2, 32-23; 3 Pal Kovács (Hungary) 5-2, 33-24; 4 Jacques Lefevre (France) 4-3, 27-26; 5 George Worth (USA) 2-5, 26-27; 6 Gastone Daré (Italy) 2-5, 25-30; 7 Tibor Nyllas (USA) 2-5, 20-31; 8 Antonio Haro Oliva (Mexico) 1-6, 15-34.

Team sabre result: 1 Hungary (Tibor Berczelly, Aladár Gerevich, Rudolf Kárpáti, Pal Kovács, Bertalan Papp, László Rajcsányi) matches 3-0, hits 29-13; 2 Italy (Gastone Daré, Aldo Montano, Renzo Nostini, Vincenzo Pinton, Mauro Racca, Carlo Turcato) 2-1, 24-24; 3 USA (Norman Armitage, Dean Cetrulo, Miguel de Capriles, James Flynn, Tibor Nyllas, George Worth) 1-2, 24-23; 4 Belgium (Robert Bayot, Georges de Bourguignon, Ferdinand Jassogne, Eugène Laermans, Marcel Nys, Edouard Yves) 0-3, 12-29. Match results – Italy 10 Belgium 6, Hungary 10 USA 6, Hungary 10 Italy 6, USA 10 Belgium 5, Hungary 9 Belgium 1, Italy 8 USA 8 (59-61)

Emeritus at the University of Music and Interpretative Art in Vienna and earned a worldwide reputation for having "developed a breathing and movement technique that maximises energy, frees the body of tensions, and lets the voice flow freely". She worked with such eminent figures as Zeffirelli, Bernstein and von Karajan and was still supervising masterclasses throughout the world when beyond her 90th birthday.

Maria Cerra came desperately close to winning the only non-European individual medal of the tournament.

Elek and Lachmann continued to compete with great success and at the 1952 Olympics were second and third to the Italian, Irene Camber, who had been eliminated by barrage at the Wembley semi-finals. Lachmann was sixth at the 1956 Games, one place ahead of Müller-Preis. World titles were won by Müller-Preis again in 1949 and 1950, and by Elek in 1951, Camber in 1953 and Lachmann in 1954. There was no women's team event at Wembley, but there had been a World Championship event at The Hague the previous month which Denmark had won from Hungary, France, Austria, the USA and Great Britain.

The British performances in fencing at Wembley had been reasonably encouraging. John Emrys Lloyd had earned an excellent fourth place. Ronald Parfitt and Mary Glen Haig had reached finals. None of these achievements, though, would have given any real hint of a golden era to come. At the 1956 Olympics Gillian Sheen, who had won her first national title in 1949, became Olympic champion. Allan Jay emulated Emrys Lloyd by placing fourth in the foil and the British team was fifth. In 1958 Bill Hoskyns was world épée champion. The following year Jay won the world foil title. At the 1960 and 1964 Olympics Jay and then Hoskyns took the épée silver medals. Britain also won the épée team silver in 1960.

Individual foil (women) result: 1 Ilona Elek (Hungary) bouts 6-1, hits 31-15; 2 Karen Lachmann (Denmark) 5-2, 24-11; 3 Ellen Müller-Preis (Austria) 5-2, 24-16; 4 Maria Cerra (USA) 5-2, 23-16; 5 Fritzi Filz (Austria) 4-3, 20-12; 6 Margit Elek (Hungary) 1-6, 10-26; 7 Velleda Cesari (Italy) 1-6, 15-27; 8 Mary Glen Haig (Great Britain) 1-6, 10-27.

Chapter 24

IF BRITAIN HAD NOT BEEN PREPARED TO HOST THE GAMES OF 1948 ...

A lifetime's Olympic memories for Dame Mary Glen Haig

THE LIFE OF Dame Mary Alison Glen Haig, born on 18 July 1918, has been one of exceptional distinction. As a fencer she reached the final of the Olympic women's foil in 1948 and subsequently also competed for Great Britain at the Games of 1952, 1956 and 1960. She was awarded the MBE in 1971 and the CBE in 1977 and was appointed Dame Commander of the British Empire in 1993. She was elected a member of the International Olympic Committee in 1982. She held senior executive posts in administration at King's College Hospital and then at the Royal Northern Orthopaedic Hospital. Her recollections of her 1948 Olympic experience remain crystal clear some 60 years later.

"On the eve of my first Games I remember hurrying out of King's Hospital in South London for the British team quarters, which for us was not some purpose-built Olympic village but some rather grotty rooms behind Victoria Station, containing little more than a few camp-beds. Then I suddenly stopped and thought there probably wouldn't be any food where I was going. So I ran back into King's and persuaded the cook – because I didn't have my ration-book with me – to put some sugar and milk into little pots for me.

"When I finally got to our room I hadn't been there long when I sniffed the smell of meat being grilled, rushed down the stairs, and discovered that some French girls – of course, they would be organised in this way – were cooking. I joined the queue, and because they had so much they gave us some for our supper, too.

"We all finally settled down on our camp-beds, determined to get some sleep before the big day, the opening of the first post-war Olympics at Wembley. Except we were woken up halfway through the night by our team-mate Gytte Minton moving about. We switched on the light and there she was, standing fully dressed in her complete new British uniform. 'What on earth are you doing?' we asked, and then she confessed that she had lain awake for hours, worrying she might forget something, until she decided that the only solution was to get dressed and ready hours before it was necessary.

"Of course, the Games opening ceremony at Wembley Stadium was very splendid. Now, with all my subsequent experience, including three more Olympics as a fencer, and my work with the International Olympic Committee for many years, I'm convinced that if Britain had not been prepared, in spite of barely recovering from the war, to host those 1948 Games, the whole movement might have foundered.

"Still, looking back to when one was young, there's always some slightly bizarre or cheerful memory as well. One concerned Emrys Lloyd, the most experienced British fencing captain, a London solicitor who had already competed at Los Angeles in 1932 and Berlin in 1936. On the way to Wembley he'd taken off his official team beret and sat on it for safety. Of course, when he got up he forgot it at first and then found that someone had presumably pinched it for a souvenir. I think, studying the film of the march past the King there's just one bare British head ...

"By far the biggest thrill for me, I'm ashamed to admit, was that our wonderful West Indian sprinter McDonald Bailey used to dabble, among other things, in what was known as the 'rag trade', and Mac, as we all called him, gave some of us girls an absolutely smashing cocktail dress – no clothing coupons needed, first class, perfect fit. I wore it as often as I could, and I'm sure the other girls did, too.

"Competitively, I suppose I should have been pleased that I qualified for the Olympic final in the women's foil at the Wembley Engineering Centre, which was overall the biggest ever international fencing competition the sport had seen. There was no way, over the three days, that I was going to beat the individual winner, Ilona Elek, of Hungary, who – full marks to her – had won the Olympic title in 1936, but quite honestly with my experience I could and should have won the 1948 bronze medal from Müller-Preis, of Austria. I needed my coach, but he couldn't be there.

"I owed all my fencing ability to my father, William Charles James, who was perhaps the only surviving member of the regiment which went missing, possibly all killed, after landing at Gallipoli in the First World War. He was wounded on the beaches, and so he could never fence competitively again, but he could still coach me. But while I was fencing at Wembley he was officiating in the fencing in the modern pentathlon at Aldershot. Every official, every volunteer, went where they were needed most because, quite simply, we were hosts to the whole world.

"When the Games were finally over, the British team went to Buckingham Palace, and I was last of all to meet the Queen. She leaned forward and said quietly, 'Your uncle is very proud of you.' My uncle was a member of the Royal household. Then I found myself facing the splendidly upright figure of Queen Mary, parasol and all. I was wearing my brand new blazer with its British flag when she asked, 'And which country do you represent?' Oh yes, I certainly didn't have any difficulty answering that."

Chapter 25

SWEDISH STRENGTH, SLAV STERILITY

Football. Various grounds and Empire Stadium, Wembley. 26 July–13 August.

BRITISH FOOTBALL SEEMED to be in good order. A Great Britain team had walloped the Rest of Europe 6-1 at Hampden Park in 1947. In May of 1948 England had run rings round Italy in Turin, winning 4-0, and had then beaten Switzerland 6-0 at Highbury. But all that success was achieved in the professional game. Matters were rather different among the amateurs – not least the question of what exactly constituted an amateur.

British teams had won the Olympic football tournaments of 1900, 1908 and 1912, but this was in the early days of international competition and some of the results were decidedly unusual. Denmark scored 26 goals in their three matches in 1908, but only two of these were in the final and so they had to settle for silver. Holland beat Finland 9-0 for the bronze medals in 1912. From 1920 onwards Britain had not won again at the Olympics – and this was scarcely surprising as they had not even taken part until 1936. The reason for the absence was the vexed question of "broken time payments".

This was the money which the international ruling body, FIFA, had agreed could be paid to amateurs in compensation for wages lost whilst playing. The problem was that Britain, Eire and France did not agree with the decision, and so the British stayed away until relenting for the Berlin Games, where their performance was not too inspiring, as a 2-0 win over China was followed by a 5-4 defeat against Poland. The British Olympic Association report, written by the secretary of the Football Association, Stanley Rous, pointedly referred to the fact that the team "had but little opportunity for training or practice", whereas the Poles "had practised together for six weeks".

The conflicting rules regarding "amateurism" were succinctly summarised by Edgar Kail, the amateur football correspondent for the London *Daily Graphic* newspaper, and who had himself been a leading amateur international, playing 18 times for England between 1921 and 1933. "The amateur status acceptable to Sweden, Russia, Switzerland, Italy and the South American countries would not be tolerated by the English FA," he wrote. Furthermore, the concept of a Great Britain team was almost entirely one of Olympic convenience, as all amateur international matches in Britain were played by teams representing each of the home countries. Stanley Rous had concluded his 1936 post-mortem by insisting, "There must be some organisation between the four British Associations if Association Football continues to figure in the programme of future Olympiads and Great Britain takes part". The inference was crystal clear: there had not been too much co-ordination between England, Wales, Scotland and Northern Ireland in the lead-up to Berlin.

During the 1947–48 season England's amateurs had beaten Ireland 5-0 and Wales 7-2 but had not played Scotland. Then from May onwards valiant efforts were made to forge a Great Britain team from these disparate elements, with trial matches at Blackpool on 8 May and at Hampden Park, Glasgow, on 29 May, under the managership of Matt Busby, whose 24-year reign in charge at Manchester United had begun in 1945. Internationals were played against Holland (lost) and France (won), and of the 22 players eventually chosen from these reasonably comprehensive preparations 10 were from England, eight from Scotland and two each from Northern Ireland and Wales.

There had been only four Olympic tournaments between the wars as football had not figured on the 1932 programme at Los Angeles. Titles had been won in 1920 by Belgium, in 1924 and 1928 by Uruguay, and in 1936 by Italy, but neither Belgium nor Uruguay, who had also won the 1930 World Cup with nine of their 1928 Olympic players, sent teams to the 1948 Games, and nor did previous medallists such as Argentina, Norway, Spain and Switzerland. The line-up was Afghanistan, Austria, China, Denmark, Egypt, Eire, France, Great Britain, Holland, India, Italy, Korea, Luxembourg, Mexico, Sweden, Turkey, Yugoslavia and the USA. Some of these entrants were entirely unknown quantities, and not least among them the Chinese team which included 11 players from Hong Kong and three from Malaya and was captained by 41-year-old Fung Ching Hsiang.

The likeliest form-guide had been provided by a match between the full England professional side and the Swedish amateurs at Highbury the previous Autumn which the hosts – including such legendary names as Frank Swift, Tom Finney and Wilf Mannion – had won 4-2, but the Swedes had impressed mightily with their skills and teamwork. The report of the match in *The Times* emphasised that England were flattered by the score, and that it was "only a very fine run and shot by Mortensen two minutes from the end that finally gave their victory of four goals to two a confident look about it". The correspondent added that after England's early domination "Sweden's second-half display was an eye-opener ...

the real strength of Sweden's rally lay in the close collaboration and positional play of the team as a whole". All but one of Sweden's team that day were in the Olympic squad. Earlier evidence of Swedish talent had been provided the year before when the IFK Norrköpping club side had visited England and had beaten Charlton Athletic, Sheffield United and Newcastle United and drawn with Wolverhampton Wanderers.

The International Olympic Committee may well have had their own reservations about the FIFA decision regarding "broken time" payments. Certainly, they felt constrained to send out a reminder under the name of Dr Ivo Schricker, secretary to the executive committee, to all member countries in May 1948 of exactly what it was that had been agreed. The key sentences in the IOC's 1947 resolution regarding football amateurism read as follows: "An amateur is one whose connection with sport is and always has been solely for pleasure and for the physical and moral benefits he derives therefrom, without material gain of any kind, direct or indirect. This definition is liberal in so far as it admits the reimbursement of actually lost salary and of real expenses of the athlete." The circular finished with a hopeful appeal to human nature: "This definition is based upon the loyalty of the athletes and the honesty of the officials."

Whether or not the concept of "moral benefits" was uppermost in the minds of the footballing hierarchy, the draw for the Olympic first round was made with every good intention at FIFA's headquarters in Zurich on 17 June, but between then and the opening matches six weeks later five of the entered countries pulled out, which rather threw affairs into a tangle. Two matches needed to be arranged to reduce the numbers from 18 to 16 for the first round, and so Afghanistan and Eire suffered the dubious privilege of being eliminated before the Olympic Games had even been officially opened. On 26 July Holland beat Eire 3-1 at Portsmouth's Fratton Park ground and Luxembourg beat Afghanistan 6-0 at Brighton & Hove Albion's aptly-named Goldstone Ground.

The other venues to be used for the preliminary matches were spread throughout London's professional and amateur clubs: Arsenal, Brentford, Crystal Palace, Dulwich Hamlet, Fulham, Ilford, Tottenham Hotspur and Walthamstow Avenue. The semi-finals, third-place match and final would all take place at the Empire Stadium.

Despite the reshuffle, the first-round matches still seemed oddly imbalanced. Sweden and Austria were drawn together in what was described by the veteran *World Sports* correspondent, Willy Meisl, in his BOA report, as the "shadow final". Sweden won 3-0 and the *Manchester Guardian* correspondent enthused of the Swedes: "One could not wish for more intelligence or stylish back play, for keener tackling or neater passing, or for a better shuttle-service between half-backs and forwards." Korea won 5-3 against Mexico, and there were decisive victories for Italy against the USA (9-0), Yugoslavia against Luxembourg (6-1), and Turkey against China (4-0). The other winners were Denmark in extra time over Egypt (3-1), Great Britain over Holland (4-3) and France over India (2-1). "The British", said

Meisl in commendation of Matt Busby's coaching, "had improved enormously. It proved conclusively that with proper organisation and planning British amateur football could still produce great teams, as it did in the past."

When Britain then beat France 1-0 in the quarter-finals to join Sweden, Denmark and Yugoslavia in an all-European last four, hopes were running high, and in all probability too high. Meisl was to later reflect that "far too much was suddenly expected of the British amateurs". Sweden had predictably slaughtered Korea 12-0. Denmark had beaten Italy 5-3. Yugoslavia had beaten Turkey 3-1.

In the first semi-final Sweden were already 4-1 up on Denmark at half-time, including a goal described as "possibly without parallel in soccer annals". The scorer was the Swedish inside-left, Carlsson, as the Danish goalkeeper was well beaten – but the goal-area was occupied by the Swedish centre-forward, Gunnar Nordahl, who had cleverly leaped into it to avoid being caught offside. The British held the Yugoslavs in check in the early stages of their match but were 2-1 down at half-time and conceded another goal thereafter. Plenty of goals were scored in the subsequent third-place match between Denmark and Great Britain, played in pouring rain on a soft and slippery Wembley pitch, and the Danes eventually won 5-3 to take the bronze medals. The same two teams had met in the 1908 and 1912 finals, and both matches had also been won by two goals – but to the favour of the British, 2-0 and 4-2.

"There is hardly any doubt that the two strongest national sides met in the final and that the best team won," concluded Willy Meisl. "The first half produced probably the best play of the entire tournament." Sweden and Yugoslavia were level 1-1 at the break, but the Swedes had the better of the second half and eventually won 3-1, with the last of their goals coming from a penalty. Meisl was full of praise for the winners: "Sweden fielded a well-balanced side in which the outstanding stars blended splendidly with the rest. The strength of the side lay in its cohesion. It was really a unit built up of 11 parts which worked in unison without friction or hesitation."

Meisl also had much to say about the Yugoslavs and analysed their style of play in great detail, using some phrases which followers of professional football more than six decades later might find painfully familiar: "They demonstrated what has become known as the 'Viennese School' of soccer, with far more insistent orthodoxy than did the Viennese themselves. I would describe their game as 'standing soccer'. They over-do the useful back pass. Even with one or two players in promising forward positions, the ball was constantly passed back, and the nearer they came to the opponent's goal the more they elaborated their pattern-weaving until the chance had gone. The Yugoslav game is extremely attractive and utterly exasperating – the more so as some of their players lack the discipline and restraint which is indispensable in sport, above all in international competition. They played football of almost unlimited potential in a sterile way."

Sweden's team included three Nordahl brothers – Bertil, Gunnar and Knud – who were a mechanic, a fireman and a policeman by occupation. There were two other firemen, another policeman, another mechanic, two print workers and two clerks among the Swedish team. Sweden were to place third to Uruguay and Brazil in the 1950 World Cup, and despite losing more than 20 of their best players to professional clubs in Italy, France and Spain the Swedes took the bronze medals at the 1952 Olympics with Erik Nilsson, Karl Svensson and Ingvar Rydell again in the team. Hungary won the gold that year and Yugoslavia again the silver, including in their team Bobek, Zlatko Čajkovski, Mitič and Vukas from the 1948 squad. After being beaten finalists for the third successive Games in 1956 Yugoslavia eventually won gold in 1960.

Until the 1984 Games, which were affected by a widespread Eastern European boycott, and where France won the title, all the Olympic gold medals in football were to go to state-aided teams: Hungary in 1952, USSR in 1956, Yugoslavia in 1960, Hungary again in 1964 and 1968, Poland in 1972, German Democratic Republic in 1976 and Czechoslovakia in 1980.

The supreme irony of the outcome of this 1948 Olympic tournament was that the Swedes and the Danes were both coached by Britons (George Raynor and Roy Mountford respectively), and this was nothing new because British coaches had been helping continental teams ever since 1912, when Willy Garbutt enterprisingly took a job with the Genoa club in Italy. Garbutt had played 134 League games for Reading, Arsenal and Blackburn Rovers in the years 1905 to 1912, and he stayed in Genoa until 1940, when the onset of war forced him home. Garbutt had been assistant to the long-serving Italian team manager, Vittorio Pozzo, at the 1924 Olympics.

When Austria won the Olympic silver medals in 1936 the team was under the guidance of one of Britain's best-known football strategists, Jimmy Hogan, who had previously coached in Hungary and was to be forever regarded there as having laid the foundations for a style of football which would dominate the game in the early 1950s. George Raynor was described in a biography of Hogan, written in 2003, as "another enormously gifted manager-coach". He had been a talented player himself as a professional for 17 years and was recommended to the Swedish authorities by the FA secretary, Stanley Rous, who would play a major part in the administration of the 1948 Olympics and served as secretary of the ground committee for the football tournament. Raynor continued to coach Sweden throughout the 1950s, and after his team had reached the 1958 World Cup final he was so highly thought of that the King of Sweden created him Knight of the Order of Vasa and the Brazilian team management presented him with a gold medal. When he returned to England his only management post was with a Third Division team, Doncaster Rovers, and he ended his working life as a storeman at a Butlin's holiday camp. A prophet without honour?

The Wembley organising committee's report further underlined the continuing influence of the country which had created the game. The author was Bernard Joy, who had been the last amateur to play for a full England side and had been a member of Great Britain's Olympic team in 1936. Now the football correspondent of the *Evening Standard*, he wrote: "The Swedish play was modelled on that of the best modern English professional teams. While Denmark had the fast open style of English football, they retained the looser marking and carefree shooting so typical of the amateur."

The lesser teams also helped to make the 1948 Olympic tournament a refreshingly entertaining and trouble-free one, compared with the disputes and crowd invasions which had marred some of the interwar matches. Joy commented, well, joyfully: "Added spice came from the barefooted Indians, the deceptively lazy Mexicans, the close passing of the Chinese and Koreans, and the ball jugglery of the Egyptians. With varied temperaments, the keenness to win, and different ideas on body-checking, occasional incidents were inevitable. What few there were were easily outweighed by the sporting way in which the 18 matches were played."

At the 1908 Olympics Great Britain had beaten Sweden 12-1. Times had changed somewhat.

The Danish captain, Knud Lundberg, became an accomplished writer and the author of an enthralling and prophetic novel with an athletics theme. *The Olympic Hope*, published in 1958, was his story of the Olympic 800 metres final of 1996, and in 171 pages Lundberg described every step of the race. Two Americans, a Russian, a Georgian, a German and a Dane were the competitors and genetic engineering played a major part in deciding the outcome.

Football results: 1 Sweden, 2 Yugoslavia, 3 Denmark, 4 Great Britain
Final: Sweden 3 Yugoslavia 1
Sweden: Lindberg; K. Nordahl, E. Nilsson; Rosengren, B. Nordahl, Andersson; Rosén, Gren, G. Nordahl, Carlsson, Lindholm.
Yugoslavia: Lovrič; Brozovič, Stankovič; Zlatko Čajkovski, Jovanovič, Atanakovič; Cimermancič, Mitič, Bobek, Željko Čajkovski, Vukas.
Third place match: Denmark 5 Great Britain 3
Denmark: Nielsen; V. Jensen, Övergaard; Piilmark, Örnvold, I. Jensen; Plöger, Lundberg, Praest, J. Hansen, Seebach.
Great Britain: Simpson; Neale, Carmichael; Hardisty, Lee, Fright; Boyd, Aitken, McIlvenney, Rawlings, Amor.
Semi-finals: Sweden 4 Denmark 2; Yugoslavia 3 Great Britain 1

Number of appearances by players:
Sweden: Sune Andersson 4, Henry Carlsson 4, Rune Emmanuelsson 0, Gunnar Gren 4, Egon Jonsson 0, Börje Leander 2, Torsten Lindberg 4, Nils Lindholm 4, Erik Nilsson 4, Stellan Nilsson 0, Bertil Nordahl 4, Gunnar Nordahl 4, Knut Nordahl 2, Stig Nyström 0, Kjell Rosén 4, Birger Rosengren 4, Ingvar Rydell 0, Karl Svensson 0.
Yugoslavia: Aleksandar Atanakovič 4, Stjepan Bobek 4, Miroslav Brozovič 4, Željko Čajkovski 4, Zlatko Čajkovski 4, Zvonko Cimermančič 1, Miodrag Jovanovič 4, Ljubomir Lovrič 1, Prvoslav Mihajlovič 2, Rajko Mitič 4, Franjo Sośtarič 3, Branislav Stankovič 4, Kosta Tomaševič 1, Franjo Völfl 3, Bernard Vukas 1.
Denmark: John Hansen 4, Karl Aage Hansen 3, Ivan Jensen 4, Viggo Jensen 4, Knud Lundberg 2, Ejgil Nielsen 4, Dion Örnvold 4, Knud Börge Övergaard 4, Axel Pilmark 4, Johannes Plöger 4, Carl Aage Praest 4, Holger Seebach 2, Jörgen Sörensen 1.
Great Britain: Andrew Aitken (Queen's Park) 1, William Amor (Reading) 1, Alan Boyd (Queen's Park) 1, Andrew Carmichael (Queen's Park) 1, Frank Donovan (Pembroke Borough) 2, Eric Fright (Bromley) 4, John ("Bob") Hardisty (Bishop Auckland) 4, Thomas Hopper (Bromley) 1, Denis Kelleher (Barnet) 3, Peter

Kippax (Burnley) 3, Eric Lee (Chester) 4, D. Letham (Queen's Park) 0, Kevin McAlinden (Belfast Celtic) 2, Douglas McBain (Queen's Park) 3, James McColl (Queen's Park) 2, Harold McIlvenney (Yorkshire Amateurs) 4, Gwynne Manning (Troedyrhiw) 0, Jack Neale (Walton & Hersham) 4, R.W. Phipps (Barnet) 0, Jack Rawlings (Enfield) 1, Ronald Simpson (Queen's Park) 2, J. Smith (Barry Town) 0. Note: Letham, Phipps and Smith are not included in the list published by the Games organising committee of players who actually took part, as opposed to those entered, although they were certainly among a final group of 22 nominated from the trials.

Chapter 26

BRITAIN'S BEST TAKE THEIR GERMAN PRISONER'S ADVICE

Gymnastics. Empress Hall, Earls Court, 12–14 August.

THE OLYMPIC AUTHORITIES and the international federation had insisted that the gymnastics events should be held at the Empire Stadium. "Inadvisable", warned the officials of the Amateur Gymnastics Association, who knew rather more about the vagaries of an English summer. Plans went ahead regardless for an outdoor tournament, just as it had been in Berlin, only for local opinion to be proved right. Torrential rain fell throughout the day and night preceding the gymnastics events "Indoors, if wet" became the emergency alternative all too familiar to village-fete organisers the length and breadth of Britain. The stadium infield was under water.

The Empress Hall, at Earls Court, was pressed into service, and proved a blessing in disguise. The spectators were far closer to the action than they would have been at Wembley. After each gymnast had performed, the judges simultaneously held up cards showing the marks which they had awarded, and these could be seen by all. There was no scoreboard – rationing of building materials, perhaps? – but the crowds didn't mind. Their only objections were to the well-meaning loudspeaker announcements which intruded on the efforts of the competitors.

"Make do and mend" had been the watchword for months before the gymnastics began. There was no up-to-date apparatus available in Britain, and all the visiting teams were asked to bring their own. The British Olympic hopefuls met in the basement of a London brewery and practised on home-made equipment of incorrect width and unsafe construction. One end of the beam on which the gymnasts attempted their routines was attached to a wall and the other end rested on a convenient beer-barrel. It probably helped that the two leading members of the British team were film stuntmen and were accustomed to taking risks. One of them, Frank Turner, later became a regular stand-in for Burt Lancaster and Roger Moore.

Yet there is an even more remarkable aspect to this improvised approach to the Games. One of the coaches to the men's team was a 26-year-old German prisoner-of-war, Helmut Bantz, whose name is not to be found in any of the official reports. Bantz was understandably asked to keep a low profile, but he eventually got the chance to prove himself in public. He was the leading scorer in the German teams which placed fourth at the 1952 Olympics and fifth in 1956 and tied for the vault gold in the latter year, where he was also sixth in the individual combined exercises behind three from the USSR and two Japanese.

Gymnastics has a history as long as any sport at the Games, stretching back to Ancient Greece, and was on the programme when the Olympics were revived in 1896, with competitions for men in five exercises – parallel bars, pommelled horse, rings, horizontal bar and vault. The modern form of gymnastics had been developed in Germany in the late 18th century and early 19th century, and Britain's Amateur Gymnastics Association was celebrating its 60th birthday at the time of the London Games, having been founded in 1888. World Championships for men had been held intermittently from 1903 to 1922 and then every four years after that. Women's events had been introduced in 1934.

The Olympic titles for the men's individual combined exercises had been won by Italy in 1908, 1912, 1920 and 1932, by France in 1900 and 1906, and by Austria (1904), Yugoslavia (1924), Switzerland (1928) and Germany (1936). Team titles had been won by Italy in 1912, 1920, 1924 and 1932, and by Norway in 1906, Sweden in 1908, Switzerland in 1928 and Germany in 1936. The only women's event held so far had been for teams in 1928, won by Holland, and in 1936, won by Germany, and attitudes towards the appropriateness of gymnastics for women differed sharply from country to country. Susan Noel, in her "Women in Sport" column in *World Sports*, previewed the forthcoming Olympic competition in the issue for March 1948, tipping the Czechs to win but pointing out: "The Swiss girls are also excellent gymnasts, but a certain restraint is kept on their competitive work because of the feeling in Switzerland that heavy muscular work is unsuitable for women. The French and Belgians, on the other hand, are all for following in the footsteps of the men, and although perhaps they are apt to neglect finish and style on occasions they undoubtedly achieve very good results."

The last World Championships before the London Olympics had been in 1938 when the men's winners had been Jan Gajdos, combined and floor, and Alois Hudec, rings, for Czechoslovakia, and Michael Reusch, horizontal bar and parallel bars, and Eugen Mack, vault, for Switzerland. The pommelled horse title had been shared by Reusch and another Czech, Vratislav Petraček. The Czechs had won the men's team title for the seventh time and had also dominated the women's events, taking the team title and having winners in all four individual events. Vlasta Dekanová won the combined and the beam and Matylda Pálfyová the vault (tied with Marta Majowska, of Poland) and floor.

There would be a full programme of events for men at the London Games but again only a team event for women – though, curiously, unofficial individual exercises would also be staged for the latter. The 16 countries entered for the men's events were Argentina, Austria, Cuba, Czechoslovakia, Denmark, Egypt, Finland, France, Great Britain, Hungary, Italy, Luxembourg, Mexico, Switzerland, USA and Yugoslavia. Of these Austria, Czechoslovakia, France, Great Britain, Hungary, Italy, USA and Yugoslavia were among the 11 in the women's events, plus Belgium, Holland and Sweden. The Swiss would have two pre-war gold-medallists, Hermann Hänggi and Eugen Mack, among their squad of coaches.

The tournament had been due to open at the Empire Stadium on the morning of 9 August, and when that proved impossible it was quickly agreed that the start would be postponed for three days to prepare the Empress Hall, which would still be in use for weightlifting in the meantime. There was no alternative but to hold men's and women's events simultaneously in order to get through the extensive gymnastics programme, and the men's free exercises and women's team event were accommodated on platforms at opposite ends of the hall. It all made for a rich feast for the spectators, even if it proved indigestible at times with so many appetising plates set before them.

The format for the men's team event was that there would be compulsory and voluntary programmes for each of the six disciplines – free exercises, pommelled horse, rings, parallel bars, horizontal bar and vault – and that the scores on each apparatus would also decide the individual placings. Remarkably, at the end of the three days, involving 123 gymnasts in a never-ending panoply of activities, Finland won the team gold by the narrowest of margins over Switzerland, with 1,358.3 points to 1,356.7, representing a difference of about 0.1 per cent! The margin between the individual gold medal, won by Veikko Huhtanen, of Finland, and the silver, won by Walter Lehmann, of Switzerland, was 0.7 of a point out of a possible maximum of 240. Lehmann was a bookkeeper by profession and so no doubt had kept a practised eye on the scores throughout.

Huhtanen was 29 years old but by no means the senior member of the Finnish team, of which the average age was almost 34. The father figure was Heikki Savolainen, now 40, who had first competed in the 1928 Games, winning bronze for the pommelled horse, and had won a silver and three bronzes in 1932 and another bronze in 1936. Here at Wembley he would win gold in the team event and for the pommelled horse, and his Olympic career would extend to 1952 when he won yet another team bronze at 44 years old. A team-mate, Einari Teräsvirta, had also won two bronzes in 1932. Huhtanen, Teräsvirta and a third member of the team, Aleksanteri Saarvala, who had won the horizontal bar gold in 1936, had all been born in Viipuri, now renamed Vyborg and part of the USSR, having been annexed during the war. The most experienced of the Swiss was the pre-war world champion, Michael Reusch, who had additionally won two Olympic silvers in 1936 and would add a gold and two silvers in London.

Oddly, the only one of the first three in the men's individual competition to win outright any of the six events was the bronze-medallist, Paavo Aaltonen, of Finland, who took the gold in the vault, though there was a three-way tie between him and his team-mates, Huhtanen and Savolainen, on the pommelled horse. Nor did any of the leading six overall figure at all prominently in the floor exercises, which were won by Hungarian Ferenc Pataki.

Switzerland would provide the 1950 world combined exercises champion in the person of Lehmann, the silver-medallist in London, who would win five of the six titles on the various apparatus – the sixth going to the Finn, Aaltonen, on the horizontal bar. There would be further Olympic gold medals in 1952 for Switzerland (horizontal bar, parallel bars) and Sweden (floor), for the former German prisoner-of-war, Bantz, in 1956, and for Finland in 1960 (pommelled horse), but by then the era of almost total dominance by the USSR and Japan was solidly established. One or other of these two countries was to win every team title from 1952 until 1984.

Men's team result (the first six in each team to score, individual points/positions listed for each competitor):

1 Finland 1,358.30 points (Veikko Huhtanen 229.70/1, Paavo Aaltonen 228.30/3, Kalevi Laitinen 225.65/8, Olavi Rove 225.20/10, Einari Teräsvirta 225.00/12, Heikki Savolainen 223.95/14, Aleksanteri Saarvala 222.10/17, Sulo Salmi 217.45/31)

2 Switzerland 1,356.70 (Walter Lehmann 229.00/2, Josef Stalder 228.70/4, Christian Kipfer 227.10/5, Emil Studer 226.60/6, Robert Lucy 223.30/15, Michael Reusch 222.00/18, Melchior Thalmann 220.60/21, Konrad Frei 217.20/32=)

3 Hungary 1,330.85 (Lajos Tóth 225.20/10, Lajos Sántha 224.30/13, László Baranyi 222.40/16, Ferenc Pataki 221.30/19, János Mogyorósi-Klencs 218.95/27, Ferenc Varköi 218.70/29, József Fekete 218.60/30, Gyözö Mogyorósi 214.30/38=)

4 France 1,313.85 (Raymond Dot 220.80/20, Michel Mathiot 220.40/22, Lucien Masset 219.95/24, André Weingand 219.80/25, Antoine Schlindwein žž216.50/34, Alphonse Anger 216.40/35=, Marcel Dewolf 214.40/36=, Auguste Sirot 214.10/40=)

5 Italy 1,300.30 (Guido Figone 225.30/9, Luigi Zanetti 219.00/26, Savino Guglielmetti 217.20/32=, Domenico Grosso 214.10/40=, Quinto Vadi 214.00/42=, Danilo Fioravani 210.70/51, Ettore Perego 206.30/57, Egidio Arnelloni 195.05/72)

6 Czechoslovakia 1,292.10 (Zdenek Ružička 226.20/7, Pavel Benetka 220.30/23, Miroslav Málek 212.90/47, Vladimir Karas 212.20/48, Leo Sotornik 210.80/50, František Wirth 209.70/52, Vratislav Petraček 203.30/65, Gustave Hrubý 193.10/74)

7 USA 1,252.50 (Edward Scrobe 213.90/44, Vincent D'Autorio 211.30/49, William Roetzheim 209.10/53, Joseph Kotys 208.50/55, Frank Cumiskey 205.15/62, Raymond Sorensen 204.55/63, William Bonsall 201.70/69, Louis Bordo 77.00/119)

8 Denmark 1,245.40 (Paul Jessen 214.30/38=, Tage Grönne 213.50/45, Freddy Jensen 208.35/56, Arnold Thomsen 206.25/58, Wilhelm Moller 201.75/68, Poul Jensen 201.25/70, Gunner Olesen 193.30/73, Børge Minerth 156.30/100)

9 Austria 1,212.15 (Ernst Wister 218.90/28, Karl Bohusch 214.40/36=, Hans Friedrich 205,80/59, Willi Schreyer 205.40/61, Johann Sauter 203.10/66, Robert Pranz 164.55/99, Gottfried Hermann 132.30/114, Willi Welt 2.00/123)

10 Yugoslavia 1,194.80 (Konrad Grilc 213.05/46, Josip Kujundzić 208.90/54, Miro Longyka 200.40/71, Drago Jelić 191.80/75, Ivan Jelić 191.75/76, Styepan Boltižar 188.90/78, Jakob Šubelj 178.50/88, Karel Janež 152.45/103)

11 Luxembourg 1,150.45 (Jey Krugeler 214.00/42=, Josy Stoffel 203.35/64, Polo Welfring 189.25/77, René Schroeder 188.00/80, Jos Krecké 180.55/84, Pierre Schmitz 175.30/90, Jos Bernard 172.40/91, Georges Wengler 166.70/96)

12 Great Britain 1,114.40 (George Weedon 205.60/60, Frank Turner 202.60/64, Ken Buffin 188.65/79, Alec Wales 180.80/83, Percy May 171.45/92, Jack Flaherty 165.30/98, Glyn Hopkins 134.80/111, Ivor Vice 134.50/112)

13 Egypt 1,057.95 (Ali Zaky Attia 187.55/82, Moustafa Abdelal 177.70/86, Mohamed Roushdi 177.35/87, Ala Khalaf 177.15/88, Ali El-Hefnawi 169.55/93, Mohamed Aly 168.65/94, Abdel Al Mahmoud 167.50/95, Ahmed Khalil El-Giddawi 148.85/107)

14 Cuba 950.7 (Rafael Lecuona Asencio 187.70/81, Fernando Lecuona Asencio 166.35/97, Angel Aguiar Garcia 156.15/101, Raimundo Rey Carcano 152.05/104, Baldomaro Rubiera Fernández 151.15/105, Roberto Villacian Alemany 137.30/109, Antonio Diáz Corpion 136.75/110)

15 Argentina 863.85 (Arturo Ainos 176.85/89, Pedro Lonchibucco 154.20/102, Enrique Rapesta Wilson 148.90/106, César Bonoris 139.65/108, Jorge Soler 134.30/113, Roberto Nuñez 109.95/115, Jorge Vidal 37.30/123)

16 Mexico 343.85 (Jorge Castro Valdes 103.90/116, Ruben Lira Ariles 98.95/117, Dario Aguilar González 81.80/120, Everardo Rios Peña 55.20/120, Nicolas Villareal Sánchez 40.00/122)

Men's individual combined exercises result (the leading eight positions – scores and positions in sequence for horizontal bar, parallel bars, horse vault, pommelled horse, rings, floor exercises)
1 Veikko Huhtanen (Finland) 229.70 points – 39.20 (3), 39.30 (2), 38.40 (6), 38.70 (1=), 37.80 (11=), 36.30 (34=)
2 Walter Lehmann (Switzerland) 229.00 – 39.40 (2), 39.00 (5), 38.10 (7=), 37.60 (11), 38.40 (4), 36.50 (29=)
3 Paavo Aaltonen (Finland) 228.80 – 38.40 (12=), 38.80 (7=), 39.10 (1), 38.70 (1=), 37.30 (17=), 36.50 (29=)
4 Josef Stalder (Switzerland) 228.70 – 39.70 (1), 39.10 (3=), 36.90 (38=), 37.70 (8=), 38.30 (5=), 37.00 (16=)
5 Christian Kipfer (Switzerland) 227.10 – 38.60 (9=), 39.10 (3=), 37.90 (14=), 37.20 (14=), 37.80 (11=), 36.50 (29=)
6 Emil Studer (Switzerland) 226.60 – 38.80 (4=), 37.80 (21=), 38.00 (10=), 37.70 (8=), 38.30 (5=), 36.00 (41=)
7 Zdenek Ružička (Czechoslovakia) 226.20 – 37.90 (17=), 38.80 (7=), 36.60 (46=), 36.30 (30=), 38.50 (3), 38.10 (3)
8 Kalevi Laitinen (Finland) 225.65 – 38.10 (14), 38.10 (16=), 38.00 (10=), 36.90 (19=), 37.40 (16), 37.15 (13)

Men's individual exercises (the leading eight positions in each exercise)
Horizontal bar – 1 Josef Stalder (Switzerland) 39.7pts, 2 Walter Lehmann (Switzerland) 39.4, 3 Veikko Huhtanen (Finland) 39.2, 4= Raymond Dot (France), Lajos Sántha (Hungary), Aleksanteri Saarvala (Finland), Emil Studer (Switzerland) 38.8, 8 Einari Teräsvirta (Finland) 38.7.
Parallel bars – 1 Michael Reusch (Switzerland) 39.5, 2 Veikko Huhtanen (Finland) 39.3, 3= Christian Kipfer (Switzerland), Josef Stalder (Switzerland) 39.1, 5 Walter Lehmann (Switzerland) 39.0, 6 Heikki Savolainen (Finland) 38.9, 7= Paavo Aaltonen (Finland), Zdenek Ružička (Czechoslovakia) 38.8.
Horse vault – 1 Paavo Aaltonen (Finland) 39.1, 2 Olavi Rove (Finland) 39.0, 3= János Mogyorósi-Klencs (Hungary), Ferenc Pataki (Hungary), Leo Sotornik (Czechoslovakia) 38.5, 6 Veikko Huhtanen (Finland) 38.4, 7= Walter Lehmann (Switzerland), Sulo Salmi (Finland) 38.1.
Pommelled horse – 1= Paavo Aaltonen (Finland), Veikko Huhtanen (Finland), Heikki Savolainen (Finland) 38.7, 4 Luigi Zanetti (Italy) 38.3, 5 Guido Figone (Italy) 38.2, 6 Frank Cumiskey (USA) 37.9, 7 Michael Reusch (Switzerland) 37.8, 8= Josef Stalder (Switzerland), Emil Studer (Switzerland) 37.7.
Rings – 1 Konrad Frei (Switzerland) 39.6, 2 Michael Reusch (Switzerland) 39.1, 3 Zdenek Ružička (Czechoslovakia) 38.5, 4 Walter Lehmann (Switzerland) 38.4, 5= Josef Stalder (Switzerland, Emil Studer (Switzerland) 38.3, 7 Vladimir Karas (Czechoslovakia) 38.2, 8 Heikki Savolainen (Finland) 38.1.
Floor – 1 Ferenc Pataki (Hungary) 38.7, 2 János Mogyorósi-Klencs (Hungary) 38.4, 3 Zdenek Ružička (Czechoslovakia) 38.1, 4 Raymond Dot (France) 37.8, 5 Tage Grönne (Denmark) 37.65, 6= Pavel Benetka (Czechoslovakia), Leo Sotornik (Czechoslovakia) 37.6, 8 Vladimir Karas (Czechoslovakia) 37.4

Considering the primitive conditions in which they had trained, the British contingent was not disgraced. In his authoritative history of the sport in Britain, published in 1988, Jim Prestidge was to conclude: "The preparations to train a men's and women's gymnastic team were indeed hectic. In spite of the shortages of apparatus, training facilities and coaches, British gymnasts gave a creditable performance."

The team's coach at the Games was a 40-year-old Welshman, Arthur Whitford, from the Swansea YMCA club, who had won the British title a record 10 times between 1928 and 1939 and had competed in the 1928 Olympics. George Weedon, the leading Briton, was one of the film stunt-men in the team, and the most experienced member was Jack Flaherty, also 40, who had taken up gymnastics as a 16-year-old and had been British champion in 1938. He had the highest British individual placing on any apparatus, with 30th on the horizontal bar. At least being present in the Olympic arena was an improvement on 1936, when it had been decided after a series of trials that it was not worth sending any male gymnasts to Berlin. Britain's only Olympic medals were but distant memories – a silver in the combined exercises in 1908 by Walter Tysal and a bronze in the team event in 1912.

Britain's women had won the team bronze in 1928 – albeit a long way behind Holland and Italy – and the most senior of the 1948 team members, 37-year-old Clarice Bell, from Bradford, had taken up the sport the year of that Olympic success. Under her maiden name of Hanson she had been British champion on five occasions from 1933 to 1939 and again in 1948 and had competed at the 1936 Olympics, where the team had finished a distant last of eight. For whatever reason, perhaps injury of illness, Mrs Bell did not actually compete at Wembley, though her name appears in the BOA list of team members. Pat Hirst, aged 29, had been an international since 1938 and had won the British title in 1947 and 1948 and would do so on six further occasions to 1956.

As forecast five months previously by Susan Noel in *World Sports*, Czechoslovakia won the women's team title from Hungary and the USA, and it was as much a triumph of courage in adversity as it was of physical and technical superiority. One of the Czech team-members, 22-year-old Eliska Misáková, was taken ill three days after her arrival in London and was found to be suffering from meningitis. She was confined to an iron lung for four days at Uxbridge Isolation Hospital but died on the day that the gymnastics events began, and yet the Czech team went ahead with their performance. Not only that but Eliska's older sister, Miloslava, was the second scorer, in fourth place overall. The Czech flag was bordered in black when it was raised at the victory ceremony.

For a very different reason, the appearance of Czech women gymnasts and officials in London marked a page of Olympic history. Marie Provaznikova, one of the two women officials serving on the technical committee at the gymnastics events, became one of the first Olympic participants from Eastern Europe to defect to the West. The Communist party had come to power in her country only six months before, but her explanation that "there is no freedom of speech" was a refrain that would be heard again from Olympic "refugees".

The sporting significance of that recent change of regime is that the success of the Czechs in winning six gold medals, two silvers and three bronzes at the various Olympic sports in 1948 cannot be attributed in any degree to the state-support system which was to become endemic throughout Eastern Europe in the years to come. Whatever long-term plans might have been formulated by the new Czech government regarding promotion of political ideals by sporting achievement, there had not been enough time for them to start working to effect at the London Olympics. At the 1952 Games the benefit of state aid became all too obvious when the first three places in women's team gymnastics were taken by the USSR, Hungary and Czechoslovakia.

Two of the medallists had been born in countries other than the ones they represented: Kövi, of Hungary, in Rumania, and Elste, of the USA, in Bremen, in Germany. Elste was not actually the only German-born woman to win a medal at

---

Women's team result (all to score; individual points/positions listed for each competitor):

1 Czechoslovakia 445.45 points (Zdenka Honsová 54.85/1, Miloslava Misáková 53.40/4=, Vera Ružičková 53.00/7, Božena Srncová 52.95/8, Milena Mullerová 52.50/10=, Zdenka Veřmiřovská 50.00/24=, Olga Silhanová 49.95/26, Marie Kovářová 49.60/28)

2 Hungary 440.55 (Edit Perényi-Weckinger 54.25/2, Mária Kövi 53.40/4=, Irén Kárpáti-Karcsics 53.20/6, Erzsébet Gulyás-Köteles 52.25/12, Erzsébet Balázs 52.10/13, Olga Tass 51.45/15, Anna Fehér 49.15/30, Mária Sándor 39.10/74=)

3 USA 422.63 (Helen Schifano 51.70/14, Clara Schroth 51.05/17, Meta Elste 50.90/20, Marian Barone 50.30/21, Ladislava ("Laddie") Bakanic 50.10/22=, Consetta Lenz 49.10/31=, Anita Simonis 47.80/40, Dorothy Dalton 47.65/41)

4 Sweden 417.95 (Karin Lindberg 52.70/9, Kerstin Bohman 51.40/16, Ingrid Sandahl 51.00/19, Göta Pettersson 50.10/22=, Gunnel Johansson 49.10/31=, Märta Andersson 49.05/33, Ingrid Andersson 47.10/47, Stina Haage 39.10/74=)

5 Holland 408.35 (Jacoba Tonneman 52.50/10=, Helena Gerrietsen 49.50/29, Jacoba Wijnands 47.25/44, Johanna Ros 45.75/54=, Anna van Geene 45.45/57, Klassje Post 44.80/62, Geertruida Heil-Bonnet 42.55/67, Barendina Meijer-Haantjes 38.30/78)

6 Austria 405.45 (Gertrude Fesl 51.05/18, Gretchen Hehenberger 50.00/24=, Gertrude Kolar 48.65/37, Irmintraud Ruckser 48.35/38, Gertrude Gries 48.00/39, Gertrude Winnige 45.60/56, Edeltraud Schramm 45.10/60=, Erika Enzenhofer 38.95/76)

7 Yugoslavia 397.90 (Vida Gerbeč 49.00/34=, Drogana Djordjevič 47.60/42, Rusa Vojsk 47.20/45, Draginja Djipalovič 47.15/46, Tanja Žutič 45.25/58, Draginja Basletič 42.70/66, Zlatica Mijatovič 40.35/72, Nide Cerne 24.70/85)

8 Italy 394.20 (Laura Micheli 53.65/3, Elena Santoni 47.55/43, Lizia Macchini 46.30/48, Wanda Nuti 45.75/54=, Liliana Torriani 45.10/60=, Renata Bianchi 43.25/65, Norma Icardi 40.70/71, Luciana Pezzoni 28.20/83).

9 Great Britain 392.95 (Cissie Davies 49.90/27, Joan Airey 49.00/34=, Patricia Hirst 48.70/36, Patricia Evans 46.95/48, Dorothy Hey 46.15/49, Audrey Rennard 45.20/59, Irene Hirst 43.60/64, Dorothy Smith 26.35/84)

10 France 384.65 (F Vaillee 48.80/33, Jeanine Touchard 47.70/40, C Palau 46.70/49, G Guibert 46.65/50, Colette Hué 46.45/51, Martine Yvinou 43.85/63, Irène Pittelioen 42.10/68, Jeanette Vogelbacher 41.40/69)

11 Belgium 353.60 (Albertine van Roy 48.75/34, Denise Parmentier 40.55/71, Yvonne van Bets 39.70/73, Jenny Schumacher 38.45/77, Caroline Verbraecken de Loose 38.20/79, Marie-Thérèse de Grijze 36.20/80, Anna Jordaens 29.70/81, Julienne Boudewijns 27.90/83)

the 1948 Games because the Dutch swimmer, Hannie Termeulen, had been born in Wiesbaden and the Austrian fencer, Ellen Müller-Preis, in Berlin.

Had there been an official individual competition the winner would have been Zdenka Honsová, of Czechoslovakia, from Edit Perényi-Weckinger, of Hungary, and 17-year-old Italian Laura Micheli. This was an era of women's gymnastics long before the emergence from the Eastern European nations of youthful sprites such as Korbut and Comaneci, and Micheli was a rarity, though she was still considerably the senior of one of her team-mates, Lizia Macchini, who had celebrated her 12th birthday a month before. The silver-medallist was aged 25 and her team-mate, Erzsébet Gulyás-Köteles, was the mother of a two-year-old boy and had taken up the sport 10 years before, remaining active until 1958. One of the Czech team, Zdenka Veřmiřovská, had also won silver in 1936 and was now 35 years old. Also among the Berlin competitors had been Drogana Djordjevič, for Yugoslavia, and Consetta Lenz, for the USA, who by 1948 was a mother of two. A notable absentee from the London Games gymnastics was Poland, for which country Helena Rakoczy would win the world titles in combined exercises, vault, beam and floor two years later.

The unofficial women's competitions in London which were held for the rings, beam and vault brought some success for Britain, with a third place for Joan Airey, and, coupled with the overall 27th ranking for Cissie Davies in the team event, these were encouraging results.

The individual exercises were introduced for women at the 1952 Olympics and the USSR took six of the first eight places overall, with the other two going to Hungary. The only gymnasts from the 1948 Games to obtain top-eight places in 1952 were three of the Hungarians – Perényi-Weckinger, Gulyás-Köteles and Tass – and the Swede, Lindberg, and none of them placed higher than fourth. The Hungarian trio, plus Kárpáti-Karcsics, won team silver.

The overall impression of the gymnastics contests in London formed by the arena manager, EA Simmonds, the honorary secretary of the Amateur Gymnastics Association who contributed the articles for both the BOA and the organising committee reports, was a favourable one. "Gymnastics has been maintained at the high level seen in previous Olympic Games," he concluded. "Not only was the standard of the sport high, but the physique of the men's teams coming from the devastated areas of Europe was little short of marvellous".

There was clearly something amiss with the standards of judging, and you have to read between the lines to divine that from Simmonds's summaries, though he was by no means alone among the various contributors in being diplomatic in his comments. Without exception, writers in the organising committee's report glossed over the problems at the Games, seemingly content to record the fact

---

Unofficial women's invididual exercises. Rings: 1 Zdenka Honsová (Czechoslovakia), 2 Laura Micheli (Italy), 3 Edit Perényi-Weckinger (Hungary. Beam: 1 Honsová, 2 Irén Kárpáti-Karcsics (Hungary), 3 Micheli. Vault: 1 Karin Lindberg (Sweden), 2 Helen Schifano (USA), 3 Joan Airey (Great Britain).

that the international ruling bodies of the various sports had taken note of the shortcomings – and were presumably doing something about them.

"Each country had to give a declaration as to the competence and integrity of their judges," Simmonds wrote, "but so that every aspect of the judging might be considered in retrospect it was decided at the meeting of the Federation that all judges' marks would be published throughout the world. In this way it would be established if any were unnecessarily severe, too easy, or of unreliable judgement, and in such cases they would not be allowed to judge in future. It is of interest that, whereas the rules allow each nation to nominate an observer at the scoring table, none were in fact so appointed." It is not entirely clear what the writer meant by this last remark, and there is no indication whether any disciplinary action was taken, but it all seems to suggest that there *were* judges in London whose abilities were called to question.

In his BOA contribution, Simmonds listed several modifications which could be made to the judging system, the rules and the technical arrangements, without making any great issue about them, but his closing comment that "it would seem that there is much work to be done before the next Olympic Games" clearly indicates the size of the task. None of this could be blamed on the makeshift set-up at the Empress Hall, which worked as well as could be expected – and far better than many people had feared.

Chapter 27

BRITISH GET ORGANISED AT LAST, BUT THE INDIANS WIN AGAIN

Hockey. Various grounds and Empire Stadium, Wembley. 31 July–13 August.

INDIA HAD GAINED its political independence from Britain in 1947, but so far as outstanding sporting achievements were concerned Indian players had stood on their own two feet for the previous 20 years or so, winning the Olympic hockey tournaments of 1928, 1932 and 1936, remaining undefeated in 10 matches, and scoring 102 goals to three. Britain had led the way in the past, as in so many sports, with the first organised matches played in the 1870s and the foundation of the Hockey Association in 1886, but a club was to be formed in Calcutta only two years later.

It rained, of course, during many of the hockey matches in London in 1948, and as the Indians were accustomed to playing on hard, dry, bare surfaces they should have been inhibited by the weather, but if they were it was not at all obvious. Having scored 29 goals to nil at the 1928 Games, 35 goals to two in 1932, and 38 goals to one in 1936, they settled for a relatively modest tally this time round of 25 to two. With every claim to being the finest team in sporting history – in any sport – India would take the gold medals again in 1952 and 1956 and only finally succumb to their neighbours from Pakistan by 1-0 in the 1960 final after winning 30 successive matches and scoring 196 goals to eight.

Great Britain had won at the only two Olympic Games at which hockey was played before the advent of the Indians, in 1908 and 1920, but had not even sent a team in later years for reasons which were never fully explained. In his contribution to the British Olympic Association report of the 1936 Games, Colonel Bruce Turnbull, member of the International Hockey Board (IHB), had merely observed: "The absence of an entry from Great Britain again caused the greatest disappointment, but it is doubtful if they could have done more than give the winners a good run for their money. The continental teams are disappointing in tournament play and none of them played up to the standard we know them to be capable of producing."

There could be no question of missing out again, but there were bureaucratic problems to be solved before ever thinking about selection of a team, and it was maybe these which had accounted for the British absence in pre-war years when there were medals – though not, of course, gold – apparently ready for the winning. There was no British ruling body because each of the four home countries was independently affiliated to the Fédération Internationale de Hockey (FIH), and the British-based IHB was responsible only for framing rules and was a separate entity from the Federation in its own right. The domestic hockey season in Britain usually ended at Easter, and so the cricketers who took over the grounds in the summer had to be asked politely to "play away" for a few weeks so that facilities could be made available for the Olympic matches and practice in the London area.

The unprecedented venture into summertime hockey, despite the inevitable rain, caused Hylton Cleaver to muse in the *Evening Standard* after the Games concerning the advantages of making that a permanent arrangement, though he admitted it was unlikely to happen. "I wondered during the Olympic Games of 1948 whether it would ever be an accepted thing in this country to play hockey in the summer," he wrote. "The most cogent reason offered against this is that summer hockey entails too much rushing about in hot weather, but does it demand more than first-class lawn tennis or fast bowling at cricket?

"Hard grounds don't matter, and if anything are an advantage. The finest hockey-players in the world are the Indians, whose grounds are brick hard. As a result the ball comes off the ground slap on the blade of the stick, which just puts the edge on their play. This is not what the ball does on typically heavy pitches in winter here. Perhaps a better reason for not playing hockey in summer is that many hockey-players like cricket, too, and many hockey grounds are appropriated in summer for the other game."

Great Britain's Olympic team preparations were reasonably comprehensive – at least by British standards. Trial matches were held in June and July at Weston-super-Mare and at Motspur Park, in Surrey, and a squad was selected of nine players from England, six from Scotland and four from Wales. After beating a combined Oxford & Cambridge Universities team 8-1, the prospective Olympians were described as being "a machine-like combination", which presumably satisfied the military-minded requirements of the manager, Lieutenant-Colonel GS Grimston, and the trainer, Quarter Master Sergeant Instructor S Blacknell. The final warm-up, at Thorpeness on 24 July, brought a 6-0 win over Eastern Counties. Everybody knew only too well that the Indians would be a very different proposition, and as Britain's assistant team manager, CE Newham, was an ex-president of the Indian Hockey Federation that message would no doubt have been spelled out loud and clear.

There were 16 nations originally entered for the Games tournament, but with less than two days to the start of play it became apparent that without any forewarning Czechoslovakia, Hungary and Poland were not going to appear. The remaining 13 were divided into two groups of four teams and one group of five teams, with the winners of each of the first two groups and the two leaders of the third group to go through to the semi-finals. The International Federation decided that Great Britain, Holland, India and Pakistan would be the seeded teams. The group matches were played in the evenings at the Lyon's club at Sudbury, the Guinness club at Park Royal, and the Polytechnic ground at Chiswick. The Empire Stadium would be the venue for the semi-finals (Monday 9 August) and the final and third-place match (both on Thursday 12 August).

Group A consisted of Argentina, Austria, India and Spain, and the defending champions had no trouble against Austria (8-0) and Argentina (9-1) but were surprisingly held to 2-0 by a Spanish team which obstinately packed its defence throughout the game. Group B involved Afghanistan, Great Britain, Switzerland and the USA, and after an unexpected goalless draw with the Swiss the home team qualified readily enough by disposing of the USA (11-0) and Afghanistan (8-0). Group C contained Belgium, Denmark, France, Holland and Pakistan, from which Pakistan won all four matches and Holland also got through.

Some of the teams which had appeared in the group matches had a distinctly makeshift look about them. There were no more than 300 players in Afghanistan and just 90 in the USA! The Argentinians had never previously played any international matches and Austria had great difficulty in putting a team together so soon after the war. The Pakistanis were also making their Olympic debut, but as the country had only recently been separated from India, the skills and experience of their players were scarcely those of novices. Though eliminated, Belgium, Denmark and France all played "sound, scientific hockey", in the words of CF Newham, who wrote the official report for the British Olympic Association.

The semi-finals and final at the Empire Stadium were tremendous successes: "both matches produced magnificent hockey", said Newham. The Dutch, having lost 6-1 to Pakistan in their group match, were transformed, holding India to 2-1, and according to Newham "most of the 10,000 spectators in the stadium considered the Dutch team a shade unlucky not to force a draw". Great Britain beat Pakistan 2-0, and "both teams were completely done at the end of a great game in which they gave of their best".

The attendance for the final was 25,000 – four times as many as had ever seen a hockey match in Britain prior to the Olympic tournament – and Newham, presumably suffering some divided loyalties, described concisely India's 4-0 victory as follows:

"The heavy ground favoured the British game, but the Indians proved to be the more adaptable team in conditions which prevented both from producing their highest form. The British defence, which had not previously conceded a goal, could find no reply except resolute determination to the brilliance of the stick-work and high-speed tactical moves of the Indian forwards and halves. The British halves were so pre-occupied with defence that they could not feed their forwards, and when the latter did break through at times they found a very competent defence ... Great Britain fielded the best team she could find, well trained and superbly fit, but the Olympic champions since 1928 set the seal on their supremacy." The average age of the Indian team was 20; that of the British team was 30. In their five matches Britain used only 12 of their 19 players.

Pakistan and Holland drew their third-place match before the Dutch, who fielded the same 11 players in all their matches, easily won the replay. "It had been a memorable Olympic championship in every way," reflected Newham, "not least in its demonstration of the growth of the game in quality and popularity." There were now 32 nations affiliated to the International Federation, whereas at the original Olympic tournament in 1908 four of the six teams had been from England, Wales, Scotland and Ireland. Another significant development was that a British Hockey Board had at last been formed and affiliated to the International Federation.

Eighty years after an England team had won the first Olympic hockey tournament Great Britain would become gold-medallists in Seoul in 1988 against rather more stern opposition than their predecessors of so long ago had faced.

Seven of India's players were to win further Olympic gold medals: Grahanandan Singh, Keshava Datt and Kunwar Digvijay Singh in 1952; Balbir Singh, Leslie Claudius, Randhir Singh Gentle and Ranganandhan Francis in both 1952 and 1956. Eight of the Dutch team won silver in 1952: Boerstra, Derckx, Drijver, Esser, Kruize, Loggere, Teil and van Heel. Another of India's Wembley gold-medallists, Latifur Rehman, played for the Pakistan teams which were fourth in 1952 and second in 1956.

The 30-year-old captain of Britain's team was described by *The Times* as "probably Britain's most talented post-war all-round amateur sportsman ... a man for his Corinthian age, the age of the amateur, and he flourished prodigiously within it". He was Norman Borrett, who played in 30 international hockey matches for England from 1939 onwards and scored six goals in Britain's Olympic match against the USA and four against Afghanistan. Before the war, Borrett had represented Eastern Counties at schoolboy rugby union and had played first-class cricket for Essex, once scoring 63 for Young Amateurs v Young Professionals at Lord's.

From 1946 onwards he won the English amateur squash title for five successive years. He also played Minor Counties cricket for Devon from 1947 to 1958 (scoring 2,408 runs at an average of 36), got down to a four handicap at golf, and qualified for the Wimbledon tennis tournament but could not find the time to take part. A Cambridge graduate, he became a schoolmaster at Framlingham College, where he was in the habit of keeping a rifle in the classroom. He is reputed to have one day spied a rabbit from the window, fired at it, and then resumed the lesson with the words "Now, where were we?" He became president of both the Hockey Association and the Squash Rackets Association.

One of his team-mates, Micky Walford, was another versatile sportsman and an even more accomplished cricketer, playing for Somerset from 1946 to 1953 whilst he was a master at Sherborne School. He was a fine batsman whose highest score was 264 against Hampshire in 1947 and who during his career made 5,327 runs at an average of 33.71. He had also played rugby union for Oxford University. Two days after taking part in the Olympic hockey final Walford was at Chelmsford for the Essex v Somerset match and scored 21.

Hockey result: 1 India, 2 Great Britain, 3 Holland, 4 Pakistan.

Final – India 4 Great Britain 0.

India: Pinto; Randhir Singh Gentle, Trilochan Singh; Vaz, Amir Kumar, Keshava Datt; Fernandes, Jansen, Balbir Singh Dosanjh, Kunwar Digvijay Singh, Kishan Lal.

Great Britain: Brodie; Sime, W.Lindsay; Walford, Reynolds, R. Lindsay; Peake, White, Adlard, Borrett, Griffiths.

Third-place match: Holland 4 Pakistan 1 (after a 1-1 draw).

Holland: Richter; Derckx, Drijver; Langhout, Loggere, Tiel; van Heel, Boerstra, Bromberg, Kruize, Essre.

Pakistan: Mohamed Anwar Beg Moghal; Mohamed Niaz Khan, Mohamed Abdul Razzak; Shah-Rukh Shahzada, Hamid Ullah Khan Burki, Mohamed Khawaja Taki; Abdul Qayyam Khan, Abdul Aziz, Iqtidar Ali Shah Dara, Mohamed Ul-Hussain Shaikh, Ahmed Masud.

Semi-finals: India 2 Holland 1, Great Britain 2 Pakistan 0.

Players and appearances:

India: Akhtar Hussain (1), Amir Kumar (4), Balbir Singh Dosanjh (1), Leslie Claudius (1), Walter de Souza (1), Lawrie Fernandes (4), Gerry Glacken (0), Grahanandan Singh (2), Patrick Jansen (5), Jaswant Rajput (1), Keshava Datt (5), Kishan Lal (5), Kunwar Digvijay Singh (5), Latifur Rehman (1), Leo Pinto (3), Randhir Singh Gentle (3), Ranganandhan Francis (2), Reginald Rodrigues (1), Trilochan Singh (5), Maxie Vaz (4).

Great Britain: Robert Adlard (5), Norman Borrett (5), David Brodie (5), Ronald Davies (1), W.O. Greene (0), William Griffiths (5), E.J.E. Hitchman (0), G. Hudson (0), H.T. Lake (0), Robin Lindsay (5), William Lindsay (5), John Peake (5), Frank Reynolds (5), George Sime (5), D.B. Thomas (0), Michael Walford (5), Peter Whitbread (0), William White (4), A.H. Young (0). Note: Greene, Hitchman, Hudson, Lake, Thomas, Whitbread and Young are not included in the official list published by the Games' organising committee of those players who actually took part, as opposed to those entered, but they were certainly among the group of 19 originally nominated from the trials.

Of the Great Britain team, England provided Adlard, Borrett, Green, Griffiths, Hudson, Lake, Peake, Reynolds and Walford; Scotland provided Brodie, Robin and William Lindsay, Sime, White and Young; Wales provided Davies, Griffiths, Hitchman and Thomas.

Holland: Andries Boerstra (6), Henricus Bouwman (6), Peter Bromberg (6), Henri Derckx (6), Johan Drijver (6), Rius Esser (6), Jan Hendrik Kruize (6), Jenne Langhout (6), Hermanus Loggere (6), Antonius Richter (6), Edouard Tiel (6), Willem van Heel (6).

Pakistan: Abdul Aziz (7), Abdul Ghafoor Khan (3), Abdul Hamidi (3), Abdul Qayyum Khan (1), Ahmed Masud (6), Azziz-ur-Rahman (0), Milton Muhammad d'Mello (1), Hamid Ullah Khan Burki (6), Iqtidar Ali Shah Dara (7), Mohamed Abdul Razzak (6), Mohamed Anwar Beg Moghal (6), Mohamed Khawaja Taki (2), Mohamed Niaz Khan (6), Mohamed Ul-Hussain Shaikh (4), Mukhtar Bhatti (3), Rahmet Ullah Shaikh (5), Sayed Mohamed Khurrum (1), Sayed Mohamed Saleem (1), Shah-Rukh Shahzada (6).

Chapter 28

TESTING MAN'S VALOUR IN EMERGENCY

Modern Pentathlon. Aldershot and Camberley, 30 July–4 August.

WILLIE GRUT COULD lay claim to being the best all-rounder at the 1948 Olympics. He was an outstandingly talented horseman, swordsman, marksman, swimmer and runner, and combining all these accomplishments he won the modern pentathlon gold medal by much the greatest margin before or since. There was only one proviso to be made about his supreme abilities – he originated from a small and privileged group of sporting society.

As was the case with the equestrian dressage event, the modern pentathlon in 1948 was restricted to those serving in the armed forces, though there was no limitation regarding rank, and Captain Grut, of the Swedish artillery, happened to have rather more mental and physical weapons at his disposal than any of his uniformed rivals. It had ever been thus in his country because Sweden had almost entirely dominated Olympic competition in the sport since it had been introduced at Stockholm in 1912. Swedes took the first four places that year, with the future US General George Patton fifth, and then the first four places again in 1920, the first three in 1924, and the first two in 1928 and 1932.

If that seemed to be a very gradual whittling away of Swedish dominance, then the result in Berlin served to prove it. The winner there, in the militaristic fashion of those flawed Games, was a German, Lieutenant Gottfried Handrick, who was promptly promoted to Captain, with an American second, and an Italian third, and the best of the Swedes only fourth. He was Sven Thofelt, who had been the winner in 1928 and also fourth in 1932, and who furthermore appeared as a specialist épée team fencer in 1936, winning a silver, and again in 1948, where he won a bronze.

Britons had occupied minor positions in past Olympics. Regimental Sergeant Major George Vokins was seventh in 1924 and Captain Brian Horrocks (the General-to-be) 19th; David Turquand-Young, of the Territorial Army, was sixth in 1928; Lieutenant Digby Legard was eighth in 1932. Yet Hylton Cleaver was almost certainly right in his post-Games assessment when he wrote in the *Evening Standard*, "I doubt if the average Englishman had ever heard of the modern pentathlon until the Olympic Games of 1948. Even then, most people seemed to think this was a semi-decathlon and meant taking part in five field or track events". Cleaver then penned a splendidly swashbuckling description of what a modern pentathlon entailed:

"The basic conception behind this test of man's unconquerable virility and valour in emergency is that some servant of the King is sent away on horseback to carry dispatches. He rides what amounts to a 3½-mile hunter trial on a strange horse, which is supposedly shot from under him. He draws his pistol, shoots his way through, and dives into a tidal river 300 yards broad. On the other bank he uses a sword, which he grabs from the enemy, and ends with a desperate run on foot. This demands much of what Dick Turpin and Shackleton had between them." Another British writer, Reginald Crunden, had captured a similar mood in previewing the Olympic modern pentathlon: "It appeals above all to the youth of a post-war age who previously found their niche in a Spitfire or a commando raid."

Such fanciful adventures are closer to reality than might be supposed because one of the British team, Lieutenant Geoffrey Brooke, had been aboard the battleship *Prince of Wales* when it was sunk by the Japanese off the coast of Malaya in December 1941. He had managed to get to Singapore and had escaped from there in a tanker-vessel which was also sunk. Reaching Sumatra, he crossed the island on foot, with occasional lorry rides, and then spent five weeks in an open boat sailing the Indian Ocean to safety. He was awarded the Distinguished Service Cross after that escapade and the modern pentathlon must have seemed to him like child's play by comparison.

The British championships in 1948 had attracted an encouraging total of 60 entries and the winner had been Lance-Corporal Albert Martin, of the Royal Inniskilling Dragoon Guards, who did not win any of the individual events but was never lower than sixth. The third member of the Olympic team would be Flight Lieutenant Jack Lumsden, of the RAF, and the appointed manager was the former Lieutenant Legard, now a Major, and also of the Royal Inniskilling Dragoon Guards, who had competed in 1936 as well as 1932. Legard has a rare claim to fame as he had also taken part in the Nordic combined skiing at the 1936 Winter Olympics at Garmisch-Partenkirchen. Then at the age of 42 he had been a member of the British team in an unofficial pentathlon at the Winter Olympics in St Moritz earlier in 1948, involving downhill and cross-country skiing, shooting, fencing and horse-riding, in which the versatile Willie Grut had placed second.

A conventional international modern pentathlon had been held at Thun, in Switzerland, in the summer and had been won by Grut, with Sweden also the leading team, scoring 11 points to 22 each for Hungary and Switzerland, 23 for the USA, 26 for Italy and 27 for Great Britain. In another major competition in 1947, in Stockholm, Grut had again been first, ahead of the Hungarian, Karácson, and Sweden had scored 103 points under a different system to 147 for Hungary, 193 for Finland, 197 for Switzerland, 207 for the USA, 257 for France and 294 for Great Britain. Would any self-respecting bookie have taken odds against Sweden? Yes, of course he would!

There were 45 competitors entered in total for the Olympic modern pentathlon, with three each from Argentina, Belgium, Brazil, Finland, France, Great Britain, Hungary, Italy, Spain, Sweden, Switzerland, Uruguay and the USA, plus two each from Chile, Czechoslovakia and Mexico. A team event would not be introduced to the Games until 1952.

The horse-riding opened the competition and was held at Tweseldown Racecourse, also a venue for the specialist equestrian competition, on Friday 30 July. The fencing took place the next day in the Army School of Physical Training gymnasia at Aldershot. The remaining events began on Monday 2 August, followed on successive days by the shooting on a specially constructed range at Bisley, the swimming at Aldershot Borough Council's open-air 50-metre pool, and the cross-country running in the grounds of the Royal Military Academy at Sandhurst.

In the modern pentathlon the competitors do not ride their own horses but are allocated mounts. Some 50 horses were borrowed from the services in Germany, and then put to graze for three months to strengthen them up, and a dozen or so more were hired or were lent by supporters of the Modern Pentathlon Association of Great Britain. The horses were then schooled by a specially formed mounted squadron at Aldershot – but there would still, of course, be some element of luck in the draw. As it happens, only nine riders completed clear rounds within the time limit, as compared to 25 in Berlin on what was said to be an easier course, but this may have been because the time limits had been made stricter with a speed of 500 metres a minute now required, rather than the previous 450 metres a minute.

Willie Grut led after the riding from Major George Moore, of the USA, with Lumsden third and Martin 12th. Grut (9min 18.2sec), Moore (9:22.7) and Lumsden (9:29.0) were comfortably ahead of the rest. The slowest time, including penalties, was 16:13.2 for Lieutenant Hernán Fuentes Besoain, of Chile. The next day's fencing was immensely hard, with the 44 remaining competitors required to meet each other in turn, and the bouts continued from nine o'clock in the morning until seven o'clock in the evening. Grut and a Brazilian, Lieutenant Morrot Coelho, each had the greatest number of wins (28) and Moore was next (26 wins), thus retaining second place overall.

One of the Hungarians, Captain László Karácson, had astonishingly managed 21 wins and 11th place in the fencing despite having fallen and broken his collar-bone in the previous day's riding. He had spent the night in hospital and then returned to fence left-handed with his right arm bound to his side. Brooke was the best of the Britons in 13th place. A Belgian, Lieutenant Mollet, had cracked a rib in the horse-riding event and was unable to start the fencing.

After two events the leading 10 were Grut with 2 place points, Moore 5, Hegner (Switzerland) 13, Morrot Coelho and Premoli (Argentina) 16, Floody Buxton (Chile) 18, Baugh (USA) 19, Gärdin (Sweden) 23, Wirth (Argentina) 26, and Riem (Switzerland) 28. For Great Britain, Lumsden was 14th (37), Martin 21st (43) and Brooke 26th (52). Those readers particularly interested in military protocol might like to know that of the above Hegner, Premoli, Floody Buxton, Baugh, Gärdin and Wirth all held the rank of lieutenant and Riem was a second lieutenant. Of the 45 original competitors, two were majors, 15 were captains, 20 were lieutenants, two were second lieutenants, two were sergeants, and there was an Adjutant, a corporal, a lance corporal and a guardsman.

The winner of the rapid-fire pistol shooting was the Swiss, Bruno Riem, with 194 points, though this was well short of the maximum 200 scored by Charles Leonard, of the USA, at Berlin. Riem's team-mate, Schmid, was second and Frigyes Hegedüs, of Hungary, third (both 193). The Hungarian had been placed 45th and last overnight after being disqualified in the riding when his horse came to an exhausted halt. His injured team-mate Karácson, whose speciality was shooting, managed to score 173 despite using his left hand instead of his customary right. It was the bravest of efforts for a man who knew it was all ultimately in vain because he would obviously not be able to attempt the swimming event the next day.

Grut scored 190 for fifth place to still lead overall from Moore, Riem and Gärdin. Martin remained 21st, but Lumsden had slipped to 26th and Brooke to 28th. The points scores now were Grut 7, Moore 26, Riem 29, Gärdin 33, Larkas (Finland) 36, Hegner 37, Floody Buxton 38, Curcio (Italy) 43, Baugh 47, Morrot Coelho 49.

The rain, which had begun the previous day, continued throughout the swimming and so the performances for the 300 metres distance in the open-air conditions were inevitably affected. Even so, the remarkable Grut won his third event with a time of 4:17.0 which had only been beaten twice before in Olympic competition. The next fastest was a Hungarian, István Szöndy, at 4:21.1, and a mere four others broke 4:35, though there were 15 under five minutes, compared with 10 in Berlin. In any case, Grut already had an Olympic "record" to his credit because the previous highest number of wins in the individual disciplines was two by the Swedish gold-medallist of 1924, Bo Lindman. Curiously, no other Olympic champion had ever won a single one of the five events.

Thus Grut led at the start of the cross-country – and he led so commandingly that it was no longer a matter of whether he would win but whether he could finish in the first nine and thus beat the Olympic record of 18 place points set by fellow-Swedes Gustaf Dyrssen in 1920, with three second places and two at sixth, and by Lindman in 1924, which had been made up of ninth, first, third, fourth and first in that sequence. The leading 10 were Grut 8, Moore 43, Gärdin

44, Hegner 50, Larkas 55, Baugh 58, Gruenther (USA) and Vilkko (Finland) 62, Riem 65, Floody Buxton 68. Gruenther, who had been born in the Philippines, had moved steadily up from 24th place after the riding to 14th after fencing and 11th after shooting. Vilkko had been in 18th place after the fencing but was then fourth in shooting and produced the third best swim of 4:24.0. The British had Martin in 28th place (97 points), Lumsden 34th (112) and Brooke 41st (130).

The running course was 4,000 metres in length over rough going of bracken and woodland paths, with a testing hill about one-third of the way round. The runners set off at intervals and the Scandinavians were very much at home in this setting, which must have seemed so like their familiar sport of orienteering, with the resounding winner being Wehlin, of Sweden, in 14:09.9, though he was well down the overall scoring and that sufficed only to move him up from 29th to 17th. Vilkko and another Finn, Platan, who had placed last in the shooting, took second and third places in 14:21.9 and 14:24.6, promoting them from seventh and 16th respectively overall to fourth and 10th. No one else broke 15 minutes, but among the next fastest were the key figures – Moore fourth in 15:07.5, Gärdin fifth in 15:08.7 ... and then Grut eighth in 15:28.9 to win the gold medal by the modern pentathlon equivalent of a "street" and to beat Lindman's points-scoring record from 24 years before.

The British trio completed the cross-country event in style, with Martin 11th, Brooke 15th and Lumsden 20th. This was to be a traditional strength for Britain's modern pentathletes in the years to come, but Lance Corporal Martin and his colleagues could scarcely have thought that two fellow-countrymen, Jim Fox and Adrian Parker, would win the cross-country at the 1972 and 1976 Olympics respectively and finish fourth and fifth overall, and nor could anyone in 1948 have possibly contemplated that Fox, Parker and Robert Nightingale would together be the Olympic team-winners for Great Britain those 28 years later. Another Briton, Richard Phelps, would also be fourth in the 1984 Olympics and in 1993 became world champion.

Szöndy, of Hungary, who was 18th overall, won the bronze medal in 1952 and Vilkko, of Finland, was seventh at those Games. The rules regarding eligibility were changed by then and the sport opened up to all comers, with another Swede, Lars Hall, promptly becoming the first civilian winner in 1952 and then successfully defending his title in 1956.

Grut, who had joined the Swedish army at the age of 19 and had five times won the national modern pentathlon title, was interviewed after the Games by Laurence Wilkinson, for the *Daily Mail*, and explained that he had begun his sporting career as a swimmer, winning a Swedish schools' title at the age of 14. He described his daily routine, which he had followed for 12 years, as follows: 6.30 a.m., 30 minutes' horse-riding; 9.15–12.30, working in the Swedish war office; 12.30, 30 minutes' running; 1.00, lunch; 1.30, 20 minutes' pistol practice; 2.15–5.15, work in office; 5.15, fencing (every other day); 6.30, dinner; 8.30, bed.

Grut was aged 33, married with two children, and he was surprisingly frank about his decision to retire from the sport: "I shall be glad to be finished with it all. In Sweden an engineer who invents something beneficial or an agriculturist who increases the productivity of the soil gets only a paragraph in the paper. A man who kicks a ball gets himself splashed over six columns. I don't approve of that." Grut, whose father had designed the stadium for the 1912 Olympics in Stockholm, later became secretary-general of modern pentathlon's international ruling body.

Modern pentathlon result (positions in each of the five sports in brackets in the sequence riding, fencing, shooting, swimming, running)
1 Willie Grut (Sweden) 16 place points (1, 1, 5, 1, 8), 2 George Moore (USA) 47 (2, 3, 21, 17, 4), 3 Gösta Gärdin (Sweden) 49 (6, 17, 10, 11, 5), 4 Lauri Vilkko (Finland) 64 (17, 38, 4, 3, 2), 5 Olavi Larkas (Finland) 71 (26, 3, 7, 19, 16), 6 Bruno Riem (Switzerland) 74 (19, 9, 1, 36, 9), 7 Fritz Hegner (Switzerland) 79 (7, 6, 24, 13, 29), 8 Richard Gruenther (USA) 81 (24, 13, 13, 12, 19), 9 Nilo Floody Buxton (Chile) 85 (11, 7, 20, 30, 17), 10 Viktor Platan (Finland) 86 (4, 28, 44, 7, 3), 11 Enrique Wirth (Argentina) 93 (9, 17, 25, 29, 13), 12 Frigyes Hegedüs (Hungary) 95 (45, 13, 3, 24, 10), 13 Hale Baugh (USA) 96 (10, 9, 28, 9, 40), 14 André Lacroix (France) 97 (27, 17, 18, 29, 6), 15 Giulio Palmonella (Italy) 98 (14, 26, 15, 21, 22), 16 Louis Pichon (France) 100 (36, 5, 9, 32, 18), 17 Sune Wehlin (Sweden) 102 (31, 34, 22, 14, 1), 18 István Szöndy (Hungary) 105 (28, 44, 11, 2, 20), 19 Roberto Curcio (Italy) 105 (22, 7, 14, 26, 36), 20 Albert Martin (Great Britain) 108 (12, 31, 23, 31, 11), 21 Augusto Premoli (Argentina) 109 (5, 11, 35, 33, 25), 22 Alberto Moreira López (Spain) 112 (23, 31, 19, 5, 34), 23 Luis Riera Caballer (Spain) 114 (18, 24, 42, 4, 26), 24 Hernán Fuentes Besoain (Chile) 117 (43, 13, 6, 23, 32), 25 Diulio Brignetti (Italy) 118 (38, 34, 12, 6, 28), 26 Alberto Ortiz (Uruguay) 119 (20, 41, 17, 34, 7), 27 Werner Schmid (Switzerland) 119 (42, 17, 2, 28, 30), 28 Christian Palant (France) 119 (40, 24, 8, 16, 31), 29 Karel Bártu (Czechoslovakia) 124 (30, 38, 27, 15, 14), 30 Aecio Morrot Coelho (Brazil) 125 (15, 1, 33, 39, 37), 31 Carlos Mercader (Uruguay) 125 (16, 28, 34, 35, 12), 32 Horacio Sibiru (Argentina) 127 (13, 28, 30, 18, 38), 33 Alejandro Quiroz Galvez (Mexico) 130 (29, 31, 16, 27, 27), 34 Jack Lumsden (Great Britain) 132 (3, 34, 37, 38, 20), 35 Gracida Rojas (Mexico) 134 (8, 40, 43, 10, 33), 36 Manuel Bernabeu Prada (Spain) 141 (41, 17, 39, 20, 24), 37 Geoffrey Brooke (Great Britain) 145 (39, 13, 41, 37, 15), 38 Aloysio Alvez Borges (Brazil) 146 (33, 26, 36, 8, 43), 39 Otto Jemelka (Czechoslovakia) 150 (25, 17, 31, 42, 35), 40 Louis Fauconnier (Belgium) 155 (32, 17, 26, 41, 39), 41 Charles Vyt (Belgium) 156 (21, 34, 38, 40, 23), 42 Ruben Orozco (Uruguay) 164 (35, 41, 25, 22, 41), 43 Humberto Bedford (Brazil) 205 (37, 43, 40, 43, 42). Did not finish – Raoul Mollet (Belgium), László Karácson (Hungary).
Had there been a team competition the order of finishing would have been as follows: 1 Finland 19 points, 2 Sweden 21, 3 USA 23, 4 Switzerland 40, 5 Italy 59, 6 Argentina 64, 7 France 68, 8 Spain 81, 9 Great Britain 91, 10 Uruguay 99, 11 Brazil 111.

Chapter 29

"NEVER HURRYING, JUST ROWING LIKE A MACHINE, IGNORING THE OPPOSITION"

Rowing. Henley-on-Thames, 5–9 August.

I T WAS A masterpiece of understatement. "Bushnell and myself, of Great Britain, won safely." That was the sum total of the description of the double sculls final by Richard Burnell in the British Olympic Association's official report of the Games, and the coverage which had appeared on the Tuesday morning after the race in *The Times* was only a shade more expressive. The headline was brief and to the point: "British Victories At Henley". Of the 23 paragraphs which followed only one and a half were given over to the exploit of Burnell and Bert Bushnell and that of their fellow gold-medallists from Britain, Jack Wilson and "Ran" Laurie.

But then the whole gold-medal-winning enterprise was typically British. Burnell and Bushnell had belatedly come together as a result of a hastily improvised decision made less than five weeks before the Games rowing began, and a trial race to ensure selection had been held only nineteen days before. A couple of months earlier Wilson and Laurie had re-formed a racing partnership which had been in abeyance for a decade. To complete the picture, it should be pointed out that Burnell was actually the rowing correspondent of *The Times* and was presumably expected by his editor and his readers to be suitably modest about his achievement.

Bushnell had originally hoped for a place in the single sculls, but at the Henley Royal Regatta on 3 July – which would more or less decide the composition of the Great Britain team – he was beaten by five lengths by the Australian, Mervyn Wood, and the Olympic selectors opted instead for a young sculler in his first serious season – the bearer of an appropriate name – Anthony Rowe. Burnell and his double-sculls partner, RF Winstone, had lost in the heats to the eventual winners from Belgium. Bushnell and Burnell were then invited by the selectors to join forces with only a fortnight or so's training available to them and challenge for the double sculls place. Hylton Cleaver, the authoritative rowing writer, had astutely anticipated just such a development earlier in the year when he wrote: "Double sculling is simply another form of single sculling, and I commend to Bushnell's notice the suggestion that he find himself a partner and include the double sculls on his calendar, just as lawn tennis champions enter for singles and doubles at Wimbledon. The ideal would be for Burnell and Bushnell to pair up."

There was a great tradition for Burnell and Bushnell to follow because the double sculls had been won for Britain in Berlin by Jack Beresford and Leslie Southwood, both of whom had resumed rowing after the war but at the ages of 49 and 42 respectively did not for one moment consider themselves as Olympic contenders. In any case, the expertise of Beresford, whose father, Julius (originally named Wisniewski), had won a coxed fours silver medal at the 1912 Olympics, would be available as one of the officially appointed panel of eight coaches, and he had a vast amount of first-hand knowledge to pass on. In the annals of British rowing into the 21st century only the achievements of Sir Steve Redgrave supercede Beresford's three Olympic gold medals and two silver medals from 1920 to 1936 in single sculls, double sculls, coxless fours and eights.

Bushnell and Burnell won their Olympic place by beating the 1947 Henley winners, WEC Horwood and DCH Garrod, in the qualifying trial over the Henley course on 17 July. The newly-formed pair were both steeped in rowing history: Burnell's father, Charles, had won a gold medal in the eights at the 1908 Olympics, while Bushnell's family owned a boatyard at Wargrave, near Henley. Yet such was the complexity (some might say hypocrisy) of the rules then in effect regarding amateurism that Burnell was eligible to compete even though he had been writing about rowing for *The Times* since 1946, whereas Bushnell was not allowed to work in the family business and still row as an amateur and so had instead joined the Thorneycroft engineering firm.

The story of how rowing provided another of the total of three gold medals won by Britons at the Games is even more exotic. Wilson and Laurie had won the coxless pairs at Henley in 1938 while on leave from the Sudan Government Service which they had both joined two years before. In the course of their subsequent duties in Africa – which were frequently demanding and sometimes downright hazardous, even life-threatening – they occasionally rowed together for the fun of it on the nearest convenient river, but there was no competition to be had.

On one occasion Laurie received news that Wilson had been cut through with an assegai by a crazed woman, but on arriving post-haste at the hospital expecting to find the victim at death's door Laurie discovered the bed empty and the redoubtable Wilson not only up and about but playing tennis! One of Laurie's duties was to conduct negotiations with the armed Abyssinian partisan patriots who were opposing the Italians in 1940, and while engaged in that task he met up with Wilfred Thesiger, described as "the last of the great British eccentric explorers", who clearly thought very highly of Laurie, though his praise in his autobiography was characteristically limited to the phlegmatic observation that "I found his presence reassuring at this time of increasing anxiety".

Wilson and Laurie had returned to England on six months' leave in the early summer of 1948 and had lost inauspiciously in the heats at the Marlow regatta to an Australian pair but had then won again at Henley, beating the same opponents with what Richard Burnell described in *The Times* as "not only an exhibition of oarsmanship but also of how a pair should be rowed". Like Burnell, who had been a member of the Oxford Boat Race crew in 1939, and whose father had been a member of the winning Oxford crew every year from 1895 to 1898, both Wilson and Laurie came from an Oxbridge background, as did so many others among Britain's oarsmen in 1948. Wilson had been born of English parents in Rhode Island, in the USA, and from Shrewsbury School he went up to Pembroke College, Cambridge, and rowed in the winning Boat Race crew in 1934, 1935 and 1936 alongside Laurie, who was at Selwyn College. The 1934 time of 18min 3sec was a record which would stand until 1948. Laurie was a member of the Great Britain eight which was fourth at the Berlin Olympics, and but for the fact that he was already in Sudan it is likely that Wilson would have also been selected.

Hylton Cleaver, prominent among many others, had pointed out the necessity for long-term preparations for the 1948 Games. The previous year he had warned: "The Olympic regatta is not due till August 1948, and prior to that we shall have another Henley. Either we must pick our Olympic crews in the spring and keep them in training for that one regatta, or we must again leave selection till after Henley and leave too little time for preparation." Neither of the prospective gold-medal pairings – for differing reasons – had managed to follow Cleaver's sensible advice, and one can only conclude that in both cases great natural talent and supreme competitiveness were the qualities which carried the day.

However, Cleaver's words proved prophetic so far as the eights event was concerned. He had voiced the contentious opinion that the best crew of 1947 should have been nominated well in advance for the Olympics, and that was the crew of Jesus College, Cambridge – with Chris Barton in the key position at stroke – which had won all the events open to them, including the Grand Challenge Cup at Henley, where they had beaten the Leander club which had provided another eight in its entirety at the Berlin Games. In 1948, Cambridge broke the Boat Race record of 14 years before by 13sec in 17min 50sec, with Barton again at stroke, and he was promptly selected as captain and stroke of the Olympic eight to be based on the Cambridge crew.

All this seemed wise planning, but differences soon arose between Barton and some of the crew members regarding rowing technique, and the Olympic selectors took the only step open to them, which was to try and re-assemble the previous year's Jesus College crew. The plan did not work because the spark seemed to have flickered out and the Grand Challenge Cup at Henley was won instead by Thames Rowing Club, who beat Jesus College in the semi-finals and a Leander crew containing a number of the Cambridge "Olympic rebels" in the final. Further complications followed because the Thames club won the fours at Henley with oarsmen who were also in the eight and it was decided that the four would be kept together for the Olympics.

A scratch eight was then press-ganged for the Games under Barton's leadership, consisting very largely of the Cambridge men (six, in fact) who had begun practice with him three months before – but who, of course, had lost much valuable training time with him thereafter.

The wonder of it all is that this crew managed to win the silver medals on so little cohesive training together, but maybe they were partly carried along by an inbred sense of history. Had it not been for the public-school and Oxbridge rowing legacy, Britain would have experienced a very much less successful Olympic Games in 1948. The manager of the team was Ewart Horsfall, who had rowed in Great Britain's Olympic champion eight of 1912 and the silver medal crew of 1920. Horsfall had been educated at Eton and Magdalen College, Oxford, exactly as had father-and-son Charles and Richard Burnell.

Writing in *The Times* of 13 July, Richard Burnell exercised cautious optimism regarding the comeback by Wilson and Laurie: "Their victories in the 1930s have become rowing legend, but it did look at one time as though they had left too long a gap in their racing careers. It is too early to say what opposition they will face next month, but it is certain that they will not easily break their winning tradition." By 26 July, 10 days before the Olympic rowing was to begin, Burnell had the vastly more encouraging news to convey that in practice Wilson and Laurie were "going even better than ever", adding as a self-effacing footnote that Bushnell and Burnell were showing "excellent form".

A record number of 27 nations took part in the rowing events – 18 of them from Europe, but also including Argentina, Australia, Brazil, Canada, Cuba, Egypt, South Africa, the USA and Uruguay – and Britain's two gold medals and a silver made them the most successful, ahead of the two golds and a bronze for the USA, whose oarsmen were so much better prepared. The double triumph also revived a time-honoured British tradition – two gold medals had been won at each of the Olympic rowing regattas of 1908, 1912, 1924 and 1932.

The Henley course was of worldwide fame, of great scenic beauty and of unparalleled historical significance, having been the venue for an annual regatta (barring the war years) ever since the Grand Challenge Cup had been first contested in 1839, but it has to be said that as an Olympic setting it left a great deal to be desired. The distance to be raced was restricted by the contours of the river to 1,929 metres, instead of the regulation 2,000 metres, though this could be regarded as being of no more than academic importance. What was far more serious was that even with a widening of the course from 24 metres to 36 there was still only room for three crews abreast instead of the customary six in championship racing. This not only detracted from the classic spectacle of a number of crews racing together but entailed holding a total of 87 races over the four days for the 85 entries in the seven events! Nevertheless, the regatta ran as smoothly as the weather-beaten rough water would allow, and the appropriately named chairman of the Henley management committee, Harcourt Gold, was subsequently knighted for his efforts.

At the 1936 Olympics Germany had won all the titles except for the double sculls (Great Britain) and the eights (USA). The British had also had a silver in the coxless fours and Italy had won two silvers and France two bronzes. At the first post-war European Championships, held on Lake Lucerne in 1947, France had won the single sculls and coxed fours, Italy the coxless fours and eights, Hungary the coxed pairs, Denmark the coxless pairs, and Holland the double sculls. Britain, hampered by lack of equipment and foreign currency restrictions, made little or no impression with their severely limited entry and the Thames RC coxless four which had won at Henley could only place fifth.

The six boat tents, landing stages and changing marquees which had been in use for the Henley Regatta were left standing for the Olympics, and a 4,000-capacity temporary stand was put in place, together with a 150-seater press box built on piles in the river just beyond the finish-line and a broadcasting facility set up by the BBC on the stewards' barge. Instead of the traditional Henley method of sending off crews by the command of an umpire in a barge, the starters, drawn from Belgium, France, Holland and Switzerland, were installed in a tower and as they gave the command, "Partez!" they pressed a button which electrically set the three stopwatches at the finish in operation. A photo-finish camera was provided as back-up but was not required for any of the races.

During the practice week beforehand the weather had been glorious, but in true Perfidious Albion manner it deteriorated as the opening day approached and Thursday 5 August dawned cold and rainy. The coxed fours opened the proceedings with eight heats of two crews in each, and in succession Portugal, Hungary, Italy, USA, Austria, Denmark, Switzerland and France duly won through. The losers, including Great Britain, would have a second chance, as in all the events, with the provision of a series of repéchage heats from which four would go through. In other words, 12 races lasting some 1 hour 25 minutes in total, plus all the time in between manoeuvring boats into position, would have the effect of reducing the number of crews in one event from 16 to 12! It was an unwieldy system which Richard Burnell, in his BOA report, admitted was hard to defend, but in the circumstances there seemed to be no alternative.

Next came the first round of the coxless pairs in which Switzerland, Great Britain (Wilson and Laurie), Austria and Brazil were the winners of the four heats, though the British seemed to be struggling to beat the Italians by only half a length. In the single sculls, where there were just 14 competitors, the three previous Henley winners – Séphériadès (France), Kelly (USA) and Wood (Australia) – all qualified with ease, as did Rowe for Great Britain. The coxed pairs qualifiers were Yugoslavia, Italy, France and Argentina; those for the double sculls were France, Denmark, Belgium (the Henley winners) and the USA; and those for the coxless fours were Italy, USA, Great Britain and Holland. In the eights it was Great Britain, Italy, Canada and the USA that came through.

The whole of the wind-blown second day was given over to repéchage heats. In the double sculls Burnell and Bushnell had been beaten surprisingly and rather easily in the first round by a French pair described by Burnell as "light and lively", though it later transpired that this was a deliberate ploy on the part of the British to get themselves a more favourable draw, and they then comfortably disposed of Holland and Argentina and were joined by Italy and Uruguay in the semi-finals. In the coxless pairs the winners were Italy, Denmark and the Australian pair, Grace and Bromley, who had beaten Wilson and Laurie at Marlow but had been required by their selectors to reach the Henley final in order to qualify for the Games. Hungary and Italy went through in the coxed pairs, but the British were eliminated. South Africa and Denmark survived the repéchage heats for the coxless fours, as did Finland, Norway, Cuba and Great Britain in the coxed fours and Portugal, Switzerland and Norway in the eights.

On the third day of racing, Saturday 7 August, the weather was awful. A strong headwind was gusting and there were rainstorms of near-tropical intensity lashing the course, the competitors and the onlookers. There was no turning back from now on, as there would be no further repéchages: for the buffeted and bedraggled oarsmen it was do or die. The coxed fours, which opened the programme, necessitated a prolonged second round of six heats, from which emerged Italy, Switzerland, USA, Denmark, France and Hungary (who beat Great Britain).

The first of the semi-finals were for the coxless pairs and Wilson and Laurie were back to form, beating Brazil, and joined by the Swiss and Italians for the final, with the Australians eliminated. Towards the end of the morning the conditions were at their very worst and produced what Burnell described as "the regatta's most dramatic race". It brought together for their single sculls semi-final Kelly, Rowe and Risso (Uruguay), and it was Risso who had unexpectedly produced much the fastest time so far with 7min 24.4sec in his repéchage. Burnell described the race in splendidly vivid terms as follows:

"It was confidently expected that Rowe, of Great Britain, who had raced so well against Wood at Henley Regatta, would give Kelly a hard fight. Kelly set a tremendous pace in his determination to dominate Rowe, who had no choice but to try and go with him. In terrible conditions of wind and rain Kelly did succeed in battering down Rowe, but he finished himself in the process. Risso, of Uruguay, who can have had little expectation of victory, and was therefore sculling, comparatively speaking, within himself, suddenly found himself level with Rowe and only a length or so behind Kelly. A splendid spurt up the enclosures gave him a 0.4sec victory."

The Reverend GIF Thomson, reporting the next day for the *Daily Mail* in a manner far from ecclesiastical, wrote excitedly of having been witness as "human excitement and meteorological disturbance jostled each other". Hylton Cleaver, reflecting three years later, thought this was "the most dramatic sculling race I ever saw", and his description of the closing stages rowed in what he remembered as a hailstorm brings alive all the excitement and tension of the occasion even when read some 60 years later: "The river was boiling, but through this liquid shingle Risso made his boat leap at every stroke. Kelly fought to hold him off but was fast collapsing, and when in this incredible way Risso managed to catch up six lengths in 20 strokes, and win on the post with a most dramatic last drive of his sculls, Kelly sat ashen-faced and motionless. For a long time he could not reach the landing-stage, and when he did so by painful stages he fainted." The next year Kelly won at Henley and beat Risso in Amsterdam ... but it wasn't the Olympics.

The conditions were such that the fastest time of the three semi-finals was 8min 5.4sec by the Italian, Catasta. The other semi-final was won by the Henley champion, Wood, who comfortably beat his French predecessor as Henley Regatta winner, Jean Séphériadès, who was to be world champion the next year. When he came to write his reminiscences of his rowing career in 1961, the Frenchman told an endearing tale about his experiences at Henley in 1946, which seemed to sum up the spirit of the sport in that age.

"On the Wednesday the first round brought me up against an Australian sculler. At the start he was in his place before me and he said that he hoped I was in good form. I thanked him, wished him the same ... and then won easily. Not only was he the first one to congratulate me, but that evening his wife brought three eggs for me to the hotel, which were of great value in that year of 1946 when there was still rationing from the war. 'For you,' she said. 'My husband was eliminated, so he has less need of them than you.'

"I could not return the favour, but the final of the competition gave me the opportunity to make a similar gesture. My opponent in the final, Jack Kelly, hit a course marker with his boat when we were rowing alongside each other and lost his rhythm. I stopped rowing and signalled to him to go back to the starting line. There was no merit in what I did. In rowing you do not win because of an accident. That is not the way that things are done."

The Frenchman's opponent from Australia in 1946 was not, as it happens, his future Olympic conqueror, Wood, but another sculler named Marks.

Danish crews – perhaps re-enacting their ancient past as fearless Viking mariners braving the high seas – seemed unaffected by the weather and won their semi-finals in the doubles sculls, coxed pairs, coxed fours and coxless fours. Hungary and Italy also won their semi-finals of the coxed pairs, and the Danes (staving off a late effort by Great Britain) and Italians were joined by the USA in the coxless fours. Great Britain (Burnell and Bushnell) and Uruguay were the other qualifiers in the double sculls. USA, Great Britain and Norway were the successful crews in the eights. Thus for finals day the line-up by nations would be the following:

Single sculls – Australia, Italy, Uruguay.

Double sculls – Denmark, Great Britain, Uruguay.

Coxless pairs – Great Britain, Italy, Switzerland.

Coxed pairs – Denmark, Hungary, Italy.

Coxless fours – Denmark, Italy, USA.

Coxed fours – Denmark, Switzerland, USA.

Eights – Great Britain, Norway, USA.

The finals were held on the afternoon of Monday 9 August, and at last the sun broke through and the wind had abated to a reasonable level and had swung round so that it was blowing across the course. The correspondent for *The Times*, who was, of course, more than usually interested in the weather conditions, reported next day that there had gathered for the occasion "an enormous crowd in glorious sunshine". The opening event was the coxed fours in which the Swiss led from the start, but at 750 metres the Danes were only a few feet behind and the US within a quarter of a length. At 1200 metres the US had moved to second and then at 1400 metres into the lead, holding on to win by three seconds from the Swiss.

It was the first occasion in nine Olympic finals in this event that a crew from outside Europe had won, and no other would do so until New Zealand in 1968. Great Britain were to be the winners in 1984.

Then came the coxless pairs and the first hopes of a British medal – or, to be honest, a British victory because Wilson and Laurie had been regarded as the favourites from the outset, summed up by Burnell's view that "their supporters had been searching vainly to see whence any opposition was to come". Switzerland's Kalt brothers led, as their team-mates had done in the previous race, but at 1000 metres there was very little in it between the three crews – maybe a third of a length – and the British challenged and then gradually moved away to win by a length as the Italians tired and finished a further two lengths down.

The athletics events in the Empire Stadium had finished two days before with further silver medals and none of those elusive victories for Britain – in all, six silvers and a bronze. The swimming events had also been completed, with a single honourable bronze for Britain. On the cycle-track at Herne Hill there were hopes of a gold medal in the sprint event being decided that same day. But this, at last, was the victory which all of Britain had craved. The Cantab men – William George Ranald Mundell Laurie, of Monckton Combe School and Selwyn College, Cambridge, and John Hyrne Tucker Wilson, of Shrewsbury School and Pembroke College, Cambridge – had saved the day. "Their Olympic

---

Coxed fours result: 1 USA (Warren Westlund *stroke*, Robert Martin, Robert Will, Gordon Giovanelli, Allen Morgan *cox*) 6min 50.3sec, 2 Switzerland (Rudolf Reichling *stroke*, Erich Schriever, Emile Knecht, Pierre Stebler, André Moccand *cox*) 6:53.3, 3 Denmark (Erik Larsen *stroke*, Börge Nielsen, Henry Larsen, Henry Knudsen, Jörgen Ib Olsen *cox*) 6:58.6.

performance," said Burnell, who was presumably watching from the towpath or some other vantage point as he awaited his own race, "was a beautiful example of British rowing at its best."

It was Great Britain's third win in the coxless pairs in seven Olympic finals. The first success in 1908 had been rather a hollow one as there had been only four entries and the Leander I crew beat Leander II for the title. In 1932, in Los Angeles, Hugh Edwards and Lewis Clive had beaten New Zealand and Poland in more competitive circumstances.

Mervyn Wood, of Australia, was now clear favourite for the single sculls, with the USA's Jack Kelly out of the reckoning. Kelly's father, John, had beaten Britain's Jack Beresford for the single sculls gold in 1920, and Kelly Jnr would finally win a bronze medal in 1956. Wood confirmed his status with by far the largest recorded victory in Olympic singles sculls history after being held by the Italian, Catasta, for no more than the first minute or so's rowing. Then, in the words of Jack Beresford, who was writing in the organising committee's official report and knew a thing or two about sculling, Wood's "power and stride overwhelmed his opponents and he finished easily, many lengths ahead". Still, the Uruguayan, Risso, was no doubt happy with his unforeseen silver.

Wood, a police officer in Sydney, was not the first Australian to win the Olympic single sculls because Henry Pearce had done so in 1928 and 1932, when a Uruguayan, Guillermo Douglas, was third. Pearce had been denied entry at Henley even as an Olympic champion because he was a carpenter by trade and therefore not a "gentleman", but he moved to Hamilton, Ontario, where he was given a job as a salesman by Lord Dewar, of the whisky distillers, and this made him eligible for Henley. There he won the single sculls in 1931 by six lengths.

Wood's victory was Australia's second at the 1948 Olympics, following Jack Winter's success in the high jump. Altogether, Australia won 13 medals at the Games, compared with a previous highest of seven in 1900, and this marked the first emergence of the country as a growing power in sport. Wood, who was second in the 1952 Olympics when the USSR won the event for the first of four consecutive Games, had started rowing at the age of 13 at Sydney Boys' High School and was still only 19 when he had been a member of the Australian eight at the Berlin Games. He did not touch a boat at all between 1940 and 1945 but returned to win four Commonwealth Games gold medals and a further bronze in the double sculls on his fourth Olympic appearance in 1956. He rose through the police ranks to become New South Wales Commissioner and died in 2006 at the age of 89.

The coxed pairs title went to Denmark ahead of Italy and Hungary, who had all met in the same first-round heat which had been won by the Italians. At 1200 metres Italy still led, but 100 metres later Denmark had edged ahead and then drew steadily away to win by three lengths, with Hungary far back. Denmark

---

Coxless pairs result: 1 Jack Wilson *stroke* & Ran Laurie (Great Britain) 7min 21.1sec, 2 Hans Kalt *stroke* & Josef Kalt (Switzerland) 7:23.9, 3 Felice Fanetti *stroke* & Bruno Boni (Italy) 7:31.5.

had previously finished fourth in this event at the 1908 and 1936 Games and maintained a respectable tradition after their Henley success by taking the bronze medals again in 1952 and 1968. In that latter year Italy won for the first time since 1906 and were to do so again in 1984.

It was Hungary's first appearance in an Olympic coxed pairs final, and though it was not a particularly auspicious occasion for their crew there was an interesting sequel for one among them. Their cox escaped to the USA after the Hungarian uprising in 1956, and with his name now Americanised as Bob Zimonyi he was the cox at the age of 46 to the Vesper Boat Club eight, from Philadelphia, which won the Olympic eights title in 1964.

Italy sped away at the start of the coxless fours and led Denmark by two lengths at 750 metres. The Danes had now moved from the centre of the river to the edge and were in their turn almost two lengths ahead of the USA and pressing the leaders. In the final drive for the finish the Italians still had enough left to win by 1½ lengths, with the USA another length behind. Italy and Denmark had also met in the first round with the result and margin much the same. Italy had won the bronze medals in 1928 and 1932 and had placed fourth in 1936. The Danish oarsman, Ib Storm Larsen, was one of four rowers all with the same surname who won rowing medals for Denmark in 1948.

Next came the double sculls, and hopes for further British success were raised sky-high as Burnell and Bushnell led from the start. The Danes did their chances no good by colliding with the marker buoys, allowing the Uruguayans into second place, but then staged a spirited recovery and at 1200 metres were only 1¼ lengths down and sculling strongly. The British now needed to respond and did so with great power and determination, holding off the challenge and eventually winning by four seconds.

It was really rather daft of the British Olympic Association to leave the coverage in their official report of that event entirely to one of the perpetrators of it; especially as this was very much out of keeping with the style of the publishers, *World Sports*, which had already set a high standard for the quality of its monthly reporting of international sport since before the war and was to continue to do so over very many years until its demise in the 1970s. Richard Burnell, in classic British stiff-upper-lip fashion, was bound to play the whole thing down, but reducing the event to a one-sentence throwaway mention was taking matters

---

Single sculls result: 1 Mervyn Wood (Australia) 7min 24.4sec, 2 Eduardo Risso (Uruguay) 7:38.2, 3 Romolo Catasta (Italy) 7:51.4.

Coxed pairs result: 1 Denmark (Finn Pedersen *stroke*, Tage Henriksen, Carl-Ebbe Andersen *cox*) 8min 00.5sec, 2 Italy (Giovanni Steffe *stroke*, Aldo Tarlao, Alberto Radi *cox*) 8:12.2, 3 Hungary (Antal Szendey *stroke*, Béla Zsitnik, Róbert Zimonyi *cox*) 8:25.2.

Coxless fours result: 1 Italy (Giuseppe Moioli *stroke*, Elio Morille, Giovanni Invernizzi, Franco Faggi) 6min 39.0sec, 2 Denmark (Helge Halkjaer *stroke*, Aksel Bonde Hansen, Helge Schröder, Ib Storm Larsen) 6:43.5, 3 USA (Frederick Kingsbury *stroke*, Stuart Griffing, Gregory Gates, Robert Perew) 6:47.7.

much too far. It has to be wondered why an expert journalist like Hylton Cleaver, for example, or the master rower, Jack Beresford, could not have been called upon to add their comments on this particular race, and so save Burnell the embarrassment of singing his own praises.

The correspondent for the *Manchester Guardian* wrote of "Burnell supplying the horse-power and Bushnell the expertise, verve and watermanship". Astoundingly, the official film of the Games showed nothing at all of this race.

Though short of training because of business commitments, Burnell and Bushnell met the defeated Danish pair again the following year at Henley and at the European Championships and were beaten on both occasions ... but it wasn't the Olympics.

USA had won the eights at five successive Olympic Games. In succession the US Naval Academy (1920), Yale University (1924), the University of California (1928 and 1932) and the University of Washington (1936) had provided the winning crews en masse. Now the University of California was carrying the flag again, and there seemed little reason to suppose that they would fail in their duty, particularly as they had been the only crew to beat six minutes in the preliminaries. The Leander club had won for Great Britain in 1908 (including Charles Burnell) and in 1912 (including Ewart Horsfall), but even Horsfall's most optimistic managerial viewpoint could hardly envisage another success 36 years later.

Nor was there. The Great Britain crew – actually Cambridge University – went out fast and led for the first 500 metres, but by halfway the USA were in front, and then it was relentless progress to the end. Jack Beresford explained lovingly in the organising committee's report how the Americans did it: "They went off the mark in a steady rhythm, never hurrying, just rowing like a machine, entirely ignoring the opposition. Racing against the watch the whole way, their final 'row in' was a joy to watch. The beat went up quite gradually, and a perfectly-balanced tremendously-strong eight fairly swept home."

The British never faltered, but they were beaten by 10 seconds and chased home by the Norwegians. For Richard Burnell, this US performance was one of the outstanding achievements of the Olympic regatta. "Just as Wilson and Laurie exemplified the best of English rowing, so did this American eight show all that is best in their way of rowing," he enthused. "They were beautifully together, and immensely powerful, with that strong finish which seems to be the main feature of American rowing."

The correspondent of the *Manchester Guardian* bemoaned Britain's lost opportunity in this eights event: "The material was available, but it was so mishandled there was first a split in Cambridge loyalties and then a defeat for two Cambridge crews at Henley. At last, a fortnight before the Games, the eight

---

Double sculls result: 1 Richard Burnell *stroke* & Bert Bushnell (Great Britain) 6min 51.3sec, 2 Ebbe Parsner *stroke* & Aage Larsen (Denmark) 6:55.3, 3 William Jones *stroke* & Juan Rodriguez (Uruguay) 7:12.4.

was finally selected." Such sentiments were widely shared among the rowing *cognoscenti*, but in all conscience it is difficult to envisage a British victory in any circumstances. US crews were to win the eights again in 1952 and 1956, though it would surely have been impossible for anyone at Henley that Monday afternoon in August of 1948, however far-sighted they might have been, to visualise that German crews would win in 1960 and 1968 – and that in 1972 and 1976 there would not even be a US crew in the final.

Jack Beresford had taken part in every Olympics from 1920 to 1936, but the enthusiasm had yet to wear thin. Writing from his standpoint as coach and umpire, rather than competitor, his fondest memories of the Games regatta at Henley were of the victory ceremonies: "Weary shoulders were braced, tired legs straightened, as those lithe figures stood to attention in honour of their country. For weeks and months these young oarsmen had trained, had dedicated every moment of their lives that they might at Henley give of their best to strive to win the greatest rowing honours of the world."

Eights result: 1 USA (Ian Turner *stroke*, David Turner, James Hardy, George Ahlgren, Lloyd Butler, David Brown, Justus Smith, John Stack, Ralph Purchase *cox*) 5min 56.7sec, 2 Great Britain (Chris Barton *stroke*, Maurice Lapage, Guy Richardson, Paul Bircher, Paul Massey, Brian Lloyd, David Meyrick, Andrew Mellows, Jack Dearlove *cox*) 6:06.9, 3 Norway (Kristoffer Lepsöe *stroke*, Torstein Kråkenes, Hans Egil Hansen, Halfdan Gran Olsen, Harald Kråkenes, Leif Naess, Thor Pedersen, Carl Henrik Monssen, Sigurd Monssen *cox*) 6:10.3.

Chapter 30

"Now, Dick, Yesss ..." was the cry. In a flash Olympic Gold was won

Bert Bushnell describes a triumph at Henley

THE FIRST CHALLENGE for Bert Bushnell when he took up rowing in the late 1930s was to face up to the restraints of the existing amateur code imposed by the sport's officialdom, and even some 70 years later at the age of 86 he readily recalled in a feisty manner, "There were lots of stupid old men who turned their faces against anyone who worked in or about boats, and if I wanted to compete in amateur rowing it was impossible for me to work in the family boat business. So I had to work at becoming a qualified engineer until I retired from rowing, and only then could I return to the family firm."

Athletics, not rowing, was the first love for Britain's gold-medallist. "I ran in the London Athletic Club schools' meeting at the White City for Henley Grammar School but didn't get through my heat of the 100 yards," he relates, "but eventually I did the 100 yards in 'evens' at Palmer Park, Reading, where I was coached by Sandy Duncan, later general secretary of the British Olympic Association."

Bushnell never gave up basic running as training, even after competing on the water for the first time at the Maidenhead Regatta of 1939. "During the war I was moving all over the country using my engineering skills on motor torpedo boats, and as it was so very boring living in 'digs' on your own I would go regularly for a five-mile run," he says, and he kept up this regime after the war. At the 1946

Marlow Regatta he was invited by visiting Argentinians to go to South America to train and race: "I went there during the winter of 1947 and was unbeaten in races, but I also learned so much more about training, including the importance of having regular daily massage. During my six weeks there, I also kept up my five-mile runs."

Back in England, Bushnell received invaluable coaching from Dan Cordrey, one of several Englishmen who during the 1930s and even earlier worked full-time on the Continent with oarsmen and scullers of other countries. Cordrey had coached Gustav Schäfer, of Germany, to the single sculls gold medal at the 1936 Berlin Olympics, and so dedicated had Cordrey been to his German employers that he had even followed their orders to hide in a Berlin railway siding the specially-built boat in which Dick Southwood and Jack Beresford were to row in the double sculls event for Britain. Fortunately, it was found with two days to go, and the Britons won the gold in front of the waving swastika flags. Cordrey, who had married a German woman, was forewarned by his employers to leave the country on the very eve of war breaking out.

"Meeting him after the war was vital to my technical advance as a sculler," Bushnell remembered. "He wanted to make me think and feel what I was doing. Competitors in all sports have so much advice shouted at them over the years, but what you need most of all is just one phrase which continues to ring in your mind like a bell. Dan wanted me to recover on my blade – to reissue with your wrist cocked, like a maestro playing the piano, almost like a dog raising a paw, he suggested. What he said stayed with me for ever."

Another major influence was the Australian, Mervyn Wood, the Olympic single sculls gold medallist. Wood was staying at the Leander club at Henley before the Games, and Bushnell would cycle home to Wargrave after his morning's work and then be driven over to Henley by one of his parents to work with Wood, but the serious ambition of competing in the Olympic single sculls was frustrated when Bushnell was chosen, instead, for the double sculls with the Old Etonian and Oxonian, Richard Burnell.

Bushnell described their preparations thus: "Dickie – I don't think anyone else ever called him that – presented me with a physical and technical rowing problem because he was about 6ft 2in and 13½ stone, while I was no more than 5ft 10in and 10st 12lb. In the six weeks we had together before the Olympics we obviously had two hours daily of race training, but it was also vital that I had to re-rig the boat so that in spite of the serious physical differences between us we were able to reach together. It took time – hours and hours – but eventually we got better and better together, and thankfully we reached our peak just two days before the Olympic regatta began."

Then a careful strategy was worked out for the heats. "The Danes seemed far the best from the start," Bushnell explains, "and since we were on their side of the draw we would have to race them twice if we weren't careful. So we deliberately made sure that we only just got through to a repêchage and ended up on the other side of the draw from them. Then we won our semi-final easily from the Americans, while the Danes went much faster, unnecessarily, in theirs ahead of Italy.

"In the final on the Monday – sun shining at last and the wind across the course dropping a little – we were about a third of the way down the Henley course when it looked to me at stroke, and maybe also to Dickie, that the Danish bow man was going. Instantly I shouted out, 'Now, Dick, yesss ...' and absolutely no more than two seconds later he was shouting, too, 'Yes, now ...' and in what seemed a flash we had taken first a length and then a length-and-a-half off them, and we were away, well away, and safely home, all of it accomplished."

Neil Allen, who reported on 14 Summer and Winter Olympic Games from 1956 to 1996, readily admits that when he first listened to Bert Bushnell's wonderful description of his gold-medal triumph he found at first he could not speak. "Sorry, Bert," Neil Allen said, "Just got a lump in my throat."

The octogenarian champion replied, "That's all right, young 'un. You take it easy."

Chapter 31

59 BULL'S EYES OUT OF 60 – BUT STILL ONLY 23RD

Shooting. Bisley Camp, Surrey, 2–6 August.

S HOOTING HAD FIGURED among the nine sports contested at the first Modern Olympic Games of 1896 in Athens, and a bewildering variety of ever-changing events had been held since – 22 of them in all, including one in Paris in 1900 where live pigeons were the targets and the four competitors from Australia, Belgium, France and the USA disposed of 77 birds between them. Needless to say, this particular event had not been repeated and would certainly not be on the programme for 1948. World-championship competitions had been even more diverse, involving 58 different rifle events and 12 different pistol events since they had begun in 1897 and 1900 respectively.

The four competitions to be held at the Bisley Camp range, near the Surrey towns of Guildford and Woking, were ones which had stood the test of time. The rapid-fire pistol, free pistol and free rifle events originated from 1896 and the small-bore rifle from 1908. The USA had been much the most successful country in these disciplines, with nine wins, and titles had also gone to Belgium, Brazil, France, Germany, Great Britain, Greece, Italy, Norway, Sweden and Switzerland. At the 1936 Games Willy Rögeberg, of Norway, had fired the first perfect score of 300 with the small-bore rifle and Thorsten Ullman, of Sweden, had set a world record of 559 for the free pistol, improving by 12 points on the record which he already held. Both men were competing again at Bisley.

It was the opinion of Britain's ruling body, the National Rifle Association, that Bisley was "regarded throughout the shooting world as the mecca of rifle shooting". The various ranges were evocatively known as Stickledown, Short, Century, Short Siberia and Long Siberia, and the site had been established in 1890, though an annual meeting had been held by the NRA for 30 years before that on Wimbledon

Common. The most magnificently titled of the competitions was The Rajah of Kolapore Imperial Challenge Cup, which had been contested ever since 1871 by teams representing "The Mother Country" and "The Dominions".

The free pistol event was the first to be held on 2 August. The designation "free" meant that the 50 competitors were entitled to use pistols with stocks specially made to fit the bone structure of the hand. The competition began at 9 a.m. and lasted until 1 p.m., with each of the entrants firing 60 shots in six series of 10 at a target of 50 centimetres in diameter, with a black bull's eye of 20 centimetres. There was a break of half an hour midway through. The Swiss, Rhyner, had a substantial lead by that stage, having scored 96 in the third series for a total of 277. Next best were Vázquez Cam, of Peru, and another Swiss, Schnyder, both with 271, and then Ullman, the defending champion and world record-holder from Sweden, with 269.

Rhyner slipped to an 85 in the fourth series, whereas Vázquez Cam had a 91 to level the totals. Rhyner edged ahead again in the fifth series with a 91 to a 90, but Vázquez Cam finished in grand style with a 93 and Rhyner fell out of the medal reckoning with an 83. The silver and bronze medals were decided by the narrowest of margins as Schnyder, Ullman and the American, Benner, all had scores of 539. Schnyder and Ullman also had 60 hits on target, but the former had more shots which had scored the maximum 10 points, 21 to 16. Benner had 58 hits and so was fourth, but he was to return in 1952 and win the gold.

Vázquez Cam had showed marvellous consistency throughout the competition, with a highest series of 93 and a lowest of 89. His was also an historic victory because Peru had never previously acquired an Olympic medal of any description in any sport and would not do so again for a further 36 years until another marksman, Francisco Boza, won silver in the Olympic trap event in 1984. Ullman, already 40 years old in 1948, would eventually make five appearances in this event at the Olympics; first in 1936, third in 1948, sixth in 1952, sixth again in 1956, fourth in 1960. He also won world titles in 1935, 1937, 1947, 1952 and 1954. The Swiss marksman in fifth place at Bisley, Rhyner, would be world champion in 1949.

The next day it was the turn of the competitors in the small-bore free rifle event, and this had the largest entry of any at Bisley – 71 from 15 nations in Europe

---

Free pistol result: 1 Edwin Vázquez Cam (Peru) 545pts, 2 Rudolf Schnyder (Switzerland) 539, 3 Torsten Ullman (Sweden) 539, 4 Huelet Benner (USA) 539, 5 Beat Rhyner (Switzerland) 536, 6 Angel Leon de Gozalo (Spain) 534, 7 Ambrus Balogh (Hungary) 532, 8 Marcel LaFortune (Belgium) 532, 9 Eino Saarnikko (Finland) 530, 10 Sture Nordlund (Sweden) 527, 11 Frederick Grüben (Argentina) 527, 12 Sándor Tölgyesi (Hungary) 525, 13 Walter Walsh (USA) 525, 14 Lajos Börszönyi (Hungary) 525, 15 Heinz Ambühl (Switzerland) 524, 16 Oscar Bidegain (Argentina) 523, 17 Quentin Brooks (USA) 523, 18 Klaus Lahti (Finland) 522, 19 Ignacio Cruzat Santa Maria (Chile) 520, 20 Väinö Skarp (Finland) 520, 21 Guy Granet (Great Britain) 519, 22 John Gallie (Great Britain) 517, 23 Uno Berg (Sweden) 517, 24 Jacques Mazoyer (France) 519, 25 Martin Gison (Philippines) 514, 26 Albert von Einsiedel (Philippines) 512, 27 Salgado Gandara (Peru) 512, 28 Silvino Ferreira (Brazil) 511, 29 Marcel Bonin (France) 511, 30 Gunnar Svendsen (Norway) 510. Note: there were 20 other competitors, including Peter Marchant (Great Britain), 44th with 484pts.

and also from Argentina, Australia, Brazil, Cuba, Iran, Lebanon, Mexico, Peru, Philippines and USA. The requirement here was for 60 shots to be fired in a prone position at a 20-centimetre diameter target from 50 metres range in six series of 10, with 15 minutes allowed for each series. As was explained by AJ Palmer, secretary of the National Small Bore Rifle Association and a judge at Bisley, "every conceivable aid was permitted" for the .22 calibre rifles, including sights, though these were not allowed to be telescopic.

Nine men had perfect scores of 100 in the first series: Cook, Tomsen (both USA), Kongsjorden (Norway), Nielsen (Denmark), Horber (Switzerland), Martins Guimaraes (Brazil), Koch (Sweden), Johnson (Puerto Rico) and Gilbert (Great Britain). Only the two Americans and Horber repeated the feat in the second series, and then only Cook and Horber in the third series, with Tomsen missing one bull's eye. Such was the accuracy of shooting that even though Horber completed the competition with successive scores of 98, 99 and 98 he slid right down the placings to 12th. Cook dropped one point in the last series and Tomsen scored his third successive 100 to effect a tie, but Cook had the very slightest edge, and therefore the gold medal, with 43 shots hitting the inner area of the bull's eye, which was only three-eighths of an inch in diameter, to Tomsen's 42. Tomsen has the distinction of having been born in Kiev, in Czarist Russia – but only just. His birthdate was 4 March 1917 and the Russian Revolution began eight days later.

The decision regarding the bronze medal was also arrived at only after examining the inner hits, as three men tied with 597, and Jonsson, of Sweden, got the verdict over two Norwegians. Martin Gison, of the Philippines, had suffered the same experience in this event in Berlin, placing fourth with an equal score to those of the silver- and bronze-medallists, but his return to the Olympics in 1948 was a triumph over much greater adversity. He had been captured by the Japanese during the war and had survived a death march. At Bisley he placed 43rd, and also 40th in the rapid-fire pistol, but his was truly a story which lived up to the maxim that it was the taking part which counted. Willy Rögeberg, the Norwegian champion and record-holder from 1936, was eighth on this occasion and only the third-placed representative of his country.

The rapid-fire event for all pistols or revolvers of .22 calibre was held on 4 and

---

Small-bore free rifle result: 1 Arthur Cook (USA) 599pts, 2 Walter Tomsen (USA) 599, 3 Jonas Jonsson (Sweden) 597, 4 Halvor Kongsjorden (Norway) 597, 5 Thore Skredegaard (Norway) 597, 6 Enrique Baldwin Ponte (Peru) 596, 7 Albert Ravila (Finland) 596, 8 Willy Rögeberg (Norway) 596, 9 Harry Cail (USA) 596, 10 Uno Berg (Sweden) 595, 11 Gustaf Nielsen (Denmark) 595, 12 Otto Horber (Switzerland) 595, 13 Antonio Martins Guimaraes (Brazil) 594, 14 Veijo Kaakinen (Finland) 594, 15 John Chandler (Great Britain) 593, 16 Onni Hyninnen (Finland) 593, 17 Cesar Jayme (Philippines) 593, 18 George Jones (Great Britain) 592, 19 Erland Koch (Sweden) 592, 20 R Gauthier-Lafond (France) 592, 21 Victor Gilbert (Great Britain) 591, 22 Albert von Einsiedel (Philippines) 591, 23 François LaFortune (Belgium) 591, 24 Lucien Genot (France) 591, 25 George Johnson (Puerto Rico) 590, 26 Oscar Lozano Soto (Mexico) 590, 27 M Bouchez (France) 589, 28 Manuel Braga (Brazil) 589, 29 Jan Hendrik Brussard (Holland) 588, 30 Gustavo Huet Bobadilla (Mexico) 588. Note: there were 41 other competitors.

5 August, with 30 shots required of the 59 contestants on each of the two days. The shots were to be fired in six series of five to a strict time formula: two series of eight seconds; two series of six seconds; and two series of four seconds. A row of five targets, each of them 1.60 metres in height and 45 centimetres wide, was mounted on an electrically controlled frame and marked with 10 scoring areas. When the competitor said, "Ready", the targets were turned edgeways on for a few seconds and were then swung automatically into position for the required period of time, during which one shot would be fired at each of the five targets. This device was the invention of an RAF officer and was well thought of by the competitors.

The quality of the event was exemplary, as confirmed by AJ Palmer in his article for the British Olympic Association's official report. He wrote: "To score a total of 60 hits required superb marksmanship and timing, especially in the four-second series when split-second co-ordination of the senses was essential. That no fewer than 22 did so indicates the high standard and the intensive training of the marksmen." Those with 60 hits were ranked ahead of those with 59 hits, and so on, in order to decide the leading positions, and the gold medallist in this event was unquestionably one of the most courageous in the entire history of Olympic sport. Károly Takács had been a member of the Hungarian pistol team which won the world title in 1938, and then while serving as a sergeant in the army he had lost his right hand as a result of a grenade explosion during an exercise. His arm was replaced artificially and he taught himself to shoot left-handed, competing again in the World Championships in Lucerne a bare year later and winning another team title.

At the end of the first day at Bisley, Takács and Ullman, the free pistol bronze-medallist two days before and also the rapid-fire bronze-medallist in 1936, led at 286 points. The 1947 world champion, Diaz Sáenz Valente, of Argentina, was only one point behind, and then came Heusala, of Finland (283), Lundquist, of Sweden, and Rasilo, also of Finland (both 282). On the second day it was the nerves of Takács which stood up best to the strain of the competition – and to the shock of an accident which could have cost him the gold. His pistol accidentally went off into the ground after reloading, which was at first counted as a valid

---

Rapid-fire pistol result: 1 Károly Takács (Hungary) 60 hits/580pts, 2 Carlos Enrique Diaz Sáenz Valente (Argentina) 60/571, 3 Sven Lundquist (Sweden) 60/569, 4 Leonard Ravilo (Finland) 60/563, 5 Väinö Heusala (Finland) 60/563, 6 Lajos Börszönyi (Hungary) 60/562, 8 Birger Buhring-Andersen (Norway) 60/559, 9 Michelangelo Borriello (Italy) 60/557, 10 Charles des Jamonières (France) 60/555, 11 Konstantinos Mylonas (Greece) 60/554, 12 Charles Willott (Great Britain) 60/554, 13 Bob Chow (USA) 60/553, 14 Ernesto Montemayor Rodriguez (Mexico) 60/550, 15 Walter Boninsegni (Italy) 60/549, 16 Odd Bonde Nielsen (Norway) 60/546, 17 Luis Palomo Pujol (Spain) 60/546, 18 Francisco Bustamente Cruz (Mexico) 60/538, 19 Hernando Hernández Hernández (Cuba) 60/532, 20 Rudolf Schnyder (Switzerland) 60/531, 21 Roberto Müller (Chile) 60/528, 22 José Maria Ferreira (Portugal) 60/524, 23 Philip Roettinger (USA) 59/554, 24 Claes Egnell (Sweden) 59/558, 25 John Layton (USA) 59/548, 26 Rafael Cadalso Fernández (Cuba) 59/548, 27 Henry Steele (Great Britain) 59/545, 28 Hans Aasnaes (Norway) 59/544, 29 Jaakko Rintanen (Finland) 59/543, 30 Pedro Simão (Brazil) 59/540. Note: there were 59 competitors, including Henry Swire (Great Britain), 39th with 58 hits/538pts.

shot, and it was only as the outcome of lengthy deliberation by the jury of appeal that he was allowed to fire again. Undeterred, his score of 294 was seven better than Diaz Sáenz Valente, who had won the previous year's world title. Takács was to successfully defend his title in 1952, when Diaz Sáenz Valente was fourth, and also to place eighth in 1956. Earlier that year Diaz Sáenz Valente had been killed in an aircraft crash.

The free rifle event was held on a specially-constructed 300-metre range, with the 36 competitors required to fire 120 shots in the prone, kneeling and standing positions at a 100-centimetre target which contained a 10-centimetre bull's eye. The regulations required that rifles should not exceed 9mm in calibre or nine kilogrammes in weight, and metal sights, special hand-grips and tailored stocks were allowed. The competition was drawn out over four and a half hours, and so patience was as much a virtue as accuracy. In the prone position Grünig, of Switzerland, led Leskinen, of Finland, by one point, 390 to 389 out of a maximum of 400, but the Finn dropped too many points in the kneeling position, scoring 368, and Grünig's score of 375 now gave him a two-point lead over another Finn, Janhonen, the reigning world champion. At the standing position Grünig outscored Janhonen 355 to 351 to win the gold, while the Norwegian, Rögeberg, came through from sixth place with the equal best score of 357 in this final phase to take the bronze.

The selection process for the Swiss in this event was rather more intense than most. The new champion had beaten tens of thousands of his fellow-countrymen to qualify because there had been an entry of 168,000 for the national 300-metre championship! There were 3,460 shooting clubs in the country. By contrast, their French neighbours had been at something of a disadvantage in the war years because possession of a weapon risked the death penalty during the German occupation. Three former world champions represented France at Bisley in various events – Jacques Mazoyer, Marcel Bonin and Lucien Gerrot – but none of them placed higher than 24th.

Shooting was one of those Olympic sports which was to undergo a transformation by the time of the 1952 Olympics. At Bisley the gold medals had

---

Free rifle, three positions result: 1 Emil Grünig (Switzerland) 1,120pts, 2 Pauli Janhonen (Finland) 1,114, 3 Willy Rögeberg (Norway) 1,112, 4 Kurt Johansson (Sweden) 1,104, 5 Kullervo Leskinen (Finland) 1,103, 6 Olavi Elo (Finland) 1,095, 7 Halvor Kongsjorden (Norway) 1,093, 8 Holger Erbén (Sweden) 1,091, 9 Otto Horber (Switzerland) 1,080, 10 Emmett Swanson (USA) 1,079, 11 Marcio Ciocco (Switzerland) 1,078, 12 Pablo Cagnasso (Argentina) 1,075, 13 Ricardo Grimau (Argentina) 1,074, 14 Abel Ortiz (Argentina) 1,072, 15 Odd Sannes (Norway) 1,070, 16 Arthur Jackson (USA) 1,067, 17 Walther Fröstell (Sweden) 1,067, 18 Frank Parsons (USA) 1,057, 19 Gustaf Nielsen (Denmark) 1,057, 20 Enrique Baldwin Ponte (Peru) 1,052, 21 Uffe Schutz Larsen (Denmark) 1,047, 22 José Nozari Espinosa (Mexico) 1,013, 23 Jean Fournier (France) 1,001, 24 Edouard Rouland (France) 991, 25 Bob Maslen-Jones (Great Britain) 981, 26 John Knott (Great Britain) 966, 27 S Lesceux (France) 952, 28 Jocelyn Barlow (Great Britain) 949, 29 José Reyes Rodriguez Mireles (Mexico) 944, 30 Reginald Parker (Australia) 926. Note: there were 36 competitors.

been won by Hungary, Peru, Switzerland and the USA and the most medals by Sweden with three bronzes. In Helsinki four years later three of those four titles and eight of the 12 medals went to Eastern European countries, and the USSR had the most medals (a gold, two silvers and a bronze). Great Britain's marksmen had made no great impression on their home range at Bisley – Victor Gilbert, of the Ham and Petersham club, having dropped to 21st place after being one of the early leaders in the small-bore rifle event – but Squadron Leader Charles Willott made some small amends in the rapid-fire pistol. From being 19th after the first day, he put together a score of 281 to move up to 12th. It was 24 years since Britain had won a shooting gold, and that had been achieved in a running deer team event which had been abandoned thereafter, and the next gold was still another 20 years away, Bob Braithwaite winning the clay pigeon event in 1968.

Chapter 32

ALWAYS AFRAID OF LOSING ... THE TRAINED SEAL KNEW NO FEAR

Swimming. Empire Pool, Wembley, 30 July–7 August.

I N THE WATER or on the track, the accession to gold had a familiar look about it. Bob Mathias was not the only precocious champion from the USA. On the same days as Mathias was winning the decathlon competition in the Empire Stadium, another 17-year-old, Jimmy McLane, was setting up his own title bid not much more than a discus-throw's distance away in the Empire Pool. While Mathias laboured from morning till night on the Thursday and Friday of that Olympic week running, jumping and throwing, McLane spent exactly 40 minutes 9.9 seconds swimming back and forth to qualify for the 1500 metres freestyle final.

Those 40 minutes or so were taken up with the formalities of the heats and semi-finals of the event, and when it came to the final on the Saturday a surge of power eight lengths from the finish was quite sufficient to take McLane into a 15-metre lead and onwards to the gold. His time of 19min 18.5sec, it has to be said, was not exceptional, and so the Olympic record of 19:12.4, set by a 14-year-old Japanese, Kusuo Kitamura, in Los Angeles in 1932, comfortably survived. More significant still, news emerged a few days later from Tokyo of an astounding exploit which further served to put McLane's performance, commendable as it was, in the shade.

Japanese competitors, of course, had been banned from the 1948 Olympics, and their absence – and that of others from Germany and the USSR – perhaps makes swimming the sport at the Games for which the thought of "what might have been" is most apposite. In Berlin in 1936 Japan had won three men's gold medals, including the 1500 metres freestyle, to the USA's two, and on the eve of the 1948 Olympics it was a Japanese, Tomitaksu Amano, who after 10 years still held the world record for that distance at 18:58.8. Coinciding precisely with the Wembley events, Japan staged a meeting of its own, clearly intended to prove a point, and amongst a profusion of fast times a 20-year-old political science student, Hironashin Furuhashi, achieved 18:37.0 for the 1500 freestyle, with Shiro Hashizume close behind in 18:38.8.

Furuhashi was coached by the 1936 Berlin breaststroke champion Tetsuo Hamuro, and was said to be training as much as seven hours a day. He also beat the existing world records for 400 and 800 metres freestyle (4:33.5 and 9:35.5), and it is difficult to imagine that he would not have won two individual gold medals at Wembley, and maybe a third in the relay. A year later he was to reduce the 1500 metres record to 18:19.0 in the USA, and that achievement was described by *Time* magazine as being "roughly as good as running a mile 12 seconds faster than anyone else". As the world record for the mile then stood at 4min 1.3sec, this was giving Furuhashi's swim a value equivalent to a sub-3min 50sec mile 26 years before it was actually achieved! He was hailed by WJ Howcroft as "unquestionably the greatest swimmer of all time".

By the time that Japan returned to the Olympics in 1952, Furuhashi was past his best and finished last in the 400 metres freestyle, while at 1500 metres US ascendancy was re-established by a Hawaiian of Japanese origin, Ford Konno, ahead of Hashizume, though Furuhashi's world record still stood. The absence of some medal challengers at Wembley is a theme to which it is necessary to return, but on the principle that Olympic champions can only beat those who are in the pool alongside them, and not those who remain on the other side of the world for whatever reason, it is more appropriate for the time being to concentrate on the happenings in the Wembley pool.

Swimming in 1948 was conducted on a very much smaller scale than it has become 60 years or so later. There were merely six events for men at Wembley: 100, 400, 1500 and 4x200 metres freestyle, 200 metres breaststroke, 100 metres backstroke. There were five events for women: 100, 400 and 4x100 metres freestyle, 200 metres breaststroke, 100 metres backstroke. Races at other distances were yet to be introduced to Olympic competition – 200 metres freestyle and 100 metres breaststroke for men, 800 metres freestyle and 200 metres backstroke for women came in 1968, 200 metres backstroke in 1964. The butterfly technique was still regarded as being a variation of the breaststroke and would not be held separately until 1956. The 4x100 medley relay would be added in 1960 and the 4x100 freestyle and the individual medleys from 1964 onwards. Introduction of races at 50 metres was still 40 years away.

Now that swimming is regarded as being one of the major Olympic sports, it seems odd that the programme of events at Wembley should have taken place at almost precisely the same time as that of the athletics in the stadium nearby. Sessions were held morning, afternoon and evening and the schedule of finals was as follows: 31 July – Men's 100 metres freestyle; 2 August – Women's 100 metres freestyle; 3 August – Men's 4x200 metres freestyle relay, Women's 200 metres breaststroke; 4 August – Men's 400 metres freestyle; 5 August – Women's 100 metres backstroke; 6 August – Men's 100 metres backstroke, Women's 4x100 metres relay; 7 August – Men's 200 metres breaststroke, Women's 400 metres freestyle, Men's 1500 metres freestyle. The diving competitions and the water polo final and third-place match were also staged at the Empire Pool during the week.

There were 33 countries entered for the swimming events and the USA, inevitably, provided the strongest men's contingent, including three who had set world records earlier in the year: Alan Ford, 55.4sec for 100 metres freestyle; Joe Verdeur, 2min 30.0sec for 200 metres breaststroke; and Allen Stack, 1min 4.0sec for 100 metres backstroke. The most notable of the Europeans was the 19-year-old Frenchman Alex Jany, who had established a world record of 4min 35.2sec for 400 metres freestyle and had been enthusiastically described by Howcroft in that pre-Furuhashi era as "the greatest all-round swimmer the world has seen". It was at the previous year's European Championships in Monte Carlo that Jany had achieved his 400 metres time, beating by seven seconds the existing record of Bill Smith, who would represent the USA at Wembley. Jany had also won the 100 metres freestyle and later set a world record for that distance of 55.8 which Ford subsequently improved.

The Americans were much less dominant in women's swimming, and the post-war standard, generally, was rather lower than the men's in relative terms. Of the five Olympic events for women the existing world records were held by three Danish swimmers and two Dutch, but the only one set since 1940 was by Petronella ("Nel") van Vliet, of Holland, at 200 metres breaststroke, with 2min 49.2sec earlier in 1948. She had beaten 11 world records at various distances in the past two years and was the title-winner at the 1947 European Championships, where all the four other women's events were won by Denmark. The outstanding US woman was Ann Curtis, who held world records for the 440 and 880 yards freestyle.

Britain's hopes rested for the most part with Roy Romain and Cathie Gibson, who between them provided the most graphic of contrasts in build. Romain was a moustachioed 6ft 4in (1.94m) tall law student at King's College, in London, who would be 30 on the eve of the Olympics. In 1947 he had become only the second British man after Jack Besford at backstroke in 1934 to win a European title by taking the 200 metres breaststroke with the butterfly technique in a time of 2:40.1. This ranked second in the world for the year to Joe Verdeur, and even though the American had now moved 10 seconds ahead with his world record, Howcroft expressed great confidence in Romain's potential, saying that he had the "ideal physique for the exhausting butterfly stroke". The slightly-built 17-year-old Miss Gibson, who came from the highly successful Motherwell club in Scotland which provided three members of Great Britain's swimming team and three more for water polo, had first emerged as a prodigy at the age of 12, and had placed second to Karen-Margrete Harup, of Denmark, in the European finals at both 400 metres freestyle and 100 metres backstroke.

The age range in the British team was also well illustrated by Norman Wainwright and Jack Wardrop. Wainwright, from the Hanley club, in Staffordshire, had won 21 national titles at various freestyle distances since 1935 and had set British records from 150 yards to one mile. He had competed in the 1932 and 1936 Olympics, placed third at the European Championships in the 1934 1500 metres and 1938 400 metres, and would be 34 when he appeared again at Wembley. Wardrop, a 16-year-old team-mate of Cathie Gibson's at Motherwell, would go on to a glittering career as one of Britain's finest swimmers of the 1950s, setting four world records and winning 11 national titles. Both he and his twin brother, Bert, would be Olympic finalists in 1952.

As in so many other sports, Britain's Olympic successes dated from a much earlier era. No men's titles had been won since the 1908 London Games, though Henry Taylor has his place in Olympic swimming history, with four gold medals in 1906–08, setting a world record of 22:48.4 for the 1500 freestyle in the latter year. The only win by a British woman had been by Lucy Morton at 200 metres breaststroke in 1924 when the current record was held by another Briton, Irene Gilbert, at 3:20.4.

First day, Friday 30 July

The original intention had been to build a new open-air pool at Wembley for the Games, but it was decided that this would be too costly, and so the indoor Empire Pool was refurbished instead. With its 8,000-seat capacity, the venue proved perfectly adequate, and it seems surprising that in such a cost-conscious Games thought should ever have been given to a budget-consuming alternative.

The first round of the 100 metres freestyle for men began the afternoon's activity at 2 p.m. and the winner of the opening heat was Jany, in 58.1sec, with his time being equalled in the fifth heat by Walter Ris, of the USA. The world record-holder, Ford, and the third American, Keith Carter, also won their heats, and others among the 16 who went through to the evening's semi-finals were three from Hungary, two each from Australia and Sweden, and one each from Argentina, Brazil, Egypt, Great Britain and Mexico. Ford had the added merit of being the first man to have swum 100 yards in under 50 seconds and had beaten a 16-year-old record for the distance held by the legendary Johnny Weissmuller. The valiant swimmers from India were somewhat slower, finishing last in each of their three heats. The three heats of the women's 200 metres breaststroke were really rather inconsequential, as only six of the 22 competitors were eliminated, including all three Americans, but the world record-holder, Nel van Vliet, did set a Games record of 2:57.4.

The 100 metres freestyle for women began the evening session at 7 p.m. with the five heat-winners including the European champion from Denmark, Fritze

Carstensen (née Nathansen), and Ann Curtis, for the USA. Denmark and the USA had all their three swimmers into the next evening's semi-finals and Britain's Patricia Nielsen, aged 18, and Lillian Preece, 20, also went through. Youngest of the qualifiers was an Australian, Marjorie McQuade, who had celebrated her 14th birthday only a fortnight before, and who caught Howcroft's keen eye, as he wrote in the *World Sports* report of the Games of "an amazing performance for a schoolgirl". It was in her heat that occurred the first of several instances where the judging of positions did not comply with the times awarded, and this failing would have more serious consequences later in the week. Among those eliminated was a 20-year-old Hungarian, Zsusza Nádor, who a few days later slipped secretly away from the Hungarian team headquarters, thus becoming one of the first Olympic defectors. She was to compete for Britain in the 1950 Jewish Maccabiah Games in Israel.

The men's 100 metres semi-finals were conducted in two heats, with the first three in each, plus the two other fastest, to go through, as would be the case in all the events. As it happens, it was neatly the first four in each of the races who were to advance on this occasion, but this was a sensible method of qualification, which allowed for any possible imbalance in the draw, and it could readily have been copied by the athletics administrators to good effect. Carter, the third-string American, surprisingly won the first heat from Jany, having started very fast, and according to Howcroft this was a deliberate ploy devised by the immensely experienced US coach, Bob Kiphuth, to upset the Frenchman, whose delicate temperament had been remarked upon when he had visited the USA the previous year. Ris won the second heat in 57.5 to equal the Games record. The three Americans and the Frenchman were to be joined by two Hungarians, an Egyptian and a Swede in the final the following afternoon.

Second day, Saturday 31 July

The afternoon's semi-finals of the women's 200 metres breaststroke proved the benefits of the qualifying system as Elizabeth Church, the Amateur Swimming Association national champion from Northampton, went through in fifth place in the second of the races, having produced the eighth fastest time overall. The world record-holder, van Vliet, broke the Games record again with 2:57.2, narrowly ahead of the Hungarian, Eva Novák, at 2:58.0. Two other Dutchwomen, a second Hungarian, an Australian and a Belgian completed the roll-call of qualifiers.

Then came the first of the finals – the men's 100 metres freestyle. The eight concerned were Carter, Ford and Ris for the USA, Jany for France, Kádas and Szilard for Hungary, Olsson (the European silver-medallist) for Sweden and El-Gamal for Egypt. The three Americans, plus Jany and Kádas, had all swum in the 57.5 to 58.0 range in the heats, while the other three had not broken 59.0. Ford and Jany were the fastest, at least on paper, and Jany seemed to be proving that statistics don't lie when he led at halfway, but then Ford surged past him and Ris finished strongest of all, taking the lead in the last 10 metres to win the gold. Jany faded to fifth and Kádas came through for the bronze. The winning time of 57.3 was well outside the world record; nevertheless, Howcroft described the race as "an epic final, the greatest of all time".

Ris was a 24-year-old student from the University of Iowa and was the first American winner of this event since Johnny Weissmuller, later to gain screen fame as Tarzan, took the second of his titles in 1928. Standards had not advanced that dramatically in the intervening 20 years because Weissmuller had won Olympic gold in 58.6sec and held the world record at 57.4 for 10 years from 1924. The Egyptian, El-Gamal, though last, merits a footnote as the first male swimmer representing an African country to contest an Olympic final, though he was not actually the first African-born swimmer to do so, as will be noted in due course.

More freestyle events followed that evening: the semi-finals of the women's 100 metres and the heats of the men's 400 metres. Greta Andersen, of Denmark, the European bronze-medallist who had improved to the third fastest ever time of 1:05.6 earlier in the year, equalled the Olympic record of 1:05.9 in the first of the women's semi-finals to establish herself as favourite for the next evening's final, though Ann Curtis was clearly not at full stretch in winning the other semi-final in 1:07.6. The two other Danish women, two Dutch and two Swedes were the remaining finalists. The six heats of the men's freestyle were won in sequence by McLane (USA), Yantorno (Argentina), Hale (Great Britain), Mitró (Hungary), Kadás (Hungary) and Smith (USA). McLane's time of 4:42.2 improved the Olympic record, and Jany also got through to revive French hopes, but among those who went out was Roy Botham, from a well-known South Manchester swimming family, who had been an outstanding junior 11 years before and had served during the war in the RAF. Smith had a long wait for the last finisher in his heat, a Pakistani, Karim Ali Sultan, eventually completing the course more than 2½ minutes later in 7:16.9.

Third day, Monday 2 August

The heats of the men's 4x200 metres freestyle relay were held in the afternoon and served to prove that the next day's final would be between the Americans and the Hungarians. They met in the first heat and Hungary won in a time of 8:53.6, only a couple of seconds outside the Olympic record from 1936 held by Japan, but the US management – in what was to become a time-honoured tradition – put out a team of reserves to ensure an easy qualification in second place. The other finalists would be Argentina, Brazil, France, Mexico, Sweden and Yugoslavia, but not Great Britain, whose team, including the veteran Wainwright, could only finish fifth.

---

100 metres freestyle (men) result: 1 Walter Ris (USA) 57.3sec, 2 Alan Ford (USA) 57.8, 3 Géza Kádas (Hungary) 58.1, 4 Keith Carter (USA) 58.3, 5 Alex Jany (France) 58.3, 6 Per-Olof Olsson (Sweden) 59.3, 7 Zoltán Szilárd (Hungary) 59.6, 8 Taha Youssef El-Gamal (Egypt) 1:00.5.

The evening session featured the final of the women's 100 metres freestyle, with Andersen, Carstensen and Harup for Denmark, Heijting-Schuhmacher and Linssen-Vaessen for Holland, Ahlgren and Fredin for Sweden, and Curtis for the USA. Carstensen led by a metre at the turn, and just as in the men's race it was not until the last 10 metres that the gold was decided by Andersen's finishing effort, as Curtis came through even more strongly and just failed to catch her rival. Andersen's time of 1:06.3 was slower than in her semi-final, but she would have had no concerns about that. Danish pre-eminence in women's swimming was a new phenomenon and hers was the first Olympic gold medal in the sport for her country.

The men's 400 metres freestyle semi-finals completed the evening's schedule, and curiously neither of them was won in a time which approached McLane's of the previous evening. Four went through from each semi-final: McLane and Smith for the USA, Mitró and Kadás for Hungary, Jany, Yantorno, Hale and Marshall (Australia). Jack Hale, from the Hull Kingston club, had won nine ASA freestyle titles in the past two years and also the long-distance championship in London's Serpentine lake, and his career would continue until 1954. He had set a British record of 4:46.2 for the slightly longer 440 yards. John Marshall was a portent of things to come from Australia, because he was still only 17 years old and had won four freestyle events at his national championships.

Fourth day, Tuesday 3 August

In the afternoon's heats of the women's 100 metres backstroke, the Olympic record was broken by Denmark's European champion, Harup, with 1:15.6, and not much slower was Judy Joy Davies, of Australia, at 1:16.4. Only eight of the 24 competitors were eliminated, and all three Britons were among those who advanced. The evening was given over to the finals of the men's 4x200 metres freestyle relay and the women's 200 metres breaststroke.

The relay produced one of the best races and the only world record of the Games. The USA team was restored to full strength, swimming in the order of Walter Ris, Walter Wolf, Jimmy McLane and Bill Smith, but they were challenged resoundingly by the Hungarians. Ris held off an unexpected response from the unheralded Nyéki by only a metre after the first stage. Then Mitró went ahead of Wolf by less than half a metre. McLane took back an advantage of two or three metres over the European 100 metres bronze-medallist, Szathmáry. On the anchor Smith at last pulled his team safely away from Kadás. The times were brilliant – 8:46.0 for the winners and 8:48.4 for the silver-medallists, compared with the previous world record of 8:51.5 set by Japan at the 1936 Olympics. The

---

100 metres freestyle (women) result: 1 Greta Andersen (Denmark) 1min 06.3sec, 2 Ann Curtis (USA) 1:06.5, 3 Marie-Louise Linssen-Vaessen (Holland) 1:07.6, 4 Karen-Margrete Harup (Denmark) 1:08.1, 5 Ingegärd Fredin (Sweden) 1:08.4, 6 Irma Heijting-Schuhmacher (Holland) 1:08.4, 7 Elisabeth Ahlgren (Sweden) 1:08.8, 8 Fritze Carstensen (Denmark) 1:09.1.

race would have been an even more enthralling three-way battle had the Japanese been there because the next year they improved the world record to 8:45.4. Credit, also, to the US "B" team of Gibe, Dudley, Gilbert and Rogers, whose time of 8:55.9 in the heats would have easily won the bronze medals.

Hungary had placed only third in the previous year's European Championships, though it had been an even closer race than at Wembley with Sweden winning from France and only half a second separating all three teams. The prominent showing of Hungarian swimmers at Wembley before the Communist Party gained the monopoly of power in the country the following year and instituted state aid for sport should not be surprising. There was a strong tradition of swimming expertise, dating back to the inaugural Modern Olympics of 1896 when an 18-year-old, Alfréd Hajós, had won the 100 metres freestyle, to be succeeded four years later by Zoltán Halmay.

In the women's 200 metres breaststroke final, van Vliet, the Dutch holder of the world record, of whom it was said that "there is scarcely a male swimmer in Holland who can beat her", faced Hungary's Székely, a chemistry student who had finished only half a metre behind her in the previous year's European Championships, and the bronze-medallist de Groot, also from Holland. The others were Novák (also Hungary), Hom (again Holland), Hansen (Denmark), Lyons (Australia) and Church (Great Britain), who had made a promising international debut the previous year at the age of 17 with fifth place in the European Championships. A German woman named Krey had swum a time of 2:57.6 and would be missed. Nancy Lyons, aged 17, had beaten the world record for the 100 yards breaststroke earlier in the year, having only recently made the transition from the conventional breaststroke style to the butterfly stroke. Elizabeth Church was the first British swimmer to figure in a final at these Games.

Van Vliet and Novák, who had been fourth in the European final, disputed the lead for the first three lengths, but then Lyons came storming through from fifth to second place and failed by only a foot to catch the Dutchwoman for the gold. The winning time for van Vliet, who used the orthodox breaststroke style, was eight seconds slower than her own world record, but a much smaller margin than that caused some controversy over the fifth and sixth places as de Groot was timed in 3:06.2 for fifth and Church one-tenth faster for sixth. Fortunately, there was no question of a medal being in stake, and it seemed to be the sort of marginal disparity between man-made times and placings which was bound to occur on

---

4x200 metres freestyle relay (men) result: 1 USA (Walter Ris, Walter Wolf, Jimmy McLane, Bill Smith) 8min 46.0sec (world record), 2 Hungary (Imre Nyéki, György Mitró, Elemér Szathmáry, Géza Kádas) 8:48.4 (European record), 3 France (Joseph Bernardo, Henri Padou, René Cornu, Alex Jany) 9:08.0, 4 Sweden (Martin Lundén, Per-Olof Östrand, Olle Johansson, Per-Olof Olsson) 9:09.1, 5 Yugoslavia (Vanja Ilič, Čiril Pelhan, Ivan Puhar, Branko Vidovič) 9:14.0, 6 Argentina (Horacio White, José Durañona, Juan Garay, Alfredo Yantorno) 9:19.2, 7 Mexico (Ramón Bravo Prieto, Angel Maldonado Campos, Apolonio Castillo Diaz, Alberto Isaac Ahumada) 9:20.2, 8 Brazil (Sérgio Alencar Rodrigues, Willy Otto Jordan, Rolf Kestener Egon, Aram Boghossian) 9:31.0. Note: In the heats Bob Gibe, Bill Dudley, Edwin Gilbert and Eugene Rogers represented the USA and Augusto Canton represented Argentina.

occasions. There was no automatic timing equipment in place at the Empire Pool, though, of course, even such incontestable evidence as that could provide had been ignored by the officials at the nearby athletics events.

At the 1952 Olympics Székely and Novák were to take the gold and silver ahead of Great Britain's Helen Orr (known as Elinor) Gordon, from the Hamilton club in Scotland, who was a semi-finalist at Wembley at the age of 14 and would win an Empire Games title in 1954 and be an Olympic finalist again in 1956. After the 1952 Olympics the breaststroke and butterfly were separated and a 100 metres event was held for the latter technique until 1968, when comparisons of the respective winning times at 200 metres would show how superior one was to the other – 2:44.4 for breaststroke, 2:24.7 for butterfly. The butterfly alternative had been well developed by male swimmers from 1928 onwards, as will be explained in due course, but the women were slower on the uptake, and the one exponent of it at the 1936 Games had been a Brazilian, Maria Lenk, who had been eliminated in the semi-finals but had set a world record of 2:53.0 three years later.

Fifth day, Wednesday 4 August

The fastest heat in the 100 metres backstroke for men was won by Stack in 1:06.6, but the standard varied enormously and another of the swimmers from Pakistan, Jaffar Ali Shah, was a long way last in his heat in 1:30.2. The European champion was Georges Vallerey, of France, who had been born in Casablanca, and he seemed a very serious threat to the Americans, having set the world's fastest time for 1947 of 1:06.8. The women's 4x100 metres relay heats formed the other part of the afternoon's prosaic entertainment, requiring only Argentina, Belgium and Canada to be eliminated. The evening promised rather more in the way of excitement in the form of the men's 400 metres freestyle final and the semi-finals of the women's 100 metres backstroke.

The eight men who lined up were Smith and McLane (USA), Kádas and Mitró (Hungary), Yantorno (Argentina), Marshall (Australia), Jany (France) and Hale (Great Britain). Here again there was a notable absentee in a Soviet swimmer named Ushakov, who had recorded a time of 4:43.8. Smith, from Hawaii, led from the start and at halfway was at least five metres ahead of McLane, closely followed by Marshall and the two Hungarians. The order remained the same for the rest of the race with Smith's winning time of 4:41.0 beating the Games best from 1936 and almost exactly equalling the world record which he had set in 1944 and which had subsequently been surpassed by Jany.

Smith had suffered typhoid at the age of six and his rehabilitation had been

---

200 metres breaststroke (women) result: 1 Nel van Vliet (Holland) 2min 57.2sec, 2 Nancy Lyons (Australia) 2:57.7, 3 Eva Novák (Hungary) 3:00.2, 4 Eva Székely (Hungary) 3:02.5, 5 Adriana de Groot (Holland) 3:06.2, 6 Elizabeth Church (Great Britain) 3:06.1, 7 Antonia Hom (Holland) 3:07.5, 8 Jytte Hansen (Denmark) 3:08.1. Note: de Groot was officially placed fifth and Church sixth despite the contradictory evidence of the times.

aided by a Japanese-born swimming coach in Hawaii, Soichi Sakamoto, who famously had his group training seven days a week from the age of 13 onwards and one year had used an irrigation ditch for their workouts when the local pool was closed. Ford Konno, the Olympic double gold-medallist of 1952, was to be among the numerous other eminent swimmers coached by Sakamoto.

By the time of the 1968 Olympics the women's world record would be more than 10 seconds faster than Jany had achieved in 1947. The young Frenchman was never a serious challenger for a medal, much to the chagrin of his supporters. The son of a Toulouse pool manager, he was perfectly built for the sport at 1.80m (5ft 10in) tall, with size 13 feet and hands described as being "as large as 10-inch dinner plates", but his Olympic career would be confined to relay bronze medals at Wembley and in Helsinki four years later. His problems at Wembley seemed to be gastronomic, rather than physical or mental. Renowned for his gargantuan appetite, he was said by his team-mate, Monique Berlioux, to be pining for *"le Midi, sa mère et le cassoulet"*, which roughly translates as "his home, his Mum and his favourite stew". The English diet of potatoes and cucumbers, with which he was provided at the team headquarters, apparently reduced the usually cheery Jany to *"une profonde mélancholie"* – which needs no translation. Jany soon recovered his appetite and his peace of mind because he beat the Americans, Walter Ris and Bill Smith, in the France v USA match in Paris the following week.

Marshall's bronze was an early return on the investment in a concentrated nationwide training programme which had been instigated by Bill Berge Phillips, the honorary secretary and treasurer of the Amateur Swimming Union of Australia from 1941 to 1967, who managed the team at Wembley and was one of the chief judges. Working from his solicitor's office he developed the scheme alongside an inspirational coach, Forbes Carlile, and it would be tempting to see this as the foundation-stone of the countless Australian swimming successes in years to come. In fact, as early as 1912 Australia had won an Olympic title in the pool when Fanny Durack took the women's 100 metres freestyle, and then in the 1920s one of the all-time great swimmers had emerged in the person of Andrew (Boy) Charlton, who had won the 1924 1500 metres freestyle at the age of 16 in a world-record 20:06.6 and was second in 1928, plus achieving silver and bronze at 400 metres.

By the 1950s, Australia was to vie with the USA as the world's major swimming power, and the coach largely responsible for this upsurge was Forbes Carlile, but he was no autocrat – rather a man of wide interests and a generous spirit. He was in charge of the Australian team at Wembley, and almost 60 years later he is remembered with great affection by a 14-year-old whom he

---

400 metres freestyle (men) result: 1 Bill Smith (USA) 4min 41.0sec, 2 Jimmy McLane (USA) 4:43.4, 3 John Marshall (Australia) 4:47.7, 4 Géza Kádas (Hungary) 4:49.4, 5 György Mitró (Hungary) 4:49.9, 6 Alex Jany (France) 4:51.4, 7 Jack Hale (Great Britain) 4:55.4, 8 Alfredo Yantorno (Argentina) 4:58.7.

befriended at the time. The boy in question was Terry Warner, and he relates the tale thus:

"My school, Willesden Technical College, in north-west London, was used to house competitors from Australia, New Zealand and Korea, and the college had a gymnasium, outdoor jumping pits and a rough 440 yards grass running-track. Students not on holiday were encouraged to make friends with the athletes. I knew nothing of the Olympic stars or champions, apart from Jesse Owens and Fanny Blankers-Koen, as there was no TV and most 14-year-olds didn't read newspapers.

"Close to the school, and also close to Wembley Stadium, were five public swimming baths and these were used for training by the Olympic swimmers. During visits with other students I met up with Forbes Carlile, and I realise now that he was interested in the poverty and the run-down state of this area of London, just as he was in the swimmers. I spent many hours listening and talking to him, within the limits of a 14-year-old. With the small amount of knowledge I had of athletics he realised my keenness and gave me tickets to the stadium. I went alone, a trolley-bus ride from my house in Kensal Rise, and during my second visit I saw the final of the 100 metres, which was the only race I really wanted to see.

"Forbes Carlile met my parents and sent a huge hamper to the family on his way home to Australia. During his trip back by boat I received letters from him telling me about his training routines for his swimmers and reporting on the joys of the long ocean journey. I used the letters in my English thesis for the following year at school."

From the women's backstroke semi-finals, the eight who qualified for the final were the three Dutch competitors, two Americans, and one each from Australia, Denmark and Hungary. No one had come within five seconds of the Dutch-held world record from 1939, and among those eliminated were all three Britons, including the European silver-medallist Cathie Gibson, and Frenchwoman Monique Berlioux, who was to become director of the International Olympic Committee in future years and a distinguished writer about swimming and Olympic history in general. She had actually been selected for the cancelled 1940 Games; so just being present at Wembley was probably reward enough.

The inconsistencies regarding results had a significant bearing here because Great Britain's Helen Yate should have been in the final as she was given a time of 1:18.6, one-tenth faster than van der Horst, of Holland, who was awarded the automatic qualifying third place ahead of her. Yate, from Plymouth, was aged 27 and had been ASA 100 yards backstroke champion in 1938 and 220 yards freestyle champion the next year. She had then served for seven years in the Women's Royal Naval Service. She would not conceivably have challenged for an Olympic medal, but what a pity that she lost her one and only chance of being a finalist through an official oversight.

Sixth day, Thursday 5 August

The 1500 metres freestyle heats were held in the morning and afternoon with McLane, Marshall, Mitró and Hale from the 400 metres final again involved and among the qualifiers. The fastest time was 20:01.1 by Marshall and the slowest was 25:37.4, by another of the dogged Pakistanis, Anwar Aziz Chaudhry. The women's 400 metres freestyle heats followed on and should have been a formality, with only three of the 19 starters to be eliminated. Instead, there was high drama as the 100 metres winner, Greta Andersen, suffered stomach problems and fainted in the course of her race and had to be rescued from the pool. Fortunately, she was only temporarily indisposed and would swim again later in the week.

The evening's events were the 200 metres breaststroke, with the heats for men, and the 100 metres backstroke, with the women's final and men's semi-finals. Joe Verdeur, the world record-holder, a dentistry student of Lithuanian descent, had much the fastest breaststroke heat time of 2:40.0 to beat the Games record from 1936, and Great Britain's Roy Romain was among those who accompanied him through to the semi-finals. Having been unable to sleep properly at the team headquarters, Romain had been allowed to go back to his home comforts in Walthamstow. Encouragingly, both 19-year-old John Brockway and Bert Kinnear, who had been fourth in the European Championships, got through to the backstroke final for Great Britain, though Stack remained the obvious favourite after his semi-final win, and his compatriot, Cowell, seemed to be the most likely challenger. Argentina, France, Mexico and South Africa would also be represented in the final.

The women's backstroke finalists were Galliard, van Ekris and van der Horst for Holland, Mellon and Zimmerman for the USA, Davies for Australia, Harup for Denmark and Novák (Ilona, not Eva) for Hungary. According to WJ Howcroft's authoritative account in the British Olympic Association's Games report, this was supposed to be the most open event of the week, but Harup, who had placed fourth in the 100 metres freestyle final, soon changed that opinion. She gave what Howcroft eloquently described as "a splendid exhibition of the art of waiting in front ... a beautiful stylist, Miss Harup was never led in the heat, semi-final or final". It was Denmark's second women's gold of the week in swimming, but this was not a feat which would be matched by their Danish menfolk. Not a single male swimmer had been entered from that country.

Seventh day, Friday 6 August

The semi-finals of the men's 1500 metres and women's 400 metres freestyle

---

100 metres backstroke (women) result: 1 Karen-Margrete Harup (Denmark) 1min 14.4sec, 2 Suzanne Zimmerman (USA) 1:16.0, 3 Judy Joy Davies (Australia) 1:16.7, 4 Ilona Novák (Hungary) 1:18.4, 5 Hendrika van der Horst (Holland) 1:18.8, 6 Dirkje van Ekris (Holland) 1:18.9, 7 Muriel Mellon (USA) 1:19.0, 8 Greta Galliard (Holland) 1:19.1.

took place in the morning. Marshall and then McLane won the men's races, and Hungary yet again had two finalists, Mitró (the European champion) and Csordás. The other two Americans, Heusner and Norris, also went through, together with Stipetič, of Yugoslavia, who had been third in the European Championships, and 17-year-old Donald Bland for Great Britain. Bland's team-mate Jack Hale had unfortunately been unable to take his place in the semi-finals because of a muscle injury. Harup, no doubt buoyed by the previous night's gold medal, broke the women's 400 metres freestyle Games record with 5:25.7, though this was still far short of the world record of 5:00.1 which had been held by another Dane, Ragnhild Hveger, since 1940. Miss Hveger broke a multitude of freestyle and backstroke world records (41 to be precise), was the Olympic silver-medallist in 1936 at the age of 15, and but for the war would surely have won several Olympic titles. She made a comeback at the 1952 Games while still the world record-holder and placed fifth.

The afternoon's 200 metres breaststroke semi-finals for men reinforced Joe Verdeur's position as favourite; he won his semi-final in 2:40.7 and Ahmed Kandil, of Egypt, the other in 2:43.7. Verdeur's team-mates, Sohl and Carter (fourth at 100 metres freestyle), also qualified, as did Davies (Australia), Jordan (Brazil), Bonte (Holland) and Cerer (Yugoslavia). It was a grievous disappointment for British fans that Romain, far from his form at the European Championships, where Cerer was second, was well beaten. For reasons which are not readily apparent, almost all swimmers at Wembley were several seconds slower than their best, but Romain was more than nine seconds down, and maybe it was a matter of the pressure of public expectation weighing heavily on him.

In last place in Romain's semi-final was 32-year-old Alfred Nakache, of France, but it was a miracle that he was there at all. His is one of the most astonishing stories of survival against all the odds through the war years. Born in Algeria, he had been the lead-off man for the French team which placed fourth in the 1936 4x200 metres and had set a world record of 2:36.8 for the 200 metres breaststroke in 1941. His life after that had been harrowing because he was Jewish, and in 1944 he and his family were deported from Toulouse to the Auschwitz concentration camp where his wife and two-year-old daughter died in the gas chambers. He was then sent to Buchenwald and was one of only 47 survivors when it was liberated in April 1945. Although 1.85m (6ft 1in) tall his weight had dropped to 42kg (less than seven stone), and yet he survived the experience, returned to Toulouse, where he was taken in by the Jany family, and within a year was French champion again. If ever there was any justification needed for reviving the Olympics so soon after World War II, then the presence of Alfred Nakache in the Wembley pool provided it. He died in 1983 at the age of 67.

The two evening finals were the men's 100 metres backstroke and women's 4x100 metres relay. Cowell gave his more favoured fellow-American, Stack, a fine race for the backstroke title and was only one-tenth down at the finish, while France got another bronze through their European champion, Vallerey, who also thus became the first African-born swimming medallist. Sadly, within 18 months, he contracted a mysterious kidney disease from which he never recovered and he died in 1954 three weeks before his 27th birthday. Welshman Brockway and Scotsman Kinnear, representing Britain, were in the last two places but not outclassed; Brockway, from the Maindee club in Newport, was a mere touch away from fourth place and Kinnear would go on to an accomplished coaching career in later years.

The teams for the women's relay were Brazil, Denmark, France, Great Britain, Holland, Hungary, Sweden and the USA. Denmark had won the 1947 European title from Holland and Great Britain, and in the Wembley heats first Denmark (4:33.5) and then Holland (4:31.3) had broken the Games record of 4:36.0 set by the Dutch in 1936. The Danes, with Andersen and Harup bidding for their second gold medals, led from the start, but at the final change Carstensen, the European champion, had only a metre lead on Termeulen, for Holland, with Curtis and Gibson starting some three metres behind for the USA and Great Britain.

Termeulen, a future Olympic 100 metres silver-medallist, chased hard, "threshing behind her in a cataract of foam", to repeat Howcroft's vivid description, but Carstensen seemed to have ensured a Danish win ... until 10 metres from the end when Curtis, the 400 metres silver-medallist, who had looked to be safe for third place at best for the USA, charged through in lane six to snatch the gold. Her time of 64.4 for her 100 metres stint was two-tenths better than the world record set in 1936 by Willy den Ouden, of Holland, but could not count officially. Den Ouden's record would last 20 years until beaten by one of the greatest of all swimmers, Dawn Fraser, of Australia. Great Britain, having previously won a gold (1912), three silvers and a bronze in this relay event, was a commendable fourth. The youngest of the swimmers was Rodrigues, of Brazil, who would not be 14 until 17 days later.

The next Olympic relay final for women in Helsinki in 1952 would bring many of the 1948 finalists back together. The Hungarians, Temes and Novák, together with Eva Novák, would be in the gold-medal team which set a world

---

100 metres backstroke (men) result: 1 Allen Stack (USA) 1min 06.4sec, 2 Bob Cowell (USA) 1:06.5, 3 Georges Vallerey (France) 1:07.8, 4 Mario Chaves (Argentina) 1:09.0, 5 Clemente Mejia Avila (Mexico) 1:09.0, 6 Johannes Wiid (South Africa) 1:09.1, 7 John Brockway (Great Britain) 1:09.2, 8 Albert ("Bert") Kinnear (Great Britain) 1:09.6.

4x100 metres freestyle relay (women) result: 1 USA (Marie Corridon, Thelma Kalama, Brenda Helser, Ann Curtis) 4min 29.2sec, 2 Denmark (Eva Riise, Karen-Margrete Harup, Greta Andersen, Fritze Carstensen) 4:29.6, 3 Holland (Irma Heijting- Schuhmacher, Margot Marsman, Marie-Louise Linssen-Vaessen, Johanna Termeulen) 4:31.6, 4 Great Britain (Patricia Nielsen, Margaret Wellington, Lillian Preece, Cathie Gibson) 4:34.7, 5 Hungary (Mária Littomeritzky, Judit Temes, Ilona Novák, Eva Székely) 4:44.8, 6 Brazil (Eleonora Schmidt, Maria Leão da Costa, Talita de Alencar Rodrigues, Piedade Coutinho-da Silva Tavares) 4:49.1, 7 France (Josette Arène-Delmas, Gisèle Vallerey, Colette Thomas, Ginette Jany-Sendral) 4:49.8. Disqualified – Sweden (Gisela Thidholm, Elisabeth Ahlgren, Marianne Lundquist, Ingegärd Fredin). Note: Elvi Carlsen (Denmark) and Marie Foucher-Cretau (France) swam in the heats.

record of 4:24.4. Also appearing again would be Vaessen, Schuhmacher and Termeulen for Holland (winning silver medals), Andersen for Denmark, Preece for Great Britain, Arene and Jany for France, Lundquist and Fredin for Sweden. The most lasting fame was to be achieved by Andersen in a very different aquatic setting, swimming the English Channel in 1957 and then establishing a record of 11hrs 1min for the crossing from Cap Gris Nez to St Margaret's Bay the following year, by which time she had become an American citizen.

Eighth day, Saturday 7 August

The swimming events were completed during the afternoon with the finals of the men's 200 metres breaststroke and 1500 metres freestyle and the women's 400 metres freestyle.

The breaststroke finalists were Verdeur, Sohl and Carter for the USA, Davies for Australia, Jordan for Brazil, Kandil for Egypt, Bonte for Holland and Cerer for Yugoslavia, and all but Bonte would be using the butterfly technique. Invention of the butterfly stroke is attributed to a German, Erich Rademacher, twice European breaststroke champion and who had won the silver medal at the 1928 Olympics in the traditional manner (plus gold at water polo) but had realised that by bringing his arms back above the water, rather than through it, he could swim more efficiently and still abide by the rules then in force. The first American to have demonstrated the butterfly in competition was said to be Henry Myers in a race at the Brooklyn Central YMCA pool in 1933. At the 1936 Olympics the traditional stroke used by the Japanese winner, Tetsuo Hamuro, had prevailed. The only concession which swimming's governing body FINA had made since then to the advent of the butterfly was to decree that each swimmer could use only one or other of the styles in the course of a race, and not both.

Leading all the way, Verdeur won in 2:39.3, again an Olympic record but far off his world record, to maintain an unbeaten sequence which had now lasted almost four years. Carter took second place by three metres from Sohl to complete the first clean sweep of medals in any of the races in the Wembley pool and the first in any swimming event since a Japanese 1-2-3 in the 1932 men's backstroke – but thereby hangs a tale. The timings showed that Australia's John Davies had swum two-tenths faster than Sohl and should surely have been given the bronze medal. The previous day a similar fate had befallen Davies's track-sprinting compatriot Shirley Strickland, who had been deprived of the 200 metres bronze in the same circumstances. Fortunately, Davies – like Strickland – lived to fight another day and won the gold in Helsinki four years later. From the 1956 Games onwards breaststroke and butterfly were separated, as they had been for the women, and the winning times that year were again startlingly different – respectively, 2:34.7 and 2:19.3.

Though last, Bob Bonte subsequently set world records for the rarely-swum 400 and 500 metres breaststroke to become the first Dutch male swimmer of genuine international class. He worked as a hairdresser in his father's shop.

Verdeur was a university student, but his was not a particularly privileged existence as he paid his way by stoking a furnace at night. Whether or not this heavy work helped, or he was just naturally gifted, he had a very distinctive style in that he was so supple that, disconcertingly for the spectators, he appeared to dislocate his shoulders with each turn of his arms. Missing from Wembley were three men who might well have challenged him for the gold because the Soviet Union had claimed world records by Leonid Meshkov (1:05.1 for 100 metres) and Semyón Boychenko (2:29.8 for 200 metres). Germany also had a fine exponent of the conventional breaststroke in Herbert Klein, who had been the national junior champion in 1941 and then returned to competition in peacetime. He went on to break the European record in 1949 with a time of 2:36.4 and win the 1950 European title. He was then third at the 1952 Olympics, but at the next Games in Melbourne he was among a number of competitors disqualified while differences of opinion still remained among judges regarding what was acceptable as a breaststroke.

Two of the three Americans in the women's 400 metres freestyle final, Ann Curtis and Brenda Helser, had already won gold medals in the relay. Curtis also had a silver medal from the 100 metres freestyle and Harup, of Denmark, the gold from the 100 metres backstroke and silver from the relay. Harup, Helser and the Belgian, Caroen, were the leaders for six of the eight lengths until Curtis made her move, and whereas in the 100 metres final she had left it too late to catch the Danish winner, Andersen, who would have been a contender this time but for her mishap in the qualifying round, no mistake was made and Harup was beaten by four metres. Curtis had a best time for the event of 5:07.6 earlier in the year, but some 10 seconds slower on this occasion was quite sufficient to win.

If any miscalculation had been made, it was perhaps by Great Britain's Cathie Gibson, back in seventh place at 200 metres but who gained enormous ground (or should that be "water"?) to take the bronze medal. The times suggest that even with a better distribution of effort she would not have got gold but might have got silver. At least, and at last, it was a medal for Britain, and it broke a mould. At the 1924, 1928 and 1932 Games British women had been fourth in this event and there would not be another British medal at the distance until Sarah Hardcastle won silver and June Croft bronze in 1984.

Ann Curtis, from San Francisco, whose mother came from County Kildare, in Ireland, was 5ft 10in (1.80m) tall and aged 22. She was the only woman to have thus far been honoured with the "James E Sullivan Memorial Trophy" presented to the outstanding US amateur sportsman or sportswoman of the year, and she was to win 31 national titles during her career, only ever being beaten once. She had started competing at the age of nine, and her coach, Charlie Sava, who she had joined when she was 14, was full of praise for her dedication. "Nobody ever worked harder to get where she is," he said. "Since she got there she's kept right on plugging because she's always afraid. Real champions are always afraid they'll lose."

The final event of this Olympic gala was the men's 1500 metres freestyle, bringing together McLane, Heusner, Norris (all USA), Mitró, Csordás (both Hungary), Marshall (Australia), Bland (Great Britain) and Stipetič (Yugoslavia). The Hungarians led initially, but at 400 metres McLane was in front by 10 metres. Marshall had moved up to second place and by 1000 metres had caught McLane. Maybe the effort to close the gap was too great because after another couple of lengths McLane drew away again and won with some ease. Mitró took Hungary's fourth medal, while young Bland swam exactly the same time as he had in the semi-finals for seventh place.

McLane and Marshall were to come together as students at Yale University the following year under the guidance of Bob Kiphuth, the Olympic coach of 20 years' standing, though it was Marshall who moved into the ascendancy. He broke 26 world records, including 15 in a single month, but by the time of the Helsinki Olympics all that effort could have taken its toll. He was last in the 1500 metres freesyle. McLane was fourth in that race and seventh at 400 metres. Marshall competed again in the 1956 Games, placing fifth in the 200 metres butterfly, but he was killed in a car crash soon afterwards at the age of 26.

McLane's talent had been developed at the club set up by the Firestone tyre company in Akron, Ohio, and his coach there, Harold Minto, had said of him that his strength was in his kick which "goes deep and resembles the back-wash of a Mississippi steamboat".

The USA had won all six men's gold medals, plus four silver and a bronze, and the remaining medals had been shared among only three countries – Hungary, Australia and France – and they might have had nothing at all if Japan, Germany and the USSR had been in attendance. In the women's events Denmark and the USA had each won two golds and two silvers, Holland a gold and two bronzes, Australia a silver and a bronze, Great Britain and Hungary a bronze each. Of the American medallists, Alan Ford, Sue Zimmerman and Brenda Helser retired soon afterwards and Ann Curtis turned professional to race a trained seal in an "aquacade" set up by the 1936 Olympic backstroke champion, Adolf Kiefer. At the 1949 US Championships the six-man team

---

200 metres breaststroke (men) result: 1 Joe Verdeur (USA) 2min 39.3sec, 2 Keith Carter (USA) 2:40.2, 3 Bob Sohl (USA) 2:43.9, 4 John Davies (Australia) 2:43.7, 5 Anton Cerer (Yugoslavia) 2:46.1, 6 Willy Otto Jordan (Brazil) 2:46.4, 7 Ahmed Kandil (Eqypt) 2:47.5, 8 Bjorn ("Bob") Bonte (Holland) 2:47.6. Note: Sohl was awarded the bronze medal, though his time was slower than that of Davies.

---

400 metres freestyle (women) result: 1 Ann Curtis (USA) 5min 17.8sec, 2 Karen-Margrete Harup (Denmark) 5:21.2, 3 Cathie Gibson (Great Britain) 5:22.5, 4 Fernande Caroen (Belgium) 5:25.3, 5 Brenda Helser (USA) 5:26.0, 6 Piedade Coutinho-da Silva Tavares (Brazil) 5:29.4, 7 Fritze Carstensen (Denmark) 5:29.4, 8 Nancy Lees (USA) 5:32.9.

from the Tokyo club, headed by the remarkable Hironashin Furuhashi, would win five of the six freestyle events.

A single medal was not a sufficient return for the British, according to the *Sunday Times* summary by Howard Croft: "It is too early to hold an inquest, but it is obvious that the training scheme has not fulfilled the hopes of those who subscribed approximately £10,000 to finance it," he wrote. There had been two years of what Croft called "intensive preparation", but it had not been enough, and the competition would be very much stronger in four years' time.

The huge difference between times achieved in 1948 and some 60 years later is glaringly obvious. The men's 100 metres freestyle world record was 55.4sec in 1948 and the improvement to 47.84sec by Pieter van Hoogeband, of Holland, at the 2000 Olympics represents an advance of 13.6 per cent. The women's 100 metres freestyle record was 17.5 per cent better when Britta Steffen, of Germany, achieved 53.30sec in 2006, compared with the 1min 04.6sec which had stood from 1936 to 1956. The men's 400 metres freestyle improved 19.5 per cent from the 4:33.5 of 1948 to the 3:40.08 by Ian Thorpe, of Australia, at the 2002 Commonwealth Games, and the women's freestyle improved by almost exactly the same margin, 19.3 per cent, from the 5:00.1 which lasted from 1940 to 1956 to the 4:02.13 by Laure Manaudou, of France, in 2006.

Whatever they prove, none of these figures should be construed as detrimental to the champions of 1948. Then there was no professionalism and no state aid. Swimming was an amateur pastime, and if anyone wanted money from it they had to take on seals instead of human beings.

1500 metres freestyle (men) result: 1 Jimmy McLane (USA) 19min 18.5sec, 2 John Marshall (Australia) 19:31.3, 3 György Mitró (Hungary) 19:43.2, 4 György Csordás (Hungary) 19:54.2, 5 Marjan Stipetič (Yugoslavia) 20:10.7, 6 Forbes Norris (USA) 20:18.8, 7 Donald Bland (Great Britain) 20:19.8, 8 Bill Heusner (USA) 20:45.4.

Chapter 33

THE MEDAL SCORE STAYS MUCH THE SAME: THE USA 10, EVERYONE ELSE 2

Diving. Empire Pool, Wembley, 30 July–6 August.

F EW, INDEED, ARE the genuine claims to a unique place in Olympic history. Whatever is done, it has in all probability been done before, but the women's springboard diving event was an exception to this general rule. Since the event was introduced in 1920 Americans had won all the 15 medals, and as the next five places in Berlin in 1936 had been taken by German and Japanese competitors it needed no long and hard contemplation of a crystal ball to forecast that the USA would be first, second and third yet again in the Wembley pool.

The men's event was only very slightly less of a monopoly during those interwar years because on a single occasion in 1928 a flag other than the Stars and Stripes had been raised to the masthead at the victory ceremony when an Egyptian, Farid Simaika, had taken the bronze medal. The acrobatic style of the Americans was best demonstrated by a diver who was actually Canadian-born: Pete DesJardins. Only 5ft 3in (1.60m) tall, he turned professional after winning Olympic silver in 1924 and two golds in 1928 and became known, evocatively, as "The Little Bronze Statue from Florida". At highboard, the USA had also won all the titles, though three of the men's medals and six of the women's medals had gone to other countries, and Simaika had pressed DesJardins close in 1928.

This was a sport which attracted the attention of the more flamboyant of Fleet Street journalists to the pool-side and John Macadam, the *Daily Express* columnist, coined a neat turn of phrase when he described the American women competitors as "the lovelies of the long drop". He was particularly enamoured of

Zoe Ann Olsen, who was to be the silver-medallist at springboard, and wrote of his sighting of her: "Your eye rises from the cool blue of the Empire Pool, carries up the 33 feet of the great diving tower, and fastens on the slim figure poised there in silhouette against the vaulted roof." He liked the others, too – "trim figure after trim figure, poised, assured, lovely". It all made for a welcome contrast to the previous month's British trials, which had been held at the North Bay Pool, in Scarborough, in weather so awful that one of the Olympic qualifiers, Kay Cuthbert, had been blown off the board as she was about to dive.

The Empire Pool was the first indoor venue to have been used for Olympic diving, and so there was no interference from the downpours which hampered the athletics events in the nearby stadium. Come rain or come shine, it made little difference to the Americans, who took all three medals in both springboard events and the gold and silver in both highboard events. WJ Howcroft, writing in the British Olympic Association report of the Games, thought that "it was possible to see the signs of a crack in the American diving armour", and certainly Birte Christoffersen, of Denmark, came very close to taking silver at highboard, but the distant third place of the Mexican, Joaquin Capilla Pérez, in the men's event was almost certainly due to the withdrawal beforehand of one of the Americans. Howcroft's conclusion seems, in retrospect, to be more in the nature of wishful thinking, though Capilla was to prove his worth by placing second at highboard in 1952 and then winning by the narrowest of margins in 1956. It took slightly longer – until 1960 – for Ingrid Krämer, of the German Democratic Republic (but representing a combined Germany), to end the US women's domination by winning both events.

Both the men's and women's highboard contests were notable for victories by divers who had overcome considerable problems of racial prejudice at home in the USA. Sammy Lee was a doctor in the US Army of Korean origin. Vicki Draves's father was from the Philippines and her mother from England. Lee, who was to become one of the most celebrated of all divers by winning gold again four years later, took the highboard title by almost eight points from team-mate Bruce Harlan, 130.05 to 122.30, and Harlan had a margin of some six points at springboard over his fellow-student at Ohio State University, Miller Anderson, 163.64 to 157.29. For each of the events there were seven judges who awarded scores in the range 1 to 10; the highest and lowest scores were excluded, and the average of the remaining five was multiplied by the degree of difficulty of the dive, based on a scale up to 2.0. For the first time at the Olympics there were two women judges, including Belle White, of Great Britain, the highboard bronze-medallist in 1912 at the age of 17, who had competed again at the next three Games, had won 15 ASA titles and the inaugural European championship in 1927, and who was to dedicate the rest of her life until her death in 1972 to officiating.

The four competitions were divided into compulsory and voluntary dives and Lee's best highboard performance was his last – a "3½ Somersault Forward" for which he was awarded two scores of 9½. Half a century later Lee wittily described his feelings as he had come out of the pool, knowing the dive had been a good one: "As I tell everyone, that's the second time in history man walked on water." His elation at winning gold continued to have a particularly emotive edge; "I hear these recent winners in the Olympic Games say, 'I did it for myself.' Well, in my day sure it was for yourself, but it was for your country, for your family, as well. The Olympic Games are something different because it's you and our system against the world. It's also a rebellion against the bigots in my own country who said I couldn't do it."

The consistent Harlan scored at least eight points for all but one of his springboard efforts, but it was Anderson who produced what WJ Howcroft said was "the best dive of the whole Games" with a concluding "Double Twisting 1½ Somersault Forward" which brought him the only two maximum scores of 10 which were awarded during the week.

The European highboard champion from Denmark, Thomas Christiansen, had started poorly and was never a challenger, eventually placing sixth, but Howcroft was warm in his praise of Lennart Brunnhage, of Sweden, and Peter Heatly, of Great Britain, in fourth and fifth places. In 11th for Great Britain was Louis Marchant, who had won four national titles between 1933 and 1938 and had then been European bronze-medallist in 1947. He was one of four male divers in the British team at Wembley who belonged to the Highgate club, in North London. No Briton had ever placed higher than the Scotsman, Heatly, in the Olympic men's highboard, and Howcroft said of him that his "performance in taking fifth place among an entry of 30 is the best news British diving has known for the past two decades. Now that Heatly has struck the knack of repeating in public the form he has shown in private he should provide a good scoring unit for his country in future international tests".

Though he subsequently won three Empire & Commonwealth titles for Scotland, Heatly, an engineer by profession, was to achieve more lasting renown as an administrator; in particular, as chairman of the Commonwealth Games Federation from 1982 to 1990 and of the Scottish Sports Council from 1975 to 1987. He received the CBE in 1971 and was knighted in 1990. In 1960 Olympic medals for Great Britain in diving were to be won by Brian Phelps and Liz Ferris. There were only four Empire divers other than those from Great Britain in the four competitions at Wembley, and one of them, David Norris, of Australia, had spent three years in a German prisoner-of-war camp.

The Europeans provided much less of an opposition in the men's springboard, as the best of them, Raymond Mulinghausen, of France, was some 15 points behind the fourth-placed Capilla, and Heatly was 13th. The silver-medallist, Anderson, had served in the US Army Air Corps during the war, had been shot down over Italy on his 113th mission, hitting his leg on the aircraft's wing as he baled out, and had spent a month in a German military hospital before it was captured by the advancing allied troops. He was to die of a heart attack in 1966 at the age of 42, and the winner, Harlan, had already by then come to a premature end, falling to his death in 1959 at the age of 33 from scaffolding which he was helping to dismantle after a diving exhibition. Anderson had finished second again at the 1952 Olympics to David Browning, a US Navy pilot who was killed in an air crash in 1956 at the age of 24.

Vicki Draves won both the highboard and springboard titles, which no woman had ever previously managed at the Games, and she was also the first Asian-American woman champion at the Olympics. Her margin of victory in both cases was narrow, and several of the European competitors distinguished themselves. Denmark's highboard bronze medallist Birte Christoffersen achieved the rare feat of competing for another country, Sweden, under her married name of Hansson, in 1956, placing eighth. Not far behind her in fourth place, and ahead of the third American, was the European bronze-medallist from Austria, Ali Staudinger. Juno Stover was the sole US non-medallist but made up for the omission by competing in three more Olympics as Mrs Irwin and winning silver in 1956.

Mrs Draves, who had married her coach, Lyle Draves, in 1946, was denied entry to a club in San Francisco because of her mixed race background when she began diving at the age of 16, and she was persuaded to use her mother's maiden name, Taylor, in competition instead of her family name of Manalo. She had met her husband in 1943, and he had been a fine diver himself in the 1930s, missing the 1932 Olympic trials because he could not afford the journey and then ineligible to contest a place at the Berlin Games after accepting a job as a pool manager. Lyle Draves had also coached Zoe Ann Olsen since 1936, and his wife forever remembered her trepidation as she came to take her last springboard dive, with the gold medal in the balance between her and Olsen, and was only calmed by the assurances of Sammy Lee:

"I am sitting by Sammy and I was so nervous that I would shake between each dive, as though I was cold. I remember saying to Sammy, 'I can't do this, Sammy. I'm not going to make it.' He said, 'You came all this distance and you're going to give up? Get up there and do what you're supposed to do!' I got up there for that back 1½, and I tell you it was like somebody else did that dive for me. I sort of sailed through it and I knew I had hit it when I was under water, and I thought, 'Oh, boy! Thank you, God!' "

In the springboard event Nicole Péllissard, of France, the European highboard champion who would also continue competing at the Olympics until 1960, was less than one point behind third place. Edna Child, from the Plaistow club, was a worthy sixth and 15-year-old Esme Harris, from Oxford, 13th for Great Britain. The more favoured French entrant here had been Mady Moreau, winner of the European title the previous year after only a few months of competition but she finished seventh at Wembley, perhaps lacking experience. Four years later, in Helsinki, she made amends in the manner of Juno Irwin by taking the silver medal and becoming the first non-American medallist ever in the event.

Standards of diving worldwide had advanced since pre-war days, and WJ Howcroft said of the springboard competitions that "not only was there an improvement in the techniques of using the board, but the increase in difficulty of the movements performed marked a further stage in the development of the sport". He also had kind words to say about the British women, particularly remarking on Edna Child's performance and on the showing of Denise Newman in 11th place, who, he noted, "was among the leaders in the highboard final when she pulled her arm muscle". Newman had returned to diving after a seven-year absence. "In our sea-bound insularity our divers are given but little opportunity of meeting foreign challengers," Howcroft had pointed out in a pre-Games forecast. Now that they had done so at Olympic level they had comported themselves really rather well.

Men's highboard result: 1 Sammy Lee (USA) 130.05pts, 2 Bruce Harlan (USA) 122.30, 3 Joaquin Capilla Pérez (Mexico) 113.52, 4 Lennart Brunnhage (Sweden) 108.62, 5 Peter Heatly (Great Britain) 105.29, 6 Thomas Christiansen (Denmark) 105.22, 7 Raymond Mulinghausen (France) 103.01, 8 George Athans (Canada) 100.91, 9 Rolf Mørch Stigersand (Norway) 97.93, 10 Zoheir Shourbagi (Syria) 97.81, 11 Louis Marchant (Great Britain) 96.11, 12 Kamal Ali Hassan (Egypt) 95.33, 13 Diego Mariscal Abascal (Mexico) 95.14. 14 Gustavo Somohano Winfield (Mexico) 91.98, 15 Franz Worisch (Austria) 90.05, 16 Haroldo Mariano (Brazil) 90.00, 17 Wilhelm Lippa (Austria) 89.04, 18 Gordon Ward (Great Britain) 88.96, 19 Ilmari Niemeläinen (Finland) 87.82, 20 Guy Hernandez (France) 87.46, 21 George Mandy (South Africa) 86.00, 22 Rauf Abdul Seoud (Egypt) 85.95, 23 Willy Rist (Switzerland) 81.78, 24 Mohamed Allam (Egypt) 77.92, 25 Ernst Strupler (Switzerland) 77.67.

Men's springboard result: 1 Bruce Harlan (USA) 163.64pts, 2 Miller Anderson (USA) 157.29, 3 Sammy Lee (USA) 145.52, 4 Joaquin Capilla Pérez (Mexico) 141.79, 5 Raymond Mulinghausen (France) 126.55, 6 Svante Johansson (Sweden) 120.20, 7 Kamal Ali Hassan (Egypt) 119.90, 8 Thomas Christiansen (Denmark) 114.59, 9 George Athans (Canada) 114.13, 10 Frank Gosling (Bermuda) 113.98, 11 Milton Busin (Brazil) 113.86, 12 Franz Worisch (Austria) 112.15, 13 Peter Heatly (Great Britain) 111.73, 14 Roger Heinkelé (France) 110.78, 15 Ismael Ahmed Ramzi (Egypt) 110.18, 16 David Norris (Australia) 109.67, 17 Diego Mariscal Abascal (Mexico) 107.78, 18 Charles Johnson (Great Britain) 105.32, 19 Wilhelm Lippa (Austria) 103.18, 20 Guy Hernandez (France) 102.89, 21 Gunnar Kemnitz (Brazil) 102.22, 22 Mohamed Ibrahim (Egypt) 97.52, 23 Peter Elliott (Great Britain) 91.23, 24 José Castillo (Cuba) 84.81, 25 Ernst Strupler (Switzerland) 80.09, 26 Günther Mund (Chile) 68.08.

Women's highboard result: 1 Victoria Draves (USA) 68.87pts, 2 Patricia Elsener (USA) 66.28, 3 Birte Christoffersen (Denmark) 66.04, 4 Alma Staudinger (Austria) 64.59, 5 Juno Stover (USA) 62.63, 6 Nicole Péllissard (France) 61.07, 7 Eva Petersén (Sweden) 59.86, 8 Inge Beeken (Denmark) 59.54, 9 Irén Zságot (Hungary) 56.62, 10 Lettice Bisbrown (Great Britain) 53.95, 11 Denise Newman (Great Britain) 53.50, 12 Maire Hider (Great Britain) 52.31, 13 Inger Nordbø (Norway) 51.55, 14 Rosa Gutiérrez de Pardo (Mexico) 41.88, 15 Gudrun Grömer (Austria) 39.65.

Women's springboard result: 1 Victoria Draves (USA) 108.74pts, 2 Zoe Ann Olsen (USA) 108.23, 3 Patricia Elsener (USA) 101.30, 4 Nicole Péllissard (France) 100.38, 5 Gudrun Grömer (Austria) 93.30, 6 Edna Child (Great Britain) 91.63, 7 Madeleine Moreau (France) 89.43, 8 Jacoba Heck (Holland) 87.61, 9 Birte Christoffersen (Denmark) 87.12, 10 Jeannette Aubert (France) 86.96, 11 Alma Staudinger (Austria) 86.93, 12 Jacoba Floor (Holland) 83.14, 13 Esme Harris (Great Britain) 74.10, 14 Kay Cuthbert (Great Britain) 72.40, 15 Inger Nordbø (Norway) 70.86, 16 Ivonne Belausteguigoitia Arocena (Mexico) 65.18.

Chapter 34

ITALY WINS THE GOLD, BUT IT WAS NOT A GAME FOR A BRITISH GENTLEMAN

Water polo. Finchley and the Empire Pool,
29 July to 7 August.

HUNGARY AND GERMANY had been by far the superior teams at the Berlin Olympic water polo tournament. They had each won all their eight matches and had then drawn 2-2 when they met. Hungary had slightly the better goal difference, having scored 57 and conceded only five, compared with Germany's tally of 56-10, and so were given the gold medals. The pioneers of the sport had been the British, who had won four titles from 1900 to 1920, and their most notable player had been Paul Radmilovic, whose father was from the future Yugoslavia, and who had won three gold medals, plus a fourth for the 4x200 metres freestyle relay, and continued competing at the Games until 1928, by which time he was 42.

Various water games had been devised in Britain during the 1870s when swimming became a popular pastime, including water football, water rugby, water handball, and a form of water polo in which the players rode around the pool on floating barrels, which were painted to look like horses, and propelled the ball with a stick. The game then began to take on its more familiar modern look, and after it was introduced to Hungary in 1889 and then to Germany, France and Belgium it became in 1900 the first team sport to be contested at the Olympics.

There was no hope of the Great Britain team reliving past glories, and though a group of 20 players had been brought together for a year's special training from clubs as far apart as Motherwell and Weston-super-Mare so little was thought of their chances that the courtesy place among the six seeded countries which they were given was voluntarily ceded to France. The other nominated seeds were Italy, Belgium, Sweden, Holland and Hungary. At the previous year's European Championships Italy had won from Sweden and Belgium, with Hungary, the champions on five previous occasions, out of the medals and Great Britain in sixth place, having lost every match. There were 18 teams entered for the Olympic tournament, also including Argentina, Australia, Chile, Egypt, Greece, India, Spain, Sweden, Switzerland, Uruguay and the USA.

The Finchley Borough Council pool was used for the preliminary matches. For the first round there were six groups of three teams each, with the first two in each group advancing. There were inevitably some one-sided matches – for example, Holland beating India 12-1 and Chile 14-0 – but the only countries which lost both their encounters were Australia, Chile, Greece, Switzerland and Uruguay. Even so, after managing a 3-3 draw with Egypt, Great Britain made an early exit, swamped 11-2 by Hungary. The qualifiers from the second round were Belgium, Egypt, France, Holland, Hungary, Italy, Spain and Sweden. It had been a long journey for the Australians for little return, but their adventures had started long before they left home. The 10 players, and 25 of the 29 swimmers, had to find their own funds to get to the Games, but one of the water-polo players, Les McKay, was a bookmaker and £2,000 was raised in a single afternoon by his Melbourne colleagues in the betting business after an impassioned appeal by team official Bill Berge Phillips. McKay carried the Australian flag at the opening ceremony.

Yet, with the semi-finals still to come, the key match had perhaps already been played when Italy beat Hungary 4-3. A ruling peculiar to water polo was that if two teams which had already met were drawn against each other again the match would not take place and the original result would be carried forward. Of the 54 matches due to be played throughout the eight days, 14 were decided in this way, and the eventual outcome was that Italy became champions by beating Belgium and then Holland by the same score of 4-2 in the final group. There was no doubting the calibre of the Italians, but some sympathy had to be felt for the Yugoslavs, who had drawn 4-4 with Italy in the first round and held Hungary to 3-1 in the second round but because of the luck of the draw did not place in the top eight.

One of the members of the Egyptian team was Taha Youssef El-Gamal, who has an unusual but not necessarily unique claim to fame, having taken part in two different Olympic sports on the same day. He had swum in the heats, semi-finals and final of the 100 metres freestyle final on 30 and 31 July and played water polo against Hungary on 1 August. The next day he played against France and also took part in the freestyle relay heats. He played in further matches against Italy on 4 August and Sweden on 6 August. At previous Games six Britons – Peter Kemp, Paul Radmilovic, Harold Annison, John Derbyshire, John Hatfield and Edward Peter – had all taken part in freestyle swimming and water polo at the same Games, as had also Erich Rademacher, for Germany, and it may be that one or more of them were also involved in both sports on the same day.

Hungary returned to win the gold in 1952, 1956 and 1964. Six of the 1948 team played again in 1952, and Gyarmati, husband of the gold-medallist breaststroke swimmer Eva Székely, eventually became the most successful of all water-polo players since Radmilovic with three gold medals, a silver and a bronze. Italy and Yugoslavia took the gold in 1960 and 1968 respectively. However, all was not well with the sport and it seems surprising that it had survived as part of the Olympic programme even as far as 1948. It had a history of conflict both in and out of the pool.

There had been a rough element to the sport ever since its invention, and at the Antwerp Olympics of 1920 spectators had attacked the British team after they had won. In 1932 the Brazilian players had set upon the referee after losing to Germany. The rules regarding fair play were difficult to enforce, and any hopes that the 1948 tournament might see a reform in behaviour were soon dashed. "Even with the best will in the world the referees could not stop the riot of fouling," wrote WJ Howcroft in the British Olympic Association report. "All too often the game degenerated into a rough house, with the defending backs wrapping their arms and legs around the opposing forwards. It was not a case of accidental fouling due to the excitement of a close game. It was deliberate planned fouling." It is said that the perfect water-polo player should have the "over-arm accuracy of a baseball pitcher, the vertical leap of a volleyball player, the toughness of a rugby player, the endurance of a cross-country runner, and the strategy of a chess player." Regrettably, the strength of an all-in wrestler also seemed to come in handy from time to time.

Even an eminent Olympic historian from Hungary was ready to admit that one of his country's most successful sports was flawed. Of the 1948 Games, Sándor Barcs was to write in 1964: "The rows that seemed to have become almost obligatory at water-polo tournaments again occurred during the match between Italy and Yugoslavia. The game itself was a hard one, and very rough at times. However, the fighting did not break out in the pool but in the grandstand. Police had to intervene and expel the spectators who had peppery tempers." By contrast, the Italy v Hungary game passed off relatively peaceably, even though patience must have been tried for the Hungarians when one of their players completely fluffed a penalty throw by dropping the ball when his side was 4-3 down.

Henri Padou, a member of the winning French water-polo team in 1924, whose son won a bronze medal in the freestyle relay at Wembley, made a spirited defence of his sport when he wrote a detailed history: "At all costs we must oppose the idea that water polo is an unfair game in which the water covers up all manner of infamy. On the contrary, it is a sport which is very well regarded. It calls for an enormous amount of work and sacrifice." He was writing in 1961, with the memory still fresh of the riot at the 1956 Olympic match between Hungary and the USSR which brought the game further into disrepute, and his efforts were not in vain. Water polo has remained on the Olympic programme ever since, with Hungary winning again in 1976, 2000 and 2004 and Italy winning in 1992. Women's water polo was introduced in 2000.

Water polo result: 1 Italy, 2 Hungary, 3 Holland, 4 Belgium, 5 Sweden, 6 France, 7 Egypt, 8 Spain.
Italy's matches – Won 6, Drawn 1, Lost 0. 4-4 v Yugoslavia, 9-0 v Australia, 4-3 v Hungary, 5-1 v Egypt, 5-2 v France, 4-2 v Holland, 4-2 v Belgium.
Hungary's matches – Won 5, Drawn 1, Lost 1. 5-2 v Egypt, 11-2 v Great Britain, 3-1 v Yugoslavia, 3-4 v Italy, 5-4 v France, 4-4 v Holland, 3-0 v Belgium.
Holland's matches – Won 4, Drawn 2, Lost 1. 14-0 v Chile, 12-1 v India, 5-2 v Spain, 5-3 v Sweden, 3-3 v Belgium, 2-4 v Italy, 4-4 v Hungary.
Italy: Ermenegildo Arena, Emilio Bulgarelli, Pasquale Buonocore, Aldo Ghira, Mario Maioni, Geminio Ognio, Gianfranco Pandolfini, Tullio Pandolfini, Cesare Rubini.
Hungary: Jenö Brandi, Oszkár Csuvik, Dezsö Fabián, Dezsö Gyarmati, Endre Györffi, Miklós Holop, László Jeney, Dezsö Lemhényi, Károly Szittya, István Szivós.
Holland: Cornelius Braasem, Hendrikus Keetelaar, Cornelis Korevaar, Johannes Rohner, Albert Ruimschotel, Pieter Salomons, Fritz Smol, Hans Stam, Rudolph van Feggelen.
Great Britain's players were Charles Brand (South Manchester), Roy Garforth (Bradford Dolphins), Robert Gentleman (Motherwell), Peter Hardie (London Otter), Ian Johnston (Motherwell), Trevor Lewis (Swansea), David Murray (Motherwell) and Reginald Potter (London Otter).

Chapter 35

AT THE LAST, THE LIFTER GAZES SADLY DOWN …

Weightlifting. Empress Hall, Earls Court, 9–11 August.

SIX EVENTS… ALL 24 Games records broken … eight world records broken. No other sport at the 1948 Olympic Games comes remotely close to weightlifting in terms of the standards achieved. The USA won four of the gold medals; Egypt won the other two; and had the USSR been there the levels of performance would have been even higher. From the 4ft 10in (1.48m) tall bantamweight Joe De Pietro to the supreme heavyweight John Davis, who was to be described as a "One Man Dynasty", human power of every dimension was witnessed and marvelled at over the three days of competition at the Empress Hall.

At the 1936 Berlin Games the events had been at featherweight (60kg maximum), lightweight (67.5kg), middleweight (75kg), light-heavyweight (82.5kg) and heavyweight (unlimited). The comparisons with 1948 of the winning overall totals spell out the story of the sport's advance:

Featherweight: 1936: Tony Terlazzo (USA) 312.5kg (world record).
                     1948: Mahmoud Fayad (Egypt) 332.5kg (wr).
Lightweight: 1936: Robert Fein (Austria) 342.5kg (wr).
                     1948: Ibrahim Hassanien Shams (Egypt) 360kg.
Middleweight: 1936: Khadr El-Sayed El-Touni (Egypt) 387.5kg (wr).
                     1948: Frank Spellman (USA) 390kg.
Light-heavyweight: 1936: Louis Hostin (France) 372.5kg.
                     1948: Stan Stanczyk (USA) 417.5kg.
Heavyweight: 1936: Josef Manger (Germany) 410.kg (wr).
                     1948: John Davis (USA) 452.5kg.

The World Championships had been promptly revived after the war in 1946 in Paris and again in 1947 in Philadelphia. The bantamweight division (56kg) was not introduced until the latter year and was won by De Pietro. The featherweight titles had been won by Andersson (Sweden) and then Higgins (USA); the lightweight by Stanczyk and George (also USA); the middleweight by El-Touni and Stanczyk; the light-heavyweight by Novak (USSR) and Terpak (USA); the heavyweight on both occasions by Davis. Only 10 of the 39 competitors at the 1947 Championships were from Europe, and the Americans won all the events, with the most notable absentees being the Soviet lifters.

El-Touni, still only 33 years old, would be at Wembley to defend his middleweight title of 12 years before. His compatriot, Shams, also 33, had won the featherweight bronze in Berlin and had now moved up to lightweight. Davis, a 27-year-old garage mechanic from Brooklyn, had been a pre-war teenage prodigy, winning the world light-heavyweight title in 1938. All the current holders of world records for total lifts, combining the press, the snatch and the jerk, would be competing – with the exception of the Soviet Union's Grigoriy Novak, whose light-heavyweight aggregate of 425kg had won the 1946 world title.

The origins of competitive weightlifting were to be found, like so many other sports, in late-19th-century England. Such had been the impact made by the Prussian-born "strong man", Eugen Sadow, when he gave a series of exhibitions of his lifting capabilities in England in 1889 that within two years a "World Championships" was held in London.

The English lead was soon followed by Austria, Belgium, Germany and Italy in setting up organising bodies, and the International Weightlifting Federation was founded in 1905 with the first European Championships held the next year in The Hague. There had even been weightlifting of sorts at the inaugural Modern Olympics of 1896, where Launceston Elliott, of Great Britain, won the one-handed lift from Viggo Jensen, of Denmark, and Jensen reversed the positions in the two-handed lift. Both Elliott and Jensen managed to raise a respectable 111.5kg in the latter event.

A comprehensive programme at various weights had been established at the 1920 Games onwards, and France had been the most successful nation since, winning nine of the 25 titles. Germany and Italy had won four each; Austria and Egypt two each; Belgium, Czechoslovakia, Estonia and the USA one each. The first Egyptian – and non-European – winner had been El-Sayed Nosseir at light-heavyweight in 1928, and he became national coach after this surprise success had earned the sport nationwide recognition and the support of Sultan Ahmed Fuad, who had been proclaimed King in 1922 at the end of Britain's protectorate rule. Great Britain's record at those five Olympic celebrations had been uniformly unimpressive, with the single exception of a heavyweight, Ronald Walker, who had placed fourth at the Berlin Games. It was said by the British journalist, Ernest A Bland, of the *Daily Telegraph*, in an Olympic review written in 1948 that "there is little doubt that biased refereeing by pro-Nazi officials" had deprived Walker of the gold.

For a sport so dominated by Europe, the entries at Wembley were encouragingly widespread: 120 lifters from 11 nations in Europe, nine in the Americas, eight in Africa and Asia, and two in Oceania.

No bantamweight event had previously been held at the Games, but it soon made an impression, and particularly so in the person of Joe De Pietro, described by Oscar State, who provided the weightlifting articles for both the BOA and organising committee reports, as "a miniature Hercules". Judging from the photographs of the competition, De Pietro must have presented a remarkable spectacle on the high-raised lifting platform in the centre of the hall because, as State wrote, "his unusually short arms barely enabled him to raise the bar above the top of his head". De Pietro may even have been as short as 4ft 6in (1.37m) or 4ft 8in (1.43m), as no two versions of his stature seem to agree.

Yet his diminutive physique gave him an advantage in the first lift, the press, in which the competitor is required to bring the bar to shoulder level, to hold it there, and then on the referee's signal to raise it to arm's length above the head, all without moving the feet. It was not until the best of his opponents had completed the three attempts allowed to them that De Pietro even began the press phase and he achieved an Olympic record of 105kg. In second place at this stage was Abe Greenhalgh, an electrician from Bolton, in Lancashire, with 92.5kg, and though he was later to slip down the order the very fact that he was at Wembley was a triumph in itself. He had spent 11 years of his life as a bedridden invalid.

The next lift, the snatch, requires the bar to be raised at arm's length above the head in one movement, and here De Pietro was not so much at ease, with a best of 90kg. Ahead of him was the Korean, Kyu Hyuk Lee, at 92.5kg, and the other Briton in this event, Julian Creus, who broke the existing world record with 95kg but was actually overweight at the instant of doing so and therefore the record was not claimed. Creus had, of course, weighed in beforehand within the 56kg limit. De Pietro now led at 195kg, with Creus and the other American, Richard Tom, who had been second to De Pietro in the previous year's World Championships, next at 177.5kg, and Thévenet, of France, fourth at 170kg.

The competition was completed with the jerk, which involved raising the weight to shoulder level and then to arm's length above the head in the competitor's own time, with movement allowed. Creus lifted 120kg to De Pietro's 112.5 and Tom's 117.5 and thus took the silver medal, though the best lift here came from Namdjou, of Iran, whose effort of 122.5 broke the Olympic record and lifted him to fifth place overall. De Pietro's overall total of 307.5 beat the world record, and the full measure of the talents of this astonishing man can be seen from the fact that in the next higher weight division only the three medallists lifted more than he did.

The achievement by Creus was memorable – the first weightlifting medal at the Olympics for a Briton since Launceston Elliott 52 years before – and Creus, like so many of his British team-mates, had an interesting life-story to tell. Aged 31, he was a Liverpool dock-worker who had first competed internationally in 1939. He had then served in the Merchant Navy during the war, and brought his wife and three children to watch him compete at the Olympics. He was to be British featherweight champion for nine successive years from 1945 to 1953 and again in 1956 and also competed at the 1952 and 1956 Olympics. Third in the World Championships of 1950 and 1951, his Olympic silver was not to be matched by another Briton until Louis Martin in 1964. Creus later emigrated to Australia. Notably missing from the 1948 Olympic event was the Soviet lifter, Asdaryev, who had set world records of 90kg for the snatch and 110kg for the jerk.

The featherweights were led after the press by Salmasi, of Iran, with an Olympic record of 100kg, followed by Wilkes, of Trinidad, and del Rosario, of the Philippines, at 97.5, and four others at 90 or better. Then in the snatch the Egyptian, Fayad, set a world record of 105kg, though the competition for the medals still seemed to be marvellously poised – Fayad and Salmasi had totalled 197.5kg and Wilkes 195, with del Rosario next at 190. Fayad soon put an end to speculation with performances in the jerk which culminated in another world record of 135kg and, in the words of Oscar State, "drew thunderous applause from the connoisseurs of stylish lifting". Mr State knew rather a lot about this sort of thing; he was a world-renowned authority, honorary secretary of the British Amateur Weightlifters' Association, and organiser and master of ceremonies of the Olympic tournament. Fayad's total of 332.5kg was another world record, and he went on to win world titles in 1949 and 1950.

Neither Trinidad nor Iran had ever previously earned an Olympic medal in any sport. Rodney Wilkes, the Central American & Caribbean champion in 1946, had first competed in 1942, when he was 17, and would continue until 1960. He went on to win the bronze at the 1952 Olympics, was fourth in 1956,

---

Bantamweight (56kg) result: 1 Joe De Pietro (USA) 307.5kg (105, 90, 112.5), 2 Julian Creus (Great Britain) 297.5 (82.5, 95, 120), 3 Richard Tom (USA) 295 (87.5, 90, 117.5), 4 Kyu Hyuk Lee (Korea) 290 (77.5, 92.5, 120), 5 Mahmoud Namdjou (Iran) 287.5 (82.5, 82.5, 122.5), 6 Marcel Thévenet (France) 280 (90, 80, 110), 7 Rosaire Smith (Canada) 277.5 (82.5, 85, 110), 8 Maurice Crow (New Zealand) 272.5 (77.5, 85, 110), 9 Keith Caple (Australia) 272.5 (77.5, 85, 110), 10 Dong Wook Pak (Korea) 272.5 (80, 85, 107.5), 11 Abdel El-Hamid Yacout (Egypt) 272.5 (75, 85, 112.5), 12 Ernö Porubszky (Hungary) 270 (72.5, 87.5, 110), 13 Abe Greenhalgh (Great Britain) 267.5 (92.5, 75, 100), 14 Einar Sündstrom (Finland) 267.5 (77.5, 85, 105), 15 Win Maung Maung (Burma) 265 (82.5, 82.5, 100), 16 Eugène Watier (France) 260 (80, 80, 100), 17 Josef Vojtech (Austria) 255 (80, 75, 100), 18 Pentti Kotvio (Finland) 247.5 (65, 80, 102.5), 19 Marcelino Salas Maravilla (Mexico) 230 (60, 70, 100).

Featherweight (60kg) result: 1 Mahmoud Fayad (Egypt) 332.5kg (92.5, 105, 135), 2 Rodney Wilkes (Trinidad & Tobago) 317.5 (97.5, 97.5, 122.5), 3 Jaafar Salmasi (Iran) 312.5 (100, 97.5, 115), 4 Su Il Nam (Korea) 307.5 (97.5, 92.5, 122.5), 5 Rodrigo del Rosario (Philippines) 307.5 (97.5, 92.5, 122.5), 6 Emerick Ishikawa (USA) 307.5 (92.5, 95, 120), 7 Johan Runge (Denmark) 305 (95, 90, 120), 8 Max Héral (France) 300 (85, 95, 120), 9 Richard Tomita (USA) 300 (85, 92.5, 122.5), 10 André Le Guillerm (France) 300 (87.5, 92.5, 120), 11 Anton Richter (Austria) 292.5 (80, 92.5, 120), 12 Ibrahim El-Dessouki (Egypt) 292.5 (87.5, 90, 115), 13 Arvid Andersson (Sweden) 292.5 (85, 92.5, 115), 14 Denis Hallett (Great Britain) 292.5 (87.5, 87.5, 117.5), 15 Bálint Nagy (Hungary) 290 (82.5, 90, 117.5), 16 Daniel Mony (India) 280 (85, 85, 110), 17 Simon Williams (Jamaica) 277.5 (87.5, 80, 110), 18 Alphonso Correia (British Guiana) 275 (75, 85, 115), 19 Henri Colans (Belgium) 275 (75, 85, 115), 20 Sydney Kemble (Great Britain) 272.5 (87.5, 80, 105), 21 Alfonso Fiorentino (Argentina) 260 (75, 80, 105), 22 Richard Rieder (Switzerland) 255 (80, 75, 100), 23 Hang Kee Choi (Korea) 85 (-, 85, retired).

and was a title-winner at the Pan-American and Empire & Commonwealth Games. Both the American competitors, incidentally, were of Japanese descent.

The world champions of the previous two years from the USA, Stan Stanczyk and Pete George, had moved up a division, and so there was no obvious favourite for the lightweight title at the Empress Hall, though the man with the most experience was Shams, the featherweight bronze-medallist from 1936. It was an outstanding competition, described by Oscar State as "some of the most thrilling lifting of the whole meeting". The first of the record-breakers was John Stuart, of Canada, who had been second to George in the World Championships, with a new Olympic best in the press of 107.5kg. Then in the snatch Hammouda, of Egypt, and Halliday, of Great Britain, improved the Olympic record to 110kg, only for Shams to surpass them both with 112.5 and "a perfect lift" (State's words) of 115.

This meant that Hammouda had now totalled 215kg and Shams 212.5 to give Egypt the two leading places. Next came Stuart at 207.5, Terpak (USA) at 205 and Halliday at 200. The first to fall by the wayside in the jerk lifts was Stuart, who failed at 130kg, and then Terpak missed at 137.5. "This gave Halliday his opportunity," wrote State, "and the British lifter and team captain succeeded brilliantly and determinedly with 140kg, thus wresting third place from the veteran, Terpak. Halliday's effort was all the more praiseworthy because he had fought back from a seemingly hopeless position after the press which had left him in 16th place."

The climax of the event as the two Egyptians contested the gold was immensely exciting. Hammouda lifted 145kg and Shams needed to succeed at 147.5 to win. State described the scene: "The big arena was deadly quiet as he approached the barbell. He crouched over it in his own peculiar style and summoned his nerves for the great effort. Suddenly he turned away and a great sigh came from the pent-up spectators. He turned back and again crouched to lift. He stooped, and then as soon as he grasped the bar he dropped it again and once more drew back. For a third time he concentrated, then swooped on the bar and with a terrific effort drew it to his shoulders. Another fierce movement from this tigerish lifter, and there was the weight triumphantly overhead." Both men had achieved the same overall total, but Shams was declared the winner because of his lighter body weight. He would be world champion in 1949 and 1951, and it was only the second time since the Olympic schedule was rationalised in 1920

Lightweight (67.5kg) result: 1 Ibrahim Hassanien Shams (Egypt) 360kg (97.5, 115, 147.5), 2 Appia Hammouda (Egypt) 360 (105, 110, 145), 3 Jim Halliday (Great Britain) 340 (90, 110, 140), 4 John Terpak (USA) 340 (102.5, 102.5, 135), 5 John Stuart (Canada) 332.5 (107.5, 100, 125), 6 Suk Young Kim (Korea) 330 (95, 100, 135), 7 See Yun La (Korea) 330 (90, 100, 125), 8 Joe Pittman (USA) 322.5 (100, 95, 127.5), 9 Michael Espeut (Jamaica) 322.5 (100, 95, 127.5), 10 Jørgen Fryd Petersen (Denmark) 315 (90, 97.5, 127.5), 11 René Alleman (France) 315 (95, 97.5, 122.5), 12 Giuseppe Colantuono (Italy) 312.5 (92.5, 95, 125), 13 Ronald Eland (Great Britain) 310 (95, 95, 120), 14 Sigvard Kinnunen (Sweden) 307.5 (85, 102.5, 120), 15 Frank Teräskari (Finland) 307.5 (82.5, 105, 120), 16 Guillermo Alvarado Cornejo (Peru) 305 (90, 95, 120), 17 Théophile Huyge (Belgium) 300 (85, 92.5, 122.5), 18 Salvador Lopresti (Argentina) 300 (90, 90, 120), 19 Asadollah Mahini (Iran) 295 (85, 92.5, 117.5), 20 Hugo D'Atri (Argentina) 295 (85, 90, 120), 21 Hugo Banda Bernal (Mexico) 272.5 (85, 80, 107.5), 22 Fernando Louro Sierra (Cuba) 185 (92.5, 92.5, -).

that one country had taken gold and silver in the same event; Czech heavyweights having done so in 1932.

Halliday was 30 years old and from Farnworth, Manchester. He was to win five British titles through to 1954 and was also twice Empire & Commonwealth champion – at lightweight in 1950 and middleweight in 1954. The most remarkable aspect of his Olympic medal success was that he had spent four years in a Japanese prisoner-of-war camp.

When Khadr El-Sayed El-Touni had won the Olympic middleweight title for Egypt in 1936 he had lifted 25kg more than his nearest rival and his world-record total of 387.5kg would also easily have won the higher light-heavyweight division. Until that achievement the international ruling body for the sport had refused to accept the lifts of his that had been reported from his homeland because they did not believe that any middleweight was capable of them. Since then El-Touni had won the 1946 world title at 377.5kg, and the 1947 event had gone to Stan Stanczyk, of the USA, with a resounding new world record of 405kg. But there would be no mighty showdown – for the simple reason that Stanczyk had moved up to the light-heavyweight division.

El-Touni thus started favourite and duly improved his own Olympic record of 117.5kg in the press to 120kg, but it was the Korean, Sung Jip Kim, who had placed third in the World Championships the year before, who actually led with 122.5. Further surprises followed in the snatch phase when the Americans, Pete George and Frank Spellman, both produced better efforts – 122.5kg for George (an Olympic record, naturally), 120 for Spellman, 117.5 for El-Touni, 112.5 for Sung Jip Kim. Spellman and El-Touni now shared the overall lead at 237.5kg, ahead of the Korean (235kg) and George (227.5kg). All of the other 21 competitors had completed the jerk, with Sung Jip Kim the best of them at 145kg, before the two Americans and the Egyptian had even announced their intentions for their first lifts.

It was now a battle of nerves as to which of them would be pressurised into going first, and it was El-Touni who conceded by coming in at 142.5kg. Oscar State surely caught the tension of the situation perfectly with his description that "at last the Americans succeeded in driving out El-Touni to make his first jerk, fearful lest another increase in the weight of the bar would be too much for him". El-Touni failed with his first lift. Spellman lifted that weight without much difficulty, and then El-Touni, to the consternation of his managers and supporters, could not lift 145kg with the final attempt available to him and so lost all chance of a medal.

Now came one of the most dramatic sequences of the entire 1948 Olympic Games.

First Spellman pushed the Olympic record up to 152.5kg with his third and final effort. He had had no failures at any weight and his total was now 390kg, beating El-Touni's exceptional Olympic record from 1936. George, only 19 years old and just graduated from high school, improved Spellman's short-lived record to 155kg but still trailed overall by 7.5kg. So he decided to go for 165kg, five kilogrammes more than the world record held by Stan Stanczyk, and which was required if the gold medal was to be won. Oscar State's words again tell the tale of the long-drawn-out preparations: "For minutes on end George paced up and down the platform, trying to nerve himself for a supreme effort, and all the while the atmosphere became more and more electric with suspense."

For those familiar with weightlifting tournaments, the situation will be pleasurable. The bar with its weights at each end lying dormant on the platform, like some captive and somnolent animal ... the man prowling back and forth, as if seeking the perfect vantage point from which to launch an attack, exhorting himself with grunts and gasps, working himself up in the manner of some deranged penitent monk into a fury of emotional – even quasi-religious – fervour. At last the lifter turns towards his prey.

"He stooped and gripped the bar with agonising deliberation," wrote State. "His knees bent as he set himself, then straightened with a tremendous heave. The bar came to his shoulders and he squatted deep under it. Could he come up with this tremendous weight? Slowly, but surely, he did, and a tremendous roar burst out to greet this partial success. Abruptly, the roar died away as George set himself for the final effort of jerking the bar to arm's length. A short dip and the bar was sent overhead. He had done it. But no, even as he started to recover from his split to the erect position, he slipped. Down crashed the bar to the platform and a groan of disappointment echoed round the hall while he stood gazing sadly down on the great weight that had so narrowly beaten him."

Frank Spellman had started competing in 1941 and then served in the Army Air Corps from 1942 to 1945. He had placed third in the 1946 World Championships and second to Stanczyk the next year, and he continued competing until 1961. Pete George went on to win the Olympic title in 1952 and was also a world champion on five occasions from 1947 to 1953. He was of Bulgarian descent, and by 1956 the world record (415kg) and then the Olympic title had passed into Soviet hands. Bulgarians would win three successive middleweight golds from 1972 to 1980. At the Melbourne Games George was second and his

---

Middleweight (75kg) result: 1 Frank Spellman (USA) 390kg (117.5, 120, 152.5), 2 Peter George (USA) 382.5 (105, 122.5, 155), 3 Sung Jip Kim (Korea) 380 (122.5, 112.5, 145), 4 Khadr El-Sayed El-Touni (Egypt) 380 (120, 117.5, 142.5), 5 Gerald Gratton (Canada) 360 (112.5, 107.5, 140), 6 Pierre Bouladoux (France) 355 (102.5, 110, 142.5), 7 Orlando Garrido Luloaga (Cuba) 355 (112.5, 107.5, 135), 8 Bill Watson (Great Britain) 350 (100, 110, 140), 9 Georges Firmin (France) 347.5 (100, 107.5, 140), 10 Joseph Sklar (Canada) 345 (105, 107.5, 132.5), 11 Lennart Nelson (Sweden) 335 (95, 105, 135), 12 Jan Smeekens (Holland) 330 (95, 102.5, 132.5), 13 Mansour Mir Ghavami (Iran) 327.5 (102.5, 95, 130), 14 Ignace Bloomberg (South Africa) 327.5 (105, 97.5, 125), 15 Ernest Peppiatt (Great Britain) 327.5 (100, 102.5, 125), 16 Klement Schuh (Austria) 320 (100, 95, 125), 17 Armando Rueda Garcia (Mexico) 315 (100, 95, 120), 18 Julio Bonnet (Argentina) 312.5 (90, 100, 122.5), 19 F Mast (Switzerland) 310 (90, 100, 120), 20 Juán Russo (Argentina) 310 (90, 95, 125), 21 Anthony Chaves (British Guiana) 307.5 (82.5, 100, 125), 22 Muhammad Iqbal Butt (Pakistan) 305 (92.5, 90, 122.5), 23 Roger Rubini (Switzerland) 292.5 (82.5, 90, 120), 24 Jørgen Moritzen (Denmark) 182.5 (87.5, 95, retired).

younger brother, Jim, kept up the family tradition with light-heavyweight bronze in 1956 and silver in 1960.

Stan Stanczyk won the light-heavyweight style in a manner royal. He led by a long way after the press, not even starting until everyone else had finished, and lifting 130kg. A Canadian, Jim Varaleau, was next best at 112.5. The snatch served to put the American even further ahead as he achieved another Olympic record of 130kg, 10kg better than Gösta Magnusson, of Sweden. Stanczyk's overall lead was now 30kg over Magnusson, and short of a disaster the title was decided. He even snatched 132.5kg for a new world record which was accepted by the judges, but he then told them that his rear knee had brushed the ground – which they had not noticed – and so the record was lost. The packed audience acclaimed this selfless act with massive enthusiasm, and it was almost an anticlimax when the champion-to-be succeeded only with the first of his three attempts at the jerk.

Stanczyk remains one of the greatest of all weightlifters, having won world titles at lightweight in 1946, middleweight in 1947, light-heavyweight in 1949–50–51, and also at heavyweight in 1950. His lightweight world-record total of 367.5kg in 1946 was not beaten until Pete George achieved 370kg for the world title in 1953. His middleweight record of 405kg from 1947 also lasted until 1953, when another great American, Tommy Kono, won the world title with 407.5. Stanczyk had started weightlifting in 1942 at 17 and was straight away third in the US championships, but he was in the army from 1943 to 1945. The 1946 World Championships had been only the 10th competition of his career, but he had beaten the two Soviet lightweight competitors, Vladimir Svetilko and Grigoriy Popov, by 20kg. After retiring from lifting, Stanczyk set up a gymnasium and then a bowling alley in Miami which he operated for 27 years.

Even so, Stanczyk's claims to fame were exceeded by the silver-medallist, also from the USA, as Harold Sakata became a successful professional wrestler and then took up a Hollywood career and achieved worldwide recognition in the role of Oddjob in the James Bond film *Goldfinger*. Of Japanese-American parentage, Sakata had been given the first name "Tashiyuki" at his birth in Hawaii. The Soviet world champion from 1946, Grigoriy Novak, would assuredly have been a medal contender here, with a press of 141kg and a snatch of 131kg recorded for him in 1947, but much less certain is whether he would have matched Stanczyk's fighting spirit, which he would have needed to do to have stood a chance of winning.

Light-heavyweight: 1 Stanley Stanczyk (USA) 417.5kg (130, 130, 157.5) 417.5, 2 Harold Sakata (USA) 380 (110, 117.5, 152.5), 3 Gösta Magnusson (Sweden) 375 (110, 120, 145), 4 Jean Debuf (France) 370 (107.5, 112.5, 150), 5 Osvaldo Forte (Argentina) 367.5 (105, 115, 147.5), 6 Jim Varaleau (Canada) 365 (112.5, 112.5, 140), 7 Juhani Vellamo (Finland) 355 (100, 115, 140), 8 Rasoul Raisi (Iran) 355 (110, 110, 135), 9 Ernest Roe (Great Britain) 355 (110, 105, 140), 10 László Buronyi (Hungary) 355 (102.5, 112.5, 140), 11 Mohamed Ibrahim Saleh (Egypt) 350 (350 (97.5, 112.5, 140), 12 Raymond Herbaux (France) 350 (102.5, 107.5, 140), 13 Wilhelm Pankl (Austria) 347.5 (95, 107.5, 145), 14 Carlos Bisiak (Peru) 332.5 (97.5, 102.5, 132.5), 15 Young Hwan Lee (Korea) 205 (100, 105, -).

There seemed as little doubt about John Davis winning the heavyweight title as there had been about Stanczyk winning the light-heavyweight. Davis had remained undefeated since winning the world light-heavyweight title at the age of 17 in 1938, and would continue to be for another five years. He had set a world-record total of 455kg in 1947, which converted to what was for English-speakers the more resonant figure of 1,003lb. Like Stanczyk, Davis had the gold medal all but won after two of the three lifts, setting identical Olympic records of 137.5kg for the press and the snatch to forge a 20kg lead over Norbert Schemansky, the second American in the event.

US team coach Bob Hoffman persuaded Davis to take an extra lift in the snatch at a world-record 142.5kg and he succeeded, though this would not count in the competition. Finally, in the jerk, Davis set another world record of 177.5kg for a total of 452.5. As Oscar State rightfully concluded, Davis had "brought this wonderful cavalcade of strength to a fitting end". Davis won again at Helsinki in 1952 and was world heavyweight champion in 1946, 1947, 1949, 1950 and 1951. He pushed the world-record total up to 482.5 kg, and none of the gloss can be taken off his marvellous carer even by the fact that the Soviet-held world record had already reached 580kg by 1964 and 645kg by 1972.

The lifting talents of Davis – prophetically christened "John Henry" by his mother in honour of a legendary Afro-American strongman – had been discovered by chance by gymnasium owner Steve Wolsky, who saw him pick up a cement block on a playground in his birthplace of Smithtown, New York, and the same year Davis became the youngest ever world champion, and would remain so for almost 50 years. He served in the army during the war, where he contracted jaundice, which continued to trouble him in later life, and won his first post-war title ahead of a Soviet lifter, Yakov Kurchenko. Davis weighed no more than 90kg (14st 4lb) when he was competing, compared with the 155kg (24st 5lb) of his Soviet successor as Olympic champion in 1964, Leonid Zhabotinsky, and is regarded by weightlifting experts as being, pound for pound, one of the greatest of all lifters.

It had been a splendid tournament – certainly the best in Olympic history to that date, and maybe even for a lot more years to come. The USA had been much the outstanding team, with four golds, three silvers and a bronze. Egypt had won the other two golds. Great Britain had won a silver and a bronze, and also had a fourth place for what was by far their finest Olympic showing. Iran and Trinidad had won historic medals. Equally significantly, top-eight places had been achieved by Canada, Cuba, Denmark, Iran, Korea, New Zealand, the Philippines and South Africa, among others. On the other side of the coin, France fell far short of previous standards with a fourth place and two at sixth.

The six official world records set during the Games were:

Bantamweight total: 307.5kg, Joe De Pietro (USA)
Featherweight snatch: 105kg, Mahmoud Fayad (Egypt)
Featherweight jerk: 135kg, Fayad

Featherweight total: 332.5kg, Fayad
Heavyweight snatch: 142.5kg, John Davis (USA)
Heavyweight jerk: 177.5kg, Davis

Heavyweight (unlimited) result: 1 John Davis (USA) 452.5kg (137.5, 137.5, 177.5), 2 Norbert Schemansky (USA) 425 (122.5, 132.5, 170), 3 Abraham Charité (Holland) 412.5 (127.5, 125, 160), 4 Alfred Knight (Great Britain) 390 (117.5, 117.5, 155), 5 Hanafi Mustafa (Egypt) 385 (120, 115, 150), 6 Niels Petersen (Denmark) 382.5 (115, 112.5, 155), 7 Robert Allart (Belgium) 377.5 (122.5, 110, 145), 8 Pieter Taljaard (South Africa) 375 (117.5, 112.5, 145), 9 Alfonso Perera Alonso (Cuba) 372.5 (105, 112.5, 155), 10 Carlos Dominguez Mavila (Peru) 362.5 (117.5, 105, 140), 11 Hugo Vallarino (Argentina) 357.5 (100, 112.5, 145), 12 Raymond Magee (Australia) 357.5 (110, 110, 137.5), 13 Leopoldo Briola (Argentina) 347.5 (110, 102.5, 135), 14 Franz Eibler (Austria) 327.5 (102.5, 100, 125), 15 Muhammad Naqi Butt (Pakistan) 320 (97.5, 97.5, 125), 16 Dandamudi Rajagopal (India) 305 (92.5, 90, 122.5).

Chapter 36

THE LORDS OF THE MAT ON WHICH THE GAME OF 'BODY CHESS' IS PLAYED

Wrestling. Empress Hall, Earls Court, 30 July to 6 August

W HO WAS THE 1948 Olympic champion immediately worth $1.37 million by 21st-century standards? Not sprinter Fanny Blankers-Koen. Not distance-runner Emil Zátopek. Nor the boxers Pascual Pérez and László Papp. Nor even Sweden's entire team of triumphant footballers. The gold-medallist who was offered $60,000 to turn professional was the freestyle heavyweight wrestler, Henry Wittenberg, then a sergeant in the New York police force with two awards for bravery to his name. He rejected out of hand the chance to cash in on his Wembley success, and one of his coaches, Walter Steinhilber, said by way of explanation that Wittenberg "had too much dignity for that kind of thing".

Wittenberg had done nothing more active in high school than play chess. He did not take up wrestling until the age of 19 in 1938 when he entered the Central College of New York. He proved to be a natural, winning his first national title in 1940, and between 1939 and 1951 he remained unbeaten through 300 recorded contests – and maybe many more, because his later recollection was that the sequence could have run to 400 or even 500. Having extended his education to earn himself a master's degree, he regarded wrestling as an intellectual exercise as much as a physical one, describing the sport as "body chess", and this view was confirmed by Steinhilber, who said of Wittenberg: "He brought intelligence to wrestling. He could think ahead of his opponents. He was a planner."

Wrestling at the Olympic Games was conducted as two separate disciplines, Greco-Roman and Freestyle; the difference between the two being that in the former a contestant is not allowed to touch or use an opponent's legs as a means of attack or defence. The sport has an ancient history, traced back to cave paintings discovered from 3000 BC, and had been an integral part of the Ancient Olympic Games. So it was naturally included in the programme at the first Modern Olympics in Athens in 1896, where a heavyweight event in the then prevalent Greco-Roman category was held. The Greek hosts failed to defend the national honour as the title went to a German, Karl Schumann, but one has to wonder at the level of competence of the contestants in view of the fact that Schumann was more in the nature of a good all-round sportsman, also winning three first prizes at the Games in gymnastics.

The International Amateur Wrestling Federation did not come into being until 1921, and other Greco-Roman weight divisions had already been added at the Games from 1906 onwards. Of 132 medals awarded through to 1936, Finland and Sweden had been the most successful nations, with 14 gold medals each, and only one – also gold – had ever gone outside Europe, when Ibrahim Moustafa, of Egypt, won the light-heavyweight title in 1928. Yaşar Erkan, of Turkey – in both Asia and Europe – had won the featherweight in 1936. Even leaving aside the 1904 Games in St Louis, which were almost exclusively contested among Americans, and those of 1908 in London, dominated by the British, the USA was still the leading nation in the freestyle events with 10 wins, to seven for Finland and five for Sweden. Great Britain had won three titles in 1908, and their most recent success dated back to 1928 when Samuel Rabin had won a bronze at middleweight.

World Championships at freestyle had been held in 1946, and Turkey had been the most successful nation with three wins, to two for Sweden and one each for Finland and Hungary. The Turks could claim a very firmly established wrestling tradition, with an annual tournament said to date back to 1362 and which was therefore the world's longest-lasting sporting event of any kind. Theirs was a particular form of wrestling known as *yagli gures*, pronounced "yaw-luh gresh", in which the contestants daubed themselves in olive oil and wore close-fitting leather trousers, grappling with each other in a free-for-all manner and for hours on end, though eventually a time limit had been introduced. The Olympics had some notable experience of long-drawn-out contests because at the 1912 Games in Stockholm an Estonian representing Czarist Russia, Martin Klein, and a Finn, Alfred Asikainen, had spent the best part of 12 hours – with a short break every half-hour – trying to pin each other down until Klein at last won by a fall.

In 1947 there had been World Championships for Greco-Roman wrestling and the USSR had won the three heaviest divisions: Nikolay Byelov at middleweight,

Konstantin Koberidze at light-heavyweight, Johannes Kotkas at heavyweight. All this trio would, of course, be absent from Wembley, and the most sorely missed would be Kotkas, who had also won the world title in 1938 and 1939, representing his native Estonia, which had then been annexed by the USSR. Kotkas, interestingly, could have additionally been an Olympic contender in 1944 at a very different sport, but one which, naturally, also required great strength. This was hammer-throwing, for which he had won the Soviet title the previous year. He had a best effort of 52.78m, which ranked him 12th in the world in 1946, and he placed fifth at the 1948 USSR Championships.

The wrestling events had originally been planned for the Harringay Arena, but the necessity to stage more than 80 basketball matches there caused a late switch to the Empress Hall. The change of venue turned out to be an advantage – just as happened when gymnastics had to be moved indoors – because the three platforms set out in the large space available, with electric scoring equipment and a detailed results board, provided a fine spectacle for the audience. George MacKenzie, reporting for the British Olympic Association, described the tournament as simply "the greatest ever" – and he should know. He had been the secretary of the British Amateur Wrestling Association since 1935 and had competed in every Games from 1908 to 1928.

For the freestyle events seven of the eight world champions from 1946 would be in action: Vilho Lennart ("Lenni") Viitala (Finland) at flyweight and Lajos Bencze (Hungary) at bantamweight, together with three Turks, Gazamfer Bilge at featherweight, Celal Atik at lightweight and Yaşar Dogu at welterweight, and two Swedes, Bengt Fahlkvist at light-heavyweight and Hans Bertil Antonsson at heavyweight. Dogu was also Greco-Roman champion in the same division, and the other Greco-Roman world champions present at the Empress Hall would be Ali Mahmoud Hassan (Egypt) at bantamweight, Olle Anderberg (Sweden) at featherweight and Gösta Jönsson-Frandförs (also Sweden) at lightweight, although the last-named would actually take part in the freestyle event. The one medallist from the 1936 Games to appear again would be a Turk, Ahmet Kireççi, who had won the freestyle middleweight bronze in Berlin but would contest the Greco-Roman heavyweight division in London.

The rules for competition then in existence were somewhat complex and therefore need explaining in fair detail. Contestants were debited "bad" points per bout on a scale of 0 to 3: no points for a win by a fall; one point for a win by judges' decision, whether or not it was unanimous; two points for a loss by judges' decision which was not unanimous; three points for a loss by a unanimous judges' decision or by a fall.

Once a competitor had accumulated five of these "bad" points he was eliminated. Bouts were limited to 20 minutes for Greco-Roman events and 15 minutes for freestyle events, and there were further regulations which decided whether bouts would continue in the normal manner or by a series of set-pieces if they had produced no fall after the first 10 minutes of a Greco-Roman contest or six minutes of a freestyle contest. A fall was registered if an opponent's shoulders both touched the mat simultaneously for however brief a time. The medals were thus decided by a process of elimination, and there were no "finals" as such, other than by chance.

No Olympic contest at freestyle flyweight had been held since 1904 when all three medals had been won by Americans – hardly surprising as they had been the only contestants. As there were no more than 11 competitors at the Empress Hall, it seemed odd that the eventual gold- and silver-medallists should be drawn against each other in the first round, and it was therefore predictable that the judges should disagree on the result of the bout between Viitala and Turkey's Balamir. Viitala got the verdict on points, but the rules allowed Balamir to go on to the second round, where both of them won. By the fourth round there were five survivors and Viitala, who by then had conceded only two points, received a bye. He then met Johansson, of Sweden, and won on points to take the gold.

The Indian wrestler, Jhadav, in sixth place, went on to win the bantamweight bronze in Helsinki in 1952, his country's first Olympic wrestling medal. Great Britain's representative here was Harry Parker, who worked as a motor mechanic for a living, and was a member of the leading North of England club, Hilltop, in Bradford. After losing his opening bout by a fall to the eventual bronze-medallist he was forced to retire in his next contest with the Frenchman, Baudric.

Of the 15 bantamweight competitors only two – Akar, of Turkey, and Leeman, of the USA – won all of their first three bouts. In the third round Leeman beat world champion Bencze, known as "Biringer" when he won his title, and this left only four men in the competition. Akar and Leeman then beat both Kouyos, of France, and Trimpont, of Belgium, and the medals were decided. Akar and Leeman had each won all of their five bouts, but they did not actually meet each other on the mat. The points-scoring structure and Akar's win by a fall against Kouyos, with only 1min 6sec to go of their contest, decided the gold and silver medals. Akar was to be world champion in 1949 and 1951.

Great Britain's Ray Cazaux, also from Bradford and a member of the College Wrestling Club, had competed at the 1936 Games at the age of 19 and was a

---

Freestyle flyweight (52kg) result: 1 Vilho Lennart Viitala (Finland), 2 Halit Balamir (Turkey), 3 Thure Johansson (Sweden), 4 Raisl Mansour (Iran), 5 Pierre Baudric (France), 6 Khashaba Digvijai Jhadav (India).
The medallists' bouts: Viitala bt Balamir pts, bt Adolphe Lamot (Belgium) fall, bt Billy Jernigan (USA) pts, bt Johansson (Sweden) pts. Balamir lost to Viitala pts, bt Baudric pts, bt Johansson fall, bt Mansour pts. Johansson bt Mohamed Abdel Hamid El-Ward (Egypt) pts, bt Harry Parker (Great Britain) fall, lost to Balamir pts, bt Baudric fall, lost to Viitala pts.

Freestyle bantamweight (57kg) result: 1 Nasuh Akar (Turkey), 2 Gerry Leeman (USA), 3 Charles Kouyos (France), 4 Joseph Trimpont (Belgium), 5 Lajos Bencze (Hungary), 6 Ray Cazaux (Great Britain).
The medallists' bouts: Akar bt Norman May (Canada) fall, bt Walter Wenger (Switzerland) pts, bt Erik Persson (Sweden) pts, bt Trimpont fall, bt Kouyos fall. Leeman bt N Bhose (India) fall, bt Cazaux fall, bt Bencze pts, bt Kouyos pts, bt Trimpont pts. Kouyos bt Sayed Hafez Shehata (Egypt) pts, bt Francisco Vicera (Philippines) fall, bt Erkki Johansson (Finland) fall, lost to Leeman pts, lost to Akar fall.

master baker by profession. He won two of his three bouts, but his defeat by a fall against Leeman relegated him to sixth place, which was nevertheless to be the best showing by a British freestyle wrestler. Asked many years later how he acquired his two prominent cauliflower ears, he replied that it was the fault of the style he had adopted against his opponents: "I go for them head down."

There were 17 featherweight competitors, but one man stood out above the rest. The world champion, Gazanfer Bilge, of Turkey, swept through round after round, winning the first five of his six bouts by falls. Apart from anything else, his supremacy saved him a lot of time on the mat as those five contests lasted a total of 41min 41sec, instead of the 75 minutes they could have occupied, had they gone to points decisions. By the fifth round his solitary challenger was Ivar Sjölin, of Sweden, also unbeaten, and eventually the two of them met with Sjölin managing to make Bilge go the full distance. Arnold Parsons, Great Britain's representative from Chingford, in Essex, made an honourable showing, winning twice before losing by a fall to the eventual bronze-medallist.

Again a Turk was the most prominent among the 18 lightweight competitors, and as he was the world champion it was not that unexpected. Atik won his first three bouts by falls, occupying 22min 2sec in all. For the fifth round there were four men left in the competition, and Jönsson-Frändfors, of Sweden, beat Baumann, of Switzerland, and Atik beat the Italian, Nizzola, to set up a neat final round of a bronze-medal bout followed by a gold-medal bout. Atik won in the most decisive fashion, putting his Swedish opponent down on the mat in just 4min 3sec. Atik was to win world light-middleweight titles in 1949 and 1951. Britain's entrant, Peter Luck, from Hornchurch, lost both his bouts on points.

Yaşar Dogu, the world light-middleweight champion from Turkey at both Greco-Roman and freestyle, opted for the latter event, and although at the start that did not automatically mean that everyone else among his 15 rivals was battling for no better than second place it must soon have begun to look that way. Dogu disposed in quick succession of an Indian, an Iranian, an Egyptian

---

Freestyle featherweight (62kg) result: 1 Gazanfer Bilge (Turkey), 2 Ivar Sjölin (Sweden), 3 Adolf Müller (Switzerland), 4= Paavo Hietala (Finland), Ferenc Tóth (Hungary), 6 Harold Moore (USA).
The medallists' bouts: Bilge bt Hassan Sadian (Iran) fall, bt Tóth fall, bt Robert Jouaville (France) fall, bt Moore fall, bt Hietala fall, bt Sjölin pts. Sjölin bt Hietala pts, bt Delmiro Bernal Contreras (Mexico) fall, bt Ibrahim Abdel Hamid (Egypt) fall, bt Tóth pts, lost to Bilge pts. Müller bt José Maria López Alvárez (Cuba) pts, bt S B Suryavanashi (India) fall, bt Antoine Raeymackers (Belgium) pts, bt Arnold Parsons (Great Britain) fall, lost to Sjölin pts.

Freestyle lightweight (67kg) result: 1 Celal Atik (Turkey), 2 Gösta Jönsson-Frändfors (Sweden), 3 Hermann Baumann (Switzerland), 4 Garibaldo Nizzola (Italy), 5 Bill Koll (USA), 6= Sulo Leppänen (Finland), Suk Young Kim (Korea).
The medallists' bouts: Atik bt Koll fall, bt Banta Singh (India) fall, bt Anthony Ries (South Africa) fall, bt Leppänen pts, bt Nizzola fall, bt Jönsson-Frandförs fall. Jönsson-Frandförs bt László Bakos (Hungary) pts, bt Ries fall, bt Koll pts, bt Baumann pts, lost to Atik fall. Baumann bt José Luis Perez Valencia (Mexico) fall, bt George Plumb (Canada) pts, lost to Lajos Bakos (Hungary) pts, lost to Jönsson-Frandförs pts, bt Nizzola pts.

and a Hungarian, all by falls, and with none of the bouts lasting longer than 7min 39sec, before Merrill, of the USA, at last held him to a points decision in the sixth round. Merrill had been unbeaten until then, and Dogu finished off the proceedings by defeating Australian's Garrard on a fall after 6min 45sec. The points system, though, gave Garrard the silver and Merrill the bronze. Don Irvine, for Britain, was beaten twice.

Dick Garrard, who had celebrated his 38th birthday two days before the Olympic wrestling began, remains one of the most durable figures in the sport. He had been in London 14 years before to win the Empire Games title. He had competed at the Berlin Olympics and went on to win again at the Empire Games in 1938 and 1950 and to take part in the Olympics of 1952 and 1956 – the latter at the age of 45. He fought 525 bouts during his career and lost only nine of them. After retiring from competition he continued to serve the sport as an official, and he received a rapturous reception when he was introduced to a packed 104,000 crowd during the 2000 Olympics in Sydney. He lived to the age of 92.

Though there were 16 middleweight competitors, the gold- and silver-medallists each needed only four bouts to decide their destiny. The Turkish representative here was Adil Candemir, and according to George MacKenzie he "had been expected to have the weight at his mercy". Even so, having won three golds and a silver, Turkey had to settle for another silver at best when Glen Brand, of the USA, threw Candemir after 13min 24sec of their fourth-round bout. Brand then beat Erik Lindén, of Sweden, on points to clinch the gold. MacKenzie's expert eye was particularly caught by Brand, whom he described as "a fine exponent of all-round wrestling". Britain's Eddie Bowey, from Wood Green, did well enough to get to the third round but then lost on a fall to the eventual silver-medallist.

Candemir went on to win the world light-heavyweight title the next year. Brand, like the bantamweight silver-medallist, Leeman, and a third member of the US team, William Nelson, was a student at Iowa State Teachers' College.

The world freestyle champion at light-heavyweight, Bengt Fahlkvist, of Sweden,

---

Freestyle light-middleweight (73kg) result: 1 Yaşar Dogu (Turkey), 2 Dick Garrard (Australia), 3 Leland Merrill (USA), 4 Jean-Baptiste Leclerc (France), 5 Kálmán Sóvári (Hungary), 6 Frans Westergen (Sweden).
The medallists' bouts: Dogu bt Anant Ram Bhargava (India) fall, bt Abbas Zandi (Iran) fall, bt Abdel Ibrahim Moustafa (Egypt) fall, bt Sóvári fall, bt Merrill pts, bt Garrard fall. Garrard bt Willy Angst (Switzerland) pts, bt Sóvári pts, bt Bhargava fall, bt Leclerc fall, lost to Merrill pts, lost to Dogu fall. Merrill bt Harry Peace (Canada) pts, bt Westergren pts, bt Byung Kwan Wang (Korea) pts, bt Garrard pts, lost to Dogu pts.

Freestyle middleweight (79kg) result: 1 Glen Brand (USA), 2 Adil Candemir (Turkey), 3 Erik Lindén (Sweden), 4 Carel Reitz (South Africa), 5 Paavo Sepponen (Finland), 6 André Brunaud (France).
The medallists' bouts: Brand bt Abbas Hariri (Iran) pts, bt Bruce Arthur (Australia) fall, bt Candemir fall, bt Lindén pts. Candemir bt Arthur fall, bt Maurice Vachon (Canada) pts, bt Eddie Bowey (Great Britain) fall, lost to Brand fall. Lindén bt Jean-Baptiste Benoy (Belgium) fall, bt Abbas Ahmad (Egypt) fall, bt Reitz pts, bt Brunaud pts, lost to Brand pts.

lived up to his reputation with four successive wins, but he was matched by Henry Wittenberg, of the USA, and the American had the edge at that stage with three wins by a fall to Falhkvist's two. With three of the original 15 men left in contention, it still needed three more bouts to decide the medals, and the judges disagreed on the winner in every case, with the verdicts going to Wittenberg over Fahlkvist ("the pity was that one of the two had to lose", said MacKenzie), Stöckli (Switzerland) over Fahlkvist, and finally Wittenberg over Stöckli. This last bout was described by MacKenzie as "a contest that will live long in the memory of those who saw it ... it was a battle of styles, of differing systems of technique. The Swiss, like so many of his countrymen, showed a preference for 'doing his wrestling on his feet' – the Swiss national style, 'Schwingen', is practically all up-standing wrestling – whereas the American showed to greater advantage in the ground work".

Wittenberg and Fahlvist were responsible for the two quickest bouts of all the freestyle or Greco-Roman events; Wittenberg beating Great Britain's Irish-born Johnny Sullivan in 47sec and then Fahlkvist beating Spyros Defteralos, of Greece, in 38sec.

Having spurned that lavish offer to turn professional, Wittenberg continued with his police career, earning three more recommendations for bravery, and retiring from wrestling in 1949, apart from a brief reappearance to win the title at the Maccabiah Games for Jewish athletes in 1950. Persuaded by his wife to return to the ring the next year, he soon got himself back into shape and won through the trials to represent the USA again at the 1952 Olympics, where he narrowly lost the gold to a Swede, Wiking Palm. Wittenberg was coach to the US wrestling team at the 1968 Olympics.

There were only nine entrants for the heavyweight competition and the decisive bout came in the fourth round when 38-year-old Hungarian Gyula Bóbis beat the world champion from Sweden, Hans Bertil Antonsson, on points, though the judges were not unanimous in their decision. This left Antonsson and the aptly-named Australian, Jim Armstrong, to fight off for the silver. Though

---

Freestyle light-heavyweight (90kg) result: 1 Henry Wittenberg (USA), 2 Fritz Stöckli (Switzerland), 3 Bengt Fahlkvist (Sweden), 4= Muharrem Candaş (Turkey), Fernand Payette (Canada), 6 Patrick Morton (South Africa).
The medallists' bouts: Wittenberg bt Pekka Mellavuo (Finland) pts, bt Johnny Sullivan (Great Britain) fall, bt József Tárányi (Hungary) fall, bt Candaş fall, bt Fahlkvist pts, bt Stöckli pts. Stöckli bt R Landesmann (France) fall, bt Karel Istaz (Belgium) fall, bt Candaş pts, bt Payette fall, bt Fahlkvist pts, lost to Wittenberg pts. Fahlkvist bt Oscar Verona (Italy) pts, bt Morton pts, bt Spyros Defteralos (Greece) fall, bt Payette fall, lost to Wittenberg pts, lost to Stöckli pts.

Freestyle heavyweight (unlimited): 1 Gyula Bóbis (Hungary), 2 Hans Bertil Antonsson (Sweden), 3 Jim Armstrong (Australia), 4 Sadik Esen (Turkey), 5 Josef Ružička (Czechoslovakia), 6 Abdul Ghasem Sahkdari (Iran).
The medallists' bouts: Bóbis bt Willy Lardon (Switzerland) pts, bt Armstrong fall, bt Ružička fall, bt Antonsson pts. Antonsson bt Esen pts, bt Sakhdari fall, lost to Bóbis pts, bt Armstrong fall. Armstrong bt Freddy Oberlander (Great Britain) pts, lost to Bóbis fall, bt Dick Hutton (USA) retired, bt Esen fall, lost to Antonsson fall.

Armstrong finished up with the bronze, he shared the distinction with Henry Wittenberg of having beaten a Turk by a fall. Antonsson was to become one of the most prolific of post-war champions, winning world titles again at freestyle in 1949 and 1951 and at Greco-Roman in 1950 and 1953. He also competed in the Olympics of 1952 (second again at freestyle), 1956 (fifth at Greco-Roman) and 1960 (seventh at freestyle).

The British heavyweight, Freddy Oberlander, lost both his bouts on points, though the second of them was a divided decision. He was a member of George MacKenzie's Ashdown club and of the Maccabi Association of London and was the owner of a paint and varnish manufacturing business which he later moved to Canada. He became a prominent member of the sport's international ruling body.

No Greco-Roman flyweight contest had previously been held at the Olympics or World Championships, and by the completion of the third round the only unbeaten competitors among the 13 who had entered were Kangasmäki (Finland), Lombardi (Italy) and Olcay (Turkey). Lombardi then beat Kangasmäki and Olcay lost to the Hungarian, Szilágyi. Lombardi still needed two more contests to ensure the gold and the points decision for the final one against Olcay was not unanimous. The Finn took the bronze and was the only man in any of the wrestling divisions to earn a medal despite losing as many bouts as he won.

For the Greco-Roman bantamweight division, the world champion, Ali Mahmoud Hassan, of Egypt, was the favourite, though Europeans had won all the medals at the four previous Olympics. Hungary had provided the winner in 1936 and their selected man this time was Lajos Bencze, who also competed in the freestyle bantamweight event at these Games. Both Hassan and Bencze had difficult wins by split decisions in their first-round bouts, and the quickest success was by the Greek, Nikolaos Biris, who threw Great Britain's Ken Irvine, from the Islington Men's Institute club, in 5min 46sec.

By the end of the third round of bouts Ali Mahmoud Hassan had won twice more by falls against an Italian and an Austrian and was the only man among

---

Greco-Roman flyweight (52kg) result: 1 Pietro Lombardi (Italy), 2 Kenan Olcay (Turkey), 3 Reino Kangasmäki (Finland), 4 Malte Möller (Sweden), 5 Gyula Szilágyi (Hungary), 6 Fridtjof Clausen (Norway).
The medallists' bouts: Lombardi bt Svend Aage Thomsen (Denmark) pts, bt Mohamed Abdel-El (Egypt) fall, bt Kangasmäki pts, bt Möller pts, bt Olcay pts. Olcay bt Clausen pts, bt Thomsen pts, bt Mohamed Abdel-El fall, lost to Szilágyi pts, lost to Lombardi pts. Kangasmäki bt Möller pts, bt Edmond Faure (France) fall, lost to Lombardi pts, lost to Szilágyi pts.

Greco-Roman bantamweight (57kg) result: 1 Kurt Petersén (Sweden), 2 Ali Mahmoud Hassan (Egypt), 3 Halil Kaya (Turkey), 4 Taisto Lempinen (Finland), 5 Elvidio Flamini (Italy), 6= Lajos Bencze (Hungary), Reidar Maerlie (Norway).
The medallists' bouts: Petersén bt Francesco Suppo (Italy) fall, bt Bencze pts, lost to Maerlie pts, bt Lempinen fall, bt Ali Mahmoud Hassan pts. Ali Mahmoud Hassan bt Kolle Lejserowitz (Denmark) pts, bt Suppo fall, bt Kurt Elias (Austria) fall, bt Flamini fall, bt Kaya pts, lost to Petersén pts. Kaya bt Jésus Arenzana (France) fall, bt Nikolaos Biris (Greece) fall, lost to Bencze pts, lost to Ali Mahmoud Hassan pts.

the original 13 remaining unbeaten. Yet it was the Swede, Petersén, who went on to win the title by beating the Egyptian in a closing contest which George MacKenzie described as "a delight to those who understand the art of wrestling". Petersén's achievement in becoming champion despite losing one of his bouts was unique at the 1948 Games. Italy's Francesco Suppo had the misfortune to be drawn against the eventual gold- and silver-medallists in his first two contests and made an early exit.

The Greco-Roman featherweight division was one of the more heavily subscribed; 17 contestants in all, including the world champion, Olle Anderberg, of Sweden, and the most experienced of any of the wrestlers, Greco-Roman or freestyle, in London, the Hungarian, Ferenc Tóth, aged 38. He also competed at freestyle at the Empress Hall, sharing fourth place, and had been fifth at freestyle in Berlin in 1936 and had won the world titles for that event in 1933 and 1937. However, by the completion of the fourth round there were still nine competitors left in, and Anderberg had lost to the Turk, Oktav, by a fall in 2min 48sec, while Tóth had been beaten by the Italian, Campanella.

In the next two rounds Oktav won twice more to take the gold after only four bouts from Anderberg and Tóth, though there was very little margin between the contestants from third place onwards and there was a four-way tie for sixth. Anderberg had beaten four of his five opponents by falls. He became world champion again in 1950 and 1953 and by way of variation won the lightweight freestyle title at the 1952 Olympics.

Sweden's nominee for the Greco-Roman lightweight competition, for which there were 17 starters, was Gustav Freij, and not their world champion from the previous year, Gösta Jönsson-Frandförs, who competed in the freestyle lightweight event instead. Freij disposed of Great Britain's Ray Myland, a licensee by trade, in the first round, with a fall after 9min 27sec, and then beat a Frenchman and a Dane to qualify among the best eight for the fourth round. Also undefeated were Ferencz, of Hungary, and the ominously-named Damage, of Lebanon. Freij threw a Turk, Şenol, in 2min 14sec and Ferencz did even better, putting the Dutchman, Munnikes, down in 1min 48sec, but Freij then beat Ferencz on points to win the gold. Damage won four of his six contests but such was the competitiveness of this event that he narrowly missed collecting Lebanon's first ever Olympic medal in any sport.

Two interesting anomalies of this event were that Eriksen, of Norway, eventually won the silver after losing his opening bout to the bronze-medallist to

---

Greco-Roman featherweight (62kg) result: 1 Mehmet Oktav (Turkey), 2 Olle Anderberg (Sweden), 3 Ferenc Tóth (Hungary), 4 Georg Weidner (Austria), 5 Luigi Campanella (Italy), 6= El-Sayed Mohamed Kandil (Egypt), Egil Solsvik (Norway), Safi Taha (Lebanon), Erkki Talosela (Finland).
The medallists' bouts: Oktav bt Talosea pts, bt Anderberg fall, bt El-Sayed Mohamed Kandil pts, bt Weidner pts. Anderberg bt Weidner fall, lost to Oktav fall, bt Talosela fall, bt Campanella fall, bt Tóth fall. Tóth bt Jan Stehlik (Czechoslovakia) pts, bt James Mortimer (Great Britain) fall, lost to Campanella pts, bt Solsvik fall, lost to Anderberg fall.

be, Ferencz, and that Freij had become Olympic champion without ever having won a Swedish title. Freij went on to conclusively prove that his Empress Hall success was no fluke by winning Olympic silver in 1952, the world title in 1953 and Olympic bronze in 1960.

The light-middleweight world champion at both freestyle and Greco-Roman was the Turk, Dogu, who had opted for the former event, and the Greco-Roman version, for which there were 16 competitors, was thrown into some confusion when Dogu's replacement, Ali Özdomir, who might reasonably have been regarded as the favourite for the title, lost his opening bout on points to a Finn and then did not reappear for the next round. Andersson, of Sweden, and Szilvási, of Hungary, each worked their way through four rounds undefeated. Szilvási then beat Hansen, of Denmark, and thus met Andersson in the most appropriate confrontation with which to finish the event. Andersson won his fifth bout to gain full plaudits from George MacKenzie – "an outstanding performance in an Olympic event". The Greco-Roman light-middleweight event had not been introduced to the Games until 1932 and Sweden had now won it on each of the three occasions it had been held.

Szilvási had made a remarkable return to wrestling after being accidentally shot in the leg in 1946 while on police duty, and he and Andersson were the dominant figures again in the same event at the 1952 Olympics, with the Hungarian winning on this occasion and Andersson taking the silver. At those same Helsinki Games a Lebanese wrestler, Khalil Tala, was the bronze-medallist.

The three heaviest Greco-Roman weight divisions were the ones to suffer from the absence of Soviet world champions, and the missing middleweight title-holder was Nikolay Byelov. The event had always been won at the eight previous Games at which it had been held by a Finn or a Swede, and this time it was another Swede, Axel Grönberg, who maintained the line of succession. He was also to win the world title in 1950 and the Olympic title again in 1952, but the man who followed him as world champion in 1953, 1955 and 1958

Greco-Roman lightweight (67kg) result: 1 Gustav Freij (Sweden), 2 Aage Eriksen (Norway), 3 Károly Ferencz (Hungary), 4 Charif Damage (Lebanon), 5 Johannes Munnikes (Holland), 6= Georgios Petmezas (Greece), Ahmet Şenol (Turkey), Eino Virtanen (Finland).
The medallists' bouts: Freij bt Ray Myland (Great Britain) fall, bt Albert Falaux (France) fall, bt Abraham Kurland (Denmark) pts, bt Şenol fall, bt Ferencz pts. Eriksen lost to Ferencz pts, bt Giacomo Gesino (Italy) pts, bt Petmezas declared loser 17min 41sec, bt Virtanen retired, bt Damage pts. Ferencz bt Eriksen pts, bt Mohamed Ahmed Osman (Egypt) pts, bt Gesino pts, bt Munnikes fall, lost to Freij pts, bt Damage pts.

Greco-Roman light-middleweight (73kg) result: 1 Gösta Andersson (Sweden), 2 Miklós Szilvási (Hungary), 3 Henrik Hansen (Denmark), 4= René Chesneau (France), Veikko Männikö (Finland), Josef Schmidt (Austria).
The medallists' bouts: Andersson bt Johan Schouten (Holland) fall, bt Hansen pts, bt Luigi Rigamonti (Italy) pts, bt Chesneau pts, bt Szilvási pts. Szilvási bt Julien Dobbelaere (Belgium) pts, bt Schmidt pts, bt Chesneau fall, bt Mänikkö pts, bt Hansen fall, lost to Andersson pts. Hansen bt Kemal Munir (Egypt) fall, lost to Andersson pts, bt Bjørn Cook (Norway) pts, bt Schmidt fall, lost to Szilvási fall.

and as Olympic champion in 1956 would be another Soviet exponent, Givy Kartoziya.

Grönberg won three of his six bouts by falls and the last of them was the decisive meeting with the silver-medallist, Muhlis Tayfur, which resulted in a unanimous points victory. There were only 13 competitors in this event but it still needed to go through six rounds before the gold and silver medals were decided.

In the seventh and final first-round bout involving the 14 Greco-Roman light-heavyweight competitors the eventual bronze-medallist from Egypt beat a Briton by a fall after 7min 4sec, but the loser of this bout would go on to gain far greater fame than either his conqueror, or for that matter the gold- and silver- medallists. As it happens, Ken Richmond produced the best showing of any British wrestler at the Empress Hall in placing fifth and then went on to win the bronze at freestyle heavyweight in 1952 and place equal fourth in 1956. Even so, his much more celebrated public feats of strength were as the strongman who struck the massive gong, the trademark introduction to films produced by the J Arthur Rank Organisation. Millions of people who went to the cinema in the 1950s would have seen him in action week after week without ever knowing his name.

Richmond's route to fifth place was an odd one because he had a bye in the second round, beat a Turk by a fall in the third round, and lost by a fall to the eventual champion in the fourth round. The gold-medallist was Swede Karl-Erik Nilsson, who beat each of the next five competitors in the event in turn, culminating with the Finnish silver-medallist, Gröndahl, and who could say whether the world champion, Konstantin Koberidze, from Georgia, would have done any better? The world title was to be won in 1950 by Muharrem Candaş, of Turkey, who had finished just outside the freestyle medals at these Olympic Games. At the 1952 Olympics Gröndahl would win the gold and Nilsson the bronze, separated by another Georgian for the USSR, Chalva Chikhladze, with the Hungarian, Kovács, again fourth.

Ken Richmond's life was worthy of a film in itself. Born in Kensington, in London, he was a dedicated pacifist from an early age and served a prison sentence during World War II as a conscientious objector. He had taken up wrestling after returning from serving as a deckhand on an Antarctic whaling ship in 1945 and was aged 22 when he took part in the 1948 Olympics. He also competed at the Olympics of 1960, won the heavyweight title at the 1954 Empire & Commonwealth Games, competed at judo in the 1955 European Championships, and later became a Jehovah's Witness missionary, spending two

---

Greco-Roman middleweight (79kg) result: 1 Axel Grönberg (Sweden), 2 Muhlis Tayfur (Turkey), 3 Ercole Gallegati (Italy), 4 Jean-Baptiste Benoy (Belgium), 5 Kaare Larsen (Norway), 6 Juho Kinnunen (Finland).

The medallists' bouts: Grönberg beat Abbas Ahmad (Egypt) fall, bt Larsen pts, bt Kinnunen fall, bt Gyula Németi (Hungary) pts, bt Benoy fall, bt Tayfur pts. Tayfur bt Klaas de Groot (Holland) pts, bt Alberto Bolzi (Argentina) fall, bt Anton Vogel (Austria) fall, lost to Kinnunen pts, lost to Grönberg pts. Gallegati bt Bolzi fall, bt Vogel pts, lost to Németi fall, bt Larsen pts.

years in Malta, and a district overseer. He was an active windsurfer into his late 60s and died in 2006 at the age of 80.

Richmond, 6ft 2in (1.88m) tall and weighing 19st (120kg), had appeared in films as an extra – including the celebrated *Henry V* from 1944 and *Blithe Spirit* from 1945 – and was invited by the Rank organisation to take over the role of their gong-beater in 1955. The sequence of him continued to be used until 1978 and his fame spread so far afield that one of the most telling tributes at his death came from John H Lienhard, a Professor of Mechanical Engineering and History and the author and presenter of a US public radio series, whose words will have a poignant echo for ageing cinema-goers: "Deeply woven into the imagery of my childhood are the MGM lion, RKO radio tower, Paramount mountain, Columbia's lady with the torch, and 20th Century Fox's monumental statue of the number '20th'. All these remain in updated versions, but the British J Arthur Rank studio which is no more had the greatest logo of them all."

At the risk of spoiling some fondly-held illusions, it ought to be added that the impressive screen gong was made of plaster and papier mâché and Richmond mimed his wielding of the hammer to the sound of a small hand-gong being struck offstage!

The third of the USSR's Greco-Roman world champions whose non-appearance was regretted was the heavyweight, Johannes Kotkas, but the Estonian would eventually get his chance at Helsinki four years later at the age of 37 – and would win the gold medal in the most emphatic of fashions by throwing four successive opponents, including the silver-medallist in 4min and the bronze-medallist in 2min 43sec. Kotkas would surely have been the man to beat in 1948, but the winner in his stead was an outstanding wrestler in his own right in the imposing form of the Turk, Ahmet Kireççi, who had been the middleweight bronze-medallist in Berlin in 1936.

With only nine men taking part, Kireççi had a key win by a fall against Tor Nilsson, of Sweden, in the second round and then a points success in his fourth and final bout with Fantoni, of Italy, to decide the title. He beat all of the next three placed competitors.

Greco-Roman light-heavyweight (87kg) result: 1 Karl-Erik Nilsson (Sweden), 2 Kaelpo Gröndahl (Finland), 3 Ibrahim Orari (Egypt), 4 Gyula Kovács (Hungary), 5 Ken Richmond (Great Britain), 6 Erling Lauridsen (Denmark).
The medallists' bouts: Nilsson b Kovács fall, bt Mustafa Çakmak (Turkey) fall, bt Lauridsen pts, bt Richmond fall, bt Orari fall, bt Gröndahl pts. Gröndahl bt Karel Istaz (Belgium) fall, bt Umberto Silvestri (Italy) retired, bt Peter Einziger (Austria) pts, bt Lauridsen fall, lost to Nilsson pts. Orari bt Richmond fall, bt Albin Dannacher (Switzerland) fall, lost to Kovács pts, lost to Nilsson fall.

Greco-Roman heavyweight (unlimited) result: 1 Ahmet Kireççi (Turkey), 2 Tor Nilsson (Sweden), 3 Guido Fantoni (Italy), 4 Taisto Kangasniemi (Finland), 5 József Tarányi (Hungary), 6 Moritz Inderbitzen (Switzerland).
The medallists' bouts: Kireççi bt Inderbitzen fall, bt Nilsson fall, bt Kangasniemi pts, bt Fantoni pts. Nilsson bt Len Pidduck (Great Britain) fall, lost to Kireççi fall, bt Inderbitzen fall, bt Fantoni fall. Fantoni bt Kangasniemi pts, bt József Tarányi (Hungary) fall, lost to Nilsson fall, lost to Kireççi pts.

Turkey had been the most successful nation, winning four freestyle and two Greco-Roman titles. Sweden had won five Greco-Roman titles. The other gold medals had gone to the USA (two), Finland, Hungary and Italy. George MacKenzie gave credit to Turkey's national training programme: "The Turkish victories in the Greco-Roman style were somewhat unexpected for it is freestyle wrestling in Turkey which has always been highly popular, and if its exponents were not greatly skilled the deficiency was well made up by their great strength. 'Strong as a Turk' is an almost proverbial expression, and the Turkish wrestlers at the Empress Hall proved themselves worthy of the saying. Not only were they strong but their technique evidenced the advantage taken of the skilled instructors whose services had been deployed during the preceding two or three years. The condition of the men was magnificent. Never has a better trained team of wrestlers taken part in Olympic contests."

Perhaps never, too, was a team of wrestlers so well received on returning home. The November 1948 issue of *World Sports* carried a splendidly laconic report from its Turkish correspondent, as follows: "Public subscriptions raised considerable funds. Valuable presents poured in, including masses of gold watches and tie pins. Life pensions, furnished houses, all these were prepared and heaped on the victors. The Lord Mayor of Ankara offered every Olympic victor who would choose to live in the Turkish capital a villa as a present. However, a short time after the first frenzy had subsided warning voices were heard mentioning something about the 'amateur law', of which neither the Lord Mayor, nor apparently the Turkish people generally, had ever heard. Very little exact information has been reported about the distribution of the collected tributes, but it can be safely assumed that most of the Olympic medallists will receive some comforting reminder of their triumphs in the Earls Court wrestling events."

The 16 British competitors went back home presumably unannounced to their humble abodes in Bolton, Bradford, Chingford and elsewhere, having between them produced a fifth and a sixth place. In the Greco-Roman events seven of the eight entered had lost their first two bouts by a fall and thus been eliminated at the earliest stage. At freestyle the record was rather better: five wins in 19 bouts, and four of the team had each lasted long enough to take part in their third bouts. George MacKenzie, as one of the team coaches, would have appreciated that it had been a case as much as anything else of "showing the flag", and he would have been delighted to have known that a bronze medal was only four years away.

Chapter 37

IT'S A BRITISH GOLD – BY 14 SECONDS AFTER MORE THAN 95 HOURS!

Yachting. Torbay, South Devon, 3–12 August.

I T WAS AN unlikely connection, but Napoleon could take some of the credit for Olympic yachting being awarded to Torbay on the South Devon coast. Napoleon's activities on the Continent put an end for many years to the leisurely Grand Tour of the European capitals taken as a matter of course by 19th-century English gentry, and so convivial resorts such as Torquay were developed to provide an alternative respite. Even Napoleon himself was a visitor – albeit an unwilling one as a captive aboard the warship, HMS *Bellerophon*, for two days before being sent off to Plymouth and then into exile on the island of St Helena.

The first recorded yacht race in Torbay had taken place in 1811 for "boats of not more than 25 feet in the keel and to carry no more than 60 yards of canvas", while Napoleon was still working up his plans for the next year's march on Moscow. The Royal Torquay Yacht Club was formed in 1875, but one of the early regattas was marred when it was discovered that the first marker-buoy was not in place as the craft responsible for carrying out the duty was manned only by "two boys without orders". An international regatta to celebrate the coronation of King George VI had been held rather more successfully in 1937, and there was every expectation that the Olympic races would also go off to the satisfaction of all.

One of Britain's leading yachting experts, John Scott Hughes, was particularly enthused by the prospect. Writing five months before the Games opened, he provided a good reason as to why the choice had been made of a venue more than 200 miles from London: "Torbay has some special qualities which are not found in combination elsewhere; at any rate, not in British waters. For one thing, it is a splendid expanse of open water, freer than most yachting centres of tide, currents and obstructions of one sort or another which may be turned to helpful advantage by the seaman with local knowledge." Recognising, too, the sociability associated with sailing even at such a serious level, Scott Hughes added meaningfully: "The towns close at hand – Torquay itself, Paignton, Brixham and historic Dartmouth – afford the accommodation and entertainment which visiting yachtsmen would wish to enjoy."

Torquay, however remote from London, had been in the thick of it during the war as a military training centre and had suffered 700 air-raid alerts and considerable bomb damage and fatalities. Yet all these tribulations were not without their less onerous side-effects. The roof of the billiards room at the yachting club had been rendered unsafe, though maybe the greater concern for the members was that rationing caused the supply of whisky to be limited to two single measures or one double per imbiber per day – and not even that on Tuesdays and Fridays.

Five classes were to be raced during the Olympic regatta – International 6-metre, International Dragon, International Star, National Swallow and National Firefly. The largest 6-metre class, for a five-man crew, had been held at every Games since 1908 and won on three successive occasions by Norway (1920–24–28) and by Great Britain in 1936. The three-man Dragon was introduced in 1948 and was to remain an Olympic event until it was discontinued after 1972. The two-man Star had been contested in 1932, won by the USA, and in 1936, won by Germany. The two-man Swallow was also a new event and was not held again after 1948. The one-man Firefly replaced the Finn, which had been held since 1920 and won twice by Holland and once each by Belgium, France and Sweden. The Firefly was a 12ft dinghy and an odd choice because it was actually designed for a two-man crew.

Of the 25 countries which had confirmed entries, the Czechs and Hungarians failed to arrive. The only ones taking part in every class were Argentina, France, Great Britain, Italy, Sweden and the USA, and there were three newcomers to Olympic yachting – Australia, Cuba and Eire – though some of these latter mariners perhaps came more in hope than expectation. It was said of Bob French, the Australian entry in the Firefly event, that he had not seen a boat of this type until he arrived at Torbay. A world championship series for the Star class had been held uninterrupted from 1930, even through the war years, and won on each occasion since 1940 by the USA until the Bahamas pairing of Durward Knowles and Sloan Farrington broke the monopoly in 1947. Knowles and Farrington would represent Great Britain at Torbay as "colonial" recruits in the absence of their homeland having an Olympic Committee, and coupled with the Berlin achievement of a 6-metre gold, a Finn bronze and a Star fourth place, this gave some considerable promise of British success on the Atlantic waters. When the yachting began on 3 August, Britain had yet to win a gold medal in any sport at the 1948 Games.

Extensive trials had been held throughout the summer to select the British representatives. Knowles and Farrington had won four of the five Star-class races held in Torbay and it was understandably proclaimed by *The Times* of the helmsman, Knowles, that "this kind of thing is expected of him" and that he "may be expected to win" the Olympic title. Selected for the Swallow class was one of Britain's most experienced yachtsmen, Stewart Morris, who had been the reserve at the 1936 Games when Peter Scott had won the Finn class bronze. Scott (later Sir Peter Scott, the world-famed naturalist) was in his turn the reserve on this occasion and was to be present at Torbay in his capacity as chairman of the Yacht Racing Association of Great Britain's Olympic Committee. Writing beforehand for *The Sunday Times*, he risked overburdening Morris with expectation in proclaiming that he "has shown such brilliant form that he should win the gold medal with ease".

The qualifying helmsman in the 6-metre class was James Howden Hume, and it is no disrespect to him to suggest that the reserve for this Olympic place would equally well have graced the sylvan waters of the bay, even though he would not have been in his most favoured habitat. Captain GET Eyston was accustomed to a rather greater velocity in his mode of progression, having set three land-speed records in his streamlined car, *Thunderbolt*, culminating in 357.5 m.p.h. on the Bonneville Flats, in Utah, in 1938.

George Eyston was a daredevil sportsman in the grand Victorian tradition; a man of independent means who took up motor racing in 1921 and then speed-boat racing and wrote an autobiography in 1933 entitled *Flat Out*, in which he pronounced: "Motor racing is a man's game, calling for iron nerves and quick action. To those of us who practise it, the starter's flag is a lovely sight and the boom of the maroon in speed boat racing is music ... it would be ridiculous to say that motor racing is not a risky business, but empires have been won because men have taken risks."

The Olympic regatta would comprise seven daily races held on 3–4–5–6 August and then on 10–11–12 August, with the three-day break used for overhauling boats, gear and rigging. The best six results would decide final placings, based on points scored according to what was an apparently complex but logical mathematical formula: $101+1000\log A-1000\log N$, where "101" is the number of points awarded for last place, "A" is the number of boats entered, and "N" is the finishing position of the boat in question. Thus the points for a win in a 6-metre race involving 11 competitors, would be 1,142, and in the Firefly class, where there were 21 competitors, it would be 1,423. This system had been devised by an Austrian scientist/yachtsman and was in use for the first time, and it has to be said that the advantages over a simple 1-to-11 or 1-to-21 method of scoring might not seem obvious to the layman.

Three alternative courses had been set out in the bay, each of eight buoys in a circle, with a ninth buoy in the centre as the starting and finishing point. Races would go off in whichever direction was most to windward and the three most appropriate buoys would be used as the turning points. The approximate distances would be 14 miles (22 kilometres) for the 6-metre and Dragon classes, 10 miles (16 kilometres) for the Star and Swallow, and six miles (10 kilometres) for the Firefly. All five classes raced on each day of competition, and only the Firefly class, close inshore, would be readily visible to spectators. It would not be until the 21st century that the relatively simple idea would be introduced of making the sails into national flags for ready identification.

Age did not seem to wither yachtsmen as it did practitioners of so many other Olympic sports, and among those gathered in Torbay were some distinguished members of the older school. Most notable among them was 59-year-old Ralph Craig, who had won two gold medals 36 years previously in Stockholm but very much as a "landlubber", triumphing in the 100 and 200 metres sprint races on the track. Unfortunately, he remained on the Torquay shoreline as a reserve, and so did not quite complete a highly unusual double, though he had surely been perfectly satisfied with having had the honour of carrying the US flag at the opening ceremony at Wembley. Magnus Konow, aged 60, who would be Norway's helmsman in the 6-metre class, had competed at the London Games of 1908, had also been a champion in 1912 in the 12-metre class, had won again in the 8-metre in 1920, and had placed second to the British in the 6-metre in 1936. Tore Holm, of Sweden, though a mere 50 years old, had two gold medals and a bronze from the Games of 1920, 1928 and 1932, and he would also be a 6-metre helmsman.

Though far removed from Wembley, the yachting competitors enjoyed all their own pomp and ceremony. They paraded through the streets of Torquay behind their national flags, and a 107-man relay brought an Olympic torch to the opening ceremony held in the meadows surrounding the ruins of Torre Abbey, which had been founded in 1196 and would have provided a particularly poignant reminder of the costs of defeat for those members of the Spanish team with a finely tuned sense of history. The last visit to Torre Abbey in any numbers by Spanish seamen had been in far less auspicious circumstances in 1588 when 300 survivors of the routed Armada were imprisoned there.

The Spanish lost again to the British on Olympic waters, but happily their respective ninth and fourth places in the Star class event were not the cause for any sort of punitive repercussions. If the account by John Scott Hughes in the organising committee's report is anything to go by, they all enjoyed themselves hugely. "It is hard to imagine a more beautiful setting than wide Torbay in shadow and sunshine, whose waters were foam-flecked and sparkling with all the shades of blue and green," he wrote appreciatively. "Then, too, there was the prolonged intensity of the racing, which held all in suspense, increasingly unbearable the longer it was prolonged. Up to the last race of the seven days' racing there was no certain winner in any class; in some classes the issue remained in doubt up to the last second of the last minute."

Nowhere was this more apparent than in the Swallow class – and there the tension was even more pronounced because the gold medal for Great Britain's favoured Stewart Morris and his crewman, David Bond, hung entirely on their managing to finish at worst fourth in their final race. This they did, but only by a margin of 14 seconds, having been in 11th place at one stage and causing what the *Daily Telegraph* justifiably described as "desperate anxiety" for their earthbound supporters. Even after the finishing line had apparently been safely crossed, the British pair had to survive a protest made against them by the Italians. It ought to be added, by way of explanation, that protests were literally a matter of course and that there had been as many as 20 a day during the Olympic racing.

The British had seemed assured of a safe passage to gold after placing third, first, third and first again in the opening four races, and at that stage leading by almost 1,000 points – GB 4,034, Portugal 3,085. In the fifth race the Portugese had won by seven seconds from Morris and Bond, and the situation changed dramatically in the sixth race when the British were disqualified after again finishing one place behind Portugal, fifth and sixth. The lead for Morris and Bond going into the last day had been a mere 100 points, 4,980 to 4,880. No gold medals were fought for longer and harder at the 1948 Olympics than those in yachting: the seven races for Morris and Bond lasted in all 95 hours 13 minutes 3 seconds. Yet the *Daily Mail* gave nothing more than the bare results in small print the day after the victory, with not a word of commendation. *The Times* allocated three crisp sentences. The *Manchester Guardian* briefly extolled Morris's "unconcerned consistency".

Morris, then aged 39, had been born in Bromley, in Kent, but was brought up amid the waters of the Norfolk Broads. He went to Trinity College, Cambridge, and his major sailing successes dated back to 1932, when he won the coveted Prince of Wales Cup for International 14ft dinghies on the first of a record 12 occasions. In 1938 he had been the European Finn title-winner in Potsdam. He had served as a commander in the Royal Naval Volunteer Reserve during the war and had been awarded the OBE for his part in the 1944 Normandy landings. He was to be an Olympic reserve again for the 1952 Olympics and continued racing, completing his Prince of Wales Cup sequence in 1965, and serving on many administrative committees, having been a member of the Yacht Racing Association Council since 1935, while managing the family hop-growing business. His 26-year-old crewman, David Bond, had been born in Falmouth, in Cornwall, had served as an aircraftsman in the Royal Air Force during the war, and later became a boat-builder.

Hylton Cleaver wrote of Morris in 1951 that he was "not only Britain's best small boat helmsman but an international yachtsman who had, perhaps, done more than any other Englishman for sailing in the years just before and just after the war". Morris died in 1991 at the age of 81, by which time further Olympic yachting titles had long since been won for Britain in the Flying Dutchman class in 1968 and 1972 and in the Tornado catamaran class in 1976. Rodney Pattisson's two gold medals in 1968 and 1972 and a silver in 1976 would make him Britain's most successful Olympic yachtsman.

The Portugese silver-medallists were the Bello brothers, who had been born in Portuguese East Africa, which was to become independent as Mozambique in 1975. They were sailing in a borrowed British boat. Portugal had never won an Olympic title in any sport at the Olympic Games and this was the first silver medal for the country, having previously won bronze medals in 1924 and 1928, with a third to come from the 1948 Games when the following year Sweden was disqualified from the equestrian team dressage event which had been held three days before the yachting finished.

As Great Britain's Star class crew of Bahamians, Knowles and Farrington, had started the Olympic regatta with as much faith placed in them by their expert compatriots as there had been in Morris and Bond, the disappointed reaction by John Scott Hughes that their mere second place to Italy on the opening day was "one of the main surprises" is perhaps understandable. The Italian helmsman, Straulino, had been born on the island of Lošinj, off the coast of what is now Croatia.

Though a placing of second again to the USA on day two seemed promising enough, with the overall lead being shared with the Americans, the British performance fell away after that. After four races the Americans led by a distance, 4,421pts to Great Britain's 3,342, and then the chance of a medal of any kind went adrift when the Britons were disqualified in the sixth race and lost their mast on the final day. The US partnership of a 56-year-old lawyer, Paul Smart, and his 23-year-old son, Hilary, won with ease, from another father-and-son crew from Cuba, whose medal was the first for their country in any Games sport since 1904, and there would not be another until 1964. Great Britain placed fourth

---

Swallow class results (each day's race positions in brackets after the points scores; disq disqualified, dnf did not finish, dns did not start)1 Great Britain (Stewart Morris, helmsman, David Bond) sailing *Swift* 5,625pts (3, 1, 3, 1, 2, disq, 4), 2 Portugal (Duarte de Almeida Bello, helmsman, Fernando Pinto Coelho Bello) *Symphony* 5,579 (1, 4, 4, 5, 1, 5, 1), 3 USA (Lockwood "Woody" Pirie, helmsman, Owen Torry) *Margaret* 4,352 (5, 9, 5, 3, 11, 1, 2), 4 Sweden (Stig Hedberg, helmsman, Lars Matton) *Chance* 3,342 (2, 3, 14, 8, 4, 12, 6), 5 Denmark (Johan Rathje, helmsman, Naali Petersen) *No Name* 2,935 (8, 7, 1, 9, 10, 7, 12), 6 Italy (Dario Salata, helmsman, Achille Roncoroni) *Enotria* 2,893 (12, 6, 10, 2, 9, 4, 9), 7 Canada (John Robertson, helmsman, Richard Townsend) *Scaup* 2,807 (7, 2, 2, 11, 14, disq, 11), 8 Norway (Øivind Christensen, helmsman, Knut Bengtson) *Nora* 2,768 (4, 10, 12, 6, 6, 3, 13), 9 France (Jacques Baptise Lebrun, helmsman, Henri Perrissol) *Red Indian* 2,729 (6, 5, 11, 10, 3, 9, 7), 10 Brazil (Vitorio Walter dos Reis Ferraz, helmsman, Carlos Rodolpho Borchers) *Andorinha* 2,630 (9, 11, 9, 12, 8, 2, 5), 11 Holland (Willem de Vries Lentsch, helmsman, Philippus Keegstra) *St Margriet* 2,494 (dnf, 13, 6, 4, 13, 8, 3), 12 Uruguay (Carlos Alberto Saez, helmsman, Juan Bidegaray Pons) *Nortazo* 2,208 (10, 8, 7, 7, 12, 6, 8), 13 Eire (Alf Delany, helmsman, Hugh Allen) *The Cloud* 1,500 (dnf, 12, 8, 13, 5, 11, 14), 14 Argentina (Gastón Gustavo Cibert, helmsman, Silvio Merlo) *Antares* 1,336 (11, 14, 13, dnf, 7, 10, 10).

– colloquially known as the "chocolate medal" on dry land, and so maybe the "sponge medal" on water.

The achievements of Knowles and Farrington, who were both born in Nassau, in the Bahamas, inspired the setting-up of the Bahamas Olympic Association in 1952, and they represented their home country in subsequent Games, placing fifth that year and winning the bronze in 1956 – the first ever Olympic medal for their country. Knowles persevered and won the gold in 1964, with Cecil Cooke as his crewman, and then was fifth again in 1968, partnered by his brother Percival ... and simply kept on sailing. He eventually competed in eight Olympic celebrations from 1948 to 1988, and was just short of his 71st birthday – regarded probably as the oldest Olympic yachtsman ever – on his final appearance. As Sir Durward Knowles, he has continued to play a major part in yachting administration and to contribute enormously to public and philanthropic causes in the Bahamas into the 21st century.

The British representative in the Firefly class was Group Captain AWB McDonald, and as this type of boat was a British innovation it seemed that there was a very reasonable chance of a medal for the sea-going RAF officer. Arthur McDonald had been born in Antigua, in the West Indies, where his father was a doctor, and had joined the RAF in 1924, serving during the war as air defence commander in Ceylon and then with responsibility for air officer training throughout South-East Asia. He was to eventually rise to the rank of Air Marshal in 1958. There were 21 Firefly entries, the largest for any single class at Torbay, and after four races the Swede, Rickard Sarby, seemed to be in command, having won twice and accumulated 3,944pts for a substantial lead. In second place was Ralph Evans, of the USA, at 2,846 and close behind in third was Paul McLaughlin, of Canada, at 2,835. Yet 11 different countries had occupied top-

---

Star class results: 1 USA (Paul Smart, helmsman, Hilary Smart) *Hilarius* 5,828pts (4, 1, 2, 1, 3, disq, 6), 2 Cuba (Carlos de Cardenas, helmsman, Carlos de Cardenas Jr) *Kurush III* 4,849 (7, 7, 7, 2, 7, 1, 2), 3 Holland (Adriaan Maas, helmsman, Edward Stutterheim) *Starita* 4,731 (3, 5, 5, 3, 4, 2, 7), 4 Great Britain (Durward Knowles, helmsman, Sloan Farrington) *Gem II* 4,372 (2, 2, 6, 4, 2, disq, dnf), 5 Italy (Agostino Straulino, helmsman, Nicolo Rode) *Legionario* 4,370 (1, 3, 3, disq, 1, disq, dnf), 6 Portugal (Joaquim Mascarenhas Finza, helmsman, Julio Leite Gourinho) *Espadarte* 4,292 (11, 6, 1, 5, 12, 5, 3), 7 Australia (Alexander Jock Sturrock, helmsman, Len Fenton) *Moorina* 3,828 (dnf, 4, 15, 6, 10, 4, 1), 8 Canada (Bill Gooderham, helmsman, Gerald Fairhead) *Ariel* 2,635 (9, 15, 4, 14, 8, 6, 10), 9 Spain (José Maria Alonso Allende y Allende, helmsman, Juan Manuel Alonso Allende y Allende) *Galerna* 2,564 (15, 8, 16, 10, 5, 7, 8), 10 Greece (Gevrilos Kalambokidis, helmsman, Khristofor Carolou, Kharalambos Potamianos, Nikolaos Vlangalis) *Nephos* I 2,532 (8, 13, 9, 12, 11, 9, 4), 11 France (Yves Lorion, helmsman, Jean Peytel) *Aloha II* 2,515 (12, 9, 8, 8, 6, 3, dnf), 12 Finland (René Nyman, helmsman, Christian Ilmoni) *Lucky Star* 2,058 (13, 12, 13, 13, 9, 11, 5), 13 Austria (George Obermüller, helmsman, Hans Schachinger) *Donar III* 1,661 (10, 16, 14, 15, 15, 8, 9), 14 Brazil (João José Bracony, helmsman, Carlos Melo Bittencourt Filho) *Buscape II* 1,644 (16, 14, 11, 11, 14, 10, 11), 15 Switzerland (Hans Bryner, helmsman, Kurt Bryner) *Ali Baba II* 1,610 (6, 10, 12, 9, disq, dnf, dns), 16 Argentina (Jorge Piacentini, helmsman, Angel Carrasco) *Acturus* 1,550 (14, 11, 10, 7, 13, dnf, dns), 17 Sweden (Bengt Melin, helmsman, Yngve Engkvist) *Lotta IV* 888 (5, dns, 17, 16, disq, dnf, dns). Note: the names of all four Greek yachtsmen appear in the official list published by the Games organising committee of those who actually took part, as opposed to those entered. So it must be presumed that they all competed in at least one race each.

three positions on various days – Belgium, Canada, Denmark, Finland, France, Great Britain, Italy, Sweden, Switzerland, Uruguay and the USA – and so the issue was still wide open.

When racing was resumed after the three-day break the weather conditions particularly affected the Firefly competitors, as was explained by John Scott Hughes in the *World Sports* official report: "The wind was of good sailing strength, although not always reliable in direction. The main consequence of this was, of course, a great fluctuation of fortunes. Especially true was this in the single-handed event. Indeed, so numerous were the mis-chances that it is not improbable that of each of the 21 competitors it might be claimed that at one time or another he led the fleet." In the end it was Evans who won from McLaughlin, and the major victim of the day was Sarby, who came in fourth but was disqualified. Evans's winning time was 13 hours 36 minutes 14 seconds, and so close was the competition that the 20th and last finisher from Spain crossed the line only 4 minutes 4 seconds later.

The penultimate day's race was won by Paul Elvström, of Denmark, who thus moved into fourth place overall, but the convincing leader was still Evans, as the scores showed: USA 4,993, Sweden 4,326, Holland 4,275, Denmark 4,120, Canada 3,975. Great Britain's Group Captain was now out of the medal reckoning, and it had been a long, hard day for the Spaniard, who shipped so much water that he eventually capsized, and despite all his efforts he could not right the craft.

The 20-year-old Dane won the final race by more than three minutes to take the gold medal, and the consolation in years to come for the American who finished fifth and thus had to settle for silver would be that he had been beaten by a man destined to become the greatest of all Olympic sailors. Elvström was to win the Firefly class again in 1952, 1956 and 1960. Of the 27 Olympic races he contested in those years he was first in 14 and was in the leading six in nine others. He continued competing at the Games until 1988, and on the last two occasions partnered his daughter Trine in the Tornado event. He also won 14 world titles in seven different classes, financially supporting his competitive career by a successful sail-making business which he set up in 1954, and was still racing beyond his 70th birthday.

No one could possibly have foreseen all this tidal wave of honours from a glance at the results for the opening race of the 1948 Games. Of the 21 starters the only one not to complete the course had been Elvström. He told an interviewer many years later that the reason for his retirement that day was because he was upset by an argument which he had during the race with a Finnish opponent, and only when he got to shore did he resolve to do better the next day. This might have confirmed the misgivings of the Danish selectors who had at first been reluctant to send Elvström to Torbay because he spoke no English, and then when they relented they apparently told him, in Elvström's own recollection, "If you will not be last, we will be happy."

He had won the Danish trials in a boat of the correct Olympic design built in their spare time by English engineers working on a bridge project in Denmark.

Elvström shares the record of eight Olympic participations with his fellow Torbay yachtsmen, Sir Durward Knowles and Magnus Konow, and 1948 is a particularly productive year for Olympians of exceptional longevity. Of the four others who have also taken part in eight Games three competed in 1948 – the d'Inzeo brothers from Italy in equestrianism and Ivan Osiier, also from Denmark, in fencing. Osiier, like Konow, had first competed in 1908, and so the Danish team of 1948 contained three members who between them would span 80 years of the Olympics. The one exception from a later era, incidentally, is another yachtsman, Hubert Raudaschl, of Austria, who competed in every Games from 1964 to 1992.

The entries for the larger 6-metres and Dragon classes were much fewer – 11 and 12 respectively. Defending Great Britain's title in the 6-metre racing was James Howden Hume, and the Norwegian and Swedish yachts, both with immensely experienced helmsmen, could be seen as obvious main rivals. The first day's result revived memories of Berlin 12 years before because the Belgians winners were sailing the same yacht in which the British had previously won the gold. One of the most remarkable achievements of the entire Torbay regatta was the second place of the landlocked Swiss. Great Britain finished seventh. None of these countries, though, sustained any real medal challenge as the USA, Argentina and Sweden more or less took charge, winning all the remaining races between them.

After five days Argentina led Sweden by 46pts and the USA by 250 – in yachting terms, a neck-and-neck (or should that be "bow-to-bow"?) struggle. The USA won the sixth race from Norway and Great Britain, with Sweden disqualified and Argentina fourth; so that on the last day the Americans started with an advantage of 252pts. Almost 13½ hours' sailing served to separate the two by a mere 19 seconds, and Argentina's victory was not enough to take the gold. By finishing second the USA won overall, but Norway was only a further 21 seconds behind, and had the American yacht finished third then their gold would have been won by only 176pts.

Firefly class result: 1 Paul Elvström (Denmark) 5,543pts (dnf, 6, 3, 12, 5, 1, 1), 2 Ralph Evans (USA) 5,408 (2, 3, 13, 10, 1, 5, 5), 3 Jacobus de Jong (Holland) 5,204 (6, 5, 17, 4, 3, 3, 2), 4 Rickard Sarby (Sweden) 4,603 (8, 1, 7, 1, disq, 11, 14), 5 Paul McLaughlin (Canada) 4,535 (5, 9, 8, 2, 2, disq, 7), 6 Felix Sienra Castellanos (Uruguay) 4,079 (13, 2, 5, 9, 10, 9, 4), 7 Jean-Jacques Herbulot (France) 4,068 (1, 7, 11, 5, 12, 2, 16), 8 Filip van der Haegen (Belgium) 3,660 (3, 14, 15, 6, 6, 4, 15), 9 Arthur McDonald (Great Britain) 3,456 (10, 4, 18, 3, 7, 8, dnf), 10 Albert Oswald (Switzerland) 2,915 (14, 17, 1, 18, 18, 13, 8), 11 Wolfgang Richter (Brazil) 2,904 (7, dnf, 6, 20, 4, 15, 9), 12 Morits Skaugen (Norway) 2,888 (19, 13, 9, 14, 14, 7, 3), 13 João Miguel Tito (Portugal) 2,603 (15, 10, 10, 8, 8, 14, 11), 14 Livio Spanghero (Italy) 2,410 (17, 15, 4, 11, 11, 17, 12), 15 Eric Palmgren (Finland) 2,396 (11, dnf, 2, dnf, 15, 6, dnf), 16 Jimmy Mooney (Eire) 2,342 (4, 8, 14, 16, 13, 18, dnf), 17 Jorge Emilio Brauer (Argentina) 2,276 (16, dnf, 12, 7, dnf, 10, 6), 18 Bob French (Australia) 2,005 (18, 11, 19, 17, 9, 12, 10), 19 José Luis Allende y Garcia Baxter (Spain) 1,829 (9, 12, 16, 13, 19, dnf, 13), 20 Herbert McWilliams (South Africa) 1,278 (12, 16, dnf, 15, 16, 16, dnf), 21 Harald von Musil (Austria) 627 (20, dnf, dnf, 19, 17, 19, dnf). Note: the organising committee official report does not list the names of the Firefly dinghies.

The US helmsman, Herman Whiton, who was to win the gold again in 1952, was one of the pioneers of US Olympic yachting, having first competed at the Games in 1928, and among his numerous victories over the years had been a pre-war one in Germany which had earned him the dubious honour of holding the "Adolf Hitler Cup". His refusal to give the Nazi salute at the victory ceremony on that occasion had caused the German organisers to keep the trophy. After his 1948 Olympic win, he sold his yacht to Magnus Konow, on condition that he could charter it back for the next Games. Ironically, a Norwegian crew, though not including Konow, was second in 1952.

Scarcely could the Dragon class have been more finely balanced after four races as Norway and Sweden were the joint leaders with 3,340pts. The Norwegians had actually led the Swedes across the line in three of those races, winning two, but a 12th place on day three cost them a clear lead. Yet the intensely exciting fifth day's racing left the overall position even more fraught. Great Britain won after 14 hours 52 minutes and 10 seconds of sailing, and the race was so close that Norway, Sweden and Denmark all came across the finishing line within the next 53 seconds ... but then Norway and Sweden were disqualified, and so with two days remaining the GB crew now led with 3,365pts, with Norway and Sweden still on 3,340.

The British and the Swedes slipped back on the sixth day, ninth and 12th respectively, and Norway's third place that day and again the next was enough for the gold. An odd feature of this class was that the gold- and silver-medallists each had a last place on their record. The very same Norwegian trio was to win again in Helsinki in 1952, and other medallists were to follow suit: Folke Bohlin, of Sweden, won gold in 1956 and Ole Berntsen, of Denmark, won gold in 1960.

The final races had been, according to John Scott Hughes in the British Olympic Association report, "a day of glorious victories and no less glorious defeats ... never did a more glorious day's sport gladden the heart of man". The Torbay setting, enthused *The Times*, had been "an arena of wonderful beauty, whose waters if not wine dark were foam flecked and sunlit and sparkling with all shades of blue and green". Then the medals were presented, the speeches made. The Olympic flame flickered out. The yachtsmen and the crowd linked hands to sing "Auld Lang Syne". The battleships, *Anson* and *George V* steamed slowly away, alongside the aircraft carrier, *Victorious*, and the visiting Belgian, French and American destroyers. One of Britain's "little ships" had performed the most daring deeds of competitiveness, just as others of its kind had carried out their miraculous errands of mercy across the English Channel to the shores of Dunkirk and back eight years before.

6-metre class result: 1 USA (Herman Whiton [helmsman], Alfred Loomis, Michael Mooney, James Smith Jr, James Weekes) *Llanoria* 5,472pts (4, 1, 1, 3, 8, 1, 2), 2 Argentina (Enrique Corrado Sieburger [helmsman], Emilio Homps, Rodolfo Rivademar, Rufino Rodriguez de la Torre, Julio Christian Sieburger) *Djinn* 5,120 (3, 3, 3, 2, 1, 4, 1), 3 Sweden (Tore Holm [helmsman], Karl Ameln, Martin Hindorff, Torsten Lord, Gösta Salén) *Ali Baba II* 4,033 (5, 2, 2, 1, 3, disq, 11), 4 Norway (Magnus Konow [helmsman], Anders Evensen, Ragnar Hargreaves, Lars Schage Musaeus, Häkon Solem) *Apache* 3,217 (8, dnf, 9, 5, 2, 2, 3), 5 Great Britain (James Howden Hume [helmsman], Brian Hardie, Henry Hardie, James Douglas Howden Hume, Harry Hunter) *Johan* 2,889 (7, 4, 8, 7, 4, 3, 4), 6 Belgium (Ludovic Franck [helmsman], Emile Hayoit, Willy Huybrechts, Henri van Riel, Willy van Rompaey) *Lalage* 2,752 (1, 8, 11, 9, 5, 7, 5), 7 Switzerland (Henri Copponex [helmsman], André Firmenich, Louis Noverraz, Charles Stern, Marcel Stern) *Ylliam VII* 2,549 (2, 6, 7, 4, 9, 6, 10), 8 Italy (Giovanni Reggio [helmsman], Giorgio Audizio, Renato Costentino, Giuseppe Croce, Gennaro de Luca, Enrico Poggi, Luigi Mino Poggi) *Ciocca II* 2,099 (6, dnf, 5, 6, 7, 5, 9), 9 Finland (Ernst Westerlund [helmsman], Rote Hellström, Ragnar Jansson, Adolf Konto, Rolf Turkka, Valo Urho) *Raili* 1,691 (9, 7, 10, 8, 6, 8, 6), 10 Denmark (Troels La Cour [helmsman], Bruno Clausen, Svend Valdemar Iversen, René La Cour, Hans Aurelius Sørensen) *Morena* 1,648 (10, 5, 4, 11, 10, 10, 8), 11 France (Albert Cadot [helmsman], Jean Castel, Claude Desouches, Robert Lacarrièrre, François Laverne) *La Bandera* 1,280 (11, 9, 6, 10, 11, 9, 7).

Dragon class result: 1 Norway (Thor Thorvaldsen [helmsman]. Sigve Lie, Häkon Barfod) *Pan* 4,746pts (1, 2, 12, 1, disq, 3, 3), 2 Sweden (Folke Bohlin [helmsman], Hugo Johnson, Gösta Brodin) *Slaghoken* 4,621 (2, 3, 2, 2, disq, 12, 1), 3 Denmark (William Berntsen [helmsman], Ole Berntsen, Klaus Baess) *Snap* 4,223 (3, 4, 3, 5, 2, 5, 2), 4 Great Britain (William Strain [helmsman], George Brown, James Wallace) *Ceres II* 3,943 (7, 7, 1, 7, 1, 9, 4), 5 Italy (Giuseppe Canessa [helmsman], Bruno Bianchi, Luigi De Manincor) *Ausonia* 3,366 (9, 8, 4, 3, 6, 1, dnf), 6 Finland (Rainer Packälen [helmsman], Niilo Orama, Aatos Hirvisalo) *Vinha* 3,057 (4, 1, 11, 6, 4, 11, 10), 7 Argentina (Roberto Guillermo Sieburger [helmsman], Jorge Alberto Sálas, Jorge Alberto del Rio Sálas) *Pampero* 2,843 (6, 5, 8, 4, 10, 2, dnf), 8 Holland (Cornelis Jonker [helmsman], Abraham Dudok van Heel, Willem van Duyl) *Joy* 2,508 (5, 6, 7, 11, 9, 4, 7), 9 Portugal (João Felix da Silva Capucho [helmsman], Antonio Guedes de Herédia, Henrique Reis Goucho Sallaty) *Argus* 2,123 (11, 9, 6, 8, 8, 6, 5), 10 France (Marcel de Kerviler [helmsman], Jean Frain de la Gaulayrie) *Allegro* 1,743 (10, 11, 10, 9, 3, 8, 8), 11 USA (Henry Duys Jr [helmsman], Richard Jessup, Julian Roosevelt) *Rhythm* 1,621 (8, 10, 5, 12, 7, 10, 6), 12 Belgium (Albert Huybrechts [helmsman], Roger Anciaux, Charles Delfosse, Georges Hellebuyck, Jacques Lauwerys, Jacques Lippens) *Dolfijn* 1,549 (12, dnf, 9, 10, 5, 7, 9). Note: five Belgian crewmen are listed among the entries and all also appear in the Belgian National Olympic Committee's official list of Olympic participants. It must be assumed that all took part on one day or more.

Chapter 38

GREAT DAYS, GREAT NIGHTS FOR THE 'ENEMIES OF NONSENSE'

THE CLOSING CEREMONY of the 1948 Olympic Games which followed on after the completion of the Prix des Nations showjumping event at the Empire Stadium needs no detailed description. These affairs in their 21st-century guise, with all their orchestrated cavortings and trumpetings, are familiar to millions of television viewers – rather too familiar, some might say; those who decry the nationalistic fervour and wonder whether the extrovert passion and emotion of the young competitors will ever temper the opportunism and connivance of their political masters, as ready to bask in the reflected glory of an Olympic success as they are to exploit the Games for easy propaganda gestures.

Of course, at Wembley six decades ago it was rather different. The simplicity of the occasion, banishing all remembrance of Nazi Berlin in 1936, and the knowledge among the tens of thousands of spectators, the phalanx of officials and dignitaries, and the few remaining competitors who had not yet already made their way home, that the Games were over and that they had gone well was enough to satisfy most needs in a less sophisticated age.

The ritual was observed. The flame was extinguished and the Olympic flag passed on to the denizens of Helsinki for raising again to the masthead in four years' time. The British press was, almost to a man, enthusiastic, even euphoric, about what they had witnessed during the previous fortnight, and such disputes as there had been were mostly – and justifiably – relegated to a footnote.

"There was a dignity in this simple ceremony as there had been a dignity since the Games opened ... magnificent in sportsmanship, superb in athletic performance, and admirable in organisation, these Games will pass into a high place in sporting history." – *David Divine, Sunday Times.*

"It is the guests as much as the hosts who make a party, but we may well feel proud of our share in the wonderful success of the Olympic Games of 1948. Incidents, fortunate or otherwise, there were many, just as there doubtless are in a diocesan conference or a spelling bee. If boxing judges had to be dismissed, it has happened before, and indeed a boxing tournament without a disputed decision is like 'A Christmas Carol' without Scrooge. Incidents are all part of the Games, and the only incident one can hardly deplore in the Games is the rain." – *Michael Melford, The Observer.*

"We can take some credit also for having entered a team for every event, including basketball and some even more recondite contests. And all this we have done quietly, with none of the nationalistic ostentation which travestied the Olympic spirit in Berlin. We can no longer expect to keep our early lead in world athletics, but we can feel modest pride that the London Games have been one of the most successful of these festivals of sport and quite the most harmonious and sensible in temper. May we not claim to be leading contenders for the honourable title, Enemies of Nonsense?" – *A leader writer, The Observer.*

"On the athletic track, as on the cricket field, we have in these times to content ourselves with being good losers, taking what consolation we can from those Olympic trophies which we won last week on the river and the sea. But our recent visitors would, it is believed, readily grant us laurels for the successful organisation of the Games and the way in which Britain's resourcefulness overcame those obvious material difficulties which faced us. Already it may be written that the experience of reviving the Games within three years of a world convulsion, and of making London the host city, has fulfilled the hopes of those who greatly dared." – *A leader writer, Daily Telegraph.*

"Great days, great nights – a fortnight of them. We shall think of them, you and I, many times in the years to come. And in our memories we can rightly include the satisfaction of a task well done. Great Britain has organised an Olympic Games which, by the verdict of the world, is acknowledged the greatest of all Olympics." – *Denzil Batchelor, World Sports.*

"There are plenty of lessons, easy to read. For a nation of players at games we did uncommonly well. We got enough placings to prove with proper coaching and facilities and food – never mind what the apologists say, our athletes don't eat enough – we can match the best. There are not enough class tracks, pools and coaches in the country, and until there are we shall continue to be seconds and thirds." – *John Macadam, Daily Express.*

"We did not do too badly." – *An editorial writer, The Listener.*

There was, though, at least one authoritatively contrary view:

"I am not so much against the Games as they were originally meant to be as I am against the form in which they now take place. Times change, and I consider they lead nowadays to more ill-feeling than friendship. In any case, I was in 1948 against our own participation in world championships, for the simple reason that it does no country any good rarely if ever to win, and that no matter how good a grace one shows in losing there comes a time when to lose persistently has a very bad effect on one's outlook upon, and enjoyment of, a game ... the reason we competed under a handicap was not only that ever since the war we have been short of food, homes and money – which is quite enough in itself – but that we persist in regarding ourselves as the only ones in step. We know that nearly every other country taking part is semi-professional, heavily subsidised by its government, and as often as not will create an uproar if defeated. But in our own quiet, phlegmatic, insular and almost arrogant way we still pursue our own ideals. No sport is subsidised. Only those who can afford to meet their own expenses can attain championship rank. We start too late to get ready, and we are obsessed by the belief that to win is not the object of taking part." – *Hylton Cleaver, Sporting Rhapsody, 1951.*

And:

"It is the ardent desire of the Finnish people that at least 64 nations, including Russia, Bulgaria, Rumania, Germany and Japan, will compete in Helsinki in 1952." – *Erik von Frenckell, President & Chairman, 1952 Olympic Games Organising Committee, writing in May 1949.*

Chapter 39

WARRIORS AND AMBASSADORS: HOW THE OLYMPIC BATTLE WOULD BE WON

The Wembley aftermath: the rise of sport in the USSR

N EVER HAD ANY country made such an impressive Olympic debut. The team from the Union of Soviet Socialist Republics at the Helsinki Olympic Games of 1952 accumulated 71 medals, which ranked second only to the USA's total of 76. The extent of the Soviet success was no great surprise and the long-term objective was well enough known – to defeat the Americans in the Olympic "war" of ideology. By 1956 a battle was already won, as if by some decisive basketball score: USSR 98 medals, USA 74, at the Melbourne Games.

"Nil to 71" between 1948 and 1952 is an impressive enough advance in all conscience, even when allowance is made for what the USSR might have won at the London Olympics, had they entered. A reasonable assessment of the various sports suggests that they could have taken 20 to 25 medals in 1948 – as many as ten in athletics alone, and others in basketball, gymnastics, rowing, shooting, weightlifting and wrestling. That tally would have earned a respectable sixth or seventh place in the medal rankings, but it was dominance, not respectability, which was the Soviet benchmark, and so the decision was made to watch and wait for another four years.

It is tempting when making a study of any of the Olympic Games celebrations since the modern revival in 1896 to talk of significant changes from one Games to the next, of unprecedented political or sociological effects, of "the end of an era", but there is perhaps no Olympiad – in its literal sense, it means the time elapsing between each Games – which justifies that claim more than the years 1949, 1950 and 1951. It was not only the USSR which made such a significant impact in 1952. So, too, did other Eastern European countries where state aid for sport had become a matter of major national policy: Hungary was third in the 1952 table (42 medals) and Czechoslovakia sixth (13).

The most dramatically successful sports for the Soviet Union in Helsinki were gymnastics and wrestling. Their gymnasts more or less swept the board; four individual golds and the team gold for the men; three individual golds and the team gold for the women. In the women's vault the first six were Kalinchuk, Gorokhovskaya, Minaycheva, Dshugeli, Urbanovich and Bocharyeva, all from the USSR, and the only reason that there weren't more of their team-mates immediately behind them was that each nation was restricted to six competitors, and therefore a Swedish entrant was a distant seventh. Of the 16 Soviet wrestlers sent to Helsinki, six won gold, two silver, two bronze, and four others were each placed fourth. The seven weightlifters from the USSR won three gold, three silver and a bronze between them.

The arrival of Soviet track and field athletes was exemplified by the result of the Helsinki women's discus: one-two-three for Romashkova first, Bagryantseva second and Dumbadze, who should have won in 1948, third. The women won two gold, four silver and five bronze in the nine events, failing to get medals only in the 100 metres and the 4x100 metres relay (and in the latter case by merely 1/100th of a second). The men won four silvers and a bronze and had fourteen other top-six placings in 16 different events, including six fourth places. The US women won only one medal – gold in the 4x100 metres relay – but the achievements of the Soviet men did not in any way, of course, compare with the Americans, who won fourteen gold, ten silver and six bronze.

In basketball, the USSR team were the silver-medallists to the USA. The Soviet boxers won two silvers and four bronzes, ranking second to the USA, whose five winners included a 17-year-old Floyd Patterson, the future world heavyweight champion. In shooting, only Norway, with two golds, improved on the USSR's gold, silver and two bronzes. Rowing brought a Soviet gold and a silver, as only the USA won more than one title. In canoeing, still dominated by Finland and Sweden, there was a bronze medal and a fourth place for the USSR. In the modern pentathlon an individual placed fourth and the team fifth.

There were also lesser performances in other sports. The footballers lost to the eventual silver-medallists, Yugoslavia, but only in a replay after a 5-5 draw. No swimmer did better than sixth, though there were four divers in top-six placings, bettered only by the USA. The water polo team was seventh. The lone finisher in the cycle road-race was 40th. None of the fencers reached the semi-finals. The best position in the equestrian events was tenth and in the yachting was twelfth. No team was entered in the hockey. Yet it was mostly just a matter of time. In 1956 the USSR won the football tournament and had bronze medals in fencing, swimming and water polo. In 1960 a Soviet rider won the cycle road-race.

This surge of success had, of course, come about only as a result of an immense input of facilities and expertise. It did not happen overnight, as there was already a very well-established sporting infrastructure in the USSR by the 1930s. Many national sporting bodies had been established and events organised in Czarist times from the latter part of the 19th-century onwards, including fencing in 1860, rowing in 1864, gymnastics in 1881, cycling in 1883, weightlifting in 1885, athletics in 1888, football and wrestling in 1897, boxing in 1898, then basketball in 1906 and handball in 1909. Yachting could be traced back to the formation of a club in 1718 under the patronage of Peter the Great.

At the 1908 Olympics in London, silver medals were won for Russia in Greco-Roman wrestling by Nikolay Orlov at lightweight and Aleksandr Petrov at heavyweight and a gold medal in ice figure-skating by Nikolay Panin. At the 1912 Games Martin Klein was the silver-medallist in the Greco-Roman middleweight wrestling division but is more memorably listed in the record books for his qualifying bout with a Finn which lasted eleven hours 40 minutes, leaving Klein understandably too exhausted to contest the final. There were three further medals at those Games in pistol and clay-pigeon shooting and in yachting, but all this achievement still did not add up to a very impressive tally for a country of such size and resources. Neighbouring Finland, tiny by comparison, and at that time a subjugated part of the Russian Empire, won 26 medals at those Games.

Even though the country was still in turmoil after the 1917 Revolution, national championships for weightlifting were established under the new Soviet Communist regime as early as the following year, for men's athletics in 1920, men's swimming in 1921, and women's athletics and swimming in 1922. Over the next five years football, shooting, cycling, basketball, boxing, water polo, canoeing, fencing, rowing, gymnastics and yachting were each in turn put on a proper national footing.

Facts and figures for athletics in the 1920s and 1930s are easy to come by, thanks to the diligent retrospective work of a worldwide fraternity of statisticians and historians whose interests know no artificial boundaries, and in particular a British enthusiast, Richard Hymans, who has produced the definitive work on the subject. The data which has been collected shows that there were some Soviet athletes approaching world class in the interwar years – but not very many. At the first national championships for men in 1920 the standards sufficient to win were very ordinary, such as 11.6sec for 100 metres, 4min 28.5sec for 1500 metres, 37min 32.5sec for 10,000 metres, 1.60m in the high jump and 41.10m in the javelin. Women's titles in 1922 were achieved with performances as derisory as 1min 10.4sec for 400 metres, 4.66m for the long jump and 16.38m (!) for the discus. Things could surely only get better.

By 1928, when the Olympics were held in Amsterdam, there were some perfectly capable winners of Soviet athletics titles. Timofey Korniyenko ran 10.9sec for 100 metres and 22.0sec for 200 metres. One of the future great "Flying Finns", Volmari Iso-Hollo, was invited as a guest and won the 5000 metres but was beaten at 10,000 metres. The javelin produced a throw of 61.77m by Anatoliy Reshetnikov, who had been competing in unchallenged obscurity ever since 1922. Not much, if any, of this information would have filtered through to the West at the time, but Reshetnikov's effort could have got him eighth place at the Olympics and so would have been regarded with some respect.

During the 1930s there were athletes who would in all likelihood have achieved something similar at the Olympics, had they been given the chance. The Znamenskiy brothers, Syerafim and Georgiy, were the eighth and ninth fastest 10,000 metres runners in the world in 1939, headed only by five Finns, a Swede and a Hungarian, and were "extensively publicised heroes who travelled widely and were lionized wherever they went", according to the eminent US expert on Soviet sport, Robert Edelman. That same year the best pole vaulter outside the USA was the remarkable Nikolay Ozolin, who had won his first USSR national title in 1928 and would continue to be champion most years until 1950.

Together with the British, but, of course, in isolation from them, Soviet women were the enterprising pioneers at the non-Olympic middle-distance events, 800 and 1500 metres; the 800 at the 1938 USSR championships had been run by Yevdokiya Vasilyeva in 2min 15.3sec, well inside the British-held world record, and this performance was equalled by Kseniya Shilo at the 1940 championships. In the women's field events, Nina Dumbadze had already twice beaten the official world record in the discus throw in 1939, and there were three shot-putters, three more discus-throwers and three javelin-throwers all among the leading ten in the world that year.

However, as there was no attempt to set up a National Olympic Committee, which was the prerequisite for competitors to be sent to the Games, it was not readily apparent to the Western world what sort of standards were being achieved in other sports. There were very little international ventures of any kind by Soviet sportsmen and sportswomen, and performances of the era are thus largely shrouded in mystery and doubt. In a study of sport behind the Iron Curtain published in 1980, Simon Freeman and Roger Boyes, who were respectively a sports feature writer and a political correspondent specialising in Communist affairs, pointed out that such limited contacts as took place adhered to a specific agenda: "In international terms the Communists used sport to seal links with foreign workers' movements, rather than truly pit their skills against Western competition. Soccer was the main tool in this; it did not need much equipment and was easily organised around local factory clubs."

The first such football match was in Moscow in 1922 when a Finnish team was beaten 7-1, and there were other fixtures with trade-union sides from France, Germany, Norway and Poland, but the only country to maintain regular links at a national level in the game was Turkey, whose team visited Moscow in 1924 and on four further occasions over the next twelve years. After the non-aggression pact agreed by Germany and the Soviet Union in 1939, there was a series of exchanges of sports teams, and according to Freeman and Boyes, "More sports contests were organised between German and Russian sportsmen during 1940 than between the USSR and the rest of the world in all of the years since the 1917 Revolution". Hitler's invasion of Soviet territory the following year put an end to all that false bonhomie.

A history of sport in the USSR published in Moscow in 1988 refers enigmatically to the fact that in swimming competition during the 1930s "Semyón Boychenko and Leonid Meshkov beat official world records; Meshkov on five occasions", but no details are given. The same source gives the peremptory information that in shooting "a series of records were set in the USSR which were superior to the official world records". It was also claimed that "by 1941, of the 35 exercises which were contested in weightlifting, the Soviet records in 27 were superior to the official World records". All sporting ambitions were controlled by the Communist Party, which had established an official policy of *rekordsmentsvo* ("record-seeking"), decreeing that "Soviet athletes must not only improve All-Union records but beat world records as well". The downside was that sporting heroes, like all Soviet citizens, could easily fall foul of the system, and Nikolay Kovtun, a pre-war high-jump champion, was imprisoned for eighteen years and his records liquidated.

Though Soviet sporting progress was inevitably affected by the Second World War, it was, for example, only at the very height of hostilities with the Germans in 1941 and 1942 that the national championships in the most important of Olympic sports, athletics, were not held, and by the time that a team was sent to the European Championships at Oslo in 1946 the members of it had profited from three full years of training and competition and won titles in the men's 200 metres and the women's 100 metres, 200 metres, shot, discus (Dumbadze) and javelin. The fact that the Soviet athletes were strictly speaking ineligible to compete because their country was not affiliated to the international ruling body, the IAAF, was blithely ignored by the organisers and the other competing countries. After all, who was going to deny access to the brave Soviet allies who had fought off the German onslaught?

Even at the height of the war there had been some remarkable Soviet athletics achievements. A fine distance-runner, Fyeodosiy Vanin, who would have been a strong contender in the 1948 Olympic marathon, ran 10,000 metres in 30min 35.2sec in Moscow in September of 1942, and only seven other countries had ever produced anyone faster at the distance. During 1943 and 1944, Yevdokiya Vasilyeva improved her 800 metres record to 2min 14.0sec and Nina Dumbadze the discus record to 49.88m.

Track and field athletics had a particular appeal for the Soviet regime, as was explained by Robert Edelman, who made some 25 visits to the USSR from

1965 onwards for research and to spectate at different sporting events. "The highly technical nature of track made it seem more consistent than soccer with the goals of a 'scientific' version of socialism," Edelman concluded. "The precise measurements of time, distance and height revealed success or failure just as production statistics had come to demonstrate the success or failure of Soviet construction." Furthermore, as Edelman pointed out, "The fundamental skills of track and field were closely tied to military fitness".

The way in which the Soviet Government from the 1920s onwards had actively encouraged the public at large, and gifted individuals in particular, to develop their sporting talents was comprehensively explained by another American academic, William J Baker, when, in 1982, he published a detailed study of the historical development of sport worldwide. "From their distant tsarist past the Russians inherited a strong tradition of weightlifting, wrestling, speed-skating and gymnastics," he wrote. "After the Bolshevik Revolution in 1917, Communist officials socialised those traditions by taking sport out of the hands of private clubs and making it available to all Russian citizens. They instigated a new program of sport and physical exercise to overcome old class prejudices, to improve the health of the Russian people, to integrate diverse geographical sections of the country, and to build up the Red Army.

"In 1931 they devised a system of awards for all-round physical development, offering a coveted GTO badge ('GTO' in Russian script is the abbreviation for 'Ready for Work and Defence') to each adult citizen who passed a series of stiff practical and theoretical tests on physical fitness. Soon a badge was similarly created for schoolchildren. Also in the 1930s Soviet officials distinguished between a program of physical activity for all and a more specialised program to produce elite competitive athletes. The post-war system of sport in the Soviet Union built on these pre-war foundations.

"It was a system created and controlled by Government. The All-Union Physical Culture Council, founded in 1930, was replaced early in the post-war era by the Committee of Physical Culture and Sport, an arm of the Central Committee of the Communist party. Facilities, equipment, coaches and material incentives ultimately derived from party headquarters. So did programs of physical exercise for pre-schoolers, elementary and secondary school children, university students, police and military personnel, trade unions, and even farm collectives. Each group formed a link in the organised chain of Soviet life, a life in which a high premium was placed on health, physical strength and agility, and athletic excellence.

"With the onset of the Cold War, Soviet officials looked on their athletes as both warriors and ambassadors. In an international arena symbolically charged with prestige, Russian athletes could 'defeat' their country's ideological enemies. Sport, no less than economic development and military strength, was a key element in the Soviet drive for 'world supremacy'. In December 1948, within months of the Soviet blockade of Berlin, the Central Committee of the

Communist Party called on all schools, universities and sports societies 'to spread physical culture and sport to every corner of the land, and to raise the level of skill so that Soviet sportsmen might win world supremacy in the major sports in the immediate future'."

Professor Baker claims that from October 1945 until July 1947 cash prizes were paid directly by party officials to sportsmen and sportswomen who broke world or national records, or who placed in the first three in the USSR championships, on a sliding scale according to the importance of the sport. These bonuses were then replaced by salaries paid as university grants, or for police and military appointments, or as physical-education instructors, in order to comply with amateur regulations.

The Soviet sporting model was one which by 1949 was being copied by almost all of the Iron Curtain satellite countries – Bulgaria, Czechoslovakia, East Germany, Hungary and Poland – and by Yugoslavia, China, North Korea and subsequently Cuba, and within the next three years there were world titles for Czechoslovakia in archery, canoeing, figure-skating, ice hockey and table-tennis; for Hungary in fencing, figure-skating, speed-skating, table-tennis and wrestling; for Poland in gymnastics; and for Rumania in table-tennis. Between the Olympics of 1952 and 1988 – the latter being the last Games before the fall of the Berlin Wall – Communist-led regimes were to increase their share of medals from 31 to 51 per cent.

Clearly, the Soviet authorities had felt that the time was right immediately after the end of World War II to make an entry into international sporting events on a wide scale, even if not at Olympic level, because they had affiliated to numerous world ruling bodies over the next four years: basketball, football and weightlifting in 1946; figure-skating, speed-skating, swimming, volleyball, water polo and wrestling in 1947; athletics, gymnastics and skiing in 1948; boxing in 1949. At the 1946 world weightlifting championships, in Paris, Grigoriy Novak won the light-heavyweight title. At the 1947 European Greco-Roman wrestling championships the USSR won three of the eight titles.

The first display of post-war Soviet sporting skill in the West had been provided as early as November of 1945, with the goodwill visit to Britain of the Moscow Dynamo football team. When the autobiography of the legendary England winger, Stanley Matthews, was published more than 50 years later, he still enthusiastically recalled the impression which the exotic visitors had made: "From the moment Moscow Dynamo touched down at Croydon Airport to the time they left for home they captivated football fans the length and breadth of Great Britain. Dynamo arrived with the reputation of being a real crack side, but I doubt if anyone had ever seen them play."

Matthews, then serving in the Royal Air Force, went to watch the Dynamo match against Chelsea at Stamford Bridge and remembered: "The Dynamos started to live up to their name. They proved themselves to be very fit and fast. They combined speed with a great deal of skill, and in the end a pulsating match ended in a 3-3 draw. The scenes at the end had to be seen to be believed. The crowd were in raptures and roared their approval as the Russians left the field."

The seal of approval for the Soviet way of doing things in sport, which effectively put an end to the concept of amateurism, was to come in the fullness of time from the least likely of sources – the American millionaire, Avery Brundage. He had been elected president of the International Olympic Committee in 1952 and had been arch-defender of the principles of amateurism ever since becoming president of the US Olympic Committee in 1929. When he gave the opening address at the 59th IOC Congress in Moscow in June 1962, he must have surprised and delighted his hosts when he proclaimed of sport in the USSR: "No other country has made such a tremendous advance in such a short period. It has undoubtedly been due to the strong and broad foundation which has been laid in the last 40 years ... no country applies more intensively the theory of Baron de Coubertin that a national programme of physical training and competitive sport will build stronger and healthier boys and girls and make better citizens. In striving for victory and new records, it should never be forgotten that it was a national programme of this kind for all countries that was the main objective of the Baron de Coubertin when he initiated the campaign to revive the Olympic Games. The Games were not to be an end in themselves. They were to be the means of stimulating a broad programme of physical training and competitive sport for all youth."

The far-reaching changes that sport underwent between the Games of 1948 and those of 1952 are unparalleled, and it seems appropriate to end this appraisal of the rise of Soviet sport after the Wembley Olympics with the views of an expert whose ideology was totally contrary to that of Brundage. Sándor Barcs was a prominent sports administrator in Hungary, where state aid revolutionised athletics and football during the 1950s, and in a book published in Budapest in 1964 he made the following witty observation:

"The meeting in Helsinki in 1952 marked a new era in the history of the Olympic Games – the epoch of giant Olympics, but it was certainly not in the way that de Coubertin had imagined it. The Helsinki Olympics far outgrew the significance of sports events. The Games became an international and a social matter. In fact, they were a world event, in which victory and not participation was the most important. As far as pure amateurism was concerned, perhaps that should not even be mentioned! Everyone behaved as if he did not know, but everyone knew, and everyone knew that the person he just happened to be speaking to also knew. So it is perhaps best not to broach the subject of amateurism. The important thing was that the participants all took the Olympic oath of amateurism, and the rest is best left unsaid."

Bibliography

The following list represents a selection of the books and publications referred to in the course of research. Unless otherwise stated, the place of publication was London.

British Olympic Association Official Report of the Xth Olympiad 1932, edited by Captain FAM Webster (British Olympic Association, 1932)

British Olympic Association Official Report of the XIth Olympiad 1936, edited by Harold Abrahams (British Olympic Association, 1937)

50 Years of Sport, edited by Ernest A Bland (Daily Mail Publications, 1947)

Olympiad 1948, HJ Oaten (Findon Probus, 1948)

Olympic Games 1948: British Olympic Association Official Report, edited by Cecil Bear (World Sports, 1948)

Olympic Story, edited by Ernest A Bland (Rockcliff, 1948)

The Sports Book, edited by James Rivers (Macdonald & Co, 1948)

Report of the United States Olympic Committee, edited by Asa S Bushnell (US Olympic Association, New York, 1949)

Get To Your Marks! Ross & Norris McWhirter (Nicholas Kaye, 1951)

Sporting Rhapsody, Hylton Cleaver (Hutchinson's Library, 1951)

XIVth Olympiad London 1948: The Official Report of the Organising Committee for the XIV Olympiad 1948 (the Organising Committee, 1951)

Olympic Games 1952: British Olympic Association Official Report, edited by Cecil Bear (World Sports, 1952)

Modern Track and Field, J Kenneth Doherty (Bailey Bros & Swinfen, 1954)

Zátopek The Marathon Victor, František Kóžik (Artia, Prague, 1954)

First Four Minutes, Roger Bannister (Putnam, 1955)

Olympic Odyssey, edited by Stan Tomlin (Modern Athlete Publications, 1956)

The Olympic Games Book, Harold Abrahams (James Barrie, 1956)

1957 British Athletics Record Book, Ross McWhirter, Ian Buchanan and Norris McWhirter (McWhirter Twins, 1957)

The Olympic Hope, Knut Lundberg (Stanley Paul, 1958)

Encyclopaedia of Sport, edited by Charles Harvey (Sampson Low Marston, 1959)

Fencing: Ancient Art and Modern Sport, C-L de Beaumont (Kaye & Ward, 1960)

Encyclopédie des Sports, edited by Jean Dauven (Librairie Larousse, Paris, 1961)

Rétrospectives Olympiques, Otto Mayer (Pierre Cailler, Geneva, 1961)

Running Wild, Gordon Pirie (WH Allen, 1961)

The Olympic Games: Citius, Altis, Fortius (International Olympic Committee, Lausanne, 1962)

Héros Olympiques: Les Francais aux Jeux, Robert Parienté and Gérard Edelstein (La Table Ronde, Paris, 1964)

Encyclopaedia of Track and Field Athletics, Melvyn Watman (Robert Hale, 1964)

Meet the Olympians, Dimiter Mishev (Medicine & Physical Culture, Sofia, 1964)

The Modern Olympics Story, Sándor Barcs (Corvina Press, Budapest, 1964)

La Galaxie Olympique, Nicole Pellissard-Darrigand (J & D Editions, Biarritz, 1966)

Post-Victorian Britain 1902–1951, LCB Seaman (Routledge, 1966)

Olimpiai Jatékok 1896–1968, Endre Kahlich Andre, Lászlo Papp and Zoltán Subert (Sport, Budapest, 1968)

The Sports Illustrated Book of the Olympic Games, edited by Charles Osborne (Time-Life Books, New York, 1968)

Champions in the Making, Payton Jordan and Bud Spencer (Pelham Books, 1969)

The Olympics 1896–1972, Ross McWhirter (Esso, 1972)

Lexikon der 12,000 Olympioniken, Erich Kamper (Leykam-Verlag, Graz, 1975)

Sport in Britain: Its Origins and Development, Professor HA Harris (Stanley Paul, 1975)

Les Grandes Histoires des Jeux Olympiques, Francis Le Goulven and Gilles Delamarre (PAC Editions, Paris, 1976)

Pursuit of Excellence: The Olympic Story, edited by Ben Olan (Grolier Enterprises, Danbury, Connecticut, 1979)

The Official Centenary History of the Amateur Athletic Association, Peter Lovesey (Guinness Superlatives, 1979)

The Olympic Games, edited by Lord Killanin and John Rodda (Macdonald & Jane's, 1979)

Sport behind the Iron Curtain, Simon Freeman and Roger Boyes (Proteus Books, 1980)

Histoire des Jeux Olympiques, Daniel Costelle (Librairie Larousse, Paris, 1980)

The Games, edited by Marshall Brant (Proteus Books, 1980)

The History of the Olympics, edited by Martin Tyler and Phil Soar (Marshall Cavendish, 1980)

Sports in the Western World, William S Baker (Rowman and Littlefield, Totowa, New Jersey, 1982)

The Guinness Book of Athletics Facts & Feats, Peter Matthews (Guinness Superlatives, 1982)

The Olympic Games: Athens 1896 to Los Angeles 1984, Peter Arnold (Optimum Books, 1983)

Olympiské Hry, Karel Prochazka (Olympia, Prague, 1984)

British Society since 1948, Arthur Marwick (Penguin Books, 1985)

Now The War Is Over: A Social History of Britain 1945-51, Paul Addison (BBC & Jonathan Cape, 1985)

Changing Horizons: Britain 1914–80, WO Simpson (Stanley Thomas, 1986)

Guinness Track & Field Athletics: The Records, Peter Matthews (Guinness Books, 1986)

The Complete Book of the Olympics, David Wallechinsky (Penguin Books, 1988)

The Sport: Sport for All and Sport for One, Boris Javin (Nóvosti Press, Moscow, 1988)

A Statistical History of UK Track & Field Athletics, edited by Andrew Huxtable (National Union of Track Statisticians, 1990)

British Olympians, Ian Buchanan (Guinness, 1991)

Track & Field Performances Through the Years: Volume 2 1937–1944, Rooney Magnussson, Don Potts and Roberto Quercetani (Association of Track & Field Statisticians and International Athletic Foundation, Monaco, 1992)

Serious Fun: A History of Spectator Sport in the USSR, Robert Edelman (Oxford University Press Inc, New York, 1993)

Australia and the Olympics, Harry Gordon (University of Queensland Press, 1994)

All-Time Greats of British and Irish Sport, Peter Matthews and Ian Buchanan (Guinness Publishing, 1995)

The Guinness Encyclopaedia of International Sports Records and Results, Peter Matthews (Guinness Publications, 1995)

Track & Field Performances Through the Years: Volume 3 1945–1950 by Nejat Kök, Rooney Magnusson, Don Potts and Roberto Quercetani (Association of Track & Field Statisticians and International Amateur Athletic Federation, Monaco, 1995)

American Women's Track and Field: A History 1895 through 1980, Louise Mead Tricard (McFarland & Co, Jefferson, North Carolina, 1996)

Canada at the Olympics 1896–1996, edited by Jack Batten (Infact, Toronto, 1996)

Olympic Facts and Feats, Stan Greenberg (Guinness Publishing, 1996)

Europe: A History, Norman Davies (Pimlico, 1997)

The Road from Berlin to London, Les Crouch (unpublished thesis, 1997)

Dictionnaire International du Cyclisme, Claude Sudres (Cofidis, Wasquehal, France, 1998)

Whitaker's Almanack of International Sports Records and Results, Peter Matthews (The Stationery Office, 1998)

La Grande Histoire des Jeux Olympiques, Henri Charpentier and Euloge Boissonade (Editions France-Empire, Paris, 1999)

The Modern Olympic Century 1896–1996, Ekkehard zur Megede (Deutsche Gesellschaft für Leichtathletik Dokumentation, Berlin, 1999)

Stanley Matthews: My Autobiography – The Way It Was (Headline Book Publishing, 2000)

The Olympic Games: Fundamentals and Ceremonies, edited by Franklin Servan-Schreiber (International Olympic Committee, Lausanne, 2000)

Whitaker's Olympic Almanack: An Encyclopaedia of the Olympic Games, Stan Greenberg (The Stationery Office, 2000)

The Verdict of Peace, Correlli Barnett (Macmillan, 2001)

The History of the US Olympic Trials: Track & Field 1908–2000, Richard Hymans (USA Track & Field, Indianapolis, Indiana, 2002)

The Iron in his Soul: Bill Roberts and Manchester's Sporting Heritage, Bob Phillips (The Parrswood Press, Manchester, 2002)

Zátopek! Zátopek! Zátopek! The Life and Times of the World's Greatest Distance-Runner, Bob Phillips (The Parrswood Press, Manchester, 2002)

Progression of World Best Performances and Official IAAF World Records, Richard Hymans (International Association of Athletics Federations, 2003)

Prophet or Traitor? The Jimmy Hogan Story, Norman Fox (The Parrswood Press, Manchester, 2003)

British Athletics 1946–49, Michael Sheridan (published by the author, 2004)

3:59.4: The Quest for the Four-Minute Mile, Bob Phillips (The Parrswood Press, Manchester, 2004)

Great Britain's medallists at the 1948 Olympic Games

R EMARKABLY LITTLE IS known about some of the British medallists in 1948. In some cases, despite the determined researches of Ian Buchanan, of Great Britain, and Bill Mallon, of the United States, two of the world's leading Olympic experts, even the dates and places of birth and the full first names have still not been discovered. The information given below consists of full name, familiar name, dates of birth and death, and brief biographical details of achievements prior to the 1948 Games. Further detail about the subsequent careers of many of those listed below can be found in the relevant chapters of this book.

Gold (3):

Rowing, Coxless Pairs:

John Hyrne Tucker (Jack) Wilson, b Bristol, Rhode Island, USA, 17 September 1914. William George Ranald Mundell (Ran) Laurie, b Grantchester, Cambridgeshire, 4 May 1915; d 19 September 1998 aged 83. Both Wilson and Laurie were members of the record-breaking Cambridge crew in the 1934 Boat Race and won the 1938 Henley coxless pairs. They joined the Sudan Colonial Service and did not compete together again until 1948. Laurie also took part in the eights at the 1936 Olympics.

Rowing, Double Sculls:

Richard Desborough Burnell, b Henley-on-Thames, Oxfordshire, 26 July 1917; d 21 January 1995 aged 77. Rowing correspondent of *The Times*. His father won gold in the eights at the 1908 Olympics. Burnell jnr and Bushnell formed their partnership less than a month before the 1948 Olympics.

Bertram Herbert Thomas (Bert) Bushnell, by Woking, Surrey, 7 May 1909. Engineer. His family owned a boat-building business with a branch at Henley-on-Thames and working for that might have prejudiced his amateur status.

Yachting, Swallow class:

Stewart Harold Morris, b Bromley, Kent, 25 May 1909; d 4 February 1991 aged 81. Manager of family hop-growing business. Reserve for the 1936 Olympics. European champion in 1938. Member of the council of the Yacht Racing Association since 1935. Served as a Commander in the Royal Naval Volunteer Reserve during World War II and awarded the OBE in 1945 for wartime service.

David John Were Bond, b Falmouth, Cornwall, 27 March 1922. Served as an aircraftsman in the RAF during World War II. British Aircraft Corporation employee.

Silver (14):

Athletics (men), Marathon:

Thomas John Henry (Tom) Richards, b Upper Cwmbran, Torfaen, South Wales, 15 March 1910; d 19 January 1985 aged 74. Nurse. Made the first of 10 appearances for Wales in the International cross-country championships in 1934 and ran his first marathon in 1939.

Athletics (men), 4x100 metres relay:

John (Jack) Archer, b Nottingham 10 August 1921; d 29 September 1997 aged 76. Served in the RAF during the war. Won the European 100 metres in 1946. Broke a leg playing rugby union in 1947. Member of Notts AC.

John Arthur (Jack) Gregory, b Sea Mills, Bristol, Gloucestershire, 22 June 1923; d 15 December 2003 aged 80. Was also qualified to represent Eire. Gained an England cap as a rugby union wing-threequarter in 1947. Member of Crusaders AC, Dublin.

Alastair McCorquodale, b Hillhead, Glasgow, 5 December 1925. Manager of family printing business. Retired after the 1948 Olympics, having competed for only two years. Member of London AC.

Kenneth Jeffrey (Ken) Jones, b Blaenavon, Torfaen, South Wales, 30 December 1921; d 19 April 2006 aged 84. Schoolteacher. Won the first of 44 caps for Wales as a rugby union wing-threequarter in 1947. Member of Newport Harriers.

Athletics (women), 100 metres:

Dorothy Gladys Manley, b Manor Park, Essex, 29 April 1927. Typist. Converted from high jumping to sprinting earlier in 1948 by her coach, Sandy Duncan. Member of Essex Ladies' AC.

Athletics (women), 200 metres:

Audrey Doreen Swayne Williamson, b Bournemouth, 28 September 1926. Women's Royal Army Corps officer. The 1948 Olympics was her only appearance for Great Britain. Member of St Gregory's AC, Cheltenham.

Athletics (women), 80 metres hurdles:

Maureen Angela Jane Gardner, b Oxford, 12 November 1928; d 2 September 1974 aged 45. Married her coach, Geoff Dyson. Member of Oxford Ladies' AC.

Athletics (women), High jump:

Dorothy Jennifer Beatrice Tyler, b Clapham, London, 14 March 1920. Also second in 1936 Olympic high jump. Member of Mitcham AC.

Boxing, Middleweight:

John A (Johnny) Wright, b 19 May 1929. Navy seaman. Member of Polytechnic BC.

Boxing, Light-heavyweight:

Donald E (Don) Scott, b 23 July 1928; d February 2006 aged 77. Military policeman. Member of Premier BC, Derby.

Cycling, Sprint:

Reginald Hargreaves (Reg) Harris, b Birtle, Lancashire, 1 March 1920; d 22 June 1992 aged 72. Served in the army during the war. World amateur sprint champion in 1947. Member of Manchester Wheelers.

Cycling, Tandem sprint:

Reg Harris (see above).

Alan Bannister, b 3 November 1922. Clubmate of Harris's.

Cycling, Road team:

Robert John (Bob) Maitland, b Birmingham, 31 March 1924. Member of Solihull Cycling Club.

Cyril S Ian Scott. Member of Middlesbrough Cycling Club.

Gordon W Thomas, b 18 August 1921. Member of Yorkshire Roads Club.

Hockey:

Robert Edward Adlard, b 15 November 1915. Played for England.

Norman Francis Borrett, b Wanstead, Essex, 1 October 1917; d 10 December 2004 aged 87. England. Also played first-class squash.

David LS Brodie. Scotland.

Ronald Davies, b 28 December 1914; d 24 October 1989 aged 74. Wales.

William Salterlee Griffiths, b 26 June 1922. Wales.

Frederick Robin Lindsay, b 11 January 1914. Scotland.

William LC Lindsay, b 11 April 1914. Scotland.

John Morris Peake, b 26 August 1924. England.

Frank O Reynolds, b 21 August 1917.

George B Sime. Scotland.

Michael Moore (Mickey) Walford, b Norton-on-Tees, 27 November 1915; d 16 January 2002 aged 86. England. Also played first-class cricket.

William Neil White, b Troon, Ayrshire, 2 May 1920; d 19 February 1990 aged 69. Scotland.

Rowing, Eights:

Christopher Bertram Ronald (Chris) Barton, b 21 November 1927. Stroke of the 1948 Cambridge Boat Race crew which broke the 1934 record.

Ernest Augustus Paul Bircher, b 11 November 1928.

Jack Gilroy Dearlove, b 5 June 1911; d October 1986 aged 75.

Michael Clement Lapage, b 15 November 1923.

Charles Brian Murray Lloyd, b 11 March 1927.

Paul Mackintosh Orgill Massey, b 12 March 1926.

Alfred Paul Mellows, b 8 June 1922.

David John Charlton Meyrick, b 2 December 1926; d March 2004 aged 77.

Guy Colquhoun Richardson, b 8 September 1921; d 27 October 1965 aged 44.